Family Stories

...and How I Found Mine

J. Michael Cleverley

CLEARFIELD

Published for Clearfield Company
by Genealogical Publishing Company
Baltimore, Maryland
2020

ISBN 9780806359090

To My Parents

Margie and Owen

Who Gifted Me the Past

And the Itch to Explore It

Table of Contents

Maps

Map A   United States

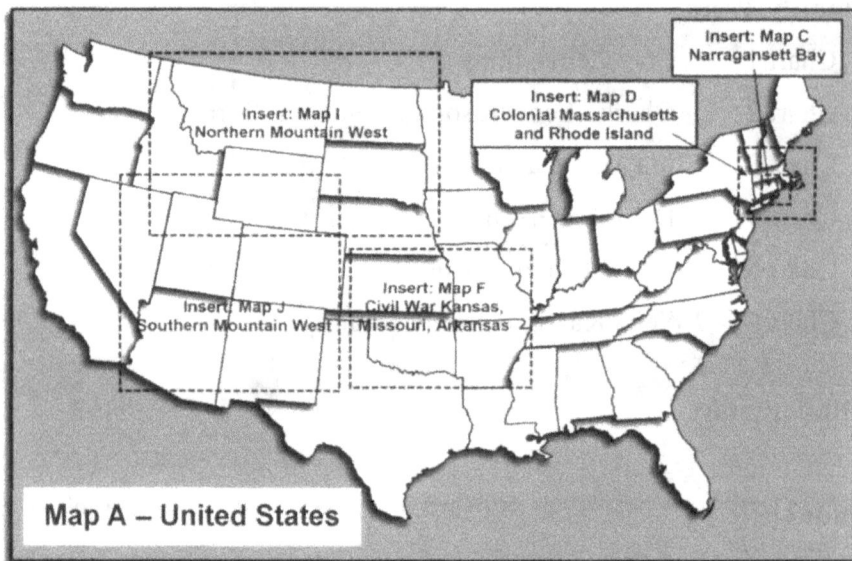

Map A – United States

Acknowledgments

Above everything else, my voyage in search of family was propelled by family. My wife, Seija, was with me from beginning to finish. In addition to selflessly tendering unlimited patience, endurance, and encouragement, she made conceptual suggestions that early on focused my ideas on how to structure the narratives. My sister, Jeannine, spent countless hours, days, and weeks going through chapter drafts, discovering typos and errors, but most important of all, helping me zero in on a style that accomplished my aim of relating my stories.

I have been blessed with talented and supportive children, Kristiina, Kaarina, Mikael, and Markus. They encouraged the writer and helped refine his prose. Markus, Mikael, and his wife, Rachel, proofread chapters. And two of my teenaged grandsons, Asher and Kai, asked if I would email them a PDF copy of a draft to read in advance, the best kind of cheer any writer could hope for. Distant cousins, in some cases whom I had never met in person, came to my rescue on many occasions to offer additional insight and information to include in my project. Cousin **Peggy Lent and her mother Ora's** vast research was invaluable in pinning down countless elusive details. Another, Alice Walker, provided me piles of information to use in one of my chapters.

There are many institutions dedicated to preserving our past. The role they play is crucial for people, like me, who seek to walk in the footsteps of ancestors living long ago. I have deep appreciation for the National Park Service. Its rangers, without exception, were knowledgeable about the sites they were entrusted to preserve and present and went out of their way to assist me in my project. They, themselves, can be considered a proud part of America's heritage. And how could I not mention the capable people who work the desks of libraries everywhere. These people are treasures waiting to enrich researchers. They opened new worlds, everywhere I went.

Despite all these generous contributions, I realize that any project that combs the past will inevitably have shortcomings and errors. For all these, I take responsibility and seek new opportunities to update and fix anything I may have missed.

Preface

Most books about family history are either a "family history" or a "how-to-do family history." This volume is neither. It starts with the idea that most people today want to know more about their family than simply genealogical basics: names, dates, places, and relationships. They would like to learn the stories of their ancestors. How did they live, what were good days and bad? What were their adventures, and what were their failures? That is what I wanted to find when I started a search for my family's stories.

This book describes what five years of morning-to-evening research, and travel throughout the United States and to different corners of Europe, taught me. On one level, it is an anthology of stories about remarkable people at pivotal points in history. On another, it is a set of case studies. These are stories I found, and how I found them. It traces my own successes – and failures – in unearthing all I wanted. Reflecting back, when my journey to the past was over, I knew I had found much more than I ever expected.

Everyone's possibilities are unique, and their family's history is unique, as well. One thing I learned was that what worked for me, may not work as well for someone else, and vice versa. I had opportunities to travel, and some people may not. My mother Margie's sixty years of genealogical research gave me a head start. Others may have to launch their searches from ground zero. But one thing we all have in common is a heritage, and you do not have to reach back to 1066 to find family stories that inspire us. Our own parents and grandparents, and cousins and aunts and uncles, may have a treasure of stories for us to find.

Because everyone's family stories are individual, I tried to steer clear of formulas and templates for finding them. I did not want my book to be a recipe for finding one's stories. Simply: here is how I found mine. You will discover from my experience ways to find yours, too. I envisage your journey will track mine especially in this sense: some stories were easier to find than I expected; some were harder than expected; and sometimes, serendipitously from the blue, a fascinating story popped up that I could never have hoped for.

The Inheritance
Margie Lea Leonardson Cleverley

"Here I go!"
Margie Lea Leonardson Cleverley
with a smile, on her last night

It was the call we expect all our lives, yet dread when it finally comes. Why did it ring just like any other? We had just got off a long flight from Athens where we had spent a few weeks at our apartment overlooking the turquoise Mediterranean near Cape Sounio. My wife, Seija, and I stretched our cramped legs and bodies into a brisk pace along the corridors of one of JFK's many terminals. As I switched on my cell phone, it immediately buzzed alive. It was my sister Lorilee. Mother had taken a turn for the worse. Lorilee said we should come home. It was time to say our final goodbyes.

The news took us by surprise. Only three days before, we had talked at length with my mother Margie by phone from Greece. It had been a good conversation, and she seemed fine then. I phoned one of our sons to tell him what was happening, and during the time we were taking the final leg of our trip to Virginia, he found us tickets for a flight from Washington, DC during the early hours of the next morning.

After a short sleep, a long flight to Salt Lake, and a four-hour drive, we arrived in Pocatello, Idaho. Mother's bed was in the middle of the family room, and around it sat my siblings. In the corner, my uncle and his son sat vigil. I had not seen either of them for many years. Mother gave Seija and me a loving smile. She was glad we had made it on time.

We saw immediately that this was the last stop of her mortal travel. She was breathing hard but seemed happy. Dad had passed away only nine months before, and she had told us she was anxious to join him on the other side. We had a warm conversation, and when we departed for the motel, she looked up at me, smiled with a gleam in her eyes, and said with a not a little excitement, "Here I go!" That night she joined Dad, the love of her life.

Two days later, Seija, and I sat on the floor of Mother's study, one that doubled as her guest room. Scattered around us on the floor were boxes, files, and packing materials. Mother had bequeathed me her family history files. During six decades of enthusiastically pursuing her great passion, she had amassed a great deal of genealogical materials: notes, copies, pedigree and family group sheets, correspondence, photographs, audio cassettes, typed and hand-written stories, and histories. I had not shared this same passion with Mother, but recognizing hers, I had taken a genealogy class during my first year of college. The following summer I had helped her organize a filing system that she had used extensively over the subsequent decades. Perhaps for that reason, or perhaps because like most mothers, she knew something about her son that I did not, she left me those files.

Seija and I spent two days going through the filing cabinets. The amount of material was immense. As Mother aged and her files proliferated and thickened, it had become increasingly difficult to keep things weeded, relevant, and organized. After a first take at slimming down the files, we packed them into boxes and drove them over to the local UPS store. The tab came to almost $1,000, but the heavy boxes were soon on their way to our home in Virginia. When they finally arrived, we were there waiting for them. I stacked them on a trolley which I pulled in several trips up the stairs to my second-floor study. There, I carefully stacked them along the wall in the back of a walk-in closet.

They sat in the closet for a year, and then another year, and then another and another. I hated to walk into that closet, because the first thing I saw were the unopened boxes. I humored myself to think that one day I would open them. I even purchased a large wooden file cabinet and cartons of folders for the organization and re-organization of new files, whenever that happened. But the boxes stayed in the closet and the cabinet sat full of empty folders.

2

I knew the brown taped boxes held 60 years of Mother's burning dedication to the past. I suspected they might even have some treasures in them as well. They remained there, however, until one New Year's Day when Seija and I sat at dinner with our children and grandchildren. As was our custom, we started around the table sharing our New Year's resolutions. When it was my turn, I announced with pent-up guilt that this year I planned to dive into Mother's family history to re-organize and re-file it. The next day I started by opening the first brown box.

One-by-one, I unfolded Mother's worn manila file folders, pulling out their contents piece-by-piece, sorting and relabeling, and carefully replacing everything into new file covers. I discovered that these folders were filled with passion and indeed some treasures. I found such things squirreled into the files as a satchel and account book from the grandfather of my Great-Grandmother Lent. In it, he had kept business and family records that told of everyday life on the American frontier. Far off grandfathers and grandmothers whom I had once heard about came to life in photographs that revealed real people to me. And there were Mother's notes to herself and to whomever would one day finger through her files, with her descriptions of dreams she had had, amazing experiences she had encountered, and hints on where to go next. Mother's obsession began to take hold of me, too, just as I am sure she knew it would.

I traveled from one family to the next, spilling the contents of one folder after another onto my desk. It was more than a simple sorting exercise. Everywhere, I found something meaningful. These families were connecting to me. They were becoming my family. There I sat, an end product of long past lives that were occasionally glorious, often taxing and trying, and sometimes infamous. A treasure trove of tales was hidden in these folders.

It occurred to me that behind each of us, there are a thousand stories of our people, their aspirations, their successes, their follies, and their tragedies – if only we knew them. These narratives make up a collective forge that casts our own sagas. As any pedigree chart visually displays, our ancestral family – our parents and their progenitors – eventually funnel down to a single point with our name on it. We are the latest episode among these stories.

My mother Margie's decades of work made it possible for me to know something about these people. Her efforts had produced scores of accounts from our family's past. She had bequeathed me the barebones of many of them. There was just enough to whet my appetite. I was intrigued to learn more of the plots and the storylines. Inside me began a wanderlust to take a journey to the past, to find the real people and real tales of those who came before me. More than just *names*, *places*, and *dates*, I wanted to know *how* they lived.

Margie's files gave me a head start, and by the time I had made it once through them, my ship was already leaving port on an odyssey to find my thousand stories. I knew they would have to be unearthed in a menagerie of times and places. Some might be just waiting to be found. Others would require sweat and digging. My thousand stories were scattered over a thousand years and two continents, an impossible journey to make.

Part of the trip would be possible right in front of my computer screen; other segments would demand more. I decided to focus my collections on key moments in history – the Norman Conquest, Puritan New England, the American Revolutionary and Civil Wars, the American migration West – to experience those critical conjunctures through the eyes of my ancestors. I decided from the beginning that the final part would be from where two rivers met: my Finnish wife's and my own.

If I wanted to bring these people back to life, however, I would need to visit where they lived, walk the paths they followed, and sometimes even eat where they ate. In other words, I would have to pack my bags. I had spent a career as an American diplomat traveling from to country, almost like a nomad. Now I would embark on another wayfaring adventure, not just from place to place, but as a nomad traveling back through time.

As I began mapping out this journey, I was reminded of an experience we had when living in London during the mid-1980's. One-night, Seija and I woke up in the middle of a storm. Our distressed thick-furred white Samoyed, Frosty, had climbed onto our bed. It was October, and storms were not a rare thing. What intrigued me, however, was how the rays of light seeping through the bedroom curtains ebbed and flowed with an unaccustomed flickering. Outside the house stood an iron light post whose lamp radiated nighttime brightness into our room. It was normally steady. We were so used to its every evening presence that the sputtering glow this stormy night was enough to bring me to the window.

I stared at the solid pole as it waved back and forth in a way I would not have thought possible. It was swaying in a tempest, and its light fluttered with it. Earlier in the evening I had watched the nightly BBC weather forecaster tell that a woman had called to say she had heard a hurricane was on its way. "Don't worry," he pronounced, "there will be no hurricane." I saw now he was wrong about that. A massive storm was blasting its way through southern England. Today, a few decades later, the night is still remembered as "The Great Storm of 1987."

Early the next morning, my wife and I leashed Frosty, and the three of us crossed the street into nearby Hyde Park. The sight was appalling. Even Frosty was unnerved. Thousands of stately trees lay on their sides, with their broad root systems extending for yards in every direction. The ground, already saturated from several days of earlier rainfall, held little in place as the heavy winds pulled up the trees, roots and all, and threw them down again. When they had stood upright, the trees were invincible pillars with their wide brown trunks supporting vast spreads of branches and leaves. Now, standing beside these felled proud trees, we observed the hundreds and thousands of normally hidden roots that for decades, or much longer, had propped them up with strength and confidence.

The site seemed so allegorically related to us, and to Frosty, too. With his thick white fur and slight butternut tinge, his perfectly symmetrical black eyes and nose, pointed ears and curved tail, he was one of the most magnificent dogs we had ever seen. Both his parents had been English champions. His roots (and a lot of daily brushing) made him the handsome dog he was. My roots extended in every which-direction and "English champions" were rare, but all these roots anchored my own story. Seija's roots extended deep into her culturally rich Finnish-Karelian tribe and explained much of her colorful personality. These roots, normally not seen, propped us up.

Now, many years later, as I contemplated embarking on such an ambitious journey, I thought about how intriguing it would be to pull my roots from the ground for a few moments of revelation and marvel. Maybe this is what makes exploring one's family history so addictive. Under each of us are thousands of these roots that we normally do not see but exist as surely as we do. Each of them has a story to tell.

It is hard to comprehend how extensively our family root network spreads. An article in *The Atlantic* a few years ago told how a simple mathematical progression describes the enormous scope of our ancestral roots. We are all born to two parents (2^1), and they were born to four (2^2), and those grandparents, in turn, came from eight (2^3). Each generation increases the number of our ancestors by a factor of 2, or, in other words, doubles the previous number of grandparents.

We can quite reasonably assume four generations per century, and with each generation, the number of ancestors doubles. Going back 100 years, we will have 14 ancestors, including parents; another 100 years, 254 including all those who came between now and then. All other things being equal, 400 years back we can potentially number as many as 33,000 ancestors, all living in the early 1600s.

Quickly, the numbers become absurdly large. Extending our progression back 1,000 years – to the time of William the Conqueror and his wife Matilda – we would theoretically have one trillion ancestors. Presumably, that is more than the number of human beings who have ever lived – so obviously, the progression begins breaking down with time as lines cross over and join with other lines of common ancestors. However, if we only have $1/10^{th}$ of 1 percent of that number, we will still have a billion ancestors one thousand years ago, at least according to the theoretical progression.

That number, too, is greatly inflated beyond reality, but whatever the real number is, it is massively large and has some implications for us. Statisticians estimate that extending back 1,000 years, every European living today is theoretically a descendant of every European living then. Since there has never been a free mixing of populations in Europe, this may not be exactly the case. Each European country and its people are still quite distinct. On the other hand, it is not hard to imagine that if every English woman and man living today pulled up their roots for 1,000 years back, each of them would most likely find King William and Queen Matilda somewhere among them.[1]

If the ancestral lines of those living today all begin to merge 1,000 years in the past, why then are we interested in family history? What is the point? As my quest for stories proceeded, I learned ever more clearly the reason was in the stories, themselves. Each of these ancestors, generation by generation, century by century, had their own unique story. The stories, good or bad, sad or happy, enrich us as we learn them. As segments of our own intricate root system, they can even prop us up with strength and confidence, just as the stands of noble trees had stood for centuries in Hyde Park.

One of Homer's great stories that has captured people for thousands of years was that of Odysseus, told in his epic *The Odyssey*. After the Trojan War, Odysseus and his men board their ship and sail off toward their homes on the island of Ithaca. It is a long and eventful voyage, and the book follows their adventures. Getting to Ithaca turns out to be an anti-climax, however. The Odyssey is not about arriving home, but about how they get there. So it is with our family history. What matters is not the last stop, but the search for it. Exploring our 1,000 stories is about the journey, not the destination.

What Homer recounts is what I discovered when I began the search for my one thousand stories. I had no intention or even the possibility to trace all those who made my life a reality. The stories that I could find, and my journey to discover them, were ultimately my goal. As it turned out, the tales and accounts were more colorful and endearing than I imagined. But the journey to find them was equally thrilling, with unexpected twists and turns, full of excitement and victory, and often frustration and disappointment. The past is a foreign land, I found, and whoever who travels there

7

may be smitten with its exotic landscape but never catch sight of as much of it as they want. Sometimes the fog of the past is simply too dark to see far, and occasionally, as I learned, there are people there who do not want to be found.

PART I
MEDIEVAL TALES

Chapter 1

The Wife of a Conqueror
Matilda of Flanders

O twofold light of November, it is
a little plot,
A small pile of ash, but nevertheless a
source of glory and grace.

Medieval poet Fulcoius
lamenting Matilda's passing (1083 AD)

If most people of English descent could trace their families back
1,000 years and likely discover William the Conqueror and Queen
Matilda (and just about everyone else of their times), it seemed to
me that the 11th century was a place I should visit. Indeed, I found
that moving back along the family trees that Mother had started,
William and Matilda were my grandmother and grandfather
through several different lines, about 40 generations ago.

William and his remarkable wife Matilda were one of history's
great power couples. William the First was the founder of a Britain
that has dominated Western history over the ten centuries since he
invaded the Anglo-Saxon kingdom. All subsequent English royalty
descended from William and Matilda. There have been reams of
writings about his life. Quite surprisingly, however, not a lot has
been said about the capable and multi-talented woman who ruled
alongside him. For that reason and more, I was curious to learn
Matilda's stories.

Young Matilda, Wife and Duchess of Normandy

William, Duke of Normandy, and his men angrily spurred their
big mounts from Normandy toward Bruges, a Flemish center that
today is part of Belgium. The year was about 1049. This was not a
neighborly visit to Flanders. William had been publicly insulted,
and he aimed to bring the guilty party to account. Even so, it was a
little delicate. If he was after a man, it would have been easier. The

11

sword he swung with uncommon expertise would have accomplished the job quickly. But it was a young woman in her teens responsible for his embarrassment. And it was not just any young lady. She belonged to one of the most powerful families in Europe. Just the same, she would pay.

William was also referred to as "William the Bastard." *Bastard* in this case was not a profanity, but a reference to his being born illegitimately. When people called him bastard, however, they normally were sneering that he was not the legitimate Duke. His father, Robert, fathered William with Herleva, the daughter of a local tradesman who worked near Robert's castle in Falaise. Robert remained with Herleva, but they never married, perhaps because of the difficulties of their different stations. He was a duke and she was low born. Robert named William his heir before his own sudden death on the way back from a Holy Land Crusade. The boy was not even ten years old when he inherited the duchy. He remained forever thin-skinned to any reference to his illegitimacy.

William aimed to punish the young girl who had spurned him with exactly that, *bastard*. Matilda of Flanders, the teenaged daughter of Baldwin V, Count of Flanders, was young, beautiful, educated, and had one of Europe's most impressive pedigrees: her uncle was King of France, and her grandfather was king before him. On her father's side, she descended from a long list of nobility and royalty, including the noted Anglo-Saxon King Alfred the Great. She was also an eligible match for marriage. All this had caught William's eye when looking for a bride to further establish himself as the Duke of Normandy.

When William's envoys had proposed a marriage with Matilda, her father Baldwin reacted positively. It was a perfect political arrangement to have the rulers of two adjoining principalities linked in marriage. When Baldwin informed his daughter, however, Matilda flatly refused, saying she would never marry "a bastard." Daughters of noble families rarely declined an arranged marriage, but Matilda was unbending and obstinate in her rejection. She was not private about it, either. Gossip of her repudiation embarrassingly spread across both Flanders and Normandy.

William had lived a difficult childhood. He had seen two of his guardians murdered in front of him, and he was a warrior at heart. Matilda's public rejection, because he was illegitimate, was an unacceptable humiliation.

William, his horsemen rode about 200 miles along the windy medieval roads to Flanders before finally entering Bruges. They found Matilda worshipping in the family chapel near the palace. He waited for her outside until she emerged. Grabbing her by the hair, William struck her and threw her to the ground, ruining the elegant gown she wore. With that, he thought, he had made a point that no one, not even Matilda of Flanders, would humiliate William of Normandy. The audacity of his attack on Matilda would send the message to everyone in Normandy and Flanders. He "sprang to the saddle, and setting spurs to his good steed, distanced all pursuit." Matilda's servants helped her to her feet and to her bedchamber.

Matilda's father Baldwin, infuriated by William's violent attack on his daughter, prepared for war against Normandy. But as he did so, he found Matilda once again stubbornly opposing his plans. She emerged from the ordeal to declare to her father that she would marry no one else but William. "He must be a man of great courage and high daring," she is reputed to have said. Instead of sending an army to Normandy, bewildered Baldwin arranged for messengers to approach William about the marriage. An agreement was swiftly reached, and a splendid wedding took place with grandeur. By contemporary accounts, William and Matilda were to become the power couple of their age, living happily (mostly) ever after.[1]

A year after Matilda consented to marry William, Count Baldwin and his wife Adela escorted their daughter with "honor and gifts" to Eu, a Norman city on the border with Flanders. Preparations for a splendid wedding were well underway. When they arrived, Matilda's party was met by William, his mother Herleva, his two half-brothers Odo and Robert, a host of dignitaries, and, not least, his retinue of nobles, knights, and soldiers.

The marriage couple dressed in rich matching gowns with crosses, cameos, and precious stones, all meant to flaunt the magnificence of the occasion. William wore his helmet, lest anyone forget he was a warrior. Like today, Matilda's father gave her away, there was an exchange of promises, and the ring was blessed. The bridal chamber was also consecrated to remind everyone that the purpose of a noble marriage is to produce heirs. Next, Matilda and William were led to the chamber in a great procession.

Later, during the wedding feast, one account relates that Matilda's father turned to her and asked what had changed her mind about William. She replied, "I did not know the duke so well then as I do now."[2]

The entire wedding was done "with great pomp and much joy and jubilation," as one 12th century historian recorded, and, "...when the wedding guests dispersed... they went back to Rouen [William's capital in Normandy], where, for the whole fortnight following, there was such rejoicing as was beyond description."[3]

Matilda was barely 18-years old. According to William of Jumieges, a writer who knew her, she was "of a beautiful body and a generous heart." Almost all contemporary accounts agree. They mention how she was "renowned equally for nobility of blood and character," and "endowed with fairness of face, noble birth, learning, beauty of character, and – what is and ever will be more worthy of praise – strong faith and fervent love of Christ."

Another wrote that she was "a model of wisdom and exemplar of modesty without parallel in our time." Even Pope Gregory, when he once wrote to Matilda, made mention of, "...your chaste and honest life, your charitable deeds to help the poor and of your means and the perfect love you give to the Lord and your fellow creatures." Like William, she was strong willed, confident, and ambitious. She could be a cold pragmatist. Well educated, cultured, and refined, however, she was also quite his opposite. One biography calls her one of the most remarkable women in history.[4]

William was about 23 years old, a little older than Matilda. He was smitten by Matilda and totally endeared to her until he died. She completed him. He was brilliant, probably the best military commander of his day, and a great leader, but William was not cultivated like his wife. He was from Viking ancestry. His 3rd great-grandfather was Rollo, a Viking war lord who settled in Normandy.

William did not lose battles, could be grossly cruel, and was ambitious enough to conquer none other than Anglo-Saxon Britain from the base of his relatively small duchy across the Channel. One chronicler wrote, "Nations foreign and far-distant feared nothing so much as his name."[5] By the time William married Matilda, he had become one of the most respected and dreaded rulers in Europe. One of his best traits was a willingness to let his wise but gentler wife soften some of his rough edges. Like Matilda, he was also deeply religious.

A match like William and Matilda caught the attention of all of Europe's ruling families. With Matilda's noble heritage, linking her to many of the day's elite families, and William's sheer military prowess, the couple seem indomitable. Pope Leo XI made up an excuse to forbid the marriage. It was "incestuous," he claimed. In fact, they were distantly related. Viking war lord Rollo was also one of Matilda's ancestors, but the connection was five-generations back. What really concerned Leo XI was the power the marriage consolidated in central Europe. It joined Normandy and Flanders with a family connection, and on top of that, Matilda's uncle was King of neighboring France (see Map B).

Matilda and William ignored the pope's injunction. Typical to both their characters, they plunged into the wedding without the pope's approval. Afterwards, they tried to change his mind. It took them over ten years to do that, and they succeeded only after each agreed to build abbeys. The priories, a women's abbey and a men's abbey, still stand in Caen, France.

Matilda and William set up court in Normandy. Thanks to Matilda, the court became a center of culture and refinement as well as a center of political power. William never got completely away from his basic roughness, but she introduced etiquette and ceremony, poetry and literature. She and William became literary

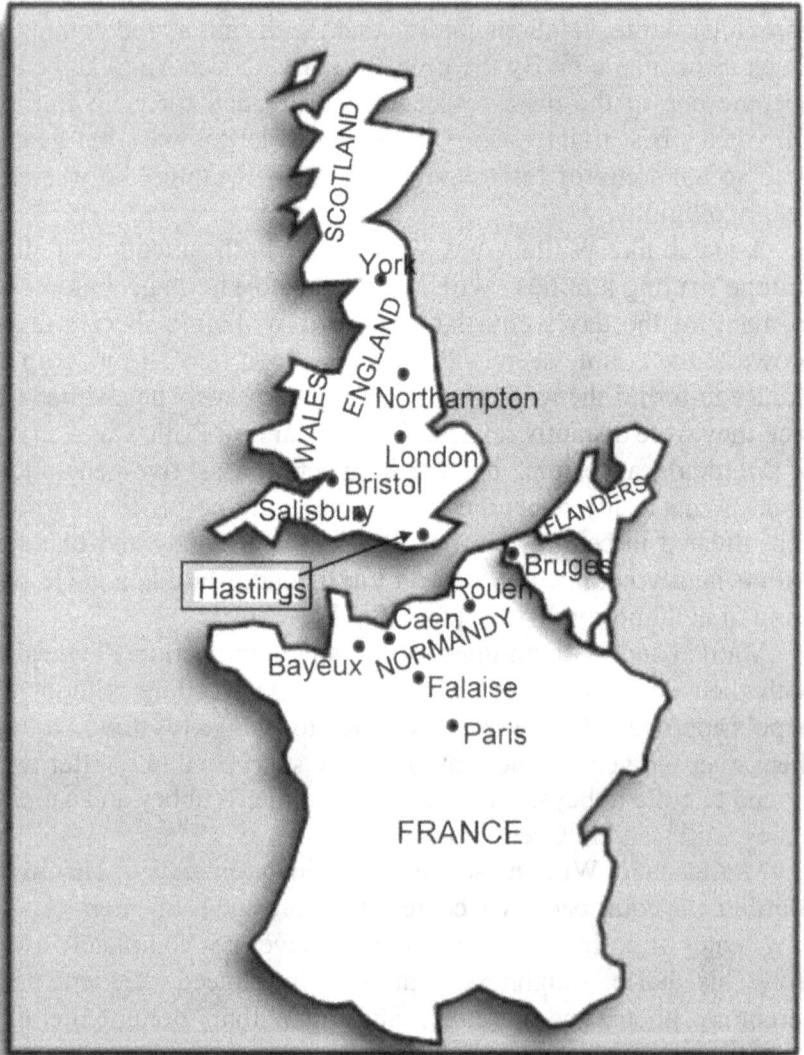

Map B – Medieval Britain and Normandy

patrons, and one chronicler noted that their court was surrounded with "illustrious men excellently versed and learned in letters."[6]

Whether wearing a simple robe, gathered at the waist by a belt and a cloak, or presenting herself glamorously in courtly apparel, Matilda took over the daily routines of court life. They ate breakfast in private each day, and then joined the rest of the court for "dinner" at about 11:00, and supper between 5:00 and 6:00. She made sure a large array of dishes was available for everyday meals. She also supervised great feasts, pageants, and representational occasions. Along the way, Matilda tempered her husband.

Matilda, Regent of Normandy

The year after Matilda and William were married, they were visited by an old acquaintance, Robert of Jumieges, the Archbishop of Canterbury in England. Years before, when Robert was an abbot in Normandy, he had first met the Anglo-Saxon Edward, then in exile from England. When Edward returned to England to be eventually crowned king and called "Edward the Confessor," he took Robert with him. Now, Edward the Confessor, the King of Anglo Saxons had sent his top churchman to convey an important message to William, another Norman he had known in Normandy and a relative, as well. Robert told William and Matilda that Edward had named William his heir to the English throne. Edward and his wife were childless and had no natural heir. William would be crowned King of England when Edward died.[7]

Time went by and fourteen years later, Anglo-Saxon Earl Harold Godwinson now knelt before William in Normandy. Harold's story is a little involved, or at least not totally agreed (see the footnote), but the gist of it was this: When Harold's ship blew off course, he shipwrecked onto a Norman beach and was taken captive by a Norman Lord. William rescued Harold, whether by force or ransom, and brought him to his court. There, Harold, head bowed before William, offered fealty to the Duke and said the purpose of his voyage was to re-confirm his aging brother-in-law Edward the

17

Confessor's promise that William would be his heir. This moment was later immortalized in a scene on the Bayeux Tapestry. In William's and Matilda's minds, they would be the next King and Queen of England.[8]

However, everything did not turn out quite that way. A few months later, after Harold returned to England, Edward the Confessor took mortally ill. While Edward lay on his deathbed streaming back and forth into consciousness, he said only a few words to the four people present before dying. Harold, one of them, came out and told everyone that Edward had designated himself as successor to the throne. Harold organized his own coronation for the next day. Whether Harold's claim was true was troublesome to many. But to William, the matter was clear. He saw Harold as an imposter, worse still one who was now stealing the English throne for himself only a few months after he had pledged loyalty to William. William lost little time in launching preparations to equip an army to cross the Channel and seize the crown he considered rightfully his.[9]

Matilda threw herself in full support of William's plans. She could not join the army's invasion, but she decided to make her own unique contribution. Gathering a force large enough to defeat a kingdom the size of England was an enormous undertaking. William's army would have to cross the Channel inside small vessels patterned after Viking ships. While he mustered soldiers and sailors, he had to build the craft to transport them. Matilda saw a role for herself: she decided to use some of her own personal fortune to construct the flagship from which William would command the invasion armada. She kept it secret, a surprise for him.

The Duchess summoned shipbuilders and carpenters to plan the construction of her ship. It would be the largest of the fleet, carrying more men than any other. Four-cornered sails, painted in red and yellow, would billow in the wind to propel it with the help of oarsmen. Matilda's planning was meticulous. She loaded the vessel with emblems to evidence the grandeur of a campaign led by one of Europe's most powerful rulers. She ordered builders to sculpt the figurehead of a golden child for the ship. The child's left hand held an ivory horn pressed to his lips. His forefinger gestured toward England. Since Matilda was expecting, the figure might also have suggested the newborn she knew was soon to arrive. Some, on the other hand, have thought the child figurehead meant to symbolize the birth of the Norman dynasty in England.

Matilda garnished the vessel with still more symbols. She ordered that the prow be ornamented with a lion's head signifying bravery and strength. Her faith and religion were evidenced with a banner that Pope Alexander II sent from Rome in support of the invasion. As the ship sailed toward England, the Pope's banner would stream in the wind above. She named her ship the *Mora* which meant "mansion" or "habitation. Some later historians, in fact, claim that "mora" was an anagram of "amor," *love*. Above all, it was a gesture of respect for her husband, a work of love.

How Matilda kept her ambitious project a secret from William is hard to know, but she did. The work continued unnoticed and untold, as other shipbuilding reached a climax. When it was finished, Matilda, surely bursting with pride and the anticipation, had the beautiful vessel sailed to William. When the *Mora* arrived during the summer of 1066, he was assembling his fleet at the mouth of the River Dives. William was overwhelmed. Full of excitement and thanks, he promised her the County of Kent, one of the richest in England, once he was King. He had a lot of work – and fighting – ahead of him before that happened. However, there were probably few doubts in his mind, or in Matilda's, that the moment would come. He had never lost a battle.

Meanwhile in every shipyard along the Norman coast, axes chopped, saws hummed, and hammers clanged as craftsmen worked with the know-how of their Viking ancestors to finish the fleet. Finally, a thousand boats were ready. Each had room for 15-20 oarsmen. Seamen began loading their cargos of knights, horses, archers, and infantry. The fleet carried about 8,000 soldiers, of which 2,000 were horsemen. Around 4,000 sailors were charged with getting the swift Norman boats across the Channel. Just before sunset, on September 28, 1066, the huge armada moved out to sea.

William stood on the *Mora* at the point of the vast formation, ready to claim the English throne.

Matilda made her way back to the palace in Rouen. Her husband had his work ahead, and she had hers. Before his departure, William had designated Matilda to be Regent of Normandy. In his absence, she would rule and manage all affairs of the duchy. This was hardly a routine caretaker role. After countless hard-fought battles of the past decades, William knew that the region in and around Normandy was a turbulent, unstable place where uprisings and invasions were common. The prospect of losing Normandy while attempting to take England was hardly a remote one. There was also the possibility he might never return from the war. William trusted Matilda, not just as a spouse and confidant, but as a leader capable of managing his duchy over the months or years he might be away. This was a highly unorthodox decision on William's part. Although it was not unknown, women in that day and place were seldom given the responsibility to rule principalities.

As regent, Matilda had the power to make laws, oversee justice, levy taxes, and even mint money. William knew that in his absence, Matilda, a small woman, pregnant, and only in her mid-thirties, could be vulnerable to insubordination, if not insurrection. To bolster her position, he called a great council sometime before his departure. Standing before the grand gathering, he obliged his chief magnates to swear allegiance to her regency. William then assigned his three most trusted counselors as her advisors. He made it clear, however, that Matilda held the reins. She could accept or ignore their advice.

As the Regent of Normandy, Matilda was shrewd and effective, and the duchy was firmly under her control. Normandy in fact, was more stable under Matilda than it had been for years. She traveled from city to city where she held court grandly. She won the respect of nearly everyone. William of Poitiers, a contemporary commentator, praised her wisdom, adding that Normandy's "government had been carried on smoothly by our lady Matilda."[10]

Matilda's brilliance as regent earned William's keen admiration. For years afterwards, he continued to grant Matilda full powers during his many absences to England. Even when he was in Normandy, William had her at his side. Her name is signed next to his on an exceptionally large number of the charters where he transferred property and estates, or granted lands to subjects. It appears on 20 of the 21 officially registered acts concerning the Caen abbeys, and her seal is on 30 of the 151 acts William issued.[11]

Over the days and weeks after the flotilla set to sea, Matilda anxiously awaited news of William's landing and what was happening in England. As military families even today know, an aura of both hope and fear surrounds news from the front. One afternoon she went to the Benedictine priory of Notre Dame du Pre to pray that William was safe, and the campaign, successful. She was in a small chapel on the banks of the Seine near Rouen when a courier arrived bringing news. Soon after reaching England, the messenger reported, William's force clashed head-on with the Anglo-Saxon army under King Harold at a place called Hastings. Harold had been killed, shot with an arrow in the eye. Harold and the Anglo Saxon army was utterly defeated.

In her joy and excitement. Matilda proclaimed that henceforth the priory where she was praying would be called Notre Dame de Bonnes Nouvelles ("Our Lady of Good News"). She then made generous and well publicized bequests as a way of thanking God for William's success. One from her times described her exuberance and generosity: "The alms which this princess daily distributed with such zeal brought more succor than I can express to her husband, struggling on the field of battle."[12]

Matilda, Queen of England

William's defeat of Harold at Hastings hardly guaranteed his place as England's new ruler. He had to consolidate his rule during the years of uprisings and revolts that followed. Back and forth between Normandy and England he rushed, from one conflict and battle to another. He wisely understood that he needed more than battlefield victories to strengthen the Norman monarchy among his new Anglo-Saxon subjects.

One means of doing this, he thought, would be to establish Matilda's position as England's new queen. In the beginning of 1068, the time was right, and William brought Matilda to England for a magnificent coronation ceremony. They lived in London for a few months while they organized the event. It was her first time in England, and she was anxious to get a sense of the country and people she had always heard about. For the English, it was the first time a coronation was staged for just a queen.

In May, everything was ready. William and Matilda planned the celebration on the Day of Pentecost to represent symbolically the connection between heaven and earth. They wanted the ceremony to emphasize the divine appointment of Kings and Queens to rule their earthly peoples. On the day of the coronation, William escorted Matilda in a royal entourage to Westminster where with pageantry and fanfare they entered the grand Abbey. Matilda regally marched down the aisle where she knelt and was anointed with holy oil. In an emblematic moment, William placed a ring on her finger. It symbolized marriage to her kingdom, and her husband and king. In great ceremony, the Archbishop of York placed a crown upon her head: Matilda, 36 years old, Queen of England.

The Anglo-Saxons had never seen anything like it. It was a moment of splendor and awe contrasting so powerfully with the bloody battles fought on the fields of England over the previous two years. The new kingdom's nobility, Norman and English alike, joined in a marvelous banquet that followed the coronation. When all were seated, a "champion" unexpectedly rode fully armored on his battle steed into the hall and declared, "If any person denies that our most gracious sovereign, lord William, and his spouse Matilda, are not king and queen of England, he is a false-hearted traitor and liar; and here I, as champion, do challenge him to single combat."

No one, of course, rose to the challenge. How could they? Present were certainly some, perhaps many, who disputed Norman rule. But the audacity and astonishment of the moment eclipsed any will to oppose England's imposing new King and Queen. That was exactly what William meant to accomplish. Not even his own coronation two years earlier had been on this scale. The "champion" episode was part of Norman tradition. None of the English had experienced it before.

Matilda's spirits were high. William was pleased: "...since if God granted him this honor, he wished for his wife to be crowned with him," wrote the chronicler William of Jumieges. He expressed his pleasure royally. Before the conquest of England, William had promised Kent to Matilda, but instead gave her estates in Buckinghamshire, Surrey, Hampshire, Wiltshire, Gloucestershire, Dorset, Devon, and Cornwall, perhaps one fourth of the lands he had to disperse. She was the richest woman in England.[13]

When she was not consorting with William as Queen of England or governing Normandy in his absence, Matilda was raising a family. She and William were fruitful, and although no one knows for sure, Matilda gave birth to at least ten children. This strong woman was expecting her sixth when William left her regent of Normandy during his conquest of the English throne. The first three were boys: Robert, Richard, and William Rufus. She was expecting again at her coronation, and a few months later gave birth to their fourth son, Henry, in York before she returned to Normandy.[14]

Matilda, a Mother

It is a rare couple that never encounters dissension. That was true in William's and Matilda's marriage, as well. Discord in the medieval royal household was dangerous. In a world of absolute monarchs, marital differences sometimes blew up into state affairs that resulted in more than just a separation. Take, for example, King Henry VIII's brutality when he fell out with his wives.

At one point, a dispute between William and Matilda erupted and smoldered for some time afterwards. William's deep affection for Matilda was probably the only reason things did not end tragically. Underneath his tough surface, William was more compassionate than some thought, at least toward Matilda.

At the center of the dispute was Matilda's and William's oldest son, Robert. Seventeen years old, having grown into adolescence with the pampering of one of Europe's most powerful courts, Robert was the designated heir to the Duchy of Normandy. Matilda had a special attachment to Robert from the time he was born. He was her first-born son, and by all accounts, also her favorite. As only a mother might, she indulged Robert's many faults in character and behavior. William, on the other hand, overlooked none of them. He despised Robert for his weaknesses, debauchery, and vices, and William did not shield these feelings from the public.

It is difficult for us today to dissect a mother's love and a father's rejection, as well as all the reasons that led to Robert's character flaws, especially from our roadside viewpoint 1,000 years later. What is important, however, is that these emotions churned round and round, bouncing off each other, until they conjured serious issues in William's and Matilda's relationship. One can easily imagine the damage such a clash of affections might breed in a modern family. In a royal household, especially in William's and Matilda's times, the consequences were potentially catastrophic. William liked getting his own way, loyalty was paramount, and the definition of treason was wide and inclusive.

Robert, full of the hot blood of youth, demanded that his father install him now as ruler of Normandy. William had England to govern, he argued, and it was not too early for Robert to take responsibility for Normandy. "I ask you therefore to grant me legal control of the duchy, so that, just as you rule over the kingdom of England, I, under you, may rule over the duchy of Normandy."[15] William considered his son's demands ludicrous. In a rage, he derisively bellowed a flat refusal that drove Robert from court.

Over the next several years, the conflict between Robert and William fumed and flamed. Robert was often in exile plotting revenge, or in actual rebellion, attacking his father's Norman strongholds. He and his friends sought and readily made alliances with William's enemies. Robert's acts were treasonous, and William fought him with contempt. Matilda was in the middle. Seeing her favorite son estranged, sometimes impoverished, and ever embattled, spawned deep maternal anguish.

Eventually, her grief evolved into material support. To relieve Robert's travails, Matilda secretly provided him gold, silver, and provisions. As she did so, her sympathy and protection transformed

24

into a greater and more serious matter. Sometimes Robert used the money just to survive, but at other times it funded soldiers to attack William's men and castles. William, if he learned what Matilda was doing, would also consider her efforts on Robert's behalf treasonable, although that was not what she intended.

But it was only a matter of time before William did find out about Matilda's support for their son's rebellion. He was livid. If he had been Henry VIII, she might have been tried and executed. Not just Henry, but many kings in one way or another would have punished a wife engaged in something bordering treason. Despite the ruthlessness he sometimes showed his enemies, however, William was not Henry VIII. As the chroniclers described his reaction, William "...in a passion, [ordered Matilda] never to do such a thing again."[16] If Matilda agreed to William's demands, her compliance was short lived. Not long after she was again caught assisting her son.

William was beside himself. He brought her before the court and publicly berated her. "A faithless wife," he fumed, "brings ruin to the state. After this who in this world shall ever find himself a trustworthy helpmate? The wife of my bosom, whom I love as my own soul, whom I have set over the whole kingdom, and entrusted with all authority and riches, this wife, I say, supports the enemies who plot against my life, enriches them with my money, zealously arms and succors and strengthens them to my grave peril."

Matilda was torn with grief and knelt at William's feet to proffer a request for forgiveness. "O my lord," she sobbed, "do not wonder that I love my first-born child with tender affection. By the power of the Most High, if my son Robert were dead and buried seven feet deep in the earth, ...and I could bring him back in life with my own blood, I would shed my life blood for him and suffer more anguish for his sake than, weak woman that I am, I dare to promise. How do you imagine that I can find any joy in possessing great wealth if I allow my son to be burdened by dire poverty? May I never be guilty of such hardness of heart; all your power gives you no right to demand this of me."[17]

Despite her eloquence and penitent demeanor, Matilda's words were not exactly repentance. She told William that she was acting as a mother, and he should not blame her for that. Nor did he have the right to do so. William burst into a rage. But he let it go at that. Again, he levied no punishments against Matilda.

William's and Robert's feud continued, and one can only imagine a mother's despair during those years. At one point, it led to a battle between William's and Robert's forces that continued until at some point William and Robert faced off against each other armored and in hand-to-hand combat. William was struck in one arm and wounded. According to tradition, only then did Robert realize that the helmeted warrior he fought was his father. It is hard, however, to believe that neither knew whom they were fighting. Robert stepped back, and William withdrew. It was his first defeat.

Matilda persisted in her efforts to persuade William to reach an accommodation with his son. It took time, but she finally succeeded in getting through her strong husband's obstinate will and often impenetrable crust. In April 1080, Robert arrived at the ducal palace in Rouen for a grand reconciliation. William grudgingly forgave his son and reinstated him as heir to the Duchy of Normandy. It was functional but not a "happy ever after" ending. William never changed his feelings about Robert.

It is difficult to say how much damage the affair did to William's and Matilda's relationship, but it seems to not have been long-lasting. All three of them, Matilda, William, and Robert, traveled together later that year to England. During their stay, Scotland's Queen Margaret invited Matilda and Robert to Scotland to be godparents to her newborn daughter, Edith. The two countries had been at war on and off since William's conquest of England, and the invitation was welcome. Matilda and Robert journeyed to the Scottish court and were present at Edith's baptism. According to tradition, when Matilda peered down at the baby, the infant reached up and grabbed her veil and tried to pull Matilda toward her. The same tradition claims this was taken as an omen. In fact, baby Edith would one day marry Matilda's young son Henry. When they wed,

Edith took Matilda's name and with him reigned as King Henry I and Queen Matilda of England.

Matilda was hardly 50 when three years after her trip to England and Scotland she fell into a downward spiraling illness. She was in Normandy and knew her health was waning. As the end approached, she wrote a will and left most of her possessions, including her crown, scepter, and royal ornaments, to the abbey she had built in Caen many years before. Matilda continued to weaken, and finally the end drew near. On November 2, 1083, she confessed her sins with tears and passed away.

William was with her the entire time, absolutely consumed with grief. It was said that he wept for days on her passing. She was not very old, but life, even for a queen, was not always easy, and her many childbirths undoubtedly would have borne heavily on anyone in that time and age. With beloved Matilda's passing, all of Normandy fell deeply into mourning. The poet Fulcoius lamented her loss:

> If she could be brought back from death through
>   tears,
> Money, fair or foul means, then rest assured
> There would be an abundance of these things...
> O twofold light of November, it is a little plot,
> A small pile of ash, but nevertheless a source of
>   glory and grace.[18]

Matilda's body was taken to the abbey she had built, La Trinite. William arranged a splendid funeral that lasted two days, and then she was buried. Her tomb's black marble plaque still graces the abbey today. The epitaph engraved on the marble in gold is a reflection on her kindness that all would miss:

> ...She gave this site and raised this noble house,
> With many lands and many goods endowed,
> Given by her, or by her toil procured;
> Comforter of the need, duty's friend;
> Her wealth enriched the poor, left her in need.
> At daybreak on November's second day

27

She won her share of everlasting joy.[19]

William never got over the loss of his soul mate Matilda. For the remaining four years of his life he suffered grief, torment, and depression. He never associated with nor married another woman. Without Matilda's tempering influence, however, it is said that he ruled with tyranny.

When William died, their son Robert became the Duke of Normandy. Their third son assumed the crown of England as William II, and when he died in a hunting accident shortly thereafter, William's and Matilda's fourth son, Henry, was crowned Henry I. Their second son, Richard, had died before his parents.

Matilda was wife to one of the most powerful dukes in Europe and to a King of England. More than just a spouse, however, she stood alongside him and ruled effectively in his absence. She was mother to two other Kings of England. Equally important, she left behind a long list of her own accomplishments and refinements at the birth of England's most important dynasty. As I learned of this great matriarch, I had to agree with her biographer. Matilda of Flanders was the most remarkable woman of her time.[20]

Relying on Secondary Sources

From the beginning of my search for family stories, medieval Britain beckoned. So many of my ancestral lines found their source waters there. From childhood, I had heard the names of some of those medieval families. Medieval England, however, was not a destination I was anxious to reach. The period was more foreign to me than many others from the past. I had a degree in history, but my interests then and afterwards were always modern Europe and Western America, not medieval Europe. Still, my medieval family incessantly called, and I knew that some of the more colorful stories I sought would only be found in that far off terrain. It required a lot of reading, and I soon had a bookshelf full of books on the three centuries between William I and King Edward III.

Any family search requires a mixture of primary and secondary sources. Primary sources, of course, **are a family researcher's holy grail**, the more of them, usually, the more reliable our research is apt to be. However, when searching a period this many centuries ago we are often lucky to find even sufficient secondary sources. In the scarcity of primary sources, the farther back we go, the more we must rely on secondary. For most family researchers tracking Medieval ancestors, there is little we can do other that recognize secondary sources are less reliable, but we are lucky when we find them. This was all the more so **in Matilda's times** when the few contemporary writers we know today usually wrote their accounts in Latin or French. I spoke four languages, but no French nor Latin.

Details of Matilda's life have always been sketchy at best. There is a lot on William and many more on his times. Searching Amazon.com, I finally discovered one by Tracy Borman (Queen of the Conqueror, The Life of Matilda, Wife of William I) that was scholarly written, thorough and well researched. Borman extensively **quoted chroniclers from Matilda's own times**, in English. I found these quotes useful for describing events through the mouths of those who lived then or not long after Matilda.

On-site Visits

It is not always necessary to make on-site visits when seeking family stories. So many of mine I found behind my computer, or through interviews with living family members. Later I will relate how. But when it is possible, an on-site visit can transport you back to places where some of some of these stories took place. There you can envision their lives in a unique way.

I eventually made four trips to Great Britain in search of distant ancestors. The path to Normandy began one rainy September morning in Concord, Massachusetts, where I was tracking the exploits of family members on the first day of the American Revolution (See Chapter 5). Seija stayed in the car while, umbrella in hand, I joined a tour of the North Bridge where the first shots in Concord were fired. When I ran back to get out of the downpour, I found her talking with our son, Mika, who had called from

Switzerland. Mika said that he and his wife, Rachel, were planning our visit to Geneva a few weeks later and asked if we would like to travel with them to sightsee Normandy. It sounded exciting. Seija and I had never been there. Mika knew that the Greenes, another family I was researching, were Normans, and asked if I could find a Norman castle where one of our ancestors might have once lived. He said his four small boys would be ecstatic.

Histories of the Greene family claim that they were Normans who came with William and changed their name to Greene in England. I assumed they might have had a castle in Normandy 1,000 years ago. A lot can happen to a castle over a millennium, I realized, and there were probably few left today that were built ten centuries ago. Mother's genealogy only took the Greene line back to Sir Henry Greene of the 14th century. But one day in the British Library, I had found Sir Henry's ancestors (more about that later), and when I got home from Concord, I started moving back generation-by-generation in search of a castle we could visit.

An afternoon spent traveling the internet and combing through my notes from the British Library in London revealed that I was not likely to find a castle in Normandy where some Greenes had lived. I also knew, however, that I had lines descending from Henry I, son of William and Matilda. This was my first glimpse of far-back Matilda. I wanted to know more about her, and the more I learned, the more her stories intrigued me. I also had a castle to visit. In Normandy, there are still castles where William and Matilda once stayed.

A month later, we all were exploring the splendid Norman castle in Falaise where William was born in 1027. It his lifetime, the castle was much less undeveloped than today. After his death, his son Henry almost totally rebuilt it into the massive structure you find there now. The castle's keep survived one of World War II's greatest killing fields in and around Falaise where the allies finally defeated German resistance to the Normandy landing. Post-war repairs and renovations brought back its austere splendor. With wooden swords, shields and touched imaginations, our grandsons fought their way across the castle yard toward the keep.

Inside the keep, modern technology brought the ancient castle to life. They gave us IPads when we entered. Pointing them toward any wall, floor, or ceiling, the screens portrayed what those stone surfaces probably looked like during the castle's days of medieval splendor. As we moved the view around the room, everything was adorned with rugs, tapestries, and other furnishings like those our ancestors used to decorate them. Our imaginations slipped back 1,000 years. Even four-year old Joshua was absorbed by this castle and the images he found by pointing his IPad in different directions.

All three generations of us stretched across the 40 or so generations to catch sight of how some of our family lived then. Near the top of the tower, we peered over the old stone window ledges. The fields spanned Normandy; the towns, castles and churches, and the Channel waters separating Normandy from England had their stories to tell.

When we saw the Bayeux Tapestry in the nearby town of Bayeux, there was no end to the stories. Although called a tapestry, it was actually an embroidery, about 2 ½ feet high and over 200 feet long, and 1,000 years old. The massive work hung in a lighted showcase that curved along the wall of a long dark corridor in the Tapestry Museum. From one end to the other were the stories of William's conquest of England, embroidered in bright colors on a plain linen background by women living in William's and Matilda's day. We sauntered slowly past each scene alongside people from everywhere who, equally awed, spoke only in low tones. Warriors wearing helmets and mail shirts, horses galloping and charging, ships being built and sailing the sea, hunts, battles, castles and so on composed the extended visual record of this pivotal moment in not just the history of Britain but of the Western World.

At the time of its manufacture, no one who saw the Bayeux Tapestry had to be literate to capture the Conquest with all its vivid details. The work was made for the people of their times to learn these stories, as well as for us, too, in ours. For centuries, it was thought that Matilda, who was an embroiderer, sewed this monumental work with her court ladies. Today, it is well accepted that it was done by a group of talented women working across the Channel in Canterbury, just a few years after the Norman victory.

Not far along from the Tapestry's first scene, we saw the *Mora*, the ship Matilda had built for William to use on the fateful day his armada pulled to sea from Normandy. Just before the departure sequence, the Tapestry had an image of Earl Harold Godwinson, Anglo-Saxon King Edward the Confessor's brother-in-law. Harold is kneeling before William, about a year before William embarked on the *Mora*.

Their Times were Not Our Times

When I began searching for stories about Matilda, the medieval account of how William's and Matilda's engagement was the first one I came across. When I read it, I was both shocked and amused. It had all the makings of a fairy tale: the beautiful damsel, the brave prince or knight, some violence we do not easily understand, the couple falling in love, a magnificent wedding, and a happy-ever-after ending. When I related it to our son Markus's family, their 9-year son and 7-year old daughter followed every word. At the end, Markus quickly added that we do not believe such things are right. *"Men don't beat women,"* he said. He was right, and I was glad he said it emphatically for two pairs of small ears to hear.

I had two questions about this family story. First of all, was it true? And then, what do we make of it? In seeking an answer to the first, I learned that we do not know about the tale's authenticity. It has been told for 800 years, and that is a long time. However, the three chronicles where it first emerged were written 200 years after it might have happened, and that is a long time, too, especially in days when written histories were few and far between.

On the other hand, the fact that no one has disproved it during these 800 years makes it difficult to discount out of hand. After all, just because tales and legends have no documented proof does not necessarily make them false. Homer's story of the Battle of Troy was told thousands of years before archeologists in the late 19th century made findings that suggested the battle actually took place, although perhaps not with all of Homer's details and intrigues.

In pursuit of my stories, I saw early on a spectrum with "facts" on one side and "legends" on the other. As we peer through the dark spyglass of time, the line extending between the spectrum's polar ends often runs ever so hazily. Sometimes "legends" resurface as history when findings, such as Schliemann's discovery of Troy, provide proof that mythological events actually occurred. On the other hand, "historical facts" are often disproven, not just because new information emerges, but because explorers with different perspectives arrive to interpret the events. As one historian once put it, "...facts do not compel us to believe one way or the other because the understanding of those facts will inevitably change."[21]

In family history, even something as clear cut as a parent-child relationship recorded in contemporaneous records may not always be accurate. Not long ago, orphaned children were adopted and raised by neighboring families. Census records might show them as children of the adopting family. Illegitimate births can also easily mask the true heritage of a child listed in the records. I quickly learned that collecting stories of our past is not an exact science. What appears as reality may not always be as definitive as we think.

In this case, there are enough details recorded at the time of William's and Matilda's match and marriage to venture the basic outline: William's desire to marry a well-pedigreed wife, Matilda's beauty and character, William's coarse and aggressive nature, and their subsequent complementary and happy marriage. But what about his beating her, and her changing her opinion so profoundly about him? In our age, this may seem strange.

Something worth keeping in mind as we travel in search of family stories, is that their times were not our times. Yes, people were human and knew joy and sorrow, success and failure, love and hate, just like we see around us today. Their value structures were often different, however, and their priorities often diverge from our own. The way they experienced pain may have been different. Their faith in God and an afterlife was often stronger.

For example, until recently, people lived with death more intimately than we do. For them, the impact of a tragedy might often have been different from what it might be to us. A family could have

33

ten children and lose several of them to an epidemic within a week or so of each other. I tell later the story about a family that lost their mother and two sisters while crossing the American Plains. How they found the strength for normal and happy lives afterwards, as they evidently did, was hard for me to grasp. In fact, many things in the past are hard to understand with today's values as our reference points: public violence, corporal and capital punishment, social and gender roles, and how one's inherited, but stagnant, position in society was taken for granted. The idea of social mobility to many of them was foreign.

It is easy for us to feel enlightened, and somehow morally superior to our family members who lived in the past. Many of them, however, might have felt exactly the same way about us if they had had a chance to see our day. They might, for example, easily scorn our secularism, the widespread devaluation of religion in our society, and many other common modern values. It is thought-provoking to list things we accept in our day as common and normal that they, in theirs, would find objectionable.

Historians often compare a journey back through history to a trip to an exotic foreign land. "The past is a foreign country: they do things differently there," as one writer put it.[22] Decades of traveling to and living in foreign countries taught me that people in different places often enjoy their culture and traditions just as much as I do in my own country, however different theirs are from mine. Travelers hoping to be welcome and to get the most from their visit must be respectful of the customs of their hosts. This is just as important when traveling to the foreign times of the past. If it is not my way, it is not necessarily the wrong way, it is just different, however hard that may be to understand.

If William did beat and throw Matilda to the ground in an angry act of vengeance, that is something we cannot accept in our times. That Matilda would reverse her view of William after such treatment is nearly impossible for us to believe, something almost humorous. People living 1,000 years ago, however, might not have related to the story like we do. To them, it might have told of how a stricken and embarrassed man expressed his anger, and how a tough, head-

strong woman found his actions full of courage, and even respectable.

Our Grandmothers' Stories

The more I got into the lives of Matilda and William, the medieval Greene family (whose stories begin in the next chapter), and other grandparents of the era, the more comfortable I came to be in this exotic, though often opaque, era. As hard as it was to find details, traveling medieval times was as enchanting and rewarding as visiting any distant country. I was especially pleased to find Matilda, a woman whose life was filled with extraordinary deeds that were still discoverable. It was unfortunate, though, that finding her was possible mainly because of her husband's fame. Modern histories of the Norman Conquest – ones you would think should be more gender sensitive and complete – often cast Matilda as one of the "extras" while they spend considerably more time and pages pulling some of William's male collaborators to center stage.

Getting deeper into my search for family narrative, one of my greatest frustrations was how difficult it was to find my grandmothers' stories. It seems that the past's male bias still too often prevails. You can find a great number of personal histories of the males who populate the trees of Ancestry and FamilySearch, but not nearly enough of their spouses and mothers.

When tracking one's family, an assumption that your male lineage is superior to your female ancestry occasionally surfaces. Often, people feel closer to those ancestors whose last name they share – but if you are talking about the same last name, you are talking about paternal lines. Of course, the idea is faulty and illogical. If I am a descendant of Sir Henry Greene, and my last name is "Greene," I am no more nor less a part of the Greene family than if my last name is Smith through a maternal connection. Even in the "foreign lands" of the past, it took a father and a mother to produce new generations. Mothers and grandmothers are just as important and direct in our lineage as fathers and grandfathers. Yet these mothers and grandmothers often disappear in the search for the family story, often forgotten in the records and research.

35

It was a "mother" who got me started on the quest for family stories, but that is not why I felt a need to trace the female narratives. Having six grandmothers when I was young (I will explain that later) in no small way influenced how I thought about my maternal legacy. The six grandmothers, consciously or not, **made sure I wanted to learn as much as possible about the women's** *paths that brought me here. I resolved that the first set of stories I would relate would be of a grandmother many generations back. One of my last sets of stories is also about a Matilda, one I knew.*

Circles in History

Earlier that day we discovered the Tapestry in Bayeux, we paid a visit to the beaches of Normandy. The sand and cliffs were only about a 20 minutes' drive from the medieval town's center, its churches, and museums. Here, above the spot where the allies made their determined landing in 1944, our four grandsons climbed into and on top the huge bunkers that once housed the Germans' big guns. Their parents, Seija, and I stood looking over the cliffs of Pointe du Hok at the stretching landing areas, Utah Beach on one side and Omaha Beach, on the other.

Behind us, a vast military cemetery holding those who did not survive the heroic assault spread almost endlessly. Its white markers, in carefully aligned horizontal and diagonal rows, memorialized their final resting places. People quietly strolled along the cemetery's paths. Their imaginations, probably like ours, drifted from cross to cross wondering about the stories behind those who had sacrificed their everything on the beaches below us. Looking out to sea, we followed the waves rolling onto the shore. In my mind, I could see the thousands of allied ships that approached Normandy from across the English Channel that June morning, their cargoes primed for invasion.

A similar vision returned a few hours later in Bayeux where the Tapestry's hundreds of embroidered images told the story of the Conquest. My mind once again saw multitudes of ships moving out to sea. Then, with their square sails high and oarsmen straining, their holds full of men, horses, armor, and weapons, they launched across the Channel in the opposite direction. It happened nearly a millennium before what I had imagined earlier in the day.

The American, British, Canadian, and other allied soldiers, heavy backpacks on their shoulders, rifles in their hands, stormed the Normandy beaches. William's thousands of Normans carrying spears, swords, and bows, mounted their ships. My imagination continued to drift: how many of those who landed on the D-Day beaches had forefathers who sallied from those same shores in 1066 toward England, with William in his fine flagship "Mora" at the front?

How curious a thing, the flow of history? D-Day and the Conquest were both critical moments in the history of civilization, and in the stories of all the generations that followed. Yet they flowed in opposite directions, in a round. William departed from here. One thousand years later, his descendants returned. There are circles and loops in the tide of history, and, as I often found, in people's lives, as well.

Chapter 2

Two Knights and a Swordsman
Sir Henry Greene (Sr.), Sir Henry Greene (Jr.), and John Greene

*"I am amazed that Grene makes himself
out to know everything in the world, and
he is only a young man."*
John Stonor
Chief Justice, the King's Bench (1345)

*Among William the Conqueror's fellow Norman invaders and
their descendants was a family that took the surname Greene. By
the 14th century, members of the Greene family had reached a
station of prominence in medieval England. I knew from Mother's
work that these Greene grandfathers and grandmothers were
notable strands in our family's ancient past. The Greenes about
whom I heard so much as I grew up were on my mind from the
beginning of my pursuit of family stories.*

Chief Justice of the King's Bench

Henry Greene thrived in the rousing times of the Late Middle
Ages, days of chivalry, jousts, damsels, etiquette, art, and
architecture. It was 14th century England with civil wars, battles,
sieges, tournaments, formidable castles and beautiful palaces,
outlaws, and Britain's ascent to becoming one of the foremost
military powers in Europe. Henry's family had lived in Boughton
(or, Buckton), Northamptonshire, for over 100 years (see Map B).
The Greene family, or "de Boketons" as they were earlier known,
had produced a long line of knights.[1]

His was a privileged childhood. His father, Sir Thomas Greene,
was the High Sheriff of Northampton, a position in those times
"esteemed equal even to the care of Princes," the Earl of
Peterborough noted in his masterwork family history.[2] As High
Sheriff, Sir Thomas was the King's representative in the county. In
wartime, he mustered fighting men and raised funds to support the

King. He could arrest and imprison people and send some of them in chains to London. As the title "Sir" indicates, Sir Thomas was a knight, a non-hereditary title bestowed by the King for life only. Generation after generation of Greenes had been knights, evidencing continued loyalty and exemplary service. Sir Thomas also served in Parliament under Kings Edward II and Edward III. There, he joined with noblemen, prelates, and other representatives of England's shires and boroughs to pass and confirm laws as well as act as the highest court of the land. Thomas was still a young man when his wife, Lady Lucy de la Zouche, gave birth to Henry in 1310.[3]

The family was well-known in Northampton. They were not nobility, though many of their near ancestors were. Henry's mother, Lucy, was from the noble Zouche family who were important in Normandy even before William's conquest of England. On his father's side, too, were noble families. Ten generations back, King William and Queen Matilda, themselves, were among Thomas's far grandparents. Over the generations, the Greenes had been one of those knightly English families who, through careful intermarriages with the younger sons and daughters of noble families, reached their ancestry into the Great Barons of England. During the centuries that followed, their heirs linked large numbers of lower Gentry to England's old royalty. In turn, these descendants bestowed royal lineage to masses of their own descendants, including many in America, my own included.[4]

Henry's childhood drifts back and forth through the foggy spots of time where it is often hard to find many details. However, in his days, sons of knights at the age of seven were normally sent for education and training to another knight's family, usually the home of an uncle on their mother's side. Seven-year old Henry might well have moved to one of his uncles' or relatives' estates to get his education. Training varied from place to place, but a knight was foremost a warrior in Henry's times, and much of a future knight's education was spent learning weapons and how to sword fight, ride, and joust.

Sons and daughters from a prominent family often had their own private tutors as well. That was probably Henry's case. He was a smart and confident boy with talent and potential. When he was 14 years old, his father was elected for the first time to Parliament in about 1324. We can imagine him sometimes traveling with his father to London where Sir Thomas would take his seat in the highest council of the land.

It was not long before Henry was living in London permanently, studying to become a lawyer in the company of some of London's most prominent attorneys. Perhaps law was Henry's aspiration, but more likely his father recognized his intellectual talent and set him on this track. However it was, it was a big departure from managing the family estates, something that tasked generations of Henry's forefathers.[5]

By the time he was 21, Henry was already a promising young attorney who attracted the attention of many around him. A few years later, he appeared as "counsel in the bench," where he represented clients. Henry was precocious on a spiral to the top of the legal world. He was also cocky, and evidently annoying to some. Once, England's Chief Justice took a shot at him for his brashness, "I am amazed that Grene makes himself out to know everything in the world, and he is only a young man."[6]

Henry may have rubbed the Chief Justice wrong, but he was gaining a reputation for his legal skills. Among others, the Royal Family noticed him. In 1345, he was appointed "King's Serjeant-in-Law." The King's Serjeant-in-Law was a member of an elite order of barristers who acted as prosecutors in criminal cases and representatives of the Crown in civil ones. At one point, King Edward III's mother, Queen Isabella, brought Henry into her service. The King and his mother had gone through difficult times when her consort, Roger Mortimer, tried to steal the reins of power from young King Edward. Edward eventually forgave her for her role in that (after he had executed Mortimer). Now she was in her early 50's, and she and King Edward were close. Perhaps Isabella brought Henry to the King's attention.

Henry served Isabella well, and she was generous in expressing her gratitude by granting him a manor estate at Brigstock (Northamptonshire). Her grandson and the King's eldest son, Crown Prince Edward, also hired Henry and put him on an annual retainer to sit on his council. Edward was a popular prince and commander of King Edward's knights and footmen. He is known in history as the Black Prince, perhaps because of the black armor he wore and the black background on his coat of arms. Henry now represented the Black Prince whenever a legal matter arose, and cocky, or not, he was on a roll.

These were heady days in the reign of England's great King Edward III. Edward was not just another medieval king. He wanted to become England's "perfect king," and when he reached his prime, many truly thought him England's greatest king. While Henry Greene's reputation was spreading through London, Edward III was at the apex of his Age, and England, itself, was on the ascent. Edward introduced new arms, ideas, and strategies based on the careful deployment and use of long bowsmen. Time after time, his outnumbered army decimated the French in France. He introduced arts and architecture. One of his many construction projects turned Windsor Castle into the most splendid residential castle in Europe. And he remodeled Parliament to make it into a functioning and effective legislative body, divided into a House of Lords and House of Commons that met regularly.[7]

Edward III brilliantly led the way with new movements and innovations that changed much of Henry Greene's world. Time, for example. In a day when many had difficulty seeing the value of a new invention called the "clock," Edward grasped how important it was to standardize time measurements. When Henry was young there were sundials, but no clocks. The day was divided into 12 hours of daytime and 12 hours of nighttime. Since daytime began at sunup and the length of daylight varied between winter and summer, at different seasons of the year one daytime hour might be twice as long as a nighttime hour, and vice versa. By the time Henry reached full adulthood, his and everyone's lives were beginning to be calculated in standardized days, hours, and seconds. A tower

41

went up above the palace at Westminster, and the first Big Ben gave all of London a keener sense of time.

Edward was also changing the language people spoke. William the Conqueror and subsequent generations of Norman rulers all spoke French.   Henry Greene's family was French speaking, whereas common people conversed in the English inherited from their Anglo-Saxon ancestors. Not everyone of Henry's class spoke English, even as a second language. Edward III, however, was an admirer of the use of English, and under him, the upper stratum of society began to change over en masse to English. By the time Henry's children were being schooled they were probably being taught in English. While Henry was on the bench, Edward issued a decree that pleas could be made in English, the "tongue of the nation." From then on, Henry heard arguments in either language.

At the opening of Parliament in 1351 Edward said, "We desire always to do right to our people and to correct wrongs and defaults wherever they may be found in our realm." In Edward's view, the rule of law should guarantee justice to every subject. He was also determined to stamp out corruption in his court, and proclaimed that corrupt officials found guilty would be executed. When a case of corruption came out against Chief Justice William Thorp, Edward had him arrested and tried. Thorp was found guilty, but Edward showed mercy, and he narrowly escaped an early death.   That Edward noticed and was ready to take Henry Greene into his service at the highest levels, shows the esteem Henry enjoyed in perhaps the greatest royal court of his time.

While Henry Greene's prominence grew, he started a family. His bride, Catherine Drayton, was also from another well-known Northampton family. They had changed their surname to Drayton from De Vere, an aristocratic Norman family going back to William the Conqueror's time. Seven generations back, her grandfather, Aubrey de Vere, had been Great Chamberlain to Henry I, a ranking position that, among other things, oversaw the King's court. Aubrey was also the first Chief Justice of England. Henry and Catherine had five children, two daughters and three sons. They named their oldest son Thomas, after Henry's father, the second son, Henry, after his own father, and their third son, Nicholas, after Henry's half-brother. Catherine brought with her a grand estate in Drayton, not many miles from Boughton. [8]

Henry added more to his estates by purchasing the Northamptonshire village of Norton (today's Greene's Norton) where generations of his and Catherine's descendants were to be born. One of them was one of England's most fascinating and remarkable women: Queen Katherine Parr, Henry VIII's last wife, the only one not divorced or executed. About the same time, Henry Greene was granted right to start a fair in his hometown of Boughton. The Boughton Fair became one of England's finest and grandest. [9]

During the years Catherine was carrying and giving birth to these children, the terror of their times stole ashore to quickly spread across all of England. The Great Plague, also called the "Black Death," began its rampage in 1348, bringing devastation among everyone, old, young, rich, poor, throughout both city and countryside. Some parts of England were left completely empty, the people dead of the plague, and their livestock, gone from the lack of feeding and care. The plague was often unforeseen and rapid: a child could be well at one minute and within hours dead. It began with a fever and the spitting of blood. Then followed boils and black swollen lymph nodes in the armpits and groin.

I was unable to find how the Greene family survived the plague. At a monastery in Peterborough, not far from their homes in Northamptonshire, 32 of the 64 monks perished from the scourge. The only way anyone knew how to avoid it was to, "Go quickly, go far, and return slowly," in other words, to isolate themselves as much as possible from places where people met. [10] That was possible for many of the gentry and higher classes who, like Henry, Catherine, and their children, had landed estates in the country. But it was not an option for the bulk of the population. We can only presume that was what they did. The family removed to one of their more isolated estates and remained there until the disease subsided, about a year after it first appeared. They did survive, and they also outlasted the next epidemic in 1361 that killed 15 percent of the English population.

By 1354, the plague was over, if only temporarily. The family was growing and Henry, flourishing. That year he reached the summit of the realm when King Edward appointed him, at the age of 44, a justice on the King's Bench. The King also knighted him Sir Henry Greene. It did not hurt that Sir William Shareshull, the mentor for whom he had interned, was Chief Justice. The Crown paid Sir Henry 120 marks (about £80) a year. As a member of the King's Bench, Sir Henry investigated and heard cases primarily in the Midlands near his family home.

In 1361, Edward received a particularly grievous complaint from his cousin Blanche, Lady Wake. The matter was delicate and had a history. A few years before, Lady Wake had charged that after her husband's death some men had burned houses on her property. King Edward, who was determined to stamp out the all too prevalent gangs of ruffians, was especially displeased. The matter was complicated, however. Thomas Lisle, the Bishop of Ely, was behind the attack. To take action against a senior cleric in a church that believed it enjoyed immunity was not done easily. The pope took an interest in cases like this.

An original trial had ended when the court found the bishop responsible and ordered him to pay Lady Wake £900 in damages. King Edward also formally rebuked the bishop. Now Lady Wake made a new charge. The bishop's men, she said, had murdered one of her servants in a nearby wood. More than annoyed at the news, the King sent Sir William Shareshull and Sir Henry Greene to adjudicate the case.

After hearing the arguments and weighing the facts on the King's behalf, the justices found enough evidence to pronounce Bishop Lisle guilty of Blanche's charges. Once again, it was awkward, with the King and his justices weighing against the dignity of the Church and one of its bishops. The court's decision had to be sound, and it was. Edward ordered all of Thomas Lisle's personal possessions forfeited. He also commanded him to beg forgiveness from Lady Wake. Rather that complying, Lisle rejected the verdict and fled to France. The pope was hardly happy with the verdict and took out his displeasure on the justices. Sir Henry was excommunicated from the Church.[11]

I never found whether Sir Henry Greene regretted his excommunication, but it obviously did not bother Edward. That same year, in 1361, the King appointed Sir Henry to succeed William Shareshull as Chief Justice of the King's Bench. In England, there were three high courts, and the King's Bench was the most important. The Court of the Exchequer heard cases regarding financial arrangements with the Crown. The Court of Common Pleas took personal appeal cases from people suing over debt, theft, fraud, and similar matters. The King's Bench handled criminal cases and appeals from the lower courts.

Sir Henry was at the pinnacle of England's judicial system. Under him, a team of royal justices traveled the country holding court and hearing cases. It was an big occasion when they arrived in a town. The accused and hundreds of local officers were involved in the trials held over the following days. Justice was administered rigidly and visibly in medieval England: the gallows were a busy part of the community, traitors' heads were impaled on city gates, and pillories were ready for fraudulent traders.

The Lord Chief Justice also played an important role in Parliament, one of whose tasks was to serve as the highest court in the land. As Lord Chief Justice, Henry made the opening speech of Parliament in the fall of 1362. It was King Edward's 50th birthday, and to mark it, the King convened this Parliament almost entirely from "commoners," representatives below the nobility. In commemoration of the jubilee, wrongdoers were granted a general pardon. More importantly, this Parliament passed the first piece of legislation that officially recognized the English language. English was henceforth the "Tongue of the Country." Sir Henry's opening address was in English, the first time ever.

A few years later, something derailed Sir Henry's career. In 1365, he and the Baron of the Exchequer were arrested for "enormous derelictions." They were both fined and Henry never returned to office. This is another of those moments obscured by the fog of time, and it appears that no one over the centuries has learned the details. Was he guilty of corruption? some anomalous act the King did not like? or simply political intrigue? The answer to this question seems to have eluded historians. Henry's penalty, however, was a simple fine, and the Latin expression inscribed on his transfer of authority suggests it happened with honor. It would seem that the matter had less to do with corruption than politics. Although not disgraced, Sir Henry was out of office not to return.

Four years later Sir Henry Greene passed away leaving an enormous estate to two of his sons, Thomas and Henry. He was buried in a tomb inside the Catholic Church of his hometown of Boughton. Although the Pope had once excommunicated Sir Henry, something must have happened to restore his position. Atop the tomb were sculpted Henry's and Catherine's effigies. Neither the church nor the tomb exist today. In Halstead's Genealogies, however, I found a handsomely drawn print that depicts their resting place. The couple lie magnificently, Henry, his bottom half covered in a knight's armor, and Catherine wearing the beautiful long flowing gown of a Lady. Henry's cleanly shaven face appears strong, intelligent, and resolute. Catherine's is smooth, beautiful, and calm.

The Beheaded

All good stories have a villain or two, and no set of stories should be complete unless there is at least one among the main characters. When I started my journey in quest of family stories, I wondered when and where I would meet a desperado, thug, or rogue. Young Sir Henry Greene Jr. might fit this bill, although it is hard to understand why he turned out that way. Sir Henry had risen at a relatively young age to possess vast properties. Working in the service of Edward III's son, John of Gaunt, he was near the heart of power of one of Europe's mightiest kingdoms. But apparently his ambitions were even greater.

Sir Henry's and Lady Catherine's son Henry,[12] like his father, was born in Boughton, Northamptonshire. If his mother and father had followed tradition, Henry was also probably trained and educated in an uncle's home, perhaps in the home of his Mother's brother Simon de Drayton. If so, he might well have lived at least for some amount of time at Drayton House while growing up. There, he would have also been well acquainted with his cousin John who bestowed the Drayton estate to Sir Henry and Catherine with the stipulation that it would go to Henry Jr. when his father was gone. The family also spent time at their home in London. By the time he was ten, his father was well known among the royal family and employed in the King's court.[13]

Born in 1347, young Henry's life, too, was one of privilege and status.[14] But his times were a time of war. During the last decades of the 1300's and first part of the 1400's, England and France were engaged in a long series of battles and wars, since known as the Hundred Years' War. The long war entered still another phase during the summer of 1369 when Henry and his older brother Thomas were old enough to take up arms. Both joined an army that Edward III sent to France under the command of two of his sons, Edward the Black Prince and John of Gaunt. Edward was Crown Prince and John was King Edward's third son, about seven years older than Henry. Henry would eventually serve John of Gaunt.

For whatever reason, the lure of battle often attracts men and boys, and nowhere was that truer than during Medieval times. The upper stratum of English society was essentially a warrior class. Henry and his brother Thomas, sons of a long line of knights, were probably eager to join the King's army. Active duty would be a useful waypoint on the road to getting their own knighthoods. Eager or not, however, the King expected lords and knights to mobilize their families and men when the kingdom went to war.

The two brothers were soon in France, but as it turned out, they were there only a few months before receiving word of their father Sir Henry's death. Both Thomas and Henry immediately returned and were home by December to be with their family and to handle inheritance issues. Normally, the oldest son acquired the family fortune when his wealthy father died. The rest of the family fared best they could in other ways, through marriage to rich spouses or by taking good professions in law, business, the army or navy.[15]

Henry was a second son, only in his early twenties when his father passed away, but the arrangement with his mother's family ensured he inherited the Drayton House estate. Not long before that, he had also made a propitious marriage when he wed Matilda Mauduit from another powerful Norman family that arrived with the Conquest. Matilda, who went by the name Maud, was the heiress to her wealthy grandfather Sir Thomas Mauduit's many estates. Henry's fortune was made. He and Maud's vast holdings made the young couple wealthy and notable. They set up their home at Drayton House and got a charter to hold a weekly market and an annual fair at Lowick on Whitsuntide in the middle of May. Lowick was part of the Drayton estate.[16]

It is not clear when Henry returned to join the King's men in France, but by spring 1373 Henry was in England, knighted like his father and grandfathers before him. He was the second Sir Henry Greene, and was then working for John of Gaunt, the Duke of Lancaster. The young Sir Henry served as a knight in the campaign John launched into France that summer.

John of Gaunt's army of 9,000 mounted men cut a 600-mile long swathe of havoc, destruction, and mayhem across France. The devastation was intentional and aimed to undermine and discredit the French king's control. By the end of the year, John's men, Sir Henry among them, reached Bordeaux. However, the long march through France took its toll also from John's army, and when they pulled into Bordeaux, they were tired and undernourished. Many of their horses had died, and knights and cavalrymen, unable to carry the weight of their equipment, had thrown their armor into rivers to keep it from the French.

Gaunt and his army lost one third of its men in action and another third to disease but had little to show for it. Even worse, the men stumbled into a plague-ridden town when they reached Bordeaux, and many more perished from the Black Death. In April 1374, Henry and other survivors of the expedition hobbled their way back to England. Gaunt's campaign had been a disaster. By the time it was over, however, Sir Henry and John of Gaunt knew each other well. After this, Henry appears to have remained from time to time in John's service and was eventually on an annual retainer.

To Sir Henry, being part John's inner circle must have seemed smart. After all, next to the King, John of Gaunt was probably the wealthiest man in England. Besides that, John was soon at the center of power. Edward III, now in his old age, grew increasingly weaker, and a few months before he passed away, his eldest son and heir, Edward the Black Prince, also died of natural causes. The next in line to the throne was the Black Prince's son Richard, who was only ten years old in 1377. John was the boy king's uncle.

Young Richard became Richard II, but John of Gaunt was by necessity the real power behind the throne. John managed much of the Crown's affairs until Richard was old enough to assume fully his royal role. This was not an easy job. Questions about John's loyalty inevitably arose along with a persistent fear that he might try to usurp the crown from his young nephew. As he grew, moreover, Richard did not mature well. Ten years old was a tender an age to assume a throne.

Richard II, a far cry from his grandfather who strived to be England's perfect king, grew up to be "unstable, extravagant, headstrong, suspicious, temperamental..., and cruel," as one modern historian describes him.[17] This led to uneasy tensions between young King Richard and his uncle John, who often found himself having to prove and defend his loyalty. Intrigues ripened after 1384 when Richard, at the age of 17, assumed his full role as King of England. During these years Henry Greene rotated through this troubled political world, aspiring to a stronger role in royal affairs, much like his father had enjoyed.

At just about this same time, a Friar of the Carmelite Order named John Latimer urgently approached King Richard who was in Salisbury for a session of Parliament. Latimer told Richard that there was a widespread conspiracy against the King's life. John of Gaunt, harboring ambitions to take the throne for himself, was at the center of the plot to overthrow the King. Newly empowered King Richard launched into a mad frenzy and called for John to be arrested and executed. When he finally calmed down, he ordered Latimer to write down this accusation in front of witnesses.

Gaunt then was sitting in Salisbury's cathedral waiting for the royal procession's arrival as part of a solemn service. When the King did not appear, John made his way to the Earl of Oxford's chamber where Richard had gone after the meeting in Parliament. As John entered the room, Latimer shouted "There is the villain! Seize him and put him to death, or he will kill you in the end!"[18]

Astounded, John defended himself eloquently enough to convince the King that the accusations were false. Richard would have put Latimer to death on the spot, but Gaunt urged him to try Latimer before a court. They needed to find who was behind him. Gaunt was right to believe that there was a plot. The Earl of Oxford, Robert de Vere, had secretly orchestrated the friar's accusations. De Vere, who had been close to young King Richard over his adolescent years, now wanted Gaunt out of the way.

However, Latimer refused to say and stayed with his story that Gaunt was plotting against Richard's life. He gave the names of two witnesses, but when they were interrogated neither appeared to know anything about a plot. When Latimer continued to refuse cooperation, Richard and John sent him to the dungeon of Salisbury Castle to await a trial they would convene the next day.

As guards took the Latimer from the King's lodging, a group of men stood waiting at the door. The men, Richard's half-brother Lord John Holland, Sir Henry Greene, and two other knights, took custody of the friar. They were certain they could get the conspirators' names. There were ways to acquire information, none of them pleasant. What followed was a night of viciously brutal torture that even exceeded the normal atrocities used to get confessions. When John Latimer refused to give them the names they wanted, the horrors continued until the friar was dead. The next morning, his broken body was paraded about the town to show what happens to those making false accusations and guilty of treason.

Was Sir Henry involved in this ugly affair on John of Gaunt's or King Richard's behalf? Or were they both behind it? Not surprisingly, the record is silent about that, but Sir Henry would not have been working on his own. He may have been following Gaunt's orders. Records show that Sir Henry was doing business on behalf of John of Gaunt in other cases during those same times.[19]

Whether as a result of the John Latimer case, or for other reasons, Sir Henry soon came to the attention of young King Richard. Sir Henry was a member of Parliament, and Richard believed he could be useful to him in that capacity. In March 1397, Richard retained Henry and two other knights, Sir William Bagot, and Sir John Bussy, to work as agents of the Crown. The King liked the three, and they swiftly rose to become Richard's key advisors. Three months later, he lavished Henry with salary of £100 a year to serve on the King's Council. The position was otherwise lucrative with spoils to be gained.

Disregarding his grandfather's efforts to impower Parliament, Richard strove to be an absolute monarch, ruling with few or no restrictions from Parliament. Opposing him in this, a number of Lords was determined to check what they considered the King's megalomania and imbalance. (Some modern researchers believe Richard suffered from schizophrenia.)

Sir Henry and his two colleagues were useful in Richard's ongoing struggles against these opponents. Sir John Bussy was Speaker of the Parliament that met that autumn, and Sir Henry Greene and Sir William Baggot, as members of Parliament, assisted him in manipulating the body to get King Richard's agenda through. In return, the King rewarded them with large parcels of land he confiscated from rivals. Bussy and Greene were even granted a London inn that the King seized from one of the those opposing his autocratic style.

This was only the beginning of the new personal wealth Sir Henry's royal service was affording him. These riches, widely considered ill-gained, brought with them a curse of their own. The richer the three men grew, the more unpopular they became. Their names quickly took on a sinister tone throughout England that extended long after their deaths. Shakespeare even made Sir Henry Greene one of the villains in his play Richard II that disparaged Richard II's reign.[20]

Into this medieval affair now entered Henry Bolingbroke, John of Gaunt's son and heir, a man Richard feared. Bolingbroke was the King's cousin with a potential claim to the throne. To head off the possibility that Henry Bolingbroke might exercise this claim, King Richard and his advisors forced Bolingbroke into a ten-year exile from Britain. As part of the arrangement, the King promised Bolingbroke that his property and estates in Britain would remain Bolingbroke's own possessions during the exile.

Grieving deeply his son's banishment, Gaunt took ill and died in 1399. From Paris, Henry Bolingbroke learned of his father's passing and that he had inherited his father title, Duke of Lancaster, as well as his fabulous wealth. Then more news arrived. The King had expropriated all of Bolingbroke's lands, including those to be inherited from his father, and re-distributed them to the King's own supporters. Richard had also extended Bolingbroke's exile from ten years to life. Sir Henry Greene, as a member of the committee that justified the King's confiscation of the Bolingbroke estates, was in the center of all this.[21]

Neither Richard II, Sir Henry, nor the other advisors may have fully appreciated the dramatic implications of what they had set in motion. They had just stocked Bolingbroke with a quiver-full of reasons to seek Richard's overthrow. Richard left the country for Ireland to manage a situation brewing there. In his absence, the King made Sir Henry Greene a leading member of the government under the Duke of York.

Henry Bolingbroke, vowing not to accept the seizure of his and his father's properties, gathered men and prepared a return to England to regain lands and inheritance, one way or another. After sailing from France, Bolingbroke stepped off the ship in Ravenspurn, on the east coast of England, at the head of about 60 men. He knelt and kissed the soil, then mounted and led his men toward London, gathering more followers as they went. Richard II was so unpopular that people flocked to Bolingbroke, and he soon had a formidable army marching south behind him. Along the way, noblemen and clergy rallied to his support. And to further Bolingbroke's swelling popularity, the Archbishop of Canterbury announced that anyone giving him allegiance would be remitted of their sins and achieve "a sure place in Paradise."[22]

With the King still in Ireland, his caretaker, the Duke of York, was paralyzed and panic-stricken when Henry Bolingbroke's invasion drew closer. York called Sir Henry Greene, Bussy, Bagot and others of the King's Council together to consider what to do. They discussed the obvious solution of getting a force together to oppose Bolingbroke's advance. Except for Greene, Bussy, Bagot, and a couple others, however, it was clear there was no resolve in the council nor in Parliament to resist Bolingbroke's army.

Unlike just about everyone else, Greene and the other advisors were not in a position to extend a welcome to Bolingbroke's crusade to end Richard's tyranny. They had been at the center of the King's machinations, most recently trying to seize Bolingbroke's own inheritance. Panicking, they realized their best option was to get out of London. Their hope was to travel west to meet Richard's return from Ireland. Greene, Bussy, and Lord Scroope rode quickly toward Bristol; Bagot went to Chester and then to Ireland. Greene and his two companions arrived in Bristol safely.

In Ireland, King Richard had heard of Bolingbroke's arrival and was rushing to get back to England. Sir Henry and his two colleagues took control of Bristol Castle in the name of the King and hoped they could hold out there long enough for his return. Unfortunately, by now almost everyone, including the Duke of York, was joining Bolingbroke's ranks. The mass of followers continued west toward where Sir Henry's party was holed up in the fortress. When it reached Bristol, Bolingbroke's army was overpowering. His men massed around the castle in a siege.

Inside, Sir Henry and his colleagues started planning their defenses, but as they looked from the castle towers at the masses of armed men before them, they knew that their situation was hopeless. There was no way they would resist the siege. The three decided to surrender and lay themselves at Henry Bolingbroke's mercy. Sadly for them, their role in seizing Bolingbroke's inheritance did not endear them much. Worse, still, their unpopularity among the people made clemency a long shot.

They ordered the doors to the castle swung open and the two knights and lord presented their surrender to Bolingbroke's captains. The next morning, they were arraigned before the constable and marshal. Greene, Bussy, and Lord Scroope were accused of misgoverning the King and realm, and of treason. There was not much of a trial. Few were willing to testify on their behalf when they faced the charges. Nor was Henry Bolingbroke sympathetic. The three men, in his view, were among the King's key conspirators and had achieved gain at his and many others' expense.

Their fate was sealed when news arrived that King Richard at the head of an army had just landed in nearby Wales. The matter needed to be done and over. Sir Henry Greene, Sir John Bussy, and Lord William Scroope were found guilty. They were taken out and, on July 29, 1399, beheaded. Before his execution, Sir Henry, in his distress, admitted that for ten years he had kept a man in Wiltshire from his property and gave the wronged man his best ox-team. Few mourned their loss. In fact, a Bristol poet even wrote a long poem that lamented Richard II's sorry reign. So strongly were the King's counselors hated, that the poet mentioned all of them, including Sir Henry, by name.

Shortly thereafter, Henry Bolingbroke defeated Richard II and imprisoned him in the Tower of London. Bolingbroke was eventually crowned Henry IV. Although Bolingbroke had sequestered all of Sir Henry Greene's property at the time of his execution, the new king later relented. Henry IV returned Sir Henry's original family properties (i.e., those not "ill-gained" during his service to Richard II) to support his widow and children. Among the properties returned was the Drayton House estate which stayed for generations in the family. Henry IV even appointed Sir Henry's son, Ralph, as Sheriff of Northamptonshire. Ralph, too, became a knight of the realm and served faithfully both Henry IV and his son, Henry V. [23]

The Fog Banks of History

I started my journey into Greene family history by reading several books about the early Greenes and their descendants. The

*George Sears Greene volume (*The Greenes of Rhode Island, with Historical Records of English Ancestry, 1534-1902*) gave me an incredibly ambitious introduction to the family. Lora Sarah Nichols La Mance wrote another important volume,* The Greene Family and its Branches from A.D. 861 to A.D. 1904.[24] *She deserves much credit as a woman researcher and author at a time when there were so few of them. I also found important information on the family from Horatio Somersby's book (*The Greene Family in England and America: With Pedigrees*), that, although apparently somewhat controversial, tracked well with much of the later research I did. I also discovered a 19th century historian, George Baker, who is an often-quoted source of information on the early Greene family (*George Baker,* The History of Antiquities of the County of Northampton, *vol I).*

However, as I reached back into the history of the 1300s, I found that the Greene family's stories appeared and then disappeared along the foggy medieval landscapes. Here and there were references to Sir Henry Greene or his son, Henry, Jr., but initially I found only fragments that hinted of larger, bolder events in their lives.

Traveling through this spotty terrain reminded me of experiences we had when living in Milan, Italy. During those years, we often drove back and forth on the autostrada that sped along the pre-Alpine hills toward Venice. The area was well-known for its patches of dense fog that would unexpectedly roll off the pre-Alps and across the Lombardy plain to suddenly envelope the fast and bustling motorway with an impenetrable mist. Chain accidents were common, and we had to be ready to brake quickly whenever visibility abruptly dropped to only a few yards. We might be enjoying picturesque roadside scenery one moment, and an instant later find ourselves in a bewildering fog unable to see anything for the next ten minutes. Then, light quickly reappeared, and the old-world countryside was crisp and clear again.

That is what so often occurred in my attempts to pull together a picture of the Greenes' lives in medieval England. Everything at one moment was as clear as day. Suddenly, another dense fog would obscure the picture, and as I traveled along, it rotated back and forth between light and thick mist.

Despite often longing to spy more clearly through the fog of the past, the outlines of Sir Henry Greene, Sir and Jr. began to take form. On Google Books, I located medieval chronicles (such as Raphaell Holinshed, Chronicles of England, Scotland, and Ireland, vol II; Sir Thomas More, History of King Richard III, and of course, Shakespeare's Richard II) that offered general contemporary accounts of their times and sometimes even provided an anecdote or two about these Greenes. On Ancestry.com I discovered histories written by some of the Greenes' modern descendants. A few of these went on for pages and were well written, but inevitably while venturing through the Middle Ages, the fog often obscured these writers' best efforts, too. Scouring through them, I found inconsistencies and often mistakes.

I also found that studying a good social or general history of the times our ancestors lived was always helpful for putting their lives in context. The farther back I went, the more important this type of an approach was. Several books succeeded splendidly in teleporting me in spirit if not in body back to those distant times. Ian Mortimer, The Time Traveler's Guide to Medieval England, Ian Mortimer, The Perfect King, The Life of Edward III Father of the English Nation, and Allison Weir, The Princes in the Tower were a few of them

When visiting a medieval Greene home in England, its curator told me that the granddaddy of source material on the Greene family was a volume called Halstead's Genealogies. The book was written in 1685 and today only 24 copies exist in the world. The name of its author, "Robert Halstead," was a pen name for its real writer, the 2nd Earl of Peterborough, who, himself, had Greenes among his illustrious ancestors. I made note of the work as well as of other often quoted antique sources that might be useful.

The British Library

I had this source list in my pocket one day when I entered the British Library in London. It was one of many libraries I visited in

56

search of my ancestors' past. The information I found in these places not only produced some of the stories I wanted, but they often offered insights that allowed me to follow up at home. This was especially true following this visit.

The British Library is the world's second largest, and I hoped I might find some of these rare sources in its stacks. I crossed the library's large entrance hall to the receptionist desk. When I asked her how to get started, she peered down her nose with a look that told she knew I did not know what I was doing. She referred me to a registration desk downstairs, where I explained to a clerk that I was on a project and wanted to access some materials in the library. He told me that I needed to register, something I had already been told once. Then, pointing to a computer terminal, he said I first had to get reference numbers for books I wanted to read. After that he would decide whether I would be registered.

Fortunately, I had my list with Halstead's Genealogies *at the top of it. Ten minutes later, I came back to the registration desk with reference numbers for all the books I was seeking. Satisfied that I had performed that task properly, and without even looking at my list and its reference numbers, he next sent me to a cubicle to fill out an application. I was back again a few minutes later with the completed papers in my hand. He took it with my Virginia driver's license and told me to take a seat. "An interviewer will be with you soon," he muttered, and went on with his work.*

I sat in a chair against the wall waiting for the interview and remembered how in high school I joked that one evening I had to "check" my date out after her father gave me a good grilling when I arrived. I felt this was that kind of moment. I would have to go through a grilling before I could get a library card to access the materials I wanted. Eventually my turn came, and an interviewer, much more congenial than I expected, went through everything with me from my project to my background. When assured I was a legitimate researcher, she signed the application and sent me to get a picture ID badge. Afterwards, I found the proper desk to order the volumes I wanted and was told to return another day to get them.

Finally, two days later, I was sitting in one of the immense reading halls of this magnificent library when a librarian rolled his cart to my table. On top was a copy of the rare book that the Earl of Peterborough penned 330 years earlier, *Halstead's Genealogies*. It was worn but truly beautiful, about 2 ft x 1 ft in size and 4 inches thick. The volume was filled with detailed prints of Greene family knights and tombs, copies of wills, deeds, and so on, in their original English, French, and Latin languages. Many of the families extended back to William the Conqueror's time, and beyond to Normandy. The Earl also summarized some of the stories of the Greenes and their affiliated families.

I took out my phone, opened its optical reader app, and started taking pictures of the **Genealogies'** pages, glad that taking photos was allowed. Soon, however, a fellow patron came over to complain that my camera was making too much noise when it clicked. I fumbled to find the setting that turned off the sound, and we seemed to get along better after that, silently of course. As the pages turned, and my camera took quiet photos, some of the fog banks I had encountered earlier began to thin.

Medieval Family Places May Still be There

Before starting on one of our trips to England, I researched locations where some of the stories occurred. However, I was not optimistic that places where people like Sir Henry Greene and Lady Catherine Drayton lived nearly 700 years ago still existed. I was wrong. One evening while googling I discovered Drayton House near Northampton (see Map B). The historic old estate was more a palace than a house. Sir Henry and Lady Catherine Greene, I read, had owned Drayton and lived there in the 14th century. Their son, Henry, and his wife, Maud, lived there, as well.

The online history of the property told how in about 1300, Catherine's brother, Sir Simon de Drayton, built the first portions of this beautiful home. When Sir Simon passed away about 50 years later, he left it to his son John, who in the early 1360's bestowed it to his uncle and aunt, Sir Henry and Lady Catherine Greene. The entrusted estate was to go to Henry, Jr., when Sir Henry died. I later *found in* Halstead's Genealogies *a copy of the original document where John transferred Drayton House to his cousin, Henry Jr., upon the death of Sir Henry, Sr. Absent this stipulation, the estate under normal inheritance law and custom would probably have gone to Sir Henry's and Lady Catherine's first son, Thomas. With this arrangement, however, the house and property were granted, and the Greenes were the new residents and proud owners.*

Now, seven centuries later, I was elated to read how the old house had spread out from its original hall to include several Baroque and Neo-Classical wings built much later. Different websites explained that the original central tower, surrounded by lavish later additions, was still standing and in everyday use. The Drayton House estate was just one of many that Henry and Catherine might have considered home, but it was Catherine's family estate, and it was not far from where Henry was born. It was good fortune to find Drayton House still there, situated elegantly as the private residence of the Stopford Sackville family whose ancestors had lived in it continually since 1770.[25]

Timing was perfect, and I hoped there might be an opportunity to visit Drayton House during our upcoming trip. Unfortunately, the house was private and not open daily to the public. I decided to write a letter to the house's current owner, Charles Stopford Sackville, describing the project I had underway. A few weeks later, his response kindly offered us a chance to tour Drayton House. We immediately got in touch with a long-time friend of ours, Mary Lou, who lived not far from the estate. She generously invited us to spend a few nights in her visitors' cottage during our visit. We planned the rest of our trip to England around this marvelous opportunity.

A few months later, we drove our rental car through Mary Lou's quaint village and up to her artistic home. We had first met her when living in Britain during the 1980's. She was originally from South Africa and once owned a London modeling agency. Her husband, Bill, had been a talented graphic designer whose well-honed British wit kept us in good humor. Their friendship over the years helped make us the Anglophiles we were.

It was a delight to see Mary Lou again. She made us comfortably at home and accepted our invitation to join us when we visited Drayton. Early the next morning the three of us rambled along the narrow roads, with charismatic houses, green fields, and pastures on either side, until we finally turned onto the 5,000-acre Drayton House estate. There were pheasants in the fields and sheep and cattle grazing near the gardens. It was a working property, a living home, far from just another old historical country estate.

Drayton House had a curator, Bruce Bailey, who welcomed our visit. As we walked around the house and through its medieval halls and corridors, Bruce explained how the property had developed and grown over the centuries. The rooms, the stairs, the halls, and the furnishings were splendidly preserved and maintained. Looking through the windows, we admired the expansive green meadows and beautifully laid out gardens that swept around the mansion.

The Great Hall harkened back to times when the Greenes dined there. Even though it was now adorned in a later epoch's style, it was still easy to imagine the days when distinguished guests from the shire, or from London's center of power, visited and shared an evening with the lords and ladies who hosted them. On the walls hung large portraits of monarchs, many of whom had visited Drayton House. The outside stone walls were built high enough to protect against invaders during medieval society's disturbances.

The Stopford Sackvilles, we learned, descend from their ancestor Lord George Germaine who was the first of their family to own Drayton House. What a surprise. Lord Germaine was a familiar name to American colonists who, like our family members, fought in the American Revolution. As Secretary of State for North America under King George III, Germaine managed Britain's handling of the American revolt. From London, he formulated British policy toward the Colonies and very much micromanaged the British military campaign, many say to its detriment, during the American War of Independence.[26]

As we wandered through the old mansion, it occurred to me that here was another great historical round. Germaine, who prosecuted the war against America, and Sir Henry Greene, whose descendant Nathanial Greene was one of the most effective American generals against Germaine's armies, both owned and lived in Drayton House. George Germaine and Nathanael Greene had this in common: without both of them, there might not have been the American victory at Yorktown. Germaine's bungling prosecution of the superior British army and Greene's effective generalship molded the last stage of the war to the colonials' advantage. It occurred to me that fine old homes such as Drayton House have their own stories and souls that reflect the people who once lived in them, almost as if Sir Henry and Lord Germaine might have carved their names on neighboring walls of the old house.

Expect a Horse Thief or a Bank Robber Along the Way

When Sir Henry Greene (Sr.) traveled from Drayton House to become one of the important men in Edward III's court, he set a high mark for his son. Henry the younger may have expected or thought he deserved to rise at least to the level his father had. Ingratiating himself with whoever held power, first John of Gaunt and then John's brother, Richard II, may have seemed the natural path toward his destination. For some, perhaps, the pursuit of wealth and power never lessens, no matter how much they accumulate. Short cuts became easier to rationalize.

In the past's "foreign country," I realized the importance of not judging too harshly the characters I met there, at least not by the standards of our times. Even among his contemporaries, however, Henry's methods were questionable. His role in John Lattimer's gruesome torture and death might have been acceptable in Richard II's and his brother John of Gaunt's courts, but contemporary and later chroniclers seem appalled. Sir Henry and his colleagues grew even more wealthy by supporting Richard's devious rule but remained despised and remembered for evil all over England, even in Shakespeare's Richard II written nearly two hundred years later.

As I dug into Henry Jr.'s stories, I remembered how in a genealogy class I took as a college freshman, the professor gave us a list of things NOT to do. One of the first was not to research ancestors just to find the kings, queens, and nobles among them.

*Expect to find a horse rustler or bank robber along the way, he said,
and do not regret it when you do.*

The Fugitive
*The next story may fit the criteria of folklore, a story, maybe true,
maybe not, that comes from family tradition. This is the tale of John
Greene, the Fugitive. It is full of intrigue, and one wants to believe
it. The account appears in many family histories of the Greene
family. In addition to simply being a good story, the character John
Greene has often served as the link between the 14th century Greenes
of Northampton and the 16th century Dorset Greenes, two of whom,
both named John Greene, left for Puritan America in the 1630's to
father many lines of Americans.*

*One account of John the Fugitive originates from Lora La
Mance's book.[27] Mrs. La Mance says that the Dorset Greenes from
England brought the story of John Greene with them when they
migrated to America. She wrote her book at the end of the 1800's,
and by then the John Greene tale would have been traveling through
the American family for at least 200 years. Since I have not been
able to pin down details about this John Greene, and given the long
time between when he lived and when La Mance actually wrote
about him, I was definitely on the doubter's side of this question –
until I started delving deeper.*

A year after the **Sir Henry Greene Jr.**'s beheading, Ralph, the
oldest of the six Greene children, petitioned King Henry to return
their inheritance. The King accepted Ralph's plea and returned
everything except the properties Richard II had awarded him to
Maud and her children. Ralph soon gained the favor of both Henry
IV and his son, Henry V. Eventually knighted, Sir Ralph served as
Sheriff of Northamptonshire twice and was also a member of
Parliament.[28]

The family was soon flourishing again, and Sir Ralph was one
of the richest landowners to represent Northampton in Parliament.
Ralph died quite young, however, probably as a knight during Henry

V's second campaign in France. Since he had no heir, the entire estate went to his brother John, Sir Henry's second oldest son. The inheritance passed in a rather complicated path from generation to generation after that. Ralph's and John's brother Thomas, however, does not appear in Halstead's wills and other documents.[29]

About 100 years later lived a man named John Greene, said by Mrs. La Mance and some others to be one of Thomas's descendants. John, they wrote, was an accomplished swordsman, a true expert in the use of his weapon, and considered to be the finest in all England. In the York and Lancaster families' ongoing feuds and the civil war known in history as "The War of the Roses," John was a Yorkist, a divergence from his earlier family ancestors who under Sir Ralph had committed themselves to the Lancaster kings Henry IV and V. In July 1483, Richard III, the last Yorkist king, came to spend a week at the Earl of Warwick's castle not far from the Greene family home in Northamptonshire. During the stay, King Richard met and took a liking to John Greene. John was soon in the King's service.

A cloud shadowed Richard III's reign, however, and once John Greene was in his employ, he fell into the intrigue. Richard's brother was the great Yorkist king Edward IV, whose story many people today may know from the TV series *The White Queen*. When Edward died, he left two young sons, one of whom, also Edward, was heir to become the next king. On his death bed, Edward IV turned to his brother Richard and asked him to care for the boy until he was old enough to assume the crown.

Richard readily agreed, and Richard was proclaimed "Lord Protector of the Realm." Unlike John of Gaunt a century before, however, Richard coveted the crown and not long after had both of Edward's sons imprisoned in the Tower of London. Richard eventually convinced Parliament to declare his late brother's marriage invalid, making both boys illegitimate. With that, the boys were no longer heirs to the crown, and Richard was rightful king. He was immediately crowned Richard III.

One day, Richard III ordered John Greene to carry a letter to Sir Robert Blackenbury keeper of the Tower of London. In this clandestine message, the King commanded Blackenbury to assassinate secretly the two young princes held in the Tower. John sped off on the errand and eventually handed Blackenbury the royal dispatch. Sir Robert was appalled by the message and refused. He said so in a reply John Greene relayed to the King.

Refusing an order from the King was normally rare, but the awkwardness of the situation made it difficult for Richard to take action against Blackenbury. The King was not deterred, however, since the matter continued to trouble his legitimacy. As long as the princes were alive, his claim to the throne was in question. The next month, Richard found someone else capable of the deed. The boy princes mysteriously disappeared and have been the subject of speculation and investigation ever since.

John continued to work for King Richard until two years later Henry Tutor killed Richard in battle. Few tears were shed for Richard, and Henry Tudor became the new king, Henry VII. With Henry's victory, the War of the Roses ended, but Greene feared retribution for his service to Richard III and fled to Europe.

After a time as a fugitive, John returned to England in disguise under the name John Clarke to see his family again. This seemed to work well, until one day he engaged in a duel. When those present saw how skillfully John wielded his sword, they recognized who he was. John rushed an escape back across the Channel, and there he stayed until the King died, and his son, Henry VIII, took the throne. He then returned to purchase an estate not far from Salisbury in Gillingham, Dorset, home of the Dorset Greene family.[30]

As a man who held Richard's trust, was he involved with the murder of the princes in early September 1483? No one knows for sure. It appears that he was not present at the Tower the night the princes disappeared and presumably killed. However, we know Greene was associated with, and had probably even worked for Sir James Tyrell, Richard's henchman thought to be responsible for the murder. Only a few months after the murder, moreover, John Greene along with Tyrell and another of the perpetrators, Miles Forrest, received generous grants from King Richard. The King also appointed John Greene as receiver of the Isle of Wight and overseer of the Port of Southampton, and Escheator of Southampton. More interestingly, only three weeks after the princes' deaths, he received from the King a general pardon for all offences, and his neighbors in Warwickshire were all granted one, too, maybe to make sure they kept quiet about anything they might know.

It is possible, of course, that John's greatest crime was simply having inside knowledge of what had happened. According to Sir Thomas More, John seems to have been well aware of the message ordering the princes' deaths. When the boys disappeared from the Tower a few weeks later, he would have had no doubt of their fate. Moreover, John and those who knew him well were pardoned in advance to keep them from talking. This also explains why, according to tradition, he was quick to escape from Britain the moment he heard Richard III had been toppled. Someone with his knowledge would have been, at least for a time, on the bad side of Henry VII, who was married to the princes' sister. John Greene was not officially banished, and he could legally come back to visit, as tradition says he did. However, for all practical purposes, John was probably a fugitive for several years while Henry VII was alive. Tradition tells that he returned to England sometime after Henry VII's death in 1509.

Sir James Tyrell, who is generally considered to have overseen the murder, and his accomplice John Dighton also fled to France. Tyrell was eventually brought back and executed. John's knowledge of the murders and his association with the perpetrators probably would have been enough to convict him, too, of treason. The punishment for treason was hanging until not quite dead, followed by drawing and quartering.

A few years later, Sir Thomas More penned his history that detailed the tragic story of the princes in the Tower. When writing of the affair, More noted with disgust that Dighton was then still walking free in France. He also knew John Greene's name. Sir Thomas obviously received his information from sources who personally knew something of the murder, and there were not many people who did. Who knows? John Greene could have been one of More's sources. [31]

65

Do Not Totally Ignore Family Traditions

Another class I took as a student had to do with folklore: tales, true or not, that survive generations of telling. Folklore was another of the topics on my genealogy class's *DO NOT* list: *do not use family histories short on concrete facts.* I footnote that one, however. Folklore is a lot of fun – that is one reason the tales travel from person to person, sometimes for millennia. As I noted earlier, concrete facts are too often in short supply in history generally, and especially in genealogy. Family traditions and national traditions, too, for that matter, may be no less true simply because we cannot pin down the written sources as well as we want. I have no problem recording family traditions as long as we openly tell that we cannot verify the veracity of the accounts. They sometimes add excitement to the family narrative, but should necessarily be kept in their own box, at least until we can get more convincing facts together.

So I added to my own *DO NOT* list: *Do not totally ignore family traditions.* Most of us have a family story or two about glorious or inglorious things that once happened in the family. It is important to consider them seriously. If one cannot prove or disprove them, maybe with time, someone else may. In the meantime, it is worth keeping these traditions alive, for they may be true.

So far, this story of John Greene remains a family tradition with some circumstantial evidence behind it, but as yet not sufficiently proven. Even amidst the dense fog surrounding his story, it follows some of the most dramatic and infamous moments in English history. One of the problems with the story is that genealogists have not found detailed vital records for John Greene. It has not been possible to anchor the story in official birth, marriage, and death records. La Mance admits that some of it is based on tradition – when the Greenes reached America, the family told their descendants that the family in Dorset began with John. Because of the lack of written evidence, however, the story has sometimes been doubted.

As I researched it, however, I found elements that seemed to have facts behind them. For example, Sir Thomas More, writing *only about 15 years after the events, told of a John Greene who was involved in Richard III's murder of the Princes in the Tower. Sir Thomas relates the story this way,*

> *"Whereuppon he [Richard III] sent one John Grene, whom he specially trusted, unto sir Robert Brakenbery constable of the Tower, with a letter and credence also, that the same Sir Robert shoulde in any wise put the two children to death. This John Grene did his errande unto Brakenbery kneling before our Lady in the Tower, who plainely answered that he would never putte them to death to dye therefore, with which answer John Grene returning recounted the same to Kynge Richarde at Warwick yet."[32]*

So there was a John Greene involved with the affair of the Tower Princes. It is also clear that in King Richard's inner circle was a John Greene, whom "...he specially trusted," as More writes.

In fact, Richard III knew John Greene even before the tradition says they met at Warwick Castle. When Richard was still the Duke of Gloucester during his brother Edward IV's reign, John Greene worked for him in some capacity, among other things overseeing the stables. He may have served in King Edward's household, as well. His service is not likely to have been in just a trivial capacity, or Thomas More would not have bothered to mention his name.[33]

The Greene family in Gillingham, Dorset, reaches back at least to the time their family tradition says John came to Dorset. Parish records only extend to about 1560, and that year they show that a John Greene was buried there. Was this the Greene tradition's John, or perhaps his son? The first Greene entry from Gillingham Manor Rolls is for a J. Greene in the time of Edward IV.[34] Could this be tradition's John Greene, or his father, or uncle?

With these questions in mind I went to the library of the Society of Genealogists in London but was unable to resolve them. However, I found a John Greene who was knighted by Henry VII for his service in helping put down an invasion of London by Cornish rebels. A Robert and Richard Greene were also knighted during the decades around John Greene. Robert Greene and Richard Greene were the names of the Dorset Lords of Gillingham, and various genealogies place the title "Sir" in front of their names, denoting their knighthood. The records I found had no other knights named Robert or Richard Greene "from the Earliest Time to the Present Day," and it is possible they were the Gillingham lords. Along with John, were these the men of the family traditions, in some combination of grandfather, father, son relationships? The names, times, and places were right. Rummaging through the old library stacks at the Society I found nothing to prove definitively that they were, but the possibility is a real one.[35]

The obscurity of time clouds John Greene's story more than many of the others I discovered. John definitely needs a few rays of light from new research. However, the story is based on an enduring family tradition that goes back to only a few decades following the actual events. And we know that at least one of the most respected chroniclers from John's own time, Sir Thomas More, verified some key elements of a story that cannot be discarded for being implausible or out of touch with the events it portrays. Somewhere, John the Fugitive sits on a hazy segment of that spectrum ranging from myth to established fact, just like so many other stories that centuries later we accept as a description of our past. I decided that for the time being I will take it on its face value.[36]

Tracking Far-off Terrains

In some ways, my search for stories of Henry Sr., Henry Jr., and John the Fugitive produced much more than I expected, and in others, much less. I learned a lot about their lives and even visited where two of them lived. What I was able to write down about them exceeded anything else I found written in one place. Going back 700 years to track the lives of people who were not royals is hard to do, something I realized before I started looking. I was satisfied, however, to find who these grandfathers and grandmothers were and some of the things they did.

Missing, I realized, was insight into their emotional and spiritual lives. How did they feel? What did they think? How did

Sir Henry and Catherine deal with the dreaded plague? What exactly were the motivations that led to the ruin of Sir Henry Jr.? Without passage into their intellectual worlds, I could not find the fully 3-dimensional characters for whom I was searching.

Emotions clearly do not survive the centuries as well as actions do, at least not this many centuries. However, that was not the case when I started tracking early American ancestral families who lived 400 years ago. As the next chapter shows, these people often wore their feelings on their lapels. I was even fortunate enough to find some of their most cherished thoughts in their own words, written for posterity to remember. Perhaps this was a result of the invention of the printing press that made it much easier for people to record stories and even some of the words of those about whom they wrote.

PART 2

THE BIRTH
OF A
NATION

Chapter 3

The Struggle for American Values
Ida May and Charles Leonardson, the Homesteaders
John Greene, the Gentleman Surgeon
Samuel Gorton, the Firebrand
Obadiah Holmes, the Martyr
John Greene, the Trader

"However we are set apart as a forlorn people in the eyes of, & by the world, yet doubt I not, but our God hath singled us out for ends and uses... that it may be told unto our childrens children that noble work that he hath wrought for us... "
Samuel Gorton
From a Boston prison to his wife Mary (1643)

The wanderlust that drove my search for ancestral stories was born during my first encounters with the past. I listened to every word as my Grandfather Leonardson wove history into his conversations with friends and relatives. He was from a long line of farmers who had not attended university, but who were intelligent and thoughtful people. I had two great-grandmothers living within a block of our home. As I looked up at them, their wrinkled faces beaming smiles at me and their worn hands seemingly wanting too many hugs, I saw in their eyes another world. I neither knew nor understood it, but I realized it was somehow connected to mine. I was the eldest child, and my mother was the eldest child in her family, and her parents, the eldest in theirs. It was possible for me to feel linked to several generations that laddered back into the past.

My family was like the community around it. On my father's side were 19th century Mormon immigrants from Great Britain and Scandinavia. My mother's ancestors were hearty ever-westward-moving families who had been in America as long as there were Europeans here. The town of Idaho Falls and its surrounding fertile mountain-plateau farmlands was settled by these Mormon pioneers,

Mid-Westerners, and Easterners. As in my family, the two-sides of the communal neighborhood, mainly Protestant and Catholic families, and Mormon adherents, got along well with each other.

Into these fertile valleys, my great-great-parents arrived carrying with them a rich heritage full of family stories.

The Homesteaders

Just as my childhood benefited so greatly from having great-grandmothers living around me, so my Mother, Margie, was nurtured in her earliest years by her great-grandmother Ida May Dawley Leonardson. Margie was the oldest great-grandchild, and her father's house was located next to the Idaho homestead built forty years earlier by Ida May and her husband, Charles Leonardson. By the time Mother came along, Ida May was a widow, thin and stooped. But her photos still reveal how she peered with a steady gaze that conveyed the indomitable spirit of an extraordinary woman who had spent most of her life on the American frontier.

Rattlesnake-infested fields and an orchard separated Mother's childhood home from Ida May's. Margie and her cousins loved to sneak off for adventures in Ida's house where they were awed by the bedroom trunk holding a sword Ida's father carried in the Civil War. They fed lumps of sugar to her Shetland pony, jumped on Ida's bed, and, in short, got away with nearly everything. Margie wrote of Ida, "She saved me from getting more than one spanking... We lived just through the orchard from her on the south. I would run away and go up to her place. My dad would come after me. She would say, 'Now, Wayne, don't you touch that girl!'" The homestead was peacefully situated in a remote high mountain valley community called Medicine Lodge, and Margie regretted the day her parents moved away, and her protector remained behind. "So my carefree days were over," Margie continued. "We left our beloved Medicine Lodge and my Great-Grandmother Ida May Dawley Leonardson... It was an end of an Era."[1]   Ida May was my Mother's first connection to her past. Later in life when she shared these happy childhood days with us, it was clear that her memories were surrounded with the security of belonging.

Ida May had her own family stories and traditions. When she was still small, her father and mother migrated from Rhode Island to Illinois and then to Kansas and on to Nebraska. Life was poor and simple. Times were hard. Ida May did not have a pair of shoes until she was 12 years old. Her father built a frame house that was just nearing completion when lightning burned it to the ground. Not deterred, Ida's father put up another house on the same foundation. Lightening may not strike the same spot twice, but they learned that this was not true about tornadoes. Just after it was finished, a tornado swept the house up and crashed it to the ground a mile away.

With the resilience of those who lived on the frontier, Ida May's parents endured through good days and poor. For a while they lived in a sod house. For her, however, childhood was hardly dreary. She loved to dance and party, and she enjoyed many friends. Ida May was also quick to learn. When she was just 15 years old, she was teaching school in a schoolhouse that she walked six miles each morning to reach. She met her husband Charles, a schoolteacher from a nearby Kansas settlement, at a 4th of July celebration. They wrote back and forth to each other for about a year and got engaged in about 1879, just before "Charlie" and three companions left for adventures farther West. The young men were looking for work, land, and a place to raise families – like the things sought by many others then flocking across the American continent.

The four young men left their homes by team and wagon, pushing from Nebraska into Wyoming. "We camped each night on a different creek in which fish were plentiful and very easily taken on any kind of bait," one of them later told.[2] Running short on cash, Charlie took a job in a Rock Springs, Wyoming, mine while the other three drove into Montana. Then two of them, brothers Johnnie and Sandy Beal, moved across into Idaho where they spent the winter in a cabin on Blue Creek. It was a severe winter, typical to the Idaho-Montana border region. One morning, Johnnie took off on snowshoes to mail a letter to Charlie. Along the way, he wandered into a heavy blizzard. It was a desperate situation and made even worse when one of his snowshoes broke. Johnnie Beal never made it to the post office.

Later that spring, as the snows melted, a rider found the boy's body with the letter still in his pocket. The man took the envelope and mailed it. In his letter, Johnnie had urged Charlie not to come to Idaho. By the time Charles received the letter in 1881, he was already working in Silver Bow, part of a rough and tumble Montana mining town named Butte. He had written Ida to join him, and a few months later she did. They were married without much ceremony in a hotel. They remained working there, and their first son, Arthur, was born in Butte.

Charlie paid no attention to his pal Johnnie Beal's plea to avoid coming to Idaho. There was land to be had there, and a rough Montana mining town was not where he wanted to raise his family. In 1883, the young but hearty couple and their small son, Arthur, boarded a train and traveled just across the Idaho border to a stop on the line called Camas Creek. In Camas, Charlie and Ida May climbed off and spent their last $450 for a team of roan horses, Major and Jonny, and a wagon. "The wagon proved to be most reliable" part of their investment, another of their sons later joked.[3]

The homestead was a ranch not far from where the Beal's had spent that tragic winter. The young family first built a small one-room cabin that was adequate for the moment. With sweat and toil, Charlie cleared sagebrush off the land, and Ida May gave birth to two more sons. The cabin was now too small, and Charlie wrote to his brother in Wisconsin to come help build a four-room house in a cottonwood grove on Medicine Lodge Creek. The mountain climate sometimes brought setbacks and losses, but Charlie's and Ida May's new home gave them shelter, and they were soon raising horses, cattle, and hogs, along with hay, grain, and potatoes. They had the first and largest dairy in that part of Idaho. As the years passed, their house was the scene for parties and dances. Charlie provided the violin music.

Living on the frontier was always tricky, especially in the high Idaho desert where harsh winters and hot dry summers challenged any ranch or farm operation. It is a mistake, though, to think that a rough life was necessarily a plain and simple one. Charlie, with his talented charismatic personality, plowed a wide swath through his community. His daughter later wrote, "He could figure out any problem in algebra or geometry without a pencil or paper." In this isolated countryside, she said, he was a doctor, a lawyer, a marriage counselor, and sometimes even a minister. He played the violin by note and by ear, led the singing in church, and played for dances at the local hall. Charles was on the school board and would only hire teachers who could play and teach the organ.[4]

The Leonardson Ranch Company prospered and remained in the family after Charlie's death in 1916. Ida May lived another twenty years, long enough to see the ranch lost at the beginning of the Great Depression. Their first son, Arthur, was my great-grandfather. When a boy, I was fortunate to know Great-Grandfather Leonardson and his bride, Mary Emma. I was nine years old when they both died the same day in a tragic car accident in Montana, not far from where Arthur was born. I have always been glad there are a few places in my own memory that transport me back to this settler family and their New England roots.

Mapping my Search

Over the years, I have several times visited the spot on that high Rocky Mountain desert where Charlie Leonardson and Ida May Dawley homesteaded their ranch in the late 1800s. The sweet smell of sagebrush still drifts over the spring meadows and there is always an invigorating rush from the thin mountain air. But their summers were hot, winters cold, and it was dry – so dry and remote that the ranch house was eventually abandoned. The last time Seija and I visited the old homestead, there was nothing left of it except an old apple tree. My parents took a sprig from it to grow a tree of remembrance in their own yard. We enjoyed apples and apple butter from that tree until Mother and Dad joined her great-grandparents who planted the original one.

The trail into one's family past usually begins with those family members still around us. My mother Margie embarked on hers by writing down her own memories of Ida May, the stories she had heard of Charlie, and many others. Aware that memories are never complete and only weaken with time, she interviewed her parents, grandparents, uncles, and aunts, often many times, to augment her memories with theirs. Margie also sought out family histories, letters, and records written by Ida May's children. All of this she carefully filed in a folder labeled "Charles Leonardson and Ida May Dawley." A generation later, I integrated this material into a single narrative, trying to emphasize the similarities among all these recollections.

I regretted not having asked Mother more than I did. In retrospect, there are many questions we could have asked if we had known then what we do now. But the important thing is to gather as much information as we can as early as possible from older family members. I was four generations from Charlie and Ida May, still close enough to profit from first-hand accounts of this illustrious pioneer family.

Over the decades, Margie built pedigrees extending back from her initial family interviews. Accessing vital records and the work of other genealogists, she eventually extended the trees hundreds of years. They went back to Colonial New England, a place full of record-keepers. There was no shortage of information on the people who lived there.

Before moving West, ten generations of Ida May's family had been in Rhode Island, from the beginning of the 1630's. Her ancestors helped found the Rhode Island colony. I often overheard some of their tales in Mother's conversations when I was growing up. I was anxious to learn details of these nearly 400-year old stories. The more I dug into the lives of these remote grandfathers and grandmothers, the more I was surprised how readily their colorful accounts jumped onto my pages. Ida May's heritage was richer than I could have imagined. I found many new stories that would have endlessly enchanted my mother Margie, if only she had lived to hear them.

I expanded my search by copying a list of the founders of Rhode Island found in a Wikipedia article "Early Settlers of Rhode Island." Although Wikipedia could be called a lay-researcher's encyclopedia, it is much more than that. True, its articles are submitted by its readers, but the site's quality control is quite remarkable, and the people who submit material are often first-rate researchers and academics. Also, at the bottom of Wikipedia entries is normally list of sources and associated weblinks. When I was fortunate enough to find an ancestor (or a place or event associated with an ancestor) listed in Wikipedia's massive data base, these references alone often launched me on a fruitful journey. Often, they led me to books and websites that were valuable resources.

With this list of founders in hand, I next sorted through Mother's genealogy pedigrees that extended into 17th century Rhode Island. When I compared my list of founders to the names I found on Mother's pedigrees, there were several hits: Obadiah Holmes, both John Greenes, Samuel Gorton, and more.

The following stop on my road was a copy of John Osborne Austin's The Genealogical Dictionary of Rhode Island that my son's family gave me one year for Christmas. I found many family genealogies and summaries on pages where in 1888 Austin effectively crafted so much information on so many people into such a short space. Mother, for all her extensive research, was not aware of some of these ancestors nor of Austin's genealogies, but piecing together the connections I found in Austin's three generation-tables, I discovered new grandfathers and grandmothers that we had missed before. I also saw that Margie's research tracked closely with what I found in Austin's compilations. That gave the work credibility in my eyes.

With Austin, I was off and running. Once I had a general skeleton of their stories, I was able to focus on details. (There are similar genealogical dictionaries for other parts of the New England colonies as well as regions elsewhere. They are not always 100% accurate – what compilation is? – but they are the result of years of serous research by dedicated genealogists.)

Where Time and Place intersect
Even with so much new information in hand, however, everything came a piece at a time. Much had been long forgotten, other parts were totally lost, and the fragments that came to the surface needed synthesis into coherent stories. But new tales were

78

taking form, and I knew that I needed more context to tie them together into a narrative that did justice to the extraordinary lives these people led.

I also recognized that any story, and any person for that matter, has two defining coordinates: time and place. Everyone lives and everything happens at the junction of a time and a place, precisely where the two intersect. Time is totally transient, and in our minds, at least, may even seem to pick up speed the farther it moves along. Places, however, remain fixed in one configuration or another, forever. We can only revisit time in our memories, imaginations, histories, and perhaps in our genes. Places are usually accessible. It had been 400 years since these families etched out their multihued lives, but the places where their stories unfolded were still somewhere, and maybe we could find them. I wanted to see and experience these places.

I planned our trips meticulously and had long lists of locations to visit in every place we stopped. Some spots were the usual ones: museums, historical sites, and so on. Others I found through the internet, such as the addresses where they lived and graveyards where some were buried. But I also set aside time to follow-up on what I learned as my wife and I explored the towns where they lived.

Each visit revealed how Ida May's early American people were *from an extraordinary generation of women and men who sensed the enormity of their New World narrative. Their unlimited tenacity, their unwavering awareness of destiny, and their uncompromising sense of right gave prominence to their lives. I chose to concentrate on four families whose remarkable lives particularly fascinated me: John Greene, Samuel Gorton, Obadiah Holmes, and another John Greene. There were others, such as Chad Brown, the first appointed* **pastor of America's first Baptist Church, and John Coggeshall, the combined Rhode Island colony's first governor. For the sake up** *brevity I decided to save their stories for another time.*

Dealing with Perishability

When gathering the information on the families I was tracking, I realized almost immediately that the material I was collecting was vulnerable to loss, either physically, or simply due to my being unable to locate it when needed. To protect against this inherent perishability, I needed as much as possible to have redundant systems to preserve them: one of them paper and the other digital. The paper went into my file cabinet's folders, each file devoted to one couple, a grandfather and grandmother. These couple/family files were organized in groups with the same surname. The file cabinet was a fairly conventional way of organizing family data.

The digital files contained much of the same information and had many advantages, not the least of which was the ability to access quickly documents, photos, and so on, and to email them to other family members. But there were also disadvantages: the eventual obsolescence of file formats, vulnerability to computer crashes, and the susceptibility to over-filing and crowding. (I will talk more of this in a later chapter.)

To offset some of these problems, I used only software (such as MS Word) that I expected to be around for a while and to be automatically updated. For a modest price, I also ordered cloud storage that automatically uploaded all my files to the cloud. I labeled and subdivided my cloud storage into broad categories: "Written Histories," "Photographic Histories," "Video Histories," "Audio Histories," and so on, each with its own layers of sub-folders. I wanted to be able to find something quickly when I needed it, and logically ordering the folders was the key to this. I also wanted the files to run both directions, into the past and the future, allowing my own children and grandchildren to one day find what was available. To me it was important that the stories I was finding would be preserved and easy to locate by my own posterity.[5]

"What Cheer, Netop?"

The one thing that most people know best about Rhode Island is that it is America's smallest state. However, the role this small state played in America's early cultural and political development was immense though now often forgotten. It was among the five original New England colonies, along with Plymouth, Massachusetts Bay,

New Haven, and Connecticut. Of the five, Rhode Island became the crucible where many of the ideals that distinguished the American experience were born and tested: pluralistic democratic governance, freedom of speech and religion, separation of church and state, equality, diversity, and tolerance. For most of New England's first 100 years, the other four colonies fought to constrain those nascent features of our experiment. They considered Rhode Islanders heretics for disagreeing with them.

The Plymouth colony was the beginning of New England. There, an unusual group of colonists made an audacious start. They were ordinary men, women, and children willing to suffer almost anything for the freedom to worship their religion and embark on a new path toward prosperity. Weavers, wool carders, tailors, and shoemakers, none of them much experienced in building a community in the wild, climbed off the Mayflower in the late fall of 1620. "It is not with us as with other men," they told, "whom small things can discourage, or small discontentments cause to wish themselves home again."[6] The Pilgrims' resolve was tempered when the ensuing winter took the lives of half of them. By spring, only 52 of the original 102 were left.

One cold autumn morning we shivered when visiting the captivating re-enactment park at "Plimoth Plantation," just a few miles south of today's Plymouth. A Wampanoag Native American re-enactor sat around a bonfire in her full costume, the fur leaving parts of her arms and legs bare. Not seeming to mind the cold, she succinctly described the problem to us: "When they arrived, we thought they would never have come if they didn't know what they were doing. By the end of the first winter, we knew they didn't." Only with the Wampanoags' generosity with food and know-how did these English Pilgrims find a foothold in their New World.

Ten years later, on the heels of the Plymouth Colony, John Winthrop led a robust fleet of eleven ships carrying 700 people to establish another colony just north of Plymouth in the area around today's Boston. They called it the Massachusetts Bay Colony. They, too, hoped to worship their religion without the persecution they had endured in England. Over the following decade, the "Great

Migration" that Winthrop led brought 20,000 people across the Atlantic in nearly 200 small vessels. In 1640, the Great Migration ended almost as abruptly as it began. By then, many of Grandmother Ida May's Puritan ancestors were in the New World.

The Massachusetts Bay colonists have been called "Puritans" because they wanted to cleanse the errors they saw in the Church of England. On the other hand, many of the Plymouth colonists were "Separatists" with no inclination to remain part of the Church of England fabric. The Connecticut Colony, settled in 1636, came about primarily as a result of land hunger on the part of some of the Massachusetts Bay arrivals. The New Haven settlement was born in 1638 when a group from Boston, hoping to set up a trade center, ended up instead establishing a farming community. In truth, however, the religion of these four colonies flowed from the same well. Religiously they were greatly in harmony, Puritans and Separatists alike, meeting each week in Congregationalist churches that still dot the picturesque countryside in New England.

As strange as it seems to us today, neither the leaders of Plymouth nor Massachusetts were after freedom of religion, if that meant letting people follow their own consciences. The path to heaven was clearly marked in their minds. To them, any deviation in the everyday lives of the colonists was to be caught early and corrected as completely as possible. The irony was that a movement that attracted non-conformists was also sure to draw individualists who might easily stray from Puritan thought. This quickly created the need for an escape mechanism to re-locate "heretics." The Puritans had no interest in establishing a place of banishment, but if there were a place the banished could go, that was helpful.

Sooner or later, most of Ida May Dawley's ancestors were in the "banished" category. The consistent unorthodoxy among so many of her grandfathers and grandmothers is a family tradition, a penchant, a weakness, or a strength, depending on how you look at it. I remember university professors who liked to call my research papers iconoclastic, and I was proud of that, even though sometimes my teachers were not. I cannot remember many from my modern family on Ida May's side who seemed satisfied to just follow the crowd. On the other hand, few of them failed to cherish liberty and tolerance, the hallmark of Ida May's independent ancestors. Individual freedom and an early form of populism constituted the unorthodoxy for which Ida May's forefathers fought and sacrificed. It was a continuing thread in their stories that I began to find.

Ida May's individualist ancestors followed a remarkable man named Roger Williams into a new wilderness settlement that eventually became Rhode Island. Roger Williams was born sometime between 1599 and 1603, the son of a London merchant tailor. After being educated at Cambridge, he was ordained a clergyman in the Church of England. He was dissatisfied, however, and associated with the English Puritan movement. When John Winthrop began planning to lead a group of Puritans to New England, Williams followed him to Massachusetts. He was welcomed there and offered the pastorship of the first Puritan Church in Boston. Roger Williams thought himself more a separatist, however, and refused. Instead, he moved to Plymouth where he hoped to feel more comfortable among Separatists.

Roger Williams was intellectually and spiritually restless in Plymouth, as well. In 1633 Williams was summoned to Boston to appear in court for his attack on the establishment he published in a tract. His tract disappeared and was probably burned. With this wrinkle smoothed out, he moved to Salem to take over the pastorship there. In Salem he had many followers, but he was soon espousing many of the same arguments as before. In a matter of months Roger stood again before the Court, accused of heresy.

In October 1635, the Court convicted Roger Williams of heresy and sedition. It ordered him banished. In a January blizzard, he escaped just ahead of the constables, and trudged 55 miles in deep snow to a place on the colony's west coast, near present day Raynham, Massachusetts. He was only able to survive when Wampanoag Chief Sachem Massasoit sheltered him for three winter months. Williams never forgot Massasoit's generosity. The mutual friendship with the Native American tribes lasted several decades.[7]

When the spring thaw came, Roger Williams, with five friends from Salem who had followed after him, began to look for a site for their own settlement, a place outside the control of the Massachusetts and Plymouth colonies. One morning while rowing on Narragansett Bay, a group of Indians saw the men and yelled, "What cheer, Netop?" which meant "What's the news, Friend?" These kindly words, still gracing Providence's city seal, became the defining motif of the new colony Williams founded just west of Plymouth and Massachusetts Bay.

When he found a site he thought would work well for the new colony, Roger Williams approached Miantonomi and Canonicus, chief sachems of the Narragansetts, and offered to purchase the land. The 5,000-member Narragansett tribe was by far the largest and most powerful in the area. Canonicus had had his fill of the Puritan Europeans and wanted none of them on his lands. Williams, on the other hand, had carefully nurtured friendship with the Narragansetts and other tribes and even mastered their languages in order to know them better. "It was not price nor money that could have purchased Rhode Island. Rhode Island was purchased by love," Williams explained. "'Tis true he recd presents and Gratuities many of me: but it was not thouhsands nor ten thouhsands of mony could have bought of him an English Entrance into the Bay." [8]

Soon, followers, friends, and newly banished souls from Salem and elsewhere in the Massachusetts and Plymouth were flocking to join Williams in the town he called Providence. Ida May's forbearers were among them. In the spring of 1638, Roger Williams, organized a congregation of the Baptist church. The first Baptist church in the New World met in the Williams's home. Typical of his spiritual restlessness, Williams only served four months as the Baptist leader before doubts led him to an early departure. He had come to believe that a church could not be established unless it could trace its origins to the apostles. No mere man could start a church, he decided. Ida May's ancestor Chad Browne took over as the chosen pastor of the new church. [9]

The Gentleman Surgeon

Among those in the small group that gathered with Roger Williams for baptism that day in 1638 was a surgeon named John

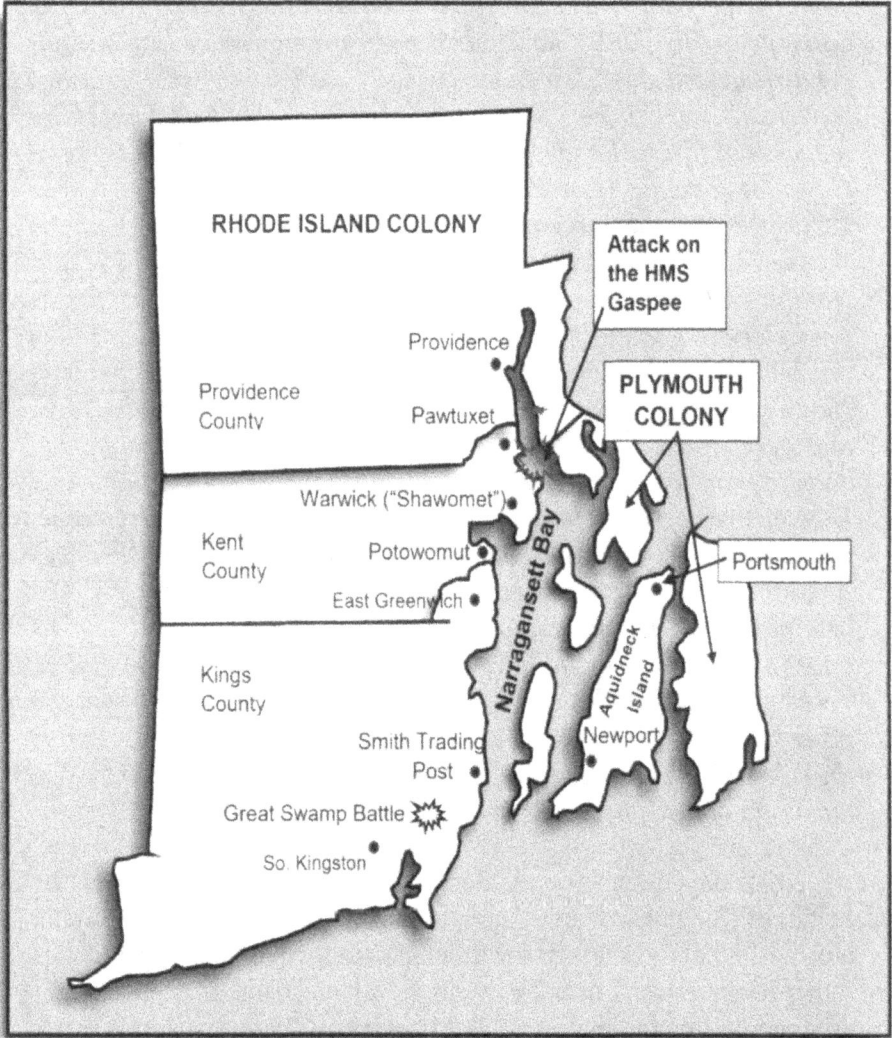

Map C – Rhode Island and Narragansett Bay

Greene. When he arose from the water, Dr. John Greene was one of the original members of the first Baptist Church in America. John, a surgeon, had immigrated from an established practice in Salisbury. His gentry family had been prominent in England for centuries, and his descendants were to become distinguished Americans. When he passed away, he left behind an impressive legacy, not just to Rhode Island. His descendants include a broad range of famous Americans, from the great Revolutionary War General Nathanael Greene, to inventor Thomas Edison, actor John Wayne, American President Warren Harding, and religious leader Nathan Tanner.

Before I get more into his story, however, I will make an important clarification. There were at least two John Greene's in New England's earliest history. Both of them lived in Rhode Island and were married to women named Joanne, also spelled Joane and Joan. And both were my great-great grandmother Ida May Dawley's ancestors. Her father's mother was Lydia French Greene, who descended from Dr. John Greene. Ida's mother, Frances Angeline Greene, came from the other Rhode Island John. The two original Rhode Island John Greenes are said to be second cousins once removed, although I have not yet found sound evidence of that. To keep them straight, I will call one "Dr. John Greene" and the other "John of Quidnessett" because that is where he lived. This is the story of Dr. John Greene. John of Quidnessett, an Indian trader, makes an appearance later in the chapter.[10]

Dr. John Greene was a Gentleman born around 1595, at the height of Queen Elizabeth I's reign, in Bowridge Hall, a manor lying atop a hill that overlooked the quiet Dorset town of Gillingham. His father Richard was Lord of Bowridge Hall and came from an ancient aristocratic lineage that ascended back to William the Conqueror's time, with Sir Henry Greene, Chief Justice of England in between.[11] One of his father's distant cousins, Katherine Parr, a few decades before, had been Henry VIII's last wife and Queen of England. His mother Mary Hooker's family, too, was full of political and clerical leaders. John was the fourth son in a large family.[12]

As Lords of the manor, the Greene family was part of England's gentry, the sub-noble class that ran the Elizabethan countryside. The realm had only 50 peers – dukes, earls, barons, and so on – and its 500 knights and 15,000 gentlemen were the gentry backbone of the Tudors' rule and economy. Families like the Greenes were in the mainstream of local and national society. With their vast herds of sheep (there were twice as many sheep as Englishmen) and fields worked by local peasants, the gentry's manors were crucial to the country's well-being. England was still mainly rural. Only a fourth of its people lived in the country's 25 cathedral cities and just over 600 market towns. The largest city near Gillingham was Salisbury, a city that impressed the kingdom with its magnificent cathedral.

When it came to inheritances, England followed primogeniture rules which in practice meant that the first son inherited the family estate and title. As the fourth son, there was little chance John would succeed to become Lord of Bowridge Hall. Like other second, third, and fourth gentry sons, he needed to find a profession. Of the possibilities, there were three common professions or vocations: the law, the church, and medicine. All three could generally produce a healthy income, although medicine was the least rewarding.

The medical profession was divided into three branches: physicians, surgeons, and apothecaries. Physicians treated illnesses; surgeons dealt with injuries, wounds, and ulcers; and apothecaries handed out medicines and ointments. Of these, surgeons were by far the most effective. The field of medicine still lacked sound theories of disease and how it was transmitted, and care by a physician usually started with leaches. But surgeons bound wounds, and there were plenty of wars where they learned how to do it. John chose to become a surgeon.

Dr. John Greene would have trained in medicine either at one of England's two universities of the time, Oxford or Cambridge, or as an apprentice surgeon. Since John was of a landed gentry family and known later to be well educated, he probably followed the university path. If he did, he left for university in his early teens, as was normal for his time. There he joined about 3,000 other students studying for degrees. After reading toward a Bachelor's degree, he could have taken a Master's and Doctorate in medicine, a course of study that sometimes took up to ten years to finish. A "John Green" was "licensed to practice medicine" from Cambridge University in 1615. There is not enough information on the university roster to know for sure that this "Green" was our John, but I would like to think it was.[13] He was in his early twenties when he married his first wife, Joane Tattershall, in 1619. In his time, men commonly married at about 28, so he was somewhat younger than average. But he had a profession, and at least some family resources as well.

John did not return to Gillingham, but set up his home and practice in Salisbury, about 25 miles away. Salisbury, with about 6,000 inhabitants, was one of England's largest cities during Elizabethan times. Its cathedral boasted then, and still does, the tallest spire in England. John was married and his children were christened in the newly expanded Parish Church of St. Thomas & St. Edmund, another stately Anglican church, often forgotten in the shadows of the cathedral, only a few blocks away. Toward the rear of St. Thomas's still stands the old font where their priest baptized sons James, Ida May's ancestor and the great grandfather of Revolutionary War general Nathanael Greene, and John, Jr., a future 10-consecutive term Deputy Governor of the Rhode Island colony.

When their children were baptized, the parish records referred to John as a "gentleman." A gentleman in Elizabethan times was normally someone who had income from land that he did not have to farm himself. John came from a landed gentry family, but whether he had income from that land is hard to say. However, he was a noted professional in the important city of Salisbury, and he probably had enough wealth for people to call him a gentleman or "Mr. Greene, Surgeon, late of Salisbury," as rolls of the ship taking him to America recorded.

As an educated man, John also spoke Latin and apparently enjoyed reading it. When his brother Richard died, he willed John half of his Latin books. Years later when his other brother Robert passed away, his will read: "I bequeath to my brother John Greene in New England, all my Latin books if he come for them." It would have been a long trip from Rhode Island to pick up some books, and

Dr. Greene did not make it. By that time, he was getting too old for the hard Atlantic passage.[14]

Either during his university years or after he settled in Salisbury, John got caught up in the religious fervor of the time. His extended family was split in the conflict between the Anglicans and Puritans. Richard Hooker, his mother Mary Hooker's first cousin, was perhaps the greatest Anglican theologian of his time. John and Joane, however, held Puritan sympathies and were on the other side of the ongoing religious feud. As Charles I's and his Archbishop Laud's persecution of the Puritans became unbearably severe, many chose to depart England for the Puritan colony in Massachusetts. John, Joane, and their six children joined them. On April 6, 1635, they traveled to London and boarded the *James* bound for Boston.

The *James* was a 200-ton vessel, about twice the size of the small Mayflower that carried the Plymouth pilgrims fifteen years earlier. Nevertheless, the *James* was hardly spacious. The deck below teemed with animals and every nook and cranny was filled with provisions. Most of their fellow passengers were laborers and craftsmen. A small group of them was also from Salisbury. A typical ship passage was expensive, about £60-80 for a family of six. The Greenes and their children numbered eight, so their fare must have approached £100. To put this into some perspective, a typical English worker might earn £40-60 for a year's labor. In addition to this fare, the family would have needed funds to buy or build a house and start their new life. I expect John and Joane carried a sizeable amount of cash with them.[15]

The *James* pulled out of London's port of Hampton and started its voyage across the Atlantic. After 58 days – many of them long sea-sick days – the vessel sailed into Boston on June 3. John and Joane and their large family of young children – John (14 years old), Peter (13), James (9), Thomas (7), Joan (5), and Mary (2) – gladly walked down the plank from the narrow quarters of the cramped ship.[16] At the bottom, they stood once again on dry ground in the new city of Boston, itself hardly five years old.

They did not stay there, however. Salem, about 25 miles north of Boston, was a popular location for new arrivals, and, with some of their fellow passengers, John and Joanne traveled to Salem to find a home. Salem is generally remembered as the seat of the infamous witch trials a few years later, but when the Greenes reached the town they entered one of the Bay Colony's most thriving communities. They purchased a house and over the summer months started their new life. On Sundays, they attended the church where they met the pastor, Roger Williams. They were impressed with him and quickly became followers. By this time, Williams was already deep into his disagreement with the Massachusetts Bay authorities and that winter was banished from the colony.

Along with many others of Roger Williams's followers, John and Joane were outraged at their pastor's forced exile. They spent the winter in Salem, and sometime during 1637 crossed Narragansett Bay to become among the first twelve families to receive a parcel of the land Williams had purchased from the Narragansetts. John and Joane got Home Lot number 15, just four down the street from Roger Williams's lot. The family acquired or built a new house, and John began a practice as a surgeon. Their oldest son, John Jr., would soon be old enough to have his own family and was also allotted a parcel, just five lots down the street from his parents.

It is a challenge for us today to understand the hardships that people like the Greenes faced when they built their homes and communities in the New World. For John and Joane, the strain was soon compounded with the second re-location, from Salem to Providence, an area of pristine wilderness where only a small handful of Europeans had ever lived. Food and shelter, clothing and sanitation, travel and staying in touch: everything depended on back-breaking work and know-how.

We can imagine how hard it could be to travel from our century to the time and place where they found themselves. Yes, we can rationalize that in those days, unlike today, people knew how to use their hands to build and survive in crude conditions. Instead, we calculate on computers and IPADs, get our work done with machines and equipment, and travel with cars and planes.

For a Gentleman and his well-bred wife from Salisbury, however, it probably was almost as challenging to move from a privileged home in England to the wilds of America as it might be for us to slip through time to 17th century New England. The work was hard, and the climate was harsh. New England was settled during a period known as the "mini ice-age" and much colder than it is today. Gentlemen and Ladies, who had never toiled in the fields nor done hard household or manual labor, had to learn how to farm. They not only had to learn how to till the soil, but to actually do it: felling trees, plowing the earth with muscle-powered implements, milking cows by hand, keeping a household, raising children in primitive circumstances, and preparing the fields for next year's harvest. They needed not only to know how to build a house, but actually to be the carpenter who ensured it was sound and kept them warm and dry, no matter how severe the weather.

Such work often came at a price. John and Joane were in Providence only a short time before Joane's health deteriorated. She had given birth to a large family and had traveled halfway around the world to a land barely more than wilderness. Joane died not long after they arrived in Providence.[17] John was left a widower with six children, at least three of whom were under ten years old. Life without both spouses fully engaged in the family's business was virtually impossible in the everyday circumstances early colonists faced. As was customary and expedient, John looked for a new wife and soon wed Alice Daniels.

Alice's Home Lot was just three lots south of Roger Williams's, and John's was four lots north, indicating they were both some of the earliest settlers in Providence Plantation. She had arrived in 1630 on Winthrop's ships, was among the first settlers of Massachusetts Bay, and knew John Winthrop. She also lived in Salem and followed pastor Roger Williams, meeting and getting acquainted with the Greenes along the way. Alice and John shared a mutual interest in medicine. She worked as some sort of apothecary, although as a woman she would not have had an opportunity for formal training like Dr. John did. In 1637, the plantation's second year, Alice, along with the other first settlers, paid two shillings, for her lot.[18]

Alice was remarkable. She was literate and a "freeman" in a strongly patriarchal Puritan society. She had some amount of wealth or she would never have been admitted as a freeman and granted parcels of land in Salem and Providence. Alice must have been strong-willed, for it took a lot of courage as a single woman to leave everything behind in Salem. Starting completely anew in the Narragansett wilderness was challenging for a man, a family, and especially for a woman on her own.

Initially, Alice was married in England to a man named Richard Beggarly. Once in Massachusetts, however, she filed for a divorce, accusing her husband of adultery. Most people in Salem must have believed her, or Alice would not have enjoyed the prominent position she held in Salem – a town never known for its love or tolerance toward anyone whose reputation was not sound, nor even toward many whose reputations were beyond reproach. But the Massachusetts colony's fathers did not grant her the divorce she sought "till she might send into England for further proof."[19]

During its early years, the most prominent person in Salem was the Reverend Samuel Skelton. Rev. Skelton had been recruited to be the colony's minister even before the Bay Colony was established, and he was in Massachusetts before Winthrop's fleet sailed into the waters of the new colony. Rev. Skelton's wife unfortunately passed away shortly after his arrival. Samuel, too, died four years later. Roger Williams was appointed to Skelton's position at the Salem Church.

Following Skelton's passing, Alice was appointed administrator of his estate. She wrote a letter to Gov. Winthrop telling him she was willing to take on this responsibility, but she told him she did not want to have charge of Skelton's young children. Apparently, her wish was granted, and she handled the estate while the orphan children were placed with others. Putting it all together, it is easy to close your eyes and see Alice in the new colonies as a powerfully talented person capable of making her own way through an unimaginably difficult place and time, doing things few men in this strictly ordered community would be asked to do.

When Alice married Dr. John Greene. Massachusetts Governor John Winthrop complained about it in his journal entry of December, 1638, saying, "One Greene (who had married the wife of one Beggerly, whose husband is living, and no divorce, etc., but only it was said, that he had lived in adultery and had confessed it)." Apparently, the Providence authorities granted or recognized the divorce. Attitudes in Providence Plantation may have been much freer than in Massachusetts, but Providence Plantation did not condone adultery nor bigamy. In Providence, moreover, John and Alice were among the community's most prominent couples.[20]

Not long after Dr. Greene arrived in Providence, he got involved in an intriguing case before the colony's freemen. A young couple from Salisbury, Joshua Verin and his wife Agnes, had traveled from England to the New World on the *James* with the Greene family. Upon reaching Massachusetts, the Verins also settled with John and Joane in Salem.

Verin, too, was attracted to the charismatic Roger Williams. When Williams was banished a few months later, Verin was among the small group that followed him and spent that winter in the Wampanoag Indian village. He was also with Roger Williams when he settled at Providence. In May 1637, however, Joshua faced complaints of domestic abuse and curbing the freedom to worship.

Roger Williams's wife held in her house regular religious gatherings where she invited Joshua's young wife Agnes and other women of the community to join. Agnes much enjoyed the meetings and was often there. But this sat poorly with Joshua who complained she was neglecting her housework. He forbade her from attending. One day, after she returned from another of the meetings, he gave her a beating that was brutal and scandalous. People of the community saw what had happened, and Joshua was brought before the town's governing committee of the town's landholders.

In his hearing, Joshua Verin was accused of suppressing his wife's freedom of conscience and was thus guilty of violating the town's cardinal principle of religious tolerance. In the debate that ensued, one of the town fathers, William Arnold, stood in Verin's defense. Arnold claimed that when Verin agreed to the community's freedom of conscience, he did not mean to "breach the ordinance of God such as the subjection of wives to their husbands."

This claim ran counter to John Greene's sense of justice and propriety. He rose to his feet and responded with an argument that the town's governing landowners could not ignore. Dr. John pointed out, perhaps with a grain of humor, that if "they should restrain their wives, all the women in the country would cry out of them." Whatever Verin's and Arnold's theoretical notions of the proper "ordinance of God" toward subjecting wives, the reality, as John contended, was that this frontier province could not run roughshod over its women. He was arguing that if they accepted Arnold's view, they would be oppressing not just Verin's wife, Agnes, but every woman in the community. Arnold continued to drive the idea that a husband's subjection of his wife was God's order, and replied to Dr. Greene, "Would you now break an ordinance and commandment of God to please women?"

This was an intriguing case, with several interesting facets. Why did they try Verin on the principle of religious intolerance, but not for wife-beating? Beating one's wife was not necessarily a crime in the 17th century. That may be a reason why the town fathers, offended by Verin's cruelty, approached the case from another angle. At its core, moreover, there were two strong sides to the case: the right of the community to impose its democratically chosen commitment to freedom vs. the right of a family to govern itself according to commonly accepted practice, and according to a religious belief that God appointed men to rule their families. The community's founders, in their strong defense of personal freedoms, decided that the colony had a responsibility to protect those freedoms even if it encroached on one of its members' attempts to govern his household as he saw fit.

John Greene's view on this prevailed. In reaching their decision, the community elders punished Joshua Verin by taking away his right to vote. Angry, Verin departed with Agnes for Boston. Williams wrote Massachusetts Bay Governor Winthrop to explain:

"Sir: we have long been afflicted by a young man boisterous and desperate... so because he could not draw his wife, a gracious and modest woman, to the same ungodliness with him, he hath trodden her under foot tyrannically and brutishly; at the last the major vote of us discard him from our civil freedom or disfranchise him."[21]

Williams knew that Governor Winthrop would sympathize with Joshua's right to subject his wife, but he probably hoped the Winthrop would at least follow the matter in order to protect Agnes from further brutalities. From Winthrop's account of the affair, in fact, he was on Joshua's side. Hearing of the Providence debate was probably the first time he came across Dr. John Greene. It would not be the last time, however. Dr. Greene, who may have treated Agnes after her violent beating, was not only sympathetic to her case. He was also a defender of the ideas of conscience and freedom Winthrop never learned to appreciate. John was a bitter critic of the Puritan repression of these freedoms. I saw this once again when tracking more of his dealings with the Massachusetts authorities.

The summer after the Greene family located in Providence, John made a trip back to Massachusetts. He planned to sell the house they had left behind in Salem. The family had voluntarily departed Salem, and they were not banished exiles like some of their Providence neighbors. So John returned to Massachusetts without fear of imprisonment, or worse. However, at one point during his trip, he found himself publicly criticizing the Bay colony's leaders, saying "that the magistrates had usurped upon the power of Christ in his church, and had persecuted Mr. Williams and another, whom they had banished for disturbing the peace."[22] Word traveled quickly through the colony, and John's criticism soon made its back to Boston's leaders who had him arrested on August 1, 1637.

The news travelled the opposite direction, as well. When word reached Providence that Greene was in a Boston jail, Roger Williams rallied to his support and wrote a letter to Governor Winthrop asking him to release Dr. Greene. But Williams's appeal did not help. At John's trial in September, he was fined £20 and imprisoned until the fine was paid. At first, he refused to pay it. Twenty pounds was a lot of money. Still, he could not ignore the fact that his family in Providence was suffering while he wasted away in the Boston jail. John finally recanted his words and allowed to return to Providence. The Court forbade him from ever returning.

When John got back to Providence, however, he did not leave things as they were. A few months later, he wrote a letter to Boston authorities reinstating his criticism of the Boston Court. His letter, once again, charged the magistrates with "usurping the powers of Christ over the churches and men's consciences." The Court responded by ordering him not to come within Massachusetts's jurisdiction, "under pain of imprisonment and further censure."

With that, they had banned him twice. The Boston authorities knew that John Greene was not speaking alone and that many others in Providence shared his sentiments. They therefore ordered that anyone from Providence within their jurisdiction had to issue an oath disclaiming John's accusation against the court. If someone refused, they, too, would be banished. This was not the end of it. John and the Massachusetts magistrates would clash again.[23]

Dr. John Greene was not the only individualistic, strong-willed citizen in Providence Plantation. There were others. However, unlike John, a few of them led by a man named William Arnold focused their energies primarily on getting wealthier, however they may. They started by trying to increase their share of the up-to-then equal allotments of the land Williams bought from the Indians. At the same time, their Massachusetts Bay neighbor regularly took an aggressive stance toward Providence, claiming Roger Williams's small colony of "heretics" did not have its own charter from the Crown and therefore was not legitimate. That the Bay Colony coveted Rhode Island's frontage along Narragansett Bay was no secret. Massachusetts had none of its own on either side of Narragansett Bay. These things made fertile ground for intrigues, and there was plenty of infighting among various Providence factions, often fueled by Massachusetts.

In 1641, a man named Samuel Gorton and his family moved to Providence. Gorton had a reputation. He had been banished from Plymouth colony, and Massachusetts Bay authorities despised him as much as their Plymouth friends did. Just before arriving in

Providence, he had also been violently thrown out of Portsmouth on Aquidneck Island in Narragansett Bay. Because of his notoriety as an outspoken character whose acid-tongue stirred up things wherever he lived, there were some in Providence who wanted to block his right to own property there. This opened up an additional level of controversy that only added to the contentious times.

John Greene and Samuel Gorton, however, bonded from the beginning. Gorton's story comes next, but for now the Gortons enter Dr. John Greene's life when the two families, together with some friends, decide to organize a new settlement that would one day be called Warwick, Rhode Island. To do this, the Greenes, the Gortons, and ten other families approached the Narragansett tribe with an offer to buy a plot of land immediately south of Providence, at a place called Shawomet (see Map C). Chief sachems Canonicus and Miantonomi agreed to the deal, and the families signed it with the Narragansett tribe on January 12, 1642. This new site, the families hoped, would allow them to settle with like-minded neighbors, away from the contention in Providence.

Unfortunately, this would not be as easy as they hoped. William Arnold's Providence party also coveted the Shawomet lands. By egregiously counterfeiting a portion of Roger Williams's original deed and bribing some minor Narragansett chiefs to say they had sold the land to him, Arnold was able to make it appear that he had a legitimate claim to the Shawomet parcel. The faction's greed for the real estate coincided with Massachusetts's desire for a foothold on the west side of the bay. When Arnold turned to the Bay Colony for support in his attempt to seize the land from the Shawomet families, Boston's leaders saw an opportunity. As Governor Winthrop confided, "We thought it not wisdom to let it slip."[24]

Siding with the Arnold faction, the Massachusetts Court forbade the Shawomet purchase. But the families were stubbornly convinced they were in the right. Ignoring the Court's extraterritorial demands, they finalized the transaction with Sachems Canonicus and Miantonomi. The Boston Court was enraged at how these obstinate families had flaunted Massachusetts's authority and grew determined to put these heretic settlers where they belonged, in jail or on the gallows. Hardly below the surface, the affair was a convenient excuse for Massachusetts to expand into territory not granted to it in its Royal Charter.

Right in the middle of this squabble, John Greene approached Narragansett Chief Miantonomi to purchase still another parcel of land, south of the one the tribe had sold earlier to Roger Williams. Miantonomi and his uncle Canonicus also agreed to John Greene's offer. The three of them knew that the sale would further aggravate the Boston Court, but the Narragansetts' friendly relations with Providence Plantation did not extend to Massachusetts. The chiefs well understood that these lands were outside Massachusetts's colonial charter and they, too, totally disregarded its magistrates' attempts to thwart the sale. On October 1, 1642, Miantonomi sold Dr. Greene 700 acres at a place known as Occupasuetuxet on Narragansett Bay. The site was directly south of the settlement of Pawtuxet. This piece of property remained in the Greene family for the following 140 years, when it was sold to one of Chad Browne's descendants.[25]

In response, Massachusetts's leaders sent a message to the Shawomet settlers threatening legal action and more. When the families continued to dispute the Court's authority over their lands, the Boston Court began plans to force them out. In May 1643, it ordered a military mission organized to remove them from their new homes and to bring the men back to face charges in Boston.

Granting the settlers one more chance to comply voluntarily, the Court also sent a warrant to the settlers summoning them to appear before the Court in Boston. It was William Arnold, the Greenes' old nemesis from Providence and leader of the faction trying hook-or-crook to obtain new land, who delivered the warrant. For Greene, Gorton, and the rest of the Shawomet settlers, Boston could not have chosen a worse character to be its bearer. Arnold's presence made the collaboration between Boston and Arnold's Providence faction transparent and obvious.

The Shawomet neighbors shot back a response so hot it must have warmed the courier's bags all the way to Boston. The long letter was infused with scriptures that unambiguously compared

Boston's leaders to the priests of Balaam in the Old Testament and the Pharisees, in the New. It began by saying "…We could not easily give credit unto the truth" of the claims of the warrant because it was William Arnold who delivered it.

That was not the only reason the settlers rejected the Court's demands. Their retort scorned the Bostonians who drafted the warrant: "We thought that men of your parts and profession would never have prostrated their wisdom to such an act." It accused the magistrates of having eyes "dazzled with envy," and ears "open unto lyes." On and on it went, adding the ultimate insult to the Puritans' self-righteousness, "Countrey men, for wee cannot but call you so, though we find your carriage to be so farre worse than these Indians."[26] John Greene and the other eleven men among the settlers all signed the letter, but it was surely Samuel Gorton who wrote it. He was the master of such acerbic language. In my mind I can see John and Samuel having a good laugh after the letter was sent.

Boston's magistrates did not laugh, however. By July, preparations for a military expedition were well underway, and the Court sent a letter to the settlers threatening violence. The missive concluded that the Boston Court was sending "commissioners" and a 40-man armed "guard" that would settle the matter. A posse of forty soldiers may not seem terribly large to us, but an invasion of only twelve homes by forty armed soldiers led by a Captain known for his ruthlessness was a dreadful thing for those who faced it.

Trying to calm the situation, people in Providence asked Chad Browne to form a committee with two others to arbitrate a resolution with the Massachusetts colony. The Boston Court, however, was not interested in a peaceful settlement. Winthrop rejected any arbitration, since, in his words, "They were no state but a few fugitives living without law or government, and so not honorable for us to join with them in such a course." The Shawomet settlers were simply, "…men not equal to us."[27]

By September, the military mission marched from Boston and was underway. Its objectives targeted the capture of Samuel Gorton for his stubborn and vocal resistance to the Massachusetts colony – or heresy, as they put it – and John Greene for his land purchase of a few months earlier. To make the operation even more productive, their orders included a provision to confiscate all of John Greene's livestock and to bring the animals back to Boston. Livestock was still relatively rare and expensive. They obviously coveted Dr. John's herd that he probably had brought from England.[28]

The military party paraded out of Boston, and as it proceeded its commissioners wrote another letter in which they demanded to speak with the men of Shawomet. If the Rhode Islanders were not willing to repent, the commissioners threatened, they and their armed company would "look upon them as men prepared for slaughter."[29] Capt. Cooke and the commissioners were not just playing for dramatic effect. They were deadly serious. Not surprisingly, the message terrorized the settlement's families who knew that Massachusetts authorities were capable of any violence in justification of orthodoxy, and, in this case, to obtain an outpost on the west side of the Bay.[30]

When the armed men approached Providence, John and Alice and others still living in Providence escaped to their new lands in Shawomet. Cooke and his company, bolstered with Native American allies, marched after them in pursuit, right through Providence and on to Shawomet. On September 28 they halted just before entering the village. Faced with an ominous attack, Shawomet's women and children began fleeing to the forest. The men barricaded themselves into one of the buildings whose walls they quickly reinforced to stop bullets from the raiding party. (The next story telling about Samuel Gorton tells of the disastrous attack on Shawomet.)

Alice may have been already feeble or sick at the time of the attack. Before the soldiers began their assault, John and his son, John Jr., quickly departed the settlement to take Alice to a nearby Indian village where they stayed with her. She was a brave and strong woman, but further weakened from stress and exposure, Alice passed away that night among the Indians who gave them shelter. Remembering that tragic day, Samuel Gorton wrote of Alice's death and how other women, too, died, or, being "great with child," suffered miscarriages.[31]

100

John buried Alice where she died, in Conimicut. He had already lost one wife amidst the hardships of this new land, and now another, this time as a result of aggression from his Massachusetts neighbors. There is no small irony in this dreadful moment when industrious families, such as John's, found sanctuary with the local Indian tribes when faced with the violence of other White colonists. In the end, the Massachusetts raid on Shawomet was not merely a covetous adventure to promote Massachusetts's land holdings, illegal as it was. The shameful episode brought immense tragedy to some of the community's people, especially to John Greene and one of his neighbors, Robert Potter (another of Ida May's ancestors), who also lost his wife to exhaustion and exposure.

What I was finding in Dr. John Greene's stories, was somewhat different from what I had heard and read about in many histories. Dr. Greene has usually been portrayed as a member of a patrician English family who migrated to New England. There he joined with Roger Williams to help found Rhode Island, and father a line of many prominent Americans. This was all true, but now I saw something different. John was a man who had left the comfortable life of a surgeon in one of England's most splendid cities, a man who now knew hard manual work and who strained every day to etch out a life for his family. He put two wives to rest in the midst of these struggles.

Traveling from England to enjoy freedom from oppression in a new land did not work out exactly the way he expected. When he stood up for what he believed, there were still many who tried to push him down. Even removing to the fringes of New England's fledgling colonies failed to get his family far enough away from the tyrannical forces of his day. Native Americans sheltered him and his son John the night Alice passed away, in the middle of an invasion by his European brothers and sisters.

Attending Alice's last moments and grieving her loss, John was away from Shawomet when the Massachusetts troops launched their siege. He and his son escaped their neighbors' long march in chains back to Massachusetts. The Boston magistrates issued a warrant for the arrest of Dr. Greene, his son John Jr., and two others who had slipped through their fingers. The latter two men eventually left voluntarily for Massachusetts. John and John Jr. refused and remained "fugitives," another expression of his stubborn contempt for the Boston's claims to jurisdiction in Rhode Island.[32]

At the time the Massachusetts soldiers were marching through Providence, Roger Williams was getting ready to journey back to England. He knew his colony was perpetually vulnerable to neighbors who claimed the mere purchase from the Indians did not legitimize the Rhode Island settlements. In Williams' mind, he had to secure a royal charter, and he was determined to do this in London. When the Massachusetts colony refused to allow his passage from Boston, he took a longer journey via Manhattan to find ship passage. Roger Williams victoriously returned a year later with a new charter for Providence, Newport, and Portsmouth. He also carried a Parliamentary rebuke of the Massachusetts authorities for how they had treated the Rhode Island colonists.

Unfortunately, the new charter was vague about the Shawomet settlement, and Massachusetts kept pressure on the Shawomet families to stay away from their newly constructed homes. When Gorton and the Shawomet men finally returned from their incarceration in Massachusetts, they decided that they, too, would launch a delegation to London to obtain official recognition of their community. John Greene, Samuel Gorton, and fellow Shawomet settler Randall Holden agreed to take on this mission. They were a good team. Both Greene and Gorton were educated and articulate enough to assert their case in London's halls of power. They were totally confident they had right on their side and their arguments would prevail. In August 1645, the three followed Roger Williams's path to New Amsterdam and sailed from Manhattan to London.

They arrived in London after two months at sea. They went to work immediately and were totally successful in their mission. During his stay, John Greene accomplished even more than get the Crown's recognition for his Shawomet community. While in London, he met a woman named Phillip (probably pronounced Fil-LEEP). He married Phillip, and she became his third wife. In many of the histories of Dr. John Greene there has been some confusion about his three consecutive spouses. Going carefully through the old documents, it is clear that Joane was his first wife and the mother of John's children. Joane died soon after they arrived in New England. Alice, his second wife, died during the Boston invasion of Shawomet and was buried in Conimicut. Phillip, whom he married in London, is mentioned in his will and elsewhere as his widow.[33]

Dr. John Greene, Phillip, and Randall Holden arrived in Boston on September 16, 1646, with a document from the Earl of Warwick legitimizing their claim to the land in Shawomet. Samuel Gorton stayed behind in London. To the chagrin of the Massachusetts Court, they also carried a letter authorizing free passage through Boston on their way to Shawomet. John and Phillip made their way to Shawomet and, finally free from the previous harassment, began again constructing a home. In honor of the Earl of Warwick's support, Shawomet was renamed "Warwick," as it is called today.

Phillip was a delightful person. When she and John arrived from England, she fit marvelously into the Providence community, and was one of those people who could turn hardship and peculiarity into laughable fun. Sometime after she and John returned, Samuel Gorton mentioned her in a letter he wrote to one of her former London neighbors, Edward Calverly, who lived by the east end of Christ Church in Newgate Market, London. Gorton told that she had written a humorous report of the Rhode Island she found.

I have not found her account, but what Gorton wrote paints the picture well enough: "Your auld neighbor, our loving friend Mrs. Greene, hath writ a letter of advise to you [that] made me laugh not a little, which I heartily wish may come to your hands. She laies out the bencfights of these parts better than I could have advised to have done. She takes well with the country and cheerfully performs her place, hath the love of all, non[e] can open their mouth against her, which is a rare thing in these parts."[34] Such was a rare thing in those parts and days.

Warwick grew in stature to become one of the five towns in Colonial Rhode Island: Providence, Newport, Portsmouth, Pawtucket, and Warwick. Each acknowledged English sovereignty and was suspicious of their Massachusetts and Plymouth neighbors, although Pawtucket and Aquidneck Island's Portsmouth and Newport kept closer ties with Massachusetts. All were democratically governed and essentially all landowners were eligible to vote. All practiced religious toleration. From these five cities, Williams shaped a single colony.

As Dr. John Greene grew older, he held numerous positions in the colony. From 1649 to 1657, he was Warwick's deputy to the Rhode Island General Court. John was magistrate for the Rhode Island General Court of Trials in 1656. He passed away in 1659 leaving a family that became prominent in colonial affairs. Both his sons, John Jr. and James, were to hold many civic positions in Rhode Island.

The Childhood Behind a Story

During my search for Dr. John Green and his family, I planned trips to places I had discovered he once lived. I started in England, where my wife and I spent a week exploring the areas where he grew up, married, and started his family. One warm afternoon, we drove to Bowridge Hill where John spent his childhood. A stone marked "1727" was mortared into the outside wall of the old farmhouse that now stood on the site. Another one on the gate read "Bowridge Hill Farm." Sculpted stones from a much earlier era lined the path that led through this Bowridge Hill Farm gate to the house's front door. In the field behind the house were piles of massive blocks, the remains of a previous structure, apparently the Bowridge Hall manor house. Long in ruins, it had a past that someone did not want to completely forget. I had already learned that the Greene family had not been associated with the farm since the late 1600's, so I did not expect to find any descendants there.

We knocked at the door, and no one answered. We explored the barn, but no one was there either. Around the farmhouse echoed sounds of the country: machines hummed in the distance, tractors vibrated in far off fields, and the hill beyond the ruins dipped down to homes of a recent subdivision. Wheat and barley waved in the fields, much as they would have done 400 years ago when the Greenes managed their manor holdings. The farmstead was nearly three centuries old, yet it was not built for a century after John last wandered its surrounding hills. But at least for a moment, as my wife and I stood in the lane, all that time felt not so long ago. This far back ancestor, John, and his stories seemed just over the ridge.

We started the car and drove back the few miles to Gillingham. One of the many questions in my mind was: Why did John want to be a surgeon, when becoming a lawyer, politician, or clergyman usually offered many more bonuses? Of course, there are many reasons young people and their parents choose professions. Students oft times simply select a field that appeals to them, and medicine attracts many for that reason. Sometimes, however, there is someone who encourages young people toward a particular career, an informal mentor for example. Once their interest is touched, they turn in that direction.

This thought came to mind when we toured the Gillingham Parish church, St. Mary the Virgin, just two or three miles from Bowridge Hall. A group of young and middle-aged adults, seated around a table near the altar, greeted us as we entered the old church. It was a socializing afternoon for them, and they warmly invited us to join in. We were happy to chat for a few minutes.

For this group, the church was a functional part of their lives, and their interest in the old structure's long history did not run very deep. However, they pointed us to a laminated card that summarized the building's past. We took the card and started down the aisles. Their greetings made us feel at home as we wandered around the ancient naves and through the chancel, following point-by-point our self-guided walking tour. We saw the baptismal font where John must have been christened and baptized as a baby.

Then, as we turned a corner in a remote part of the chancel, we saw behind a set of folding chairs and tables the tombs of two men lying side-by-side. According to our laminated tour guide, these were John and Thomas Jessop. John was the vicar, and Thomas, his brother, was the physician in Gillingham. My eyes fixed on Thomas's tomb. During my visits to tens, even hundreds, of churches in Europe, I had never found the tomb of a doctor in any of them. Dr. Thomas Jessop was clearly popular in his community.

105

Thomas went to Oxford in 1560 and graduated as a Doctor of Medicine in 1569. He was the physician that John Greene would have known as he grew up. Was this revered community doctor, whose generation wanted him remembered, someone who influenced John in his decision to become a surgeon? It is impossible for us to know, but it is easy to think he might have been. There he lie, an effigy of him sculpted atop his resting place, a handsome man with a beard, his high laced collar sweeping around his neck, and his left arm resting on his buttoned tunic.[35]

The National Park Service

Our next trip started in Providence, Rhode Island, where John's family settled down soon after arriving in the Massachusetts Bay Colony. I hoped to find the Providence Plantation Home Lots where Dr. John Greene and his family once dwelled, a few houses down the street from Roger Williams. When googling the internet for colonial sites in Providence, I found that the National Park Service had a visitors' center in the downtown. I learned then and many times afterwards that a National Park Service facility is always a good place to start a directed trip into the past. The Service administers several well-preserved national history parks and centers that smoothly transport us back through our history. A visitors' center bookstore, with its rows of book focused specifically on this time and place, is a must to browse for relevant sources.

When we arrived in Providence, we were thrilled to find the visitors center sitting in a beautiful park, directly across the street from where those early 17th century Home Lots once stood. It was a cool, wet morning, and my wife, Seija, and I scurried from our car into the center to get out of the rain. When we entered, we saw that the stormy weather had ensured that we were the only visitors there. John, a friendly Park Ranger, greeted us and asked if he could be of help. When I explained that we were searching for some families that lived in Providence 400 years ago, his eyes lit up, and he smiled. "Well, what were their names?" he asked.

John was not just a 9-5 manager, but someone who visibly breathed the history he was there to explain. When I asked about

Dr. John Greene, he gestured to a spot kitty-corner from the center. "That's where the Greenes' home once stood," John told us. Then he showed us a painting of how the houses likely appeared when the Greene family lived there. The simple dwellings with their steeply sloped roofs lined the river and adjoined large garden plots important for keeping the families fed year around.

John had stories to tell, especially when I asked about Dr. John Greene's second wife, Alice Daniels. He later emailed me a photograph of the painting of the home lot houses, more details about Alice, and references to places where I could find still more information. John's help was typical of the enthusiastic support I received everywhere from National Park rangers who went out of their way to help me locate the people and stories I was after.

John pointed us in the direction of other places to visit. When I mentioned the parking problem, he winked and said we could leave the car in the center's visitor parking for an hour or two. "We don't check the lot too often," he smiled.

The next day, in Warwick, we searched until we found the Greene family cemetery near the site of his Warwick home. Rhode Island carefully preserves and catalogs these old family cemeteries. Because they are so old, they sometimes are found beyond the backyards of houses filling developments that sprang up over the centuries. Nevertheless, they are fenced and cared for – you just have to do a little looking to find them.

In the center of the Greene cemetery was a large tombstone commemorated Dr. John Greene. The spot was one bookend. The other was his birthplace at the Bowridge Hill Manor in Dorset where we had visited a few months earlier. In between these bookends was an illustrious volume full of hardships, adventures, victories, and explorations. This volume included the beautiful old church in Salisbury, England, where he and Joane celebrated the baptism of their children, and their home in newborn Providence, across the street from today's National Roger Williams Memorial.

Now, where their Providence home once sat is an Episcopal Church and an adjoining modern residential building that climbs up the hill behind it. Dr. John's family cemetery is in the yard of the

Narragansett Bay Baptist Church in Warwick. We stood there that spring afternoon, a layer of snow resting on its many stones. It seemed to me that the two sites appropriately depicted his migration from England's Anglican tradition to a New World home where he was one of the founders of the Baptist Church in America, and a voice in favor of the political and religious foundation on which the United States one day would be built.

The Firebrand

I have referred earlier to one of Ida May's most remarkable colonial ancestors, Samuel Gorton. As the tales of these plucky Rhode Islanders unfolded, Samuel kept weaving his story in and out of the others. Chroniclers of his times and even more recent historians usually refer to Samuel in sour terms. He was the guy New Englanders loved to hate. Even when I mentioned Gorton to Ranger John at the National Park Service Visitors Center in Providence, John looked at me and smiled with an "Ah, that rascal!" look in his eyes. "Yes," he chuckled, "Gorton was a real character."

It is hard to overestimate how Boston's rich academic community's writers have influenced views throughout the United States on many things, including our country's history. Since Boston's rulers hated Gorton's "irreverence" and outspoken "heresies" with limitless passion, their descriptions have cloaked Gorton's reputation since Massachusetts began keeping records. He disturbed their Puritan sensitivities.

Yet Samuel Gorton was an overwhelming presence in the early colony. His influence in the development of the fundamental religious and political principles Rhode Island bequeathed newly born America is huge. In fact, one biographer, with perhaps a little embellishment but also with some truth, wrote that the founding of Rhode Island was due to Roger Williams; the preservation of Rhode Island was due to Samuel Gorton.[36]

I am not sure my mother, Margie, ever discovered Samuel Gorton because I never heard her mention him. If she had known of Samuel, I am sure she would have talked a lot about her outspoken ancestor. Living in her world of 19th century populist values, Ida May would likewise have been proud of her firebrand ancestor. I found Samuel to be the one I loved to love. How to understand him was my first challenge, and I think I got closer to achieving that when I learned of his first encounter with the Plymouth authorities.

Samuel Gorton's disillusionment with what he found in New England set in within months of his arrival. He had had high expectations when he left a comfortable life in Britain. He especially yearned for a country where he was free to worship and live according to the whims of his sharp intellect and conscience. "I left my native country," he wrote, "to enjoy liberty of conscience in respect of faith toward God and for no other end."[37]

He was living in Plymouth in 1637 where he and his wife Mary had rented part of a house from a man named Ralph Smith. Like Samuel, Mary was from a wealthy and refined English background, and it must have been a shock to enter the primitive colonial environment. In Plymouth, everyday life demanded hard manual labor from just about everyone. To help with the adjustment, Samuel hired a widow named Ellen Aldridge to work as a servant in their home.

One Sunday, they all attended church together. At some point during the service, Ellen smiled. Smiling at church was forbidden, and her offense was observed. Today, it seems unbelievably absurd, but Plymouth's governor Prence demanded she be punished and then deported as a vagabond to wherever she had come from. To escape the shame, Ellen fled to the woods where she spent the days. At night, she returned to the Gortons' home for shelter.

When the case came to court on November 5, 1638, Ellen was nowhere to be found, but Samuel appeared in her defense. He argued the crime was not recognized in English law, and he appealed for her protection. Gorton added that she was not a vagabond, but a woman of good report who made her living through honest work.

I was not surprised that someone, in this case her employer, would speak in Ellen's defense. The Plymouth Court, however, saw it as an attempt to thwart its authority. Worse, Gorton waltzed around the authorities with his brilliant command of English. When a magistrate exaggerated a point, Gorton said he was "speaking hyperbolically." The magistrate, not understanding the word hyperbolically, turned to one of the Elders. The Elder said simply that Gorton just told the magistrate that he was lying. They wasted little time charging Samuel Gorton with contempt.

A few days later when Gorton appeared before the court to answer the charges against him, the courtroom heated up further. Samuel's strident manner never minced words nor trimmed his impatience with what he considered foolishness, and that was obvious in his argument before the court. He said that magistrates should not be parties and judges, but the place of the prosecutor was on the floor, where he was, and called the people present to look and see how their liberties were being abused.

Gorton's behavior brought some sharp reactions. Smarting from his insubordination, he was charged with "contempt, and his misdemeanor in the open Court toward the elders, the Bench, & stirring vp the people to mutynie in the face of the Court."[38] The Court fined him £20, a hefty sum of money, enough to show how much he had irritated the Court. It also tells that he obviously was a man of some means in order to pay such a fine. The Court also gave him fourteen days to be out of the colony. Smith, his landlord, was also agitated and evicted the Gortons from their home.

To Samuel Gorton, the Court proceedings were a farce. He knew English law well, and from the unbelievable initial charge against the woman who worked for him, to his own harsh sentence, this was not what he hoped to find in the new land he had chosen. His family was turned out of their home in the middle of one of early New England's worst winters, a year when many colonists froze to death. Mary was nursing a small child at the time, and they somehow found her temporary shelter in Plymouth until she could later join Samuel.

When I worked through Samuel Gorton's confrontation in Plymouth, I realized that to understand this man, the trial in Plymouth was the spot where everything began. For him, the episode was a big event. As he stated it himself, his sole purpose in coming to New England was to find freedom to worship with conscience and faith. His entire life was turned upside down over the ludicrous prosecution of a widow working in his household for something as innocent as smiling in a church service. He believed he was smothering from the same pettiness that he thought was left behind in England.

For the Court in Plymouth, however, the Gorton affair was relatively inconsequential. He had slandered the magistrates, been thrown out of their colony, and had disappeared from their sight. Life went on in the same way as before. That was the problem. Samuel could not stand by silently as civil and religious authorities thrashed their way through the lives of small or innocent people with little regard for their welfare. In his tightly keyed value system, this was evil not to be endured when there were simple solutions – such as freedom and democratic decision-making – that respected the value of the individual and resulted in better social outcomes.

From the time he left Plymouth, Gorton was determined to battle and, if possible, quash the little mindedness he saw around him. As long as there were those he considered bullies or despots, he would fight them. He became the ultimate fighter on such battlefields, wherever he went. The leaders in Massachusetts and Plymouth could neither understand nor condone his behavior. Nor he, theirs. He probably caused the rulers of Massachusetts Bay more grief over a greater time than any other colonist, and they did the same to him.

This was how Samuel Gorton's new life in the Puritan colonies began, and it set his direction for the rest of his life. Gorton was prickly to begin with. At his best, he never suffered fools lightly, there was never a shortage of fools in Puritan New England, and he never hesitated to tell them what he thought. Especially, in those days, he carried a chip on his shoulder when it came to authority, courts, and legal processes.

111

Samuel, nevertheless, was banished and forced to leave in a winter tempest. He recalled with bitterness, "When the snow was up to the knee and rivers to wade through up to the middle, and not so much as one Indian to be found in that extremity of weather to afford either fire or harbour,... we lay divers nights together, and were constrained with the hazard of our lives to betake ourselves to Narragansett Bay." [39] He finally made it to Portsmouth where Anne Hutchinson and her followers had recently carved their village from the woods.

Samuel Gorton was baptized in 1593 in the town of Gorton, near Manchester. His father was a London merchant and member of the guild. Samuel grew up in a privileged family, was well educated, had tutors, and learned classical languages. He was extremely well versed in English law. He did not leave his home until he was nearly 25. In the true style of the English gentry class, physical work was foreign to him. He admitted himself that he had not "engaged in any servile employment until he settled in the colonies." [40]

Sometime before 1630, Samuel Gorton married Mary Mayplet, the daughter of a London gentleman. Mary, too, was educated and, "...as tenderly brought up as any man's wife in the town," Samuel wrote. Her brother became physician to King Charles II. Trying to get away from the stifling religious environment of Stuart England, he and Mary set sail for Boston and arrived there with two or three children in March, 1637. They landed right in the middle of the fervor surrounding Anne Hutchinson's trial. Gorton did not join in that turmoil, but perhaps it convinced him that the slightly more liberal Plymouth Colony might be a better place to settle. By June, Samuel and Mary were living in Plymouth where initially he was favorably described as "courteous in his carriage to all." That was before Plymouth's rulers took his maid to court. [41]

When Samuel Gorton trudged into Portsmouth from his frosty escape from Plymouth, Anne Hutchinson's group had already been there about a year. Anne Marbury Hutchinson might have been the best known, the brightest, and most remarkable woman in Puritan New England. Growing up in England, she was educated and married well. Her husband, William, was a prosperous merchant and, like her, at home with Puritan thought. Over the years she gave birth to fourteen children.

The family landed in Boston in 1634, and William was soon a central figure in the city's merchant community. Anne became a midwife. They built a large two-story house, one of the largest in central Boston, and bought 600 acres in what is now Quincy. Bay Colony founder John Winthrop called Anne, "A woman of a ready wit and bold spirit." Anne thrived in the city's intense religious environment, and her home became a central week-day meeting place where she led discussions with friends about the previous Sunday's sermon. Soon, Anne was giving the sermons in her home.

Soon, too, Boston's church fathers objected to Anne's new ideas, for example that people could develop a direct relationship with God and the Holy Spirit, without the intermediation of civil and religious authorities. In 1637, after a trial where Winthrop served as both judge and accuser, Anne Hutchinson was banished from the colony. Many joined Anne's and William's journey into exile. On the northern tip of Rhode Island's Aquidneck Island, they founded the town of Portsmouth. Unfortunately, William died unexpectedly not long after they arrived.[42]

Eventually, alone, threatened by Massachusetts's machinations to wrest Aquidneck away from Rhode Island, and wondering what might happen to her if they did, Anne departed with her family. They traveled south and in 1642 took refuge on Long Island in the Dutch New Netherlands colony. They were not very long on Long Island when Indians raided her home, killing Anne and all her children except Susanna. Boston's clergymen were delighted when they heard the grisly news, calling what happened the "just vengeance of God." Whatever foolishness such men babbled then, Anne Hutchinson remains today one of America's first great female intellectuals and leaders.[43]

While Anne Hutchinson was still in Portsmouth, one of her followers, William Coddington, had begun promoting a claim that he was owner and proprietor of the new Portsmouth colony. He was an ambitious and often opportunist man who had set himself up as a quasi-Old Testament style judge and ruler, much to the irritation of many of the rest of the community. Roger Williams, who had purchased the island from Narragansett Chief Miantonomi, thought he was granting the land to the Hutchinson party under the leadership of Coddington, and had marked the grant to "Coddington and his friends." Nevertheless, Coddington considered it his personal property.

The resulting conflict among the Portsmouth families was one made to order for Gorton. Responding to his already deeply nurtured annoyance of fools, especially autocratic ones, he jumped into the fray to take sides with Anne Hutchinson against Coddington. In response to the squabble, Coddington and a small group of followers departed Portsmouth for the southern section of Aquidneck Island where they established Newport. By April, only four months after he had arrived in Portsmouth, Gorton was organizing a democratic form of government for the new community. His model was modern, based on universal suffrage with no religious tests nor political qualifications. Every permanent inhabitant was a citizen. The group acknowledged allegiance to the King and threw out the Puritan laws.

Intrigue in Aquidneck was never in short supply. Coddington quickly gleaned the Massachusetts colony's support for his claim to all of the island. The Bay fathers, in turn, hoped to pull Aquidneck from Rhode Island into Massachusetts. Coddington also quietly convinced several of those in Portsmouth to oppose Gorton's new government. It was not long before Coddington showed up again in Portsmouth ready to hold court as the colony's rightful judge and ruler. Samuel's mood was of nearly uncontrollable exasperation. Coddington and his followers saw him as the most vocal spoiler of their ambitions. They looked for any excuse to deal with him forcefully and did not have to wait long.

One morning, a woman's cow wandered onto Samuel Gorton's field to graze. The owner eventually came after the animal only to meet Gorton's servant girl, who like her master, entertained trespassers poorly. Some harsh words were exchanged, and the two were soon rolling on the ground pulling hair in a down and out cat fight. The woman is said to have received the worst part of it, but it was the girl who was arrested and bound over to Coddington's court. Samuel demanded to defend his maid before the hearing. It was a very similar circumstance to what had happened not long before in Plymouth. Coddington was delighted.

Samuel Gorton saw the hearing as a travesty and stormed into the court in a gloves-off rampage. He jeered at the judges and accused them of being skilled followers of Old Testament idols. He jumped to his feet and flared through the courtroom telling the judges they might consider themselves judges, but in fact they were "Just Asses." As he argued he waved his arms, brandishing a handkerchief, which at one point flicked the ears of Coddington's deputy governor and the accuser in the trial. The man angrily asserted that Gorton had done it on purpose, and with no pause, Samuel shot back that he would not touch the man's ears with a pair of tongs.

Coddington had all he needed to arrest Gorton. He cried out, "You that are for the King, lay hold on Gorton."

Gorton shouted back, "All you that are for the King, lay hold on Coddington."

Unfortunately for Samuel, Coddington had brought along an armed guard. The guards promptly subdued and arrested him. Coddington saw the opportunity to get rid of this saucy opponent. He ordered Samuel Gorton whipped and banished. They chained Samuel, bound him to a whipping post, and flogged him. But his rage was hardly subdued. After the flogging, and as Coddington began to leave, Gorton, bare chested, back bloody and shredded, and dragging his chains, hobbled after him. He grabbed Coddington, held up the shackles, and snarled, "You loaned me these chains, and definitely should have them back!"

Gorton, however, was defeated, at least for the moment. Samuel and Mary, with twelve or thirteen families following them, left Portsmouth and made their way to sanctuary in Providence. There, the Gortonites, as they were called, were initially accepted and treated kindly.[44]

In Providence, Samuel and Mary came to be best friends with Dr. John and Alice Greene. They had a lot in common. John and

Samuel were about the same age, and both were educated and from prosperous English gentry families. Years later, John was to call Samuel "my Beloved friend," and John's son, John Greene, Jr., attested Samuel's will when he died. One of the Greenes' daughters married the Gortons' son. Most importantly, they had similar temperaments. Although John's personality was not as tumultuous as Samuel's, the two of them saw the world in similar ways and wanted many of the same things from it. The destinies of the two families were soon intertwined.[45]

Over the years, it has been easy for some commentators to say Gorton took contention with him wherever he went. However, as often as not, he found conflict waiting for him, not because of him. The fact was that Rhode Island, peopled with free-spirited individualists, was also peppered with disputations. These conflicts caught the neighboring colonies' attention, particularly in Massachusetts where their dislike for "heretics" merged with their lust for coastline on Narragansett Bay. It is true that Samuel never hesitated to throw himself into a dispute. His strong sense of moral right fueled his burning paradigms of how political and religious life should be organized. He was repulsed by tyranny, and never failed to oppose it. Some have believed Gorton thrived on conflict. That is doubtful when you look at his life as a whole.

Providence was a community divided and full of disagreements. The biggest involved the group who considered themselves among the original settlers and therefore deserving of more land than the equal distribution Roger Williams allocated. These families, lived just south of town in Pawtuxet and were referred to as the "Pawtuxet Party." Samuel and Dr. John both sided with Roger Williams and many other Providence families against the Pawtuxet Party.

The Pawtuxet group especially resented Samuel Gorton and the Gortonite families from Portsmouth because of the extra support they lent their opponents. Samuel, moreover, quickly gleaned new adherents from his Providence neighbors, making things even worse from the Pawtuxet Party's point of view. Sensing a power shift, the Pawtuxet group did not allow the newcomers to use the Providence Commons, and its spokesman, William Arnold, argued to refuse admitting Samuel Gorton to the community. Gorton had "shewed himselfe a railing and turbulent person," Arnold ranted.[46]

It came to a climax one November morning when Pawtuxet men tried to seize some of the cattle of Francis Weston, a member of the Providence community who, they said, owed them money. When they started taking livestock from Weston's cornfield, he called furiously for help. Dr. John Greene, Randall Holden, and others rushed to Weston's aid, yelling "Theeves, Theeves, stealing cattle, stealing cattle!" Hearing the commotion, Samuel Gorton and some of his friends also sprinted to the rescue, and "being too strong for the other party, provoked them so by injuries, as they came armed into the field, each against [the] other; but Mr. Williams pacified them for the present."[47]

It was a riot, and a few days later, the Pawtuxet Party wrote to the governor of Massachusetts begging the colony to "Lend us a neighbor-like helping hand, and send us such assistance... to helpe us to bring them to satisfaction, and ease us of our burden of them." The plea found a sympathetic ear in Boston, whose leaders eyed access to Narragansett Bay. As John Winthrop saw it, "The place [Narragansett Bay frontage] was likely to be of use to us, especially if we should have occasion of sending out against any Indians of Narragansett and likewise for an outlet into the Narragansett Bay, and seeing it came without our seeking, and would be no charge to us, we thought it not wisdom to let it slip."[48] The Boston Court wrote the Rhode Islanders a letter that threatened the colony with violence if any were used against members of the Pawtuxet Party. From then on, the Pawtuxet people aligned themselves with Massachusetts, and in return, Massachusetts was glad to extend its "protection."

The Boston Court's threat was not hollow. It first and foremost pointed at Samuel Gorton. Governor Winthrop had written that Samuel "was a man not fit to live upon the face of the earth," and a minister remarked, "that if they had Gorton at Boston... he would hardly see his own house any more." A friend, John Warner, returning from Boston, related what he had heard there and advised Samuel to get away from Providence.[49] Another man, named

Collins, who had just spent several months in a Boston jail for heresy, also visited the Gortons' home and urged them to join Anne Hutchinson's party that was planning to remove to the Dutch New Netherlands settlement. Collins said he believed the Massachusetts rulers would soon make an attempt on Samuel's life.

Weighing the matter, Samuel Gorton and his followers finally decided they needed to re-locate to a better place. However, he was a loyal Englishman, not about to turn from the English Crown to the Dutch. In his mind, "He had neither been false to his King nor country nor to his conscience."[50] In light of the Indian massacre of Anne Hutchinson's family on Long Island not long thereafter, the Gortons' decision to stay put in Rhode Island was a fortunate one.

Samuel and his wife had had enough. As described earlier, they decided to join with the Greenes and ten other families to buy land in Shawomet from Chief Miantonomi where they would establish their own community. They hoped that the completely new settlement could be governed without interference, intrigues, and the aggressive meddling of their Massachusetts neighbors. In December 1642, they made the purchase. By January they had a deed from Miantinomi and his uncle Canonicus and had drawn up rules of governance. In May, they were planting crops on their new lands.

That same May, the Boston fathers made their decision to launch a military mission to arrest Gorton, Greene, and the other heads of families in Shawomet. The Boston Court bribed two minor Narragansett sachems to say the Shawomet lands belonged to them and not Canonicus. Gorton and the others had usurped the property without their permission, the Court claimed. It was a sham organized by the Pawtuxet Party who got paid four pounds for delivering the two sachems to the Boston Court. One of the sachems was best known for trying to burglarize a house by shimmying down its chimney until he got stuck.

In a reply to the Court's order for the Shawomet men to appear in Boston, Gorton fired a blistering response back to Boston. "We told them," he described, "that we being so far out of their jurisdiction, could not, neither would we acknowledge subjection unto any in the place where we were." True to form, Samuel's letter was brusque and ridiculing. It began insultingly enough: "To the great and honoured Idol Generall now set up in Massachusetts." Gorton then referred to Old Testament-style heathens, calling the Boston magistrates a generation of vipers, companions of Judas Iscariot, and the murderers of Anne Hutchinson.

Setting aside Gorton's abusive verbiage, if that is possible, he was absolutely right about being outside the Massachusetts colony's confines and the reach of Boston's law over him or his neighbors. Maybe that is one reason the Massachusetts Court hated Samuel Gorton so much. He was usually right, much to their annoyance, and expressed himself in words that singed their egos. To no one's surprise, Gorton's reply only further enraged the Boston magistrates who finished up preparations for their military operation.[51]

In September, when Massachusetts "commissioners" led the posse of soldiers and Indian allies through Providence to Shawomet, some of the women and children ran from their houses into the woods while others rushed down to the sea where boats waited to ferry them to safety. Friends from Providence arrived to assist their neighbors' escape to the boats. It was still early fall, but that evening was perilously cold when the craft began to draw away from the shore for fear of being captured. The women and children plunged into the frigid water to get to the receding boats. It is easy to imagine the panic that spread through the families when they saw the intruders arriving armed and ready for battle.

Mary Gorton was 'heavy with child,' and Samuel took her arm. They were leading their children toward the waiting boats along the shoreline when suddenly militiamen broke out of the trees a hundred or so yards away. The soldiers pointed their muskets toward the terrified people who were running and wading toward the craft. Samuel shouted to the families and the boatmen to stay beyond musket shot. At the same time, he called to the men in the village to grab their weapons. Some of the people of Providence took hold of Mary, and Samuel reluctantly let go of his pregnant wife's arm while they ushered her and the children into the water and a waiting boat. He then scurried back to join the other men.

119

Mary's craft pulled out into the bay, and Providence neighbors began rowing their way farther from the inlet and then turned north toward Providence. She and her family finally made it to safety. The baby she was carrying would be named Susannah and was born to be one of Ida May's distant grandmothers. For others, however, exposure to the cold took a grim toll. I mentioned earlier how Alice Greene died following that dreadful night, and others suffered miscarriages.

Meanwhile, Samuel Gorton and the other men barricaded themselves into one of the newly built log houses. He was the last one in. The Massachusetts soldiers now turned on the Providence neighbors, threatening them, too. Nevertheless, the people from Providence managed to temporarily calm the moment and succeeded in arranging a meeting between Capt. Cook and some of the besieged settlers. The first question they asked Capt. Cook was the obvious one, why were they here? Cook replied that the Shawomet families had "intruded" upon the people of Massachusetts, referring apparently to the Pawtuxet Party who were all of a sudden now considered Massachusetts subjects. More importantly, Cook said, his men had come because the Shawomet people held "blasphemous" ideas for which they needed to repent.

Gorton and his neighbors responded that the soldiers were out of their territory, and proposed arbitration. The Captain promised to relay this offer and sent off messengers to get the opinion of Boston authorities. While they awaited the reply, the Shawomet men returned to their fortification. Soldiers surrounded the building, broke into all the homes, and stole whatever they wished, included the livestock, about 80 cattle in all. They also took the hogs and goats, most of which the Massachusetts soldiers and Indians ate during their siege.[52]

Finally, the messengers returned. Shooting their weapons into the air, they announced their arrival, and then renounced the truce. They also turned some of the 80 head of Shawomet cattle over to members of the Pawtuxet group. A few moments later, the soldiers began firing into the log house where Samuel and his neighbors were fortified. Its thick logs fortunately stopped the bullets, but the siege continued for several days. When Sunday arrived, the barricaded men hoped for a Sabbath Day rest. Instead, Cook's men attempted to set fire to the house. When the Shawomet men extinguished the flames, Captain Cook sent to Boston for reinforcements to support their attack.

During the siege, Gorton and the others never returned fired, and they suffered no wounded. It was clear to them, however, that the situation could not go on indefinitely. Parleying again with Capt. Cook, they offered to return with his party to Boston if they could go as freemen. Cook cunningly agreed. As soon as the Shawomet men filed out of the log house, he reneged, seized their arms, and shackled them all. Cook lined them up and told his men, as Gorton related, "If any of us step aside, out of the place designed unto us, that they should run us through." His soldiers paraded them in irons through Providence and back to Boston.[53]

The file of prisoners was a sight for everyone along the road to Massachusetts. The returning men – soldiers proudly in arms marching double file, their Indian allies in native dress, and prisoners struggling in chains, one assigned to every five or six soldiers – arrived in Boston like Prokofiev's triumphal procession of the hunters, Grandfather, Peter, and the Wolf. They first marched to the home of Gov. Winthrop, who in a grave voice heartily thanked his troops. The Shawomet men were then jailed without bail and accused of being "a blasphemous enemy of true religion of our Lord Jesus Christ."[54]

For the next two or three weeks, the authorities tried to save Gorton's and the others' souls from damnation, and, if not that, to glean enough evidence to hang them. Much to the Puritans' dismay, the prisoners refused to attend church unless they could speak in the service. Finally, the captors agreed to let Gorton say his piece, perhaps hoping that given enough rope he would hang himself. The meeting began with a sermon by the famous Puritan minister John Cotton. He preached about how the Apostle Paul's condemnation of idols hurt the silversmiths' sales of their Roman Goddess Diana shrines.[55]

Gorton then stood and continued the discussion on Cotton's topic. It was Christ who dwelled in the church that Paul represented, Gorton stressed. He then cast an enflaming condemnation of Puritan society. In the Massachusetts colony, he slammed, all their "Ordinances, Ministers, and Sacraments" were merely for show and pomp, little better than the silver shrines Paul condemned. It was very close to the line, but not quite enough to hang him, like many there hoped.

The men were all assumed guilty so there was no need for a verdict, just a sentence, and finally the day arrived in November 1643. Many of the magistrates and deputies voted to hang them, but overall there was a small majority of deputies against capital punishment. After some debate, Samuel Gorton and his colleagues were instead sentenced to hard labor throughout the several towns of the colony.

Upon pain of death, they were also forbidden to express their views. Dangerous as it was, however, it presented an opportunity for Gorton to travel through "Babylon" preaching the gospel to its subjects. He and the others vocally went about their work, irons on one leg, coolly ignoring the threat of death, and freely sharing their religious ideas with everyone who would listen. And along the way, they drew an increasing group of followers.

The more the Gordanites found popularity, the thornier was the situation for the Boston Court. One historian has likened it to that of a man who caught a wildcat by the tail and could not figure out how to let go. The Boston fathers soon realized that their people would not support harsher punishments for the prisoners. The Court, "not knowing what to do with them, at length agreed to set them at liberty," said Winthrop. He and the other leaders wanted to be rid of the prisoners as soon as they could and gave Gorton and his followers 14 days to depart Massachusetts.[56]

Samuel relished the moment and played it to its best, at first refusing to let them take off his chains. He demanded that Boston's prominent men join the constable in releasing him. There was a short standoff, but finally the constable rounded up some personalities, and Samuel "reluctantly" allowed them to unchain him. For two or three days afterwards, he and his followers enjoyed some notoriety around the city, "The people shewing themselves joyfull to see us at liberty," he said. The Magistrates, overflowing with indignation, finally gave them two hours to be out of the colony. Samuel Gorton, though a little worn, was quickly on his way with his companions. One of the men did not come home. "Francis Weston, through cold and hardship in prison, fell into consumption and in short time after dyed of it," Gorton wrote.[57]

During the Boston drama, Samuel's pregnant wife Mary was home alone with her small children. The oldest, Samuel, Jr., was only about 13 years old. Baby Mary was only two, and the second of Samuel's children, John, who was also one of Ida May's direct ancestors, was about three. Between Samuel and John were two sisters. In other words, it was a young and large family. The children certainly helped their mother as best they could, but only Samuel, as a budding teenager, was old enough to assume any male responsibilities. Without a father, and no in-laws or extended family to help, Mary was almost totally dependent on her neighbors for support during the time Samuel was being paraded about Massachusetts in chains. Neither was there a public safety net to care for people in need.

When Samuel and the other men returned from Boston, they did not move back into their new homes in Shawomet. Massachusetts adamantly held on to its ill-gotten foothold on Narragansett Bay's west shore. The Shawomet men knew they had turned the Magistrates' triumphal capture into a charade, but they realized that a next time could turn out much worse.

They were in the right, Gorton knew. When he reunited with Dr. John Greene, they figured the only way to resolve their legitimate claim to the property was to argue their case in London. They began planning the journey. Before they left, Samuel did some business with the Narragansett tribe with whom he and his Shawomet neighbors had always been on friendly terms. The Narragansetts were aware of Boston's hostility toward the Rhode Islanders, and perhaps bemusedly had heard of the Shawomet men's adventures as prisoners of the Boston Magistrates.

The Narragansetts also detested the Boston Court, especially now following the death of Sachem Miantonomi. Just before Gorton's incarceration in Boston, Sachem Miantonomi had fallen prisoner to a rival Mohican tribe. Gorton had sent a message to Mohican chief Onkus demanding the Mohicans release his friend Miantonomi to him. The Mohicans instead turned to Boston for a decision on what to do with the Narragansett chief. After meeting on this, the Commissioners of the United Colonies replied that he deserved to die, something the Mohicans happily made happen with a hatchet to his head at about the same time Boston troops were besieging the Shawomet blockhouse.[58]

Not wanting to leave it at that, the New England commissioners wrote a letter to Miantonomi's uncle, Chief Sachem Canonicus, taking credit for the execution, "... so that the Indians might know that the English did approve it," and sent a dozen or so musketeers to the Mohicans to help protect them against possible Narraganset reprisals. Upon learning of his death, the entire Narragansett nation wailed, blackened their faces, and went into days of mourning. Miantonomi had been a close friend to Samuel Gorton, Dr. John Greene, and Roger Williams, and they, too, grieved for his loss. As too often happened, however, the Massachusetts forefathers failed to realize how their bad-tempered decision would have devastating long-term consequences, in this case perhaps eventually contributing to one of America's bloodiest wars.[59]

Just after Samuel Gorton returned home from his imprisonment in Massachusetts, Narragansett messengers paid him a visit. They wanted Gorton and some of the other Shawomet men to accompany them to Chief Sachem Canonicus. Samuel and about six of his friends followed them in boats down the bay. Approaching the large village, a mass of well-armed warriors stood on the bank to meet them, and then acted as an escort. The white men at first were apprehensive, thinking that Massachusetts agents might have organized another betrayal, or somehow convinced Canonicus that Gorton was behind the murder of the Sachem's nephew.

Their concerns soon disappeared. "Multitudes of Indians, as we passed along, coming forth and seemed joyfull," Samuel Gorton

124

wrote of this spellbinding moment. When they arrived, "Canonicus and his chief Counsellor took us aside to consult with us." Canonicus was sympathetic to what Gorton and the others had just gone through. He expressed joy at Samuel's and his comrades' release. While he entertained the Shawomet men, Canonicus talked of the wrongs his Narragansett nation had suffered. He "told us that their condition, might (in great measure) be paralleled with ours."[60]

The chief sachem had called a meeting of the Narragansett tribal council to decide how to respond to the loss of Miantonomi. The large Narragansett tribe was a force to deal with, fully capable of mounting terrible retribution on the Massachusetts, Plymouth, and Connecticut colonies. However, Gorton would not support retaliation. Instead, he wisely used his influence to move things in another direction. His plan was for Canonicus to sign an "Act of Submission" proclaiming the tribe's subjection to the English Crown and requesting redress for Miantonomi's death. Gorton promised to take it personally to London.

After further discussion, the sachem agreed to Gorton's strategy. Samuel drew up a draft of the Act, and Canonicus, Miantonomi's brother Pessicus, and Canonicus's son Mixan made their marks on behalf of the tribe. It deputized Gorton and three others to act on the tribe's behalf in the matter.

Gorton knew that returning to England with an Act of Submission from the Narragansett tribe would please Britain's colonial administrators. Hopefully, it would help bring Massachusetts's excesses under control. The Narragansett lands would also be subject to the King, creating a perpetual bulwark against the Massachusetts colony's efforts to ride rough-shod over Rhode Island. Not least of all, it prevented an immediate Indian War that would wreak bloody atrocities on both sides.

It was a fine piece of diplomacy, but obviously not to the liking of Rhode Island's neighbors. When the Boston Court heard of the Act, it summoned the sachems to appear. They refused. The Court then sent messengers urging the tribe to repudiate the Act. Canonicus let them stand outside his wigwam for two hours in the rain, said a few words to the men without even getting up, and then let them wait another four hours to see Pessicus. The frustrated emissaries returned to Boston with nothing accomplished.

Meanwhile Samuel Gorton and his two companions departed for the long journey across the Atlantic. Their ship to England pulled out of the port of New Amsterdam, today's New York, in the last part of 1645. The passage went smoothly and soon after arriving in London early the next year, Gorton, Greene, and Holden appeared before the Parliamentary Commission for Plantations in America. They came prepared with a detailed, documented written account of all that had transpired against them and the Narragansetts.[61]

The Parliamentary Commission for Plantations in America, chaired by the Earl of Warwick, was astounded when it heard of the Massachusetts colony's many intrigues. In the end, Warwick wrote a mandate to all Britain's New England authorities ordering them to allow the Shawomet families to return "to live freely and quietly" in their homes. The three men (especially, Samuel Gorton and Dr. Greene) may have known some of the members of the Commission. Winthrop later complained, that they were "favored by some of the commissioners, partly for private respects."[62] The Earl of Warwick also gave the three men letters of free passage, allowing them to transit Boston on their way home without fear of arrest or worse.

Greene and Holden wasted no time and immediately returned to New England, the mandate in hand. Word of the Commission's decision preceded him, and their Shawomet neighbors knew of their victory before they arrived. It was a politically smart move to rename Shawomet "Warwick" in honor of the Earl of Warwick's support for their community.

Boston's rulers blamed Samuel Gorton for having their wings clipped and responded by sending their own representative to make an appeal before the Commission. When Boston's man argued their side of the case, Massachusetts lost on every point. Gorton, who had stayed on in England to argue against the appeal, was victorious in his appearance, arguments, and rebuttals.[63]

With that behind him, Samuel stayed in London having the time of his life as a minor notoriety. The religious oppression that led to his departure from England a decade earlier was gone for the time being. The ever-changing political winds of 17th century Britain had reversed, and he could freely preach his ideas to heart's content. For him, it was like returning to Zion from far away Boston's Babylon.

During his stay, Samuel Gorton was a popular figure and was "...persuaded to speake the word of god publiquly in divers as eminent places as any were then in London... and I was lovingly embraced wherever I came in the word uttered, with the most eminent Christians in the place." If his Massachusetts enemies could only have seen him. Or perhaps they had foreseen this Samuel Gorton, and that is one reason they worked so tirelessly to hold him down. He became a sought-out preacher and spent much time at Thomas Lamb's church in London's Bell Alley.

After four years, Samuel was ready to return to his family in the wilds of Shawomet. When Gorton's ship slipped into Boston harbor in May 1648, the Court immediately ordered him arrested, "to prevent the infection of his pestilent doctrine." When he pulled out his letter of passage from the Earl, the Court grudgingly gave him a week to get out of the colony. He made his way home to find the family that had got by for such a long time without him.

Some have claimed that following his return from London, Gorton's career was "something of an anti-climax."[64] Maybe so. He never again was the adversary known throughout New England for his belligerence. That earlier Samuel Gorton grew formidably intractable when provoked. His victories in London brought most of these provocations to an end.

In many ways, however, Samuel's greatest and most lasting impact was yet to come. Over the remainder of his life he served continuously in many key political roles in Warwick and the Rhode Island General Assembly. When allowed to swim freely in a functioning democracy, thoughts gushed from his mind, some of them breathtaking for his time. His leadership was critical to the young colony's political development and influenced America's nascent culture of human rights.

These political ideas were ahead of prevailing views over much of the next 250 years of American history. The General Assembly and Court of Elections of the Providence Plantations met in

Warwick in 1651 and passed an Act for the Emancipation of Slaves. Samuel Gorton authored and promoted this act – the first emancipation legislation in the colonies. It read: "Let it be ordered, that no blacke mankind or white being forced by covenant bond, or otherwise, to serve... longer than ten years... [and after that] to sett them free."[65] Although he himself was not a Quaker, he was an uncompromising advocate of religious freedom and a continual supporter of the new Quaker sect's members who suffered oppression, torture and execution in Massachusetts.

Samuel Gorton's influence spanned across space and time. His mutual affection with his Native American neighbors was an asset to the Rhode Island colony, at the same time it was a grievance to the Boston Court. He believed women should be allowed to stand behind a church pulpit. And he rejected the right of civil authorities to extend their jurisdiction to religion, saying they will consistently try to enforce their own convictions and persecute those who might dissent. The breeds of the fine cattle Mary's family had sent from England soon improved his herds and others throughout Rhode Island.

Samuel Gorton believed that there was a silver lining behind all the suffering he and Mary experienced. As he saw it, they were fulfilling a divine destiny. While chained in his Boston jail, he penned a long response to a letter from Mary. He ended it this way, "However we are set apart as a forlorn people in the eyes of, & by the world, yet doubt I not, but our God hath singled us out for ends and uses... that it may be told unto our childrens children that noble work that he hath wrought for us... Your loving husband in bonds, and yet free, Samuel Gorton."[66]

Samuel Gorton lived long enough to see the long-standing peace with the Narragansetts destroyed through the Plymouth and Massachusetts colonies' inept handling of their relations with the Native American tribes. The tragic downward spiral led to the "King Philips" Indian war. All of Warwick was destroyed, including Samuel's and Mary's own home. Tradition says that as the war spread to Rhode Island, friends among the Narragansetts rowed him and his family across the bay to safety.[67]

128

During his later years, the values Samuel Gorton cherished were comfortably instilled in the world that surrounded him. His wars were over, and he became a respected senior statesman. But for the most part, people in Massachusetts wrote the histories, and when he appeared in them, Gorton was always the rascal.

Samuel died in December of 1677. Ida May's ancestral lines reach Samuel and Mary through both their daughter Susanna and their son John. Susannah's grandson, Jabez, was grandfather to Revolutionary War General Nathanael Greene – a Quaker.

Timelines

Before taking to the road, I would spend days and weeks piecing together the narratives of Samuel Gorton and the others whose stories I was exploring. Although I never uncovered a complete account of any of these swashbuckling Rhode Islanders, the amount of material I did discover often surprised me. As material began to accumulate and stories to take form, I found it helpful to start a timeline for each set of the characters, starting with the birth and continuing vertically down the page to the death of the ancestor I was following. Each important event was marked on the timeline.

It was always important to add a parallel column of associated events. For example, I put Samuel Gorton's and Dr. John Greene's timeline columns next to each other so that at a glance I could see how their lives intersected. A third column was labeled "Rhode Island History." By comparing it to Gorton's and Greene's timelines, a broader picture began to take immerge. I footnoted each entry in order to simultaneously organize my sources. Stories began to emerge with some details.

A Warm Evening Around the Fire with Ancestors

Among the many virtues of the New England colonists, their tradition of keeping records and recounting stories was quite remarkable. Combing through books and histories was producing real stories of real people who suffered tragedies and celebrated life, perhaps more than we do today. I soon began to feel comfortable with some of my grandfathers and grandmothers, as if they were becoming friends. I knew them a little, and after all, that was what my search for their stories was all about.

As much as I was able to piece together their histories from books, our visits to the spots where they lived provided pigments that converted their tales from black and white to color. During one spring trip to Rhode Island, we kept busy traveling from one location to another. One night we were in Newport, a picturesque city that has always charmed Americans, from pirates and patriots to the country's wealthiest families. Seija and I were long saturated with fast-foods and needed something more. When we looked through TravelAdvisor's "10 Best Places to Eat in Newport," one restaurant caught my eye with its photograph of a warm fireplace surrounded by cozy tables. It was April and should have been warm, but it had been a cold trip, even snowy. The vision of a wood burning hearth convinced us, and we made an early dinner reservation for 5:00 at the White Horse Tavern.

The GPS took us through Newport's old town streets to find a red barn-like structure in the style that restaurant owners often use to create authentic looking, pleasing places to eat. The White Horse Tavern immediately seemed to us the perfect choice. We parked the car in a lot behind and walked around the corner toward the main entrance. On the side of the tavern was a plaque that read:

White Horse Tavern
1673
'America's Oldest Tavern'
Yearly Gathering Place of the
Members of the Colonial Assembly

I read it twice and then turned to Seija to see if she saw it, too. We raised our eyebrows and proceeded up the steps and into the anteroom. We saw at once that if we were looking for some "technicolor," here it was, the real thing. With a 5:00 reservation we were just ahead of the crowd and were cozily seated next to the briskly burning fire.

Soaking up some timely warmth from hearth stones that had warmed centuries of visitors, we learned that before becoming a tavern in 1673, the building had been a private home, the largest

130

structure in Newport. It was built barely a few years after the town had been cleared from the surrounding wilderness by John Coggeshall and others of Newport's founding fathers and mothers. When needed, the home and tavern had served as a meeting place for the Colonial Assembly until the middle of the 18ᵗʰ century when a permanent structure was built. Like other quality colonial taverns, the White Horse had been a place to eat, drink, meet, and stay.

By now we were absorbing more than just heat from the hearth. I realized that we were sitting in one of those places where the time and place of some of our stories intersected. Dr. John Greene's sons, John and James, held responsible positions in the colony and surely many times sat in the same room we were now enjoying. Obadiah Holmes, pastor of Newport's Baptist Church, must have known this old building well. Samuel Gorton, in Newport often on business and visits, would have sat within these walls. Governor John Coggeshall died before the original house was completed, but his granddaughter Humility and her husband Benjamin, son of John Greene of Quidnessett, were both our ancestors and probably no strangers here. John Greene of Quidnessett, himself, lived only a few miles away during and after his trading post years, and came to Newport from time to time for business and family. He was once even jailed in the city. John would have known this hearth.

While it was impossible for us to visit the times of our grandfathers and grandmothers of 400 years back, we were sitting in a spot where many of their paths must have crossed at one time or another. In the back of my mind, I could hear their laughter and busy talk, and see these men and women descend the old staircase linking the upper floor with the room where we sat by the fire.

Antique Books in Your Study

Visiting places like The White Horse Tavern added much to my search, but even so, our travel was always predicated on thorough research done before. So much of my quest of these families took place right in my own study. Soon after I began researching Samuel Gorton, for example, I discovered a reference to a book he wrote in 1646 while he, John Greene, and Randall Holden were in London

131

appearing before the Parliamentary Commission for Plantations in America. The book portrayed for the English public the Massachusetts Bay Colony's attack on his Shawomet settlement as well as other Massachusetts improprieties in New England.

Was it possible, I wondered, that a copy of Samuel Gorton's book might still be around and accessible? Obviously, it was not likely to be sitting on the shelves of the local library. I started googling for Gorton's book and was surprised when I found a facsimile available to order at a reasonable price. Such an obscure work as this could now be purchased because of the many recent efforts to digitalize antique and out-of-print books. This volume belonged to a collection of books gathered from 400 years of America's past, called Sabin Americana *and made available in digital format by Gale Print Editions.*

Unknown to many, the rapidly evolving technology of book printing over the past couple decades has revolutionized the publishing world. Gale Print and Google Books are just part of this wave. It is now possible to access a library of long out of print volumes right from our home computers. As I googled and read, I also found a number of references to digitalized copies of books that were available free on the internet and relevant to my ancestral stories. Google Books was especially valuable for located old texts. Not always, but often you could download from Google Books a PDF copy of books with valuable information on the people I was following. I bought a cheap thermo binding machine and started binding the PDF copies into my own collection of antique books.

The technology has also progressed to the point that it is economical to print a book only when ordered: "print-on-demand." Gorton's book had been scanned, digitalized, and stored in a computer bank. It was available print on demand. Once I placed my on-line order, the company printed a copy of it for me. I had it in my mailbox a little over a week from the time I ordered it – another example of how on-line technologies have made family history research possible in ways never dreamed of only a few decades ago.

When Samuel Gorton's book arrived, in its original type set and appearance, I had before me the history, complete with letters and documents, of Boston's attack on the homes in Shawomet – in his own words. The 111-page volume had the mindboggling title, Simplicities defence against seven-headed policy, or Innocency vindicated: being that seven-headed church-government united in New England: or, that servant so imperious in his masters absence revived and... *When I read the title, I was not sure what to make of it (and I will not even try to explain it here).*

What was important, though, was that within a few days of learning of it, I was browsing through a book written nearly 400 years ago by one of my ancestors, in its original words, print, and style. His past was there, in his own voice, in all its rich details. I was able to illustrate his stories with the color he, himself, used to tell them.

Amazon has also transformed the book world through its Kindle and e-books. While I read Samuel Gorton's account of the Shawomet events in my print-on-demand copy of Simplicities [etc.]..., *I found it easy to follow the same story through Massachusetts Governor John Winthrop's eyes. Both Volumes I and II of his original journals were available on Kindle for only 99 cents each. For that price, they could be downloaded onto a Kindle device, or via the Kindle app onto my phone and computer. I read the journals on my computer, and while I did so, I used Kindle's search function, punching in "Samuel Gorton" or "Canonicus" to go right to the spots where Winthrop wrote about them. Of course, if you wanted to go to the New York Public Library, or the New England Historic Genealogical Society library in Boston, you might possibly read them there, too. But I did it comfortably at home, in my study.*

Sensing the Past

Often when visiting a place where an ancestor lived, I had the uncanny feeling that I knew it. Maybe I did because I had studied it before visiting; or maybe somewhere in the depths of my genes, a memory lingered from the past. More than once I asked myself, do animals and humans have genetic memories? Migrating monarch butterflies and spawning salmon suggest some kind of memory. I found a discussion of this topic, but who could ever prove it?

We found Samuel Gorton's family plot not far from Dr. John Greene's. It made sense since they were close friends and built the settlement together. The Gorton farm site had long ago been sub-divided, and the blocks were covered with modest 1950's-style homes. The fenced-off Gorton family cemetery was just beyond one of the back yards. A miniature American flag flew over Samuel's headstone. I took a photograph, then paused for a moment of reflection. I wished more people knew about this man whose ideas of freedom and individual liberty had vexed so many in his times, yet left so much for us in ours.

After visiting Samuel's gravesite, we climbed into the car and drove a couple blocks to an intersection with a road running along the coastline. When turning right onto the coastal road, I saw through the corner of my left eye an inlet or cove. I sensed immediately this was a place I knew. It had to be the spot where Samuel's wife Mary and their children, along with many other families, fled into the cold waters to reach boats waiting to take them out of the reach of the Massachusetts invaders.

I pulled the Jeep over and crossed the busy street to take a closer look. In sharp contrast to the bustling traffic was a quiet virginal piece of parkland that slipped down to the shoreline. In the middle stood a sign that read: "Warwick Neck, first known as Mishawomet Neck and deeded to Samuel Gorton and his followers in 1643." It continued, "This cove overlook has been restored and maintained with native plantings."

The Martyr

In addition to Chad Browne who was pastor of America's first Baptist Church in Providence, Ida May had another prominent Baptist in her family. Obadiah Holmes was the second pastor of the Baptist Church in Newport, Rhode Island. Obadiah Holmes enjoyed a fascinating story of his own and is known in New England history

134

not so much for what he preached, but for his values and stubborn defense of them. During one of our travels to Rhode Island, we visited the Museum of Newport History where we found Obadiah Holmes in a display on the theme, "A Refuge of Religious Tolerance."

Obadiah was another of Mother's ancestors whom she apparently did not have a chance to discover. I never heard her make reference to him. He was a new character whom I quickly found to have qualities that I admired. Not the least of these was his desire to leave a record of his life and beliefs in letters, many of them written to his family. Obadiah did not want the values he cherished forgotten, and he saw that they were not. His voice, too, remains today in his own words.

Immediately to the right of one of downtown Boston's most famous landmarks, the Old State House, and diagonally across the square from the site of the Boston Massacre, stood a whipping post. In the 1600's it was the site of vicious punishments meted out not just to criminals, but to dissidents, both men and women. These dissidents were punished as heretics. The Boston Court would try these people in what by today's standards could hardly be considered fair and objective trials. The victims were then condemned to harsh and sometimes fatal punishments.

There, at this whipping post one September day in 1651, Obadiah Holmes's hands were tied to the post above him, and he was flogged until streams of blood ran across his bare back and down his legs to puddle on the ground. It was a severe flogging, and he was unable to sleep on his back for several weeks. He was spared a second flogging only when his friends spirited him out of Boston and back to his home in Rhode Island. His crime was discussing his Baptist beliefs one Sunday morning in the private Massachusetts house of an elderly Baptist adherent.

Obadiah was born in England and christened at Didsbury, near Manchester, in March, 1610. He was bright and privileged – three of his brothers went to Oxford. In his view, however, he consumed more wild oats than his brothers. In his later years, Obadiah regretted the wild days of his youth. He told of his good parents who taught their children religious values, writing "Three sons they brought up aright... most of their care was to inform and instruct them in the fear of the Lord, and to that end gave them much good counsel, bringing them often before the Lord by earnest prayer, but I the most rebellious of all did neither hearken to counsel nor any instruction, for from a child I minded nothing but folly, and vanity... continuing in such a course for four or five years; and then began to bethink me that counsel my dear parents and my dear mother had given me, many a call many a time with tears and prayers, ...my rebellion ...then looked me in open face, and my dear mother being sick it struck me my disobedience caused her death, which forced me to confess the same to her."[68]

Obadiah's mother, whom he feared he had neglected, died in the fall of 1630. Two months later, he married Katherine Hyde in Manchester's Collegiate Church. After his marriage to Katherine, religion became a powerful engine in Obadiah Holmes's life. There was also a religious fervor and upheaval in the air, especially in the Puritan center where he lived, and he was influenced by all these things.

Obadiah was a seeker, very much like Roger Williams. "Not long after this there was in me a great love to the Lord, but alas! I was deceived by my own heart... and the ministers," he told, "... left me short of understanding him as I should." In their disillusionment, he and Katherine finally decided to leave everything behind, "...and adventure the danger of the seas to come to new England." They and their young son Jonathan sailed from Preston in 1638. It was a difficult stormy voyage that lasted six weeks before the ship finally slipped into the quiet of Massachusetts Bay. They docked in Boston and made their way up the coast to Salem where they received an acre to build a house. The family was admitted members of the Salem church in the spring of 1639.[69]

Obadiah and Katherine began putting together their new home, and along the way, Katherine brought several children into the world. To support them, Obadiah took up a business brand-new in the Massachusetts colony. He and two of his friends applied to the

136

town of Salem for a loan of £30 to set up a glass manufacturing operation. With the loan and two more acres from the town to locate the plant, they began producing glass for window frames. Obadiah and his partners were probably the first glassmakers in North America. He also surveyed and set property boundaries for a neighbor, he witnessed the will and appraised the estate of another neighbor, and often served on juries. Although he was not educated like his brothers at Oxford, and in spite of what he considered a wild childhood, Obadiah was well educated for his times.[70]

The Holmes family stayed five years in Salem before they sold their interest in the glass factory and applied for land in Rehoboth, a newly established town in western Plymouth Colony. Their departure from Salem stemmed from Obadiah's continuing search for a spiritual home. He wrote that in their newly found homeland, "...I tried all things in several churches and for a time thought I had made a good choice or change, but in truth it little differed from former times and my spirit was like a wave tossed up and down, as not yet come to dig so deep as I should, or to consider the only ground of a well-grounded hope." His search, and the divergence from Puritan orthodoxy that flowed with it, eventually brought him to the attention of the church fathers. He was excommunicated from the Salem Church and banished from Massachusetts. He and Katherine moved to Plymouth and in 1646 received lot 37 in the allocation of new forested plots around Rehoboth.[71]

Obadiah and Katherine became members of a church led by Samuel Newman, one of Rehoboth's founders. Newman had attended Oxford and after graduating became a clergyman in the Church of England. Because of his Puritan sympathies he was persecuted for nonconformity until he migrated to New England a few years before the Holmes family met him. In 1648, Obadiah was made a freeman of Rehoboth, a status that granted him the right to vote.

The next year, another conflict arose. Obadiah sued Samuel Newman for slander and asked for £100, a huge sum, in damages. At issue was Newman's accusation that Obadiah perjured himself during testimony to a grand jury. Obadiah won the case but agreed to forget the sum when Newman publicly apologized and paid court costs.

Below the surface, however, something else was happening. Obadiah was not in agreement with Rev. Newman's sermons and began meeting with a small group of similarly minded people. They sympathized with Baptist beliefs and called themselves "Schismatists." Since they had no meeting house, they met privately on Sundays in someone's home. Among other things, the group opposed the Congregational and Anglican churches' practice of child baptism. Obadiah's group thus became controversial and vulnerable, for in Massachusetts, opposition to infant baptism was unacceptable. Following their beliefs on baptism, Obadiah and his friends eventually got in touch with Dr. John Clarke, the pastor at the Newport Rhode Island Baptist Church. Clarke and a companion traveled to Rehoboth to meet with the Schismatists and baptized all of them by immersion into the Baptist faith.

Obadiah's and his followers' nonconformity was a breach of Plymouth's and Massachusetts's religious custom and law. A petition, signed by 35 people in Rehoboth, all of colony's Congregational ministers, members of a neighboring church, and by the Court in Massachusetts Bay Colony was filed against them in June of 1650. In response to the complaint, Plymouth authorities prosecuted them for their Baptist beliefs, specifically accusing them of meeting "uppon the Lord's-day from house to house." The court that heard the charges initially gave a relatively mild sentence, ordering them to refrain from their activity.

Today's Americans are often surprised to learn of the deep intolerance that permeated the Puritan colonies. After all, for most of the colonists, religious freedom was the motivation for coming to Plymouth and Massachusetts in the first place. However, personal liberty, as we know it, did not exist in Puritan America. Communities might have liberty, but not individuals. Puritans promoted "soul liberty," their reason for migrating to New England. But soul liberty was the freedom of their community to practice Puritanism without restraint – and only Puritanism.

Puritans were quite comfortable persecuting, whipping, maiming, and even executing people who deviated from their own beliefs: Catholics, Quakers, Baptists, whomever. The idea that people who had suffered from Anglican Church oppression in the Old World came to America only to be no different toward dissenters, seems hypocritical if not un-American. That is exactly how Obadiah, too, felt, and he resisted. He had not departed his homeland and family, only to suffer once again the same restraints and reprisals. Holmes and two others obstinately refused to comply with the Plymouth Court sentence.

In October, the Court again entertained the same charge against Obadiah Holmes and his group. This time the Court excommunicated the men from the church at Rehoboth, banished them from Plymouth Colony, and ordered them to pay a £10 fine. In Boston, the Massachusetts Bay Colony Court followed the heresy trial closely, even though it had no jurisdiction in Plymouth. The Massachusetts brethren openly prodded their Plymouth neighbors to prosecute the heretics vigorously. "We earnestly intreate you to take care... of suppressing of errors as of the maintenance of truth," the court wrote. They were eventually displeased that Plymouth's penalties were not stronger.[72]

Obadiah's family and his followers began preparations to move into exile. It was only eight miles from Rehoboth to Providence where they could worship as they pleased, but instead they chose to go to Newport on the southern tip of Aquidneck Island. They were drawn there to commune with Dr. John Clarke, Newport's Baptist pastor who had baptized them the year before. Obadiah and his family quickly settled in and were soon prominent members of the Baptist congregation and close friends with the Clarkes and others of the growing port city's leading families.

Many people in Massachusetts and Plymouth adhered to Baptist teachings but did not openly practice their beliefs for fear of official reprisal. The Newport church tried to stay in touch with these people and respond to their needs as best it could. One of these Baptists was William Witter, an elderly and blind man, too old to travel to Newport to attend services. In July, 1651, Dr. Clarke, Obadiah

Holmes, and a third companion, John Crandall, decided to travel to Witter's home in Swampscott, near Lynn, Massachusetts. It was about a 90-mile journey, and a slow one over the rough undeveloped roads through what merely twenty years before had been pristine wilderness. The men hoped that the trip might also offer them a chance to spread the gospel, as they believed it, among the people they met along their way.[73]

It was a risky trip, especially for Obadiah who had been banished from Massachusetts and recently from Plymouth, as well. The men probably thought making a visit to a remote spot like Swampscott would attract little attention. They safely made their way through Boston, however, and continued northeast toward Salem. It was Saturday evening when they finally arrived at William Witter's home to spend the night. The next morning Dr. Clarke was conducting a worship service inside the home when unexpectedly two constables interrupted the gathering with a warrant to arrest the three visitors. They had been discovered, or perhaps followed. Remote villages, too, have curious eyes and ears, maybe more effective than in the city. The three were taken into custody and led away to be confined at the Anchor Tavern.

Sunday afternoon the prisoners were forced to attend the Puritan service in Lynn. On the way to the meeting, Clarke told the constable that if they had to join the service, they would protest with "both word and gesture." When they entered the meeting house, the three took their hats off, sat down, and then put them on again. The constable yanked off their hats. They followed with a silent protest by reading instead of listening. Afterwards they were taken back to the tavern. When morning came, the prisoners were marched to Boston to await the next Court. Their behavior in the church service did not help their case.[74]

After a week or so in jail, Holmes, Clarke, and Crandall were arraigned. It was a mock trial. Dr. Clarke described it: "In the forenoon we were examined; in the afternoon, without producing either accuser, witness, law of God or man, we were sentenced." During the examination, John Endicott, then governor of Massachusetts Colony, lost his temper and shouted they "deserved death, and that he would not have such trash brought into their jurisdiction."[75]   He challenged them to have their religious discussions with Puritan ministers instead of "weak-minded" persons, but when John Clarke eagerly accepted the offer, the authorities backed off. Crandall was sentenced to pay £5 pounds or receive a flogging; Clarke, to pay £20 or be flogged; and Obadiah Holmes, to pay £30 pounds or be whipped. For many people, £30 was an entire year's salary. For Obadiah, it was more than the value of all his belongings except his land and livestock.

When Clark protested the stiff sentences, Endicott again declared they deserved death and were "worthy to be hanged." Endicott's angered response was not exaggerated. Puritan society mixed private order and public violence with little temperance. Institutional savagery lived alongside the very orderly lives that typical Puritans led. The worst punishment in Massachusetts was burning at the stake, a sentence suffered by only two people – both Black women.   The next was hanging, a sentence much more common and sometimes meted out to religious dissidents, such as Mary Dyer, a Quaker whom Endicott sentenced to hang for her beliefs in 1660. Then came maiming – cutting off ears, branding in the face, and slitting nostrils, for example.   Lastly there was flogging, a punishment that could be severe, bringing the victim close to death.[76]

Of the three Newport visitors, Obadiah Holmes received the harshest sentence.   He had previously been banished and the magistrates also believed he had received too light a punishment from the Plymouth authorities the previous fall. Obadiah described what happened when the sentence was announced: "Upon the pronouncing of which I went from the Bar, I exprest my self in these words: I bless God I am counted worthy to suffer for the name of Jesus." At that point, the Puritan Pastor present struck him and said, "The Curse of God or Jesus goe with thee."[77]

When local friends learned that the Boston court had ruled that Obadiah and his companions could avoid flogging if they paid fines, they donated money to cover the fines.   Dr. Clarke and John Crandall accepted the generous offers and paid their fines. Obadiah

Holmes, however, had difficulties with this. He had committed no offense, he felt, and why should he waste others' money to pay off a crime not done. He described his dilemma: "Although there were that would have payd the money if I would accept it, yet I durst not accept of deliverance in such a way, and therefore my answer to them was, that although I would acknowledge their love to a cup of cold Water, yet could I not thank them for their money if they should pay it."[78]

The three men were carried off to prison, and about a week later Clarke and Crandall were released. It was a moment of despair for Obadiah: "... I was deprived of my two loving Friends; at whose departure the Adversary stept in, took hold on my Spirit, and troubled me for the space of an hour, and then the Lord came in, and sweetly releeved me, causing me to look to himself, so was I stayed, and refreshed."[79]

Dr. Clarke returned to Rhode Island and reported to Roger Williams what was going on in Boston. Williams immediately penned a bitter letter to Endicott, saying, "It is a dreadful voice from the King of Kings and the Lord of Lords: 'Endicott, Endicott, why huntest thou me? Why imprisonest thou me? Why finest? Why so bloodily whipped...'" The letter went on in that tone. Roger Williams, though banished, was still respected among many of Massachusetts' rulers.[80] However, there is no record that Endicott responded. He did not call off the whipping.

The day of the flogging arrived on September 2. Many friends visited Obadiah that morning proffering him wine and strong drink to temper the pain. He refused it. He offered a private prayer, and when the keeper came for him, he said he was in good spirits. Obadiah picked up his New Testament and followed the guard to the place of execution just outside the Congregational Church in the center of Boston. The "executioner" and one of the Magistrates, named Encrease Nowell, were waiting for him. A large crowd stood around the well-used whipping post.

Before being strapped to the post, Obadiah asked if he could say a few words. Nowell refused him, saying "It is not now a time to speak."

142

Disregarding Nowell, Obadiah turned to the crowd and addressed them anyway. "Men, Brethren, Fathers, and Countreymen," he began, "I beseech you give me leave to speak a few words, and ...because here are many Spectators to see me punished, and I am to seal with my Blood, if God give me strength that which I hold and practice in reference to the Word of God, and the testimony of Jesus..."

Nowell told him to be quiet and commanded the executioner to begin. When they started taking off his clothes, Obadiah resumed. He described the moment saying, "that I made as much Conscience of unbuttoning one button, as I did of paying £30... I told them... that I am not come to be baptized in afflictions by your hands, that so I may have further fellowship with my Lord... for by his stripes am I healed."[81]

The executioner raised his hand high in the air, and with a large overhead motion, thrust the whip down onto Obadiah's back and began the flogging: 30 strokes with a 3-corded whip, resulting in 90 lashes in all. The whip fell with power, tearing into his back, but Obadiah kept speaking, "Though my Flesh should fail, and my Spirit should fail, yet God would not fail... and with an audible voice I broke forth, praying unto the Lord not to lay this Sin to their charge."

His spiritual anguish and surge of moral courage somehow completely overcame the physical pain. He related, "As the stroakes fell upon me, I had such a spiritual manifestation of God's presence, as the like thereunto I never had, nor felt, nor can with fleshly tongue expresse, and the outward pain was so removed from me, that indeed I am not able to declare it to you... although it was grievous, as the Spectators said, the Man striking with all his strength (yea spitting on his hand three times, as many affirmed)."

Obadiah Holmes grew quiet as more blows fell. Astonishingly, he did not cry out in pain. This disconcerted the authorities who had hoped to make him an example through the spectacle of the public whipping. When it was finally over and they released him from the post. He poured oil on their fire when he remarked, "You have struck me as with Roses. Although the Lord hath made it easie to me, yet I pray God it may not be laid to your charge."

The crowd went wild. Some of them thronged around Obadiah, and when two of them took him by the hand, they were arrested for "contempt of authority." The two men were eventually ordered to pay 40 shillings or be whipped themselves. Obadiah returned to the prison where a friend "poured oyl into my wound, and plaistered my sores." Then he was released.

That night Obadiah Holmes received word that the embittered Magistrates were issuing another warrant for his arrest. His friends spirited him from Boston toward Newport. Along their journey, they heard that a constable had arrived the next morning at the house where Obadiah was staying only to find him gone. Word of his return to Rhode Island spread before him. Obadiah's wife Katherine and their eight children along with many from Newport and Providence were on the road when he was still four miles out of town, "...where we rejoiced together in the Lord." Obadiah's wounds were so severe that for weeks he had to lie upon his knees and elbows to avoid letting his back touch the bed, but he felt triumphant. His Lord had preserved him.[82]

With the ordeal behind, Obadiah and his family continued farming their land north of Newport, and he joined Dr. Clark in ministering to the Baptist fold. Not long after, John Clarke accompanied Roger Williams to England to seek a new charter for Rhode Island. With his departure, Obadiah assumed Clarke's position as pastor. John was in England for twelve years and Obadiah officiated in his absence. When he returned to Newport, the two of them jointly managed the Baptist congregation.

Baptists at the time did not believe in a paid clergy, and Obadiah received no remuneration from his pastorship. Instead, he farmed his land to sustain the family. On their 100-acre farm he grazed cattle and sheep and grew an orchard, garden, and feed crops. He supplemented his farm income as a weaver, making cloth from his own wool. Always, however, a sense of spiritual mission propelled his life. He took his ministry to Long Island, and, despite the Boston flogging, he risked another trip to Massachusetts.

Toward the end of his life, Obadiah penned letters to his family to express his love for them and for the God he followed with so much courage. To Katherine he wrote: "My most dear wife my heart hath ever cleaved to thee ever since we came together and is knit to thee in death which is the cause of these lines as a remembrance of Gods goodness to us in continuing us together almost forty [fifty] years... And now, my dear wife... it will be but a little while before thy day will end and thy time will come to sleep with me in rest."[83]

One of Obadiah's and Katherine's children, Mary, married Chad Browne's son, John, and from their family descended a tree that eventually reached Ida May whose unyielding spirit fought the harsh elements of the 19th century Idaho frontier as boldly as her forefather confronted the Puritan Magistrates. Another of Obadiah's and Katherine's descendants was Abraham Lincoln who had his own courageous battles and victories... and martyrdom.[84]

The Words of a Grandfather

During one New England visit, we continued Obadiah's path from Newport to Boston. In Newport, we found Obadiah Holme's final resting spot on his old farm in the countryside of Aquidneck Island. The road there still travels through the fields and farms where livestock graze in their pastures, and crops push through the ground that was once cleared with so much sweat. Keeping us closer to our own times, a modern house sat on the edge of the Holmes family cemetery. In the driveway, a huge sea-going craft rested on its trailer, waiting for a few warmer days before its summer launch into Narragansett Bay.

Downtown Newport, Seija and I knocked on the locked door of the local Baptist congregation. Finally, someone arrived. When I described my interest in Obadiah, the gentleman helpfully related what the congregation might have been like 350 years ago. He told me a reference to a very good book written not long ago. I immediately ordered it from Amazon, and when it arrived, I was happy to find that it included Obadiah's own writings and letters to his family and others not long before his death.

Finding the words of a grandfather who lived centuries ago at first seems like searching a haystack for a needle. Scouting the trails left by men like Obadiah Holmes, however, I was repeatedly surprised to discover first-hand stories waiting to be discovered. There was often a reason for this. These people foresaw the importance of bequeathing their stories to later generations.

Old Histories

Another reason we can sometimes reach back centuries to discover our ancestors' words is that many authors in the 19th century were curious about people like Obadiah. Their works can often introduce us to far-off grandfathers and grandmothers. For example, during the early and mid-19th century, many counties in the United States commissioned histories of their origins, and more than once I found reference to ancestors in these name-rich records. In the 1800s, history writers, often more personal than today, sometimes wrote as much detail about people as events, and made efforts to preserve what they found.

Fortunately, through internet searches and sites such as Google Books, I learned that a good number of these 19th century histories are easily available. I googled, followed leads, downloaded, and ordered from on-line antique book and re-print stores. The appeal of historical fiction has always been that we like to hear historical characters speak, when ordinary histories are often short on personal narratives. Luckily, I was able to find Obadiah's words as he or others recorded them. His words sketched out his many colorful stories.

Preserving Our Own Words

While thoroughly enjoying a chance to meet my ancestors this way, a bothering thought emerged. If Obadiah and others like him had not written their letters, accounts, and ideas, I would not have them on my bookshelf. And although Obadiah did write things down, we still would not have access to them if there were not long-lasting media formats to preserve his stories. The letters themselves were on paper, and his children and children's children carefully preserved them. Two hundred years later they were printed in books that sat on library shelves, until someone, 150 years still later, decided to digitalize or re-print them.

146

What about us? How many of our words will people 400 years from now find? The first time I asked myself this question, I answered, "Probably a lot." "After all," I thought, "we live in the Information Age". On further reflection, I had to admit: "Maybe nothing."

Most people no longer write letters on paper or any other medium that endures the years. We write emails and text messages that eventually will be deleted. We take photographs stored digitally, nearly all of them destined for eventual deletion. Or we might even take family videos, also designed for extinction unless someone continually updates the medium in our ever-evolving information environment – from Super 8's to VHS recordings, to digital recordings, to MP3 formats, and whatever comes next. Despite the Information Age's glorious possibilities, it is quite possible that our descendants will have much less first-hand contact with us than we have with our families who came before us.

To me, bequeathing family stories, including my own, to future generations is as important as finding them. How to do this in the age we live in is challenging and worth a lot of thought. I once drove by a cemetery in Finland that extended a mile or two along the left side of the road. On the right side was a sanitary landfill. It occurred to me that on the left side went our earthly remains and on the right side everything else: all we collected and saved over our lifetimes, including our computers and their hard drives. After the trip to the graveyard and landfill, not too much remained but fleeting family memories. Fortunately, Obadiah did not have a computer. He wrote things down by quill, and we have some of what he said today. Something to consider. Most on this later.

Universal, Ever-Current Messages

In downtown Boston, we lingered across the street from where Obadiah courageously faced his flogging. The wretched whipping post in front of Boston's Old State House is no longer there. Today, the busy intersection is covered with inches of asphalt. A parked service truck prevented us from standing where the whipping post had brought torment to who knows how many. The spot was opposite the site of the Boston Massacre, and any memory of the old whipping post is conveniently lost among the glories of a Revolution that took place a little more than a century later.

Massachusetts eventually mustered penitence for its 17th century brutalities. Boston has a place dedicated to religious tolerance. A few blocks from the whipping post, on the south lawn of the new Massachusetts State House, is an inspiring statue of Anne Hutchinson done by the famous American sculptor Cyrus Edwin Dallin. Anne looks toward heaven with her left hand on her heart and her right hand protecting her young daughter Susanna, the only child to survive the family's Long Island massacre. On the other side of the entrance to the State House is a statue of Mary Dyer whom John Endicott hanged for her Quaker beliefs. These two women lost their lives largely on account of the Puritans' violent intolerance, suffering more than even Obadiah.

The monuments brought a moment of quiet and reflection that Saturday morning we visited them. They bear testimony of one of the colony's bleaker moments and of those many people, mostly no longer remembered, who were maimed, flogged, or executed because they believed differently. We paused with the realization that some of the issues and some of the messages we receive from our family's narrative are ever current and universal. The past may be a foreign country, but some messages never change.

The Trader

At the time Samuel Gorton and Chief Sachem Canonicus signed the Act of Submission agreement, the area south of Warwick was mainly Indian Territory (see Map C). A few years before, in 1637, a man named Richard Smith had purchased land there and started a trading post at a place then called Cocumscussoc. The spot was later called Wickford and today it is in North Kingston. Smith was the first White settler to set up permanently in the heart of this Indian country. Richard Smith owned the trading post, but he did not live there until about 1650. To run the trading post he hired a man

148

named John Greene, known among those seeking family stories as "John Greene of Quidnessett."

When Richard Smith started his trading post on the western shore of Narragansett Bay, he and his brother, John, resided on the other side of the bay in Plymouth colony's Taunton. The two were followers of the Rev. Francis Doughty. When Doughty was banished from Plymouth, they moved with him and a small group of other followers to Aquidneck Island and then the following year, in 1641, to Long Island in the New Amsterdam colony. There, the group received a huge tract of 13,322 acres in what is now Queens.

They surely had no idea what an immense fortune that property would be worth one day. However, their world was consumed not with the future, but with the present. Not long after they arrived, Wappinger warriors raided their small settlement, killing several people including Richard's brother, John. Despite the tragedy, Richard stayed put. He bought a sloop, the *Welcome*, that he ran between New Amsterdam and his Cocumscussoc trading post exchanging goods for furs that he shipped back to Holland. Smith soon owned houses in Manhattan and on the East River and served on the "Eight Men" advisory council to the colony's Dutch director.[85]

In the meantime, the Cocumscussoc trading post built up a thriving trade relationship with the Narragansetts. In summer, they erected their wigwams along the coast nearby, where the women planted corn, beans, squash, and pumpkins, and the men hunted and fished. During winter, they retreated into the protection of the forests. It was wild country, but a road called the Pequot Path, or Post Road, ran nearby connecting the New Amsterdam colony to Boston.

The Smith trading post traded with the Indians and others who traveled past it by foot or by sea. At one point, Roger Williams, himself, built a trading post about a mile away. Chief Sachem Canonicus, "with his own hande," laid out the spot. Another man named Wilcox also started up a small trading operation.

149

In his own absence, Richard Smith needed an agent to oversee things. After the trading post went into business, he hired a young man named John Greene to manage it. John Greene arrived in Quidnessett among the first white people to settle in that part of the great American wilderness. It is said he traveled there from England after a stopover in St. Christopher in the British West Indies, a place he found too "Godless" to stay.

They called the new trading post "the Blockhouse." Around it spread the thousands of members of the Narragansett nation. The Blockhouse was made of logs, brick, and heavy timber, most of it brought from Taunton in boats. No one knows exactly what the trading post looked like, but today's researchers believe it was a cluster of buildings surrounded by a stockade. It was a home, a fort, a trading post, and an inn. Travelers, Whites and Native Americans alike, ate and lodged there free of charge. Roger Williams was a close friend and a regular visitor at his own nearby trading post, which became a favorite retreat for him. Often, he canoed down from Providence with his wife or one of his children to spend the weekend.

John Greene bought and sold the Blockhouse's goods with strings of beads called "wampum," a Narragansett word meaning "white strings." Wampum was originally made by the Indians for gifts, but it eventually became the tender used to buy and sell even high-priced things such as land and property. Wampum came in either white or purple and was made from shells, each piece usually 1/4-inch-long and about 1/8-inch-wide. It took seven days to make one fathom (6 feet) of white wampum and twice that long to make purple. Purple wampum was thus twice as valuable as white. In 1635, a fathom of purple wampum was worth about one-half pound British sterling, the equivalent of about $575, in 2003 dollars. A beaver pelt sold for one fathom.

When John Greene was building up Smith's trading post, beaver pelts were plentiful, and Richard Smith made a lot of money trading for furs. His was the first American fortune made in the fur trade. During a day at the Blockhouse, Narragansetts would bring in beaver pelts to trade with John for firearms, ammunition, woolen cloth and cloth garments, iron and copper cooking utensils, knives, hatchets, blankets, and "strong water." In 1651, Roger Williams sold his trading post, two big guns, and a small island to Richard Smith. Smith also bought out Wilcox to become the sole trader on the bay's west coast. Over the 1650's, pelts became scarcer, however. By the 1660's the beaver were gone.[86]

Sometime after John went to work at the Blockhouse he married a woman named Joan. I could never find anything about Joan, where she was from, or even her maiden name. By the time the Smiths returned from New Amsterdam to set up a more permanent residence at the Blockhouse, about 1650, the Greenes had their own home at the post complex and raised their children there.

There is some question over how many children John and Joan had, but one of the younger sons was a boy named Benjamin. Benjamin would one day marry John Coggeshall's granddaughter, Humility. They came from different backgrounds, Benjamin from a trading post in Narragansett country, and Humility, whose grandfather had been Rhode Island's first governor, from the "urbane" – as urbane as it went in New England during those days – shipping community of Newport. Benjamin and Humility were also among Ida May's ancestral grandfathers and grandmothers.[87]

When the beaver were gone, the Indians' big "cash crop" disappeared and the value of wampum strongly depreciated. As a result, the Narragansetts could no longer afford the goods to which they were now accustomed and were soon under pressure to sell their one remaining asset, their lands. Seeing what was happening, the Rhode Island Colonial Assembly passed a law in 1658 forbidding Whites from purchasing land from the Indians without prior approval. The Assembly likely was concerned both with the plight of their Native American neighbors, and with efforts of the other New England colonies to exert control over Rhode Island territory through buying up Narragansett lands. The ban on purchasing the Narragansetts' property became a major source of conflict between the Rhode Islanders and their neighbors. John Greene of Quidnessett was in the middle of the mêlée for years thereafter.

It began with a company of land speculators under Humphrey Atherton. The group also included Richard Smith and eventually John Greene of Quidnessett. Ignoring the new Rhode Island law, the speculators purchased the entire region around the Blockhouse trading post, about 12,000 acres, from the Narragansetts. Since the purchase was a violation of Rhode Island law, its validity depended on which of the colonies' jurisdictions covered the land, and a huge jurisdictional battle was born. Atherton was from Boston, and most of the others were from either Massachusetts or Connecticut, a fact that these two colonies thought bolstered their claims. As the purchase entangled the competing interests of Rhode Island, Connecticut and Massachusetts. A land squabble ensued. It lasted a long time.

The Narragansett tribe was the first victim. In September 1660, the New England Confederation of Massachusetts, Plymouth, Connecticut, and New Haven – but not Rhode Island – fined the Narragansetts for disturbances in eastern Connecticut and Long Island. Unable to pay the sum, the tribe accepted Atherton's offer to get rid of the fine if they mortgaged their lands to him and his group. Six months later, Atherton refused the Narragansetts' attempt to repay the mortgage and instead claimed title to all of the tribe's territory, about 400 square miles. It was a land grab, one of the most confused, petty and time-consuming boundary disputes in New England's history.[88]

John Greene of Quidnessett was a leader among the land purchasers, a position he sometimes must have regretted. At one point, Connecticut officers arrested him and two others and jailed them at Hartford. The colony claimed the men were acknowledging Rhode Island's jurisdiction. To get out of the fix, John Greene and Richard Smith then petitioned Connecticut to make their property part of that colony. This, in turn, insulted the Rhode Island courts which immediately ordered the arrest of John Greene.

One fine day, Rhode Island officers seized John Greene from his home without anyone witnessing their coming or going. People at the Blockhouse and his own family were anxious because of his disappearance. The officers took John to Newport and jailed him the Blockhouse and his own family were anxious because of his disappearance. The officers took John to Newport and jailed him there. When Richard Smith finally understood what had happened, he penned a letter to the Newport Court saying, "Three days since they came to John Greene's house at Aquidnessett with a warrant from theyre Court... and forecabley fetched him away to Rhode Island where he yet remaynes. His goeing was also not known to any here..." The Newport Court finally let John go, but the dispute ran on another seven years until an agreement was finally reached. The Rhode Island Court gave full possession of the lands to Greene and his partners if they acknowledged Rhode Island's jurisdiction. They agreed to that and became Rhode Islanders, once again.[89]

This was a time of growing tensions that eventually led to a devastating Indian war called King Philip's War. Relations were already tense as Plymouth's continued expansion pinched Wampanoag lands to ever smaller areas along Narragansett Bay's east coast. The match that ignited the flames sparked when the Plymouth colony wrongfully executed three Wampanoag men, one of them Philip's brother-in-law. With the executions, New England quickly spiraled toward devastation. In June 1675, Philip's Wampanoag tribe gathered for a war that began when Philip's warriors started slaughtering cattle and pilfering houses in Swansea in the Plymouth colony. Connecticut and Massachusetts soon sent soldiers to assist their fellow colonials while other tribes joined Philip's rampage. Throughout Plymouth and many parts of Massachusetts, the countryside was on fire.[90]

The Narragansett tribe camped near John Greene's home in Quidnessett followed Wampanoag Chief Philip's rebellion closely. At first, they considered it a local affair between Philip and his allied tribes, on one side, and Plymouth, Connecticut, and Massachusetts, on the other. Since Miantonomi's death, the Narragansetts had scorned these colonies, especially now when Miantonomi's son, Canonchet, was their Chief Sachem. However, they were determined to stay neutral. They had enjoyed strong friendships with Roger Williams, Samuel Gorton, Richard Smith, both John

Greenes, and most of their Rhode Island neighbors, and saw no interest in changing that.

As soldiers from Massachusetts and Connecticut joined the Plymouth men on the other side of the bay, the Narragansetts realized how quickly the war was spreading. Even some Rhode Islanders left to join the New England mobilization. The Narragansetts asked Williams why Rhode Islanders did not let Philip and Plymouth fight it out between themselves. Williams replied that all the colonies were King Charles's subjects. Englishmen felt it a duty "to stand to the death by each other in all parts of the world."[91]

Still, Rhode Island was very hesitant to jump into the fray against Philip and his allies. For one thing, Rhode Islanders had often received more support from the Indian tribes than from their fellow colonists. For another, they lived in a place where one of the mightiest tribes in New England remained neutral. And not least, it was becoming apparent that the other three colonies were conspiring to use the war as an excuse to invade Rhode Island. Doing so could award them the lands long coveted, but never yet seized.

Rhode Island instead worked from the beginning to restore peace. In the middle of June, just before Philip's attack on Swansea, Samuel Gorton accompanied Deputy Rhode Island governor John Easton to meet Chief Philip. Their mission was to dissuade his tribe from the warpath. Easton, who was a Quaker, had done an independent investigation of the murder, the subsequent trial, and the execution of Philip's brother-in-law. He had concluded that the Plymouth trial was a travesty. Gorton and Easton suggested that Philip pursue arbitration, and they promised that Easton would go to New York, now under England's control, to see if Governor Andros would agree to arbitrate and redress Wampanoag grievances.

Philip remained unconvinced that justice was available under the English. He also had been around long enough to know that Rhode Islanders, no matter how sincere or supportive, were in no position to speak for their Plymouth cousins. In his view, "Tract after tract is gone. But a small part of the dominions of my ancestors remains. I am determined not to live till I have no country." The war broke

154

The Narragansetts were in winter camp, a few miles south of Quidnessett John's home. Up until now they had remained outside the conflict. If the Narragansetts had joined Philip in the early days of the war, it would have meant disaster for the colonies. The combined Indian forces might well have overrun all of New England including Boston. However, among the combined colonies' troops, they earned little credit for their peaceful stance.

Instead, the colonial forces gave the Narragansett tribe an ultimatum to turn over any and all of Philip's Wampanoags sheltered in their camp as well as any Pocassets who might have found refuge in the Narragansett tribal areas. The Narragansetts refused. They were neutrals in the conflict and had no responsibility to surrender anyone. Beyond that, they wondered why they should give up their Native American cousins to New England where prisoners could be sold into slavery or hanged. Canonchet's refusal to comply was all the excuse the Massachusetts, Plymouth, and Connecticut forces needed to march through Rhode Island toward an attack on the Narragansett tribe.

By December, 1,000 soldiers, five percent of the region's entire male population, were moving south through Providence, and then Warwick toward the Narragansetts' winter camp. The leader of this invasion, mammoth for its time and place, was Josiah Winslow. The advance continued until the men reached the Quidnessett settlement where they camped at the Blockhouse, now being called "Smith's Garrison." It was deep winter, and the temperatures had dropped to sub-freezing.

The Narragansetts saw the invasion coming. In response, they attacked Jireh Bull's nearby garrison which was earmarked as a staging point for the arriving English forces. The Indians killed 15 people and burned the garrison to the ground. It was clear to both sides that the battle ahead would be an ugly one. With the tribe camped in a fortified and secluded village, deep in a giant swamp land, Winslow's army at first did not know how or where to attack them. Eventually, an Indian turncoat agreed to lead the soldiers, and soon the invasion force was trudging from the Blockhouse through deep snow toward the Narragansett camp. (See Map C) Among them were four of Richard Smith's nephews.

The next day, Sunday, was not a rest day for the otherwise pious Puritans. They charged directly toward the Narragansett village. When they reached it, they encountered a huge wooden fortress Canonchet's people had constructed to protect themselves from an attack. For the next several hours, the Narragansetts defended themselves well against the Puritan onslaught, but when their ammunition drew low, the invaders finally entered the fortification whose tepees were filled with cowering women and children. The fighting raged on. Finally, Canonchet regrouped his braves and moved them into a fire line in the surrounding brush before finally escaping into the swamp. Nightfall approached, and Winslow, in a treacherous move, gave the order to burn the tepees. As they burned, a ghastly massacre of women and children huddled inside ensued.

After the horrific battle, known as the "Great Swamp Fight," Winslow's men started carrying their wounded back to Smith's Garrison. The Quidnessett Greene family was probably there at the Blockhouse, helping care for wounded as they wandered back from the terrible battle. The dead were piled into a mass grave. Casualties on both sides were beyond anything before seen. More than 20% of the English soldiers were either killed or wounded, double the rate of American forces on D-Day. Connecticut forces suffered a 30% casualty rate, about the same as Confederate losses at Antietam. Somewhere between 350 and 600 Narragansett men, women, and children were killed that day.

Yet there were still thousands of Narragansett warriors under Canonchet, angrily making their way north to join Philip. The combined Native American forces sowed terror and their own atrocities among villages and towns throughout Massachusetts, Plymouth, and Rhode Island. In just about every way conceivable, the Winslow campaign into southern Rhode Island was a debacle. The idyllic life in the wilderness countryside the Narragansett people shared with their Rhode Island neighbors was shattered forever. It was only days before the Narragansetts, who had eaten, drunk, and traded for decades there, burned the Blockhouse, too, to the ground.[93]

In was a dreadful springtime in 1676. Every town was under threat. There was no way for Rhode Island's quiet communities to remain outside the war. The united colonies' invasion ended with the entire west coast of Narragansett Bay torched and overrun. In March, a New England company of 80 men stumbled into an ambush where Canonchet's warriors massacred 65 of them. Two days later, Canonchet hit Rehoboth with 1,500 warriors. The town's inhabitants watched from their garrisons as 40 houses, 30 barns, and 2 mills went up in flames. The next day the Narragansetts fell on Providence. Most of the city's 5,000 people had evacuated to Aquidneck Island, but 20 determined men, including 77-year old Roger Williams, remained holed up in a garrison.

The same month they burned Providence, Indian parties rampaged through Warwick. Every building in the community was torched except one, a large stone house. Everyone fled, including the late Dr. John Greene's children and grandchildren, most of them boating across the Bay to Portsmouth on Aquidneck Island. John Greene of Quidnessett, his family, and the others had fled the Smith trading post when the retreating army marched back to Massachusetts and Plymouth. Canonchet's warriors took over everything. The Blockhouse compound along with every other house south of Warwick were also burned to the ground. None of the evacuees could safely return until 1677, almost two years after the war began.

A few days after the Indians ransacked Providence, Connecticut troops captured Narragansett Chief Sachem Canonchet. They offered him his life if he would persuade Philip and others to stop fighting. He refused, saying it would be fruitless to try. When they told him he would be sentenced to death, he bravely replied, "He liked it well, that he should die before his heart was soft or had spoken anything unworthy of himself." These were among his final words. [94]

Both sides languished as the slaughter renewed, but attrition hurt Philip's bands more. On July 3, 1676, near Warwick, Connecticut troops caught up with a band of weary Narragansetts who were prepared to surrender. The soldiers attacked them, anyway. Over 170 were massacred without the loss of a single Connecticut man. Such tolls bore down until Philip, himself, was finally killed.

When considering the proportion of casualties to the number of people involved, King Philip's War was America's bloodiest. There were about 70,000 colonists and Native Americans living in New England when the war started. By its end, thousands of them were dead. World War II took about 1 % of America's male population. The casualty rate in the Civil War was 4-5 %. During King Philip's War, the Plymouth Colony lost close to 8 % of its men.

The Native Americans suffered even more. Of their 20,000 people on the eve of the war, 2,000 died in battle, 3,000 died of sickness or starvation, 1,000 were shipped from the colonies as slaves, and another 2,000 fled to neighboring Indian tribes. The Native American peoples in the four colonies were decimated, never to recover fully. Of the proud Narragansett tribe, only about 500 were alive when the war ended.[95]

The war changed much in Rhode Island. Richard Smith, Jr., whose father died in 1666, built Smith's Castle on the site of his father's trading post. There were no longer Native American customers or suppliers. Samuel Gorton returned to find all of Warwick devastated except the lone stone building. One more time, Samuel and Mary were without a home. He and his family rebuilt it, and he moved in before passing away later that year at 85 years of age.

John Greene of Quidnessett lived even longer. He died at 89. He spent the final years of his life trying to resolve the conflicting colonial claims surrounding lands he and his partners had acquired before the war. Two of his sons, Captain Edward and Lieutenant John Greene perhaps got their ranks serving in the King Philip's War. His son Benjamin was too young for the Army.

When in 1676 the urgent message from the General Assembly arrived in Warwick warning everyone to flee an imminent Indian attack, Dr. John Greene's son, James, and his second wife, Elizabeth Anthony, escaped to Portsmouth where Elizabeth's family lived.

After the war ended, they, too, returned to burnt-out ruins. Rather than re-build their former home, James and Elizabeth decided to relocate on a piece of land in Potowomut, south of Warwick. There they erected a new house on a hill with a beautiful overlook across the water. In Potowomut, the family also built a forge and iron works. But this gets us into another set of stories that I will save for later.[96]

Something important about Samuel Gorton, Obadiah Holmes, Dr. John Greene, and the others, was they viewed the struggles they encountered in terms of a larger world than just their own. Whatever they suffered, in their view, was part of constructing the New World they had chosen. If there were times when they privately regretted leaving England for the North American colonies, there was never any sign of that in their histories and statements. Just the opposite. I never found any indication of regret, but instead an enthusiasm for the journey they were traveling.

Ghost Stories?

Learning about John Greene of Quidnessett began with several searches of Wikipedia, Google Books, and Amazon. There were a few hits on the 17th century American colonial name "John Greene," but most of them referred to Dr. John Greene. One search, however, identified the book by Lora Sarah Nichols La Mance, published in 1904, that was available as a re-print from Amazon.com. I promptly ordered a copy.

Browsing through the old work's pages, I learned she was a descendant of John Greene of Quidnessett. She had spent a lot of effort and time tracing her Greene family ancestors. Even with all she had done, however, I did not get to know him as well as the other three ancestors in this chapter. There were so many unknowns. Still, she left coordinates, and as I planned our trip to New England, I knew where to find the place he lived most his life.

It was a cool Spring day when we drove to the place in Rhode Island where the Blockhouse once stood. It was not difficult to imagine it lying in a clearing with crops growing in surrounding fields and livestock grazing the meadows. On one side was the sea, and behind the Blockhouse extended dense woods, although not the pristine wilderness full of the abundant game John Greene knew in his day. Then, the forest's broad tall trees had never been cut nor harvested. There were so many wolves and wildcats in the woods, that even in Providence and Aquidneck, the most developed parts of Rhode Island, the legislature offered a bounty for their pelts. It was hard for us to grasp the feeling John and his family must have had when they looked at that wilderness that flowed westward without stop, farther than they or anyone, red or white, knew.

At the Smith trading post, civilization was still far away. In a deposition he made forty years later, John remembered it this way:

> "Richard Smith that I then lived with, did first begin and make a settlement in the Narragansett, and that by the consent and the approbation of the Indian Princes and people, and did improve land mow meadows severall yeares before Warwick was settled by any English man; and I, being present did see and heare all the Narragansett Princes being assembled together give by livery and seizing some hundreds of acres of land about a mile in length, and so down to the sea; ...many hundred Indians being present, consenting thereunto."

For all the place's roughness and challenges, it must have been magnificent to behold the noble, proud peoples who had mastered it from time immemorial. But one's eye today cannot help pausing at his use of the word "seizing."[97]

As I mentioned earlier, Narragansett warriors burned the "Blockhouse" during the King Philip's War. It was re-built by Richard Smith's son in 1678 and came to be known as Smith's Castle. But it never again served as a trading post. The war destroyed forever those days, as well as most of the Native Americans who lived near the site. Today, Smith's Castle is a carefully kept historic landmark.

The week we planned to be in Rhode Island was still off season for tourist attractions. Before embarking on our travel, I learned from the Smith's Castle website that the house was seasonally closed *and would not be open during our visit. I called their management office to explain my project and ask if there were any possibility for a quick private visit. The manager was more than gracious and kindly agreed. We reserved a time to meet.*

When we arrived, snow from the previous day's fall thinly layered the peaceful enclosure. Yellow daffodils poked their heads through the white cover. A clearing behind the house reached out to the bay inlet. Roofs of Old Wickford's original colonial homes peered above the trees alongside the bay front. It was a pleasant place where we realized at once we hoped to one day again return.

To the side of the old castle was a mound. Our guide told us it was a grave where some of the colonial soldiers killed during their attack in the Great Swamp were buried. At least 40 of them still lie in that quiet meadow between Smith's Castle and waters of the bay. As I looked at the old mass grave, it occurred to me such brutalities as this war ran counter to the ideals for which people like the Gortons, Greenes, and Holmeses suffered and fought their own battles.

I mentioned several times how all stories lie somewhere along a spectrum between myth and fact. Knowing where they fit on that line is one of the challenges of family history. How about "ghost stories?" Where do they fit? This may seem a preposterous question, and perhaps it is. But they sometimes add a flash of color to our research and in Colonial America you cannot completely ignore them. Ghost stories about these old places abound in Rhode Island, even today. Obviously, we are never going to substantiate them, nor will we even try. But properly labeled, they may sometimes have a place in our story collections.

While visiting Smith's Castle, we heard an incredible one. Our guide said that a few years earlier, the foundation that supports Smith's Castle undertook a major renovation of the old structure. To protect the furniture, most of which dates back to the late 17th century, the curator made arrangements to have everything removed until the work was completed. They hired three men to transport the furnishings to a place of storage. One of them, quite by coincidence, was named "Richard Smith," the name of both the original founder of the Blockhouse settlement, as well as of his son who built Smith's Castle.

As the men brought things from the house to the van, each load was photographed to establish a visual record. Everything fortunately went well, the renovation was completed, and preparations were made to return things to the rooms where they had been earlier. When the curator pulled out the earlier photographs to check off the items, she was astonished to discover that the man named Richard Smith did not appear in any of them. The photos showed the other two men carrying their loads. But Richard Smith showed up nowhere where he should have.

Our guide looked at us, smiled, and said, "All I can say is that I have seen the photographs. The man we knew as Richard Smith appears in none of them.

Chapter 4

Road to Rebellion
Brothers and Cousins

"We fight, get beat, rise, and fight again."
Gen. Nathanael Greene
in a letter to the French Ambassador (1781)

Ida May Dawley's father Henry had a great-grandfather, Joseph Greene, who was one of a gang of brothers and cousins who contentiously defied the British even before the Revolutionary War. Among them was Nathanael Greene who during those days was grooming himself to become a soldier, something he did well enough to become a celebrated general in the Continental Army. Among the adventures was sacking and burning His Majesty's warship Gaspee *during the winter of 1772, a much more daring and dangerous adventure than the better-known Boston Tea Party that occurred a year and a half later.*

First Blood of the American Revolution

Mid-winter days off the New England coast are seldom anything but harsh, and this one in February 1772 was like the rest. Rufus Greene sheltered himself from the elements by staying in the cabin of the *Fortune* as it lay at anchor in Narragansett Bay, some distance offshore North Kingston, Rhode Island.

The *Fortune* belonged to "Jacob Greene & Co.," an enterprise owned by Rufus's cousins, sons of the late Nathanael Greene, Sr. Below deck in the hold were 12 hogsheads of West India rum, about 1400 gallons, along with 40 gallons of Jamaica spirits and one hogshead of brown sugar. The cargo belonged to one of the Jacob Greene & Co. brothers, young Nathanael, Jr., who in a few years would become one of America's most famous soldiers. Now, however, he was busy managing parts of his family's business.

One last point about the cargo: it had not cleared His Majesty's Customs in Newport, making it technically smuggled contraband.

163

Those days, however, smuggling to avoid the Crown's customs collector was business-as-usual for many Rhode Islanders, more an issue of pride than wrongdoing in most Rhode Islanders' minds.

Rufus Greene, Jr., was captain of the *Fortune*. Along with another cousin, Griffin, he worked for the Jacob Greene family enterprise. Rufus's father, Rufus, Sr., was a brother to Nathanael's father, Nathanael, Sr. Rufus, Jr., was 24, tall, brown-haired, and slim. His older brother, Joseph, was my grandfather eight generations back. This cold morning, Rufus was aboard the *Fortune* alone. Everything was quiet enough.

Or, at least so may have seemed. Unknown to Rufus, the *HMS Gaspee*, a Royal Navy two-masted schooner with cannon, rested on the horizon watching the *Fortune*. Lt. William Dudingston, commander of the *Gaspee*, peered through his telescope over the waters that lay between the two vessels, deciding the best way to detain the ship for inspection.

The job was not the young blue-uniformed officer's duty of choice. He would have preferred something better than patrolling unfriendly colonial waters looking for Yankee smugglers, especially along the coast of Rhode Island whose shippers detested customs duties. Still, he had his own ship and a small crew to command. If it was not the most romantic job in the Navy, Dudingston performed it with exuberance, stopping everything from row boats to ferries. His aggressive enforcement of the customs laws had made him as unpopular as he was enthusiastic, and he sometimes felt physically endangered when in New England ports. He played it tough, though. Not long before, he had been sued in Delaware for beating a fisherman while one of his men held the man helpless.

Moving the *Gaspee* closer to the *Fortune*, Lt. Dudingston ordered a boat into the water and commanded an officer named Dundass to lead the boarding party. Rufus quickly saw the approaching boat and came on deck to greet them. Whether he immediately knew that they were Royal Navy is unclear, but at least Dundass seemed to pretend they were not. He asked if the *Fortune* had room to take on more cargo, and his men climbed on board. When Dundass demanded to see the hold, Rufus responded that he had no extra room. The British officer then ordered Rufus to open the hatches. Rufus, impatient, replied gruffly that the hatches were open. Dundass then ordered Greene to return to his cabin. Now sure of what was going on, Rufus barked back, "By what authority?"

Dundass drew his sword and waved it at the insolent young Rhode Islander, "If you do not go into the cabin, I'll let you know." He then grabbed Rufus by the collar and shoved him into the master's cabin, but Rufus did not stay put. Determined to resist the capture of his vessel, he rushed out to prevent them from lifting the *Fortune's* anchor. In a quick movement, Dundass seized Rufus again, jammed the companion leaf – a wooden door separating the two decks – over his head, and knocked him flat over a chest. Confining the stunned Rufus to the cabin, Dundass ordered his men to tow the *Fortune* to the *Gaspee*. Once alongside the schooner, the Royal Navy had possession of the *Fortune* and its cargo.[1]

Dundass pulled Rufus Greene on board and escorted him to Dudingston. The captain questioned Greene for a while and then ordered him locked in the gangway. Before they took him below deck, Rufus demanded to know whether Dudingston had a commission to seize vessels. Dudingston curtly dismissed him, answering only that he did.

The next day Rufus was released on the mainland while the *Fortune* was accompanied to the headquarters of the British fleet in Boston. In Rhode Island waters, a seized ship and its cargo were too hot to hold on to, and Dudingston wanted to get rid of the *Fortune* quickly. He feared that if he took the vessel to Providence, the best outcome might be a colonial court order to return it to its owner. More likely, as had happened before, a seized vessel would simply turn up missing from port one morning and shortly be seen sailing again for its original owners.

Spiriting the *Fortune* to Boston, on the other hand, carried its own risks. Under colonial law, the lieutenant had no right to transport the *Fortune* to any other colony than the one where it was seized. Dudingston thought he was choosing the safer bet. But there was no local sympathy for Royal officers who confiscated vessels belonging to Rhode Islanders. The Rhode Island courts promptly issued a warrant for his arrest. Even as an officer of the Royal Navy, he thereafter could not go ashore in Rhode Island for fear of being detained.[2]

One of the first to hear of the *Fortune's* capture and transfer to Boston, of course, was Nathanael Greene, owner of the confiscated cargo. That the goods were in fact illegal outraged him no less. Up to this point he had not engaged in the continued bickering between Britain and its American colonies. The loss of the *Fortune* changed that. Everything now was personal. The Greene brothers' filed suit against William Dudingston and asked for £600 for damages sustained when he seized the vessel and its cargo. By summer, they had won their suit, but that did not change their newborn opposition to the Crown authorities.[3]

The warrant for his arrest and the judgment against him personally did not cool Lt. Dudingston's fervor for enforcing Britain's Navigation Acts. He stepped up his patrols, sailing the *Gaspee* all over Narragansett Bay in search of vessels that might be smuggling. His zeal echoed London's efforts that year to up the enforcement of the navigation laws. The duties on the colonies' trade were Parliament's way of getting the New Englanders to pay the Crown's debts from the French and Indian War, or Seven Years' War as it was called in Europe.

Dudingston, loyal to London's policies and even smart operationally, was fatally flawed in New England's incendiary political climate. Colonists were frustrated over being taxed, with no say in Parliament about the war, or the taxation to pay for it. Smuggling was passive resistance, patriotic, and lucrative to boot. To colonial traders and leaders alike, Dudingston's new energy to catch smugglers made him and his vessel too unpopular to tolerate. After the capture of the Greene brothers' sloop, and the *Gaspee's* subsequent daily raids, a group of prominent Rhode Islanders began looking for reprisal. They did not have to wait long.

In June, a Rhode Island captain named Benjamin Lindsay was peacefully sailing a coastal packet named the *Hannah* up Narragansett Bay. Loaded with cargo and passengers, the *Hannah* was on its way from Newport to Providence. Lindsay had filed his

166

cargo manifest in Newport for the New York-origin merchandise, and everything on board was legal and proper.

Somewhere along the short voyage, however, Dudingston shot a cannon across her bow and ordered the *Hannah* to stop for inspection. Lindsay ignored the signal and raced his ship in the direction of Providence. The *Gaspee* launched into hot pursuit. The *Gaspee* was a quick 8-gun schooner, 60-70 feet long, and carried a crew of about 20. It was small and swift, one of a new generation of Royal Navy ships commissioned to enforce the customs laws in the North American colonies – the original coast guard cutter.

The two vessels tacking back and forth into the north wind, sped up the bay. The *Gaspee* was closing, when just off Warwick, Lindsay spirited the *Hannah* through some shallows. When Dudingston tried the same maneuver, the *Gaspee* hit a sandbar hard and stuck fast in the mud. With the tide running out, the *Gaspee* in a few minutes was awkwardly helpless in one foot of water on one side and two feet on the other (see Map C). While Dudingston wallowed in frustration, Lindsay triumphantly hurried on to Providence. Once in port, at just about sunset, he jumped ashore and ran to find a man named John Brown.[4]

In Providence, John Brown was at the top of the shipping community pyramid, one of Rhode Island's richest men, and owner of a fleet of ships. He was a descendant of Chad Browne (Chapter 3) and lived down the street from where Chad's original home had stood over 100 years before. Brown's own residence was a magnificent mansion that President John Quincy Adams once said was the finest home he had ever been in. It still stands there in all its splendor, open for visitors to taste the opulence that the shipping trade, smuggling and all, brought New England families like the Browns. Up the hill from his house spreads the campus of Brown University that he was instrumental in founding and which carries his family name. He had laid the cornerstone to the college's oldest building two years before the day Lindsay came looking for him.

It did not take Lindsay long to find John Brown and relay the *Gaspee's* predicament. Brown was delighted to hear the despised vessel was dead aground, unable to move anywhere, and quick to grasp the opportunity the moment offered. Twelve years earlier, Brown, himself, had been stranded on the same bar and remained grounded there until the next morning when the tide came in. He knew this was what many in Providence had been waiting for.

Brown's plan, for lack of a better term, was a "pirate raid." He hired a drummer boy to go up and down Towne Street sounding an alarm meant to call a gathering of like-minded men. That night, shippers, sailors, merchants and others, as many as 500, crowded into downtown Providence inns. Headquarters was set up in the Sabin Tavern where they began to plot the raid. John Brown brought along several of his saltwater captains. One of them, Abe Whipple, was well experienced at capturing merchant vessels, having been a privateer[5] in the Caribbean.

Rufus Greene was also there, as were others who had suffered from the *Gaspee's* raids. Nathanael Greene was at home hosting a dinner party, and his brothers were also conspicuously absent – probably intentionally. An attack on one of His Majesty's vessels was not only audacious, it was dangerous. The Greene brothers, being the obvious perpetrators of anything done that night, all needed alibis. But consequences seemed not to bother many others as the evening's plans and preparations unfolded.

About 10:00 the meeting was over, and a group of 60 men marched down the dark streets to the wharf. Rufus Greene was with them as they boarded eight longboats, the largest ones in the harbor. He represented the family in avenging the seizure of the *Fortune*. More than revenge, however, the party intended to send a powerful message to London that the people of Rhode Island would not tolerate unfair laws, financial losses, and confiscations of their property. This was also the aim of Boston's patriots who mounted the Boston Tea Party a year and a half later. For whatever reason, the Boston Tea Party has always shared much more attention than the operation that night in Narragansett Bay. Yet, the *Gaspee* raid was more daring, more profound, and more dangerous. These men were mounting an attack on an armed vessel of the Royal Navy.

Five rowers took over each of the longboats' oars wrapped in canvas to hush the rowing. All the men involved swore to reveal no one's identity. With long careful strokes they pulled, and the boats slid silently across the quiet waters toward where they knew the *Gaspee* lay motionless. One of John Brown's ship captains manned the rudder of every longboat. No one talked. They held their weapons in their hands. The boats slipped forward until about midnight the *Gaspee's* silhouette stood as a ghost on the horizon. The longboats fanned out into a line and continued their slow approach.

At about 60 yards, a *Gaspee* lookout saw the approaching longboats and through the misty darkness and commanded them to identify themselves. There was no response, only quiet. The oarsmen continued pulling their boats closer. He called again, but in return received only the same silence. The crewman disappeared, and a few moments later Lt. Dudingston emerged on deck, a sword in one hand and a pistol in the other.

"Who goes there?" he shouted.

Former privateer Abe Whipple feigned, "I am the sheriff of Kent, and I want to come aboard!"

The lieutenant yelled back that he intended to admit no one at this hour of the night, sheriff or not.

Whipple boomed back, "I am Sheriff of the County of Kent... I have got a warrant to apprehend you... So surrender!"

The longboats maneuvered forward until they were under the bow, and Dudingston sounded an alarm to the crew. It was too late. The crew did not have time to get on deck before Rufus and the others were all over the *Gaspee*. Lt. Dudingston alone discharged his pistol and raised his sword, and one of the boarding party returned the fire. A single shot hit the lieutenant in the arm and groin. He fell. No more shots were fired, and instead the raiders used their barrel staves to beat and knock down the *Gaspee's* crew.

It was midnight dark, and the crew could not see the attackers' faces well. Only one of the *Gaspee's* men left a first-hand description of the attackers: "The captain, who was called the captain of the gang, was a well-set man, of a swarthy complexion, full face, and hoarse voice, and wore a white cap, was well-dressed, and appeared rather above the common rank of mankind." That must have been John Brown.[6]

Dudingston lay bleeding on the deck. Whipple would have finished him, but Brown forbade it. Instead, he asked Dudingston to command his crew to surrender. When they did, the lieutenant was taken to his cabin where one of the raiders, a young Providence man who had studied medicine, expertly dressed his wounds. Brown and Whipple rifled through the ship's records before the attackers with their prisoners climbed down the *Gaspee's* sides and back into the longboats.

Retreating now, the raiding party broke into two groups, one of them heading directly back to Providence, the other seeking a nearby shore where they left the crew members and their wounded captain. Before the last of the raiders climbed off the sloop, they set it on fire. From the shore, the crew watched it burn, until the powder magazines exploded. Its planks and cannon fragments scattered across the water. The *Gaspee* would no longer harass Rhode Island shipping.

By noon the next day it was hard to find anyone in Rhode Island who had not heard about the previous night's raid on the *Gaspee*. It was equally difficult to find someone who could identify the attackers. Solidarity with the attackers had no seams. While this might seem remarkable, it is good to remember that of all the British colonies in North America, Rhode Island owed its heritage to settlers who in one way or another had been victimized by central authority, either political or ecclesiastical. Rhode Island was built by non-conformists who valued their freedom and individuality. The Greene family descended from these individualists. So did the Browns. In Providence, the Gaspee Affair was a celebrated act of defiance, something imbedded in the colony's sense of character. The identities of the attackers were safe, as the British frustratingly found out. To this day, the raid is still celebrated each June in Rhode Island.

The morning after the raid, Rhode Island's Deputy Governor Sessions rushed to find the *Gaspee's* crew. He realized the gravity of the attack and made sure there was every appearance that local

170

authorities were taking it seriously. Sessions found Dudingston bedridden in a cottage near the shore with the bullet still lodged in his wounds. He promised medical help and made sure medical assistance was sent. Before a doctor arrived, however, the real Kent County Sheriff showed up to arrest Dudingston for the seizure of the Greene family's *Fortune*. Dudingston was in no shape to leave with the sheriff, but he accepted the arrest warrant and continued to wait for help.

The next official to arrive was the royal customs agent who was anxious to save Dudingston from any abuse at the hands of local authorities. Then, finally, medical care arrived. The lieutenant was treated, and after some convalescence, recovered. A month later, the Providence court forced him to pay the Greenes the compensation for which they had sued him. With some poetic justice, at least in the Greenes' eyes, Dudingston found the money to pay them from customs coffers.

In the meantime, Admiral John Montagu, the British commander of naval forces in North America, engaged in an angry exchange of correspondence with Rhode Island's governor. In London, as fully expected, the Crown was infuriated and demanded the attackers be arrested and shipped to England for trial and punishment. King George, himself, signed a royal proclamation offering £500 for information leading to the arrest of the attackers. He promised another £500 for the capture of the individuals called "the head sheriff" and "the captain" – who many knew to be Whipple and Brown. Finally, any participants who turned informant were promised a pardon. Even £1,000 was not enough to break the Rhode Islanders' silence. A couple of bystanders tried to collect the reward money, but their testimonies were quickly neutralized with subtle and not so subtle pressure from fellow Rhode Islanders.

A royal panel of inquiry trudged on in its investigation of the *Gaspee* Affair for nearly a year. There were suspicions that Nathanael Greene had participated in the attack, and many expected him to be hauled before the inquiry. However, Nathanael had his house party alibi from the night of the event.

Rufus Greene was also widely considered one of the ringleaders in the *Gaspee* attack, and the panel of inquiry asked him to testify. He gave his testimony through a written deposition. He and his supporters wanted to avoid the possibility that if he appeared in person someone from the crew might identify him as one of those present that night. In fact, one crewmember testified someone named "Greene" was one of the raiders. He also said he had met "Greene" in Dudingston's cabin the day after the *Fortune* was seized. This was clearly Rufus, but the panel members would not accept this as evidence without getting the attacker's first name, saying the colony was full of people named Greene. Nevertheless, Rufus's deposition played an important role in the inquiry when he detailed the abuse of power and rough treatment British officers had often given colonial shippers.

Cousins Rufus and Nathanael survived the inquiry. After months of fruitless testimony and deliberations, the panel finally closed down and reported it could not identify any of the 60 men who participated in the attack. The witnesses who came forth had been discredited. The Rhode Island authorities had acted properly, the report told London, and Lt. Dudingston's intemperate and reprehensible zeal, "exceeding the bounds of his duty." Privately, some members of the frustrated commission accused Rhode Island, in the words of one judge, of being "a downright democracy," an intended reproach that citizens of the colony had been proud to embrace for over 100 years.[7]

It was not a bad outcome for the Greenes. Nathanael and his brothers were compensated for their loss of the *Fortune* and its cargo. Rufus got off free, even after one of the crew members virtually identified him in court as one of the *Gaspee's* raiders. And the family received much recognition and sympathy in the community.

Nathanael, in fact, received an extra unexpected benefit from his successful suit against Lt. Dudingston. When staying with his relative, William Greene, during the trial, he met a charming and vivacious 16-year old young lady who was a ward in William's home. Caty Littlefield eventually became Nathanael's wife, one who a few years later would delight George Washington's headquarters whenever she came to visit her husband, Major General Nathanael Greene.[8]

On the Road to War

Nathanael's opposition to the British deepened after the seizure of the *Fortune*. He did not personally join the attack on the *Gaspee*, although it is easy to believe that behind the scenes he was part of the operation. Cousin Rufus, captain of the family's *Fortune*, was the one *Gaspee* attacker identified by the British. Now, Nathanael was already determined to be a player in the now not too-far-off conflict with Great Britain.

It was a strange place for a Quaker whose faith espoused pacifism. Nathanael's Grandfather Jabez was the first of the Greene family to join the Quakers. Nathanael's father, Nathanael, Sr., was a strict Quaker leader who saw little value in books beyond the Bible and supported only enough book-learning to take care of the family bookkeeping. Precocious Nathanael, Jr. suffered greatly from this constraint. There were few things he enjoyed more than reading a book. He saved to buy them, and he devoured them one after another, actively self-educating himself. He worked the machines at his father's mill, reading as he went.

Nathanael became so successful in managing the mills that his devout father overlooked the "worldliness" of his books and turned over a new mill operation in Coventry to his supervision. He would travel all the way to Boston to pick up a new book and soon had a respectable library of his own. By then, he was in his late 20's and his relationship with Caty Littlefield, whom he met during the *Gaspee* trial, was serious. Caty moved into Spell Hall after they wed in July 1774.[9]

Nathanael Greene saw armed conflict with Britain on the horizon and was not the only one who did. There were many others, especially among his extended family, who believed that the colonies needed to prepare for a stormy confrontation. Redcoats already occupied Boston. The same thing could happen in Rhode Island. Quakers or not, Nathanael and some of his brothers and cousins started to consider organizing and training a militia group. The idea already had momentum, but what brought it to a head was a near riot in September 1774, when a mob of Crown supporters decided to burn East Greenwich, Rhode Island.

It was just after the Boston Tea Party. Dumping British tea into Boston harbor had provoked the British Parliament. Coming so soon after the *Gaspee* Affair – where none of the perpetrators was identified let alone prosecuted – it appeared to London that it was time for a serious crack-down. Over the next few months, Parliament drafted a series of acts that the colonists termed "The Intolerable Acts." One of them (The Boston Port Act) shut down the Port of Boston to all shipping and trade. The closure brought much of the city's economy to a standstill.

This was too close to home for many Rhode Islanders, some of the thirteen colonies' most active shippers and traders. A movement to support their Massachusetts neighbors swiftly spread across the colony. The town of East Greenwich was a pioneer in the support movement and was one of the first to begin taking contributions of money and provisions for the people of Boston. When one local justice, a Crown sympathizer and Tory, publicly opposed the collection as an attempt to subvert Parliament's authority, residents of East Greenwich threatened him and his family, and promptly hanged him in effigy.

Rhode Islanders were fiercely independent, but there were also sympathizers for Parliament in its rapidly growing frictions with the colonies. In response to the events in East Greenwich, some of these Crown supporters gathered into a mob intent to burn the town. To stop a violent clash with East Greenwich opponents, the colony's Deputy Governor sent the sheriff and militiamen to disband the throng. The sheriff managed the job peacefully by getting the Tory-leaning judge to switch his earlier stand by proclaiming, "I am a Friend to the Liberty of my Country, and disapproved of Measures which have been calculated to tax America without her Consent."

To Nathanael Greene, his brothers and cousins, and many others, the episode demonstrated too well the fragile peace with Parliament and its supporters. The events in East Greenwich pointed out the colony's prevalent instability, internally and in its relations with Great Britain. Alarmed, they concluded time had arrived to organize a well-trained militia unit that was ready to confront potential opponents and defend, if necessary, the interests of those who suffered from Parliament's oppression.

A week after the East Greenwich episode, a group of 49 men from East Greenwich, Warwick, and Coventry – these were Greene family stomping grounds – met at Sullivan's Tavern in East Greenwich to organize what they called a Military Independent Company. There were ten Greenes there: cousin Nathanael, his brother Christopher, cousin Griffin, cousin Joseph (Rufus's brother and my ancestor), and a number of Joseph's brothers and brothers-in-law, to name just a few. They drew up a charter that stated:

> "Deeply impressed with a sense of the shameful neglect of military exercise, and being willing and desirous of repair and revive that decayed and necessary spirit of regular discipline at this alarming crisis, we, the subscribers, do unanimously join to establish and constitute a military independent company…"

Forty-five of those present signed the charter, including all of the Greenes.

Rhode Islanders were not alone in seeing a need to organize effective militia units. When representatives from all the colonies met the next month at the First Continental Congress, colonial legislators decided to re-vitalize their militias. It was then that the Military Independent Company submitted a petition to the Rhode Island Assembly for recognition. Thirty-five men signed the petition. Ten of them were Greene brothers and cousins. The Assembly agreed and transformed the Military Independent Company into the Kentish Guards, named after Kent County where they were located. The Kentish Guards were authorized to expand to 100 members.[10]

The Kentish Guards quickly organized itself. First, they elected officers. Nathanael hoped to become one of the Guard's officers and lobbied to be chosen. He had no formal training, but his inexhaustible independent reading had consumed everything he could find on military topics. He was easily the most military-versed member on the unit's roster. At the urging of his cousin Griffin, Nathanael ran for lieutenant, but when the votes were tallied, he lost. Many were not sure he looked "presentable" enough. One of his legs was longer than the other, and he limped.

Instead, Nathanael's brother, Christopher, was elected 2nd Lieutenant; Richard Fry was 1st Lieutenant; and James Varnum was Captain. Varnum was a close friend to the Greenes. As their attorney, he had successfully represented Nathanael and his brothers in the suit against Lt. Dudingston of the *Gaspee* for reparations. When East Greenwich opened its collection for the people of Boston, Nathanael's contribution of nearly three pounds was topped only by Varnum's.

Nathanael was embarrassed for losing, especially when the reason many voted against him was his limp. He urged his friend Varnum to continue, but resigned from the Kent Guards, pledging to financially support them. Someone talked him into rejoining, however, and he re-considered. All that winter, three days a week, he faithfully attended Kentish Guard meetings where they worked to build themselves into an operational military company. Such meetings, in fact, were going on all over New England where companies of militia and minutemen were on fast courses to prepared for a conflict they increasingly believed was coming.

The Greene boys got their first real military training at the new Kentish Guards meetings. As a Quaker, Nathanael did not even own a musket. Many of the other Kentish Guards probably did not have guns either. However, they had proud uniforms made up of red coats with green facings, white pantaloons, and white vests. They started buying cartridge paper and were soon making their own bullets. Those without muskets, like Nathanael, looked for ways to get one.[11]

Nathanael solved this problem during a visit to Boson where he went to collect on a debt owed his father. The city was full of British soldiers who often could be seen drilling, marching, and maneuvering. While he watched the British troops' precision and discipline, it occurred to him that the Kentish Guards needed a professional trainer if they wanted to become an effective unit. He seized the opportunity when he met a British sergeant who had deserted his unit. Nathanael convinced him to return with him to **Rhode Island as the Kentish Guards' new drill instructor.** He also found the musket he was seeking, maybe from the same British deserter. When they left Boston, Nathanael concealed his new **musket under the straw of a farmer's cart and walked** inconspicuously down the road behind the cart. After reaching Rhode Island, the sergeant took the task of drilling the Kentish Guards with the same type of discipline British soldiers knew.

It was not long before his Quaker community focused on the **propriety of Nathanael's participation in a military organization.** The Quaker fathers had already censured Nathanael and Cousin Griffin for deeds they considered inconsistent with Quaker principles. Now that the two of them were visibly active in a military organization, they were irretrievably out of step with the faith. By April 1775, Nathanael had departed ways with the Quakers. It was his own decision, but he maintained an attachment to the Quakers.[12]

Over the winter of 1774-1775 the Guards trained and drilled. When in the spring of 1775, British troops attacked Lexington and Concord, the news spread like wildfire throughout all of New England. Like elsewhere, the Kentish Guards instantly mobilized to support the people of Massachusetts in their face-off against the British. Donning their bright uniforms and shouldering their muskets, the men were earnest and ready to employ the drills they had practiced for this moment. With no delay, the Kentish Guards began a march toward Boston, Nathanael slightly limping as a private in the rank and file. At dawn on the 20th of April, the day after the fighting in Concord and Lexington, they paraded through Providence on their way from Warwick.

The Kentish Guards unit did not make it very far, though. They had only reached the Massachusetts border when a messenger from Providence arrived with bad news. The loyalist governor of Rhode Island, Joseph Wanton, had ordered them back. Reluctantly, most of the proud Kentish Guards turned around, perturbed that the governor had denied them the mission for which they had been training so intensively.

Not too surprisingly, however, Nathanael, two friends, and one of his brothers disregarded the Governor's command to return. Finding horses to carry them, they launched off on their own toward Boston. They had not gone far before learning that the bloody confrontations of the day before was a rout that ended with the British making a forced march back to their barracks in Boston. No one was yet certain what was coming next. The Greene party turned around and returned to Warwick.

The fighting might have eased for a day or two after the Redcoats' bloody retreat, but this was only the beginning, not the end. When the Massachusetts Colonial Congress called for help from neighboring colonies, the Rhode Island General Assembly ignored Governor Wanton and joined up. Three days later, on April 22, when Nathanael, his brother, and friends were getting home, the Assembly agreed to raise 1,500 men to send to Massachusetts. Looking around for a capable general to lead their legion, they jumped over Gen. Simeon Potter, a French and Indian War veteran, as well as Kentish Guards commander James Varnum, to choose Nathanael Greene as the new commander.

It was a surprise move for a man who at that moment was only a private in the Kentish Guards. This time, however, choosing officers was not a popularity contest. The Assembly sought the colony's best military leader, and Nathanael had already established a reputation for being that. He was from a prominent, prospering family and had already shown himself to be one of the captains of Rhode Island's industrial and commercial community. Self-educated though he was, Nathanael Greene was intelligent and probably knew more about military organization and strategies than anyone in the colony. As much as anyone, he was responsible for polishing the Kentish Guards. He had drilled with them three times a week for months. As the head of the 100 men working at his forge – a large industrial workforce for his day – he knew how to lead. He was young, just 33, and full of energy.[13]

Newly minted Maj. General Nathanael Greene assumed command of Rhode Island's Army of Observation and began preparing for deployment for what in Boston had become a siege of the British army. When Gov. Wanton refused to support the mobilization and to ratify Nathanael Greene's and the other officers' commissions, the Assembly went forward without him and a few months later, removed him entirely from his position. The army was ready to march by the beginning of June.

The Kentish Guards assembled with the army and wore their attractive uniforms as they marched into Providence in close drill formation, fifes and drums playing. John Brown, the key figure in the *Gaspee* attack, invited the Guard to Sunday Services in the grand newly built Baptist Church, and they all came.[14]

Cousins at War

With Maj. General Nathanael Greene at the lead, Rhode Island's Army of Observation and its contingent of Greene cousins and brothers marched into Boston in June 1775. He was dignified, fit, perceptive, and brilliant, standing about five feet ten or eleven, not as large as George Washington, but still tall for his time. The Rhode Islanders were part of a concentration of New England militias that had encircled the downtown headquarters of the British army.

No matter how determined they were, a bunch of militiamen with families faring for themselves on farms and shops at home, were not a long-term match for professional soldiers of the world's greatest empire. The colonists knew this better than anyone, and following Lexington and Concord, the Continental Congress agreed to raise a Continental Army. A Virginian, George Washington, was nominated to head it.

When Washington arrived in Boston on July 3 to take charge of the Army on Cambridge Common, he immediately began to organize the disparate units into a single command. Harvard moved out of its building and sent its classes to Concord in order to give the new Continental Army rooms and space. Washington replaced officer commissions from the colonies with Continental Army commissions. Nathanael Greene had caught his eye, and

Washington made him a Brigadier General in the new Army. Nathanael's older brother, Jacob, took full control of the family business, and Nathanael's wife, Caty, stayed behind in Spell Hall. Thus, began Nathanael Greene's illustrious adventures in the American Revolution.[15]

The siege of Boston continued for several months until the British army succumbed to the colonials' pressure and retreated to their ships for an attack on New York City. The Kentish Guards as a unit returned to Rhode Island where they were a militia on call in various military capacities to support Continental Army operations in Rhode Island. Joseph Greene and some of his brothers and brothers-in-law served in the Kentish Guards for several years.

Many of the Kentish Guard men, however, transferred into the Continental Army. It has been said, that the unit furnished more officers of importance than any other pre-war militia organization. Its commander, James Varnum, advocated for allowing African Americans to serve their country as part of the mobilization. He was successful in this, and as a result, Rhode Island formed an all-Black unit, the 1st Rhode Island Regiment, with eight companies under his command. The 1st Rhode Island with its racially mixed men was made up primarily of slaves, freed and not, who joined to become free. The 1st Rhode Island, known as the "Black Regiment," is considered the country's first African American unit.

After Varnum's promotion to Brigadier General, it came under the command of Col. Christopher Greene, Nathanael Greene's friend and 3rd cousin. Many months later, on October 22, 1777, 1,200 Hessians hit the 400 men of Greene's Black Regiment at Fort Mercer only to be decimated. The Hessians lost 400 men; the Rhode Islanders took only 37 casualties. Later, in 1781, Christopher and some his Black bodyguards were surrounded and killed by British loyalists. His body was brutally hacked to pieces and left in the woods, some say, because he commanded a Black American unit.[16]

Joseph Greene's younger brother Rufus, captain of the *Fortune*, was not part of the Kentish Guards. Instead, Rufus joined other brothers and cousins, including some of Nathanael Greene's brothers, to fight the war at sea. Attacking, looting and capturing

British ships, Rufus and cousins Cable Godfrey and Capt. Samuel Godfrey were all privateers. Jacob Greene's company, including General Nathanael, owned privateer vessels as did Cousin Griffin.

Although the privateers were pirates in the eyes of the British, in Rhode Island, they were legalized and legitimately preyed off British military and cargo shipping. Privateering gave a big advantage to the Colonies by replacing much of the need for a navy. Private owners carried a good share of the expense and risk for defending the coast, but they also often profited well from it. When a privateer captured a British vessel, the captain and his crew were allowed to keep up to half of the cargo for themselves. The rest of the booty went to the United Colonies.

For Great Britain, the war was a far-off conflict. Its troops, fighting in a foreign land, required large amounts of food, ammunition, and other supplies that had to be shipped long distances daily. At one point or another, all this had to move through American waters where the privateers sat quietly waiting for British supply ships. It was one of the British war effort's greatest vulnerabilities, and Yankee ships thoroughly exploited it.

Rufus and his cousins were part of the many Rhode Island privateers who effectively sailed up and down America's eastern seaboard and well into the British West Indies, disrupting the English supply lines as they went. They exacted a high price from the Crown. It has been estimated that 66 % of British West Indian trade was lost to Yankee privateers in 1776. The huge losses drove up insurance premiums to 50% for vessels sailing alone without warship escorts. By 1778, Rufus and his fellow American privateers had captured or destroyed 733 ships – a heavy blow to British supremacy of the seas in its American campaign.[17]

The Cradle in My 9th Great-Grandfather's House

One day in Rhode Island, we spent a morning in Warwick visiting Spell Hall, the home of Revolutionary War General Nathanael Greene. The old house still stood proudly where Nathanael built it in 1770. He had just taken over the Coventry foundry that was part of his father's complex of mills on Potowomut Peninsula. The Potowomut point extended into Narragansett Bay, and the sea connected the mills and their heavy products, anchors and the like, to neighboring destinations. Being close to the bay also allowed Nathanael and his brothers opportunities to join in the local practice of skirting British customs duties for cargoes, such as contraband rum.

Spell Hall was decked out with period furniture, much of it not original to the house, but still dating to the time when he lived there. It was a quiet weekday, and there were no other visitors. That was lucky for us, because we had the two guides on duty to ourselves. The men were excited about their volunteer jobs with the General Nathanael Greene Homestead Association. Both were retired military officers, one a Navy Corpsman and the other was on his second career as a lawyer after his first in the Army Special Forces.

In other words, our guides were not the typical ones found at historical sites, but they were perfect for a visit to the home of one of America's most famous generals. As they laid out Spell Hall's history, traditions, and gossip, the events and stories they recounted were often more macho than normal, sometimes flamboyant and a couple times even a little bawdy. They handsomely brought the old house to life. As we went room-by-room through the large well preserved two-story-and-attic home, we found ourselves laughing and enjoying the tour while learning more about this incredible man and his wife. Like all our stories, the tales were satiating and authentic, life itself.

Our ears perked up when one of our guides told us still another ghost story. The house has always been said to be haunted, he divulged. I asked him whether he believed that. He looked up with a strange smile. "I was always dubious about it," he answered matter-of-factly. However, on a few occasions when alone in the house, he admitted, he had heard what seemed to be the latch on an upper bedroom door opening and closing. He did not think much of it, until one afternoon he decided to go up to investigate. Indeed, what had been a closed door, was now open. In addition to that, an antique baby carriage that had been on the far wall had rolled to

182

the other side of the room. What was strange, he explained, was that the floor was not level, and the carriage had rolled up hill before reaching the wall opposite from where it normally stood. "You can make what you want of that story," he laughed in an off-the-record voice. I did not know what to make of it, but the story was one I was sure to remember.

As we were finishing up our tour of Spell Hall, I mentioned to our retired officer guide that I had read somewhere that the house where Nathanael Greene was born still exists.

"It does, not too far from here," he answered.

"Do we need to make reservations to visit?" I asked.

"No, I don't think so. It's privately owned," he continued. "You might just stop by and see if anyone's at home," he added while writing down the address. "Tom can tell you about it if he's there."

"The house was built by General Greene's Great-Grandfather, James Greene," he remarked as he gave us the slip of paper.

The words flashed in my mind. Here we were, zipping back in time from great-grandfather to great-grandfather to great-grandfather. James Greene, who had come as a boy to Massachusetts Bay colony with his parents, Dr. John and Joane Greene, was my ancestor, too, a 9th great-grandfather During our visit to Salisbury, England, the year before, we had seen the font where he was baptized in the 1620's. His home was one of those in Warwick burnt to the ground during the King Philip's War. James and his family had returned in the 1680's to build a new one. I did not know James's house was still standing.

When we got to the car, we plugged the address into our GPS navigator and drove through the wooded townscape and countryside until eventually the "your destination" alert sounded. We turned off the road onto a secluded tree-lined lane that twisted up to a large white two-story home. I would never have guessed that the residence comfortably resting at the end of the long driveway was over 330 years old. Three centuries, perhaps not so long in Europe, was a long time in America.

Seija, and I sat admiring the residence for a few moments, and then opened the doors and stepped out. We were still transfixed with the magnificent old home, one that sheltered so many generations and memories, when a voice hollered, "Hello!" from somewhere through the trees. I looked but could not see anyone.

The cheery "Hello!" came again, and this time our eyes found a garden where an elderly man was energetically hoeing. He put down the tool and walked spritely over to us. Returning his friendly greeting, we introduced ourselves and told we were hoping to have a look at the home James Greene once built. I added that I was a descendant of James Greene.

"Well that's it," he said pointing at the structure. "I'm Tom, and I have been living in that house for the past 80 years," he proclaimed proudly. "Why don't you come and have a look inside."

Tom was slim and in good form for his 85-years. My wife and I appreciated the kind welcome and said we would love to come in. As we walked through the back door and into the kitchen, he apologized, "I'm sorry everything's not exactly in order. I am here by myself, and it's a big house. Be prepared that a bachelor is living here." The moment seized us too much to care what order it was in.

We entered through the kitchen into the living room where Tom asked us to sit down. Relaxing, comfortably chatting, we learned about the house. Our armchairs sloped back a little, like rocking chairs, but their legs were firmly on the floor. They were original to the house, Tom told, as was the large beautiful hearth nearby.

In another room sat a grand and beautifully carved wooden chest that Dr. John Greene's family brought from England nearly four centuries before. Above it hung a ceremonial sword that belonged to General Nathanael Greene during his southern campaign in the Revolutionary War. On the wall was Charles Willson Peale's portrait of General Greene, the one found in history books. "This one's a copy," Tom said. "I own the original that is displayed in the Rhode Island Historical Society." The air was filled with generations of Greenes.

With a storyteller's ease, Tom shared family stories with us. Dr. John Greene had purchased the land from the Narragansetts, he said, and members of his family had lived on it ever since. The original site was called Potowomut, Tom added, "...and that means 'home of the fires,' in the Narragansetts' language. Perhaps the tribe had used the point to build fires to communicate across the bay or signal directions." On the farm, called "Forge Farm," were the mills that James and his family built and operated from the late 1600s. There were once nine industrial buildings in the yard. The house had been re-modeled in the 1860's. It still included the 180-acres that James cultivated.

After we chatted a while, we rose for a tour of the house. In one of the bedrooms upstairs, we found the cradle where Nathanael Greene slept as a baby. By that time, the house belonged to Nathanael, Sr., James's grandson. Young Nathanael grew up in this house. When he was 27, he built the Spell House where we had visited earlier in the day.

In other rooms were two baby grand pianos and a harpsicord. Tom, who had studied music and philosophy at Yale when young, was a professional music teacher. After we asked if he still played, he kindly agreed to serenade us. "But I don't know how well it will go. Arthritis in these fingers," he complained. He sat at one of the old pianos to play from memory some beautiful strains that Handel composed in the Old World when Forge Farm was still young, and Nathanael Greene was still sleeping in that cradle. Having played the piano myself for most of my life, it was clear to me that Tom was a virtuoso. The years had taken none of that away from him.

We took some photos of Tom standing in front of his resplendent home. He was a worthy descendant of the proud Greene family. We were sad to leave. He had been a gracious host for two complete strangers, even if we were very distant cousins. Most of all, however, in one moment, in one setting, we had connected back through all those generations that came and went, to the time some of my earliest American grandparents built a house on a new continent.

A little over a year later, we arranged to return for a follow-up visit. This time we had one of our daughters, Kaarina, her husband Derek, and their three young children with us. When we arrived, Tom's niece Kate, her husband Rob, and their two daughters were there. It was almost like a family gathering, although I could not even begin to measure how distant cousins we were. Our 12-year old grandson, Leo, sat down and played from Grieg's "Holberg Suite" on the harpsicord.

While Seija and I chatted with Tom, Kaarina and Derek enjoyed visiting with Kate and Rob. And the children, not totally dazzled by all this history, found it much more exciting to run and chase their distant cousins in the yard, to see the old farm, and to explore the woods and fields of this place from our family's past. We easily imagined Nathanael with his brothers and cousins running through the same rooms, outside gardens, and fields.

Pension Records are Valuable

I first learned about the Kentish Guards when searching for Joseph Greene on Ancestry.com. I found a few things also in a professional genealogical survey of the Greene line done decades ago, perhaps commissioned by one of Mother's many correspondents. In a short story, one of the few I found about him, it said that he was a member of the "Kentish Guards."

I googled "Kentish Guards" to see what I could learn. Through various google entries and the Guards' own web site, I found that the group still exists with a proud and honored history. They meet regularly in East Greenwich, Rhode Island. No longer a strictly military organization, the Kentish Guards provide pageantry and re-enactment color to their historic community.

When I wrote the current Kentish Guards commander that I was a descendant of the Greene family, he replied that he was well aware that there were many Greenes in the Guards' history. He kindly sent copies of some of their newsletters that laid out how the unit came into being. As too often happens, a fire somewhere along the line had burned many of their records. As I went down the early rosters of the early Guards, I was surprised to see one Greene after another in its columns. I pulled up Greene family group sheets on FamilySearch and found that a number of its members, possessing surnames other than "Greene," were actually married to Greene daughters. The early Kentish Guards was full of brothers, cousins, and brothers-in-laws to my ancestor Joseph.

Joseph's participation in the Guards and the Revolution, itself, was at first confusing. For some reason, he seemed to have dropped out of the Guards shortly after it was first organized. He signed the original charter declaration in September 1774, but his name did not appear on the petition to the Rhode Island Assembly the next month. Since he was later remembered as a member of the Kentish Guards, I thought there must be more.

*I found the explanation by looking up Revolutionary War pension records on Fold3, an excellent online site specialized in military records. Among the records I found was the file containing correspondence about his war pension. **Joseph Greene's widow, Patience, applied in 1838 for a pension for his service during the Revolutionary War.***

*As I repeat in later chapters, military records tell a lot of stories, sometimes of the battles our grandfathers fought, and sometimes of the trials their families went through while the men were away. An **image of Patience's application** told how he had been active in the Kentish Guards from the end of 1776. This was two years after the Guards were formed. **Joseph's brother, Stephen, corroborated Patience's petition by telling in a separate statement** about his service in the Guards with Joseph. Joseph was in the unit when it was first formed but must have dropped out for a time before again getting involved after the war was in full swing. According to Patience, during the war Joseph was in his unit about three years.*

*Patience was eventually awarded $ 858.76 in pension arrears, not a small sum, to help her and her family in her old age. It was **based on 22 months and 7 days of Joseph's service**. I wrote earlier that we find so little from and about our grandmothers. It was a home run to me to hear just a little in Patience's voice about the years she struggled while her husband was in his unit fighting a revolution.[18]*

Bookends and the Volumes in Between
One day during the weeks I was compiling the adventures of cousins and brothers living on the eve of the Revolution, my wife and I were driving north from Florida toward Virginia. After

187

stopping at an I-95 rest stop in South Carolina, I checked my phone for messages. One waiting voice message told that my younger brother Larry had just passed away from a cancer he had learned about only two weeks before.

Thoughts of Larry dominated the remainder of our journey. I was eight years older than he was. That difference in age allowed me to remember the bookends of his life and some of the stories in between. I tended him as a baby, and I spoke to him by phone the morning he passed away. The years in between were full of many happy moments together.

These were just the stories I knew. Hundreds of others made up the pages of his book. After he was gone, the stories, for the most part, remained only as memories among those who knew him. His deeds were a legacy bestowed to his next generation and, to some lesser extent, to following generations of future years. But just like for all of us, the legacy quickly fades as the years pass. One of Larry's sons later wrote me and others of my siblings asking if we could relate some of our memories to help him learn more about his father's life.

So often with family histories we discover only the bookends, the birth and death dates and places, but to us, living years later, the book is often under-populated and unread, because we never discover much about the pages in between. All those hundreds and thousands of ancestors who came before us had narratives that set the stage for our own. But we know little about them. Perhaps that is why researching our family stories to reveal the lives of the people who went before us is for many such a rich and revitalizing experience. Their struggles, wins, and losses were at their core the same types of things we experience.

As we pass through the years, our stories – our books – make up the essence of our being. Blowing the dust off family narratives, often discovering them for the first time, re-kindles the ardent lights and passions of our people. Sometimes, as in the case of these Greenes, and the Barretts of the next chapter, their experiences took place along a grand panorama of creation and re-definition, such as the War of Independence. More often, however, our grandparents' lives were simply spent trying to survive and improve circumstances for their families. Or sometimes, their stories merely reveal how they discovered struggle one day, and joy, satisfaction, and fulfillment on another.

Personalities Cast their Own Hues

One afternoon, during our search for family stories, my wife and I stopped at a tea house in Malvern, England. Several decades earlier, Seija and her friend were young Finnish pantry girls, who frequented the same tea house during days off from the private boys' school where they worked. We sat there, just like they sat years ago, looking through the window and enjoying the scones. When Seija told the waitress that she used to eat the same scones at the same shop, in front of the same window 50 years before, the woman muttered, "Some things never change." and moved on. She obviously did not see the shaking importance of such a thing. Yet a small event like this sweetened my wife's memories of bigger adventures during an earlier formative episode in her life.

As we peer darkly through the eons of time at our past families' lives, little things are often no less meaningful than large ones. Big or small, however, they all contribute to our own stories. There was Matilda, Queen of England, and there was Matilda Howard Johnson, whose stories on the Idaho frontier are in one of the last chapters of this book. They both, at one level or another, are part of me.

Our own experiences and personalities cast their own prismatic hues on these stories from the past. I fondly remember a family reunion years ago when my father and his brothers each recounted their own version of the same episode they once experienced together. I recall how we all laughed with them, not just about the humorous event they described, but about how their own personalities colored the way they remembered it. That is why sisters, brothers, or extended family may see our common stories from the past differently than we do. In the end, our stories and how we perceive greatly reflect on us. Discovering them, preserving them, and telling them bring our humanity into perspective.

189

Chapter 5

Day of the Revolution
One Family on April 19, 1775

*From the plains of Concord will henceforth
be dated a change in human affairs, an
alteration in the balance of human power...*
Lemuel Shattuck
Concord (1835)

*I have often wondered how much my great-great-grandfather
Charlie Leonardson knew of his minuteman great-great-
grandfather, Jonas Barrett.[19] I had never heard a word of the
Barrett families of Ashby and Concord until I began tracing
Charlie's New England roots. When piecing together the extended
Barrett family's adventures on the first day the American
Revolution, however, I found more of their stories than I ever
expected.*

"O what an ever glorious morning is this!"[20]

It was a splendid spring morning, one that atoned for the
punishing New England winter. Shades of spring greens had swept
up from the south. The maples, oaks, and birches covering the
sturdy Appalachian Hills' thick woods were in full leaf. The
country's flowering vegetation was "uncommonly forward," people
remembered long after. Fruit trees were in early blossom. Winter
wheat was already several inches high. The blue sky soaked in the
new day's sun as if Providence intended to lay the earthshaking
events already underway against the most serene of landscapes.
Sounds at daybreak told the story of the busy countryside. The
roosters crowed, a bird chorus swelled from the trees, and cows
mooed their complaints of the early day chores.

Jonas Barrett and his wife Mary were already up and taking
control of the farm. Smoke curled into the sky from the chimney
atop their large two-story wooden Massachusetts home in Ashby.

190

The smell of burning stove kindling welcomed the day with its country aroma. Mary's pregnancy was still early enough that it did not slow her from having breakfast and other household jobs underway. Their four small daughters who had been born in rapid succession – 6 ½ -year old Mary Fletcher, nearly 5-year old Lucy, 4-year old Rebecca, and 2-year old Elizabeth – were in various stages of ending their night's rest. Mary and Jonas's baby, Jonas Jr., had finally brought a boy into the family.[21]

Managing such a large family required tremendous effort in New England of the 1770s. For the Barretts, it came on top of building and keeping a big house in a new community on the New Hampshire border. Work on the farm never ended. Mary's day began early and finished late as she laundered, wove, spun, knitted, quilted, boiled, baked, and fried to keep her family clothed and fed. In addition, Jonas and Mary's home was also an inn, adding even more to the work of keeping the family well cared for.[22]

Jonas had played an active role in the town of Ashby from the time it had been incorporated, seven years earlier. He and Mary hosted Ashby's first town meeting in their home. After that, he served as a selectman, assessor, treasurer, town clerk, constable, and on the committee to build a meetinghouse. But the couple was still young – Mary 35 and Jonas 37 – and full of energy. Like most New Englanders, they were industrious people from hard working families. in neighboring towns. The Barretts were thought of as the first family in Concord, and Mary's family, the Fletcher's, were among the founders of Concord's neighboring town of Westford.

As he went about his busy morning chores, Jonas knew the peaceful start of this new day could be deceiving. For weeks, rumors had circulated throughout the Massachusetts countryside that a force of British Regulars was preparing to march into the county. Jonas was a minuteman and was expected to have his musket nearby, wherever he went.

Like most of those living in Middlesex County, Jonas and his neighbors closely followed Boston's resistance to Parliament's oppressive measures against the Massachusetts colony. Ashby vocally and actively supported Boston. A few months earlier, the town had quickly responded to the First Provincial Congress's call on colonial towns to form minuteman companies from their militia units. Ashby ordered stores and ammunition to support possible military hostilities. When the town's minuteman company met, the men elected Jonas as second in command with the rank of First Lieutenant under Captain Samuel Stone. Feeling the peril of the times and the weight of his command, Jonas prepared with his minutemen brothers to be moment-ready for the alarm when it came.

What Jonas did not know was that the alarm they had been expecting was already on the road from Boston. While Mary, the children, and he still slept the previous night it had begun. About 10:00, Dr. Joseph Warren, a leader among Boston's patriots, saw British soldiers mobilizing on the Boston Common. Longboats were waiting nearby to convey them across the Charles River to Charlestown.

Warren arranged to have two lanterns in the upper window of Boston's old North Church beam for just a moment across the river. The signal alerted Paul Revere for his famous ride to forewarn Lexington and Concord, the targets of the British expeditionary force. As a back-up, Warren ordered a Boston tanner named William Dawes to ride with the same warning along another route from the Boston Neck.

The two horsemen rode quickly and spread the word to everyone along their way. Revere reached Lexington at about 1:00 a.m. that night. He dismounted, climbed up the steps to the front door of Rev. Jonas Clarke's home, and pounded. Sons of Liberty leaders John Hancock and Sam Adams were overnighting inside. When Rev. Clarke stuck his head from the upper window to demand what was going on, Revere called back that he needed to talk to Hancock. Hancock's head quickly poked from another window. "Come in, Revere; we are not afraid of you," he quipped.

Paul Revere hastily reported the British raid was underway. He added that everyone feared one of the force's objectives was to arrest Hancock and Adams. They needed to flee before the column reached Lexington, Revere warned. Just then, William Dawes arrived from his separate ride to join them. They talked only a short while longer. Then Dawes and Revere galloped to warn Concord.[23]

Just outside of Lexington, the two of them ran into Dr. Samuel Prescott, a young man who was on his way home to Concord from an evening spent courting his girlfriend. They told Dr. Prescott their mission, and the three of them rushed off together. They had not traveled far before stumbling into a British scouting party lying in ambush for just such riders spreading the alarm.

The patrol quickly surrounded the party, and their Captain ordered Revere, Dawes, and Prescott to follow him. Although the Redcoats had cut the reins of his bridle, Prescott carefully chose a good moment to spring his horse over a stone wall. He soon lost his pursuers on the circuitous dark roads he knew well. The doctor reached Concord before 2:00 a.m. After spreading the alarm, he enlisted his younger brother Abel to carry the alarm to the nearby towns of Sudbury and Framingham and then continued himself to Acton and Stow. Riders, musket shots, and cannon fire soon spread the call to arms in every Middlesex town and beyond.

Word of the British march toward Concord eventually reached Ashby too. When it did, it came directly to Jonas. It was about 9:00 in the morning. Jonas grabbed his musket and fired the agreed signal. It was the moment they had trained and waited for. Men dropped what they were doing and hurried from all directions to gather in front of the Barrett house, their equipment and ammunition ready. Capt. Samuel Stone was soon on the spot and shortly the company's 46 men were assembled. Benjamin, Jonas's brother, was among them. Wives and mothers swarmed about their men making certain they were provisioned as best as possible for the long march and whatever came after that. None of them knew how this day would change their lives or the world they lived in.

Jonas's daughters, little Mary and her sisters, stood in the front yard watching with wide eyes as the men formed into ranks. Their mother, Mary, probably had tears. She knew well what it meant when Jonas and the other men strode off toward the fight. Not many years before, her father Timothy and brother Joshua marched with the men of her hometown to join the British in one of their wars against the French. Serving valiantly, Timothy earned a field commission as a First Lieutenant before returning home a few years later to his cooper (barrel-making) business, store, and farm. Captain Joshua Fletcher never came back. He died in 1760 at Fort Crown Point on Lake Champlain where the men had just built one the largest British fortifications in the North American colonies. Mary knew war. She understood the sorrow that accompanied it.

Capt. Stone shouted the command. The men shouldered their muskets. With well-trained discipline the men and boys all marched off swiftly in the direction of Concord. As the column paraded proudly down the road and out of sight, Mary must have grieved what lay ahead.

First Lieutenant Jonas Barrett and the 45 others of his minuteman company had a long 30 miles ahead of them (see Map D). They also understood perfectly well the imperative of time. Neither Jonas nor the others had heard details of the British march to Concord, but they knew two things: the distance the British had to cover between Boston and Concord was much shorter than what his minutemen had to march, and the British Regular army was the best in the world. The sooner the Ashby men could get to Concord, the better.

As they hurried down the winding dirt roads, muskets slung over their shoulders, they made a motley appearance in their everyday farmer's clothes. They were not a force to take for granted, however. This was something the British army did not know but would learn by day's end. The men of these minutemen companies were a well-trained lethal force.

As with Jonas's men, each Massachusetts town's minuteman company was selected from the militia the towns had maintained since the beginning of the colony. The militias had always been ready for the frequent frontier Indian conflicts. In recent years, the wars fought between the British and French in their seemingly eternal conflicts over power and territory, had forced the towns to keep militia forces of townsmen and farmers in military readiness.

The recent Provincial Congress's call for minutemen had resulted in the creation of new minuteman companies on the town

194

level and the formation of regiments composed of the various companies. The minutemen were made up of a set percentage of each town's militia. They were specially trained and equipped, and just as Jonas and his company had done, required to assemble very rapidly under decentralized tactical control.

Minutemen companies all over Massachusetts had drilled without stop all winter and spring, many receiving as much individual training over those months as did the British Regulars in Boston. A good proportion of them, in fact, were experienced fighters who had fought under the British in the recent French and Indian Wars. They carried their guns with them at all times, even to church. The minutemen were often younger than men of the militias and expected to be in the front, where the dangers were greatest. The men marching with Jonas toward Concord were not simply loosely organized, embattled farmers joining a spontaneous uprising. They were a great deal more than that.[24]

The Road to Concord

Minutemen and militiamen units like Jonas's moved as quickly as they could toward Concord. Roads throughout Massachusetts teamed with companies rushing to the assistance of their Concord and Lexington cousins – "cousins" quite literally in many cases, and in Jonas's, as well. Jonas and his older brother Benjamin keeping step next to him were actually born in Concord, and a group of their cousins was already there, muskets in hand. By the time the Ashby men got on their way, companies from Carlisle, Chelmsford, Westford, Littleton, and Acton were already marching or had augmented Concord's own men. To the north and west, Jonah's step-cousin, Col. William Prescott, had ten companies of militia and seven of minutemen (including Ashby's) underway. By day's end, thousands of Massachusetts men, from forty-seven regiments, mobilized to meet the British attack.

The column of 46 moved with military precision as they were trained, with Capt. Stone and First Lt. Barrett at the lead. The hilly roads dipped up and down and wove between fields and dense woodlands. The 30 miles to Concord was a serious march.

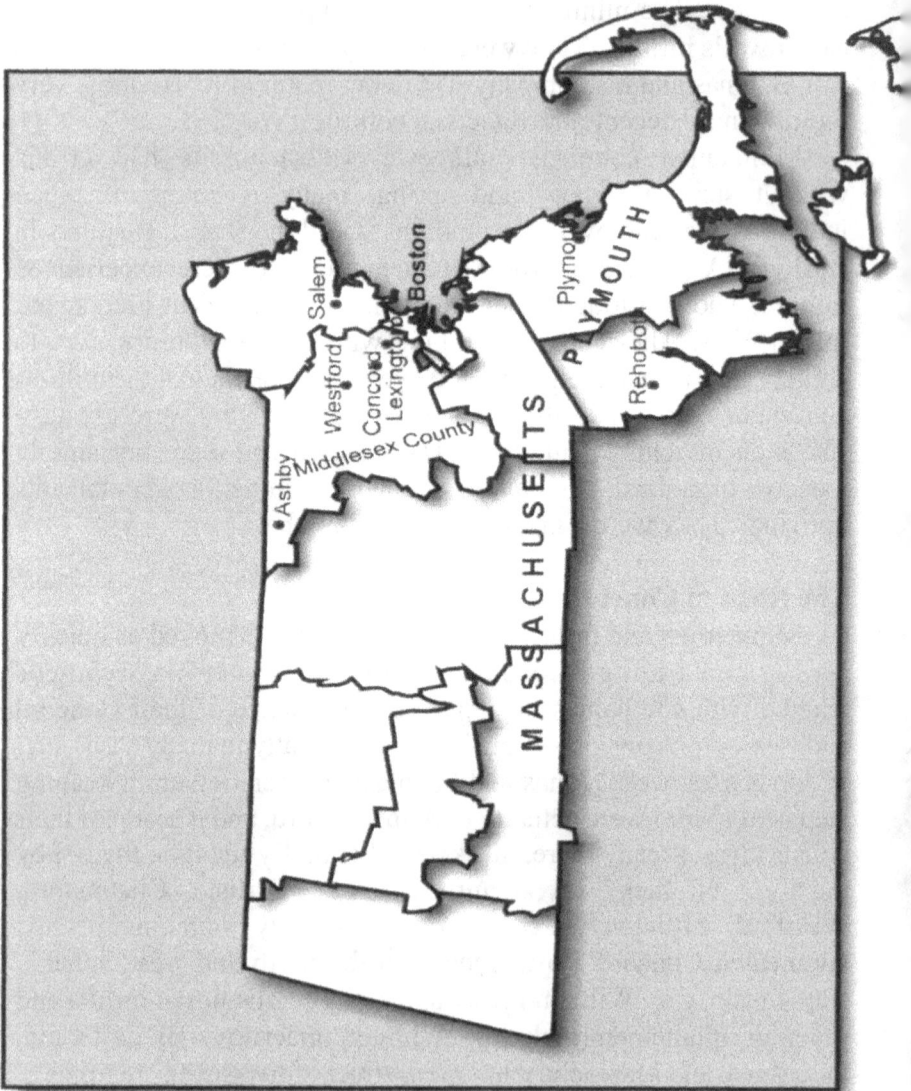

Map D – Colonial Massachusetts and Plymouth

Stonewall Jackson's "foot cavalry," ninety years later, sometimes marched 30 miles in a day, and they were famed for it. Sometimes stone fences lined the way. Often, the woods with their welcoming shade shut off the pouring sun for a few minutes. Fortunately, it was springtime, and temperatures were still moderate. The boots they wore were not yet designed to discriminate between the left and right feet. Short rests always refreshed the whole body, but especially the parts of it that met the road with each step.

While Jonas continued, there was plenty of time to think about the brewing war England and its colonies now seemed poised to fight. Behind the most recent argument was Parliament's efforts to raise revenue from its colonies without giving them a voice in Parliament. The taxation of imported tea was a case in point. The 1773 Tea Act levied a 3-pence per pound duty on tea. People in Boston reacted by turning away ships carrying the tea. Later that year, in December, a "party" of disguised Bostonians boarded one of those ships and threw its tea cargo over the side. Jonas agreed with Boston's actions. The town of Ashby, where he sat as a Selectman, sent Boston a message of support. What the Bostonians did, they declared, was "agreeable to reason and the natural rights of this free people, and the same appears to have been necessary at that time."[25]

After the Tea Party, everything cascaded downhill. Parliament's angry members responded with the "Intolerable Acts,"[26] a series of measures that closed the Port of Boston, limited the right of self-government, and permitted the quartering of British troops in private homes. The Act transformed what had been primarily a conflict between Boston and London into a broader quarrel. With a few exceptions, all the towns, including Ashby, were now forbidden to call town meetings. The British realized the town meetings had become caucuses where the people rallied politically.

The towns responded by *adjourning* rather than *closing* their meetings, meaning that they didn't have to *call* a new meeting since the previous one was still in session. They went ahead holding their meetings as before. The Bostonians also set up a network called "Committees of Correspondence" through which each town kept open communications with the others. The Committees also launched a boycott of British products.

When General Thomas Gage, the new royal governor of Massachusetts, suppressed the colony's assembly, or "General Court," the towns organized their own provincial congress. The "First Provincial Congress" had met in Concord only a few months before, in October of 1774. Samuel Stone, Captain of the Ashby minutemen, was their town's delegate to the Congress. The Provincial Congress, met again in February and March 1775, founded a Committee of Safety, and called for further re-organization of militias and minutemen companies and regiments with the aim of creating an army. It also set up the procurement of arms, ammunition, and other provisions for a force of 15,000 men, most of it to be stored in Concord. When the King declared the colony in rebellion, he was essentially right about that.

General Gage, who wore the hats of both Governor of Massachusetts and Commander of British Forces in North America, was under pressure to do something about the "rebellion." When London told him to arrest and imprison the men leading the Provincial Congress, Gage was hesitant. He knew mass arrests could easily push the colony into armed conflict, something he was still trying to avoid.

Instead, General Gage set up a spy network that soon brought disconcerting news: the number of colonial militiamen on call to resist the British far exceeded his earlier estimates. He then sent out scouting parties and organized mini raids against the rebels' arms caches, but with no real results. Gage's spies, including one in Concord whose identity is still unknown, informed him that Concord was the designated storage site for the Colonials' arms and ammunition stores, including several cannons.

Gage finally decided to launch a preemptive strike that would capture and destroy the caches in Concord. In addition to seizing the colonials' weapons, he hoped such a military excursion would also send a message that his next steps could involve blood and conflict. His Concord spy told him where the caches were hidden, and his staff began secret preparations for the military operation.

Their planned incursion, however, was not "secret" to anyone. Jonas Barrett, as far away as Ashby, expected it, and so did everyone else who followed the current crisis in Massachusetts. The rebels' own spies broadcast Gage's every action throughout the colony, and especially to everyone in Concord. That was how things had reached this point. Jonas and his Ashby neighbors could not have been more in support of this day of resistance.

The march wore on, and there was no way of knowing what was happening or had already happened in Concord. In a way, Concord was Jonas's hometown. His family had lived and toiled in Concord for five generations. His great-great-grandfather and grandmother, Humphrey and Mary Barrett, came from England to Concord in 1639 and were one of its founding families. They settled on 300 or more acres, one of the larger holdings in the area. Jonas's Great-Grandfather Humphrey, Jr. (or, Ensign Humphrey Barrett, as he was called) was a deacon of the church, a deputy and representative to the Massachusetts General Court, and commander of the community's militia company.

The Puritans, a century before, had called the region with its teaming populations of wolves and wildcats the "howling wilderness." The forests were thick, the clearing work was back breaking, and by the time Jonas's father Benjamin Barrett, Jr. was born in 1705, about a thousand people lived in hamlets scattered over a space of about 60 square miles. Some of the land was still untouched by plows.

Jonas's Grandfather Benjamin, Sr., married Lydia Minott from another old Concord family. Lydia's father James, my 9th great-grandfather, had graduated from Harvard College in 1675 and was a bit of a Renaissance man, at least on the New England frontier where he lived. James's epitaph extolled his virtues as "an Excelling Grammarian, Enriched with the Gift of Prayer and Preaching, a Commanding Officer, a Physician of Great Value, a Great Lover of Peace as well as of Justice." James Minott was a physician, a pastor, a captain, a justice of the peace, a representative to the

Massachusetts General Court, and "eminently a useful man," as a local historian later described him.[27]

I was intrigued to learn about James Minott. Coming from the Idaho countryside, I thought that I might probably be the only Harvard graduate from my family. That was not the case. Fully 300 years before I carried my books across Harvard Yard, one of my ancestors had beat me to it. I think about that now, when stepping into places where I think we are the first. I always wonder, how many have gone there before us?

Grandfather Benjamin Barrett, Sr., and Lydia had made their family business into a thriving enterprise. In 1705 he constructed a large house and a mill. They had five sons to bring up. The idea of raising children also meant taking care of them after Benjamin and Lydia were gone. It was a common problem in Concord and many others of the older communities. The town's land was soon owned and allocated, and a living had to be found for children and grandchildren who could not keep inheriting smaller and smaller parcels with each successive generation. Jonas's father, Benjamin, Jr., was the eldest and took £30 of his inheritance to set up a blacksmith operation and buy a house. When Benjamin, Sr., died young, at only 47, Jonas's Uncle Thomas inherited the mill and his Uncle James, who had not yet turned 18, inherited the farm and farmhouse where he lived with his mother and siblings (see App. 2, Chart 2: "Charlie Leonardson to Benjamin Barrett, Sr").[28]

Jonas did not remember any of this, and he wondered what his life would have been like if his own father, Benjamin, Jr., had not died when Jonas was only a toddler. After his death, Rebekah, his mother, could not realistically expect the rest of the Barrett family to support her and her four children. She did what most widowed women – and men – did in those times. She remarried quickly. Her new husband was Jonas Prescott. Jonas was older and had lost two previous wives. Rebekah was his third.

Jonas Prescott was from nearby Westford, and she with her four children moved there to live with him. For Rebekah, the marriage ensured her family a comfortable life. Her new husband was a leader in the community. His family had owned mills in Westford

200

for three generations. The Prescott's were also prominent in nearby towns, including Concord. Jonas Prescott's cousin William was a regimental commander of Massachusetts militia and in only a few months would become the heroic commander of the rebel forces on Bunker Hill. Jonas Barrett grew up in the Prescott house with stepbrothers and sisters. He spent his childhood supporting the family business in the mills built on a river with a large tranquil lake behind. His stepfather Jonas was the only father he knew.

With so many children in the family, stepson Jonas Barrett would not inherit the Prescott family enterprises. As he reached into his early twenties, Jonas looked around for other possibilities and decided to establish the farm in Ashby, about 40 miles northwest of Westford on the New Hampshire border. His extended Barrett family from Concord had owned land interests in this area for a few decades, but the surroundings were still relatively untamed. Only 12 years earlier, Indians had ravished the region killing and kidnapping some of the early settlers. Jonas bought land in Ashby in 1760, and his brother Benjamin had joined him there. Perhaps funding from his stepfather Prescott's family, and from the Barrett side, too, got them started.

About the same time Jonas was building his new house, a Concord cousin, Charles Barrett, settled just six miles northwest of him in New Ipswich, New Hampshire. It was Charles's father, Thomas, who inherited the Barrett family mills in Concord. Charles had not only learned milling while growing up, but also possessed the Barrett family's talents as businessmen and entrepreneurs. Just up the road from Jonas' new home, Charles was soon thriving. He started a farm and built a saw and grist mill. By 1774, Charles was paying the second highest amount of taxes in the town, something, I am sure, he was hardly enthusiastic about. But his business successes would eventually make him a wealthy man.

Jonas designed his own home along the lines of his grandfather Benjamin's prestigious Concord farmhouse that now belonged to Uncle James. Young Jonas put up the frames, pounded a roof, and fashioned the hand-made locks and latches. It was completed in 1764. Now, with a house and land in a new community, the only thing missing was a family. Jonas focused on that challenge next. Two years later, Jonas proudly escorted his new bride, Mary Fletcher, from Westford to preside over the new household. They rode on horseback up to the front door excited about a new future and wasted no time filling the house with a young family.[29]

The Barretts of Concord

Over the years, Jonas's extended Barrett clan had become one of Concord's most influential families. As Jonas continued toward Concord, he knew he would see the head of the family, Uncle James, when he arrived. As colonel of Concord's militia regiment, James would be in command of whatever fight developed with the British troops. In fact, Col. Barrett had been in the center of the brewing conflict for several months now. The objective of the British march to Concord was to capture things stored and hidden on James Barrett's farm.

Before the day was over, Jonas would also see Uncles James's sons: cousins James (42 years old, and captain of one of the Concord militia companies), Stephen (25), and Peter (20). There were also Aunt Lydia's son, Samuel Barrett Farrar (39, and captain of another Concord militia company), and Uncle Thomas's sons, Charles (35, who Jonas expected to be marching with the company from New Ipswich), Samuel (25), and Amos (22). These last three were double cousins to Jonas – their father Thomas and Jonas's father were brothers, and their mothers were sisters. All these cousins, too, rallied to resist the British march on Concord.

That was not all. There were even more of the extended family readying for a fight, if it came to that. The spouses of Jonas's female cousins were also prominent in the militia and minutemen: Jonas Potter (35); Capt. George Minot (33, who commanded a Concord militia company); and the commander of still another Concord minuteman company, Capt. Charles Miles (47). Col. Barrett's granddaughter, Milicent (15), and her brother, James (14), were teenagers, but old enough to play their own roles defying the British. This historic day in Concord would be like a family reunion. [30]

Then there was Philip, Col. James Barrett's young slave. Ironically, New Englanders getting ready to fight for their own liberty still condoned slavery. Philip was only 14 and too young to take part in the day's encounters. Col. Barrett's will would set Philip free when he turned 30, but he did not plan to wait that long. A year later, when only 15-years old, Philip gained his freedom by enlisting. He was soon serving with the Army at West Point.[31]

Jonas's prosperous New Ipswich neighbor, Cousin Charles, who like Jonas started out that morning for Concord, missed this Barrett "family reunion." Charles had begun with New Ipswich's militia as a sergeant and eventually had risen to captain one of its two companies. As tensions between the colonies and London grew, however, Charles was removed from command on account of his sympathies for the Crown. When the New Ipswich militia mobilized that April morning to join Concord's defense, Charles was conflicted, but just the same joined his neighbors for the march. He turned sometime during the day, however, and was eventually paid for one day's service, the shortest service of anyone in town.

When events evolved into a full-blown revolution, Charles joined the thin ranks of New Ipswich's Tories. Charles Barrett, whose father, uncles, brothers, and cousins stood in arms against the British invasion of Concord, was a Tory. The American Civil War was not the country's first war to break up families and communities along differing lines of persuasion.

Charles's opposition to the rebellion was more practical than political. He was a born businessman and doubted the colonies' efforts against the strongest nation in the world could succeed. This revolution was bad for business. In the end, he believed, everything would be worse than what had prompted the colonials' discontent in the first place. Despite this, however, the town of New Ipswich took no measures against Charles, as certainly would have happened in Concord. Town fathers simply censured his ideas as "erroneous." [32]

Uncle James Barrett had enjoyed long service as an officer in the Concord militia. Indeed, he had more experience with actual fighting than most of the British officers marching toward Concord. As a captain during the French and Indian War in the late 1750's, he

203

had served in several bloody engagements at Fort Oswego, Fort Ticonderoga, and Crown Point. Over the years since, he had been a selectman in Concord and a representative to the General Court of Massachusetts.

James Barrett's wealth came from the livestock and provisions he grew on his farm. Between 1768 and 1773, he was a major supplier of beef, grain, and more to the British army in Boston. As tensions grew, however, James increasingly became an outspoken critic of the colony's British overlords. At a town meeting the previous September, Concord heeded Boston's call to form a Committee of Correspondence and James was one of its members. The town also chose him and his brother-in-law, Samuel Farrar, to be its delegates to the First Provincial Congress the next month. When the Congress called for a reorganization of the colony's defenses, it asked James to command a regiment made up of militia companies from Concord and nearby towns and promoted him from captain to colonel.

The Congress also assigned Col. Barrett superintendent of military stores, thereby making him responsible for the large quantity of military equipment, ammunition, and provisions to be stashed in Concord. At 65, James would have preferred not to be thoroughly engaged in so weighty a task. However, he accepted and was meticulous in setting up the regiment, acquiring supplies for the new army, and hiding them from the British. Some of the most prized possessions sent to Col. Barrett were cannons. He wrote in his ledger of their arrival:

> "Two pieces of Cannon Brought from Watertown to
> ye Towns
> Eight Pieces of Cannon Brought to ye Town by Mr.
> Harrington
> Four Pieces of Brass Cannon & Two mortar from Col
> Robertsons [sic]..."[33]

Over the winter months, wagons full of supplies poured into Concord. Twenty thousand pounds of musket-balls and cartridges, 50 reams of cartridge-paper, 206 tents, and so on, were in just one of the shipments. James hid the provisions in different spots, but much of it on his farm.

Meanwhile, the Barrett mills began manufacturing firearms and gun carriages. Even Uncle James's attractive 15-year old granddaughter Millicent got involved. Before relations with the British army deteriorated, a young British staff officer on his regular procurement trips often took fun teasing young Millicent for her rebel sympathies. He once asked her how the people could revolt when they did not even know how to make cartridges. Millicent flirtatiously replied that she did not know what he meant. "Give me a piece of pine, and I'll show you how," the officer said. He whittled a stick to the proper form, then took some paper and cut it into the pattern of a cartridge. When he left, she kept the paper pattern and was soon supervising other young ladies and her brother James in producing cartridges.

General Gage's spy in Concord kept him well informed of what was going on at the Barrett farm. When the general began writing up his secret plan, he designated the farm as the location of the colonials' cache. There were supplies enough, he correctly presumed, to equip an entire army. The rebel spy network, for its part, picked up immediately what the British were planning. On April 8, Paul Revere made an earlier ride to Concord to warn its people that the patriot network had learned of British preparations to send a force there. [34]

The Square in Lexington

A week later, about an hour after Paul Revere and William Dawes rode off on their separate midnight rides, 800 British officers and men stepped into longboats and ferried across the Charles River. There were not enough longboats to do it in one trip, so the boats ferried back and forth until all the men were across. It took about two hours. Earlier that evening, Gen. Gage had given his written orders to Lt. Col. Francis Smith who would command the force. Royal Marine Major John Pitcairn was his deputy commander.

Gage wanted to strike a swift hard blow before the Concord militia could react in force. The attack would center on the Barrett farm. A top objective was to recover four brass cannons that the rebels had spirited from armories in Boston right under the army's nose. The four pieces had been smuggled from place to place until they had ended up in James Barrett's barn.

The British plan stated that the troops were not to fire unless fired upon. It also required the soldiers to respect the persons of the townspeople. Its success depended on seizing at the very onset Concord's two bridges, one of which they would need to hold in order to get back and forth to the Barrett farm. But the plan had two big flaws: the mission was hardly the surprise that Gage hoped, and it gave no details of what the troops should do if they entered into an armed exchange with the provincial militias. Both became critical issues before the day finished.[35]

Once across the river, the troops formed and began their march through Cambridge to Concord. In their colorful uniforms, they strode northwest through the night to the sound of muskets and cannons firing in the distance. The shots were alarm signals meant to awaken the towns around them with an alert that a British force was on the move. After Paul Revere's and William Dawes's quick visit, the Lexington militia, a group of men aged 16-66, began to gather on Lexington Green under the leadership of Capt. John Parker. They tried to relax as they waited for the British arrival.

Sometime around 4:00, with hardly a glow yet on the eastern horizon, a horseman rode up and warned the militiamen that he had seen Redcoats not far from the town. Capt. Parker had his drummer beat a loud roll to call the men into ranks. In the distance, British Maj. Pitcairn heard the roll and ordered his men to load their muskets. Pitcairn's advance guard exited the main Concord road into Lexington to face off against Parker's militiamen.

Parker cautioned his men, "Let the troops pass by, and don't molest them, without They being first." Some have said that the Redcoats' advance units turned off the road into Lexington by mistake. Be it as it may, the two-armed hostile sides lined up across the square from each other, the British numbering three times the Lexington men. The early morning air hung stagnant and heavy, and finally, to deflate the tense moment, Parker ordered his men to disperse. While they were doing so, a shot rang out, and once it did, the Regulars raised their muskets and fired. When the smoke cleared, eight of the militiamen lay dead and nine, wounded. Which side fired that first shot has been debated forever afterward.

Shocked, Parker's men drifted back, offering no resistance. By now, Lt. Col. Smith had reached the scene. He restored order among the Regulars and by 5:30 a.m. had them back on the road toward Concord. It was still six miles away.[36]

Concord, 3:00 A.M.

After Dr. Sam Prescott's escape from the British, he arrived in Concord sometime after 2:30 a.m., and by 3:00, the church bell had everyone awake. Since Paul Revere's first ride to Concord the previous week, the townspeople had known about Gage's plans to send troops there. For several days, people relocated, hid, and disguised weapons and supplies.

On the Barrett farm, repositioning the cache had taken a frenzied pace. Uncle James Barrett's boys, plowed land behind the farmhouse and seeded the furrows with muskets, one of them dropping the weapons behind the oxen when a furrow was opened, then others covering it, and raking it smooth. James's fourteen-year-old grandson, James, goaded the oxen to carry cartridges from his sister Millicent's cartridge production line to a swamp where the load was hidden under pine boughs.

The entire day and much of the night before the British arrival, Col. Barrett worked to get their warehoused supplies out of the troops' reach. Four cannons were carried to Stow, six to hiding places outside town, and others covered with hay, straw, and manure. Loads of provisions were taken to nearby towns or hidden in the woods. When Gen. Gage's troops began massing on Boston Common, their mission was already futile. Most of the stores were already dispersed. People that very moment were scattering what remained to still more hiding places outside the town.

The Rev. William Emerson, one of the first awakened when Prescott got to Concord, was the one pealing the church bells. When he heard the bells, Cousin Amos Barrett jumped from his bed, grabbed his things, and hurried to the town square.   He later described the morning, "As I was a minute man, I was soon in town and found my captain and the rest of my company at the post. It wasn't long before there was another minute company."[37]

At the same moment, Cousin Nathan was organizing the militia company he captained. One of its members, Thaddeus Blood, aired the excitement of the early morning, "I was called out of bed by John Barrett, a sergeant of the militia company to which I belonged. I was twenty years of age... I joined the company under Captain Nathan Barrett, at the old Court House, about three o-clock, and was ordered to go into the Court House to draw ammunitions. After the company had all drawn their ammunition we were paraded near the Meeting House."[38]

While the men joined their ranks, Reverend Emerson animated the morning by meeting and encouraging people who were now pouring into the streets. An enthusiastic patriot, Emerson would become the grandfather of Ralph Waldo Emerson who was born in Concord in 1803. He stood before the gathering crowd and cried. *"Let us stand our ground. If we die, let us die here!"*   Rev. Emerson's call fell on welcoming ears. They were fired up.[39]

Col. James Barrett, who had been sick in bed for several days before getting word of the imminent invasion, was up and firmly in charge. From the onset, he was pulled in two directions. He had already spent most of the preceding day and night spiriting equipment to hiding places. As commander of the militia regiment, and in the absence of minuteman regimental commander Col. Pierce, he was also senior officer on the field, in command of the ten companies of the minuteman regiment, as well his own regiment of militia. Competing with his job as commander was his concern for his farm, family, and the provisions concealed around the farm.

When Col. Barrett got the alarm, he rode his horse toward Wright's Tavern where he found minutemen and militiamen already filtering in. He dispatched a rider to scout the road to Lexington to get a sense of how far away the British column was. He also sent horsemen to Carlisle, Acton, Westford, and other nearby towns urging their companies to get to Concord as rapidly as possible. He then ordered his men to rest as much as they could while awaiting the Redcoats' arrival. Few wanted sleep at a time like this one.

Col. Barrett remained in the town center. In the early morning darkness, his scout returned from the Lexington Road with no information. Finally, he sent a force of three companies, about 150 men, down the road, and along the ridge overlooking it, to try to catch a first glimpse of the arriving British troops. Cousin Nathan Barrett and Capt. George Minot were two of the commanders of the reconnaissance group. Cousin Amos was among the soldiers.[40]

Meanwhile, the 800 Redcoats marched in close step, their drums marking time and fifers striking up their tunes across the fields, the sun just appearing on the eastern horizon. The troops sensed they were not the only ones filling the Middlesex County roads. A five-mile circle drawn around the center of the column would have encompassed 75 companies of minutemen and militiamen, all now funneling toward Concord. That did not count the many still farther out – Jonas Barrett's company in Ashby, for example, was just now receiving the alarm.

Britain's finest scoffed at the colonial units. Not a soldier among them understood how well the provincials were organized. They did not know, or they refused to believe, that an army had been created right under their noses. The Redcoat column was moving directly toward the center of six regiments of that colonial army. A couple of times someone from the nearby woods took a potshot at the British soldiers with no effect. The men in their red coats and tall fur hats just continued their robotic pace.

Finally, Amos Barrett's eyes glimpsed silvery pulsing reflections as rays from new morning sun flashed off the shiny rows of British bayonets down the road. Thaddeus Blood, of Nathan Barrett's company, described the sight, "The sun was rising and shined on their arms, and they made a noble appearance in their red coats and glistening arms." Someone remarked, "We must spoil their fine uniforms before night." Cousin Amos described the almost cinematic moment when the first elements of the two armies approached each other: "We staid till they got within about 100 rods, then we were ordered to about face and marched before them with our drums and fifes going, and also the British (drums and fifes). We had grand music. We marched into town..."[41]

In the opening shafts of morning brightness, the people of Concord soon saw the spectacle of two columns of soldiers filing down the narrow road in the same direction, about 1600 feet apart. The first, a group of men and boys in everyday clothes and shoes, was followed by the grenadiers with their fur hats, bright uniforms, white belts and black boots. All of them marched to their own drummers and fifers, in careful precision, both powerfully aware of the presence of the other.

It was sometime after 7:00 in the morning when the British Regulars poured into Concord. By now, the flow of Concord's own minutemen and militiamen and those from neighboring communities was strong and steady. Just a little earlier, a rider from Lexington reported that there had been British gunfire in Lexington.

"Were they firing ball?" Col Barrett asked.

"I don't know, but I think it probable," the rider reported.

That answer defined the stakes. At this moment, unity and discipline could have vaporized in an instant, but Barrett seized control with cool firm leadership. While the British troops reached the center of Concord, Barrett concentrated his assembling companies at a distance, on a hillside above the cemetery. When British skirmishers slowly started making their way up the hill toward them, he kept shifting his units northward to keep their space from the Redcoats. His plan was to defend and not attack. James then turned to his men, reminded them of the danger they faced, and cautioned them not to be careless. He charged them not to fire unless the British fired first.[42]

Passing into Concord, the British column straightaway broke into three taskforces: one took control of the South Bridge; another stayed in the town to search for and destroy provisions they expected to find there; and the third began moving toward the North Bridge. Before they reached it, Barrett moved his force across the North Bridge onto Punkatasset Hill overlooking the bridge (see Map E).

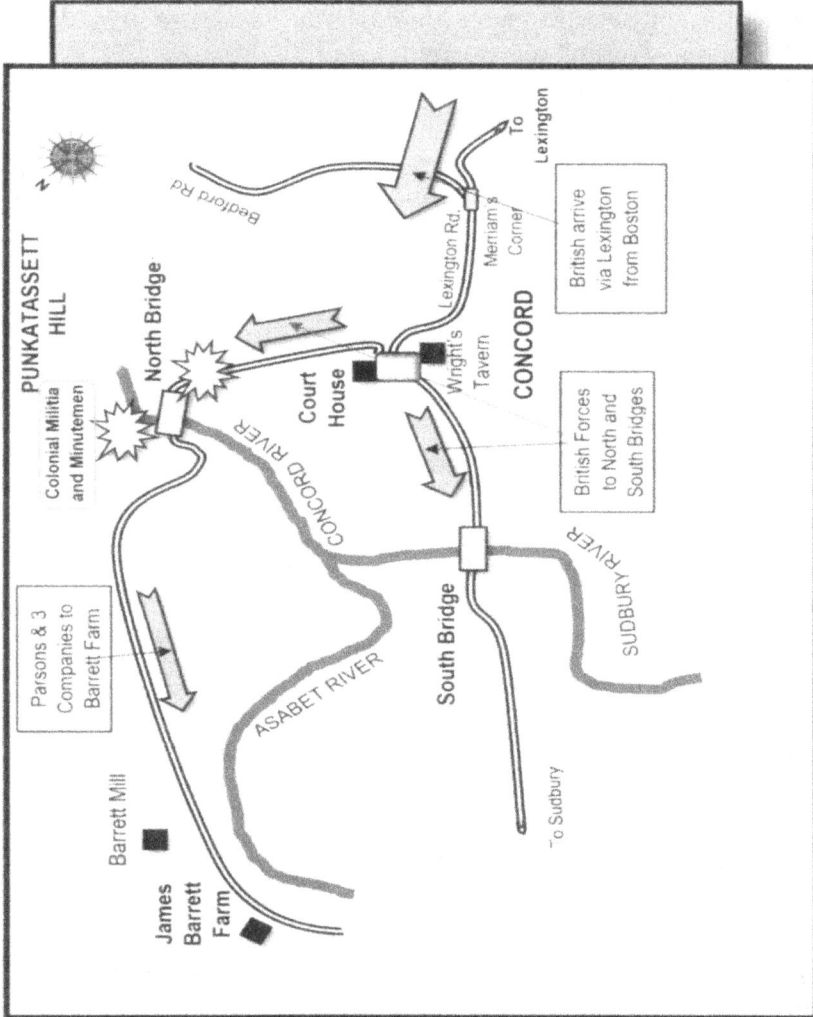

Map E – Battle of Concord

The North Bridge

Uncle James knew some of the arriving militia units would try to enter the town over the South Bridge which the British now occupied. He told his son Stephen to ride hard to intercept these units with a message to march instead from the north toward the North Bridge. Cousin Stephen galloped off.

Before the Redcoats' arrival in Concord, Barrett had had four companies of Concord militia at their ready. By this time, however, companies from Bedford, Lincoln, Acton, Sudbury, and East Sudbury were joining him. These companies had marched from their towns earlier that morning, everyone coming out to send them off, the women with cooked meat for them to carry along. On the other side, the young, mostly inexperienced, British Regulars on the road below followed their orders, but the mounting disproportionality between their numbers and the colonials above them was disconcerting.

Col. Barrett looked down from Punkatasset Hill at the British troops congregating around the bridge. The hill, where he and his men stood, sloped gently down to where the placid Concord River quietly flowed beneath it. Not far upstream, the Assabet and Sudbury rivers joined to form the Concord. A couple hundred yards away, against the tranquil riverscape, James could see red uniforms dotting both banks around the bridge that normally carried people and horse carts to and from the town.

There must have been a mix of feelings inside the farmers and shopkeepers who made up the colonial regiments. The impossibility of violence issuing from the beautiful fields below agitated against the indignation of having their homes invaded and of being bullied for so long in the halls of British power. Putting a sharp edge on the moment was the thought that just hours before, the British troops they now watched had brazenly marched into their neighbor community of Lexington in the early hours of the morning to fire their weapons. Details were still absent, but no one now doubted that the Regulars were prepared to do the same in Concord, no matter how still the countryside and its placid winding river.

Meanwhile, as much as the British soldiers tried to disparage the colonials, the militiamen were beginning to completely cover the ridge above their positions at the North Bridge. The Americans were armed and appeared determined. The British force was made up mainly of inexperienced soldiers, and every moment increased their inferiority as more and more colonials arrived to bolster their already considerable force. Among the British, fear must have stood shoulder to shoulder with hubris.

At the North Bridge, the British force then divided again, with one group of three companies staying to guard the bridge and another three-company unit crossing the bridge on their way to the Barrett farm. Uncle James was troubled that Rebecca and some of the children were where the three companies were headed. He had to warn them one more time. James turned operational control over to Major John Buttrick, deputy commander of Concord's Minuteman Regiment, and rushed off ahead of the British force to make a quick visit to his home and family.[43]

The Barrett Farm

The Barrett farm was two miles from the North Bridge on the road to Acton. The road wound between the Assabet River on the south and the wooded low hills on the north, with the between fields sloping up from the river. James had walked, ridden a horse, and driven wagons and carriages over it a thousand times since he was born. But his hurried trip up the dusty lane this day was different from any other. James galloped past the Barrett family's sawmill and grist mill and stopped a few minutes later in the small yard in front of his house (Map E)

Inside, Rebecca was surprised when her husband suddenly appeared in the doorway. James recounted the scene in Concord and told that the British column had taken up positions around the bridges. He described how the town's militia was positioned on the hill above the North Bridge, and companies from all over the county were arriving one after another to join his men. Three companies of Redcoats would soon be in their yard, he then warned. Rebecca should flee with the family, he urged

213

Rebecca understood James's concern, but stubbornly refused. "No, I can't live very long anyway, and I'd rather stay and see that they don't burn down the house and barn," she declared, heels dug in.[44] James paused and surrendered. He knew he had no time to argue and would not win this one anyway. Rebecca had married him when she was only 15 years old, very young even for then, and they had been married now 42 years. In the beginning, according to tradition, her mother had to help her with the housekeeping. Now, she was an extremely capable woman with a quick wit and full control of the farmhouse, brave, ...and she was right. The soldiers might burn the house if someone was not there.

Col. Barrett reluctantly left the farm in Rebecca's hands, checked the barn that stood alongside the house, and surveyed other hiding places to see they were secure. He then hurried his return to Punkatasset Hill. The colonel in charge of the militia forces he might be, but dressed in a worn coat, flapped hat, and leather apron, he looked like an old farmer. When he saw the British on the road heading straight towards him, he circled back toward the bridge, guiding his horse on a path through the woods onto the high ground north of the road. Twenty minutes later, he was with his troops.

The three companies of British regulars under Captain Lawrence Parsons never saw Col. Barrett as they wound down the country road to finally halt in front of the large farmhouse. It was about 9:30 in the morning. Captain Parsons pounded on the door and, when Aunt Rebecca answered it, he stiffly pronounced, "Our orders are to search the home top to bottom." He added that they would not destroy private property but would take anything that might have military use. His troops were tired and hungry, having been on the road since midnight, Parsons said. He asked for refreshment and offered to pay for it.

Rebecca said she would provide the men food and drink, but she refused the money with a tart remark, "We are commanded to feed our enemy, if he hunger."

She brought out some milk and brown cakes. When one of the soldiers threw coins into her lap, Rebecca stopped and then accepted it, loudly declaring, "This is the price of blood money!"

A sergeant stepped forward and said he wanted something stronger than milk. Aunt Rebecca flatly refused. Capt. Parsons backed her up fearing what could happen if his fatigued men started drinking alcohol. Meanwhile, soldiers continued to search the house, barn, and their surroundings. One of them stole $50 from a purse in one of the upper bedrooms.

About this time, Rebecca's son Stephen returned home from his father's mission to channel arriving militia and minuteman companies to the North Bridge. When he entered the house, a British officer grabbed him with a kick and asked his name. When the officer heard "Barrett," he said, "You must go to Boston with us and be sent to England for trial."

With a swift strong retort, Rebecca answered, "This is my son, not the master of the house, Colonel James Barrett; you may take him if you can find him."

They released Stephen, and did not bother James, Jr., who was also home sick with a lame leg. The soldiers brought some gun carriages they had found in the barn into the yard to be burned. But they searched in vain and made only a few discoveries of little importance. Then, suddenly, they heard rolls of musket fire in the distance. There was no way of knowing what it meant, and Capt. Parsons decided to get back quickly. He barked a command to form into line, and the column marched back toward the North Bridge.[45]

Atop Punkatasset Hill

After his hurried trip home, Col. Barrett was soon again on Punkatasset Hill, overlooking the bridge below as it arched up and then down to the opposite bank. The British companies had taken positions on both sides of the river. While he was gone, Maj Buttrick had been organizing the units that now, with the continuing arrival of new companies, formed two regiments, about 500 men in ten companies. The colonials well outnumbered the troops around the North Bridge. When British squads started gathering at the foot of the hill, Buttrick moved the militia down closer. The British quickly retreated to the bridge. Buttrick and his men were now about 400 yards from the Regulars.

This was a moment the British had never expected – standing below a hill covered by other British subjects, colonials though they were, on the verge of a disastrous clash. Hundreds of armed colonials in military formation stared down at them, ready to attack if ordered. For the red-coated troops, it must have seemed surreal.

Uncle James conferred with his officers, including Lt. Col. Robinson who had arrived ahead of his Westford regiment now en route. Again, he decided to await the Redcoats' next move, perhaps hoping that once they returned from his farm, they would pack up and leave. Col. Barrett and Buttrick still had not received a complete report of what had happened in Lexington, especially whether there were casualties. Meanwhile, his men on Punkatasset Hill were becoming increasingly restless. Waiting passively was not easy for them as they watched the British soldiers take control of their community.

In the center of Concord, the Redcoats were doing house-to-house searches. These troops were not as restrained as those visiting the Barrett farm. When soldiers reached the shops of Uncle Thomas, whose New Ipswich son Charles was at that moment wrestling with his Tory sympathies on the road to Concord, they pounded on the doors and pushed their way in, muskets and bayonets pointed. Inside one of the shops, Thomas had a small gun factory that produced arms and ammunition for the weapons cache. Thomas stood there, unarmed. When he tried to resist them, the Regulars threatened to shoot.

He replied dryly, "They would do better to save themselves the trouble." He was already old.

The soldiers decided to let Thomas go, replying "Well, old dada, you may go in peace."[46]

The Redcoats rummaged through the malt house of Aunt Rebecca Barrett's aged father, Joseph Hubbard, and pulled out 100 barrels of flour. "They rolled that out and knocked them to pieces and rolled some into the mill pond…," Amos Barrett recalled.[47] Others torched the Court House. When the soldiers set it on fire, a neighbor, Martha Moulton, and a servant quickly tried to put it out. She took after the soldiers to tell them that the upper Court House floors were filled with barrels of powder that would blow when the blaze reached them. This captured their attention, and Regulars were soon working alongside her trying to extinguish the flames.

Smoke from the fire curled upward over the city, its swirls slowly emerging into view from Punkatasset Hill where colonials and Redcoats continued their face-off. Though outnumbered, the Regulars still attempted to disparage the motley colonial men, but the reality was much different from what the British thought. The militiamen were not much at a disadvantage in training and equipment from their British counterparts. They had far more battle proven small unit leaders in their ranks than had the British Regulars, many of whom having never seen action. Half of the 13 Concord minuteman officers, sergeant or above, were veterans of expeditions against the French.

As close as the two sides were to each other, they were still far enough away that it was unlikely an accidental shot would kill or wound anyone. Regulars carried the old Brown Bess musket, but so did many of the militiamen. The Brown Bess shot a .75 caliber soft lead ball and could be reloaded quickly. It might hit a man once out of ten times at a range of 100 yards, so it was effective mainly at closer ranges. With 400 yards separating the two sides, there was still little danger at this point that an out of control shooter could do much damage to anyone, let alone start a war.[48]

To the Bridge

The billowing cloud of smoke from the Court House fire began to catch Col. Barrett's and his officers' attention. Until now, James had kept his options open. Without a clear view of the town over a mile away, however, there was a distinct possibility that the British were systematically burning it. Col. Barrett again parleyed with his officers and others.

During their deliberations, they agreed that the possibility the town was burning was something they could not ignore. They decided the combined colonial force should march off the hill, over the bridge, and into Concord. There was general support for this resolution, "to march into the middle of the town for its defence, or die in the attempt," as Major Buttrick put it.[49]   In Col. Barrett's words, "I ordered them to march to the north bridge and pass the same, but not to fire on the King's troops unless they were fired upon."[50]   They knew how marching right through the British position on the bridge was at best a dangerous maneuver.

It was a fateful decision. Col. Barrett gave Maj Buttrick field command to lead the companies. Buttrick and Lt. Col. Robinson wheeled the men to the right and led the column proudly two abreast toward the bridge. Meanwhile, Col. Barrett rode alongside telling the men not to shoot first, but to fire fast if they were attacked.

Their movement proceeded with care, pomp, and precision, fifers and drummers playing. At first sight of it, the Regulars were for the first time impressed with the colonial militiamen clad in farmer's britches, everyday blouses, and vests. One of them later described how the rebel advance came "with as much order as the best disciplined Troops." Barrett and Buttrick hoped that the British guarding the bridge would not resist their plan to march over it toward whatever was happening in the city.

As the colonials came down the hill, the British started pulling up planks to prevent their passage, perhaps forgetting the three British companies now marching from the Barrett farm would also need to cross the bridge. Cousin Amos captured the moment when he wrote: "Major Buttrick said if we were all his mind, he would drive them away from the bridge – they should not tear that up. We all said we would go."[51]

The militiamen loaded their guns for the first time. Buttrick placed a crack company from Acton first in order of the march. Cousin Ruth's husband, Captain Charles Miles, and Captain Nathan Barrett led companies not far behind.   The Redcoats stopped demolishing the bridge and scattered to take positions on the other side.

As well justified as the colonials' movement might have been, it destabilized whatever calm prevailed between the two sides. A few moments later, a "Crack!" sounded, and then another "Crack! Crack!" echoed through the air. Three quick musket shots rang from the British side, one after the other. These were followed by a

Redcoat volley from the front company. The blast cut down two men from the Acton company, including its commander. Buttrick shouted "Fire! Fellow-soldiers. For God's sake, fire!" With no hesitation, the militiamen shouldered their muskets and fired a deadly volley that took a heavy toll. And then they fired again.[52]

Four of the Redcoats' eight officers were wounded. A sergeant and six privates were down. The Americans easily continued their lethal fire because, besides the initial casualties, the British muskets missed their marks. Amos described it, "It is strange there were no more killed, but they fired too high."[53] The British Regulars turned and fled while the Americans swarmed across the bridge to take positions on the other side.

It all happened very quickly, and in its aftermath, the colonials were a little stunned and unsure what to do. They hesitated and stopped their march toward the town center. Shortly, they saw the main Redcoat body marching from the town toward them. Buttrick ordered his men to organize themselves behind a stone wall and said he would give the order to fire. The approaching soldiers were rattled to see so many red uniforms lying on the ground and 200 aimed, cocked muskets protruding from behind the wall. They halted for about ten minutes with their officers standing in front of the men. After the time-out, they had better thoughts and retreated back into Concord.

The colonials let them go. They still saw this as a defensive battle and were not psychologically ready to pursue the British. After the Regular troops retreated to Concord, Maj. Buttrick ordered the men back across the North Bridge to positions alongside the road at the foot of Punkatasset Hill. Their reluctance to open a full-fledged running battle with the British Redcoats would last only a few hours more.

Col. Barrett, for his part, was concerned about what had happened to his family when the Parson column reached the farm. He once again turned field command over to. Buttrick and raced back down the road toward his home. Before leaving, he ordered the provincial dead taken to Buttrick's nearby house and the wounded to his own home for care.

According to tradition, he saw Captain Parsons leading the quick return of his three red-uniformed companies whose search had been interrupted by sounds of musket fire from the North Bridge. James slowed and with little seeming interest, leisurely sauntered by the Regulars as they marched forward. They did not recognize him in his farm clothes and lost a chance to capture the day's militia leader.[54] Uncle James made it home to find nothing worse for the wear and tear. He was ready to collapse from exhaustion having spent the previous day and night supervising the concealment of weapons, and all of this day, commanding the mobilization and response to the British incursion.

Capt. Parsons and his men grew apprehensive as they approached the bridge. They had to cross to join the main force in Concord. On its far side, they could see red-coated soldiers sprawled on the ground. On this side of the bridge, the road was lined with hundreds of armed militiamen. Their only hope was that the militia would give them free passage. Eyes straight ahead, they continued their quickly paced march up the road. The militia watched as the Redcoats drew alongside, and then let them proceed across the bridge. Col. Barrett's long-standing order they not fire unless fired upon was heeded, and Parson's men slipped by.

By the time Parsons made it back to the main body, the companies assigned to the South Bridge had also retreated into the center of Concord. Lt. Col. Smith could see that their thwarted mission was now a fiasco. Not only had they failed to recover the weapons cache, but the entire countryside was literally in arms. Unrecovered wounded and dead British men in their handsome red uniforms were lying before the North Bridge, outside his reach. The mission verged on becoming worse than that – a disaster or even a massacre.

The Bloody Road to Boston

Smith lined up the now re-combined task force to start their retreat to Boston. About high noon he gave the command to march, or, in the minds of many, to escape. They departed without the sounds of their proud fifes and drums. Their dead and wounded, they left behind. It was 17 long miles back to the longboats on the Charles River.

Wish as they might, the day was not over for the British troops. When the Americans' shock from the clash at the North Bridge began to dissipate, the audacity and arrogance of the British advance on their homes and families sank in. The congregating militia and minuteman companies had followed their orders not to fire until fired upon. That moment had come and gone. Things were now far beyond that. Meanwhile, four fresh companies from Framingham and Sudbury joined them. Other units were close behind.

Looking now for an escape route, Lt. Col Smith realized his men were surrounded, with the exception of the road back to Lexington. Even that route was threatened as two new colonial regiments advanced toward Lexington along the Bedford Road. These arriving units, learning what had happened in Lexington and Concord, took up positions in the trees alongside the Lexington Road. The British would soon parade right before them. The column had not proceeded far before firing rang out. As in Lexington, there remains a controversy over who fired first, but hostilities between the two armies were now inescapable.

The shooting continued off and on until it was almost nonstop, the British marching as fast as they could along the road. The colonial men shot at them from the sides before leap frogging through the trees to be waiting when the Redcoats rounded a bend or came over a hill and into range. It was a devastating sequence of skirmishes. The battered militia from Lexington had now regrouped under Captain Parker and found their own spot to await the column. As the Redcoat formation tried to make its way by, the Lexington men took their revenge for the British massacre earlier that morning.

For Smith and his troops, it was a hard, bloody trek home, but they finally made it to the waiting longboats. Once across the river and back in their barracks, they found safety. One British tally counted 73 dead, 174 wounded, and 26 missing – about one-third of their force was casualties. The Colonials suffered 49 killed, 36 wounded, and 5 missing.[55]

It was also a long day for the Barrett cousins, uncles, aunts, and grandchildren. Before it was over, Cousin Nathan Barrett was slighted wounded. Capt. Charles Miles was wounded in the hand, but Cousin Amos made it through the day safely. Young Amos Prescott, who carried forward the warning his brother Dr. Sam Prescott brought Concord earlier that morning, was shot in the side after he returned, but he survived. However, like for everyone else in Concord, April 19, 1775, was also a watershed day that defined the rest of their lives.[56]

Minutemen and militia units continued to stream into Concord well after the fighting was over. Among them came Jonas Barrett and the tired men from Ashby. By the time they reached Concord, Lt. Col. Smith's tattered Redcoats were back in their barracks at Boston. To the Ashby minutemen's frustration, and surely their families' relief, they had missed the action. It was not a futile march for them. When they embarked, no one knew how this day and its battle would end. They might have been needed. True to their name, they were ready in minutes and prepared for whatever came.

Two days later, Rev. Emerson held a service where 700 of these soldier-patriots attended. Afterwards, in response to a false alarm, minuteman companies were dispatched to Cambridge, but returned after finding no enemy there. Within two weeks, Jonas was back home with his family in Ashby where he stayed for the next year.

The people of Concord treated the captured British soldiers well, and some of these men opted to remain in Concord. One, a British officer named Samuel Lee, married a Concord widow and spent the rest of his life as a tailor in Concord. Another Sergeant Cooper, who marched with Parson's party to the Barrett farm, married a woman in Concord and years later was often heard tongue-in-cheek grumbling that Mrs. Barrett had refused to give him some liquor when he raided her home.

When Major Pitcairn, the British second in command, was wounded, his horse bolted and was captured. Cousin Nathan Barrett bought the horse and Pitcairn's pistols at an auction. He gave the horse to Rev. Emerson for the congregation's use and the pistols to colonial General Israel Putnam. Nathan was later elected first major of regiment field officers and succeeded to his father's rank of colonel. Cousin Amos fought at Bunker Hill and went on to earn a commission as a captain in the Continental Army. Cousin James, Jr., became a prominent community leader after the war.

Col Barrett withdrew from his command responsibilities shortly after the battle in Concord and in December that year was appointed muster-master charged with raising new recruits for the great war of rebellion. He served on the committee to receive Benjamin Franklin's £100 sent by several people in England for the relief of the wounded in the battles of Lexington and Concord and the widows of those killed. Uncle James unfortunately died suddenly in 1779 and did not see the end of the Revolution. His legacy and memory are still enshrined in Concord as a patriot and the earliest battlefield commander of the War of Independence.[57]

Home in Ashby

Jonas was home for the next year. Then, in the fall of 1776, with the colonial army's operations in Canada and Washington's troops bogged down in New York, a call went out for Massachusetts men to enlist for 3-6 months to support the Continental Army. Lt. Jonas Barrett and many others in the county re-entered the service and joined General Washington in New York City.

For some, the call came so fast there was little time to prepare. A newspaper account I found told the amazing story of a teenage girl's response. When Jonas's future brother-in-law, John Locke, received orders to march, "the next day after tomorrow at sunrise," he did not have suitable pants to wear. His inexhaustible younger sister, 15-year old Eunice, resolved to solve that problem. She hurried to the pasture where she sheered a sheep. With the wool, Eunice carded, spun, washed, sized, dried, wove the cloth. Then she cut and prepared the pantaloons – all in 40 hours without sleep or rest. When she was done, young Eunice, like many women of the times, had made her own sacrifice for their cause. She wrote, "I wept until my overcharged and bursting heart was relieved." John had something to wear when he joined General Washington's army.[58]

The Revolutionary War lasted nearly eight years. I expected to find Jonas serving at other times and places, but I searched in vain for records of subsequent military service. I was puzzled I could not find more. One day, when looking again at his family's births, deaths, and marriages, I suddenly realized what must have sidelined his participation in the war whose first battle he had marched so valiantly to fight.

Jonas returned from his New York service in late March of 1777 and was paid for three month's duty. Immediately on reaching home, however, he suffered a tragedy. His dear wife Mary died only days later, in the beginning of April. I suppose she was ill when he returned.

That was not all. Nathan, the baby Mary was carrying the day Jonas left with his minuteman company for Concord, passed away three days later, not quite one and a half years old. Jonas's daughter Elizabeth was gone a month after that. They were taken by disease of one sort or another. Rarely in our modern communities does an illness sweep in and take a good share of the family all at once. But this was not uncommon then. Such calamities were part of life. Of their seven children, Jonas was left the sole parent of five.

It was four years after Mary died in the beginning of April, 1777, before Jonas married again. During these years, it would have been difficult for him to leave again for war. His new wife, Urania Locke, was a bright, well-respected woman, 21 years younger. They lived happily until he died in 1803. Over those twenty-two years of marriage, Jonas fathered another nine children.

There was a wrinkle in Jonas's later life. Not long after the war ended, before the Constitution was drafted and the United States formed, Jonas and his nephew Benjamin, Jr., got involved in an uprising called "Shay's Rebellion." Although few today have heard much about it, in its time it was a notorious revolt that resounded throughout the newly independent states.

Shay's Rebellion was born in a post-war recession that wiped out the assets of many people, especially in central and northern Massachusetts. A good share of these men were unpaid veterans. In bitter response, some of them, including Jonas, joined a movement to overthrow the government of the State of Massachusetts. Shay's Rebellion pulled retired General George Washington back into public life and fueled a realization that the country needed a written constitution to maintain its unity and stability. Two of the participants in Shay's Rebellion were hanged, and a number jailed. Fortunately, Jonas got off by surrendering his arms and taking an oath of allegiance.[59]

Starting from Scratch

I started my research for Barrett family stories almost from scratch. There was nothing in Mother's files except for a simple genealogical entry for Jonas Barrett, the father of Mary Fletcher Barrett and Thomas Chamberlain, Charlie Leonardson's great-grandparents. When I accessed FamilySearch's Family Tree, I soon had a lot of information on Jonas's genealogy that spread out in several directions.

Like Wikipedia, FamilySearch's tree is composed of user contributions, greatly coming from Latter-day Saint genealogical records. Since this is the largest genealogical data base anywhere, the tree for me was an essential jumping off point for search on any new lines. However, I found several issues to beware of. Since it is essentially a computer collation of contributor submissions, it inevitably has both human and other errors in its creation. Usually, I found that entries over the past 100-150 years were fairly accurate, but it was important to be very careful the farther back you track it.

Sources, as always, are key for giving credence to entries. Once I had Jonas's essentials from his FamilySearch entry, I could more easily get into other historical records to verify details. New Englanders from the beginning were great record-keepers. Searching for Jonas Barrett on Ancestry.com quickly got me to vital and other records that connected him to parents, his wife, and so on, until a genealogical image of him and his family emerged.

Local Histories

I never found a publication on the Barrett family with an account of their lives and deeds. Such a book is a good one waiting to be written. But early New Englanders also wrote histories, and there were several 19th century histories on the locales where the Barretts lived. I mentioned earlier the value of local histories, and that was true in this case, too. Such detailed histories written over the next 100 years preserved memories of that earthshaking dawn-to-sunset **when patriots resisted the Redcoats' invasion of Concord and Lexington.** *I started combing Wikipedia and Google Books and found some of them.*

In 1824, on the battle's 50th anniversary, the Rev. Ezra Ripley, a *pastor in Concord for 63 years, published a good account of the Battle of Concord, one both informative and full of anecdotes. Rev. Ripley knew many of the characters involved and interviewed several of them. Passages from his book are convincing as they tell* **the adventures of the people involved in the day's events.**

Ten years later, another local resident, Lemuel Shattuck, wrote an extensive history of Concord with even more anecdotes. Shattuck was one of the founders of the New England Historic Genealogical Society. His access to the town, its records, and its people so soon after the battle allowed him a **unique perspective of the war's first day.** *As he put it, "The author of the following History, having had occasion several years since to consult some of the earlier town records in Concord, discovered many important facts and documents which were wholly unknown to the public, and very imperfectly to the inhabitants of the town itself."[60] Best of all, Lemuel Shattuck talked about the people and their stories. His book has been a reference for generations of historians.*

During my searches, I found still another account that I liked written by Margaret Sidney and entitled Old Concord Her Highways and Byways. *Margaret's work was done over 100 years after the British marched to Concord, but her presentation brought a* **woman's insight into events retold in those days only by men.** *Her interview at the old Barrett farm with Augusta, Cousin Peter's granddaughter, for example, vividly conveyed the tension present when the British troops arrived to search the farmhouse, only to* *confront Uncle James's dauntless wife Rebecca. Of course, Sidney was writing a century later, and over the years, memories could have softened, or family accounts might have been embellished. But Margaret's stories are good ones, and who is to say that they are less accurate than any of the others?*

It would be difficult to uncover stories with such personal resonance without the foresight and efforts of these writers who looked toward the future by passionately re-telling the past. When I found on Amazon a reproduction of Shattuck's history, and downloadable copies of both Ripley's and Sidney's books online on "Google Books," many Barrett stories began to come together. These early historians nicely facilitated this part of my journey of discovery done at home at my desk, with the help of my computer.

Modern Histories

I found it always essential to forage the pages of modern historical work in addition to old histories. In this case, library shelves were full of general histories of the American Revolution, and all of them had discussions of the Battles of Lexington and Concord. At least Uncle James Barrett made an appearance in many of them. I took advantage of some of the latest of these (such as Walter Borneman's American Spring *and General Galvin's* The Minutemen and their World*), hoping that they would provide as modern a treatment as today's research allows.*

With the Barrett family as well as all the others I explored, it at once became clear that when studying general histories of their times, the books did not always have to mention the people I followed directly. Understanding our family stories requires understanding the events that surrounded them. For example, when I read that during the Civil War, Confederates and Indian allies raided a town a few miles from the home of one of my families, that piece of information alone began to suggest stories.

The question underlying my research was a simple one: what happened to my grandmothers and grandfathers? *Good descriptions of their times helped find answers. In other words, "visiting the living rooms" of your grandfather and grandmother starts with*

227

spending some time in your own, relaxing and reading a good book about the time and places they lived. From these books and others, I was able to piece together the family's adventures on that immortal day in Concord.

"An Old House With Stories"

Having done some homework, we traveled to Concord's North Bridge to see what else we could learn. It was April, the same time of year the minutemen and militia units once looked down from their hill positions at the faces of the red coated soldiers below. The surface of the Concord Rive ran peacefully beneath the bridge, radiantly reflecting the spring greens of newly leaved trees and shrubs along its banks. It was hard to tell it was moving at all. As many battlefields appear, it seemed the most unlikely spot for a conflict: restful, verdant, almost storybook-like.

Seija and I arrived early that morning at the National Park Service visitors center that now sits on top the hill. We took in the exhibits and I picked up some new things to read from the bookstore. When visiting historical sites, the visitor center's bookstore is always a starting point. There you can find specific accounts of people and places in books that are hard to find elsewhere, including on Amazon where you normally have to know the name of the volume to locate it. Visitors' center bookstores were often treasure troves of information for me.

Then we walked along the rises and drops down to the river. Small groups of guided tours wandered over and around the bridge, but we walked alone. I had already studied the story and did not now need a tour. We just wanted to absorb the atmosphere. The beautiful river setting had to be seen to appreciate the powerful disruption the shots fired that morning would have on America and far beyond.

A place on my mind was where Jonas Barrett lived. I found a reference to the house he built in a document a National Park Service ranger sent me about his Uncle James Barrett's home. Jonas, I learned, modeled his structure after his Grandfather

Benjamin's house, now the James Barrett house. But was Jonas's home still standing, and where exactly?

I had rummaged back and forth across the internet for months searching for more on the house, but with little luck. I knew it had to be somewhere in the vicinity of Ashby, Massachusetts. One afternoon, Seija and I were driving toward Westford from New Ipswich, New Hampshire. We had just spent the morning visiting the lavish mansion that cousin Charles Barrett built in 1799 as a wedding gift for his son, Charles, Jr.

Thinking that this might be an opportunity to find more about Jonas's old home, I chose a road that ran through Ashby. It was narrow and followed the terrain up and down, curving between fields, farmhouses and woods, and weaving through the picturesque scenery New England photobooks try to capture. I was trying to pay attention to the road, but in my mind, I watched Jonas Barrett and the Ashby minutemen that April morning in 1775. They stepped along roads like this one, their heavy muskets weighing them down. Now it was asphalted, there were no puddles to sidestep, flies to swat, no birds chirping and leaves waving – just the hum of our Jeep as we followed its navigator toward Ashby.

I had read in a 19ᵗʰ century Ashby history that Jonas's dwelling was one of the village's oldest. The town's early fathers chose it for their incorporation meeting since it was the largest in the community. We approached Ashby looking side-to-side for any old large building that resembled the James Barrett house in Concord and drove into the central commons of the tranquil old New England Town. We parked in the square that was bordered on various sides by the Grange, the American Legion, two churches, and an assortment of distinguished homes of varying periods of the town's history.

On one side was a corner grocery whose employees I expected to be from anywhere else but Ashby. I doubted anyone there could be helpful, but it was the only door open, and at least worth a try. Maybe they could point me toward the town library where we might find someone who knew of Ashby's past.

I went inside while Seija waited in the car. It was a small store, with a few counters of food stuffs and several additional aisles lined with shelves of home needs, a true country store. At first it looked like no one was there. Then off to the side of the counter, I saw a head bobbing up and down from the floor where a man was sweeping up dirt and dust. He paid little attention to me, the only customer in the store. Finally, he rose and with a curious look said, "Sorry to keep you waiting."

I responded by saying I was looking for the home of Jonas Barrett, an 18th century house that I supposed was near the center of town. He was an ancestor of mine. "If this doesn't ring any bells, maybe you could tell me where I might find the town library," I suggested.

In a seemingly apathetic tone, he asked, "How old is the house?" and I answered that I thought it was probably the oldest one in Ashby.

"Hmmm," he mused, "I was just reading about some old houses."

The storekeeper fingered through a disheveled stack of papers, newspapers, and other things piled next to the cash register. "I think I know what you mean. I might have something here." But he couldn't find what he was looking for.

I repeated, "Thank you for looking, but is the library close by?"

He mumbled, "Hmmm. I know there must be something here."

We were still the only ones in the store, and he kept sorting through the same stack of things he had already searched. Then he stopped and pulled out a large sized photocopy of a newspaper article and started reading: "James Barrett... yes, Jonas Barrett... who were you looking for?"

My eyes were big with amazement. "Jonas Barrett! That's who I'm looking for... his house."

Despite his generous efforts, he still looked disinterested. "Well here is an article about the oldest house in Ashby, Jonas Barrett's house. I know where it is. Look, I'll make you a copy."

With that, he placed the oversized sheet on large copy machine next to the cash register. The copy issued forth onto the collecting

230

tray, and he pulled the original, a copy itself, off the machine. "I don't know where I got this. Someone must have taken it off a shelf at the historical society or somewhere," he muttered, almost to himself.

My jaw dropped. In my hand I held a well written article about the Jonas Barrett house, one full of details, stories, and history, the type of information I had not been able to find earlier. At some point in the past the clipping had been trimmed at the top and had no reference to the newspaper that printed it. There was a dateline that read "March 19," but there was no year. The cash register man said, "I'll tell you how to find the house." His directions were precise.

I looked up and asked, "Can I pay you for this copy?" He made a big shrug and shook his head. I thanked him again and in astonishment wandered back to the car. "You won't believe what just happened in that store," I started.

A few minutes later we were parked in front of the splendid old residence where Jonas took his new bride Mary to live in 1766. It was a large brown dwelling on a dirt road, off today's paved streets, and surrounded by woods. There were three aged cars in the driveway. Dogs barked inside. We knocked and knocked again, but no one came to the door. Instead, my wife and I stood on the lawn, breathing in the moment, taking photographs and admiring the fine building, now just over 250 years old and in beautiful repair. It more than merited the distinction the article gave it when it wrote: "But from the days of wilderness to the atom age the house has endured and is still durable, wearing its history like a grand dame who delights but does not reveal all she knows."

Later that day, we got back to our room at a Westford B&B built by one of Jonas's wife Mary Fletcher's family when she was a girl. (How we ended there is another serendipitous story.) I sat down to sift carefully through the newspaper article to see if I could determine the year it was published. It was titled, "An Old House with Stories." I assumed it was not too old, maybe a year or two. Then I found a line that read, "In 1764 he built the house which still retains his name after 193 years." With a quick calculation, I realized the article had to be from 1957: March 19, 1957, over a half a century ago. It was on the shelf of a corner country store waiting for me to ask about it from a man who mumbled he was not sure "where I got this."

We were on a schedule and were unable to return in search of the current owners of the "Old House with Stories." When we reached our home in Virginia, however, I found a number for the Ashby Historical Society and called to see if I could learn more. After several tries, I eventually tracked down another phone number that was answered by a woman who sat on the Society's board. She knew nothing of the article when I described it, but she did know the house and gave me contact information.

A few moments later, I was in the middle of a pleasant phone conversation with the person who now owns Jonas's and Mary's home. She told me she knew nothing of the article I had found and had only the sketchiest of information about the stories it told. However, she mentioned that attached to the farmhouse were 300 acres, the same land that had always belonged to it. She said it was up for sale and asked if I knew anyone who would like to buy it. It was a tempting thought. I wished I was twenty-five years younger. I asked myself, "How would it be to live in the house your 5th great grandfather built?"

Although Jonas never again returned to the fight, he and his family remained patriotic and committed to the revolution. From the newspaper article I learned that one of the children carved "George Washington" on a beam in the attic of the house. Another, Lucy, weaved a flag on the occasion of George Washington's inauguration. Dark blue wool bunting made up the blue field. The stars were of white unbleached cotton. The red stripes were of woolen cloth "of a peculiar weave." Lucy, who was only five years old when Jonas and the men of his company marched from Ashby to Concord, was then nearly 20.[61]

PART 3

THE DUSTY
ROAD WEST

RICHARD WILSON
JULY 25, 1858
MAY 90

Chapter 6

Soldiers, Survival, Sorrow
Chester and Susannah Frasure Lent

*"On the western frontier of Missouri, the
American Civil War was fought not by armies but
by neighbors. Informal gangs of local southern
Bushwhackers fought a bloody and desperate
guerrilla war against the occupying Union Army
and pro-union Jayhawkers.*

*"Allegiance to either side was dangerous, but it
was more dangerous still to find oneself caught in
the middle."*

from the movie *Ride with the Devil,*
Universal Pictures (1999)

*During her 60 years of doing family history, Margie spent
tremendous energy tracking Chester and Susannah Lent's tragedies
during one of American history's most brutal episodes. They were
at the top of both her priority and frustration lists, and I inherited
her lists. I hoped to resolve some of the questions she battled to
answer.*

Bushwhackers, Jayhawkers, and Bleeding Kansas
On the eve of the American Civil War, Chester and Susannah
Lent lived in a hot spot. When they bought a farm in Vernon
County, Missouri, during the summer of 1857, the war's first
"official" shots in South Carolina were still almost four years away.
But Vernon and a few other counties on the Missouri-Kansas border
were already in the bloodletting throes of a growing North-South
rupture over slavery, abolition, power, and a way of life.

In all of polarized America, a debate raged over whether Kansas would enter the Union as a slave or a free state. Most of those living in Kansas were free-staters, and many violently so. But just across the border in Vernon and neighboring Missouri counties, the huge majority favored slavery. "Border Ruffians," including some of the Lents' neighbors, would cross from Missouri into Kansas to harass free-state supporters, beating, burning, and murdering. It got so bad that newspapers across the United States called it "Bleeding Kansas."

Free state "jayhawkers" from Kansas would reciprocate with raids into neighboring Missouri counties. One of the more notorious of these was a man named John Brown, who mounted murderous attacks, including one in Vernon County on the Little Osage River, only a short distance from where Chester and Susannah lived. Following his atrocities on the Missouri border, John Brown, his family, and followers left on a mission to start a slave revolt by attacking the federal arsenal at Harper's Ferry, in West Virginia. After U.S. Marines led by then Lt. Colonel Robert E. Lee caught him, he was hanged, only to become a legend and martyr in the pre-Civil War abolitionists' world. Most Americans still know his commemorative ballad, "John Brown's body lies a' moldering in the grave... His soul is marching on." [1]

Susannah and Chester Lent came to Missouri from Indiana, a northern state. They sold their farm there in January 1857, and purchased another in Vernon County a few months later. Family tradition says that they tried to be on neither side of the slavery issue, but their neighbors would have considered them "northerners" at a time when everyone was labeled one way or another.

Chester's and Susannah's upbringings were definitely northern. Susannah Frasure was born in Pennsylvania. Chester was born in Vermont, grew up in Pennsylvania, and married Susannah in Ohio before buying their first farm in Indiana. Like so many Americans of their time, they felt an uncontrollable urge to keep moving West. Now, Missouri beckoned. Among other things, setting up a new home close to the frontier offered opportunities to expand the size of their farm. The new one had 220 acres, and that was not small for then.

They arrived with six or seven children: John William (19), Mary Elizabeth (17), Maria (15), Lewis (8), Nancy Jane (5), Robison (3). Life in those days was always precious and precarious. Sometime during the process of re-settling in Missouri, their four-year old daughter, Sarah, died. A few years earlier in Indiana, they had lost two other small children, probably to a fever of one sort or another.[2]

When Chester and Susannah bought the new farm, the place was freshly settled frontier. It was situated in a fairly remote northern part of Vernon County. The first White settlers had been there only 25 years, and the county, itself, was barely two years old. It did not have a jail, and a courthouse was under construction in a town named Nevada [pronounced: Ne-vay'-da] City, in the center of the county.

The Lents were part of a brisk flow of new families. By the end of the year all the vacant land had been purchased. They were only a few short miles from a frontier village named Ballton that had a post office, mill, school, and church. About 300 people attended a celebration in Ballton in 1848. The Civil War, then on the far horizon, would irreversibly devastate the small community, but when the Lents and many more settlers arrived in 1857, it was relatively thriving.[3]

The Lents paid $1,470 for their 220 acres. The land was situated in a place that today is called the Four Rivers Area, the watershed of the Osage, Little Osage, Marais de Cygnes, and Marmaton Rivers. Near their home, the Osage River wound its way over the flat prairie to join the Marmaton River and Muddy Creek. The rivers contributed to an expanse of wetlands that made a home for abundant wildlife. In addition, their farmyard was well stocked with livestock. Three steers, two cows, four calves, and ten hogs (and probably horses, cats, dogs, and chickens) all roamed the corrals and pastures. They probably picked up some of the farm animals after arriving from Indiana, but perhaps they brought some with them. Chester and Susannah took a mortgage to pay for their new home.[4]

236

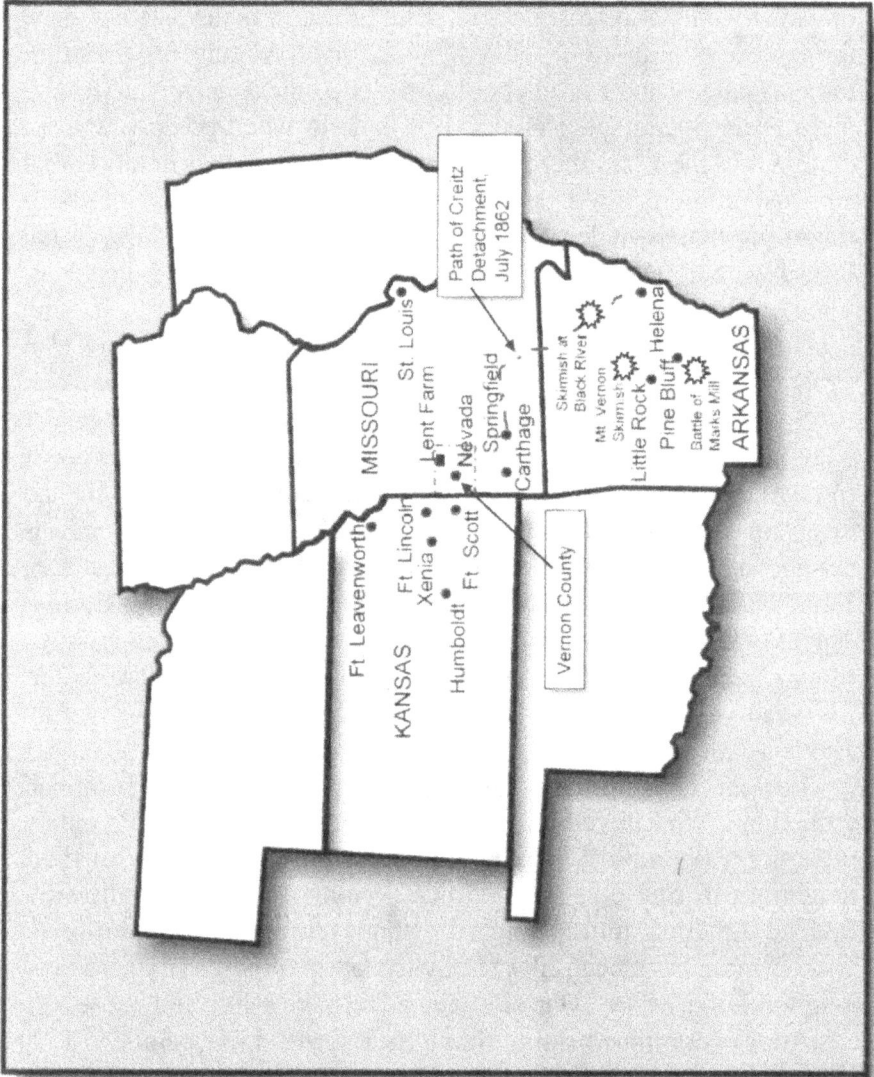

**Map F – Kansas, Missouri, and Arkansas
during the Civil War**

Maybe at another time and place, their start would have been a good one. Not long after taking up their new Missouri home, however, Chester died suddenly. The timing was devastating: new farm, new community, and young family. Among all the files, remembrances, and documents Mother and other relatives collected, there is no documented mention of exactly when or how Chester died. Over the years there were family stories and speculation that he was murdered in the cross-border raids. It is one of those traditions that is at least feasible, but most victims of the brutal forays were noted one way or another in county and other histories. There appears to be no mention of Chester's death in any newspapers or document, except the probate records that are also silent on the date and cause.

Susannah was left a widow with small children and a farm for which they owed money. On the American frontier there was never room to take much pause even to mourn tragedy and death. Life had to go on in a world that was often hostile and violent; there was simply too much work for anyone to stop. Susannah's oldest son, John William, at 20, was old enough to take some responsibility. The two oldest daughters got married during the following months. Mary Elizabeth wed a young man named Richard (Dick) Parmenter. Eighteen-year-old Maria married James Williams on the 4th of July 1860.[5]

Losing her husband and family's father left Susannah vulnerable. Whatever the family's thoughts about slavery, they were not slave holders nor heated secessionists like many of their neighbors in this polarized corner. Think of today's politically divided America, multiply that by about ten times, and then think what it must have been like for Susannah in an unfamiliar, violent neighborhood where everyone seemed to have a side and cause.

Attacks continued right around their farm. In December 1858, John Brown led his raid into the county. He kidnapped eleven slaves, took two white men captive, and stole horses and wagons. Brown's band left one man dead in his nightshirt, took the slaves to Iowa and then sent them to Canada. Almost at the same time, another jayhawker leader named James Montgomery, a Methodist preacher living just over the border in Kansas, attacked homes on the Little Osage River near the Lents' farm, taking a black woman and white man prisoners back to Kansas. Over the next year the Missourians suffered so many trepidations that the State organized a militia force and stationed it on the border with Kansas.

Life was perilous. Even trying to keep a low profile did not help when the vast majority of the people of the county were secessionists. During the presidential election of November 1860, no votes for Abraham Lincoln were recorded in Vernon County. It has been said there were a dozen people in the county who would have voted Republican, but officials made each voter declare whom they supported before casting their ballot. Lincoln supporters did not get to vote.[6]

Nor did the Lents' surname help their fragile place in the community. "Lent" sounded German or "Dutch" as locals paraphrased "Deutch." In hyper-demarcated Missouri, the German immigrant concentration living around St. Louis was a center of northern sympathizers. In the western part of the state, it was dangerous to have a German sounding name. Secessionists hated and sometimes killed people in cold blood, just because of their German last names.

It was about this time that raiders from one side or the other rode onto the Lent farm. They appeared in the distance and continued directly toward the farmhouse. It meant danger and struck fear in all of them. The smaller children ducked into barrels. Mary's young husband Dick came out to meet them. The raiders said they wanted food and whatever else they could have. Dick refused. Following Chester's passing, the Lents probably had little to surrender. One of the raiders raised his gun, pointed the barrel at Dick, and growled a threat to shoot him dead.

Before he could follow through, the boss of the band stopped his gunman. Then happened what became a common Civil War practice during the years to come. When local farm and plantation owners did not give raiding parties the provisions they demanded, the foragers burned them out. The gunmen torched Susanna's home and burnt it to the ground. Her family had little before, and now not

239

even that. That night Susanna and her children moved into the small home of Mary Elizabeth and her husband Dick.[7]

War Approaches

The artillery barrage of Fort Sumter in South Carolina during the spring of 1861 was a moment people remembered the rest of their lives. News traveled slower then, but that day it took not much longer to reach America's several states than it might today. For Americans, it was like an earthquake when they heard it. In the South it was a glorious day for most. Gone with the Wind's immortal scene portrayed it so well: southerners at an elegant plantation party cheered the courier who brought the dispatch. But Rhett Butler did not cheer. Only he foresaw the death and destruction of the months and years ahead. Nothing was ever to be the same again.

For Susannah Lent during the months preceding the Civil War, it must have seemed that things could not be worse than they were after Chester's death, the burning of their home, and the murder and plunder rampaging around them. But for her, like for everyone else in the war's path, everything did get worse. The war unleashed something dreadful especially in her neighborhood. Nowhere were Civil War atrocities worse than those on the Missouri-Kansas border. Raiders from both sides cared nothing for the rules of war and gave no pretext that they did. There was little regard for who were innocents, or who were combatants. The war was raw.

The Kansas of Susannah's day, moreover, was as close to the Wild West of American tradition as any place ever was. Over the war years all the lore – myths, and truths – intersected in the communities around her. During the 1860's, marauding Indians, shootists, robber bands, the James and Younger brothers, Quantrill's Raiders, William Cody (Buffalo Bill), Wild Bill Hickok, lawlessness and lynchings, large Civil War battles, and smaller daily skirmishes were all episodes in Susannah's and her family's Eastern Kansas and Western Missouri neighborhood.

The family's 220-acre farm bordered Bates County and was about 15 miles north of Nevada City, Vernon County seat. Today, it is part of the Busch Memorial Wetlands where 180 species of birds and a large variety of fish are found. Under other circumstances it would have been an idyllic setting to raise a family. Perhaps that promise is what lured Chester to move there in the first place. But in those years Vernon and Bates counties were a hotbed of violence and brutality.

Following Chester's death, Susannah stayed on in Missouri for a while, close to her married children. On August 1, 1860, the Census keeper visited her home in Vernon County's Little Osage Township and recorded "Susanna Lent," 45 years old, from Pennsylvania. He added "J W Lent," 21 years old, a "farmer," and then "Lewis, 11, NJ 8, and Robert [mistaken for Robison], 6." Next door to them lived their daughter, Maria, and her husband James Williams. Still a few more houses away was their other daughter, Mary Parmenter, and her husband Richard.[8]

When the anti-slavery candidate Abraham Lincoln was elected President in the 1860 presidential election, it became increasingly untenable for northerners to remain in the county. Some were calling Vernon County the "South Carolina" of Missouri. Susannah and her family knew that they had to seek a safer place to live, even when it meant abandoning their farm that was still mortgaged. She and her two daughters' families began preparations to move across the Kansas line, about 25 miles away as the crow flies.

Susannah's son Robison later told that his family moved to Bourbon County, Kansas, when he was seven years old. He turned seven on March 7, 1861, and they must have moved that spring. The winter of 1860-61 was a hard one with blizzards and heavy snows that broke what had been an 18-month drought, one so bad that people in the eastern states had sent Kansans clothing, seed, and other relief. Moving in the winter would likely have been too difficult. When older son John W. enlisted in the Army in October, he said his home was in Bourbon County, Kansas. All three families evidently moved between March and October, probably as an immediate response to the war's first shots in April. They were not alone. During that spring there was a heavy inflow of Missourians seeking refuge in Bourbon County.[9]

There were only a few miles of railroad in Kansas at the start of the war, and definitely none where they were going. For the nine members of the family, it meant loading whatever had not already been burned and plundered and walking, riding, and driving any livestock they still possessed over the rough dirt roads to Kansas. Susannah's daughter Maria was pregnant.[10] But there were now three men in the family to help: son John, and sons-in-law Richard and James. Quite possibly, other neighbors pulled out at the same time with them.

Susannah and the family may have guessed that Vernon and Bates County were destined for devastation in the Civil War tempest, but their new home in Bourbon County was not far from the storm's eye, either. Robison Lent told that the family moved to Xenia, a village about 18 miles as the crow flies, northwest of Ft. Scott, the county seat. Xenia had only been settled five years when they arrived in the spring of 1861, but it already had a general store and post office. During the Civil War, it was under the protection – as far as "protection" went in those days – of Ft. Scott, which had quickly become a big supply post for the Union Army (see Map F).

For several years Bourbon County had been a base for infamous jayhawkers such as Charles R. "Doc" Jennison and the Rev. James Montgomery, who launched bloody attacks against Missourians from their homes in Mound City, about 30 miles from the Lents' Missouri farm. Jennison was a physician who prior to the war roamed through southern Kansas driving proslavery settlers from the territory at the point of a gun. Among Jennison's and his band's victims in Bourbon County during the winter of 1860-61 were a pro-slavery man shot in his bed, an old man hanged in his own door yard, and two other men his band executed. Two were killed on the pretext that they had aided the return of runaway slaves, and another because he was "a little too conservative," as Jennison put it.

In the summer of 1861, as the Lents were trying set up their home in Kansas, Jennison and his men continued their raids up and down the border area of Missouri, plundering, tormenting and murdering citizens, Unionist and Secessionist alike. His Mound City neighbor, Methodist Minister James Montgomery, was a radical abolitionist who in 1858 participated in John Brown's attack that murdered people in the vicinity of the Lent farm. Montgomery returned from his forays, wagons brimming with plunder.

Jennison, Montgomery, and their followers were infused with the religious zeal of crusaders to end slavery. They thought themselves avengers of all the deeds Kansans had suffered at the hands of Missouri Border Ruffians. But in practice, they were little better than thieves and hoodlums. It possibly might even have been men from one of their Missouri raids who attacked and burned the Lent farm. When in Missouri, the jayhawkers did not always discriminate among slaveholders, non-slaveholders, or anyone else.

If Kansas and parts of Missouri were violently on different sides of the slavery issue prior to the war, the Civil War only accentuated the split. Two days after the shots at Fort Sumter, President Lincoln asked Missouri for 75,000 volunteers. Missouri Governor Claiborne Jackson, who sympathized with the Confederacy, refused. Lincoln asked Kansas for 16,600 volunteers. Of the 30,000 military aged men in Kansas, over 20,000 signed up. (Of these, sadly, 40% would become casualties.) On his own charge, Missouri Congressman Frank Blair resigned his seat in the House and began recruiting Missouri men for the Union.

Missouri, whose eastern, more populated counties were strongly Union, did not secede. But the result was civil war at its worst, with men from counties like Vernon, where 95% supported the South, combining into guerilla bands that furiously fought jayhawkers and Union soldiers. On both sides of the Missouri-Kansas border; every farm was a potential battlefield; every home was open for plunder; and every town was apt to get burned. This is the world Susannah and her family lived in every day.[11]

When Missouri governor Jackson refused support for the North, many Kansans began preparing against a possible invasion from Missouri. Jayhawker Jennison transformed his ruffian followers into the "Mound City Sharp's Rifle Guards" and assumed command as their captain. Kansas Governor Charles Robison called for militia companies to be organized into formal regiments. The 1st Kansas Volunteer Infantry Regiment formed at Fort Leavenworth in

May 1861, only a few weeks from the start of the war. Its men enlisted for only 90 days, a typical example of how expectations in the beginning of wars are always ridiculously short-sighted. A number of other regiments, including the 5th Kansas Volunteer Cavalry, were activated in early July.

No one waited long to go to battle. The first skirmish was on July 5 a few miles south of Nevada City. A few days later, just a few miles further south in Vernon County, the Battle of Carthage became the first large battle of the American Civil War. Still another early engagement took place in Bourbon County, the Lents' new home. On Sunday, September 1, when "Rev." jayhawker Col. Montgomery was leading church services for his men near Fort Scott, 800 Confederate soldiers swept down on a herd of Union horses grazing along the nearby river bottoms. They scattered the herders and drove 90-100 mules to their camp across the border in Missouri. When Montgomery heard what was happening, he closed the service without a benediction, calling out, "the rebel Philistines were upon them," took off his robes, and buckled on his revolvers to charge off after the rebels.[12]

In the beginning of August, Kansas's newly elected U.S. Senator James Lane arrived at Fort Scott to transform the jayhawker bands, along with fresh recruits, into a new regular army. Fort Scott was an old US Army dragoon post set up in the 1840s to protect the Santa Fe Trail. It was decommissioned in the 1850s, but with the new war, it was again bustling with activity. Thousands of troops were continually coming and going, and long trains of Union supplies were passing through. The fort's commissary department was soon stacked with supplies, and from its corrals brayed a thousand mules.

At Fort Scott, Lane began filling the ranks of several of the new regiments, the 3rd, 4th, 5th, and 7th. Among the Lane's recruits was James Butler Hickok, known in Western lore as "Wild Bill Hickok," who would later become a Union scout and spy in Missouri. Jayhawkers Jennison and Montgomery were appointed colonels and commanders of the 7th and 3rd Regiments. The 3rd, 4th, and 5th cavalry regiments became known as the Kansas Brigade, or more often as "Lane's Brigade," and Lane himself took command of it.[13]

In this mobilizing atmosphere, it would have been difficult for the men in Susannah's family, John W, Richard, and James, not to sign up. Perhaps one of them might have stayed home to help the women and children. But which one? It is always important to understand the enthusiasm people feel during the first few weeks and months of any war. If they were like their neighbors, the Lent boys were probably excited to join up with the large majority of eligible men in Kansas.

Maybe they could rely on some of their new neighbors to support their families. Maybe they, too, thought the war might be over within 90 days. Maybe the family needed the money the three of them could send home from their slim army pay. Maybe for them, like for most people, reason and common sense were poor cousins when it came to war. However it was, they joined Company K of the 5th Kansas Volunteer Cavalry as soon as the summer and harvest were over.

With the Kansas Fifth Cavalry

Not far from Fort Scott was a smaller garrison called Fort Lincoln that Senator Lane set up at the end of August 1861 (See Map F). A few weeks later, when Confederate troops starting menacing Fort Scott, Lane moved 1200 troops and most of Fort Scott's citizen population to Fort Lincoln. After the threat subsided, he brought most of the troops back to Fort Scott leaving about 300 men to defend the small fort. This was about this time the Lent boys joined up. John and Richard mustered at Fort Lincoln on October 1. James enlisted there the following week.[14]

John was 23, of medium height at 5'7", and had light hair, blue eyes and a fair complexion. His sister Mary Elizabeth's husband Richard was tall and dark, standing 6 feet tall with dark eyes and hair. Maria's husband, James Williams, at 27, was the oldest of the three, and also stood 6 feet tall with auburn hair and blue eyes. He was a new father. James's and Maria's son, James Frank, was born right after they arrived in Kansas.[15]

The three were like boys and young men all over America, North and South, that summer and fall: tall and not so tall, light complexioned and dark, single, married, fathers, and sons, young men needed at home by their mothers, wives, children, and friends. They were leaving for a war grislier than they imagined, riding tall, smiling, and hoping to be home soon with stories to tell of their adventures. And like elsewhere in America, some would not return.

In the 5th Kansas Volunteer Cavalry, one of the three regiments in the "Lane Brigade," regimental officers were often former jayhawkers who had raided Missouri homes and farms over the previous few years. The Lane Brigade men were enlisted for three years, or until the end of the war, whichever came first. They visited the warehouse at Fort Scott to get equipment and clothing to last a year. Their meager wage was $13 a month – when they got paid. Richard wrote home to Mary Elizabeth in February 1862, saying they had not been paid in six months and were yet to get their first paycheck.[16]

The 7th Kansas, under infamous jayhawker Jennison, and the Lane Brigade's three were active almost from the moment they were created. For Jennison, the war and his new command simply legitimized the raids and atrocities he had been committing over previous years. The Lane Brigade was not quite as notorious as Jennison's 7th, but during the summer of 1861, before the Lent men joined, the four regiments roamed western Missouri burning and pillaging civilian farms, homes, and towns.

Jayhawker vengeance in a blue uniform was ugly. On August 25, when Confederate General Price took his army into Vernon County where the Kansas regiments had been widely operating, they found "the country for twenty miles laid waste, the inhabitants plundered, several persons killed, and the people in much alarm for their safety."[17]

On September 22, the week before the Lent men joined their unit, the Lane Brigade rode into Osceola, Missouri to loot and impress wagons to carry their plunder. Lane supervised a drumhead court-martial and nine private citizens were shot. The courthouse and all but three houses were burned to ashes. Lane pivoted north telling the men, "Everything disloyal from a Shanghai rooster to a Durham cow, must be cleared out." One soldier from Jennison's 7th

246

Kansas wrote, "Every house along our line of march but one was burned, and off on our left flank for miles, columns of smoke from burning houses and barns could be seen."[18]

The mayhem and carnage were not one-sided. Confederates and southern-sympathizing guerillas who became known as "bushwhackers" were responsible for their own outrages. During the Lent family's first summer in Kansas, Confederate leader John Matthews organized a band of Osage, Quapaw, and Cherokee Indians into a raiding party. They rampaged throughout the nearby area killing at least 16 settlers.

In the beginning of September Matthews attacked the town of Humboldt, 40 miles west of Xenia. Most of the town's men were off to war, and the Indian marauders plundered businesses and residences almost unopposed. The raiders took all the money and valuables they found. They also kidnapped eight free Blacks who were said to have then been sold into slavery.[19]

Living close to Fort Lincoln with its small contingent of soldiers might or might not have been reassuring to Susannah. The soldiers could perhaps deter some bushwhacker attacks like those of Matthews' Indians. On the other hand, a small Bluecoat post was an alluring target for larger Confederate infiltrations. I doubt the Lent family ever knew a feeling of safety. Even in Xenia, they were near the epicenter of a guerilla war.

In addition to the warfare was the unending lawlessness typical of Wild West stories. In July 1862, a man named Rub Forbes robbed the store at Xenia. The neighborhood quickly launched a posse after Forbes and his partner, Troy Dye. Dye got away, but the posse soon had Forbes surrounded in a brush patch. When they charged, Forbes killed the head of the posse and his deputy. Finally, a company of soldiers arrived. They fired into the brush, and Forbes was dead.[20]

Later the month they joined, the Lent men went on the first big patrol, scouting out Vernon and a couple of neighboring counties. They captured some Confederate officers and men, and a herd of horses and cattle that they brought back with them to Fort Lincoln. But most of the 5th Kansas's summer and fall fighting was over for the year. They had a few rest days at Fort Lincoln near home and then went into winter quarters at Camp Denver, near Barnesville, Kansas. They were only 20 miles from their families in Xenia. All considered, it was not too bad a start.

While at Camp Denver, the regiment received new and badly needed leadership when Lt. Col. Powell Clayton took command. "New life and energy were infused into every department," wrote one of the senior officers. In March they moved to a site south of Ft. Scott where they spent their time drilling.[21]

Richard wrote Mary Elizabeth that all three were "well and harty" and that "the wether is nice and warm." They had not heard from the family. He complained, "I don't ever get any leters. I don't know but what you all are dead." He teased, "If you al are Dead I shal have to git Some one else to write." He was also concerned about how the women were getting by and asked, "I want you to give me all of the news in Particular and let me no how things Prosper and how People thinks the War is going." The family was probably still unsettled and seeking a permanent place to live, for Richard also inquired, "whether you got a Place or not" and whether people had been "loyal enough to try to help a Soldiers family and see that they have a home."[22]

It was not easy for the three of them to be away, even when not skirmishing and cheating death. But Richard's letter shows how difficult it was for the family as well. Neither side knew for sure whether the other was alive. He rightly worried that the family was struggling to find a place to live and secure enough food to eat during the long Kansas winter. Everyone also was probably beginning to realize that the war was going to be much longer and bloodier than expected.

For the 5th Kansas, winter was soon over and so were the drills. On March 17, 1862, the regiment's men and their mounts filed from their quarters south of Ft. Scott and into Missouri. A typical full-strength Civil War cavalry regiment had twelve companies of 100 men each, making it over a thousand strong. A colonel commanded the regiment. A captain was in charge of each company. Few regiments were at full strength during the war, but the 5th Kansas numbered several hundred well-armed and coordinated men on

248

horseback. It cast a formidable presence whenever it rode into a Missouri-sized town.[23]

The young Lent men had been in the 5th for over six months now. It had been relatively quiet so far, but the worst was ahead: nonstop fighting, skirmishes, and all the rest that went with them. From talking with their more seasoned colleagues over the winter months, they probably realized how the Lane Brigade's operations the previous summer and fall were not the classical kind. Civilians and innocents had been equally in the line of fire. They also knew that the Missouri bushwhackers and other guerilla units were similarly guilty of atrocities, and quite possibly responsible for what had happened to their own family before they fled Missouri. Probably to the regiment's men, one side's misdeeds cancelled out the other's.

The 5th reached the vicinity of Carthage, Missouri, a day later. Carthage, the scene of the Civil War's first large battle, was still a knot of southern sympathizers. As the regiment drew near, it learned that an assembly had been called in the town the next day to organize a guerrilla company. The following morning at daybreak Col. Clayton, a "big, fine looking fellow," sent a company under Capt. William Creitz galloping toward the town. They made the outskirts of Carthage by mid-afternoon. The rest of the regiment plodded through a blinding snowstorm to arrive close to sundown about two hours behind. Creitz's Company A had already charged the town center and rounded up about 20 "prominent rebels." Among them was a representative from the Confederate legislature of Missouri. It was a quick and relatively non-violent encounter.

The men spent nearly a month around Carthage and left a good account of themselves. One of the townspeople said, "They gave the impression of being well drilled, efficient troops." The soldiers discovered 225 bushels of wheat at a mill outside of town, and during much of their time in Carthage, they threshed and ground wheat into flour that they sent to Ft. Scott. On April 10th the men were ordered to Springfield, the capital of Missouri. They spent another month there and occupied their days with drilling and more drilling. They actually became quite good, "exceeding any other cavalry regiment at the post."[24]

249

Over the nearly eight months the Lent men had been in the 5th, the regiment had trained, sharpened up, and become professional. That was not true for Jennison's 7th Cavalry and others in the Lane Brigade. Their deprivations had grown totally out of control, and word of this had reached Washington. In February, Union area commander Hunter placed Kansas under martial law, mainly in an attempt to control the blue-coated jayhawker soldiers who were now feared by some in Kansas as much as they were in Missouri.

General Henry Halleck, commander-in-chief of all Federal armies, complained that the Kansas troops "are no better than a band of robbers; they cross the line, rob, steal, plunder, and burn whatever they can lay hands upon. They disgrace the name and uniform of American soldiers and are driving good Union men into the ranks of the secession army." One of those driven into rebel ranks was Henry Younger, originally a pro-Union Missouri stockman whose ranch was close to the Lents' abandoned farm. After Jennison's 7th took $4,000 worth of Henry's wagons and 40 saddle horses, his sons Cole and Jim Younger joined up with Quantrill's rebel guerillas. After the war ended, Cole and Jim transitioned out of the rebel army to become part of the notorious Jesse James gang.[25]

The Union Army finally decided that the only way to control Lane's and Jennison's men was to get them out of Kansas and Missouri. Jennison's 7th Kansas Cavalry was sent to Mississippi. The Kansas 5th Cavalry was earmarked for the war in Arkansas. On June 18, the main body of the 5th Kansas started their march south.

A detachment of the 5th, under Capt. Creitz, remained behind to escort a 30-wagon freight train carrying ammunition and other supplies. It was due to arrive any day from St. Louis. They ended up waiting ten days for the wagons and finally escorted the munitions train on its way. When they reached Houston, Missouri, two days later, the detachment found most the men from the 5th's Company K as well as others from Company D waiting to top up the escort. John W., Richard, and James were among Capt. Creitz's 200 cavalrymen.[26]

The next morning, they pulled out and rode 80 miles along a desolate road crossing the border to Salem, Arkansas. On the 4th of

July, they stopped in a grove, rested, sang The Star-Spangled Banner, and "jayhawked a keg of bourbon, for medical purposes." The column expected to find the rest of 5ᵗʰ Kansas waiting for them in Salem. Instead, there was only a note saying the regiment had marched south the previous week. It ordered the detachment to make haste to join them in Batesville, Arkansas, about 50 miles further south.

When the train resumed its trek on July 6, John rode in the advance with other men of his company. Just four miles out of town they surprised a force of 200 rebels. The Lent boys and the rest of the company launched into an attack, scattering the Confederate force, killing six, and taking three prisoners with no losses of their own.

The detachment was now moving deeper into the South and its men knew there was a large Confederate force between them and where they were going.   When apprised of the danger the detachment faced, the commander of Union forces in Arkansas, General Samuel Curtis, sent a messenger ordering them back to Rolla, Missouri. The messenger was captured before he ever got through. So, the men of the detachment kept riding south, unsure of the situation before them. They were a conspicuous target – the column of wagons, mules, and cavalrymen probably extended a mile in length.

The next day they found a company of bushwhackers inside a house along the roadside. The rebels were dividing up plunder they had seized from the Union army a few days before. The Lents and men of the detachment swooped in to capture the rebel guerillas before they could resist. Creitz appropriated whatever goods were useful and burned the rest. The column continued its march south with the bushwhacker prisoners walking on foot.

When the munitions train neared Batesville, Creitz heard that the 5ᵗʰ had already moved on from there as well. Instead, the town was crowded with a force of Texas Rangers. The Blue column quickly skirted the town and kept rolling night and day toward Jacksonport where Gen. Curtis and his army were supposed to be camped. But the Confederate units in Batesville learned of the Union train and were soon on the chase.

The Federal detachment kept a relentless pace forward with the Texans somewhere on their tail. They only had about 25 miles to go when at about 4:00 p.m. the next day the train reached the Black River (see Map F). The wagons needed to ford it quickly. Half the men were positioned on the far bank to protect the crossing while the wagons were loaded onto a ferry. Each of the 30 wagons was drawn by a 6-mule team, making 180 freight mules plus the detachment's own mounts. The boat was small and could only carry ten horses at a time. That made a lot of crossings. This was a moment of serious vulnerability.

They were not able to get the column across before the Texans found them. Right in the middle of the operation, a cry rang from men covering the rear, "Secesh! Secesh!" a term for "rebel" derived from "secessionist." The men waiting to cross jumped to their feet to meet the 15th Texas Rangers who were in full attack.

The Kansas men were scattered about, some even down in the river bathing. The skinny-dippers did not even have time to dress but grabbed their rifles in the buff. Clothes or no, they ferociously returned fire from behind the trees and in the ravines. One of the Kansas 5th's strengths was its superior firepower. Their Sharps Carbines, though single shot, could fire 8-10 times a minute with renowned accuracy. The unit was "a terror to the Secesh," wrote a 5th Kansas private.[27]

In the midst of the firefight, one Texan officer, a Captain Johnson (some of the men's accounts of this battle called him a colonel), shouted to the 5th to surrender. The Kansans' response was to shoot him dead. The action was intense and lasted just over an hour. For a while the rebels took over the train. The 5th Kansas men soon routed the attackers, however, driving them several miles, killing 18, and capturing their hospital, several guns and horses. One Kansas trooper drowned, two were severely wounded, and two were taken prisoner. Afterwards, the Bluecoat detachment was proud and considered it a "gallant fight." They had no time to celebrate. Once the skirmish was over, they resumed ferrying and had everything across the river by 10:00 that night.

Once in Jacksonport, the detachment discovered again they were still isolated behind the main body of troops. General Curtis's army had departed several days before. This time there was no note waiting with orders on which direction they should take. The town's southerners refused to say where the Union soldiers were headed.

John, Richard, and James and all the men of the Creitz detachment had shown they were a crack outfit well able to defend themselves, but the unit was a relatively small one carrying tons of ammunition, deep in rebel territory. They had to find General Curtis's force as quickly as possible. Capt. Creitz asked for two troopers to ride out in search of the Curtis army and to carry a verbal message asking for immediate reinforcements. John W and another Company K man, Jacob Eby, stepped forward as volunteers.

It was a dangerous mission, two union soldiers in a sea of southern troops and sympathizers. They had to move fast and not to expect help from anyone met along the road. It was just the opposite: everyone who saw them was a probable enemy. John W and Eby provisioned up and at 2:00 in the morning reined their houses southward in the direction where they hoped to find the rear of the Curtis army.

At first, the road was dark, and they were less likely to be discovered. It was July, however, and the nights were short. After only a few hours, the horizon brightened and soon sunlight flooded the entire countryside. They kept riding, but a little more warily. It was much more difficult to avoid being seen.

John W and Jacob Eby almost made it to Augusta, 35 miles away, when at some point along the winding dirt road, Confederates jumped before them and ordered them to halt. Mounted as they were, they might have tried an escape, but it must have been a vulnerable spot with more than a few muskets aimed at them. They had been going in the right direction, but were still 50 miles away from the Union Army when they were forced to surrender. After their capture, John and Eby were taken to Little Rock.

Meanwhile, the wagons with their escorts pulled out, hastily wheeling forward through hostile territory. On July 12th they came across two friendly squadrons from the Iowa 4th Cavalry, and finally on the 14th the train reached the remainder of the regiment and other units of the Union Army of the Southwest, now camped on the Mississippi near Helena, Arkansas. It was a heroic several days, with heavy fighting, all the while encumbered with a wagon train.

General Curtis's army had given up the detachment for lost, and everyone, especially their fellow troopers of the Kansas 5th, were delighted to see them when they pulled into camp. Division Commander Osterhaus personally congratulated the regiment for its remarkable bravery and skill on the difficult nearly 400-mile drive south. The men set up their tents in Helena, and soon learned that John W and Jacob Eby were taken prisoners while searching for the Curtis army.[28]

At this point in the Civil War neither side was equipped to deal with large numbers of captured troops. Instead, the two sides arranged regular prisoner exchanges. The North and South formalized the prisoner exchange process the same month John was taken prisoner, July, 1862. Under the arrangement, any prisoner not exchanged within 10 days was "paroled." John W, Eby and those taken prisoner at the Black River skirmish were all paroled. In practice this meant they could return to their regiment, but not engage in fighting until an exchange with their names on it was processed. The prisoner exchange system collapsed the next year, greatly because the South refused to return Black American prisoners.

Well before then, however, John returned to the 5th, now stationed in Arkansas. Since he was promoted to Corporal on August 2, we know John spent less than a month in Confederate hands. He was no less for the wear and tear. Prisoners in Little Rock were reasonably handled. One paroled trooper, who got back to the 5th about the same time as John, told that he was "treated as well as could be expected, although the fare was rather poor, but it was the same as they had themselves."[29]

Through the fall and winter, the 5th Kansas made contact weekly if not daily with rebel cavalry. Col. Powell Clayton turned the men into a reliable, hard fighting regiment. They also had a reputation for ruthlessness toward the local population who feared them for the merciless burning and pillaging of homes during their regular patrols to the Arkansas regions around Helena. In this way they still harbored the character that Lane had instilled into his brigade.

Maj. Samuel Walker, who commanded most of their patrols, earned them a good deal of this reputation. Before the war began, Walker was an active jayhawker and raided Missouri alongside Jennison and others of his neighbors. Walker was so hated that Missouri's governor had placed $500 on Walker's head for his jayhawking. Nevertheless, the men liked Walker. One told, "When his soldiers are hungry, he tells them to pitch in and what they find to eat, to take."[30]

Their life was hard but never dull. One day a Confederate Captain and six privates from the Texas Rangers rode into camp under a flag of truce. They were carrying a message from one commander to the other. The rebels and the boys from the 5th joined in conversations and traded blankets and spurs. After a relaxed few hours, the rebels rode out, and all were once again enemies.

Another time, a 5th Kansas patrol stopped at a farm where one of the men grabbed a turkey. The farmer's teenaged daughter was so angry at the trooper that she picked up a brick and threw it at the man, hitting him in the back of the neck. The soldier dropped the turkey. Rather than shooting someone – or burning the family out – he walked over to the girl and gave her "six or eight smacking kisses as ever you heard, in the presence of her mother and sister... After she had been kissed, she ran into the house. That is what I call returning good for evil," one of the troopers wrote home.[31]

The Lent men and the 5th Kansas mounted their horses and rode out of Helena one morning in early May 1863, to spearhead an expedition that would reveal how good the regiment's fighting ability really was. Moving through the Arkansas countryside, they destroyed every house, farm and all the domesticated animals they found. This time, however, the pillaging was done under orders, similar to Sherman's march to Atlanta or Sheridan's devastation of the Shenandoah Valley. One of task force's primary objectives was to destroy forage, food, and other supplies for Confederate General John Marmaduke who was trying to establish a presence in eastern Arkansas. Nevertheless, it was just the type of thing Maj. Walker enjoyed, and he led the burning with a vengeance. The raids are still remembered as some of the worst in Phillips County during the Civil War. The 5th Illinois Cavalry rode behind the 5th Kansas.

Gen. Marmaduke responded to the news of the Union cavalry's raids along the old Madison Road by quickly commanding several units to encircle and destroy them. He had by far the numerical advantage. Marmaduke's men caught up with the Kansas and Illinois cavalrymen when they were 130 miles out from their Helena camp. About 5:00 in the afternoon of May 11, a squad of Company K troopers were on a road near the small town of Mt. Vernon (see Map F). Sgt. Jacob Eby – the same one captured and paroled with John W. the summer before – and another man were sent to scout the road. Rounding a curve, they came face-to-face with 700 rebels marching straight toward them. The Confederates were part of an entire brigade, about 1600 strong.

The Company K men jumped from their horses and deployed in the heavy timber alongside the road, each man behind a tree. Their sergeant ordered them to start firing their Lefaucheaux revolvers to produce enough smoke to disguise the small size of their group. Soon Lt. Col. Wilton Jenkins and the rest of the men of the 5th Kansas were up alongside, 40 of them lying behind a large oak tree that a storm had toppled across the road.

The Lent men were in the trees, just to the right of the fallen tree trunk. Jenkins did not take cover but bravely sat on top his horse, squarely in the middle of the dirt road. For the moment, the 5th Kansas was alone. The 5th Illinois was in camp eating about five miles behind them. With only 325 men, the Lents and fellow Kansans were hugely outnumbered. With the first shot, Jenkins rushed a courier to get the 5th Illinois up as reinforcements.

Jenkins yelled to his men, "Reserve your fire, men, until they are close on you, and then let every shot tell." John, Richard, and James

256

did not have to wait long before the Confederates attack. The Twenty-first Texas Rangers charged screaming their Rebel yell and blasting away with double-barreled shotguns. The 5th Kansas boys waited until the Texans were only 30-40 yards away and then opened up with their Sharps carbines.

Under the withering fire, the Texas horsemen broke left and right, leaving dead and wounded on the road. They fell back just before reaching the 5th Kansas lines. The Confederates kept a constant fire toward the Union soldiers while the Texans re-grouped to charge again. All this time Jenkins sat astride his horse on the road while shots whizzed by. Once more, he ordered the men to wait. Again, the Texans charged. When the horsemen were only 30 yards off, he yelled, "Give it to them, boys, and fire low!" That they did, and the 21st Texans retreated another time from the hail of lead.

In the midst of all this, the Kansans experienced something remarkable. During the second Texas charge, a freed a slave named Buck, who was acting as a guide for the 5th, stood up in the thick of the fire. When Private Hurd took a bullet in the thigh, Buck grabbed his fallen Sharps rifle, threw off his hat, and "faught as brave as the bravest and was known to have shot at least one of the Rebels." This was the first time the 5th had had a Black American fight with them.

The 21st Texas attempted a third charge, but only made it part of the way when they realized its futility. The Kansas men would not budge, and just as the third charge was getting underway, the Illinois 5th arrived. For the moment the rebels called off the attack.

It was now dusk, and the Union cavalry mounted a long but successful night withdrawal toward the main Union Army. The Lents and their buddies of their much smaller force had won a stalemate that stymied Marmaduke's efforts to set up a base of operations. By the time it was over, the Kansans had lost only one killed and a few wounded. The Texans suffered heavy casualties especially among their officers: two captains and three lieutenants were dead. "The exact number of their losses we never knew," wrote one of the 5th's officers, but if they had not been high, the 5th would have never withstood the odds.[32]

The battles in eastern Arkansas continued one after another, with John, James, Richard and their 5th Kansas Regiment in the thick of it most of the time. On July 4, Marmaduke attacked Helena, but the Yanks beat him back. After Grant's victory at Vicksburg, Union Maj. General Frederick Steele was dispatched from Sherman's XV Corps to mount an attack on Little Rock, Arkansas. On the 15th of August, 1863, the Lent men saddled and pulled out of Helena with the rest of the 5th Kansas to join the action. At 4:00 on September 10, they raised Old Glory once again over the Arkansas capital.

After the surrender of Little Rock, Col. Clayton received a new mission to command a brigade made up of the 5th Kansas and the 1st Indiana on a 90-mile march to take Pine Bluff, Arkansas. Along the way, the 350 men of the Fifth launched a surprise attack on a rebel outpost at Tulip, near Pine Bluff. They made a furious charge through the rebel lines at the same moment artillery opened up on the camp. The brigade routed the entire 600-rebel force and captured all its arms, tents, wagons, supplies, and equipment, without losing one man. They rode their horses triumphantly into Pine Bluff.[33]

A few days later Marmaduke tried to re-take Pine Bluff with 3,000 men – against the 600 men of the Powell brigade. Early in the morning, a rebel officer carrying a flag of truce road up slowly to the Union lines and summoned Col. Clayton to surrender. Lt. Clark of the Kansas 5th met the officer to receive their demand. Looking him square in the eye, Lt. Clark rebuffed the Confederate, responding that there was no need to go to the colonel. "Anyone who knew him could answer for him, that he never surrenders."

The battle commenced and raged from nine in the morning to three in the afternoon when the rebels finally gave up with about 150 killed and wounded and the loss of 30 prisoners. The Fifth's Major Scudder proudly called the men, "the gallant 600." The Brigade suffered 37 casualties, of which 27 came from the Fifth.

Christmas brought a welcome quiet, and John W, Richard, James and the men of the 5th enjoyed what for them was a real feast, with roast turkey, pies, cakes, and more. It "...made us think of the many comforts we had left at home, and long for the time when this cruel war is over, that we can return to our homes, and not be disturbed by war's rude alarm," one of the troopers wrote to his father.[34]

The End of It

It was now exactly two years since the John, Richard, and James had joined the 5th Kansas Cavalry. They had seen the best and worst of it – by now, much more of the latter than the former. Probably, if asked about their experiences, they would have simply said they wanted to go home. James had a son, now almost two and a half years old, whom he had hardly seen. Richard's bride was still waiting for him to return. And John W must have realized how much his mother Susannah needed his help. His younger brother Lewis, who was only 12 when he left for the Army was now 14; Nancy Jane was 11, and Robison, only 9-years old.

The three of them had started and lived the war together, maybe introducing themselves as "brothers-in-law." Having experienced so much together, they must have been very close, more than just brothers-in-law. From the beginning of this adventure, they had known that the odds of all of them returning home together one day were not high. In war, glory and tragedy travel the same road. There may be good times that people reminisce about and relive the rest of their lives. But there are also the terrors that soldiers do not share with their grandchildren. Then, there are the memories that do not escape the war. They just stop, truncated, victims of one of the most tragic of human outcomes.

Initially, the 5th Kansas settled in at Pine Bluff to enjoy a short lull in the fighting. Some of the men occasionally got away from Pine Bluff. Lt. Joseph Trego of Co. D wrote his wife in January that he had "visited the St. L [Louis] Theater twice to see 'Booth' in Richard III." He was referring to the then famous and later infamous actor John Wilkes Booth.[35]

In March 1864, activity grew a little more intense, but the Fifth Kansas continued to distinguish itself. A detachment of 100 men, returning from a mission to destroy a bridge, captured a Confederate wagon train. The men reached their camp in Pine Bluff with 318 prisoners, 300 horses and mules, and 100-200 wagons they had confiscated. It only lost two killed, two wounded, and eight taken prisoners.

Fate also struck the opposite direction. In April, Gen. Steele sent a train of 240 wagons from his headquarters in Camden, Arkansas, to pick up supplies in Pine Bluff. A train this large made a long procession: the wagons, alone, could run nearly two miles in length. With its escort units in the front and rear, it was well beyond that. About 150 cavalrymen from Pine Bluff were dispatched on April 25 to meet the train, among them a small detachment from the Fifth Kansas. James Williams was one of them. Over his two years in the 5th, James had been promoted and now wore a sergeant's stripes.

Including the Pine Bluff cavalrymen, there were about 1,800 Union escorts with another 520 troops following at a short distance. Unbeknownst to the train and its escorts, a Confederate force of about 4,000-5,000 men was waiting to strike them at the intersection of Camden and Warren roads, a place called Mark's Mill. The stretched-out train was just emerging from a muddy swamp when the rebels launched their surprise attack. When the fighting began, James and the 5th Kansas men led by Lieutenants Jennings and McCarty were just arriving from Pine Bluff in support. They had one cannon with them, a howitzer.

James and the other mounted men rushed into the fight, skirmishing with the rebels at the place where the massed rebel attack smashed into the wagon train broadside. The fighting was frantic. After five hours, ammunition was low, the Union column was surrounded, and the segmented Union units began to surrender. Casualties were high on both sides. But the Union took by far the most, about 1500 casualties. Most were prisoners who were forced on a 52-mile march to a Confederate prison camp in Tyler, Texas.[36]

Both 5th Kansas lieutenants and most of their men were among the prisoners. James and a number of Kansans were able to avoid being captured, but at some point, he was seriously wounded. It is not clear whether he made it back to Pine Bluff on his own. About 190 soldiers from the battle did. But many of the Pine Bluff men were still missing. Col. Powell Clayton immediately sent help under a flag of truce, and some of the missing were found wounded on the battlefield. James could have been among them.

We do know, however, that he was still alive when they got him to medical care at Pine Bluff. With no notion of germ theory and possessing nothing like antibiotics, any medical procedure during the Civil War was necessarily crude. What could be cut off easily, was piled in stacks outside the medical tents. Beyond that, what was possible was limited. I never found how James was wounded, nor whether it was the wound or the ensuing infection that brought an end to his Civil War. For four days he suffered, with his brothers-in-law John and Richard nearby. Sgt. James F. Williams died of the wounds he suffered at the Battle of Marks Mills on April 29, 1864.[37]

We can only imagine the impact James's loss had on John and Richard. For two and a half years, they lived almost every day together. Now, they would suffer the rest of this long and dreary war without him. However deep their mourning that day, the tragedy could not have been felt more deeply than when word of his loss reached Xenia, Kansas. There, Maria and Frank, the little boy that James never had time to know, were left without a husband and father. It was sadly too common a story in Civil War America, one that played out hundreds of times a day as the war drug on.

Maria would one day re-marry, and she and her new husband would have their own children. James's son Frank died when he was about 18 years old. I have found no record of how or why. James was left with no posterity of his own, no memories to carry down from generation to generation. There were no curious great-great-grandchildren combing Civil War records to find what he did in that great war. Memories of Sgt. James Williams, who gave his life for his country, are pretty much told here, in this story.

By summer 1864, John and Richard had been in Pine Bluff over ten months. Some of the men considered it the "prettiest town" they had been in during the war. Even though many of the local townspeople saw the soldiers as part of a scorned occupying force, the men were young men, the local women were young women, and socializing was common. Over twenty of the soldiers found wives and were married there. Whatever its merits, though, Pine Bluff was surrounded by a bayou and swamp, and was a sickly place, especially during the hot summer.

By June, there was an air of excitement running through the regiment. For its men, the war was nearly over. Not that the Civil War, itself, was close to an end, but the completion date of the 5th Kansas cavalrymen's enlistment was approaching. They had mustered the summer of 1861 to serve through the end of the war, or for three years, whichever came sooner. A few men decided to reenlist and were able to return home on furlough. Most did not. The officers, themselves, did not press reenlistment. One soldier wrote his father, "They are worn out, having been in the advance and on the out-posts, in active duty all the time."[38]

The Bitter-Sweet Return Home

John and Richard knew that these years had also been difficult and dangerous for Susannah and her two daughters, Mary and Maria. Unlike most people in the North, their home was in the middle of the war. Raids and skirmishes went on almost every day in Kansas and Missouri, not just between guerillas and troops. There were also Indian bands that often violently fought with or against both sides. Only about 60 miles from Xenia, 150 Osage warriors massacred a party of Colorado men led by gunslinger Charley Harrison. Harrison and his friends had just received commissions as Confederate officers and were on their way back to Denver to lead Southern sympathizers. The Osage took scalps, but since Charlie was bald, he lost his luxuriant beard instead.

In February 1864, the Kansas 7th Cavalry under the notorious Col Jennison returned from Mississippi to camp near Xenia. Many Kansans were not happy to see them back saying, "they would about as soon the bushwhackers would come."[39] Everyone knew how Jennison's men plundered both sides the border.

Jennison showed up in his hometown, Mound City, and demanded the local doctor's home for himself. The doctor asked for $100, which townspeople collected for him, and Jennison moved in while the doctor's family moved out. Once back in Kansas, the 7th picked up some new recruits, among them 18-year old William

Cody, later known as Buffalo Bill, who wrote "…after having been under the influence of bad whiskey, I awoke to find myself a soldier in the 7th Kansas. I did not remember how or when I had enlisted."

Meanwhile, all along the Kansas-Missouri border Southern-sympathizing bushwhacker war lords attacked both soldiers and civilians. William Quantrill in a brutal raid in Aubrey, Kansas shot down unarmed civilians in cold blood. During the summer of 1863, his guerillas raided Kansas's second largest city, Lawrence, executing nearly every man and boy over 14 years old and leaving behind 150-200 dead.

In response to the Lawrence massacre, General Thomas Ewing, Union commander of the District of the Border, issued Order No. 11 that commanded citizens in northern Vernon County and neighboring Bates, Cass, and Jackson counties to leave the district. All grain and forage left in those places after 15 days was destroyed. Overnight the area became known as the "Burnt District."

"Bloody Bill Anderson," a man grislier than Quantrill and a collaborator with fellow bushwhackers Jesse and Frank James, broke off Quantrill's raiders to lead his own band on a spree of even greater atrocities throughout the Kansas and Missouri area. Early in the war, Union troops almost captured Anderson in Vernon County. He escaped, but one of his band, A. I. Baker, was caught and imprisoned for a time in Fort Lincoln, almost next door to Susannah and her daughters.[40]

Life in eastern Kansas was dangerous, and also hard. Amidst all the ravage and plunder, the cost of food was sky high. The Lent women had to pay $6 for 100 pounds of flour. Butter sold for 25-30 cents a pound, and eggs were 25-30 cents a dozen – if they had money to buy these things at all. Remember, John W, Richard, and James signed up initially at a monthly salary of $13 a month. Men in the 5th Kansas sent home as much of their pay as they could, but logistics were extremely difficult. And $13 did not go far.[41]

Susannah and her daughters had to grow as much food and raise as many animals as possible to survive. One Kansas 5th wife living near them wrote to her husband, "I have had a very good garden this summer, the children and I planted and worked it ourselves… I think I shall have nearly enuf [sic] potatoes to do us through the winter... It is very hard work and I am very tired."[42] If Susannah and the family could produce a little more than they needed, they could have extra pocket money. Lewis and Robison provided some male support. But without the adult men at home, life was meager, just surviving, and a challenge.

A single widowed mother of three children at home and the mother of two married daughters with husbands off to war, Susannah agreed to marry John Moyer in the summer of 1863. John was a farmer, and was 65-years old, much older than Susannah, only 47. Like Susannah, John was a widower. His first wife, Lydia, had died a few years earlier. He was a cooper by profession, making crates and barrels. Susannah and the smaller children Nancy Jane, Lewis, and Robison moved to live on John's farm near Xenia. There, their lives became easier and more secure.[43]

While their families struggled back in Kansas, John and Richard looked forward to getting out of the Army later the summer of 1864. At first, it was not sure whether the regiment would process out all together on the 12th of August, or by company, in which case it would start earlier. The huge losses at Marks Mill, where James was killed, made the Union presence in Arkansas much more difficult to sustain.

At the same time there was concern over a last-ditch Confederate invasion of Missouri and Kansas by Confederate General Sterling Price. With his expected offensive on the horizon, all Federal units were urgently needed back home. The Kansas 5th Cavalry started moving out of Pine Bluff in July and August. By August 22nd, the Regiment had all moved to Little Rock and were on their way back to Missouri and Kansas to fight Price's rebel army.[44]

John W. was not among them. In the beginning of July, he had taken severely ill. It is not certain what disabled him, but it was probably malaria ("ague" or "brain fever," as it was called then), diarrhea, or something similar. Surrounded by water and swamps, Pine Bluff was a devastating place in the summer. Malaria, typhoid, and dysentery killed far more men of the 5th Kansas than the rebels ever did. In Company A, for example, 28 men died during their service in the Kansas 5th Cavalry, 22 of them from diseases such as typhoid and malaria. Three of that company's men died of "chronic diarrhea" from mid-July to August 30 when John's situation also became critical.

Instead of joining the long-awaited return home, John W, on July 16, slipped away from the Army, the war, and his family. They took his body to Little Rock and buried him there a few days later. The grave still stands today in Little Rock National Cemetery. It was sorrowful for everyone, especially for Richard, who now was the only one left of the three young men who proudly started out to war together. Only a few months after James's loss, now John was gone.

When Richard and the others of the 5th Kansas reached Missouri, rebel General Price's army was on the move and everything in a state of emergency mobilization. Richard could not yet return to Mary Elizabeth. General Price's invasion with three divisions especially threatened the Missouri-Kansas border areas. Martial law was declared, and the governor of Kansas called up every man between 18 and 60. At Ft. Scott, 1,050 men were mustered into the Army. For once, Susannah's family was spared. Lewis was too young, and her new husband John was too old to report for duty.

Susannah and her family, however, were almost as close to the fighting as they would have been had they all been soldiers. Alongside the Price divisions fought bands of bushwhackers and Confederate guerillas. One night in late October, about midnight, a company of 40-60 of them attacked the village of Marmaton, less than 15 miles from Xenia. They killed every man they could get a hold of before burning the town. The bushwhackers rode out of Marmaton before troops from Ft Scott could come to the rescue.[45]

Price aimed to level Ft Scott, and Richard and the 5th were immediately fighting to interrupt the Confederates' movements in that direction. The Union units were successful. But Price's campaign was ill-fated. Reeling from relentless Union counterattacks, it eventually failed. By late fall, Price's defeated army limped across the border back into Arkansas.

In December, Richard Parmenter returned home once and for all. Joy and sorrow, and tears and laughter, must have overwhelmed the family when they saw him riding into Xenia to his wife, Mary Elizabeth, and grieving Maria and Susannah. As joyous as it was to see Richard again, it had to be a horrendous shock to see one riding back, when three proud young men rode off.

That Christmas, the war was far from over in Virginia, but in the West, the Confederacy was done. The Union controlled the Mississippi, slicing the Confederacy vertically. Sherman's march through Georgia to the sea, along with Price's defeat in Missouri, had cut the South into quarters.

The bushwhackers were also defeated or disappearing. Bloody Bill Anderson was killed that fall in a skirmish with Union soldiers selected just to find him. Quantrill was wounded in a fight with Union Soldiers after the South's final surrender. He died a few months later. Today, they and many others like them, bushwhackers and jayhawkers alike, would probably be tried as war criminals. But those were different times, and in the minds of many on the two sides, they remained heroes.

Especially for the Lent family, the war was over. For the first time in many years, they could realistically hope for a better future. Things finally could get better next year. Life could get back to normal routines. For one thing, the children could go to school. At war's end in 1865, there were over 3,000 school-aged children in the county, many of them refugees from Missouri, just like Lewis, Nancy Jane, and Robison. School rooms were fitted up, and though poorly equipped, classes began.[46]

A Trip Back to Missouri

There were still a lot of loose ends. Chester's and Susannah's abandoned Missouri farm by now had fallen into foreclosure on account of the defaulted mortgage loan. Even Chester's estate had not yet been probated. Everything had to be settled. For all practical purposes, Richard Parmenter was now head of the Lent family. Susannah's new husband, John Moyer, was too old and was otherwise occupied with his own affairs and large family. Before the war when the family was still in Missouri, Richard started the

266

process when in February 1860, he was designated administrator of Chester's estate. Now he had to finish it.

Settling the estate was complicated. Everything in war-torn Vernon County was in disarray. There was not a store left, and goods had to be purchased across the border at Ft. Scott. When people started to return, life slowly resumed. Initially, lawlessness was king. Many old feuds remained, and vigilance committees, lynchings, and hangings often resolved old scores.

However, by late 1865 the county was re-organized, and judges and a sheriff were appointed. Although the courthouse had been destroyed, the pre-war county clerk had preserved the records. When he had fled for Arkansas to join the Confederate Army, the man had taken all but one deed volume with him. After the war, they were sent back, and eventually the courts began to resolve matters left unfinished, such as Chester's estate.

Richard took charge. It must have been a bitter trip when as a civilian he returned to Vernon County. The Lents were still owed money from the buyer of their farm in Indiana, and the family owed unpaid debts for the Missouri land. The estate went into foreclosure and by the beginning of the 1870's the old Missouri farm was sold to pay the debts. As painful as it was for the family, they probably felt some relief to finally close the chapter on their years in Missouri.[47]

It was a sad chapter, but it was over. After what they had been through, there was nothing gained by dwelling on the past. It was time to look ahead: to the future of Susannah's children soon ready for their own families, to Richard's and Mary Elizabeth's plans now he was finally home, and to the efforts by widowed Maria and her son Frank to create a life without a husband and father. These were challenges, all of them born in the hardships the war had brought. But whether it was some consolation or not, their lament was not an isolated refrain. Those days, such strains were being played everywhere, North and South, but especially in Kansas and Missouri.

The Multiplying Influence of Relatives and Friends

One September morning while traveling to family history sites in England, I received an email sent through Ancestry.com. It began, "Hello, how does the family name Chester/Susannah Lent fit into your line??" That is all there was, just a short straight to-the-point question. It was from someone I did not know, Peggy Lent. She had found my name on the Ancestry site. In a quick email back, I replied that I had a lot of information on them and would get back to her a few weeks later when I returned to my file cabinets in Virginia.

During the following days, Peggy Lent's message stayed in my mind the entire time I explored the notable Greene and hardsuffering Howard families. Mother's mother, Esther, was a Lent. Chester and Susannah were Esther's great-grandparents. I was eager to refresh what I remembered of Chester's and Susannah's story in mid-19th century Missouri.

When I was finally home again, I rummaged through the papers my mother Margie had long before organized and labeled "Chester Lent." The material was voluminous, so thick, in fact, that when I had gone through her work several months before, I had made subfiles for each of their children.

Much of what I found came from correspondence between Mother and her distant cousin Ora Lent. A few years before her death, Margie had told me how she had worked with Ora on the Chester Lent family. They corresponded from opposite parts of the United States where the two of them lived and had never met. How they first made contact, I am not sure. In the pre-digital age, people found each other through writing letters to friends, occasionally calling, and always following up on referrals and hunches, and that is probably what happened.

Ora was old enough to be Margie's mother, and to Mother, Ora was a friend, cousin, and even a mother figure at a time when Mother's own mother, Esther, passed away. I found so many of Ora's letters in Mother's "Lent" files that I created a thick folder just for them: "Ora Lewis Lent Correspondence." Their notes to each other portrayed the warm relationship they shared from a distance: "Dear Margie, Was so happy to hear from you. And all the records that you sent. Really a shame that we didn't start working on the Lents together many years ago. I think that we make a very good team, don't you? Ha!"

Despite Mother's and Ora's unending efforts, they had never completely solved the Chester Lent riddle: Who was he? What was he like? When did he die and how? What were his roots? Who were his father and mother? And what were their stories? Especially in light of the powerful family traditions that survived, Chester mysteries beguiled both Mother and Ora to no end. However, they did succeed in outlining many of the fascinating, complex, sad, and often cruel circumstances that surrounded this family living on the wildland fringes of the Civil War.

I needed to write back to Peggy, and I sat down to type. Hopefully, our correspondence could at least clarify what we knew and did not know about Chester, Susannah, and their turbulent times. I had learned that Peggy's grandfather Robison and my Great-Great-Grandfather Lewis were brothers. I explained to Peggy my background and that I was drawing on work that my mother had done during her long collaboration with relatives and others. When I wrote "collaboration with relatives," Ora, who exchanged tens or hundreds of letters with Margie over the years, was in my mind.

A day or two later, I received an email back from Peggy. Responding to my comment about Margie's work and collaboration, she wrote, "Margie and Mother shared many many years of correspondence and records... and 'Chester' nearly drove them both to exhaustion." Peggy was Ora's daughter! Somehow a second generation had found each other. Ora's and Margie's partnership, that ended with Ora's passing in 2001, had somehow opened again, in a new form. Remembering my headstrong mother, I knew that she would use whatever influence possible from the next life to keep the embers burning for her treasured family stories. And now I started to think that we might be in this project together.

Peggy continued that she had extensive material on the Lents, and that she had been seeking a place where she could preserve

269

these files. Just like I was, she felt touched by how a road was now opening to keep the story of Chester, Susannah, and their family alive. She wrote, "....is it not a 'wooo-ooh' moment that here when I am finished with all that I wanted to do and was trying to figure out where my records should go... had had several talks and even tearful talks with the good Lord as to where these could go not only to honor my family, but glory to HIM also as they were His as well... and wow!! Just the day before I was going to send them off to the Arkansas [archives], there you are... that's an OPEN MESSAGE TO ME FROM HE WHO CARES ABOUT US AND OUR FAMILY...YES!!"[48] Yes. That's how I felt, too. An open message.

One afternoon a few weeks later, a large package with the return address "Peggy Lent' on it arrived on our doorstep. At first, I hesitated but then with reverence lifted it to my study. Inside were thick ring notebooks, the product of decades of loving care and preservation, that told as much about Peggy's and her mother Ora's devotion to their family as they did about the people on the beautifully done pages inside.

I resolved that these records will be explored, preserved, and expanded, and one day maybe Chester's and Susannah's complete stories will fall into place. For now, though, I needed to learn more of their world. Carefully, I again went through Mother's files and notes. As I did that, alongside them was Ora's and Peggy's work. I was soon deep into the times they lived and the places they loved and lost.

While going piece-by-piece through the notes, documents, and various scraps of paper, I, too, came under Chester's and Susannah's spell. I searched the internet and read every book I could to learn as much as possible about the Missouri and Kansas conflicts of the 1850s and 1860s. As the powerful story came vividly alive, it was easy to see their family, and more than that, to feel them as my family.

"Beyond a Reasonable Doubt"

There was a lot of material, and it took some time to get through it. By the time I did, however, we still did not have two basic questions answered about Chester – what were his origins and how and when did he die? It was strange to me that from all the time Margie and Ora had put into their research on Chester's family, we did not have answers to questions such as these. I had learned how many steers, pigs, and cows Chester managed on his farm, but I did not know who his parents were, or where they lived. Or did I?

*There was a long family tradition that **Chester's** ancestors extended back to the early New York Lent family that came from Holland in the 1600s. It was a plausible theory, though never proven, and I carefully studied the Dutch Lent family looking for clues. While immersed in all this, one of our daughters moved to Westchester County, a northern suburb of New York City. Her new home was just five minutes from a group of 17th and 18th century Lent graves. Also nearby, the old church in Washington Irving's Sleepy Hollow had many Lents in its founding congregation, and our daughter's family took us to see the Lent tombstones whose names were barely still legible.*

*The **Sleepy Hollow** church, New York state's second oldest extant church building, rests beautifully on a point next to Ichabod Crane's famous bridge. Once, when visiting our daughter's family, we attended an autumn Sunday morning service there. We sat on its wooden pews while the Dutch Reformed Church pastor delivered his sermon. Through the windows, sunrays reflected off the gold, red, and brown leaves of the ancient trees outside. "Were these Lents my people, and what were their stories?" I wondered.*

One afternoon I sat down at my computer after a week-end downpour that had shut off our electricity for ten hours. When the computer came up again, I thought I would work through all this one more time. What was I missing? I asked. Did we already have the answer to the question about Chester's origins?

*I searched the census records from 1790 to 1850. In one of Mother's folders, I found another set of correspondence from the 1980's with a person, then in her eighties, named Lavelle. Lavelle had written in 1981 that she was a Lent descendant, not from Chester but from a woman she **thought** was Chester's sister, Charity Lent. It was clear from Lavelle's lucid style that her mind was as*

271

sharp as ever. Lavelle believed the family was from New York, via Vermont.

I read through the letters between Mother and Lavelle, then one more time through Peggy's and her mother's notes, when suddenly an idea struck me. Here was something all of us had known before but had been perhaps a little slow in processing. On the 1850 census, Chester had said he was born in Vermont in 1810. We also knew Chester and Susannah were married in Holmes County, Ohio, in 1835.[49]

The 1810 U.S. Census listed only one family named Lent in the entire state of Vermont, Hercules and Elizabeth Proper Lent.[50] In Holmes County, Ohio, on the 1830 census, there were only two families named Lent. One of them was the same family who lived in Vermont when Chester was born, Hercules and Elisabeth Proper Lent. The other Lent in Holmes County was John Lent, who lived next door to Hercules and Elizabeth. John was their adult son, listed as born in Vermont.[51]

I tracked through the 1790, 1800, 1810, 1820, and 1830 censuses in Vermont and Ohio to follow how Hercules and Elizabeth's large family had evolved. Those early censuses did not list names of children, but they did list the children as male or female according to age group. The 1810 and 1830 censuses (and the 1820 census, as well) showed that one of the children in Hercules and Elisabeth's large family was an unnamed son, born when Chester was born.

The files Peggy sent me had a lot of research on Hercules and Elizabeth Lent that showed how Hercules and Elizabeth migrated from New York to Highgate, Vermont, in the 1790s, and then to Ohio about 1812. The crucial and convincing point was that this was the only Lent family living in the two spots where we know Chester lived when young, and one of their unnamed sons was a boy Chester's age. And like Chester, their children later declared on the 1850 census – the first to list birthplaces – that they were born in Vermont.

It was only common sense that Chester's parents were Hercules and Elizabeth. He was their son. Children did not wander the American frontier. They belonged to families, and the only family

272

named Lent in the two different places where we find Chester, hundreds of miles and three decades apart, was theirs. This conclusion was further supported by Ancestry.com's "ThruLines" that collates DNA links between people living today and maps their common ancestors. ThruLines showed that three of Hercules's and Elisabeth's children have today descendants whose DNA findings show me as a distant cousin. The only common ancestors between these people and me are Hercules Lent and Elisabeth Proper. In other words, Chester, my only connection to Hercules and Elisabeth, would have been a brother to the three other siblings.[52]

In retrospect, the answer was fairly obvious. However, what clouded this conclusion for Mother and all of us was the paradigm that genealogy is, or should be, an exact endeavor. The paradigm's implication is that work, to be done properly, should be done perfectly. But it was and is a faulty paradigm. In reality, there are very few data sources in family research that are exact and rock solid. Few "facts" lack some inherent margin of doubt. Nothing is 100%.

As I have mentioned earlier, even sources as reliable as civil birth records or religious christenings are not perfect. As the advent of DNA-based family research has revealed, there are not just a few cases where DNA comparisons show that the father of record had no DNA connection to a child recorded as his. In short, if we are seeking the 100% sure solution, many family history problems will go unsolved, not because we cannot find the answer, but on account of a fruitless hunt for the 100% proof.

In their attempts to resolve questions about Chester's family, a many-decade-long search by three experienced, intense people — and many others — failed to unearth the perfect source revealing his parents. For whatever reason, there was no official record of Chester's and some of his siblings' birth information, a sad reality that was not so uncommon in frontier America. People were born, and they died in the countryside, unrecorded. In the absence of these records, the answer needed to be deduced from other information available. We had been fortunate to gather enough data over the years to reach a reasonable deduction about Chester's family.

All family history is found along that spectrum ranging from fact to myth, usually somewhere in the middle. While we do our best to establish the strongest facts and sourcing possible, we need to realize that we will never reach our goal of having the 100% waterproof factual source or proof. One genealogy scholar put it well: "There is no such thing as proof that can never be rebutted. We were not there when history happened..."[53] Like in the courts, we might more realistically aim at a conclusion that is "beyond a reasonable doubt," a standard rigid enough in its own right to convict (and even execute) society's villains.

The Board for Certification of Genealogists, in its Genealogical Proof Standard (GPS), explicitly recognizes that after a vigorous study of evidence you may well reach a conclusion that may not be perfectly certain: "Meeting the GPS neither requires nor ensures perfect certainty. Genealogical proofs – like accepted conclusions in any research field – never are final. Previously unknown evidence may arise, causing the genealogist to reassess and reassemble the evidence, which may change the outcome."[54]

Good family history requires a lot of good common sense and, just like with general history, it also entails a good understanding that one day more information or insight may overturn even our best results. Relying on a beyond-a-reasonable doubt standard, I was quite comfortable placing Chester in the home of Hercules and Elizabeth Lent. I realized that I would have had to invent an unreasonable scenario to describe Chester as someone else's child. For me, the case was closed, and we had Chester where he belonged.

Civil War Records – Full of Stories

When I started tracking the Lent boys' adventures during the Civil War, I knew that this was a war documented like no other before it. In the large battles, photographers took photos of battlefields littered with the dead and wounded, men lying in ditches and sprawled over fences. Each battle's details were also recorded

274

after the war in huge compilations of records that have benefited historians ever afterwards. Since Americans fought on both sides, the archives tell of both friend and foe.

I saw this firsthand one day when I traveled to the Library of Virginia in Richmond. I had not been to Richmond many times, and I decided to drive through the center of town before going to the library. On one long esplanade, the splendor of the South still lived. Decorating the boulevard's central green were statues of their finest: Stonewall Jackson, Robert E. Lee, and so on. The lawns and well-kept houses that lined the way revealed a glory that many there have not forgotten.

When I entered the library, I knew what I wanted to find, but I was new to these types of records and not sure where to begin. The librarians gave me generous assistance. I soon discovered stacks of the published volumes of dispatches, letters, and after-action reports, such as the report of Lt. Col. Francis Drake, April 25, 1864, in The War of the Rebellion: A Compilation of the official Records of the Union and Confederate Armies. *In the index I found John W.'s name. There were detailed descriptions of the battles where the three Lent men fought.*

I learned that if you want a firsthand account of a battle an ancestor fought, this is a place to look. The accounts I located in Richmond were especially important in my search for details. Unlike my experience with the 17th century New England grandmothers and grandfathers, this family left behind little or nothing of their own words and thoughts. I found no diaries, only one letter, and nothing more. But through compilations such as these, the stories can be found, in the color of those who were present.

The Value of a Landscape View

While I rode alongside my distant uncles participating in their skirmishes and close calls – that is how I often felt when uncovering their stories – I kept thinking that these were family, but not direct grandfathers. I soon came to understand better than ever before that our family narratives flow from more than just direct ancestors.

275

We often think that biologically we are the genetic end product, the "accumulation," of our forefathers' genes. However, recent research shows that this is not exactly correct. Life is much more complex that the simple roots-to-branches tree diagram traditionally taught in biology classes. More than 8 percent of our genes are from sources outside our direct family tree on account of the "horizontal" transmission of DNA.[55]

Not to pursue that too far here, but sociologically, emotionally, spiritually, and even physiologically we are integrally connected to the living world immediately around us more than we sometimes realize. Not just our fathers and mothers, but brothers, sisters, uncles and aunts, and cousins can play important roles in our stories. It is easy to understand that in the dark years of the early 1860s, much of Suzanna's story was filled with what her son and the husbands of her daughters, then fighting in the Civil War, were doing. Their stories were her stories, and also part of mine.

I found that taking a landscape view of those around our ancestors introduced shades and nuance and was definitely more satisfying that keeping the scope narrow. Casting a broad enough net to capture those with whom they interacted can be rewarding. For example, when I scoured the internet for information about the Kansas 5th Cavalry, I found a collection of letters and diaries written by men of the regiment. The author, Alice Fry, self-published these in a book called Following The Fifth Kansas Cavalry, The Letters. *There was nothing in it from any of the three Lent boys, but the stories their saddle-mates recounted were often their stories, too. I searched internet used bookstores for the book, and in a matter of days had a copy in front of me. Many fascinating new tales and details emerged.*

When compiling the stories found in the next chapter, I was able to do the same thing by drawing on those around my family. For many reasons we may not have direct writings from the grandparents we are following. But finding material left by their fellow travelers is the next best thing, often enough to draw the outlines of the stories we seek.

Probate Records Hold Many Stories

With a solution to the question of Chester's origins, there remained when and how he died. One spring I decided to travel to the Kansas-Missouri border to find out. Seija, one of our sons, and his small six-year old daughter, Mia, joined this family history expedition. We flew to Kansas City, rented a car, and then drove south toward Nevada City. It was immediately clear that the highlight of our three-generation adventure was not just what we might find in the fields and town streets of Missouri. The real joy came from doing it together. It was a reminder that in family history, the emphasis is on the first word, "family." Linking present family to those of the past is what it is about.

Before we left, I had carefully researched records, old county plat maps, and modern maps, too, to see if I could locate the Lent farm. I found the old maps online. Many organizations, especially universities, preserve old maps in various website collections. I had also googled to find locations that sought to preserve frontier life. By the time we packed, I had a map that showed precisely the farm site as well as a list of places to visit.

It was a rainy afternoon when we traveled through the Busch Memorial Wetlands to find the Lent farm. We drove north from Nevada on I-49 for a few miles, then turned onto a narrow county road, and kept driving east. We almost made it to the site of their farm, but it had been a rainy spring, and we were driving on the border of a wetland. We pulled into a turnout at the end of the road and stepped from the car. Wide ponds of water blocked the path that would have led us directly to where Chester and Susannah had set up their Missouri home in 1857.

Still, we saw it from the distance. It was a beautiful place, especially in the springtime hues. We could see how Chester and Susannah chose to settle there. No farmhouse nor charred out ruins were left that day, just lush green fields carefully farmed by the family that now owned them. Little did the farmer know that somewhere beneath those wheat and corn fields, were the remains of dreams a family once brought with them when they moved from Indiana in the 1850s. We wished that their dreams might have come *true. For us who had studied and discussed them so much, they somehow still lingered though unfulfilled in the air above this idyllic landscape.*

As far as I could learn, Ballton, the closest village to the Lent farm, no longer existed. It did not appear on the Google maps, and as we drove through the countryside, we found only fields and farmhouses, not villages, towns, or ghost towns. But we got a good impression of what it might have been like when we visited a living history site called "Missouri Town 1855," outside Kansas City, Missouri. The outdoor history museum was set almost exactly to the year the Lents moved to live near Ballton.

Rather than the famous Wild West town reproductions, like Jackson, Wyoming, or Deadwood, South Dakota, with their facades, boarded walks, and colorful shops, Missouri Town 1855 depicted a settlement like Balltown. The buildings spread out on either side of its long street: a blacksmith over there, a school here, and a church in front of you, with abundant space and yards in between. It was a functional grouping of needed everyday services, but hardly an urban concentration. For that, the Lents would have had to travel a few miles to Nevada City, another of the places I had placed on to "to visit" list.

When we continued to Nevada City, we found it was not so well preserved, probably because it was virtually destroyed during the Civil War. But Fort Scott, Kansas, only a few miles to the west, appeared much like it might have been 150 years before. The town had built up around the fort, and many of the streets and old buildings there today still looked the part. After moving to Kansas, whenever any of the Lent family "went to town," this is where they traveled and what they saw. They spent some of the little money they had in its shops and stores.

Today, the National Park Service manages the restored and re-constructed Fort Scott. The old fort that housed the bustling troops and cavalry companies during the Civil War was built in a rectangle with a large field in the middle. But when we walked through the buildings and across the parade grounds, the fort's supply trains and patrols were long gone. The urgency that must have been the

278

order of every day in the early 1860s, was forgotten. The Black American regiments, American Indian Home Guards, and the White cavalrymen who once marched and rode through the yard were just memories. This Fort Scott was also one the Lents knew, for they lived nearby long after the fort was closed down in 1873. If they had a hometown, it was Fort Scott.[56]

Before leaving home, I had phoned the Bushwhacker Museum in Nevada, Missouri, to make an appointment with one of the museum's curators. We were scheduled to be there on a Saturday, off-tourist season. I wanted to be sure it was open and that someone knowledgeable would be there. In our phone conversation, I learned that the Museum had charge of Vernon County's historical records. All the better. A curator named Will kindly agreed to meet us during our visit.

My wife, son, and little Mia wandered the museum's colorful displays telling of the county's tumultuous history while Will listened to me tell Chester's story. After I explained to him what I was looking for, he disappeared into the back room. I was astonished when he returned with two file folders hand labeled, "Chester Lent." They contained the original probate documents from Chester's estate.

These were some of those records spirited out of Vernon County by the southern-sympathizing county clerk. They were stashed somewhere while the man served with the Confederates. After the war, they somehow were brought back home. While I combed through them, Will went through other files and newspaper indexes to see what he might find. Unfortunately, there were no further references to Chester Lent. In fact, there was no newspaper in Nevada City until well after Chester's family left for Kansas.

While sifting through the two files of documents, inventories, and receipts, one piece of paper caught my eye – an account from a Dr. Curt Boettinger who billed Chester 19 times for "Attendance and Medicine" from August to October, 1857. Once, this frontier doctor also noted giving care to a "daughter." We knew their youngest daughter, Sarah, had died sometime during or immediately after the move to Missouri, but not exactly when. Perhaps the daughter on this billing was Sarah.

The next day in September, Boettinger again billed for care to a "child," perhaps the same one. The following week he charged them extra to work during the night. A doctor's night call on the frontier suggested something very serious. There were two more charges for the child, and the rest were for someone else not noted, perhaps Chester.

This was all during the first months after they moved to their new Missouri farm. One can easily imagine one or another of the many diseases common in 19th century America inflicting them. But by the end of 1857, the doctor was billing Chester for a sack of flour he sold him on November 7. So Chester was still alive at that time.

Then, on February 10, 1859, just over a year later, Susannah signed a receipt for the sale of belongings from Chester's estate: a rifle, saddle, 10 pigs, calves, a steer, and so on. It was clear that Chester died between November 1857 and February 1859, almost certainly sometime in 1858. So, we at least had narrowed Chester's death date to a matter of months.

There had always been a family tradition that Chester might have been killed by one of the marauding bands of raiders. However, the museum curator told me that there were few jayhawker incursions into Vernon County in 1858, and he believed a death associated with a raid would have been recorded. We knew that John Brown led a murderous foray into the area around the Lent farm in December 1858, but the raid and his victims were well documented. Chester Lent was not among them.

Will agreed with my thought that probably Chester was taken by illness, disease, or a serious accident. The doctor's many visits to their home during late 1857 show that someone or several of them must have been seriously ill. So we could deduce about when he died, and the most likely cause. The full details of Chester's death remained only in the memories of his family, however, and those, too, are long gone.

Little Mia was a real trooper when we visited all these places. Wherever we went, she was patient, perfectly behaved, and *interested – certainly deserving of a reward. We decided to take her to a place we knew would highlight her day and left cross country one morning for the Wizard of Oz Museum in Wamego, Kansas. It was probably her most exciting memory from the trip. At the museum shop, Seija bought her Dorothy slippers to wear whenever walking the yellow brick road. They were quite appropriate since we later learned that the real yellow brick road that inspired Wizard of Oz writer Frank Baum was said to be in Peekskill, New York, one of those lower Hudson towns where many Lents lived in the 18th century.*

When we returned home, there were details still missing. But we had visited Chester's and Suzannah's homesite and been rewarded with a quick but revealing glimpse into Chester's and Susannah's stories. And we knew a lot more about Chester's passing. It wasn't everything, of course, but a good story is often made better if some of its strands are left unresolved. That way, something remains to perk our curiosity, to animate our imagination, and to prod us to search still more.

Chapter 7

Promised Land
Joseph and Ann Shelton Howard

*"I went on board their ship to bear
testimony against them if they deserved it, as
I fully believed they would; to my great
astonishment, they did not deserve it; and
my predispositions and tendencies must not
affect me as an honest witness."*[1]
Charles Dickens

*Joseph and Ann Howard were Mormon converts who left on
their journey to Utah from Birmingham in 1864. They were my
Father Owen's great-great-grandparents. I already knew that their
story was a powerful one. It had inspired many family histories on
account of the suffering and sacrifices they endured during that long
passage.*

Birmingham

Birmingham's population exploded over the 19th century.
When 45-year old Joseph Howard left it behind, the number of
people in this hard-working industrial city had doubled during the
25 years since he was 20. As a result, its borders reached out to
swallow farmland around it and villages in between. In the 150
years between 1700 and 1850, the once small town on the edge of
Warwickshire had become a microcosm of the Industrial
Revolution. Guns, jewelry, buttons, brass bedsteads, and silver
teapots poured from its shops and factories. By 1870 nearly two
thirds of everything written in the world was written with a pen
made in Birmingham.

The countryside around Birmingham burst with a new patch of
buildings here, and another there, until the flat green farms and
countryside shrank away like disappearing dry spots in a rain

282

shower. Birmingham's traditional big neighbor city Aston, with its mixed farming and town areas, was soon overrun and evolved into a Birmingham suburb during the time the Howards lived there and in nearby Gravelly Hill. Aston became a mix of workers' housing, small factories, and workshops. When we walked the streets where the Howards lived 150 years ago, that mix seemed hardly to have changed even though most of the old buildings had been replaced with new ones.

In the midst of this creative destruction, Joseph and Ann struggled to raise a family. On the 1861 UK census, Joseph listed his profession as a "gardener," and that is probably how he wanted to think of himself.[2] He had once farmed five acres in Gravelly Hill, but he was now working in one of Aston's workshops. At one point, he was selling coal, perhaps wheelbarrowing it from the canals and warehouses to his customers.

Life would not have been terribly easy in any case, but with eleven children it was ever challenging to make ends meet. If Birmingham was vibrant, energetic, and humming, it was also crowded and full of toil and poverty. As new families flocked to find jobs, the rapid construction of housing raced to accommodate them. Housing and everyday life for working class families, however, was always full of inconveniences and hardships. Most people lived in primitive urban circumstances.

Joseph and his family had joined the Church of Jesus Christ of Latter-day Saints (traditionally called "Mormon," "Latter Day Saint," or simply "LDS") in 1851. The faith that had come from the American frontier to Britain in the late 1830's initially had grown like wildfire. The year Joseph's family became members, the church had 52,000 members worldwide, of which 31,000 lived in Great Britain. In other words, there were significantly more members in Britain than in the United States. With time, Joseph became a member of the Mormons' unpaid lay priesthood and served as president of their central Birmingham congregation, the "Hockley Branch," for nearly ten years before they moved from Britain. He spent many of his evenings tending to the needs of his flock.

There was little open-mindedness in Britain toward people who, like the Howards, believed differently. Religious tolerance was still a new concept, often not present even in 19th century America. In Great Britain, tolerance was even rarer. Dissenters and non-conformists were regularly resented, shunned, or worse. Joseph and Ann were often isolated in their community.

Late one evening, Joseph emerged from his responsibilities at the Hockley Branch meeting house. When he turned to walk the several blocks to his home, he saw a group of men whom he had to pass. They knew who he was, at least that he was a Mormon. Taunting and grabbing him, the unruly mob punched and beat Joseph nearly to death before leaving him on the ground. On another occasion, Joseph had to give up a small coal business because customers were not willing to buy from a Mormon. This was not the life the Howards wanted for their children, and they aspired to join the exodus that many made to the seclusion of the Mormon "Zion" in Utah.

The instability of life in England's dirty industrial cities like Birmingham was another important reason for Joseph's and Ann's decision to leave. For over a century, landowners had enclosed the commons on their lands, merging small landholdings into a single large farm, and closing the common fields on which so many depended for farming and grazing their animals. Cottagers usually lost old common rights and the fuel they gathered from waste lands. Families like the Howards or their ancestors, were forced off their farms. The dispossessed swarmed into the cities in search of factory jobs to keep from starving. Their diet was meager, more often than not, bread and cheese six days a week.

With their small plot of land that produced some vegetables, perhaps a pig, and a few fowls, the Howards were luckier than many. But it was not enough. Joseph gave up his farming to find extra income. He got a job at the Webb Smelting and Refining Works. Everyone, when old enough, pitched in to support the family. By the time he was 14, Joseph Jr. was working for a factory making and shipping guns to the Confederate Army in the American South.

When deciding to migrate to America, the Howards looked for hope: hope to find food for the table and a decent home to live in; hope for opportunities that did not exist for their children in Britain's fire-breathing smoky industrial cities; and hope to follow whatever path to which their consciences led them. They had high expectations for their children. The 1861 census showed that their 8, 10, and 11-year-old children were all "scholars," or, in other words, in school. A contemporary survey showed only 40% of the children their age in Birmingham attended schools. But the Howard family saw that their children got the most education possible.

Ann and Joseph shared the same dreams as others of their faith who believed they could not realize their aspirations under the current circumstances. Many of the members of their congregation began preparations to emigrate to Utah, and Joseph and Ann did as well. When the adherents became emigrants, the number of the Mormons in Britain dropped. By 1870, it was one-fourth what it was in 1850. As the British Isles lost their Mormons, Utah became more British. Between 1860 and 1880, 22% of Utah's population was born in Great Britain.[3]

Ann and Joseph had wanted to emigrate to Utah for several years. It was always a question of how to afford it. Eventually they developed a plan. The two oldest boys would leave first, make their way to the Salt Lake Valley, and earn funds to send home to support the rest of the family's emigration. In 1861, they began to implement this plan when 18-year-old Thomas and 17-year-old William said good-bye to their parents, brothers, sisters, and friends and began their six-month journey to Utah.

To finance their trip, Thomas and William borrowed money from the Perpetual Emigrating Fund, usually referred to as the "PEF." The Church had set up the PEF in 1849 to provide assistance to mainly European converts who lacked the resources to join the "gathering" in Utah. Those borrowing for their passage were expected to pay the loan back after arrival, often through in-kind contributions or labor. Most, if not all, of the tithing the church collected in Europe was channeled into PEF accounts, and when there was a deficit between loans and pay-back contributions, the gap was filled with general tithing funds from elsewhere in the church. For two young men with a long life ahead of them and plenty of time to pay back whatever they borrowed, the arrangement was perfect.

The two boys commenced a long and difficult journey to Utah, walking and driving an ox team across the plains. Thomas' daughter wrote that their life was "...standing guard nights, hunting lost cattle, helping with the living, and burying the dead." The first winter in Utah was not much easier than their trip across the plains. They eventually found work with a man named William Muir in a community named Bountiful and began earning funds their family could use to join them.

The boys wrote to their family to tell about their passage and to invite the family to join them in Salt Lake City. I never found their original letter, but their parents', probably Ann's, response still exists. After hearing the boys arrived safely, they wrote, "We received your welcome letter, which gave great relief... Thankful that you was in good health. My dear lads it is too late this season to make any arrangements to come. You try all you can and we will do the same... and if you cannot do it of yourselves, ask your Master if he will assist you and I will recompense him for anything it requires of me." Joseph and the family continued to work and save.[4]

A year later, the family's departure from Birmingham was looking more secure. By the winter of 1863-64, Ann and Joseph were starting to get ready. Joseph Sr. and James, their oldest son still at home, each took PEF loans to cover the expenses necessary to get to Utah. There were three programs: the first type, "P.E. companies," paid the complete passage of those with no funds to contribute. The second, the "15-pound" program, required a contribution of 15 pounds for each passenger over one-year old. And the third, "cash emigrant companies," was available for those who could afford full passage.[5]

Joseph, Ann, and their children probably traveled on the 15-pound passage, because it is clear that both Thomas and William and they, themselves, had been saving a long time for the trip. This was not a small amount. In 1864, £15 was the same as 150 US dollars of the time. Or another way to put it, Ann and Joseph were traveling with 9 children for a total of 11 people. Their contribution to the trip would have been 165 pounds for everyone. A London laborer during the 1860's might earn about 50 pounds a year.

Years later when in Utah, Joseph's family made installments in kind to pay back the PEF loans, wrapping butter in grape leaves, and walking five miles to town to deliver their payment. During its 50th jubilee celebration in 1880, the Church forgave one half of all PEF debts. A few years later, the federal government's Edmunds Tucker Act disincorporated both the Church and the PEF in response to the Church's practice of polygamy. The effect was to nullify any remaining debts. By that time, the PEF had granted over 10,000 loans. In 1864, the year the Howards emigrated, over 2,500 Mormon immigrants arrived in New York. Almost half of them had borrowed from the PEF.[6]

The PEF did not just finance the migration to Utah, it made all the arrangements for the Howards' and other emigrants' journeys. It chartered entire ships, usually at low rates since the cross-Atlantic sailing vessels often lacked enough return freight from England. PEF agents were waiting at all points along the way – Liverpool, London, New York, and Nebraska. The agents shepherded the immigrants' travel to the United States, greeting the travelers, facilitating their boarding, arranging for provisions, organizing transfers, and so on.

Sometime during the winter or early spring, word arrived from the PEF that the Howards had passage to America aboard the *Hudson*, due to depart for New York from London in May. The PEF was headquartered in England's large western port city of Liverpool, and usually PEF sailings started there. But ships were scarce that year, and the PEF agents were booking where they could find ready sailings. Joseph and Ann began getting their things together and making preparations for travel to London... and far beyond. Birmingham was a rail center with a number of lines converging like wagon spokes into the center. The Aston train station was only a few short blocks from their home on Thimble Mill Lane, and from there they probably departed.

Despair from the thought of separation was especially keen in Ann's family. To them, her departing, with little prospect of returning, for a wild country reachable only by endangering her life, was too much. Her older brother, William, came to see her sometime while the family was preparing for their departure. William was still unmarried and served as an officer on a commercial sea vessel. He tried to dissuade Ann from making what he considered a foolish and dangerous trip. When she would not listen, he offered her money if she would stay. She refused. Her mind was set and their commitment, firm.[7]

The Sailing Ship *Hudson*

Joseph, Ann, and their family arrived in London at the end of May or the beginning of June 1864. Birmingham, as big and vibrant as it was, was England's second city. London, the first city, was the capital of the greatest empire in the world. It surely looked like it to the Howard family, and still does.

Whether Joseph or Ann had ever been to London before, it is hard to know, but the children probably had not. As their train chugged through the outlying towns and then into the industrialized center with its factories, smoke and fog, and centuries old buildings, it must have been a grand start for their adventure. The long sea passage and treacherous trip across the American plains were ever deep in their minds, but it was a glorious day when they first saw the London harbor filled with fleets of ships destined for everywhere in the world, including New York.

Everyone scurried to get the ship ready to sail. The *Hudson* was sailing 17 days late due to its delayed arrival from New York. Seventeen days mattered when toward the end of their trip the families made their way through the Rocky Mountains during the fall. George Q. Cannon – Mormon leader in charge of Church affairs in Britain, apostle, and step-son of future church president John Taylor – traveled back and forth between his base in Liverpool and London to personally take charge of getting the ship as fit and comfortable as possible for the arriving families.

On May 11, as soon as the *Hudson* was in port, Elder Cannon was on board making arrangements. After dining with Capt. Pratt, the *Hudson's* master, Elder Cannon wrote he was "a very gentlemanly man and is quite delighted at having our people to take on his ship." The Captain was also a relative to Mormon church leaders, Parley and Orson Pratt.[8]

After getting to the port, Joseph and Ann climbed up the gangway that connected the *Hudson* to the wharf. A long line of children filed behind them: James (18 years old), Joseph, Jr. (who had just turned 15), Mary Ann (13), Emma (11), John (10), Samuel (7), Matilda (5), her twin sister Elizabeth (5), and Tamar (just short of 3). Also accompanying the Howards was a young woman named Mary Dudley Lowe. She was a friend of their son Thomas, who was already in America, and would marry him later that year after their arrival. That made a total of 12 in the Howard party. This was their family and those who would share the great journey ahead.[9]

Arriving emigrants from many parts of Europe filled the ship until there were 863 of them. Above and below deck a flurry of activity was underway. Like the Howards, most of the passengers were families. Little children ran up and down the stairs and darted around legs while adults found old friends, met new ones, and dashed off last letters to family members and acquaintances staying behind. About 160 passengers were non-Mormon emigrants, mainly from Ireland. While people settled in, Elder Cannon appointed the leaders of his group. Detailed organization was a fundamental of Mormon ecclesiastical structures, and nowhere was it more so than among emigrant parties.

Cannon named John M Kay, a missionary returning with his wife from England to Utah, president of the party. He had three counselors, also returning missionaries. Elder Cannon and John Kay then divided the group into 14 wards, each with a president. There were three kinds of wards, and they were quartered separately: married families, single men, and single women. Joseph's and Ann's son, Joseph Jr., was asked to be president over the Sixth Ward, a single men's ward. Older brother James may also have assisted him. Joseph's job was to provide support for ward members, such as carrying food back and forth to the kitchen, dividing it among his members, making regular reports back to John Kay on conditions in the ward, and conveying regular communications from the leadership to members.[10]

The previous year, Charles Dickens had boarded the *Amazon*, another ship full of Mormons who, like Joseph and Ann Howard, were headed to Utah. Skeptical about their motivations, he wanted to interview the emigrants while they were readying to embark from London. Dickens described the passengers' optimism and organization, writing,

> "The vigilant bright face of the weather-browned captain of the *Amazon* is at my shoulder, and he says, 'What, indeed! The most of these came aboard yesterday evening. They came from various parts of England in small parties that had never seen one another before. Yet they had not been a couple of hours on board, when they established their own police, made their own regulations, and set their own watches at all the hatchways. Before nine o'clock, the ship was as orderly and as quiet as a man-of-war.'"

Dickens was impressed. He added, "It is surprising to me that these people are all so cheery, and make so little of the immense distance before them."[11]

These words probably well describe how the Howard family, too, felt during the hours before their departure. The party was up and on deck when in the early morning hours of Friday, June 3, a steam tug inched alongside the *Hudson* to pull it from dockside into the harbor. Elder Cannon disembarked in the "very wet" afternoon, "...the Saints cheering... whilst the Brethren continued in sight on the deck," wrote one of the passengers, Michael McCune.[12] The large three-masted ship, comfortable and modern for its time, slipped away from the dock.

It was a jubilant moment. On deck, around Joseph, Ann, and the children, crowded hundreds of fellow travelers from different parts of Europe: British, Germans, Danes, Swiss, and many from other countries. Most could speak only their own language, yet this voyage tied them to those around them in a common adventure. They shared a profound conviction and a transcendent dream. Somehow, language was not necessary for communicating their aspirations. Harriet Bird, one of the British passengers, wrote, "...at last we [were] able to leave all...behind us and come to Utah. We left London... sailed...down the River Thames, out into the ocean singing, 'O, Babylon, O, Babylon.'"[13] The energetic tune, "Ye Elders of Israel," is still in the Mormon hymnal, and the chorus continues, "O, Babylon we bid thee farewell; We're going to the mountains of Ephraim to dwell."

Charles Dickens probably best describes the extraordinary spirit emanating from the men, women, and children as their ship departed. After disembarking from the *Amazon*, Dickens concluded:

> "What is in store for the poor people on the shores of Great Salt Lake, what happy delusions they are laboring under now, on what miserable blindness their eyes may be opened then, I do not pretend to say. But I went on board their ship to bear testimony against them if they deserved it, as I fully believed they would; to my great astonishment, they did not deserve it; and my predispositions and tendencies must not affect me as an honest witness. I went over the *Amazon's* side, feeling it impossible to deny that, so far, some remarkable influence had produced a remarkable result..."[14]

Captain Pratt took the ship into the channel, and the long sailing commenced. On Sunday, they all gathered on deck to receive instructions and encouragement from John Kay. Captain Pratt also addressed the passengers expressing a willingness to do anything he could for their comfort. Throughout the voyage the captain was in fact sympathetic to his passengers' needs and came to be respected and popular by journey's end. On good days people met on deck and passed their time visiting and singing songs in English, German, and Dutch. Sundays, meetings were held on the main deck, or on the poop deck, the deck over the rear superstructure. It was not very long before many began suffering from sea sickness.[15]

Among the group was a passenger named George Careless. George was a musician who as a child had studied at the Royal Academy of Music and later played in famous London venues and theaters such as Exeter Hall, Drury Lane, and Crystal Palace. With his violin, Careless lightened the difficult voyage and crowded conditions by organizing music events and community singing. Careless one day would become conductor of the Mormon Tabernacle Choir and compose many songs in the LDS hymnal. "Through Deepening Trials," comes to mind and may have been inspired by the journey he and the Howards shared.

By Tuesday, Careless formed an English choir. They had plenty of time to rehearse and were soon quite proficient. One of the choir members, Mary Ann Webb, wrote, "The ship's officers enjoyed the singing very much, so the captain gave us permission to practice in his cabin." John Lyman Smith, one of Kay's counselors, organized the Germans into their own choir.[16]

Two weeks into their journey, Ann and Joseph celebrated little Tamar's third birthday and a few days later, Samuel's eighth birthday. They were not long at sea, however, before the routines and hardships of living aboard a ship began to weigh on everyone. The warm days turned considerably colder. On the 16th, when a man died from a heart attack, many assembled on deck to watch his burial at sea. The body was sewn up in a weighted bag, placed on a plank, and then tipped to fall feet first into the depths. The moment left an unforgettable impression. Joseph Jr., years later, could not forget watching the body sink deep into the water.[17]

When good winds failed to develop and slowed the already late sailing, Joseph Jr. and other presidents were asked to instruct everyone in their wards to pray for a fair wind. After a few weeks, odors on the lower deck became unbearable, and the crew sprinkled it with tar oil to "renovate" the atmosphere. More ominously, three cases of measles appeared after only three days at sea. The disease quickly spread through the ship, taking the lives of a number of the passengers, especially children. John Kay wrote, "The ties that unite us are stronger than death, and the love that warms hones upright hearts, lives and grows beyond the grave." John Kay's wife went through the ship visiting the sick, "causing many to rejoice and bless her," wrote John Lyman Smith. But tragedy had undeniably joined their passage.[18]

Life continued, with births, illnesses, and deaths, not so different from how it progressed on land. When they arrived in New York, the company's leader John Kay reported that four babies had been born, and ten, mainly children, had died during the voyage. Kay again eloquently expressed the enormous faith that made it possible for these families to endure their losses. He recorded, "...the links now broken in the family chain by death's chilly hand, shall be again welded together, and home's endearing associations shall be renewed with all the joys that animate the bosom of immortals."[19]

After weeks at sea, the *Hudson* approached the North American coastline, and new excitement interrupted the boredom of the long voyage. If they had not yet appreciated how the America they sought was in a state of civil war, they soon did. On July 8, a Confederate schooner drew up close to look over the ship and its passengers. Whether the warship had designs on the *Hudson* as bounty or to burn it, is unclear. Many of the passengers, though, believed there was an intention to do harm until the Confederates saw how many people were on board. Short of mounting a huge human tragedy and inciting an unwanted incident with Great Britain, whose flag it flew, there was little the Rebel warship could do. It sailed on, leaving the *Hudson* to continue its voyage toward New York.[20]

The first glimpse of North America sparked excitement in the same way their departure from London had done. "It was early in the morning of the 16th of July when the words, 'Land Ahoy!' were heard and it was a lively rush on the deck to witness the new land. It was certainly a picture never to be forgotten. After our six weeks and over an ocean life, to again witness land, it looked to us beautiful," remembered Charles William Symons, one of the Howards' British brethren.[21]

The Howard family and their many-languaged fellow passengers lined the rail to share the first sightings of the promised land they had talked about the entire voyage. Anyone who has taken a cruise, or even a sea-going ferry, can appreciate the hustle of the moment the ship approaches land: crew and passengers all scurrying around the ship, packing, moving their things, standing in anticipation, laughing and joking with fellow travelers, hoping not to forget something. As the shore and docks drew closer, the end of one episode merged with the anticipation and unknowns of the next.

It was Monday, the 18th of July, when the *Hudson* finally started its entry into New York City. A pilot came on board in the early morning hours to guide the ship into the harbor. The next morning, a steam-powered tug boat, the *Blance Paige*, pulled alongside to tow the large sailing vessel with the Howards and other families past Sandy Hook Lighthouse and through the narrows, until they cast anchor about 3:30 in the afternoon opposite Castle Garden. The PEF's representative in New York City, William Staines, came on board and briefed the party's leadership council about what lay ahead. He spent the night on the ship with the passengers.[22]

Riverboats, Trains, and Ferries

Joseph, the boys, and the other men worked together to unload all the party's luggage from the *Hudson*. In only a few hours' time, they had everything aboard a lighter that then moved to customs clearance at the Castle Garden facility. About noon, the passengers themselves climbed onto another lighter that carried them from the *Hudson* to immigrant processing at Castle Garden. There, the Howards went through a quick inspection by the facility's doctors to determine if they were carrying any obvious infectious diseases. Then they walked into Castle Garden's large rotunda where they were registered by the New York Commissioners of Emigration.[23]

Once through registration, the Howards waited in the facility's large central hall, surrounded by Castle Garden's circular galleries and promenades, until all the party was ready to leave. While immigration formalities were underway at Castle Garden, a steamer named the *St. John*, moved into place just offshore and started

294

loading their baggage. Once the party finished at Castle Garden, the lighter took everyone to the *St. John*, and an hour later the steamer and its passengers began their journey up the Hudson River.

It was all very efficient. The PEF choreographed the itinerary by the day and hour. Everything kept moving with little delay. For one thing, it would have been expensive and inconvenient if the party's more than 800 passengers had had to spend the night in New York. Unlike travel today, moreover, when a party of this size traveled for weeks and months at a time, birth, illness, and death accompanied them. Theirs was a life in transit and delays only complicated things. In fact, one ten-month old baby belonging to the Williams family from Calne, England, died while they were at Castle Garden. It was important to keep the travel underway.

Another reason for the PEF's premium on efficiency was the realization that it was already mid-July. The Howards and their party still had to cross the American continent, much of the way on foot. As many earlier immigrants had learned, winter storms in the Rockies generated vast hardships, often deadly ones. The moment they stepped onto American soil for the first time, empty wagon trains were already rolling eastward from Utah through Wyoming and Nebraska to meet their arrival in Nebraska. The Howards and fellow pioneers now had to move west quickly to meet those wagons.

The *St. John* pushed into the Hudson River with everyone and their belongings on board at 5:00 in the afternoon of July 20. John Kay and his counselors continued to shepherd their emigrant flock's travel toward the Nebraska frontier. The *St. John* carried its cargo up the broad river past Manhattan and through the Hudson River Valley's picture-perfect hills and palisades. People crowded on deck to watch as they passed towns, such as the legendary Sleepy Hollow on their right side, and a while later, the stone buildings and fortifications of the West Point military academy, high above on the left. Later, they slept below on top of their luggage.

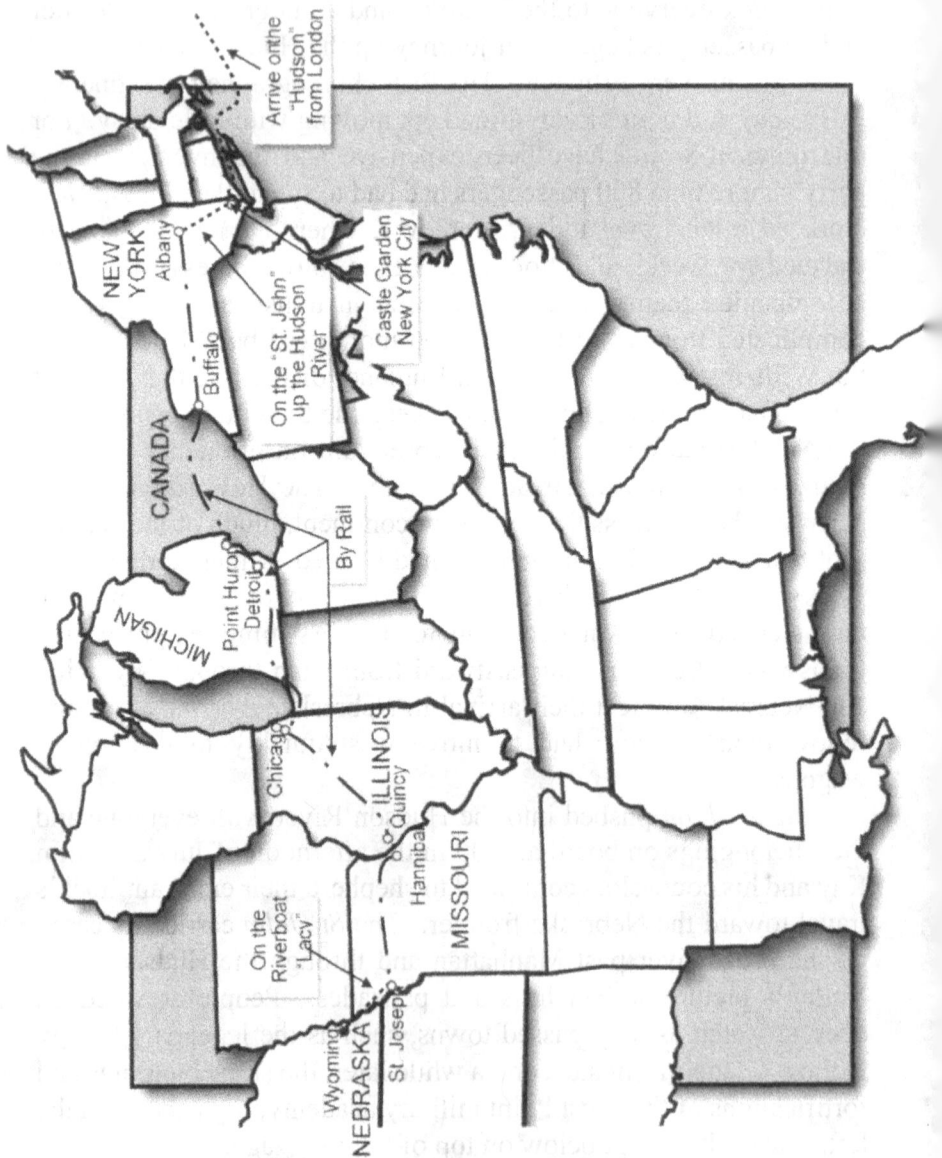

Map G - Howard Family Route Across
the Eastern United States

Labels on map: Arrive on the "Hudson" from London; New York; Albany; Buffalo; Castle Garden New York City; On the "St. John" up the Hudson River; Canada; By Rail; Michigan; Point Huron; Detroit; Chicago; Illinois; Quincy; Hannibal; Missouri; On the Riverboat "Lacy"; Wyoming; St. Joseph; Nebraska

All through the short night the *St. John* paddled upstream until they arrived in Albany, about 5:00 the next morning. The steamer, carrying over 1400 travelers, was crowded, and it was difficult for those on the lower deck to sleep. After docking, their luggage was taken to the railway station, where it weighed out at 65 tons, and the Howards and other immigrant families boarded the train for Buffalo. The train with its 24 cars departed in the early afternoon and chugged on through the next night.[24]

The pace continued with little pause. The Howards arrived in Buffalo in the afternoon and immediately transferred to a ferry that crossed the end of Lake Erie into Canada. By 8:00 that same evening, they were on another train, on the Grand Trunk Railway, steaming toward Port Huron, on the St. Clare River that separated Canada from Michigan. (See Map G) They got there about noon, on Saturday, the 23rd. The Howards had been in North America only three days and were already fairly deep into the interior. It must have been fascinating to see the vast forests, lakes the size of seas, and the relatively primitive new settlements, at least compared to England's ancient towns and quaint cottages.

The idea that they were well into their trip surely excited them. But travel by train was not easy. The Civil War North had drafted the best cars into operations farther south, and the immigrants often were cramped with little place to sleep or move about. James Sutton, one of their fellow travelers, recalled, "The cars were without decent accommodations. We had to sit on our luggage for seats. People were riding in cattle cars or any kind they could get. It was desperately hard on those who were sick and on the older people."[25] Joseph and Ann were not exactly "older people," but Joseph was 44 and Ann was 47 years old. They no longer enjoyed the young resilient bodies necessary to easily weather such arduous travel. Much of the time Joseph and three of the children were sick during this part of their journey.

They crossed the river back in the United States by steam ferry, then again made a transfer onto the Central Michigan Railroad. A few hours later, they were again on their way, toward Chicago. The travel was crude and perilous. At one point, the train even passed through a forest fire. On the ship there had been a daily routine, and regular meals. That was no longer the case in this increasingly wild land. Twenty-four hours later they arrived in Chicago. Some of the passengers jumped off the train looking for bread shops. But everything was closed. It was Sunday. The ensuing leg of the trip did not begin until the next morning, and they slept on the train.

The Civil War that had raged for over two years now was like a heavy fog that darkened the countryside the Howards were seeing for the first time. It was not just that the country was at war, but worse than that. It was a fraternal conflict with all the viciousness that entailed. Suffering and loss cloaked every community they passed. The Michigan they saw from the windows of the train sent one fourth of its male population – fathers, sons, husbands, and brothers – to fight in the war. One in six never returned.

The Confederate schooner that snooped around the *Hudson* before it arrived in New York had given a scare to many of them. But up to now, the Civil War had been little more than something on the horizon, a circumstance that occasionally complicated their trip. That changed, however, when after their connection in Chicago, the train veered south toward Quincy, Illinois, on the Mississippi River, and Missouri, beyond that. While still in Chicago, some Union Army officers boarded the train searching for deserters and harassing some of the Howards' group as they went through the carriages.

Monday morning, the immigrants pulled out on the Illinois Central Railroad. The trains were very slow, and they found themselves changing cars continually, once even at midnight. They did not reach Quincy until noontime Wednesday. The company wasted no time getting the baggage onto a ferry to cross the Mississippi.

Directly across from Quincy was a railhead on a spur built down from the town of Hannibal, Missouri. The spur connected to the Hannibal and St. Joseph Railway that spanned between the two cities on either side of the state. The plan was to cross the wide flowing river by steamboat ferry from Quincy, board the train on the opposite bank, and then travel by train west across Missouri to St.

Joseph, on the Missouri River. From there, they would travel upstream by riverboat to the Wyoming, Nebraska, settlement where wagons should be waiting to take them west across the prairie.

The travelers quickly learned that unlike where they had been so far, Missouri was right in the middle of this war. They had no sooner got off the ferry on the western side of the Mississippi, when a dispatch arrived telling that rebel raiders had burned the Salt River bridge and Shelbina Station just up the rail line. The track was cut, and their railhead was separated from the rest of the spur. They could not get out of the station. The crossing from Illinois to Missouri had left them vulnerably unprotected in the worst kind of Civil War conflict. They were told they would have to await the arrival of trains to get them on the move again.[26]

In Virginia, battlefields such as Chancellorsville where I have lived, were huge set-piece confrontations. Civilians usually had a few days' notice to try to get out of harm's way. The war in Missouri, however, was a vicious guerilla war. Confederate horse-mounted guerillas, such as William Quantrill's raiders and "Bloody Bill" Anderson's band, were especially active the summer of 1864 and were responsible for atrocities throughout the central part of the state. Unfortunately, in this type of war, Union troops, who were greatly drawn from Missouri and Kansas militias and regiments, were not always a lot better. (See chapter 6)

Joseph's and Ann's family were in the middle of a war zone. Unable to move anywhere, the immigrant party camped in the woods that night. A heavy thunderstorm rolled over the night sky and sent sheets of rain down upon the unsheltered party below. A few were able to take cover on the train platform, but there was not room for all. Most were miserable. Young Mary Ann Webb wrote about that terrible wait among unfriendly local inhabitants: "Some of us went down to the river where some men tried to drown us. They were very bitter against the Mormons."[27]

The next day, three trains were able to take the party about 40 miles to the vicinity of the burned-out bridge. From there, they moved by foot across the swollen creek below. Boards were laid down to walk on, but it took a lot of time and effort to get their luggage across and up the embankment to the tracks where they could connect with new trains. There were only three wagons and almost everything had to be carried three quarters of a mile over very rough terrain. They spent a second night again on the wet ground. Union soldiers, in readiness for another Confederate attack, stood guard. These nights were far worse than merely cold and uncomfortable. This was a tragedy. Two children died that night and were buried there.[28]

On Friday the 29th, the luggage was over the river, and by mid-afternoon the Howard family boarded one of the trains waiting to convey them forward. These were made up of freight and cattle cars, filthy, with no place to sit down, and "crammed to excess." The conditions were not something Joseph or Ann could ever have imagined from Thimble Mill Lane in Birmingham. As horrible as they were, there was no way out but to bear the squalor and discomfort.

Finally, the locomotives stoked up and started slowly across the countryside through Missouri, from Hannibal to St. Joseph's port on the Missouri River. Everyone could now see that the war was no longer a distant danger but was everywhere around them. Blackened logs from guerrilla raids lay smoldering, and armed Union men in their blue uniforms stood by the tracks to protect the railway.

Early the next morning, the Howards arrived in St. Joseph, tired and dirty. It had been an appalling ride. Besides the filth everyone suffered in the railcars, an engine and several cars had derailed. One car had caught fire and had to be cut loose. For the next two nights they sheltered in a large shed belonging to the railroad company while they awaited river boats to carry them up the Missouri River.

Soldiers and local people came to talk, and in some cases created disturbances. A group of Union soldiers tried to abduct a young Dutch girl claiming she was being taken with the party against her will. Since the entire area was under martial law, the immigrant party appealed to the Army's provost marshal for assistance. After interviewing the girl through an interpreter, he commanded the soldiers to stand off and leave the party in peace. The soldiers nevertheless stayed around threatening to burn the shed if the party did not turn the girl over to them. Finally, wearing a disguise, she climbed aboard the river boat *Colorado*, which soon left with all but the English immigrants on board.

With the rest of the English party, the Howards followed on a second river boat, the *J. F. Lacy*. Another rainstorm drenched everyone on deck. Drinking water was pulled from the unclean muddy river, and many got sick. The *Lacy* with its ill passengers arrived at Wyoming, Nebraska, in the late afternoon of August 2, 1864. The large Howard family poured off with the rest of the passengers, and everyone moved to a campground near the outfitting office. They immediately went to work getting ready for their departure. It would have been nice to take two or three weeks to rest and recuperate, but the company's leaders were anxious to get on the trail. It was already August, only a month or so before the first snows in the Rockies would start falling. For the Howard family, it had been a long trip from Birmingham.[29]

Wyoming, Nebraska Territory

In 1861, the Perpetual Emigrating Fund made a daring "down-and-back" innovation that aimed to make the long, difficult 1,000-mile wagon journey from the Salt Lake Valley to the Nebraska embarkation outpost on the Missouri River and back to Salt Lake in one season. In addition to reducing the cost of outfitting each new arriving party from scratch, down-and-back wagon trains would furnish experienced drivers and reduce a growing surplus of wagons and oxen in the valley. It was Church leader Brigham Young's idea, but at first, no one thought it could be done. The Mormon prophet's bishops, too, were concerned that the returning trains would reach the Rockies too late in the fall, risking a wintery passage. On everyone's minds were two immigrant companies pulling handcarts who only a few years before had been caught in the snows. Over 200 of them had starved and frozen to death.

Brigham Young would not give up. He met with the bishops from all his wards to work out a detailed plan for the down and back trains. Each ward would furnish a set number of men and wagons, as well as donate flour and other provisions. An 1861 trial passage, implemented with careful timing, succeeded in making it to the Missouri River and back again in one summer. It was possible, but only with precision planning, experienced leadership, and expedited passage. From then on, wagon trains equipped with provisions, also called "church trains," were dispatched from the valley in mid-spring. They were timed to be on the Missouri when the immigrants' river boats arrived.

Each church train had a hand-picked and experienced captain who was in complete command. There was at least one teamster per wagon, a commissary chief, a chaplain, a clerk, a captain of the night guard, and several night guards. A train of 50 wagons was staffed with approximately 55 men. The captain got paid one dollar a day; the others received $10 for each trip there and back. Every wagon was supposed to carry 250 lbs. of flour, 40 lbs. of both bacon and dried beef, 10 lbs. of sugar, and 4 lbs. each of coffee and yeast cake, 4 quarts of beans, and as much butter as could be obtained – but only 1 bar of soap.[30]

Months before the *Hudson* even sailed from London, preparations were rapidly underway in the Salt Lake Valley to outfit two church trains that would carry the Howards' company from Nebraska. William Hyde, from Cache Valley in northern Utah, was called to captain one of them and Warren Snow, the other. On May 1, wagons of the Hyde Company started pulling into the eastern Utah canyons to rendezvous on the mountain trails above.

Passage through the mountains and across the Plains was ever risky and dangerous, and this was true for these two eastward moving trains, as well. They moved as rapidly as they could and made good time. Following heavy rainstorms, however, the Hyde Company wagons reached the South Platte River to find it flooded a mile wide. With no time to wait for the floodwaters to recede, the teamsters innovated. They took the wagons apart, tied four wagon boxes together, sealed them with tar and rags, and "sailed" them across the swollen waters. They managed to get the oxen to swim the expanse.

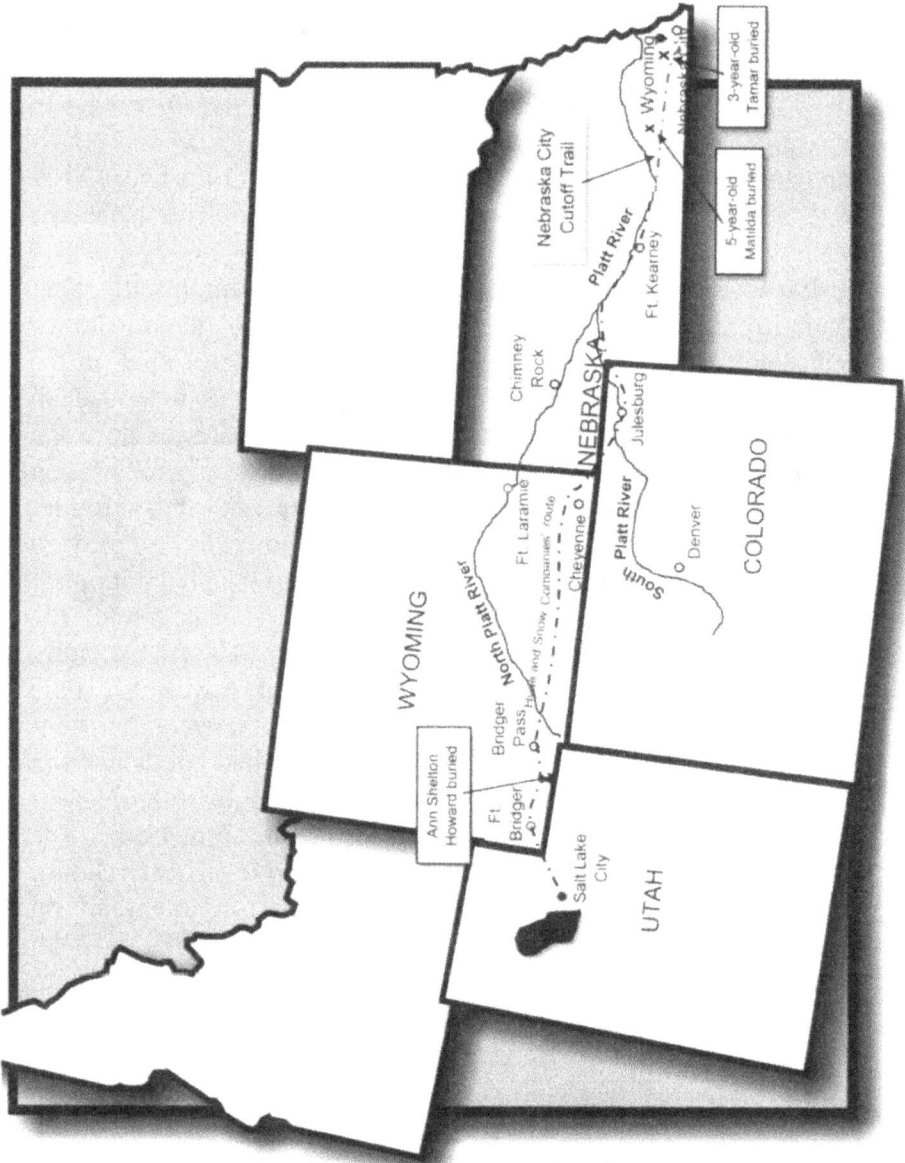

Map H – Howard Family Route Across the Western United States

The two church trains again hurried their pace at 20-30 miles a day to be at their destination on the Missouri River before the Howards' party got there. In the end, they arrived a few weeks ahead of the river boats, perhaps owing to the *Hudson's* delayed departure from London. The wagons of the Hyde and Snow companies parked and waited for the passengers to arrive. They were at a riverbank settlement called "Wyoming" in Nebraska Territory.

Early that year, the PEF chose the small Wyoming settlement, about 40 miles south of Omaha, to be its new embarkation site for immigrant parties bound for Utah. It was an isolated spot on the west side of the Missouri River, about 10 miles closer to St. Joseph than the previous jump-off point, and just a few miles north of the new thriving town of Nebraska City. Wyoming was smaller than Nebraska City but also lacked the vices prevalent in the busy frontier town. Nebraska City was close enough, however, to provide provisions, blacksmithing, and repairs needed in the preparations.[31]

When the *Lacy* arrived at the Wyoming encampment, the Howards were assigned to the Hyde Company. Almost the entire party from the *Hudson* was still together and split between the Hyde and Snow wagon trains. They were joined by others coming from elsewhere in the United States. John Kay, who had led them from London, was relieved of his responsibilities, and all authority was transferred to the two wagon company captains from Utah. The Howards received their supplies from a centrally located storehouse and camped there on the edge of the prairie waiting to embark on the great journey before them. They cooked over bonfires and slept under the stars. A spring located in a group of trees near the camp was a laundry place, and Ann and the girls did not have to wash clothes in the muddy Missouri.

The Howards' Hyde Company was one of six church trains departing from Wyoming, Nebraska, that year. The Snow company following theirs was the season's last. It is easy to imagine the eagerness filling the air while the immigrants congregated. The wagons were waiting, and freight had to be loaded, and the day they would move out toward the "promised land" was almost at hand.

The Howard family spent a week at the staging point while everyone was assigned to wagons, and the ox-drawn trains were loaded with baggage and freight. Staying put in one spot for several days in a row was a luxury the family had not enjoyed since climbing off the *Hudson* three weeks before. With all the busy preparations, however, rest from the relentless travel westward was not long enough.

The harsh conditions of the overland travel had taken a toll among the Howards and many others of their party who suffered immensely from illnesses contracted along the way. Diarrhea and dysentery were probably the most prevalent. Joseph and his son James were both sick. The Howards' daughter, small Tamar was seriously ill. John Lyman Smith, a company leader who also took ill, wrote that within 48 hours he lost 45 pounds. They expected him to die, but he survived.

Everything was under preparation for the long trip ahead. In addition to the passengers and their possessions, the wagons were also carrying freight west to Salt Lake. Many of the large wagons were painted bright colors, red and blue, not to be cheery, but because these colors contained lead pigments that sealed them better against the elements and river crossings ahead.

Each wagon was loaded with about 1200 pounds of freight. The passengers' belongings were stacked on top of that. Everything was loaded top to bottom, and there remained no space for anyone to sit or ride. Everyone but the teamster walked. A few of the immigrants were taken on as teamsters, but most wagons were driven by the men who brought the wagons from Utah.

Four to six oxen pulled the heavy cargoes. Oxen were slower but cheaper than mules and endured hardships better. The William Hyde Company, carrying Joseph, Ann, and family, had 365 people and 65 wagons. The Warren Snow party was outfitted simultaneously. It would follow close behind to afford better protection against Sioux war parties who that summer were raiding and burning all across the wagon trail routes that stretched westward. A man named Howell drove the wagon that they shared with another family.[32]

The Great Plains

When the day to push off across the prairie came, everyone gathered around the wagons, children, men, women, the strong, the weak, the ill, and even those too weak or ill to travel. Tuesday, August 9, late in the afternoon, Howell whipped the reigns, the oxen trudged forward, and the wagon jerked to a start along the rutted meandering dirt trail. At first, they headed southwest to link up with the Nebraska City Cutoff Trail that eventually would follow along the south side of the Platte River. This was the first year Mormon trains used the cut-off that led to the Mormon Trail at Fort Kearny. Overall, it was an easier beginning with fewer difficult river and creek crossings than the trail further north (see Map H).

The Howards' wagon was so full that they walked that day and every one after that. Thirteen-year old Mary Ann and their family friend, Mary Lowe, strode ahead of the wagon. Three-year old Tamar, sick and frail, travelled in the arms of her mother Ann. But they were finally moving along the last leg of their long passage, closer each day to the Zion of their dreams where two sons already awaited them.

For many, the panorama of the prairie's wide sweep, with its rolling hills and endless grass horizon, fashioned a stirring start for their journey. Sophia Goodridge wrote of the view in her diary, "...one endless sea of grass, wavy and rolling like the waves of the sea, and now and then a tree." Another young woman felt incapable of adequately portraying her feelings, "Oh how I wish mine were a painters pencil or a poets pen." She added, "My heart exclaimed how beautiful how wonderful thou art sweet earth."[33] But for the Howards, with a very sick child, weary from an already long journey, it was not so poetic. They still had two and a half months ahead of them, until late October, before the family's journey would finally reach its end in Salt Lake City's Pioneer Park.

The train only made about a mile before it stopped to sleep on a small creek surrounded with wood and grass. That night, at their first camp, two already enfeebled fellow travelers died. "We all felt very Sad they were buried," wrote a young man sent from Utah to teamster emigrants west. The next day the company started off again after organizing a committee to look after the sick and bury the dead. The train only made about four miles this second day.[34]

Three-year old Tamar, suffering from what they called "Mountain Fever," continued to weaken. By nighttime, her feeble body in her mother's arms, could last no more. It is hard to know what exactly it was, probably dysentery, diarrhea, and dehydration. They placed her small lifeless body into the ground. There was no coffin, little ceremony, just a shallow grave. They left Tamar there as the wagons pulled forward in their seemingly ceaseless procession. The rest of the family was distraught and distressed. The little grave stayed behind.

A few days later, the company was alerted that Sioux war parties were along the trail ahead. The Sioux attacks were part of a larger Indian war that began the year before and engulfed much of the eastern and central plains. The Sioux were troubled by the heavy flow of migrant trains that in addition to immigrants carried a large number of gold and silver prospectors hurrying West. The Indians fought to protect their rights to buffalo migration grounds throughout the region. Hostilities were especially common along the South Platt River, exactly where the Howards' train was headed.

Captain Hyde brought the wagons to a halt, and the company waited for the Snow Company behind them to catch up. The two trains had no military escort, and their passengers were an easy target. The people were mainly European immigrants, unused to the frontier, and few of them were armed. Most had probably never used a firearm. The trains were especially vulnerable since the Union had recently recalled some units assigned to protect the east-west trails. The Army needed the troops to defend against a major Confederate campaign in Kansas and Missouri expected to take place in the next few weeks. Once the Snow Company was alongside, the two started off again.

There were many perils, some more dangerous than Indian attacks. Disease was one. John L. Smith wrote that health in the camp was very poor. Diarrhea was prevalent. For whatever reason, travelers in the Hyde Company, the Howards among them, suffered

307

much more than was common. Perhaps it was the bad start they endured when they traveled in the cattle manure-littered rail cars across Missouri. Perhaps it came from drinking the dirty Missouri water.

On Saturday, August 20, just eleven days on the trail, Ann and Joseph said goodbye to a second daughter when they lost five-year old Matilda whose little sick body could no longer survive the strain. Matilda, like Tamar, was carefully set into a shallow grave they dug before hurrying to catch up with the wagons that did not stop for burials (see Map H). The next morning Matilda's twin sister Elizabeth trudged forward with her grief-stricken parents and family. One of the Utah teamsters wrote about the tragedy of leaving loved ones behind:

> "Such an occurrence was very sad. The whole train could not be held up for burial services, and so – three or four teamsters driving better and younger oxen would stay behind for the task of disposing of the body. They would dig a crude grave, often hitting water. If that occurred dirt and brush would be thrown in the grave, then the body, wrapped in whatever could be spared, was laid away with very little ceremony. Then those who had participated in the burial rushed to catch up with the rest."[35]

About that time, two of the Howard sons, James and Joseph, Jr., hired out to a freight train to earn extra money and separated from the rest of the company. The Howards obviously were pinching their pennies, and any additional income was important. The large family was now split: two boys were already in Utah, two more were working on a separate train, and Joseph and Ann continued with the remaining children. And there were the two little ones they had left behind in shallow graves. Under these circumstances, it is easy to understand how distressing it was for Ann to say good-bye to James and Joseph, Jr., even though she expected to see them at the end of the journey several weeks later.

The companies kept moving westward. They did not follow the traditional trail, but theirs continued along a more southerly route along the South Platte River and cut across north of Cheyenne to link up with the well-used Mormon trail in western Wyoming (see Map H). Although somewhat shorter, it, too, had its hardships.

The pioneer families pulled out of camp early in the morning and frequently halted after 2-3 miles to water and rest the cattle. At noon, the train paused for at least two hours again to graze livestock. As they walked, women and girls gathered buffalo chips for campfires. Ten-year old John Shelton Howard remembered how he and other small boys would find riding sticks and pretend to drive each other like the teamsters handled the oxen. In the afternoon there were two additional breaks, one mid-afternoon, and a later one that lasted two hours.

After the evening meal, a horn sounded, indicating it was time to turn in. There were the nighttime sounds: crying children and babies, women talking over the campfires in the rain or moaning in the pangs of birth, and all joining in song to relieve the tensions of the hard journey. After everyone turned in for the night, the natural light of the moon and universe of stars beamed down brightly, unimpeded by ground reflections of cities, streetlights, and cars, like today. And the sounds of nature – braying oxen, snorting buffalo, roaring rivers, the howling of coyotes and wolves on the trails behind and before them – drifted over the air.

Not many days on the trail, the wagons passed a still smoldering mail station that Indians had burnt to the ground. Alongside the trail a board stuck in the rubble told that a Sioux war party had killed six people there the day before. Once they saw Indians in the distance with dust rising as if they were rushing the train. The wagons were ordered to pull over to conceal themselves under the brow of a hill on the Platte riverbank. One wagon turned over, and two of its passengers, a mother and her newborn baby, were caught underneath. Both survived, but the woman remained an invalid the rest of her life. For 400 miles, the two trains sought safety by hovering close to each other along the troubled plains. They saw several small merchant trains that had been robbed and their teamsters killed, but the two companies passed safely.

The wagons trekked forward. At Fort Kearny, on August 30th, they found over 400 wagons backed up in response to the hostilities, waiting for a go-ahead to move forward on their journeys. The Hyde and Snow companies could not wait. They were already late in the season with the first snows only weeks away. They continued the next day, two-abreast. On Friday, the 2nd of September, the Howards saw several hundred troops in a "lazy camp." On Sunday, the 4th, they moved out at 8:00 a.m., and some observed Indian scouting from the hills. After three weeks' travel at about 18 miles a day, they were into Wyoming, on the rising prairie, rolling toward the ridges of the Rocky Mountains.[36]

The Rocky Mountains

Joseph and Ann probably rejoiced at the thought that their long and difficult journey was drawing closer to its end. With September, however, summer changed to fall in the high elevations. The strenuous journey continued to take its toll. No one was exempt. Everyone was vulnerable. On September 27, John Kay, the party's leader from London to Nebraska, died after being ill for several weeks. The road rising ever upward became rough. On the 28th there was a "sharp frost" on the trail. Sunday, October 2, was cold and snowing. Three inches of snow fell.

On October 7, a stagecoach caught up to the Hyde train at the head of Bitter Creek, Wyoming. Inside sat Elder George Q. Cannon, whom they had last seen when he disembarked from the *Hudson*, a few moments before it pulled away from the London docks. It was Cannon who managed the departure of the Howards and their fellow passengers. His term as head of the Church mission in Great Britain had ended, and he was on his return to the Salt Lake Valley, following fairly closely the same route across the American continent that the Howards had journeyed.

That evening Elder Cannon wrote in his journal, "We passed a large company of Saints in camp this morning travelling under Capt. Wm Hyde... There had been forty deaths in the company since they

310

started and many were still suffering from a species of typhus fever. They were exceedingly glad to see us and it was almost with difficulty that we could tear ourselves away from them."[37]

Among those critically ill was Ann Howard, 47 years old, mother of the large family, a woman who had endured so much loss on this journey. Ann was weak; her health, in sharp decline. Upon hearing that Ann was seriously ailing, Mary Lowe, who was a few wagons ahead of the Howards, came back to find her. "Mother, how are you tonight?" she asked. Ann strained, "I'll never see my dear boys again."[38]

The day Elder Cannon passed the party, Ann began to sway back and forth and was on the verge of collapsing. Joseph wrapped her in his arms. He told their teamster that Ann needed to ride, but the man refused to allow her to sit on the crowded wagon. There was an angry exchange before the wagon was brought to a stop. "Father unloaded some of their necessities and carefully lifted his wife into the wagon but there wasn't room for mother to lie down," told their daughter Emma.

Ann did not have the strength to sit up straight, and Joseph walked next to her at the rear of the wagon, propping her up. Finally, Joseph put Emma beside Ann to hold her upright. Ann grew still weaker. That night they arranged pillows for her to lean against. The next morning her journey from Birmingham came to an end.

"My mother died with her head on my lap," Emma remembered. The oxen were already yoked to the wagon and were ready to depart when she passed. Emma and her two sisters combed Ann's hair, washed the body, put on clean clothes, and sewed sheets around her. It is easy to imagine the tears flowing down the young cheeks, dripping onto Ann's hair, as the family now lost their beloved mother at Bitter Creek, Wyoming, only 23 days away from the Salt Lake Valley.

Emma described the tragic moment:

"Our clothing was sewed up in a big burlap sack which had been painted black. This paint kept the water out. The sack was opened and mother's best clothes were gotten out. Sister Jones and Sister

Lowe, who later became Thomas's wife, washed mother and dressed her and I combed her hair. While this was going on, the men dug the grave... They sewed mother up in sheets. Sagebrush was put in the bottom of the grave and she was laid on top of the brush. Then more sagebrush was put over her. The earth was packed down over her. They piled sagebrush on top of the grave and burned it to keep the wolves from digging her up. Then they piled more brush on it."

As the wagons drew away, Mary Lowe's eyes drew back across the snow-covered high desert plain, to the mound as it faded into the growing distance, "...the smoke burning up from the grave. They built a fire on all the graves to keep the animals away." Ann had joined her dear daughters, Matilda and Tamar, whose shallow resting spots the train of wagons had left behind weeks earlier. [39]

Two weeks earlier, Salt Lake's *Deseret News* had reported a telegram advising that the Hyde and Snow companies, last two of the season, were approaching Utah. The companies needed 50 yokes of oxen to meet them at the head of Bitter Creek on account of the loss of their own diseased livestock, the newspaper reported. Quickly, people in the valley mobilized to send supplies and teams. Later, when the trains were a week out of the Salt Lake Valley, the *Deseret News* included "Joseph Howard and family" among a list of members of the Hyde Company that was about to enter the Salt Lake Valley. After drawing close along the mountain approaches, the wagons of the Hyde Company carrying Joseph and his children, painstakingly inched their way down the steep grades of Parley's Canyon. It was snowing. It took them three days to reach the valley.

Thomas and William, the brothers who had traveled from Birmingham three years earlier, probably learned of their family's pending arrival from the *Deseret News* reports. The boys were waiting to welcome them when the train pulled into Pioneer Park, the disembarkation point for trains reaching the valley. They had already heard that their family had suffered a tragedy. When, in a bitter-sweet moment, they finally found their weary father and siblings, they discovered that it was their mother who had died, not their father as they had been told.

The valley's Bishops had members of their congregations meet the Hyde and Snow companies with tents, food, doctors, and other supplies for the worn travelers. Many people knew firsthand what the companies had been through and were generous. The *Deseret News* reported, "Every Ward, and almost every family freely responded to the Bishops' call."[40]

It had been an unbearably heavy journey, full of toil, sorrow and death. There is an inescapable irony in knowing that if they had left Birmingham only five years later, Joseph's and Ann's trip would have been a much different one. After 1869, all immigrants from England sailed on steam vessels and traveled directly to Utah by train across the new transcontinental railroad. The journey took three weeks over the ocean and inland, compared to the nearly five grueling months the Howards suffered.

The remarkable change in the convenience of traveling from England to Utah was probably not something they could have foreseen when sitting in their cottage on Thimble Mill Lane. Or, perhaps even if they had seen it, they might have still chosen to come when they did. It is impossible to overestimate the level of commitment and determination that motivated these families.

In a way hard to understand today, the rest of the Howard family story reveals that the journey to their promised land did not end in Pioneer Park. The wagon train's terminus was just the beginning of new productive lives that commenced almost immediately. People from our generation suffering what they went through would probably face years of post-traumatic stress and therapy. They might not even be able to mount a normal life again. But that was not the case with the Howard family.

After arriving in the valley, they moved to the community of West Bountiful, a few miles north of Salt Lake City. The first winter, they weathered in a covered wagon and subsisted on roots and weeds. It was still hard. But they soon bought farms, and started everything anew, industriously becoming prominent in both their church and community.

313

I was inspired when I learned how the Howards remained so close to each other. About two years after settling in West Bountiful, Joseph called his family together to say he would like to re-marry. He asked if they would approve of his marriage to Catherine Woodall, another English immigrant. The family agreed to the union, and Caroline was accepted into the family. Emma, who held her mother Ann's head in her lap as she passed away on the hard back of an overloaded covered wagon, wrote, "Caroline gave the children the loving care and affection of a mother which proved to be a blessing to the family."[41]

Leaving Stories for our Children

On one of our trips to England, we drove to Birmingham. The big city's aura of hustle, bustle, and transformation had not changed since our ancestors walked the same streets. Although we had been in Britain many times, and even lived there for four years, this was the first time we had visited the busy city with such an important industrial past.

Nineteenth century Birmingham was the hometown of two families I was researching, Joseph and Ann Howard, and Eli and Mary Elizabeth Taylor. The Howards were on my father's side; the Taylors, on my mother's. They both came from similar struggling working-class circumstances, and quite coincidently, probably knew each other. I wanted to walk the same neighborhoods they did, to see what they saw, or to sense what they might have felt on a good day, and a bad one. A writer once said he could write a history of the world without leaving a home.[42] I wanted to see their homes.

Before traveling, I had spent a lot of time trying to collate as much material as I could find from the internet and family files. Unfortunately, I found very few words directly attributable to Joseph and Ann Howard. To my knowledge, only one of their letters from Birmingham and no journals survived. But almost all their children in their later lives wrote short accounts of their parents and family. These sketches provided the first-hand contact I hoped for. A later generation of descendants compiled these reminiscences into a single booklet which I was able to access on a computer at an LDS

Family History Center near where I lived. Their granddaughter Tillie's children followed the example, and each penned two or so pages of recollections of growing up during the late 19th and early 20th century. I found a stapled typed copy in one of Mother's files.

These two families' efforts to convey family memories to me and others of their posterity sent a powerful message. I talk more about this elsewhere in this book, but our stories need to be communicated to later generations. I was inspired to do the same. One afternoon, I wrote an email to our children asking if they would compose a two- or three-page description of what they remember best about growing up in our home. It took a while, but eventually we had something from all four of them. We added our own recollections, included some past photographs of us and places we had lived, and published them in one of the many photobook opportunities you find online. For Christmas we gave beautifully bound volumes to all our children. It cost less than something we might otherwise have given – something that probably would have been broken or forgotten with time. Maybe our children's grandchildren will one day discover this volume with the same excitement I felt when I discovered the compilation of memories from my great-grandparents' and great-great-great grandparents' families.

Old and New Maps

During my pre-trip preparations for the UK trip, I had also spent time pinpointing where the Howards lived, walked, and worked. I surveyed all the information I had and then googled for old maps of Birmingham. I quickly pulled up an 1860s map that I studied alongside modern online street maps. With some good luck (that I consider more than luck) and a bit of work, I eventually had a set of maps in my hands the morning we arrived in Birmingham.

We drove about an hour and a half from our friend Mary Lou's pleasant cottage where we had spent the two previous nights. Somehow, we survived the narrow country roads. To avoid oncoming vehicles, we drove in the middle when not forced into hedges on the left. Finally, however, we reached the area in

Birmingham we were seeking, and, Seija and I parked our rental car in a super-sized Chinese food mall in Aston.

On the top of an 1862 letter to their two sons already in Utah, Joseph or Ann had written their address: "Thimble Mill Lane, Nechells Green."[43] In Britain "green" is another word for "park," so my conclusion was that their home was on Thimble Mill Lane and next to what showed as Nechells Park on an 1864 Birmingham map I had discovered on the internet. I looked at the map, then the Google map on my phone, and then at the street. That was exactly where we had parked the car. What must have been the location of a humble cottage in the early 1860s was now the parking lot of the largest Chinese food operation we had ever seen.

So, however unromantic it might have seemed, we had already found one of the locations we were looking for. It was not exactly what I was expecting, but I also wanted to find another of their homes. We entered the supermarket through one door and left through another so the parking security man would not know we were leaving our parked car in his lot for a few moments. Before exiting, we stopped to admire the aisles full of Chinese food with their many shoppers.

We walked north on Thimble Mill Lane and crossed one of the canals built by Birmingham's fathers to support the city's transport needs during the Industrial Revolution. I knew that the Howards once lived near a canal – some of the early family histories mentioned how they often watched boats pulled along the canals. Passing over one of the bridges, we saw how the waterway was now still. No laden boats made their way up or down the quiet waters. We continued down a Birmingham lane toward Aston's St. Peter and St. Paul Parish Church whose tall steeple towered above the congested Aston Expressway running past it. According to Joseph's and Ann's marriage license, this was where they were married.

One morning, while in Virginia researching where the Howards lived, I had opened my computer to the FamilySearch site to have a window pop-up offering me a "hint." It was a link to the 1861 British Census. Clicking on it brought up an entry for the Joseph Howard family. I was excited when I saw the census taker had

316

written down their address: "Church Lane." My 1864 Birmingham Map and my Google maps app both showed a "Church Road," but no "Church Lane." I wanted Church Lane but was willing to go with Church Road, which, as I saw on both old and modern maps, was close to the Parish Church where they were married. Still, I had my eye out for Church Road while we continued toward the Aston Parish Church.

After crossing a small street, I caught sight of a street sign through the corner of one eye. I knew what it said before I read it: "Church Lane." I turned toward the sign, and that indeed is what it said. We were walking on the street where they lived in 1861. In 1862, they had written to their sons in Utah, "My dear boys, we have left Hope Cottage. The rent is more than we can pay."[44] So they had left Church Lane to live in something less expensive on Thimble Mill Lane, a few blocks away. We stepped along the same way they had rushed, walked, and strolled each day. Hope Cottage had long ago been replaced by row houses that looked like they were built sometime in the mid-20th century, but this was the street where they lived.

As we passed under the freeway, we saw on the road's other side the large parish church. Its stone walls were still layered with black soot that had settled day-after-day when the city was still heated with soft coal. All the church's doors seemed to be locked until we found one open in a side building. We entered only to find no one. Before us was a long hallway that we followed until turning and passing through a doorway, the Gothic structure's high-ceilinged chapel suddenly soared up before us. That day the church was deserted – we were alone with not another soul in sight.

There, before the altar, young strong Joseph and tall beautiful Ann had stood one day in November 1842. Outside, in front of the main door, I could see in my mind's eye a party of friends and family congratulating the young married couple as they jubilantly emerged from the ceremony, cheerful and enthusiastic, like most just-marrieds.

It was, in fact, the beginning of a life's journey, one that was to be harder, sometimes more tragic, and sometimes more glorious,

317

*than they could have imagined. It must have been as happy a day
as any can be. How powerful it was for us, standing in the place of
that celebration long ago, to take a quick look into the past and
somehow imagine what it was like. For me, it was a moment of
connection with some of those many grandmothers and grandfathers
whose stories made mine.*

Motivations

*I was always on the look-out for motivations: what moved our
families to do what they did? When able to answer this question, I
learned as much about them as I did from their actions. Wandering
the streets of Birmingham, I could not help but wonder why Joseph
and Ann left their home, friends, and families. They knew that before
them was a perilous passage across the ever-unpredictable Atlantic
to a Civil War-torn America and the dangers of the American West.
They would have known the risks, but, undaunted, they did leave.
There must have been many answers to this question.*

*We understood one of them better during a fascinating visit the
next day to the Gadfield Elm Chapel, only 50 miles from
Birmingham. The small building today is one of the oldest Mormon
chapels in the world. In the 1840's, early missionaries baptized
nearly 2,000 converts into the Church of Jesus Christ of Latter-day
Saints from this little countryside community. Ten years later, none
of these people were left. Almost all had emigrated to Utah. They
sold the chapel, itself, to help pay for the passage of their poorer
members, and the meeting house passed through several roles
before being re-acquired and re-dedicated 150 years later.*

*In the early days of the movement, the church called its members
to assemble in "Zion," which was wherever the church happened to
be congregating at the time. For the Howards, it was in Utah, in
the dry Great Basin of the western United States. Mormon pioneers
had turned the high valley floors from sagebrush to prosperous
fields, and Salt Lake became for a time one of the largest cities west
of the Mississippi.*

*Thousands followed the church's call, not just to be near other
Mormons, but also to find opportunities to escape the squalor so*

318

many poverty-stricken people in that day's Europe knew too well. These people wanted to have a chance to have their own farms and shops and to avoid the rampant intolerance that made it difficult for many of them to worship as they pleased. At the core of most people's decision to migrate to Utah was a conviction that what they were doing was right.

Conviction is a powerful force for many people, and this was especially true for Joseph and Ann. They had a new faith, and it burned inside them. Mormonism's then strong call to gather to the still relatively unsettled Utah valleys was a beacon that pulled them and many other Mormons throughout Europe into this mass migration to Utah.

A year after our first visit to Birmingham, we returned again. This time we journeyed by train from London. As the train made its stop-and-go way towards Birmingham, we realized how much easier such travel was for us than it had been for them, even though our trip did have its own discomforts. Along the way, the engine malfunctioned, and somewhere in the countryside Seija and I had to transfer to another train. With two big suitcases, two carry-on's, and a couple of handbags, but only four arms and hands, every movement had to be done in stages. We forfeited our reserved seats for no seats on the replacement train, and there was no place for our bags, nor hardly for us.

The rest of the way to Birmingham, we stood there between cars, next to the door, wobbling and trying to keep our balance, bags on the floor. It was definitely outside our comfort zone, but it lasted only 45 minutes. For the Howards, every moment of each day was something new, beyond what they had ever experienced, and often outside their comfort zones – and this would last months, not minutes.

At the end of the Birmingham visit, we again boarded the train. We slowly moved from the super-modern New Street Station and began to pick up speed. We passed by dilapidated red brick factories, one after another. One had "Glass" painted in big letters on its side. All its glass windows were long gone, and there were holes where parts of the roof had caved in. These old buildings were

319

once the sweltering sirens whose call beckoned hordes of workers to the industrial city.

After a few minutes we pulled into another station, and across from us we saw a stopped train pointed the other direction. Its windows were crowded with people. A mother holding a small baby peered curiously from one of them, and through another we saw all its busy passengers chatting and anxiously awaiting to resume their journeys.

I imagined the crowded coaches carrying Joseph, Ann, and the rest of their family, clicking down the rails, the people dressed in their best hats, coats, skirts, and ties. The locomotive whistled, the steam, smoke, and soot drifted by the windows and through the cracks, and everyone chattered loudly to be heard over the din of travel.

Diaries and Letters of Fellow Travelers

In an earlier chapter I mentioned that to find our stories we do not have to rely simply on what forefathers and mothers may have told or written. I found that this was especially true about the Howards when I discovered a trove of documents their fellow travelers left us. The 19ᵗʰ century LDS migration West – the "Mormon Pioneers" – was a vast movement of 70,000 people, a monumental saga in settling the western United States. Over the past few decades, Brigham Young University and the Historians Office of the Church of Jesus Christ of Latter-day Saints have collected and placed online a huge compilation of diaries, letters, newspaper articles, and other primary materials. These are a treasure for any descendant of these people.

The site is available for anyone's use (see the footnotes or bibliography for links). The material is organized by travel parties. I followed the index to find to which parties the Howards belonged. Then, accessing the parties, I discovered day-to-day stories of Howards' travel from London to Salt Lake City from multiple original documents. Through the eyes of those around them, it was possible to sail with the Howards and walk alongside their ox-drawn covered wagon. I heard the voices of the men and women, and girls and boys, who traveled with the Howards during that long summer of 1864.

Ellis Island and Castle Garden

Many people tracking immigrant forefathers and mothers find Ellis Island records useful. However, America's famous immigrant reception facility Ellis Island did not open until 1892 and did not yet exist when earlier immigrants landed in New York harbor. Before that, they processed at Castle Garden. Located in what is today's Battery Park, on the southern tip of Manhattan, Castle Garden was America's premier arrival point.

Castle Garden was originally built as Fort Clinton with the mission to protect New York from a possible British attack during the War of 1812. Later, in 1855, it became the place where most immigrants first stepped onto American soil. Over 8 million immigrants passed through Castle Garden's doors between the time it opened and 1892. Among them were Joseph and Ann Howard, and family. The year they arrived, over 193,000 immigrants entered America, and of them, 180,000 came through Castle Garden.

Seija and I visited Castle Garden the summer before our first trip to Birmingham. We went there to get tickets for the Statue of Liberty. Boats departing for the statue and Ellis Island were leaving from just behind Castle Garden, which is now called by its original name, "Fort Clinton." At the time, we were not aware that this was place the Howards first entered the United States.

We purchased the tickets under one of Fort Clinton's many arches. Inside the rotunda I bought myself a baseball cap with an American flag above the inscription "National Park Service." Then, wearing my cap, we boarded a ferry crowded with people from all over the world. We embarked from the spot where, almost exactly 151 years before, the Howards had arrived. The ferry slowly pulled from Castle Garden's wharf, the trademark Manhattan skyline behind us and the Statue of Liberty growing larger before us. The statue had beckoned to millions of people who came seeking a life free from the oppression that they knew, and one full of opportunities they had not yet found.

To see the statue was a moving experience for Seija, herself an immigrant from Finland, for it symbolized the arrival that had changed her life. The Statue of Liberty was not yet there for the Howards to see, but for them, stepping ashore that summer afternoon must have been as powerful an experience as it was for Seija. After emotion-provoking visits to the statue and Ellis Island, our ferry slipped back across the water to a city that has never been anything but a world crossroad. Even today, 37 percent of New York's people are born outside the United States, more than the whole population of Chicago.[45]

The next year we visited Fort Clinton again. This time, I knew many more of the Howard family stories, and understood the significance Castle Garden had in their great journey from Birmingham to Salt Lake City. Both my wife and I were having landmark birthdays that summer, and to celebrate, our family booked passage on a sail ship tour of the harbor and Statue of Liberty. Our cheerful group of passengers, wearing shorts, T-shirts, and baseball caps was hardly reminiscent of the Howards' arrival in New York. But as the winds drew us across the landscape of New York's skyline, the statue's great uplifted hand and torch, and Fort Clinton's departure and arrival docks, the Hudson's decks, crowded with pilgrims like the Howard family, passed through our view.

Google Maps and Wikipedia: Take-along Tools

It was never practical for us to follow the Howard family's travel West from Castle Garden. However, once, when Seija and I were driving between Kansas City and Omaha, it occurred to me that we were close to the spot where the Howards launched their journey across the plains. We were on the interstate highway that followed the east bank of the Missouri. Somewhere along the way we would pass by the site their wagon train provisioned and departed from the river's other side. Seija and I decided to take a detour to see what we could find.

I studied the two good sources of information that most people these days carry on their smartphones – Wikipedia and Google Maps – and soon had the coordinates for Wyoming, Nebraska.

322

Whenever doing family history travel, carefully pre-planning is always important. However, flexibility to deviate and explore unexpected avenues should always be part of the trip. A good maps app and Wikipedia can greatly facilitate quick on-the-spot research that gives you the possibility to do this.

When we came to the I-29 exit that read "Nebraska City," we pulled off west, took a bridge across the Missouri, and let my phone's Google Maps guide us through a Nebraska City that no longer exuded the zeal the frontier river town must have had in the 1860's. Within a few minutes we turned from a modern divided highway onto a narrow country lane, and soon we were on gravel roads.

Around a turn, two wild turkeys, a tom and his hen, strutted down the middle of the roadway. We stopped to watch them, wondering whether some of their ancestors might have made some very tired pioneer travelers a happy meal that summer of 1864. The turkeys dodged into the high roadside stubble, perhaps with the same thought. The rolling grassy prairie of the Howards' times was now lush undulating north-south folds covered with the fields that made America's Mid-West the world's greatest breadbasket.

When we arrived at the place Google Maps marked "Wyoming," we found a narrow dirt lane that wound down to a farmhouse, barn, and other outbuildings. On the corner of the lane and the gravel road was a dilapidated rusty sign, barely still readable, that announced, "Wyoming Acres, Main Street." The farm below sat on a railroad line that sometime between then and now had had a stop and a post office called Wyoming. The lost spot where the Howards buried little Tamar after only two days on the trail could not have been too far from where my wife and I saw the rusty "Wyoming Acres" sign.

On the other side of the rails, the fields gently sloped downward about a mile or two to a beautifully wooded bend on the Missouri, the spot where the old town of Wyoming once stood. The river boats stopped at that peaceful mooring, and their passengers pulled off their chests and trunks full of things so precious that the families had lugged them over an unbearably long journey. There, men,

323

women, and children began preparing for the even harder leg still ahead.

I contemplated the disparity between the place heralded as "Wyoming Acres," and Birmingham's "Church Lane," where thoughts of this trip had been born. What a stark contrast there was: on one hand, the feverishly growing industrial city they left; on the other, the vast lonesome prairie that now swept before them, nearly empty for almost a thousand miles except for wild animals, hostile Sioux war parties, and fellow pilgrims. My emotions stirred deep inside, but I am sure whatever I felt was nothing compared to what the Howard family experienced the day the J. F. Lacy moored in Wyoming, Nebraska.

We turned around and drove away. I remembered how after visiting the Aston St. Peter and St. Paul Parish Church, that day in Birmingham, Seija and I wandered back to our car. We were absorbed with the streets, the homes that once stood in these neighborhoods, and the canals that were then conveyances of work and wealth, rather than today's attractions and reminders.

I cannot remember seeing another person on the streets we followed. There must have been many who passed us, rushing to stay up with the demands of their own routines and itineraries on a warm clear September day. At that moment, the streets we were walking belonged to a different time and family. We were happy. That is what we had come to find.

Chapter 8

"What was your Name in the States?"
Joseph Richard and Mary Ann Taylor Wilson

"Oh, what was your name in the States?
Was it Thompson, or Johnson, or Bates?"
19th Century American Folk Song[1]

From even before his death in 1902, Joseph Wilson's unscripted life had been an enigma to those around him, and all the more so to those who came afterwards. He left few trail markers, even to those who knew him. In spite of the serious amount of research Mother and several others had done on Joseph Wilson, discovering his stories was a challenge that required a great deal more path-breaking – and often speculation – than most others needed. Joseph was someone who tried never to be found. It took a panoply of sources to find Joseph's and Mary Ann's stories: family traditions and histories, networking with relatives, war records from the National Archives, federal and territory censuses and voter lists, the LDS Church Historians Office records, Ancestry.com and FamilySearch, and many more.

Fort Rice, North Dakota Territory, July 1872

As Fort Rice's gates swung open, Richard McGuire shouldered his Springfield rifle, bayonet fixed, and joined step with his fellow Company K friends and recruits. Or perhaps he marched with the band, instrument in hand. He was, after all, a musician according to his enlistment papers. With soldiers from the other five companies of the 8th Infantry Regiment, the men marched through the gates to form a long column facing west toward the Rocky Mountains. The fort was teaming with troops, horses, and wagons anxiously waiting their turn to pour into formation. The morning was early, but the sun was already well into the sky. The long stretched-out ranks began to take shape.[2]

The night before, Col. D. T. Stanley, the expedition's commander, had telegraphed back to General Winfield Scott Hancock in St. Paul, Minnesota: "We march at 7 a.m. tomorrow."[3] The 17th and 22nd Infantries combined with the 8th into a force of about 600 soldiers, a company of Indian scouts, 100 teamsters and other men, 120 wagons, 1 Napoleon cannon, 3 Gatling guns, and a herd of livestock. In addition to the blue-clad soldiers was a party of Northern Pacific Railroad surveyors.

A bugle called everyone to place. The ladies of the fort, mainly wives of the officers, lined up to watch their men parade out. When the bugle again sounded, their husbands cut farewells short and sped their horses to the proper places.

Finally, Richard heard the command to march, and they all started walking toward the hills that lined the western horizon. As the troops marched forward, the spectators joined in three "long, resounding cheers," and the band struck up a tune "The Girl I Left Behind Me." Linda Slaughter, the wife of the expedition's surgeon, described the decorous, but anxious moment:

"We stood with waving handkerchiefs, saluting our friends, with pleasant words as they marched gaily past us. Soon they have gone by and the long brilliant line of loyal blue winds out among the hills with the morning sun reflected from their glistening bayonets in points of light. We watch them out of sight and then walk back to the fort, with hearts full of apprehensions of dangers in the column and of fear for ourselves in the almost deserted fort."[4]

The isolated, lonesome stockade's upright log walls had protected its occupants from numerous Indian attacks over the previous few years, and now, for those few people left behind, they would afford their main defense. The women and depleted garrison would restlessly await the column's return in this high-prairie fortification on the banks of the Missouri River. That they were surrounded by hostile Sioux and Cheyenne warriors lingered constantly in their minds.

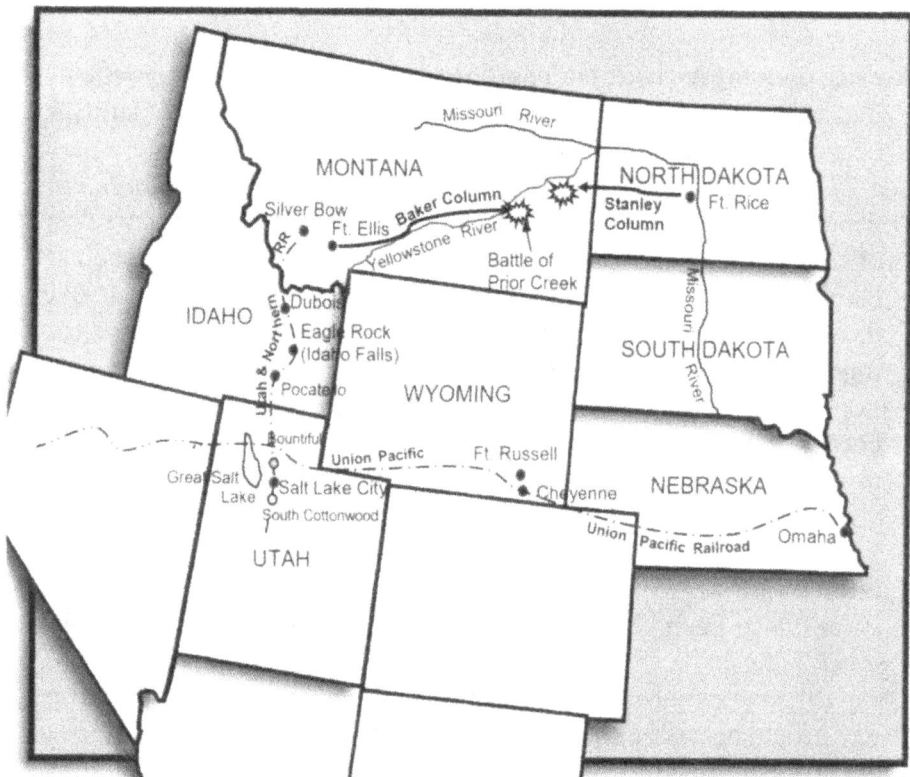

Map I – Northern Rockies and Great Plains

The march across the prairie, hills, and mountains was not short and not easy. If there was any place in the world Richard would rather be, it was not here, not on this march, not on this expedition, not fighting the Sioux, and not in this Army. Joining the Army was a mistake, and he knew it almost immediately after he did it.

In January, only six months earlier, he had gone to the Army's recruitment station on Davids Island, New York, to sign enlistment papers for three years in the infantry. The forms recorded his hazel eyes, dark brown hair, fair complexion, and height of only 5-feet, 4-inches. He was assigned to the 8th **Infantry, then the facility's** headquarters unit.

Davids Island in Long Island Sound was one of three recruitment depots in the **country, and Richard's** basic training, what there was of it, was there. After small unit tactical training, the recruits had learned basic military formations, schedules and routines, and discipline. They were toughened up with calisthenics and physical training. It all lasted only a few weeks.

Richard asked himself why he had joined. Perhaps it was because he had mistakenly thought that the Army would provide a more secure life than the one he had known. As a boy, he and his sister had left their native Ireland during the American Civil War to live with their aunt and uncle in New York City. According to the information he gave the 1900 census taker many years later, he would have been about five years old then. But he was probably much older.[5]

Life had not been easy for him as an Irish lad in New York. The day he and his sister arrived in 1863, was the very day the notorious draft riots erupted in New York City. It began as an explosion of resistance to new conscription laws. The Union wanted more men to fill its ranks in the aftermath of huge losses in Fredericksburg, Chancellorsville, and Gettysburg. The chaos quickly evolved into mass race riots. Hordes of Irish Americans, **Richard's fellow** countrymen, swarmed into the bloodiest street disturbances in American history. Only the arrival of Union troops stemmed the four days of riots that killed hundreds and injured thousands of people. Those violent days were memorialized a century later in

Hollywood's Gangs of New York. This was the city Richard and his sister found on their first day in America.[6]

Growing up in New York was not easy for the young Irish boy and his sister. As a measure of their desperation, even the Army seemed an option for something better. Perhaps with the impulsiveness of youth, or just out of pure despondency, Richard looked into an Army career. He was musical and could sing, and this pleased the recruiters. They wrote "fifer" on his enlistment documents and scrolled in big letters across the upper left-hand corner, "Musician!" They obviously were happy to have a recruit who could play in a unit band one moment and fight the next.[7]

When Richard enlisted, the Civil War had been over for six years. Recruits probably did not come not a dime a dozen when the Army's job was occupying the unrepentant South or fighting bloody Indian Wars on northern prairies or desolate southwestern deserts. If he was five years old when he arrived in the United States in 1863, as he told the 1900 census taker, he would have been only about 14 years old when he signed up. And if that was the case, Richard was lying about his age when he enlisted. Minimum age for enlistment was 18. But if he was 14, as the immigration records suggest, he would have been in his early twenties.

After a month or two, Richard was already eager to get out of the Army. His family approached their congressman, James Brooks, to ask for assistance, claiming Richard was underage and too young to be in the military. Congressman Brooks agreed to help. On April 22, 1872, he wrote a letter to the Secretary of War requesting the Army to discharge Richard from his enlistment obligation on the grounds he was underage.

Brooks asked for as early a reply as possible, probably because the 8th Infantry where Richard was now serving was being reassigned from Davids Island to Wyoming in the summer. The War Department, however, did not buy the under-age argument, and in his response of May 3rd, Secretary Belknep replied that he could not approve the petition because, "minority [is] not applicable to his case, he being over 18 years of age, thereby precluded from the benefit of the law governing the discharge of minors."[8]

Richard realized the Army was not the opportunity he sought, but he was now stuck in a three-year enlistment. Meanwhile, his unit prepared for its summer deployment to the Indian Wars in the West. As their reassignment drew closer, things grew worse when he got so ill with diarrhea that in June he was put in the camp infirmary. After two days in the hospital, however, he was released in time to join his regiment's departure for Ft. Russell. The frontier fort was just outside Cheyenne, Wyoming – a wild town on the new Union Pacific.

There was a rush to get underway. The entire 8th Infantry did not travel together. Six companies of the 8th, including Richard's Company K, were ordered to detour through Fort Rice in North Dakota to reinforce a military escort being formed to protect the Second Yellowstone Expedition. They pulled out by train in early July 1872. A few days later they reached Omaha, Nebraska, where the six companies en route to Fort Rice caught a river boat and chugged up the Missouri River toward North Dakota.[9]

Under the hot July sun, the road out of Fort Rice, if you could call it a road, was crude, long, and dusty. Flies swarmed around the livestock and pestered Richard and the rest of the men. He had been issued three pairs of shoes for the expedition, and it was clear what that meant. Along with the troops was a company of surveyors who were scouting the route for the Northern Pacific Railroad. That was the whole purpose of the Second Yellowstone Expedition. The soldiers' job was to protect the surveyors from threatened Sioux attacks. At best, the large troop escort might serve as a deterrence.

The trip west toward the extreme borders of American civilization must have been an eye opener for a young man only a few years out of Ireland. The expansive rolling prairies poured across the vastness of a place more a continent than a country. First, there was the day-and-night trip by rail to Omaha. Then, on the river, along the Missouri River banks, they had seen sporadic signs of settlement, but the territory was mainly empty and pristine.

Richard and his 8th Infantry buddies had arrived on July 21st, about a week before the expedition was to pull out. When they climbed off the river boat at Fort Rice, they had stepped into an excited atmosphere. The fort did not have enough room for everyone, and they all had bivouacked next to the Missouri. A good-sized force soon lined the riverbank. A city of tents had housed the soldiers while men wandered about talking with new friends. The first few days had been festive, almost like a jamboree.

Inside the fort, every day was full of activities. The ladies held an open house for the officers. Dinner parties and dances lit up the evenings for everyone. The presence of the large body of troops had provided, if only temporarily, a badly missed sense of security for the Fort's permanent contingent of soldiers and officers' wives. Those days were the rare occasion when even the women felt safe enough to go horse-back riding outside the fort. It had not been such a bad start for the expedition, simply too short.

The march ground on. The days were long, and Richard was weary by the time each finally ended. Reveille was at daybreak. Breakfast call was one half hour after Reveille. Fifteen minutes later was sick call. Assembly was one hour and thirty minutes after reveille. The advance commenced 15 minutes after that. They marched all day while scouts sought a suitable location for the next night's camp. After reaching the spot, there was supper, and everyone turned in at sunset when Retreat was bugled.

In front of the long column, the group of Indian Scouts reconnoitered for hostile warrior bands. Behind them, Col. Stanley took serious precautions to protect the men. The 8th was divided into two battalions; the other units formed two additional battalions. One battalion proceeded as the advance guard. Two battalions marched in the center of the column, one on each flank, and the fourth battalion made up the rear guard. Two Gatling guns were stationed with the advance guard, the Napoleon was in the center, and the rear guard had the larger Gatling gun. No one was allowed to fire their weapon at any time unless fired upon. No one was allowed outside the pickets without permission and an escort.

Richard and everyone else fully appreciated the danger they faced. Signs of hostile presence were everywhere. Frequently, braves would ride alongside the column, jeering and taunting the men, totally aware the soldiers would not fire on them first. The expedition's livestock herds were tempting, but not the source of the hostility. The Native American plains tribes were angry the Northern Pacific was being built across their lands on its way from Minnesota to meet the Pacific Ocean in Washington Territory.

Earlier that spring, Sitting Bull, who led the tribes, had sent Spotted Eagle to warn Col. Stanley that they "would tear up the railroad and kill its builders."[10] By the time Richard marched out of Ft. Rice, Sioux, Cheyenne, Arapaho, and Kiowa were camped in nearly 2,000 lodges near the Powder River on the boundaries of North Dakota and Montana.

The plan was this. The railroad's route needed to be surveyed, and it was too dangerous for the surveyors to do their work without a sizeable force protecting them. The previous year, survey teams had successfully marked out much of the route running from Duluth, Minnesota to Tacoma, Washington, but there was still a 225-mile gap to be completed between present day Billings and Glendive, Montana (see Map I).

The 1872 expedition aimed to finish the work. It had two prongs: one side moved west from Fort Rice; a second thrust, under Major Eugene Baker, snaked eastward from Fort Ellis, near today's Bozeman, Montana. The two columns were supposed to meet somewhere west of Glendive. When they did, the survey would be completed. Sitting Bull followed both sides of the expedition from his camp between the two, closely mapping their progress and watching for the first good opportunity to strike.

For the boys just fresh from New York, most days were miserable. Everyone was hungry. Their rations were meager. Meat was mostly salted pork. The colonel sent out hunting parties that received warm welcomes when they brought in game, but it took a heap of hunting to keep 700 men fed. Water was also scarce and often alkaline. Men suffered from dysentery and similar problems.

Richard, who had been ill with severe diarrhea only a month before, seemed more resilient this time. Early on, the 8th Infantry transferred ten men too sick to continue back to Ft. Rice. Seven of them suffered from diarrhea or dysentery, but Richard was not among them. By July 31st, they had got as far as Heart Butte, and from there, they followed the Heart River to Antelope Creek. In the first two weeks, Richard walked 180 miles. Overall, however, things were relatively quiet, and the weather, hot but not extreme.

Richard's prong moving westward from North Dakota was stronger and much better led than the troops from Montana. Maj. Baker from Fort Ellis was careless and vulnerable. Sitting Bull was a smart military leader, and his attention was soon glued to Baker's column. On August 14, at about 3:00 in the early morning, Sitting Bull's braves swam across the Yellowstone River to surprise Baker and his men. When they attacked, the troops awoke to a thunderous roar of gunfire echoing through the timber and across the river. Maj. Baker, drunk in bed, never sobered up enough to lead the fight, but his men did relatively well without him. The attackers were driven off by mid-morning.

The "Battle of Pryor's Creek" was a tactical victory for the blue coats, but it was Sitting Bull who won this fight. With his losses and the unknowns ahead of him, Baker decided to turn his column around and return before linking up with the eastern column to complete the surveying mission. It was not necessarily a bad assessment. Sitting Bull's forces were mounted, better armed, and determined. They knew the terrain better and were at least equal in numbers to Baker's. Worst of all, Baker was not up to the rigors of command. It was over for him.

The day before the Battle of Pryor's Creek, scouts from Richard's escort spotted about 20 warriors in the distance. The men tightened up, kept their eyes peeled, and continued their march toward the Yellowstone River. With no direct communication between the two prongs of the expedition, they had no way of knowing the fate of Baker's column.

Two nights later, just before daybreak when Richard and most of the men were still in their bedrolls, Hunkpapa Sioux war chief Gaul and 20 mounted warriors in war paint barreled out of a nearby stand of trees, yelling their war cries and firing into the camp. A few of them rode close to the sentries and then quickly escaped – a frightening wake-up call. While guarding for further attack, the troops ate breakfast and then pulled out again westward. As soon as they left camp, Sioux warriors ransacked whatever was left behind.

That day, Richard marched 14 miles down O'Fallon Creek, having made 45 miles in three days. The soldiers were now only a few miles from the Yellowstone River. At sunrise the next morning, the surveying party got up early and reached the river by mid-morning. Richard with the rest of the escort joined them later that afternoon. They still did not know Baker's fate. The scouts told Col. Stanley that a large Sioux force was near, and he corralled the wagons, unlimbered his guns, and sent out skirmish lines. But the Sioux did not attack.

When they reached the junction of the Powder and Yellowstone Rivers, they had finished their side of the survey. The men kept looking for Baker's westward column that was supposed to meet them at this spot. There was no sign. Stanley had his cannon fire a few times to signal Baker of their location. When one shell exploded over a nearby mountain, the hilltop suddenly bristled with a mounted Sioux war party nervously glaring down on Stanley's men. A few minutes later, 25-30 warriors galloped down the hill after one of the surveyors who had strayed from the body in search of agates. The party's Ree Indian scouts rushed out to rescue the man and were soon in a running battle with the Sioux warriors.

When things settled down, a tall, erect, and proud looking warrior appeared on the other side of the Powder River. He made a sign of peace. He wore nothing put paint, a breach cloth, and a worn-out stove pipe hat. It was Gaul, the Hunkpapa Chief. Gaul was handsome, well structured, and striking. Col. George Custer's wife Elizabeth, when she once saw him, wrote, "I never in my life dreamed there could be in all the tribes so fine a specimen of a warrior as Gall."[11]

Richard and the rest of the troops watched as Col. Stanley came out on their side of the Powder to face Gaul from the opposite bank. Both men laid down their arms, and Stanley invited Gaul to meet with him in the middle of the shallow river. Gaul refused. Through an interpreter, Gaul beat his chest and accused the "white dogs" of making his people poor. "I shall never make peace while the land measurers stay; go home and make no marks upon the ground," he demanded.

Stanley said he wanted peace and offered to buy the land, but Gall shouted back, "You lie!" The tension grew, and just as Stanley started to move back from the river bank, Gaul's warriors began to fire from the brush on the far side. The troops returned the shooting until the Sioux disengaged.[12]

On August 19, a telegram arrived at Fort Rice from General Hancock at his Minnesota headquarters:

> "Major Baker in command of the Montana escort down the Yellowstone was attacked on the morning of the 14th... at the mouth of Prices River by a War party of four or five hundred (500) Arappahoes and Cheyennes [sic]. Indians were repulsed. Their loss not known. Our loss is considerable. If you can do so, communicate this to Stanley by an Indian courier at once..."[13]

After the attack, Baker had got a messenger with the news back to Fort Ellis with amazing speed. From Montana, Ft. Ellis telegraphed Hancock's headquarters in Minnesota which in turn had the report to Ft Rice in North Dakota by the 19th of August. It took a full month for Goose, an Indian Scout, to carry this telegram to Col. Stanley's party, but the colonel already knew what had happened by August 20th, only a day after Fort Rice received Hancock's message. In those hills and mountains, an informal Native American chatter efficiently spread news even between enemies.

The eastern expedition's escort had done its job, but the western element was still 150 miles away and on its way back to Fort Ellis. The mission had failed its overall objective to survey the remaining wilderness for the Northern Pacific's tracks. Col. Stanley turned the column for the long and dangerous march to Fort Rice. They also heard that Sitting Bull was riding to reinforce Gaul's war party. In fact, Sitting Bull, fresh from dealing with Maj. Baker's troops, had already joined Gaul. Fortunately for Richard's party, the Sioux chief had ridden hard and not all his warriors had yet caught up with him. The Sioux were also short on ammunition.

The sun was hot in the sky by 9:00 the morning of August 22. Davids Island seemed a universe away, though just a month had passed since Richard, Company K, and the rest of the 8th had arrived at Fort Rice. Only a month, and they were already trying to escape a bloody battle with Sioux warriors in this desolate place. It was hard to believe this was even the United States. Everything was wild and rough wilderness where one's life was ever in danger of being extinguished with a hostile shot or arrow.

The camp had been up since just after 6:00, and they were already in the O'Fallon Creek Valley navigating in the general direction of far off Ft. Rice. The narrow canyon was only half a mile wide with steep hills on either side, a perfect place for an ambush. If the attack of two days earlier was going to resume, this was the likely place.

At the canyon's narrowest point, Sitting Bull and about 200 warriors surged into view in a frightening display. Col. Stanley and the men, not totally surprised by the attack at this vulnerable point, jumped to action. The wagons were tightly circled, and the infantry spread out into skirmish lines. A war party of about 100 warriors charged at full gallop toward the rear guard that was nervously readying their weapons.

The soldiers opened up the Gatling guns, ten-barreled hand-cranked early machine guns capable of shooting 350 rounds a minute. "Blam-blam-blam-blam-blam-blam!" the Gatling guns pumped, overwhelming the equestrian attackers with their hail of lead. Most of Sitting Bull's braves started firing too early, and the column's intense fire power convinced the warriors to rein in and pull back. The attackers were soon out of ammunition anyway. After a while, the war party disappeared. The troops cautiously regrouped and started once rolling eastward.

Once out of the canyon the men were safer, safe enough for Col. Stanley to dispatch two companies of the 8th and one from the 17th to escort empty wagons back to Ft. Rice. They returned three weeks later full of fresh supplies to tide the expedition over while it supported some additional exploration by the survey team. The war parties seemed to have disappeared.

336

On October 2, Stanley sent the rest of the 17th Infantry, 125 men, back to Fort Rice. He most likely also had serious concerns for the safety of the fort's skeleton crew of defenders and families. The returning soldiers were not aware that Gaul and 100 Hunkpapas were silently following them. Gaul was not strong enough to attack the party but watched for opportunities. His warriors chased five Santee scouts with dispatches all the way to the gates of Fort Rice. On separate occasions, they massacred and mutilated two lieutenants who were outside the safety of the pickets.

Finally, in the middle of October, after over 2 ½ months on the trail, Richard and his company lumbered through the gates of Fort Rice. They had marched about 650 miles through the summer's relentless heat and across a dry prairie. They were exhausted, worn, and hungry. The three pairs of shoes were done for.

Weariness was overwhelming, but worse than that was the terror of the Indian Wars. There was something especially debilitating about this kind of fighting. The Northern Pacific's chief surveyor, a former Civil War Confederate general, later wrote,

> "Although I have been in more than a hundred battles, I never dream of fighting or of war except with Indians, and for years after the death of Adair [one of the lieutenants killed on the final leg to Fort Rice], I often cried out in my sleep – Indians! Indians!"[14]

Perhaps it was the place and time, perhaps the Native American warriors' ferocity, or perhaps the fighting's ghastliness. But men did not forget this type of combat.

The grueling expedition ended in a great strategic victory for Sitting Bull. Not only did he, Gaul, and warriors from the Sioux nation prevent the completion of the survey, it took the Northern Pacific years to recover from its failure. To complete the surveying, George Custer led a much larger expedition the following summer that resulted in another violent clash with Sitting Bull.

Although Custer won this one, the specter of unmanageable Indian Wars along the railroad route unnerved New York's financial markets. Two weeks after word of the Custer battles reached Wall

Street, investors panicked. The nation's leading banker Jay Cooke, who backed the Northern Pacific, was forced to close. The country plunged into the Panic of 1873. Construction on the Northern Pacific did not resume for another six years, and the last spike was not hammered until 1883. In the meantime, Custer had another rendezvous with Sitting Bull, one he did not win.[15]

Birmingham, England, 1875

Like the rest of the army of workers invading Birmingham, Benjamin and Elizabeth Nicholls arrived in the behemoth industrial workshop of a city in search of wages to support their family. With all the construction going on in the mid-1800's, there was work for a bricklayer, Benjamin's profession. They needed a place to live and found one in a "back-to-back" tenement-style house right in the center of the city, on Holloway Head.

These days were hard. When Elizabeth passed away at only 44 years old, she had given birth to seven children, the youngest of which she delivered when she was already 42. Benjamin lived only five years after Elizabeth was gone. By then, Henry, their eldest son had also become a bricklayer. Their oldest daughter, Mary Elizabeth, was 18. She and her sisters, Mary Ann, two years younger, and Elinor, four years younger, had to fend for themselves.

Mary Elizabeth and Mary Ann soon found work and places to live as boarders. In 1861, Mary Elizabeth lived on Grant Street, and Mary Ann, on Smallbrook Street, only a seven- or eight-minute walk from each other in the same neighborhood where they were born. They both worked in factories. Mary Ann told the census taker she was a sewing machine operator. Mary Elizabeth listed her profession as a machine operator. Perhaps they worked on the same shop floor.[16]

About that time, their sister Elinor had joined the congregation of the Church of Jesus Christ of Latter-day Saints, one of several small non-conformist churches in Anglican Britain. This brought Mary Elizabeth into contact with the congregation's missionaries, and she, too, was baptized that same year. The Mormons met in a place that was only about 20 minutes' walk from where Mary

338

Elizabeth lived. The close-knitted group of believers probably provided a family and network for two girls living without the support of parents or other extended relatives.

Serving as head of the Mormon congregation then was Joseph Howard (whose story unfolds in Chapter 7). Hardly would they have known that, as serendipity would have it, the Howards would one day have a great-great grandson, who would become my father, while, Mary Elizabeth would have a great-great-granddaughter, my mother. Also living only 5-6 minutes away from Mary Elizabeth's tenement house was another Mormon, Eli Taylor, who was among the early members in Britain. Eli was married with a family including some teenaged children. He was a shoemaker and may well have conducted his business, as so many did, from his back-to-back home.[17]

By 1864, Mary Elizabeth, at 26 years old, was starting to get up in years as a spinster. That year, Eli Taylor was a 44-year old widower. He was older than she was, but it turned out to be a match. Eli and Mary Elizabeth were married. On their marriage certificate, they both wrote their professions as "shoemakers." Elizabeth signed the certificate; Eli made his mark. They wasted no time in starting their own family. Their first child was born just nine months after their wedding day and named Mary Ann, after her aunt. Over the next ten years, Eli and Mary Elizabeth had six children, not all of whom survived early childhood. Eli continued his shoemaking profession. Mary Elizabeth's job as a wife and mother was no doubt all demanding.[18]

Eli and Mary Elizabeth got by, but the twelve to fourteen-hour workdays were a struggle, and life was always balanced on razor-edge. There was little time to be sick, because a day's income lost made juggling the rent, buying food, and keeping the house warm ever precarious. If the rent was not paid, the whole family was on the street or sent to the Poor House – literally. There was no social safety net. Every day had its own calculations for spreading their meager income among the competing demands for covering basic physical needs.

Like the Howards, the Taylors aimed for a better life for their small children. Eli could not read and write, but they wanted to be sure their children could. They enrolled them in school as soon as they were old enough. Little Mary Ann was attending classes when she was six. By the time she was ten, the family began seriously preparing to leave for America. The family wanted to end this hand-to-mouth existence. America, a land of hope, would offer an easier life than what they now had.[19]

Many from their Mormon congregation had already departed for Utah in search of their own plots of land or own shops. The Howards had emigrated ten years earlier. Now, in the 1870s, the trip no longer required the perilous overland trip by covered wagon from the Midwest to the Rocky Mountains. Immigrants in the 1870's traveled from New York by rail. From Omaha, they caught the Union Pacific across Nebraska and Wyoming before dropping down into the Salt Lake basin. During the past decade, ocean passage, too, had dramatically shortened timewise as rapid steam ships replaced their masted foregoers.

Eli did not have the money to finance the trip, and just like many other Mormons, he took a loan from the Perpetual Emigrating Fund with an obligation to repay it in Utah. Timing the trip was not as crucial as it had been earlier. Without the need to beat the snows while crossing the plains, they could travel late into the year. The PEF set their departure for the fall of 1875.

In early October, they boarded the train in Birmingham and made the short 100-mile trip to the nearby port of Liverpool. It was surely a big thrill and adventure for Mary Ann and her brothers and sisters who had probably never before traveled on a train. Once in Liverpool, Eli and Mary Elizabeth found their way to the harbor and boarded the steamship *Dakota*. With them were 10-year old Mary Ann, Elizabeth (8), Ellen (6), and Eli, Jr (2).[20]

The big ship was a marvel, not just for the children. This miracle of steam technology could sail at never-before-known speeds, even without sails or wind. They found the berth where the six of them would sleep, made new friends, and learned details about their voyage. Finally, at about 8:00 the evening of October 14, 1875, the *Dakota* inched away from the big port city's wharfs.

The Mormon party included 120 Latter-day Saints, 72 adults and 45 children from Great Britain, and three from Scandinavia. Bedson Early was appointed head of the emigrant party. That evening they organized and held their first prayer meeting. When Mary Ann awoke the next morning, the day was clear, the sea was calm, and they were underway and making good time. The crossing would take only ten days. The Howards, a decade earlier, spent nearly seven weeks crossing under the sails of their vessel.[21]

The calm weather did not last long. After the *Dakota* pulled away from the English coast, a gale from the north hit the ship with heavy swells and most everyone experienced their first bouts of sea sickness. The voyagers faced strong head winds and rough seas most of the rest of the trip. Aside from the bad weather, however, the *Dakota* was as comfortable as a ship might be in those years. The *Dakota* and its sister ship the *Montana* were considered some of the best passenger ships afloat. The vessel was powerful and fast. They remained on course and on schedule.

On October 24, the *Dakota* with its 120 pilgrims drew into New York City. The day before they entered the harbor, the children watched as a pilot climbed aboard to take the big ship into port. Along the shoreline, they could see lush hardwoods in the rich yellows, reds, and browns of autumn. A doctor also came on board to do preliminary checks for immigration. They had sailed 2,813 miles. Two days later, on little Elizabeth's ninth birthday, the party was at Castle Garden, clearing immigration and customs. By 5:00 p.m., they were on their way again.[22]

The rest of the travel west would be by rail. They transferred to the train station, and after the Mormon party found space in the cars, the engine jerked the emigrants forward. Mary Ann, her parents, and siblings settled onto the wooden seats they would occupy day and night for the next ten days. Across Harrisburg and Pittsburg they sped, sometimes at the amazing pace of 40 miles an hour. The black smoke arched into the air from the engine's boiler. Sometimes steam shot up, and the shrill whistle blew to get people and cattle off

341

the tracks. The rhythm of the moving wheels pulsed hypnotically as they carried the Taylor family westward and further westward. Not all of the passengers on the cars belonged to their party. People got on and they got off. Some were pleasant; others were rough characters, who reminded them they were moving away from civilization, not toward it.

It was hard to get a lot of sleep with all the commotion. Some of their group were missionaries returning to Utah from their work in Great Britain. For them, the train was taking them home. But for everyone else, everything was completely new, fascinating, unfamiliar, and almost incomprehensibly far from their homes in England. The cost of the trip from New York to Salt Lake City was $51.00 a person. That princely sum for Mary Ann's family was fortunately covered by the PEF. Within four days they were in Iowa watching the rolling swells of prairie and then crossing the wide Mississippi River over a long iron bridge.

In Omaha, the party transferred to the Union Pacific and were soon pushing across Nebraska's unending plains. They were now well into the American frontier. In spite of the vast emptiness, it was still stop and go, with the cars pulling onto sidetracks to wait for east-bound trains to pass before they could continue. The ox trains of a decade before could make 10-20 miles on a good day. The Taylors were averaging 200 miles a day. Fast as it was, it translated to an average speed of less than 10 miles an hour due to the many stops and delays.

They passed Cheyenne, Wyoming, where Richard McGuire had soldiered three winters before, and kept chugging to ever higher elevations as they climbed across Wyoming's sagebrush desert and into the Rockies. Finally, the train began to descend into Utah. The contrast between the settled farmlands and the wild territories they had just traveled was enormous. For Mary Ann, ten years old, going on eleven, it was surely hard to put this all into an adult perspective, but she knew that this was the beginning of another world. This strange new mountain place was where her family would call home.[23]

Fort D. A. Russell, Wyoming Territory, Winter 1872

Richard and the six companies of the 8th Infantry had a few days' rest at Fort Rice. Coming off the punishing Yellowstone Expedition, it was hardly enough. The *Far West*, a river steamer under Army lease was waiting for them. Summer was over, and on a fall day, October 19th, they filed onto the steamer and pushed out into the Missouri. The steamboat company expected the river to remain totally ice-free only until about the first of November. It was urgent to get the 8th Infantry moving. The *Far West* steamed downstream. After the hardships the 8th had just gone through, even the cramped river boat quarters must have seemed a luxury.

It took only a few days to navigate the 500 miles on the Missouri to Omaha. When the *Far West* docked, Richard and the men marched through town to the Union Pacific Depot. They were still only halfway to their next stop. At least they were not walking the trip, like they did all summer. At the depot, the troops boarded a train, and for about four days and nights they rolled another 500 miles on the newly laid Union Pacific. Their destination was Fort D. A. Russell on the outskirts of Cheyenne. Across Nebraska's hilly prairies they continued until the scenery pouring by their windows turned to flat monotonous sagebrush country. Not long after that, they crossed into Wyoming, the train slowed, and the conductor announced they were arriving in Cheyenne (see Map I).

The post, the town, and the railroad had a symbiotic relationship. Fort Russell was there to protect the Union Pacific's route across southern Wyoming. Cheyenne, founded just four years earlier, first supported the construction of the Union Pacific. Now the town facilitated the trains with their loads of passengers and freight running regularly between Omaha and Utah and Nevada all the way to California. The railroad fed Cheyenne with supplies, settlers, and new soldiers, like Richard. Cheyenne's saloons and businesses catered to the men who protected it in this far off lonely corridor.

When the train finally creaked to a stop, Richard climbed off. Cheyenne was one of those "Hell on Wheels" towns that made the Wild West what it was. There was nothing like it in Ireland. It was even a far cry from New York City's raucous streets. As he looked around, up and down the muddy streets, what he saw had just five years before had been an empty grass plain where an Arapaho war party had filled the chief of a Union Pacific surveying company with five bullets and nineteen arrows. The next morning Sioux warriors had swept in to attack a nearby Mormon wagon train camped next to a company of soldiers. Before the cavalry men could get to their horses, the Sioux galloped off leaving two Mormon waggoneers dead on the ground.

A year later, Cheyenne was a boom town where hordes of all kinds of men descended to join or support the railroad construction. The place was Wild West pandemonium at its worst. Isabel Bird, a contemporary visitor, wrote how originally Cheyenne was "…mainly inhabited by rowdies and desperadoes, the scum of advancing civilization; and murders, stabbings, shooting, and pistol affrays were at times events of almost hourly occurrence in its drinking dens." With the end of the railroad construction and a generous dose of vigilantism, things had improved since then. Cheyenne was now the capital of Wyoming Territory and a major mercantile hub that at times could have over 100 wagons lining the dirt streets waiting to move goods into its hinterland.

But improvement was a relative thing. Mrs. Bird described how the town Richard met when he got off the train was an "ill-arranged set of frame houses and shanties and rubbish heaps" where the smell of manure in its muddy streets was "one of the foulest smells I have smelt for a long time." She added,

"It is utterly slovenly-looking, and unornamental, abounds in slouching bar-room-looking characters, and looks a place of low, mean lives. …beyond the railroad tracks are nothing but the brown plains, with their lonely sights – now a solitary horseman at a traveling amble, then a party of Indians in paint and feathers, but civilized up to the point of carrying firearms, mounted on sorry ponies, the bundled-up squaws riding astride on the baggage ponies; then a drove of ridgy-spined, long-horned cattle, …with their escort of four or five much-spurred horsemen,

344

in peaked hats, blue-hooded coats, and high boots, heavily armed with revolvers and repeating rifles, and riding small wiry horses."

Another woman, who arrived in Cheyenne about the same time as Richard, wrote that the main tree "in Cheyenne was not larger than a lilac-bush, and had to be kept wrapped in wet towels."[24]

Richard lined up with Company K, and the six companies of the 8th Infantry marched out to Fort Russell. Unlike Fort Rice, Russell was not under daily threat of attack. It was open, not stockaded, with the buildings arranged facing each other in a diamond shape. Its detachment of 600 men and proximity to Fort Laramie, and much the rest of the US Army just up the Union Pacific line, made Fort Russell a formidable presence. It easily protected the town, a major waypoint along the railroad stretching westward and the trail moving north from Cheyenne into the Dakota settlements.

The fort's commanders welcomed the new unit to their prairie garrison, and the 8th was sent off to its quarters. When Richard reached his barracks, he and some of his Company K buddies were assigned a bunk bed covered with straw-filled mattresses. Each barracks had its own separate kitchen built from logs. Everything was of a shaky construction, and the walls were wallpapered with tarpaper in an effort to keep out the wind and cold. This was his new home, Richard realized. Even worse, any place where the regiment might go next was likely to make this one look good.

Besides Indian skirmishes, the harsh climate was hot and dry in the summer and a deep freeze punctuated by blizzards in the winter. Loneliness grew from the isolation; the worst enemy was boredom. Some released their frustrations in Cheyenne's saloons. Taking one's cares to town, however, could be dangerous. Just before Richard arrived, Lieutenant Mason of the 5th Cavalry challenged an army civilian to a duel after the man insulted him in a saloon one night. The next morning Mason faced off with the man in a shooting that wounded both. When Lt. Mason died later that day, members of the 5th tried to pull the shooter out of the local jail for a lynching. They did not succeed, however, and a local court acquitted the man.

Pay days, especially, were followed by drunkenness, disorder, and desertion. Over the few months following Richard's arrival at post, scores of men, including some from the 8th, were court martialed and disciplined for misbehavior, but he was never one of them.[25]

There were other ways to break the boredom. Cheyenne was not all saloons. Variety theaters were also popular. The Theater Comique, Concert Hall, and Model Concert Hall often boasted full houses. On post, there was a soldiers' theater and officers' theater. The garrison also organized dances, called "hops," and sometimes balls, where over 300 ladies might be present.

All this social life, however, went only so far in lessening the strains of living in a hostile territory where the men were almost always at a state of readiness. The barracks were drafty, cold, and miserable. And after they suffered through the upcoming bitterly cold Wyoming frost and snows, everyone expected to be soon be on the trail marching toward another round of skirmishes and battles. Word was already spreading that the Oglala Sioux at the nearby Red Cloud Agency were restless and readying to attack ranches and other facilities over the following months.[26]

Nor did the dances, theaters, and even the saloons keep the men from getting sick regularly. Sanitary conditions were primitive. Ft. Russell had a 48-bed hospital when its total complement was only 600 men and officers. As in the Civil War, diarrhea and dysentery were the most prevalent diseases plaguing the troops. Even before he left Davids Island, Richard had fought a dangerous bout of diarrhea. Now, as winter proceeded, he came down with a severe case of hemorrhoids. In March, his condition got so bad that he sought help from the post surgeon. The doctor took a look at Richard and hospitalized him in the post infirmary.[27]

Richard had been in the Army just over a year and had been hospitalized now twice. He had been on a major unsuccessful expedition in the northern wilderness of North Dakota and Montana, where he had been attacked by the Sioux under Sitting Bull. He expected to be fighting another set of battles in just a few weeks. From almost the beginning of his enlistment, Richard had regretted

346

his mistake of joining the Army. When he was released from the post infirmary three days later, he knew he could take it no longer.

For soldiers serving on the 1870's frontier, desertion was always an option. In fact, nearly one third of all enlistments between 1867 and 1891 ended in some form of desertion. During the Plains Indian Wars, desertion rates averaged 25-40%. Gen. John Pope, commander of the Department of Missouri, believed much of the reason for the high desertion rates lay in boredom.

The chances of successfully walking away from the army, moreover, were quite good. On the vast sparsely populated frontier, a deserter could simply vanish. Even in the larger settlements, disappearing was not hard. The towns were always full of strangers, many of whom had backgrounds no one talked about. In 1867, the Army reported nearly 14,000 desertions, but only 3,000 of them ever surrendered or were apprehended. When deserters were caught, some were not even punished, just returned to their companies.[28]

Most of these desertions were from units that were physically isolated. Staying in the barracks produced boredom; getting out of the barracks was even worse if it meant fighting Indians. At Fort Russell, rumors of an upcoming campaign had always led to an increase in desertions. Desertion was often on the soldiers' minds. It was on Richard's mind. His piles helped make his decision.

This grim Army existence had taken Richard to the breaking point. He made up his mind. The night between Saturday and Sunday, March 16, 1873, Richard McGuire and a buddy from Company K named Charles Gallagher quietly gathered their things and walked out the door. They had just received their pay the week before and had something in their pockets to help fund their escape. Another man from their company had deserted just the week before they left. The two men may or may not have joined up with him.

McGuire and Gallagher would have to move quickly and cover their tracks. The faster and farther they traveled, the better the chance that their army days would soon be forgotten. Even in isolated Wyoming, the first thing to do was assume a new identity. "Richard Joseph McGuire"[29] no longer existed. He was now

"Joseph Wilson," "Joseph Richard Wilson," or sometimes "Richard Wilson." Gallagher must have altered his name, too.[30]

Where did they go when they fled Cheyenne? If Joseph Wilson ever told anyone, that person never passed it on. Family stories and traditions were completely silent about this. Even people like my mother and her cousin, Bonita, who had spent decades interviewing his close family and doing their own research, never discovered the answer. For them his trail appeared again only a few years later.

The fastest and easiest way out of lonely Cheyenne was on a Union Pacific rail car. On one side, the trains rolled eastward over the prairie to Omaha. In the other direction, the first destination of any notable size was Ogden, Utah, 434 miles to the west. The road northward traveled past Fort Laramie, a place where he would not want the risk of being seen and through Indian country, where he did not want to return. If Richard wanted to stay anonymous and undiscovered, he would not travel to Omaha, a city teeming with federal troops.

So, common sense says he went west, rolling up over the continental divide and then down into Utah. Utah was by far the safer destination. For one thing, the large Mormon population had no affinity for the U.S. Army. For most of them, the Army was an occupying force meant to impose federal control over their territory. Many people could not have cared less if someone was a deserter. In addition to that, the long urban area along the Wasatch mountains from Logan, on the north, through Salt Lake City to Provo, in the south, had close to 25,000 inhabitants in those days, virtual urban congestion for the West. The community was large enough for a couple of men to disappear. They must have headed toward Utah, and that is where we again discovered Richard's trail (see Map I).[31]

Salt Lake City, Utah Territory 1875

Mary Ann Taylor and her family finally reached the end of their long train journey in Ogden, Utah's second largest city. They pulled their belongings onto the platform, a whistle blew, and the Union Pacific locomotive moved forward, heading across the salt flats and Nevada sagebrush towards Sacramento. The golden spike linking the final rails of the transcontinental railroad was driven six years before in Corinne, a few miles from the Ogden station.

The family waited a while for their final transfer to the Utah Central Railroad. When the train arrived, the Taylors and others in their party boarded a car with all their things. They spent the next two hours traveling the 40 miles to Salt Lake City. It was November 3rd, 1875. They had survived the long trip across the United States on hard wooden seats.

Initially they were under the care of the Mormon wards and bishops who helped settle the new families. Mormon immigration by now had run continuously for thirty years, and there were routines to accommodate them. Eli and Mary soon found work and shelter from the coming mountain winter. In the community were many other British families, like the Howards, from Birmingham.

When the Taylor family arrived in Salt Lake City, Joseph Richard "Wilson" had been in Utah Territory two years. The first thing he had done after arriving was find work. Salt Lake City was thriving during the 1870's: its population grew by 50% over the decade, and there were plenty of jobs around. But a newcomer had to get one of those jobs. Mormon culture was close knit, particularly in those days when federal marshals and judges were tracking down polygamist men. Breaking into society was probably not always easy for a non-Mormon, especially one quiet about his background.

That might be the reason Joseph headed south of Salt Lake toward the booming mining towns of an area named Tintic that had opened just two years before. Just like mining areas everywhere in the Old West, these towns were a law unto themselves, for Mormons and non-Mormons alike. It did not matter much what or who you were as long as you were willing to do the back-breaking work of pulling the ore up and out.

Joseph told the 1880 US Census taker that his name was Richard Wilson, and the man wrote down on the Census form that Richard Wilson was a "servant." The census taker recorded "servant" as the profession of several people. A city like Salt Lake was not populated with many "servants," as we might use the word today. I take the term to mean that Richard was in someone else's employ, probably a hired hand, or someone who did odd jobs. Meanwhile, 15-year-old Mary Ann no longer lived at home. Instead, the census taker found her as a live-in servant for a family of five children.[32]

It was about that time that Joseph Richard Wilson met Mary Ann Taylor, now an attractive young woman. He was living and working near the Taylors' home in the southern Salt Lake suburb of South Cottonwood, probably doing odd jobs, and going by the name "Richard Wilson." According to at least one family history, he even did some work for her father, Eli.

Richard was much older than she was, probably in his late twenties, but their paths crossed, and he asked her to marry him. In November 1881, the two were wed. She was just short of 17 years old, a young bride, but not as young as it might seem today. There was no such thing as a secluded and uneventful childhood in her generation, at least not in Utah and other places in western America. Children matured quickly and were given responsibilities in the family from their early childhood. A wedding picture shows a slim Mary Ann, with short curled blonde hair, standing with her hand on Richard's shoulder. Richard is seated, a corsage in his lapel.

Were they married in Salt Lake City? No one yet knows for sure. Their wedding photograph does not have a photo studio's stamp on the back. Over the years, family members, including Mary Ann herself, recorded important dates in an 1880 New Testament. The first entry under marriages is: "Richard Wilson and Mary Ann Taylor was Married November 1, 1881."[33] But no place is given.

With such a beautiful wedding dress, you would assume that it might have been a family wedding in or near her mother's home. They could have been married in Utah, or, according to another family history, in Arizona. Since Utah's normally abundant archives have no entry for their marriage, and with subsequent events in mind, perhaps they were married in Arizona. Wherever it was, they made a handsome couple.

St. Joseph, Arizona Territory, 1882

Perhaps one of the least friendly spots for anyone to settle during the last years of the American frontier was on the Little Colorado

River in eastern Arizona. The climate was hot and arid. The river flooded in the late spring when crops were planted. It dried up, sometimes completely, during the intolerably hot days of late summer. Any crops surviving the floods were starved for water later in the summer. It was precisely on the Little Colorado River, however, where Mormon migration leader Brigham Young sent one of the last Latter-day Saint colonization missions he planted across the 19th century West. (See Map J)

After a horrendous wagon journey over the harsh border terrain between Utah and Arizona, the first missionary settlers arrived on the Little Colorado in 1876. They set up four settlements, one of which was first called Allen's Camp and later renamed St. Joseph (and still later called Joseph City). They struggled to survive, planting failed crops and building one dam after another, all of them washing out during the violent spring floods.

Along the way, the communities, and especially St. Joseph, were organized into a Mormon communal experiment called the United Order where people shared their belongings and production according to need. For many reasons, the experiment was not successful. By 1882, a good number of the worn and dried out original settlers had given up and returned to their earlier homes in Utah. The United Order, too, was on its last days. Instead of facilitating orderly production and distribution, it proved too trying a system for its members.

As I explain later in this chapter, I found Richard and Mary Ann living in St. Joseph in 1882, about the time they married. They must have made the grueling overland trip to the Little Colorado colony's leading settlement of St. Joseph. Perhaps they traveled part of the way on the Utah Southern Railroad that ran some distance south from Salt Lake. But there was no avoiding the forbidding wagon trail that extended several hundred miles through southern Utah to St. Joseph. If it was then winter, the weather was unforgiving at the high central Utah elevations they had to climb. It would have been a struggle for Mary Ann. Richard was experienced at roughing it through fierce climates and hard terrains, but she was not. Her trip from England was easy, compared to this.

351

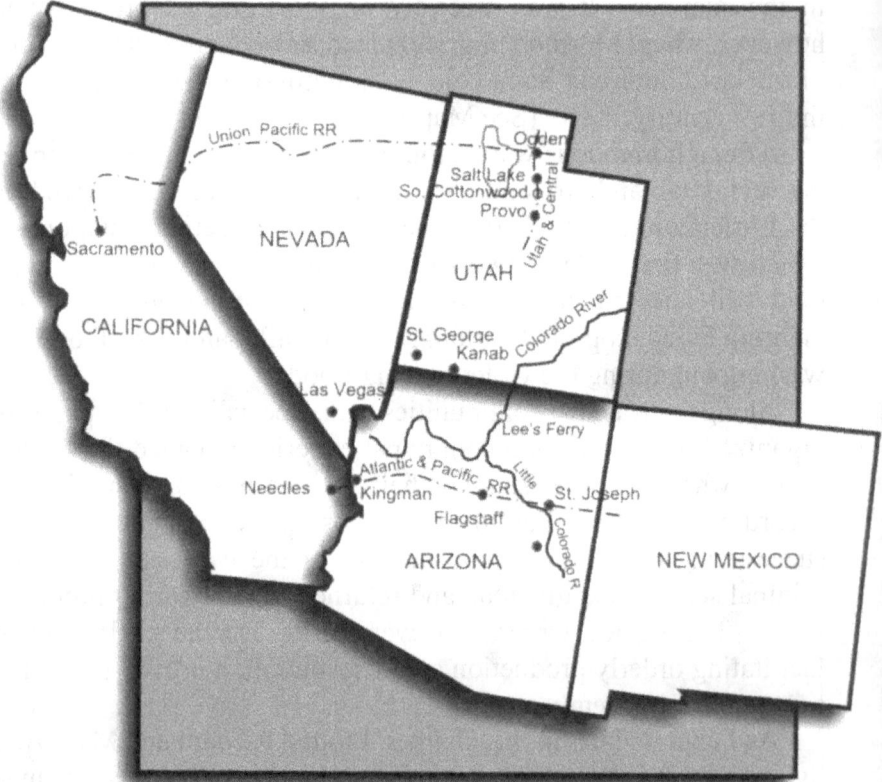

Map I – Southern Mountain West

When they got to northern Arizona, the road headed straight for the Colorado River where they forded at Lee's Ferry. The ferry consisted of a small boat positioned at a relatively quiet spot on the turbulent river. "Quiet spot" is indeed a relative term. Over the years, the crossing had taken many lives and was the most feared part of the journey. Then the trail moved southeast until it hit the Little Colorado River, where it passed over still more rugged territory before it reached the Mormon colonies. The ordeal often entailed several weeks of suffering from severe cold and snow, and at other points a total lack of water in the arid desert.

Mary Ann became pregnant sometime during or around the time of their journey. In the beginning of May, she gave birth to George W. who died the same day.[34] Whether the burdensome trip caused the loss of her baby is not certain, but it is hard to think that the hard life they were living did not play some role in the tragedy. When I searched cemetery records for St. Joseph (and for Joseph City, as it was later called), I found nothing. Their son, George, evidently was not buried in St. Joseph.

Of all the places in their world, why did they choose the St. Joseph colony, a settlement on the extremes of Arizona Territory? The colony was a highly religious order populated with pious folk who had come there only because their church had called them. In the case of Richard and Mary Ann, there is little to suggest they migrated to St. Joseph for religious reasons. Mary Ann was a Mormon, but it is uncertain if Richard had then joined the faith.

At the time they came to the Little Colorado, moreover, the community had little otherwise to recommend it. The settlement was hardly thriving; in fact, many of its settlers were actively seeking excuses to return to Utah. It was also dangerous to live in the region, especially at any distance outside St. Joseph's stockade. Bands of renegades, including the feared Apache war chief Geronimo, were regularly breaking out of the nearby reservation to raid surrounding farms and settlers. Nevertheless, the 1882 Arizona Census shows Richard and Mary Ann living in the fortification, literally alongside some of the hearty families who settled and organized the community from its beginnings.[35]

353

However, there was something happening along the Little Colorado in the early 1880s, something that provides an important key to this puzzle. It is difficult to think that the newly married couple embarked on the treacherous journey to northeastern Arizona to join a religious order in an isolated Mormon settlement. An alternative is that they went there to get work – and there was a lot of it in St. Joseph then. Throughout 1881 and 1882, crews were sweating and toiling through the desolate hot central Arizona desert to lay rails and ties for the Atlantic and Pacific Railroad. The new railroad's tracks emerged from New Mexico to extend across Arizona Territory to California. Just four days after their wedding in November 1881, the railroad reached St. Joseph. New jobs were opening to get the rails across the territory according to schedule.

One of the promoters of the Atlantic and Pacific's Arizona line was a man Richard may have worked for earlier, John W. Young, Mormon prophet Brigham Young's third son. Young had dabbled a little in the development of the Arizona settlements along the Little Colorado. He was a businessman who, for the most part, saw the development of the region as a business venture.

When the Atlantic and Pacific announced plans to build rails across Arizona, Young contracted with the railroad to build segments of the line. While it was a business opportunity, he was also interested in providing work for the struggling families of the Mormon settlements. To make good on the contract, however, he needed more manpower than was locally available. Young began recruiting hundreds of laborers from Utah to work on the construction. The men filed down to Arizona to join work crews moving westward from St. Joseph toward California where a line from the Southern Pacific would meet the Atlantic and Pacific.

John W. Young was not new to railroad construction. When the Union Pacific reached Utah on the last leg of its transcontinental construction in 1868, Young had subcontracted to prepare the grade for part of the Utah route. Three years later he was president and superintendent of the Utah Northern railroad being built from Ogden north into Idaho and Montana. During those years he also helped organize the Utah Central and Utah Western railroads, south and west of Salt Lake City. He was also president of the Salt Lake City Railroad Company that was trying to link mining areas, such as Tintic, to the main Utah Central and Union Pacific lines.

All this railroad construction was thundering ahead at full pace over the 1870s when Richard Wilson aka McGuire arrived in Utah looking for work. As I mentioned earlier, Richard's grandson and my grandfather, Wayne, related that Richard was working on the railroads. He probably was, and in 1880-81 he heard Young was looking for men to lay tracks in Arizona.

Following their desertion at Ft. Russell, Richard and his 8th Infantry buddy Gallagher appear to have arrived in Utah in search of work and anonymity. Finding the two of them, as I believe I did, in as isolated a place as St. Joseph tells that now, even years later, they were still traveling together. It makes sense they signed up for the construction and traveled to Arizona to get a job on Young's latest construction project. The men from Utah started arriving well before November 1881 when Richard and Mary Ann were married. It is likely Richard was with them. Whether Mary Ann traveled with him or joined later, it is easy to speculate that that they were married somewhere in Arizona.

Richard probably started laying the rails westward from St. Joseph sometime after his wedding. Mary Ann could have stayed in St. Joseph while he labored across the desert, or perhaps she followed along, working in the railroad camps as they leap-frogged toward California. By the time of the October 1882 voter registration in Mojave County, several months later, a Richard Wilson and a James Gallagher were in western Arizona on the other side of the territory. This James Gallagher, the same age as the one who appeared on the territorial census in St. Joseph, a few names after Mary Ann, was probably the same person. The timing also fits. The Atlantic and Pacific Railroad construction gangs had just then reached Kingman, the spot where the two registered. From Kingman, the right of way moved to the California border and in August 1883 linked up in Needles to the Southern Pacific line.[36]

Whether Mary Ann followed Richard or remained in St. Joseph, their New Testament tells that the next son was born in December

1883, and he, too, died the same day. They named him Eli R., and buried him somewhere in Arizona, but evidently not in St. Joseph. By then, work on the Atlantic and Pacific line was finished, and Richard needed something else to do. They decided to return to Utah, and Mary Ann was soon expecting again. Hard lives often exact a price, and it was Mary Ann who had to pay it. If she was not already ill, it was not long after this when she contracted tuberculosis. The bacterial lung disease in those days was common and accounted for 20 percent or more of all deaths.

South Cottonwood, Utah Territory, 1884

Richard and Mary Ann made their way back to South Cottonwood, perhaps on the new line that made the trip to Salt Lake from Arizona possible by rail.[37] The years in Arizona were hard. Mary Ann had lost two infants. There was not much to show for their trials, except, perhaps, the baby Mary Ann now carried. When in November 1884 the baby was born, it was a girl and she lived. Following the Taylor family tradition of attaching the name "Mary" to a second name, they named her Mary Emma. (Mary Emma's mother was Mary Ann; her grandmother was Mary Elizabeth.) Mary Emma was my great-grandmother whom I remember as a kind white-haired grandmother full of smiles and warmth. Another pregnancy quickly followed, and a year and a half later a second daughter was born, Elizabeth. In another heartbreak for the young family, Elizabeth died only two months later.

In Mother's files, I found a photo of the couple taken some time after they were married. It portrays them a little older than they were in their wedding photograph, but they were still a handsome couple. This time Mary Ann is seated with Richard standing next to her. Mary Ann's hair is now dark, and she is wearing a long dark dress. She is still trim but might be a few months pregnant. The picture is undated but has the name of a Salt Lake City photographer printed on the back. It was taken after their return from Arizona, probably a few months before Mary Emma or Elizabeth was born.

Mary Emma was a healthy girl, but as she grew, her young mother's strength gradually began to deteriorate. Finally, when the

356

little girl was barely five-years old, Mary Ann passed away. She was buried not far from their home in a family plot with no marker.[38] Mary Ann was still a young and beautiful woman, who had endured a lot during her 25 years. In their eight years of marriage she had delivered four babies. Only one had survived. Who knows how long she fought the crippling tuberculosis, then called consumption? An obituary in the Deseret News recorded her loss:

> November 17th, 1889, at South Cottonwood, of consumption. Mary Ann Wilson, daughter of Eli and Elizabeth Taylor; ...was a faithful Latter-day Saint, a good wife, and an affectionate daughter. She leaves a husband and one child.[39]

Noticeably missing was her husband's name.

It was a bitter thing to lose so young a wife, especially for Richard. Until he met Mary Ann, he had known few loving family members. True, Mary Ann left him a daughter. However, he was in no position to take responsibility for his five-year old. At first, he considered sending Mary Emma to live with his sister in New York City. His mother-in-law, Mary Elizabeth, talked Richard out of it and insisted that Mary Emma stay with her.

Following the death of her husband Eli, in the beginning of 1879, Mary Elizabeth had married a man named George Shell and was now known as Grandma Shell. Mary Emma lived the next five years of her life with Grandma and Grandpa Shell. To help make ends meet, Grandma Shell became a cleaning lady at the new Mormon temple when it opened in Salt Lake in 1893. It was a long commute from their home in South Cottonwood, but the modern world had arrived in Salt Lake in the form of electrified street cars that carried them back and forth efficiently. Mary Emma followed her grandmother to and from work.[40]

Camas Creek, Idaho, 1897

Sometime during the years that followed Mary Ann's death, Richard met a young striking lady named Emma Louise Holden, probably at his mother-in-law's home. Emma Louise, whom they called "Louie," was her niece, and Mary Ann's cousin. When she was just eighteen years old, a year before Mary Ann's passing, Louie had made the long journey from Birmingham, England, to visit her aunt and uncle in Utah. Louie's parents had been close to Mary Elizabeth and had even served as witnesses when Mary Elizabeth and Eli were married. Before leaving to find her aunt in America, Louie trained as a nurse in Birmingham. Richard, 15 years older than Louie, had now been the widower of her cousin for five years. They were soon engaged. A wedding was planned in the South Cottonwood Mormon chapel where they were wed in 1895.[41]

Over the previous twenty years, Richard had worked piecemeal jobs, a project here and another there. Now, however, he wanted to settle down permanently. After the wedding, he, Louie, and little Mary Emma packed their belongings and climbed aboard a Utah & Northern train that took them north from Salt Lake. They climbed off at a stop in Idaho. The station was in Camas Creek, a place soon to be called Dubois. This was where Richard had decided to settle and where they filed for a homestead. It was their new home.

Here, near Camas Creek, they sank their roots. Richard and Louie homesteaded only 40 acres, not a large piece of land, especially in the dry desert. A year later, they had a son they named Warren. Two years after that, they laid the little boy into a grave in the new cemetery just outside newly re-named Dubois. Richard had now fathered five children, and only Mary Emma had survived her early years. They tried again, and had two more children, Henry and Arthur. This time, both made it through childhood.

"He was a quiet and moody man," Louie recalled, "and I didn't always know what he was thinking." He was also musical, played the Jews Harp, and had a good voice, she told. Louie and Richard sang together not just at home, but in the homes of others. Richard's daughter, Mary Emma, remembered his tenderness, how when she was small, he took her in his arms, held her, and rocked and sang her to sleep. He had blue eyes, almost black hair, and was no longer such a young man to be the father of three little children.[42]

If Richard was finally rooted in one place, it was still a demanding life. Forty acres were hardly enough to support a family, and they were soon living on the ranch of a neighbor, where Richard

358

worked as a hired man. He went by the name Joseph Wilson – the name engraved on his Dubois tombstone. Mary Emma, as she rose into her teens, moved into town to take a job at the just constructed hotel. She lived in a private home. When the new century began, on January 1, 1900, Louie was carrying one-week old Henry Randall in her arms.[43]

It was rattlesnake infested desert. Sagebrush had to be cleared, livestock tended, hay and other crops planted and harvested. It began to take a toll. Richard frequently was ill but tried to keep up with his work. While haying, he often climbed off the stack to lie on the ground, gasping for breath. Finally, he and Louie boarded a train to travel 100 miles to Pocatello, the only nearby town of any size, to get medical help. The doctor opened him up, found cancer, and closed him again. He died a few days later, on May 12, 1902. A train brought Richard back to Dubois riding over tracks that he may have once laid. He was buried next to his son, Warren.

Richard's death left Louie nearly destitute, a young mother with two boys aged two years and eight months. However, she was strong-willed, and she was a survivor. One morning, a neighbor, George Edie, came by her house. George, a Scotsman, was a divorcee and had no children. "Now Louie, you have these two little boys to raise," he said, "I need someone to take care of my home. Now we both have a need." George offered her a bargain. He would marry her and provide for her family. In turn, he had a condition. She would produce a son for him.

Louie accepted the offer, and both made good on their parts of it. She and George kept a comfortable ranch house with scores of knick-knacks on the shelf. A spring flowed right through the lean-to porch off the kitchen. The cool water was their "refrigerator" where they stored butter, eggs, and perishables. "It was amazing to me!" my mother, who knew the place as a small girl, later recalled. When they got older, they sold the ranch to their son and moved into town where George became a judge and Louie ran the hotel.[44]

Emma Louise, Louie, "Grandma Edie," lived to be 92 years old, and was my sixth grandmother, my step-great-great-grandmother. Mary Emma, Richard's and Mary Ann's only living child, got married within two years of her father's death to Arthur Leonardson, the eldest son of one of the area's big ranching families. They became prominent in their rural community and left a large family of children, grandchildren, and great-grandchildren.

Searching for an Ancestor who does not Want to be Found

I will never forget one Memorial Day trip to cemeteries in the Snake River Valley. It was the last Memorial Day before my mother died. She, my sister Lorilee, and I filled the trunk of Lorilee's car with flowers and wire hangers bent to hold each pot erect in the spring winds that blew across the fields and high desert. We started with the grave of my father who had been laid to rest just the year before. Then, we continued northeastward up the valley toward the mountainous continental divide separating Idaho from Montana. From family plot to family plot, we drove until we arrived in the town of Dubois.

Its graveyard was quiet and pleasant, and I was happy to linger there. The desert oasis lay amidst the sagebrush whose sweet aroma drifted with the gentle breezes across the unpretentious tombstones. We planted our flowerpots on my grandparents' and then my great-grandparents' graves. At the far end, where the first stones stood, was a small one over the plot of my mother's great-grandfather. It read "Joseph Wilson, July 25, 1858 - May 12, 1902." Mother looked at us and smiled, a tear in one eye.

I knew when I started that Joseph Wilson's chapter would be different from the previous ones. I was no longer straining to see long distances through a fog of time. After all, I remembered well Joseph's daughter, who was my Great-Grandmother Mary Emma Leonardson. Before, I had searched for the stories of people who, unknowingly or not, had left hints of what they did, trails of where they went, and sometimes had even written records of what they thought. That was not true with Joseph Wilson. Mother had labored for decades trying to decipher his secrets.

Richard's biggest secrets were his real name and age. By obscuring these, he thought it would be easier to keep hidden the identity of a man who was wanted for desertion. He was right about that. Until Mother deciphered his real name, her interminable efforts to find his background never succeeded.

From tidbits and shards, she came to suspect he had changed his name. Joseph Richard Wilson was not his birth name. He never hid that he was Irish and that he had relatives in New York City. But Wilson was not the typical Irish name. At some point, there was a breakthrough. I found how it happened from a note she left in her files. Margie wrote:

> *"In the spring of 1967 I had been waiting for my Husband, Owen, to come home from a meeting. As I was lying there dozing a little, I saw a man with white hair sitting on a bench... I could not get him off my mind. When my husband came home I told him about it. I said that he looked like a fairly young man but his hair was white. Who did I know of my ancestors that had died quite young? After praying about it I decided that it had to be my Grandmother's Father, Joseph Wilson...*

> *"For many years I had wondered how I could find the true identity of Joseph Wilson. I knew that I must find his real name. ...It was Easter time. I had invited my Father & Mother for dinner. I had been praying about this problem about Joseph Wilson. The night before Easter I had a dream that his name was Joseph Richard McGuire or Frank Richard McGuire. When my Father came I told him about my dream. Tears came to his eyes. This was unusual for him as we seldom had seen him cry. He told me that they had always known that his name was Richard McGuire but had never talked about him for fear of repercussions from the government because of his desertion..."[45]*

Mother's father, Wayne, was Richard McGuire's oldest grandson and was the grandfather I knew best. He was a good-

humored but no-nonsense farmer who indeed did not cry and kept some distance from religion of any denominational sort.

Apparently, a few in the family were privy to some of Richard's secrets. Most family members, however, knew nothing about them. I found a letter in Mother's files from Wayne's younger sister, Fern. Many years after Mother's discovery, Fern wrote a perplexed letter about her grandfather's lingering mysteries and expressed great surprise about the McGuire name. She referred to an old photograph she had found, and wrote:

> *"On the back of the picture of the man and children is written Joseph Richard Mc... something that I can't make out. Mother only knew her father as Wilson. Has someone found out a name other than Wilson?"[46]*

It had been a well-kept secret, but once Mother had found the key to this lock, she was off and through the door. It did not take her long to discover Richard McGuire's enlistment records and the reason he had changed his name.

This episode reminded me of a tune that Debbie Reynolds sang in an ambitious movie, How the West was Won: *"What was your name in the States?" It was a folk tune from an Old West filled with people who for many reasons needed to remain anonymous.[47] Richard's name, like that of many who showed up in towns of the American West, had a reason to be forgotten. This was why they journeyed West in the first place, to seek a break from their past. When there was something to hide, the isolation of the West beckoned strongly.*

The National Archives, a Trailhead

I also found in Mother's "Joseph Wilson" file a letter to her from an official at the National Archives. It mentioned that her great-grandfather Richard McGuire had taken part in the Second Yellowstone Expedition. I had never heard of the expedition even though I grew up not far from Yellowstone. Initially, I could find very little about it. So I decided I would start there. It seemed right to make the Archives a trailhead for my own expedition in search of Joseph Wilson.

Early one morning I drove from my home in Virginia to Washington, DC for a day in the National Archives. I was not sure where to start, but after explaining what little I knew, helpful librarians pointed me in the right direction. What I had hoped would provide additional information about Richard McGuire turned out far more than that.

Among its other functions, the National Archives is the repository for original military records. Again, as was the case with the Lent men riding into the Civil War, going through the records of engagements, expeditions, and notes, it was possible to learn the story of where my grandfather went and what he did. The records did not necessarily have to mention him in telling his story. If I really wanted to know what Richard was doing in the Yellowstone Expedition, this was the place. It was not long before I was going through file boxes filled with handwritten notes, telegrams, and reports from infantry officers serving on the wild far edge of the 1870's American frontier.

These boxes told stories that as far as I knew no one in Richard's family now, and perhaps even when he was alive, ever knew. It was an episode almost totally forgotten. I had unearthed something new about this grandfather. Here were his first adventures in the US Army during one hot dry summer on the Northern Plains. Richard had been in the Army only a few months before engaging in running skirmishes with Sioux war parties. The experience must have played into his eventual decision to walk away from Fort Russell. That event, in turn, set the course of the rest of his life, complicating, as it did, the efforts of many to map the stories of what followed.

Still, many of the basics were still as hazy as ever. For example, how old was Richard McGuire, really, when he enlisted? Where was he born and when, exactly? When combing through my mother's files on him, I found a consistent birthday, the 25th of July, and a presumed year of birth. However, there were other years that he, himself, occasionally gave.

During the years after he deserted, what did he do? In Mother's handwritten notes from a conversation she once had with Joseph's second wife, Emma Louise, I learned how Emma told her Richard had "lived" in Tintic, Utah. People then, especially young single men, did not go to "live" in the Tintic mining towns. They went there for work. Joseph must have spent time in the Tintic area.

My grandfather Wayne, one of the very few who knew something about Richard's real history, told that Richard worked on the railroad. That, too, was a likely place for young men seeking work. During the early 1870's, a network of main lines and narrow-gauge railways was under construction from Salt Lake City to link the many new mining areas to the Union Pacific, and Denver and Rio Grande grids. The Utah & Northern Railway also soon laid tracks north through Idaho into Montana. According to my grandfather and Great-Great-Grandmother Eddie, he worked on the railroad and lived in the mining camps during his years in Utah.[48]

Networking Online

In Margie's files was a treasure of things, but the challenge was in sewing the various pieces into a narrative. I got some help when I discovered her correspondence with a cousin, Bonita. The letters began in the 1970's and continued into the 1990's. Reading through Mother's and Bonita's letters to each other, it was obvious Bonita, too, had been hot on Richard's trail for decades. She was Richard's granddaughter from his second wife. My mother was a great-granddaughter from his first.

I wondered if there was any way to resume this correspondence. Unfortunately, there was no good contact information in the file. First, of course, there was the question whether Bonita was still alive. Two decades had passed since she and Mother had last exchanged letters. If she was, how could I locate her?

I checked for any clues about Bonita on FamilySearch and Ancestry.com. Had she, for example, ever uploaded files onto Richard's FamilySearch entry? When I went one-by-one through "photos" and "memories" under his name, I was excited when I found something she had added several years before. I clicked on

Bonita's name and there was an email address. In two minutes, I had whipped off a quick note saying I was Margie's son and, like my mother, was interested in Richard McGuire. A few days later I was thrilled to get a reply via the FamilySearch website:

> *"Hi, I have all the info on him in the US and on the ship records when he and his sister came over from England. I have never been able to find him in Ireland. I have prayed that I will find him before my death. I'm so glad you sent a message as maybe with the info I have you can find him. I'm 87 years old and not very good on a computer any more. Call me... and let me know what I need to make copies of for you and mail them to you.*
>
> *Love*
>
> *Bonita "*

I called her, and we had a wonderful conversation. Bonita was alive and as sharp as ever.

Bonita, too, was baffled by the mysteries surrounding Richard. When she was young, she had lived across the street from Richard's daughter. She also knew Louie, my Grandma Edie). Even with all the times she had discussed with them, she had never been able to resolve something as basic as where in Ireland he was born.

A few days after Bonita and I talked by phone, a thick envelope arrived. Among the valuables inside was a copy of a passenger list that showed 14-year old Richard in 1863 as a passenger on the Great Eastern *sailing from Liverpool to New York with an 18-year old young lady, his sister, "Maria Anne." It immediately occurred to me that if he was 14 in 1863, then nine years later he was over the enlistment age of 18, just as the War Department claimed.*

When I asked Bonita about this, she laughed and said her grandmother told her that Richard often claimed he was younger than he was. "He wanted to impress women that he was younger," her grandma told. In fact, as I went through his various statements about his age in censuses and other documents, the birth years often varied, although the month, if stated, never changed. Giving different birth years was intentional, and not just to impress the girls. There was another reason.

From Mother's files I saw more evidence that those closest to Richard's secrets did not talk much about his history. In the letter from her elderly Aunt Fern it said that Mary Emma, Richard's daughter and Aunt Fern's mother, had never revealed much about his past. Fern wrote, "I don't know much about Grandpa. Mother said he didn't tell her much about his folks in Ireland and was cross with her when she asked questions about them."

Serendipity

Although not as easy as I would have hoped, researching Mary Ann Taylor was easier than following her husband. One of the early things I found is that her family and one from my father's side lived in the same part of Birmingham at the same time, another of the surprising coincidences that often popped up. Family history seems to teem with serendipity, I learned one day when reading The Weekly Genealogist, *a publication of the prestigious New England Historic Genealogical Society.*

The issue carried an article entitled "Serendipity in Genealogy."[49] Serendipity, I mused. That was a familiar thought. Serendipity, if that is what you call it, was a regular feature of my travels through time. The Weekly *asked if its readers had had serendipitous experiences. The next week's issue reported that of the 4,393 responses, 88% answered yes. The Weekly Genealogist went on to list a number of examples readers had sent in. None of them surprised me. They all tracked my own experiences.*

That was certainly the case with Joseph and Ann Howard, my 3rd great-grandparents on my father's side, and Mary Elizabeth and Eli Taylor, my 3rd great-grandparents on my mother's. Nearly a century separated my parents from them, and my parents found each other through completely divergent ancestral paths. Yet, the Taylors and the Howards both struggled to scrape out a living at the same time in Great Britain's sprawling second largest city. And "serendipitously," if they did not personally know each other, they surely knew about each other. Trailing my paternal grandparents

Howard and maternal grandparents Taylor took me back through history via different routes that at one point converged on the streets of 19th century Birmingham 160 years ago.

Historical Sites Stage Stories

I learned early that any contemporaneous historical sites in the vicinity of the homes of our ancestors are places you must visit. Whenever traveling, we carefully sought out historical sites not only to glean a taste of the area, but to actually discover details about their lives. While planning our first trip to Birmingham, for example, I googled for what the city offered time travelers like us. Close to the top of many lists was an entry for "National Trust: Back-to-backs." Britain's respected National Trust does excellent work preserving magnificent homes from Britain's past. Over the years we had visited many of their properties. However, I had never heard of "back-to-backs." When I read a description of the museum, I knew it was a place we had to visit.

The National Trust's "Back-to-backs Museum" in Birmingham was totally unique. Instead of manor houses or grand estates, this time the Trust had preserved working-class homes like those where the Taylor and Nicholls families lived. With Birmingham's population expanding so rapidly during the mid-19th century, housing was cheaply and hastily constructed to put roofs over the heads of the city's surging immigrants. Back-to-backs were the mold used for much of this housing.

A back-to-back was a block of four rows of narrow four-story houses connected in a quadrangle. On the inside of the rectangle was another four rows sharing common back walls with the outside rows. This made a block two rows-thick of houses with a small common courtyard in the middle. For most of the 19th century, the majority of Birmingham's population lived in back-to-backs. Today, almost all of the city's original 20,000 back-to-backs are demolished and long gone. In a far-sighted preservation effort, the National Trust set aside one full block to remind people of the dwellings where most people in Britain's industrial cities lived for decades.

We started our tour of the back-to-back by stepping into a narrow townhouse-like structure that was preserved as it existed in 1840. It was one of the museum's four renovated homes, each dating to a different era: the 1840s, 1870s, 1930s, and 1970s. Our guide told us that there was no running water, no plumbing. Water was brought in and waste carried out in buckets. In this block lived 60 people who shared three outdoor toilettes that emptied into large buckets. Parents and daughters slept in one bedroom and boys in another. In the boys' room was a second double bed used for visitors, elderly grandparents, or sub-renters.

The girls were responsible for carrying the water and waste. The laundry was washed in a shared outdoor room, each family having a reserved time once a week. Wet clothes were dried outside, but with the soot and pollution so ubiquitous, it was often cleaner to hang them inside near the fireplace where the family burned coal to cook and keep warm.

These were the routines that they went through during a typical week. Eli Taylor most likely had his shoemaking shop in his home. Shopkeepers and tradesmen like him flocked to Birmingham since it was an open city requiring no registration with the guilds. There were 2700 trades in the city, and many of these tradesmen worked out of their back-to-back residences. It was a workable arrangement that avoided the need to rent shop space. Even if life in a back-to-back dwelling was modest and sometimes crude, in many ways it was still a big improvement over the run-down rural cottages found in many villages.

Given the location of the Nichols and Taylor families, they almost certainly were back-to-back dwellers. The mid-19th century censuses told us where the Nichols and Taylor families once lived, just a few short blocks away from the Back-to-backs Museum on Inge Street. A census taker noted how one home was on the outer court. We made a tour of their 1861 addresses to find the buildings now gone. The site of one of their homes is now an already eroding shopping center near Birmingham's modern railway station. Another is covered with a modest looking middle-class home, and *still another is a rumpled field whose thin unsettled layer of soil covers the rubble underneath.*

But these were their streets. We were strolling through their neighborhoods. Thanks to the National Trust's careful preservation, we saw how their homes, in their cookie-cutter shapes, must have looked and felt. We had a good impression of how they lived and what made up a good share of each day.[50]

Local Collections: State & Territorial Censuses, Voter Lists

I found much less than I anticipated about the Taylors' first year or two in Salt Lake City. This surprised me because the Taylors' new home was in Utah, where keeping records was almost a way of life. Mormons, whose teachings emphasized a responsibility toward ancestors, chronicled and wrote histories, particularly about pioneer ancestors. I had already learned that there was no shortage of handwritten and typed family histories about the Howards' trek across the continent, even though I never found a diary of their own.

However, that did not seem to be true about the Taylors. For the first few years after Mary Ann and her family arrived in Utah, they just disappeared. Even the civil and census records did not offer a lot of help. I did learn they were living south of Salt Lake in an area called South Cottonwood. Five years passed after their arrival in Utah in 1875 before the Taylors clearly emerge again.

Even with the couple's beautiful and carefully preserved wedding photo in front of me, I was frustrated by how little detail I could find. Two entries on the family's New Testament "births" page hinted that Richard's and Mary Ann's wedding was the beginning of a hard life and sad ending. The first two boys died in quick succession, both on the same day they were born: "George W. Wilson Died May 9th 1882;" "Eli R Wilson Died December 17th 1883." There were no locations written down.

Family traditions told that both boys died in Arizona. I spent a day looking hard for any trace of these boys (and for anything on Richard and Mary Ann's wedding) in the impressive Family History Library in Salt Lake City, only to find no clues to their births or deaths in Arizona or Utah. There were no hints about the wedding, either. Even the on-duty consultant who generously tried to help could find nothing.

George W. was born six months after they were wed. Was Mary Ann expecting when they got married? If so, that might explain why they left for Arizona. On the other hand, the trim Mary Ann in the wedding photograph gives no hint of that. Was it a miscarriage or pre-mature birth? They did give their son a full name, something that sometimes suggests the child died at birth, but as I followed their paths after the wedding, a premature birth seemed the more likely possibility.

There was nothing in the letters and written family histories telling when Richard and Mary Ann left Utah for Arizona, how they got there, what they did, or even, why there? It was an intriguing, but stubborn story to uncover. I reasoned that if I had had difficulty finding them in Utah, where record keeping was an art, discovering something in sparsely settled Arizona would be a real challenge. I knew that I needed some basic facts before I could pound a peg or two that anchored the corners of this skimpy picture.

The 1880 U.S. Census recorded both of them in Salt Lake City. Family records had them back in Utah before 1890. I did a general search on Ancestry.com for "Joseph Wilson, Arizona, 1880's" and found nothing. But when I changed the search to "Richard Wilson," his name suddenly popped up in an Arizona 1882 territorial census: "name: Wilson, Richard; age: 26; birthplace: England."

Richard usually gave Ireland as his birthplace, but I had already learned that he often maintained his cover by giving conflicting statements about years and places, and by sometimes switching his first and middle names. His was the last entry on the page. The first on the next was: "name: Wilson, Mary Ann; age: 18; birthplace: England." There was just enough information here to identify the couple. Mary's Ann's name, age, birthplace, and husband matched what I was looking for.

Arizona was a rough territory in the 1880's, the home of Wyatt Earp, Geronimo, and Billy the Kid. The "Gunfight at the O.K. Corral" took place the week before Richard's and Mary Ann's wedding. Why the territory decided to do a census in 1882, precisely the year I needed, I have no idea. But there they were.

This information was not a lot, but it was enough to start piecing together a picture of Richard's and Mary Ann's lives in Arizona. I would never find all the details, but what I began to see was the probable narrative of Richard's and Mary Ann's early marriage years. Even to get that far, however, I realized that I needed still more information on the time and the place.

The 1882 Arizona census gave their local residence as "St. Joseph, Apache County, Arizona." Where was that? I had driven several times through the state and never heard of St. Joseph. Wikipedia and Google provided some quick information. From these, I found references to an old history of Arizona, written in 1896, and to two books written in the 1970s about the St. Joseph area during the 1870s and 1880s.[51] The history was available on Google Books for free-of-charge downloading. I found the other two books on AbeBooks.com, an online used book seller. Within a few days, I had in front of me more information about Richard's and Mary Ann's 1880s surroundings than I expected possible. I quickly saw that even though few people today have heard of St. Joseph, Arizona, that is not because the place lacked a captivating story of its own.

Curious for more basic information on Richard and Mary Ann, I looked another time at the 1882 Arizona census. The normal procedure for taking a census was for the census taker to go with pen and book from door to door collecting answers to standardized questions. By looking at names before and after the entry of interest, you normally find who lived around them. In those days, people often lived close to relatives and friends. I noticed one of the people near Richard's and Mary Ann's entries was a single man (or at least a man with no family listed) named James Gallagher, 29 years old, about the age as Richard.

One more Ancestry.com search produced another document with Richard's name: "Arizona Voter Registrations." It was taken later the same year in October 1882, but at the opposite end of the territory, in Mojave County, about 60 miles from Needles,

California. This time, Mary Ann's name was obviously missing since women were not yet allowed to vote, but interestingly, James Gallagher again appeared on the list to Richard Wilson's. James, it said, was from New York. I stopped for a moment to think about that. I had somewhere earlier seen the two together.

After combing my memory for a moment, it suddenly occurred to me that the 8th Infantry Muster Roll for Fort Russell, April 30, 1873, listed two men from Company K that deserted on the same day, March 16. One was Richard McGuire, and the other was named Gallagher. Both had been recruited in New York.[52]

There were a lot of pieces in this jigsaw puzzle, some of them perhaps now fitting together in a general sketch of their life in Arizona.

Adding "Why's" to Our Stories

When exploring the past, it is often easier to find "what" happened than "why" it happened. Why's are important. The "why's" are often the glue that holds together good stories, adding coherence and meaning. But they are also often so speculative and hard to get at. In my search for family narratives, the question "why?" was always in my mind.

Why did Richard and Mary Ann travel to Arizona immediately after they wed? Later, after Richard married Louie, why did they leave Utah, where they were settled and had friends, for Camas Creek, a remote place few people even knew about? Was it another effort to forestall the chance someone would learn of his past? Even over twenty years after he had deserted the army on Wyoming's desolate deserts?

In the writings Margie placed in Louie's file, my eye focused on some notes taken during a discussion in the early or mid-1950s. They were penciled on just a scrap, an old program for some event. I suspect I may have even been present during that chat. I remember Mother taking me as a small boy more than once to talk to Louie about her memories.

We called Louie "Grandma Edie" from the married name her second husband left her. When we visited Grandma Edie, she seemed so old. Over 80 years old, she was probably the oldest person I had ever met. I was fascinated by Grandma Edie's canary. Living in a desert town hardly sixty years away from its frontier days, canaries were a rare thing. It chirped and sang while Mother and Grandma talked, and the whole time my eyes were glued to its yellow feathers. In our high mountain sagebrush plain, I only knew sparrows, robins, hawks and crows, and the occasional pheasant or sage hen that Dad brought home from hunting.

Mother's passion for family history was firing up in those days. With much more foresight than most of us enjoy, she spent time with grandparents and older aunts and uncles talking about their family reminiscences. They were happy to share their memories, and she was excited to build a family history baseline from which she could work backwards toward earlier generations.

Piecing together the somewhat scattered notes taken during that visit, I found Grandma Edie's comment that when they arrived at Camas Creek, Richard told that he had been there before and knew the place. Mother later speculated that perhaps when he was at Fort Russell he had scouted that area. However, he was only at Fort Russell for a few months before walking off. There was nothing in the Fort's records to suggest any long-range reconnaissance that winter, at least not as far as Idaho,.

Not a lot of passengers disembarked the train in Camas Creek. It was a place most people stayed on the train. It was simply on the railroad's way to somewhere. The Utah & Northern Railway's station and roundhouse at Camas Creek was on its line from Utah to the mining towns of Montana. Construction of the tracks had reached Camas Creek in July 1879, and probably not a lot had changed since then.[53]

It seemed clear to me that before meeting Mary Ann, Richard had spent as least part of the late 1870s in Utah doing railroad construction. Some of that time could well have been on the big Utah & Northern project connecting the Union Pacific line from Ogden through Idaho to Montana. Why else would he have traveled that far north from Utah? He perhaps liked the area and tucked away a thought that it might be a place to settle one day. The line

373

reached Camas Creek in 1879, he was back in Salt Lake to be counted with the census in 1880, and he married Mary Ann the next year before they took off to Arizona to work on the railroad construction project there. It is speculation, of course, but I can think of no more likely reason he would once have visited this isolated place on the high Idaho desert, as Louie explained decades later.

Putting Mary Ann Taylor to Rest

Pulling together our family stories often offers a chance to show our respect to the people who in one manner or another formed our own lives. On our Memorial Day tour of family graves in 2008, my Mother, my sister Lorilee, and I made a trip to the Murray City cemetery in a southern suburb of Salt Lake City. We were searching for Mary Ann's grave site. Mother knew that it was there, but not exactly where. The cemetery office found her records and gave directions to a group plot near one of the lanes that wound among the markers. Next to Mary Ann lay others from the Taylor family, including her younger brother, Eli. No marker preserved this young woman's remembrance. Mother said her dream was to have a stone bearing Mary Ann's name erected above her grave.

In less than a year, Mother, herself was gone, but her dream remained. Lorilee and I talked about rallying some family support to have a marker made for Mary Ann. Lorilee, who lived not far from the cemetery, kindly took the lead in the project. With the donations that several members of the family sent, she soon had a stone engraved and set above Mary Ann's resting place.

A few months later, Lorilee joined Seija and me on another Memorial Day tour of family graves. This time, we placed flowers on Mother's new resting spot and on Mary Ann's, the woman none of us, not even Mother, had met. But Mary Ann's suffering and endurance left a legacy we wanted to remember.

Putting Richard McGuire to Rest

Life takes place where our dreams and memories meet. Childhood and the short years of youth normally brim with dreams,

374

some of which are soon dashed while others are happily realized. One can imagine many of Richard's dreams, especially when he and his sister stepped foot on the Great Eastern *to sail across the Atlantic toward a new home in America. Perhaps they did not know exactly what to expect, but good dreams never require detail. Their parents had gone through the Irish potato famine, and they were hoping for more than that.*

As life moved forward, however, his dreams were replaced with memories. Days were won or lost, or both, and only memories of those battles, losses, and victories remained. In Richard's case, the memories were almost truncated when he died. With no little irony, however, the mysteries born from secreting his stories kept Richard alive in the memories of many of his children and the grandchildren who followed.

With so few memories propagated, and so many of them obfuscated, the effort to illuminate this man's many heartbreaks and occasional joys was captivating and often sad – but, when the pieces of the story began to fit together, it was satisfying, too. When I finished writing down what I had found, I realized this had been one of the most demanding legs of the search for my family's stories. "So near, but so far," I often thought. Tracking Richard and Mary Ann, whose family even I knew, should have been much easier than following the trails of Puritan or medieval ancestors. That was not always how it happened.

When they slowly lowered Richard's coffin into the ground, the answers to scores of questions about the quiet unassuming man were buried with him. His fascinating stories were barely known. They hearkened to a much-dramatized period of the American West: the Sioux and Cheyenne wars on the northern plains and the Apache wars in the southwest; the unstoppable thrust of the railroads across the frontier territories; and the drudgery and grueling labor of the men and women who settled these sometimes-unforgiving new lands, mining and railroad towns, and farming communities..

Richard had been in the middle of some of those wars, worked in or around the silver mines, staked out a homestead in the dry American mountain desert, witnessed the gangs of New York, and

375

crossed the Atlantic with the masses of migrants from Ireland. As far as I could tell, his mourners on that day in 1902 would probably have never heard or guessed about all this. Perhaps his stories would not have seemed so remarkable to some of them. Many of that generation lived their own adventures, now greatly forgotten to us.

PART 4
HARD TIMES

Chapter 9

Homesick
Matilda Ann Howard Johnson

*"I suppose I cried a little. I was to cry
many times in the future, of homesickness.
One can become very sick just being
homesick."*

Matilda Ann Howard Johnson

*Margie, though not Tillie's own grandchild, was asked by Tillie
to write her life's story for the funeral, whenever it came. My father
was Tillie's grandson, but Mother was her friend and next-door
neighbor. When exploring what Mother eventually presented a few
years later at that funeral, I realized that this time my search did not
require finding the places where she lived and raised her family. I
already knew them. Now, it was more a journey through a
landscape of memories and feelings, especially my own and my
mother Margie's. On this leg of my journey I found a better
understanding of people whose lives overlapped with mine. To a
great extent, it was a re-exploration of some of the crossroads I knew
when young.*

*Tillie's family had left a lot of reminiscences, but the challenge
was to locate the various one- and two-page family histories and to
arrange them into a coherent narrative that added context and a
setting to her stories. By putting them together into a single
narrative, I found the whole was much larger than the parts.*

"Where are the Trees?"

It was a mid-1950's family reunion, and this time on the program
was a skit named "Life in the 1890s." It was meant to be a parody
about the time newlyweds Matilda (or, "Tillie," as everyone called
her) and John Johnson first came to Idaho from comfortable lives in
Utah. I saw the skit when members of Tillie's family performed it,

but I was too young to remember much other than the laughter. Years later, I was excited when I found the skit's script. From my vantage point as a collector of stories, this skit was especially important. It was one of the few instances of a drawn-out conversation between my ancestors. Events were sometimes written down. Memories were sometimes recorded. But this was a dialogue, at least Tillie's version of it.

John had already established a homestead near Idaho Falls, a fledgling town in the upper Snake River valley. He was returning with Tillie, a bride who had never been there, to start their farm. According to the 1862 Homestead Act, he could stake out and keep 160 acres of public lands if he improved it and agreed to live there five years. John had already built a small log-house as his improvement.

The skit began one snow-covered day in April 1893, as their train traveled north from the Utah settlements through the desert terrain of southeastern Idaho. Just a few lines to give the flavor:

> Tillie: So this is Idaho. My, what a dry state! I've never seen so much sagebrush in my whole life.
> John: Now, Tillie, give Idaho a chance...
> Tillie: ...Will it be anything like the folks' home in Bountiful?
> John: Oh... a little (snicker)...
> (Next Morning on Buckboard)
> Tillie: My it's a chilly day. Doesn't spring ever come around here? Just look at those patches of snow. Why you'd think it was February instead of April... If we had had to come up here a month ago we wouldn't have been able to get through the snow drifts. Who ever heard of snow in April!!... Oh, John, look at those trees over there!! Is that where we're going?
> John: Sure... Sure that's where we're going.
> (Late Afternoon)

379

Tillie: We have traveled all day and we still don't seem to be getting any closer to those trees... Look! There's a little log cabin over there in the middle of that big field of sagebrush!

John: Yep! And that's just where we're going.

Tillie: (angry and crying) But John! Where are the trees?! You said the trees were where we were going!

John: (laughing loudly) Why those trees grow along the Snake River. They're a long way from here. Can't you take a joke? This field of sagebrush is our land. But cheer up! We will make this desert blossom as a rose!

Tillie: ...I don't know how I can put my nice things in that cabin. Why the mud falls down from the walls every few minutes... and that mud roof will surely leak when it rains!... I wish I could believe you... have the faith that you do, but somehow things look pretty dark...[1]

Everyone laughed as the skit was played out. Even Tillie bemusedly smiled and chuckled, sometimes with a little more bitterness than maybe anyone noticed.

Perhaps the dialogue did not track word-for-word with what the two actually said to each other, but these excerpts are not too exaggerated. The script followed closely Tillie's recollection of the conversation. Mother was the writer, and from the notes in her files, I found that Tillie, herself, gave her most of it. The dramatization, to a great extent, followed closely what Tillie had told mother in an interview.

The skit revealed with humor and sensitivity how for young bride Tillie, arriving to a harsh life in 1890's Idaho's was not the romantic story of pioneers settling an exciting new land with joy and confidence. There were days of joy and many moments of confidence, but often it was a trying experience, full of frustration, suffering, and enduring homesickness. Even a lifetime later, Tillie still remembered keenly the deception John introduced to his new wife, the barren loneliness that ensued, and how the support and friendship that others gave helped her survive.

"Miles and Miles of Sagebrush"

Tillie Howard was the granddaughter of Joseph Howard, and the daughter of his son, James (Chapter 8). After their tragic passage across the plains, Joseph's and James's families became some of the first settlers of a community on the north edge of Salt Lake City called South Bountiful. Tillie's mother, Juliett Fackrell, came to the valley in 1852 with some of the early Mormon wagon companies. James and Juliett rented farmland and raised vegetables and fruit before homesteading a large tract of their own.[2]

Like many of her time, Tillie started her life in humble circumstances. She was born in 1874 in a two-room log house, part of the "promised land's" first native generation. James and Juliett named her after James's sister Matilda, who, as a six-year-old, died during the punishing journey West. Tillie was one of ten children in the house, the third oldest.[3]

Tillie's childhood home hummed with activity, everyone with their own set of chores and responsibilities. They raised strawberries and black currants, and Tillie's mother allowed her to keep and sell whatever remained after the family's own needs. Her father sold the berries 10 quarts for a dollar. She earned pocket money, but maybe not a lot.

In our supermarket and on-line shopping-centered lives, it is almost forgotten how in the past even smallest conveniences were the result of a great deal of effort. Take soap, for example, made then at home from fats and lye in a process that often introduced an element of danger into the house. When Tillie was about eight years old, her mother tasked her to help with the sweeping. As she brushed the small cabin's floor from side-to-side, she bumped into a large vat filled with lye being prepared from wood ashes. The vat teetered and then tipped over, splashing the caustic liquid over her head, face and arms, and, worst of all, her eyes.

Tillie's mother cleaned the skin, but for several days they kept her in a dark room fearing she was going blind. In the end, she survived, eyesight intact. Everyone considered it a blessing, but she remained frail and small for her age. They thought this was on account of the accident and nicknamed her "Teeny" Tillie.

When Tillie was nine her father took a second wife in a polygamous relationship that no one in my family ever emphasized. In fact, in well circulated histories of his life, his grandchildren completely omit this detail, one I did not know until I began gathering Tillie's stories. Tillie's father, James, and his older brother, William, were close friends who had had married sisters, Juliette and Betsy Jane Fackrell. The two brothers, according to family tradition, made a pact that if either of them died early, the other would take care of his brother's widow and family.[4]

After William was killed in a logging accident in 1872, James took Betsy Jane as his second wife twelve years later. The arrangement was not uncommon in Utah where the church still sanctioned polygamous marriages. Betsy Jane lived in a house that James built for her across the road from the one Tillie grew up in with her mother, Juliette, and father, James. Another more revealing family history, written by a granddaughter of James and Betsy Jane, tells how Juliette stood by the window, tears in her eyes, when James crossed the road to see Betsy Jane.[5]

James was industrious, and by the time Tillie turned 13 he was running his own dairy with 37 cows and 50-60 customers in nearby Salt Lake City. He drove his team of horses to make the deliveries. It was a family enterprise where Tillie and the other children all helped support. Early each morning, she milked eight cows in time to get the dairy wagon off by 7:00 a.m. That night, before sundown, she milked them again. Tillie also had the job of washing the milk cans. She hated the job passionately for the sour odor that with time milk cans begin to take even when clean. Some days she climbed onto the wagon as her father pulled the team off on their deliveries.

It was hard work for everyone, but they began to prosper. James built a new comfortable house for the family, one of the largest in the area directly north of Salt Lake City. When it was completed,

James called the family together. They bowed their heads while he addressed the Lord in a dedicatory prayer asking for peace, happiness, love, and blessings in their new dwelling. Theirs was a strict home: there were no games, playing, or work on the Sabbath Day. The family devoutly traveled two miles to church every Sunday as well as some weeknights. The dairy was nonstop, however. Its work went on seven days a week, as all dairies must.[6]

If she was small, Tillie was smart, and she was musical. Her parents recognized her abilities and arranged piano and organ lessons when she was still young. By the time she was 12, she was teaching children in their Sunday School, and when she was 15, she was already the organist in her ward congregation and its children's organization. They also saw that her schooling continued uninterrupted, eventually sending her to a church-run high school in Farmington where she also played the organ for religion class.

About the time Tillie started high school, her father was arrested for unlawful cohabitation, in other words for practicing polygamy. The church might have approved of polygamy, but the Territory of Utah, then under the control of Federal judges and marshals, did not. During the summer of 1888 James was arrested, and six month later a judge handed him a $100 fine and sentenced him to 90 days in the territorial prison. Prison is never pleasant, for prisoners or their families who are left to get by. In James's case, the family had to run the dairy. But in the Utah of those times, there was hardly a stigma attached. Prisoners, and sometimes their family members, too, considered the imprisonment a violation of their religious rights (but not always). The prisoners often saw themselves as martyrs. But sanctioned polygamy was in its last days. The year after James was released from prison it was officially banned in the church.[7]

Not all girls her age went to high school, nor even wanted to. But Tillie was in her element there, that is, until one afternoon, just two months before graduation, when her father James unexpectedly arrived in the middle of class. He had come to take her home. Her mother Juliett, extremely weak from childbirth, was not sure to survive. Tillie, their oldest daughter, would have to manage the home. For Tillie, it was a bitter day. She never forgot the afternoon she left her school and friends. But life was full of unanticipated twists and turns. Juliett eventually recovered. And interrupting her school led to bigger changes in Tillie's life than she expected.

Since Tillie would not return and only lacked two examinations to graduate, James arranged with the school that if she passed the exams, she would receive her diploma. To prepare for them, he agreed to hire a local teacher as her tutor. James quickly found a young graduate named John Johnson from a college in Salt Lake City. He lived near the Howards and taught at a local school. John began giving Tillie regular sessions.

The two were not strangers. John's family belonged to the same congregations as the Howards. However, he was seven years older than Tillie and never part of her group of friends. John was tall (6 ft. 1 in.), slim, light complexioned, handsome, artistic, bright, and outgoing. His Swedish parents had crossed the plains the same summer Tillie's father and grandparents did. John's father wanted him to be a blacksmith, like he himself, but John had other plans. After finishing school, he attended a teachers college and got his first position in the Woods Cross school he had attended.[8]

Tutoring went better than expected. Tillie passed the exams and received her diploma. But something more than that happened during John's visits to the Howard home. After high school matriculation, John asked if he could continue to call on her. Tillie was excited, but her parents did not approve. "Some of the habits of the Johnson family were not the same," as those of the Howard family, Matilda told Mother years later. Her parents "treated John quite shabbily."[9]

The Johnsons were religious hard-working folk, just like the Howard family. However, they were Swedes, not English, Tillie explained. When I read through Mother's notes from this conversation, I first wondered whether Tillie's parents' objection to John stemmed from cultural frictions between Swedish and English immigrants. Maybe not. Perhaps James and Juliett were reluctant to lose their oldest daughter at a relatively young age. Maybe James foresaw how John would take Tillie to an isolated life on a

384

homestead somewhere. James had worked all his life to ensure his own children could avoid the hardships he had gone through.

Or perhaps her parents perceived John as an exploring and wandering spirit whose desire to experience and undertake things without fully thinking them through would eventually result in a difficult life for their daughter. Tillie was a tender personality, and they may have thought she needed an easier spouse and home life than what John was apt to provide. For better or worse, right or wrong, parents often make such calculations when their children contemplate leaving home to marry.

John did not easily accept a "no." But when he called, it got so bad that Tillie was surprised he kept coming back. Her parents channeled their displeasures in her direction, as well. She finally decided that if he could take it, so could she. If he wanted to take her someplace her parents disapproved, she would simply stay home. If he was interested enough, she speculated, he would keep returning. With stubborn Swedish resilience, he did, and at some point, James's and Juliett's resistance finally crumbled. Tillie and John were soon engaged, and by March the next year, they were married. They made an exceptionally handsome couple: tall, confident and good-looking John, with slim, attractive, and radiant Tillie at his side. Both bright, both talented, they seemingly were a perfect match.

John in fact did have plans to carve out a life of their own somewhere outside the Utah valleys. He and some of his friends, the Cleverley brothers and Burtenshaws, had been to southeastern Idaho along the Snake River and wanted to pioneer this still mostly unpopulated mountainous desert. The climate in the vast mile-high valley was dry and harsh, but the volcanic soil was rich, and the hills were full of water for irrigation. The large river ran through the mountain valleys.

Jesse and Frank Cleverley moved there in the early 1880's and filed on homesteads a few miles northwest of a river crossing town called Eagle Rock. The brothers worked nearby on the Utah & Northern Railway construction two years for money to start up their farms. John Shelton Howard, John's brother-in-law (and also

Tillie's uncle, her father's brother), had marked off a homestead near the Cleverley land, as well[10] (See Map I).

During the years before getting engaged with Tillie, John filed for his own homestead in Idaho. To improve it, he decided to build a cabin, but there were no trees around the homestead. Some miles away were thick mountain forests, but John decided to get his wood from a nearby canyon. He would cut the logs and then float on them down the Snake River to a spot near his homestead. Borrowing someone's team and wagon, he could quickly get it to the place where he planned to build.

It seemed simple but was actually a daredevil endeavor as anyone who knows the Snake River will tell. At first, everything went to plan. He cut the timber, got it the river bank, secured the logs together, and jumped on top with some of his things. Down he and the logs went smoothly – at first. And then the current picked up, and from there things got worse. The torrent took his shoes, bedding, and supplies, but left him alive.

But he had his logs, and with them John built a cabin about eight miles from the river on his newly staked out 160 acres of sagebrush. Thinking of this fete, it easy to understand his persistent courage in seeking Tillie's hand. Whatever he suffered in the Howards' home probably did not surpass rafting his logs down the Snake.[11]

For all his bravado, however, John was not candid with Tillie about what faced her when they moved to Idaho. True, she could not expect John's homestead to be an easy life. But how wide the gap between living in a large home on the outskirts of Salt Lake City and a cabin in the Snake River desert was not clear to her.

Salt Lake City was rushing to modernize with services like those found in other large cities of its times: electric trolleys were already replacing horse-drawn street cars on the city's streets; miles of pipes pumped water into the homes of its residents; electric lines were running south into the suburbs; and sewers were under construction. The new home Tillie's father James had built a few years earlier did not yet have many of these conveniences, but they were coming, and the large home, itself, was refined and pleasant.[12]

John's homestead was about fifteen miles outside of Eagle Rock, just re-named Idaho Falls. The community had only about 1,500 people and was by far the largest in the southeast part of the new state. Except for areas around the riverbanks, however, the surrounding plain was arid and extended for miles with nothing but brush. "Miles and miles of sagebrush," Tillie later mused. Whether the climate was too severe to support farming was still an open question. John, perhaps, saw the place for what it might become. Tillie, when she arrived, saw it for what it was.[13]

Tillie and John were married on March 8, 1893. The dedication of Salt Lake's landmark temple was to take place a month later, and they decided to attend the dedication before departing for Idaho. The temple was the Mormon city's pride and had taken 40 years to build, nothing in terms of medieval cathedrals, but a long time by American standards. Its dedication was long anticipated. In John's mind, perhaps, the extra month would also allow Idaho's deep snow cover to melt further before Tillie saw it for the first time.

Following the dedication, they took their belongings to the depot where they loaded them onto a baggage car, climbed into the coach with the other passengers, and began clicking along the tracks northward. As the train steamed forward, it crossed into ever more uninhabited landscapes, first the hills, then the snowy passes. It finally dropped down again to a flat valley where even today one can often look to the horizon with no sign of people. The view coming off the mountains into the valley is beautiful whatever time of year you see it, but it is a lonely one for anyone who thrives on being close to family and friends.

Tillie watched from the windows of the train car hoping that something more like the home she had left behind awaited their arrival. The skit played decades later before Tillie's descendants fairly well shares their discussions along the way, and how deceived she felt when they finally arrived.

"We had a farm, but nothing to farm…"

The train from Utah slowed and rolled to a stop alongside the platform in Idaho Falls. Tillie was anxious to see the new home where her husband had promised her. They stepped from the passenger car to find a friend and relative of John's, Ed Brown,[14] waiting to meet them. It had been a long day on the train, and since it was already evening, they spent the night at Ed's and his wife Min's home in Idaho Falls.

It was April 14th in the early morning when John and Tillie climbed aboard Ed's wagon. It was loaded heavily with the young couple's possessions. John jerked the reins and the team started off in the direction of a small community that boasted only a handful of neighbors and was called Shelton. Shelton took its name from Tillie's uncle, John Shelton Howard, who lived there. He, in turn, got the Shelton name from his mother, and Tillie's grandmother, Ann Shelton.

Uncle John was a polygamist with two wives. In Idaho, he dropped the Howard surname to obscure the affair, especially among law enforcement officers, and went by John Shelton. Tillie's sister-in-law, John's sister Josephine, was Howard's first wife. Josephine, childless, lived in Utah. The second wife, Sarah Ann Downs, lived with John Shelton in Shelton and bore him eleven children.

But to be sure, Sarah hardly fit the stereotype of an oppressed polygamous mother of eleven. Sarah had a remarkable reputation as a midwife who kept a record of over 600 births she had assisted. Her skills were known widely throughout the upper Snake River Valley where it was said that nearly every family at one time or another needed her services. It was also said that she never lost a mother in childbirth.[15]

So Tillie had some built-in connections to Shelton, however good or bad the place turned out to be. Nevertheless, the trip did not get off to a good start, at least in Tillie's mind. It was well into springtime, and the road was still covered with snow. The wagon moved slowly along the drifted road. "The old Jackson Lane, as it was called then, was so drifted with snow when I first saw it, it took two span of horses to clear the way," she reminisced. Tillie asked John for some reassurance about where they were going. He wryly

388

responded, "Oh it is a nice place," words Tillie later related with a touch of sarcasm.[16]

The fifteen miles to John's farm took all day. It was evening when they finally pulled in front of the small one-room log house. Millie dryly told Mother that there was not a tree within ten miles, which was probably true. There was no water on the property, either. Drinking water had to be hauled in.

Mother wrote in her notes from that interview with Tillie: "She said that he [John] turned to her and laughed." Tillie confessed she could never forget that moment. What distressed her was not simply the primitive conditions. She felt John had deceived her by describing the place in rosier terms than what she found. And he just laughed about her surprise and grief. Tillie noted in her history, "I suppose I cried a little. I was to cry many times in the future."[17]

Their new home "had a dirt roof and was filled between the logs with mud so when it rained the mud came from all sides," she recounted.[18] Along the Shelton Road were six neighbors, one of whom was Pete Chambers, a Black American who generously helped the young couple get started. It is remarkable that a Black family was found among these homogenously white European-stock first- and second-generation immigrant families. Pete Chambers seemed to live comfortably in the community, however, welcoming and befriending new families as they arrived, loved and respected, especially by Tillie and John, in return. Across the road, the Mormon families were working on a chapel where they could hold services. Meanwhile, they took turns meeting in different homes.[19]

"We had a farm but nothing to farm with so John went to work shearing sheep, putting up hay, etc., south of here..." Tillie remembered.[20] It was one thing to feel disappointed and homesick, but quite another to fail to "put your shoulder to the wheel," as that generation called throwing yourself into a difficult situation to overcome it. That is what Tillie did. She went straight to work trying to spruce up their crude cabin.

John finally got together enough money to buy a horse. He borrowed another horse from a neighbor to make a team, and with the team, he was able to get more jobs to earn some cash. They acquired and planted tree sprouts and transported water about two miles until they could get a ditch built. They toiled until their energy gave out, and then trusted God to take them from there. When the cold Idaho winter and unpredictable frosts took their crops time after time, the church sent an apostle to bless the valley. That year the climate cooperated with the pioneer families, and every year after that their homesteads produced a living for them. God picked up after their toil could take them no further. These hearty people told the story to their children and to generation after generation. I cannot remember how many times I heard it when growing up.[21]

The couple eventually had enough to buy cloth to cover the ceiling of the log house. Tillie scrubbed the walls of the mud, they bought a bedstead, a table, four chairs, and a small stove. John nailed some boards for a cupboard, and they covered the floor with a homemade rag rug they brought from Utah. The cabin was becoming a home. "We were quite well to do," wrote Tillie, tongue-in-cheek.[22]

On the flipside, it was one thing to be "quite well to do," and another to be happy about her circumstances. Tillie suffered immensely from homesickness. She remembered the security of her parents' home, the joy and refinement of playing her piano, and the hustle and bustle of living in a growing city in the "roaring '90s" with her family and her friends around her. Often, the isolation of the semi-desert was unbearable. And the work was unending.

The young 18-year old bride was lonesome. Even the sound of the steam engine, chugging and whistling as it pulled cars up the distant tracks toward Montana, conveyed a longing for her childhood home, nestled against the mountains at the other end of the rails. Sometimes, when she heard the tell-tale rumble of an approaching locomotive, she climbed the mud-filled walls up the side of her log home. On top the roof she stood, under the blue Idaho sky, watching the far-off silhouetted train and passengers rush across the wide horizon that lined the sagebrush plain.

At summer's end, Tillie was thrilled to learn that her older brother Joseph planned to travel from Utah to visit them. Tillie and Joseph had been very close as they grew up. He escorted her to dances, and the two had always shared much in common. Joseph knew of Tillie's low spirits and hoped his visit would cheer her up. Against the homesickness she had endured over the previous months, the idea of spending time again with her favorite brother energized her. She awaited Joseph's arrival with anticipation

Joseph, 21 years old and not yet married, arrived near the end of September. It should have been a cheerful moment, but the joy of seeing him was quickly dashed when the first night he came down with a heavy fever. He complained of stomach pains and a severe headache. A rash began to appear on his skin. When after a day or two Joseph seemed to be getting only worse, they sent a team and wagon to Idaho Falls to summon the town's only doctor. "He was intoxicated when they got him here," Tillie remembered with bitterness. Joseph died of typhoid six days after he arrived. Somewhere, probably after drinking contaminated water, he had been fatally infected.[23]

Coming on top of everything else, Joseph's death was a heartbreaking blow for Tillie. His tragic loss, the arrival of this new high country's harsh winter, and the continuing isolation did nothing to restore her sagging spirits. Everything took a toll. "I had poor health for a few years," Tillie explained. "One can become very sick just being homesick."[24]

Despite that, John and Tillie worked hard. As their house became livable, they cleared the sagebrush from the fields by day and burnt the brush at night. The next year, John applied to the county for a teaching certificate. During the fall and winter, John taught children in the nearby Poplar School house.

In response to Tillie's depressed spirits, her father, James, purchased an organ in Utah and shipped it by rail to Idaho. They met the shipment at the train depot and carried the organ by wagon across the bumpy roads to their house. It was pure therapy, and Tillie's delight was still visible decades later when she wrote about it: "The first organ in this part of Idaho. A seven octave fine organ," she proudly recalled. With an organ in their humble home, Tillie earned additional money giving music lessons. When conferences were organized in the new Mormon chapel across the road, the men carried her organ there for her to accompany the congregation's hymns.[25]

During their first four years in Idaho, some things happened that complicated Tillie's efforts to get her roots firmly planted in its mountainous soil. The first year was filled with the problems of getting their new home established. Then she became pregnant. The baby was a healthy son they named John, after his father. A few months later, Tillie was expecting again. This time a little girl, Ethel, was born, not even a year and a half younger than John. Tillie now had two babies to raise in the crude conditions of the log cabin.

Then, not long after Ethel's birth, John told Tillie that the church was calling him on a mission to Sweden. LDS missions were voluntary obligations many men assumed, and not paid professions. The missionaries covered their own expenses and left their families at home to manage best they could. John had learned Swedish as a child, and hence the mission to Sweden. He would be gone two years. Tillie and the babies would be left behind to fend for themselves and, still more, to support John.

As a young and devout wife, Tillie concluded that if John felt a need to serve the mission, he should go. She would even find a way to help support him. However, there was no way she would stay on the Idaho homestead while he was gone. They agreed, and John departed at the end of October 1897. He was in Sweden by mid-November. Meanwhile, Tillie packed up the children and moved to stay with a family who lived next to her parents in Utah. "I was glad to go as I was so homesick," she told.[26]

Back at home, Tillie found a job in a small store not far from where she lived. She gave music lessons and took butter, meat, a ton of hay, and other things as payment. Her mother tended the children. She even started sending money to John in Sweden. Something she did reveals a lot about why she was so homesick among Shelton's sagebrush and mud-dripping log walls. With the first $5.00 she earned, she bought six silver knives and forks. It was refinement that she missed, and she was determined to eventually bring some of it to her Idaho cabin.

Tillie's parents realized she was poorly cut out for the hardships of Idaho and would have kept her in Utah permanently. Her father bought two acres of land with a small house on them hoping to entice John to stay near the Howards when he returned. Two years passed, and one December day in 1899 John did finally come home. He spent the winter with Tillie in Bountiful, but his dream was in Idaho, and he kept thinking of all he could accomplish when he got back to his land. When spring came, he left to fix up the log house and clear more sagebrush. Tillie, grudgingly, followed him with the children.

They soon had the log house livable again. When cleaning a dwelling like theirs, small did not mean fast or easy. Everyday housekeeping was demanding. "I remember Mother cleaning house, taking up carpet and putting it back down with straw as the pad. She stretched it with a carpet stretcher and tacks. There was a shanty at the back with custard pies set out to cool there," one of her daughters later described.

Another year passed, and Tillie was pregnant again. This time, Tillie returned to her parents' home for the birth of a second daughter they named Mayme. Tillie nearly died in childbirth and afterwards was not in a hurry to get back to the homestead. In fact, she did not return for a year and a half, and by that time she had given John another baby girl.

Tillie was expecting much of the time now and gave birth to four more children in their log cabin before John was able to complete a new home that had more room for their family of now eight children. It was made of stone, a large notable house for its time and place. They moved into the farmhouse in 1908, and over the following seven years she had four more babies. That made a total of twelve.[27]

In spite of all this, Tillie took care of herself and kept her attractive appearance. "Mother was a pretty woman. Had dark hair, very slender and neat liked to dress well," a daughter described. Her photographs tell the story. She was also known as an excellent cook, thrifty, and with just basics able to make potatoes, meat, and vegetables "taste like food for a king."

Her youngest son, wrote, "My mother was a dedicated woman who lived the golden rule and instilled these qualities in her family.

393

She worked under many hardships and handled them well." One of her children added, however, that she was always a nervous person. That offers no surprise when one thinks of the burden she carried.[28]

John was not just an ordinary man, either. He enjoyed many talents. The children adored him. "He was a wonderful writer and painter, especially drawing birds," wrote one daughter.[29] He was full of affection toward his children. Another daughter remembered how one day when her mother was gone, she wanted to go fishing in a nearby creek. "Mother would never consent to let me go," but "Dad said I could."

Once on the fishing hole, she caught something. "Suddenly I screamed that I had a hold of a big fish... When I got it out of the water, I grabbed the fish and took for home on foot as fast as I could go. I went right out in the field where Dad was working and when he saw the fish, he unhooked the horses and put them on the buggy and took me right back up there where we both fished."[30]

A son wrote about his dad, "He loved to visit and always had time to stop and visit with anyone." He also shared some regrets, "I really didn't get as well acquainted with my father as I should have done. I guess I always had the feeling of being the chore boy."[31]

Although Tillie's and John's relationship may have suffered in later years, the way she described him decades after his death to someone writing up still another short history of her life shows that she, too, had more than a little awe toward the husband who took her to Idaho. "Tall and good looking. A good singer, a very good penman. Secretary for a great many organizations. His papers were always in order. He also carved headstones for the cemetery, taught school, was very quick at figures, helped the neighbors with their problems, dug ditches, built bridges, chopped down trees, built houses, dug canals and farmed."[32]

It is difficult today to imagine how people unwound in a pre-digital, pre-video, pre-social network world. From the notes and histories, I found of Tillie's and John's family, I could see how they had no difficulty having fun together. They organized home plays and the children helped John paint backdrops for plays in the school where he taught. In the winter, "Father played games with us. We

394

sometimes made games with arithmetic, English and spelling words," wrote a daughter.[33]

On winter evenings, they sat around a potbellied stove, and "Dad rolled some apples around the top of the heater until they were warm, then peeled and divided them."[34] They sang around the piano and played card games. On New Year's Day, they had friends over and the men sat close to the radio listening to a ball game. Sometimes the visitors would stay overnight.

During the summer, there was obviously much less time for recreation when the days were full of planting, cultivating and harvesting. At threshing time, Tillie and her girls sometimes had 25 field hands to feed for breakfast, dinner, and supper. Even so, the family found time to go on picnics in the canyons and swimming in the hot springs. They played ball in the evenings after the dishes were washed. "We had our own team," one of their children remembered. A member of the local Daughters of the Utah Pioneers chapter that Tillie captained later put it, "People in pioneer days did not have to be entertained; they entertained themselves."[35]

"We paid the mortgage..."

This happy home life took a big turn one day when John was called on a second Mormon Mission to Sweden. It was late 1915. Again, Tillie realized she would be left alone and would need to provide John's support while he was gone. "I had 12 at home besides a hired man, Mr. Henry," Tillie emphasized in her own history, just to be sure her reader understood her feelings.[36] With twelve, the youngest only six months old and three under four years, there was no going back to her parents during John's absence.

Tillie would have to take responsibility for everything. John left Tillie a 160-acre farm in the valley and a dry farm to manage, a $3,500 mortgage on the house due one year from the day he departed for Sweden, and a herd of sheep to raise. Their sheep did not need to be milked twice a day, like the cows she had milked in her father's dairy. But sheep had to be sheared and lambed each year. More than that, the cold spring weeks when the ewes birthed the lambs were often a 24-hour around the clock ordeal that tried even the sturdiest sheep men. You could not afford to lose the mothers nor the newborn lambs. When you lost a ewe, you adopted the lambs until they were old enough to feed themselves.

This was a new role for Tillie, not the one she probably thought she was born to have. Tillie was the woman who took the first dollars she earned to buy silverware, the young lady who loved dancing and playing music, the bride who hated leaving her comfortable home and who had suffered homesickness ever since. However, we do not always choose the roles we play. She met the challenge head on.

Before John left, the ward congregation organized a big farewell for him in the church across the road. First there was a program in the chapel, and afterwards they threw a big party in the basement. While the music played, John took Tillie in his arms and swirled her around the dance floor. Their older children were amazed. "What stands out in my memory is the dance they had. Dad danced with Mother and I had never seen them dance before," their daughter Mayme remembered about that sweet and sour evening.[37]

In January 1916 John packed his bags and left on the train for New York. All of Europe was at war, the darkest days of World I. Even though the United States would not enter "The War to End Wars," for another year, Atlantic shipping was often prey for German U-Boats. Passenger ships were no exception. Only a few months before, a German U-boat had torpedoed the Lusitania that sunk with the loss of over one thousand passengers, more than a hundred of them Americans. John boarded the *Christianiafjord* in New York City with a missionary colleague also on his way to Sweden. When they pulled out of American coastal waters, the ship turned north to take a passage that skirted Iceland in an effort to steer clear of submarine patrols.

No U-Boat attacked their ship, and eleven days out of New York the *Christianiafjord* docked in Bergen. A few days later they arrived on a cold winter day in Malmo, Sweden. There they joined the small handful of missionaries who had remained after the church drew down its force on account of the war. For the next two years, John served as president of the Sundsvall Conference in a coastal city

396

north of Stockholm. No one knew when they could get back from Sweden, especially after the United States joined the conflict. There was no indication when and if this devastating war would ever end.[38]

If Tillie was born to belong to a gentler time and place, life never offered her that possibility. If she tearfully yearned for the days of her girlhood, she seized what life sent her and triumphed. Without a slip, Tillie took over the reins of their farming and family operation. She had a hired woman to assist her in the house and Mr. Henry, the hired man, helped with everything else. All children old enough had their own parts to play, the girls in the kitchen and the boys with the farm work. They hired men to stack the hay, shock the grain, and use a threshing machine in the fall. The farm buzzed with activity, especially when the crops grew ready for harvest. "I remember having two tables full of men (even for breakfast)," Mayme told.[39]

It truly was a time of God and toil at Tillie's house and farm. The family all toiled, and if God did not ban war from the planet, at least he let crop prices rise when his people warred against each other. "Wheat and other grain prices came up while the war was on," Mayme explained.[40] And when they did, all the work Tillie oversaw paid off well. A year to the day that John left for Sweden, Tillie paid off the mortgage.

Not only that, she also ordered a Ford Model T, said to be the first in the area. The Model T had come out in 1908, and by the time Tillie bought one, half of all the cars in the United States were Model T's. Every Model T that year was black. She paid about $1,350 for her automobile. No one was probably happier about the novel machine than John Jr. He was courting at the time, and the car came in handy for impressing his young girlfriend. John married her before his father returned, and Mr. Henry built a small house on a corner of the farm for the young couple.

Tillie oversaw all of this without a husband on the scene and paid John's upkeep in Sweden, as well. She was proud of what she did: "With the help of my children and Mr. Henry, we paid the mortgage, paid cash for a new car and did not owe a dollar when he came home. He was gone over 2 ½ years and averaged $30.00 a month while in Sweden."[41]

The 1918 flu pandemic that wrought death across the United States and throughout the world was something else that happened during John's absence. It is estimated that 10-20% of everyone infected, died from it. The flu took 50-100 million people worldwide. No place was beyond its reach, not the Arctic, remote Pacific islands, nor the isolated Idaho countryside. All of Tillie's twelve children came down with influenza. Only she was immune.

It was devastating, and during those days the entire family was debilitated. If the flu had inflicted the same proportion of losses on their family as it normally took, Tillie would have lost one or two of the children. They managed their way through it, however, and all survived. Tillie considered it a miracle: "The Lord surely blessed me to take care of them, as I did not take it." Their neighbors helped care for the family. One came to the house in the morning, another at night.[42]

The World War finally came to an end in late 1918. John would have been eligible to return home earlier that year, but with the U-Boat dangers, he stayed in Sweden until the armistice was signed in November. Ten days after the peace, John was sailing from Sweden on the *S/S Oscar II*, and just 263 miles off New York. When the ship reached port, he wasted no time transferring to the station. His train rolled across the continent until he rode the Denver and Rio Grande tracks into Salt Lake City and then steamed north to Idaho Falls. Tillie was there on the platform. To his wonderment, she drove him home in the family's Model T.

John walked in the door to find a family that had greatly changed. The six-month old was now three and a half; Mayme, who was 15 when he left, was now almost 19. John Jr. was married. Mayme described the scene: "He looked at me and said, 'Surely this isn't Mayme!' (I think I weighed perhaps 200 lbs then, Ha! All that bread and honey)," she joked. "He was somewhat like a stranger to us, but we all loved him."[43]

It might have been something hard for John to absorb. While he had felt the pain of being far away from the growing family he loved over these years, Tillie seems to have remained distant and non-responsive. It was probably difficult for him to fathom what she went through while he was gone. Tillie's triumphal achievements, moreover, were a wonder that could have led him to ask himself how she did it. Then there was Mr. Henry, the hired man, on whom Tillie had had to rely through all the burdens of John's absence. She undoubtedly displayed gratitude toward Mr. Henry for his faithful service. Without it, Tillie and the family would have been lost.

It is impossible for us to understand everything that passed through John's thinking. At some point, however, John made the fatal mistake of his marriage. When John intimated an accusation that Tillie had had a romantic attachment to Mr. Henry during his absence, Tillie's forbearance must have snapped, irretrievably broken. With false pretenses, he had brought her to a country she would have never chosen. He had left her twice to assume voluntary religious service. Alone, she had faced almost the impossible, managing twelve children and a large farm operation. She had triumphed over all the challenges John dealt her. And now on returning, her husband accused her of infidelity. It was something unconscionable, something apparently she never found the strength to forgive, at least not as long as John lived.[44]

John never traveled away again. During the fifteen years that followed, the children grew older and soon started families of their own. But his relationship with Tillie seems never to have recovered. One early October day in 1934, John and his son, Wayne, were driving a team of horses pulling a wagon full of wood. One of the team was a still temperamental colt. As John maneuvered the wagon forward, the colt bolted, spooking the team.

John frantically struggled to bring the runaway wagon back under control. Before he could, the wheels took a bump or too quick a turn. The entire wagon teetered and then flipped over. John and Wayne were thrown from the seat. Wayne cleared the chaotically tumbling pieces of wood. But John was not so fortunate. A wheel passed over his chest breaking several ribs and piercing on of his ribs. They took to a hospital in Idaho Falls. John lay there getting worse, until five days later he passed away. He was 67, not a young man to be hauling wood, but still attacking life with the same bravado that propelled him down the Snake River when rafting logs over 40 years before.[45]

Mother told me on more than one occasion that during the days John lay dying in the hospital, Tillie did not come to his bedside. It would seem that the same stubbornness that drove Tillie to succeed during the near impossible years of John's absence, prevented her from overcoming the hurt she had suffered. John's loss, in that regard, might be seen as a double tragedy. The family lost a father, and Tillie missed a chance for reconciliation, no matter how hard it might have been.

For all the candidness in the various accounts of Tillie's and John's lives, at least part of this final chapter is missing from the family histories I was able to find. Only a brief paragraph or two exists about the accident, itself, and even that arrives directly or indirectly from Tillie's own lips over twenty years later. The closest any of the children comes to it is in the words of their youngest son Wayne who wrote, "The memory of my Dad's tragedy will be with me always, but we shouldn't ponder the sad, instead we should dwell on the good."[46] In light of this couple's many accomplishments and the love the children felt for their parents, they considered it better to let dark moments be, while remembering the happier ones.

After John's tragic accident, Tillie, now 60, continued running the farm for six years. She hired a man to help with some of the work, and her sons took over much of the rest. It was not a job for an older woman, and she finally turned the operation over to the family. She moved to an apartment in Idaho Falls. From the year I was born, my parents lived for seven years next door.

Tillie spent the rest of her life in Idaho close to her family harboring memories of the adventure she and John embarked on when just married. Still, she never completely warmed up to the place. In 1952, she told my mother, with a chuckle I am sure, about how John chose to settle there: "In 1888, his friends Ben Burtenshaw, the Egan boys, and Ed Brown came with him to Idaho to visit the Cleverley's. While here they became interested in filing on some land. That's how John Johnson got tied up with this rainy, windy, good for nothing state."[47]

I remember Tillie as a warm great-grandmother, perhaps offering fewer mushy hugs than some of the others. That was fine with me. Her small home was refined with many objects on the walls and tables, such as her cuckoo clock that always captured my interest. She was then in her late 70's. Mother remembered her for her intellect. "Her mind was active – always active. I was fascinated with her thinking," she wrote. Tillie kept herself versed on local, national, and international events, mother recalled, and she enjoyed working over our Petunia beds.[48]

During Tillie's last years, she lived with her daughter Mayme and died from a stroke in 1962, at 87 years old. She wanted her posterity to know her story: from the joys of her courtship with handsome and charismatic John Johnson and her innocence on train to Idaho Falls as a young bride, to the depths of that first summer's homesickness when she climbed on top the log house just to see the train pass, to the anguish of losing her brother when he came to cheer her, to the exhaustion of being almost continually pregnant in the primitive conditions of an Idaho homestead, to the misery of feeling abandoned, to the trials of running a large family and farm on her own.

Tillie took no credit for whatever victories or successes she achieved. "One cannot look back on a life such as I have had and not know there is a Supreme Being – a Higher Power that guides and guards us," was how she saw it with words that make a fitting epitaph.[49]

All Roads Lead to Home

When traveling through my oldest memories I often hear a 9:00 whistle blowing in the distance, back behind the tall leafy hardwoods that lined the streets and homes of the town where I grew up. In the evening, it blew again, at 6:00. Sometimes, when we were closer to it, my child's eyes watched with wonder as a column of white steam shot high above the town's largest dry cleaner, and with it, the whistle echoed across the entire town.

The blast of steam marked the beginning of each workday, and in the evening, it meant that Dad would soon be home from his job selling tires at Montgomery Wards, the city's largest department store. Just a few years earlier his plane had been bolting off the decks of aircraft carriers in the Pacific. Now, he and mother and I lived in just about as quiet a small town as there was.

In the 1950's, Idaho Falls was only a few decades from its frontier origins. As I grew up, the oldest building I knew was only 60 years old. My Great-Grandmother Tillie was one of the valley's early pioneers and lived next to the small four-room house that my parents rented. The flat dry sagebrush-covered plain, tucked among the mountain ranges, was now spotted with irrigated fields. They extended for hundreds of miles along the high plateaus surrounding Idaho Falls. I did not then fully understand how my dear great-grandmother connected me to the past, but when she rode in a strange-looking antique car in the city's annual Pioneer Day parade, I sensed that she was from a world I did not completely know. But as I got older, I recognized that Tillie's life was for me a crossroads along the path to the past.

Life is full of crossroads, as is the world. From the days of William the Conqueror and his capable Matilda, people have used the phrase, "All roads lead to Rome." Rome was the center point where the roads converged and crossed. This great city was the center of the Empire, the place one must cross to get from one world to another.

My wife and I once lived in Rome, in a house nearly as old as the first ones built in Idaho Falls. From its terrace along the ridges of Gianicolo Hill, we looked off across the Tiber River at Renaissance Rome on the left and the ancient Roman Forum and Coliseum, on the right. Our villa, built in the beginning of the 20ᵗʰ century, was just about the newest building in sight. On its thick stone walls, its builder engraved in big letters Deo et Laboribus, Latin for God and Toil.

My search for family stories had taken me to many diverse times and places, but just like in Rome, the roads from all of these led to the same place, the place where I was born. In family history, "All

Roads lead to Home." All the paths from the past converged at the place and time I was born. I was at the end of these roads. The same is true for everyone. Each of us stands at the edge of the hinterland where our ancestors lived. Their lives all funnel down to ours. The back side of the pedigree chart, as it moves from the past to present, gets narrower and narrower until it ends with us. Tillie's life was a waypoint along my ancestral road, closer than most of the others. Like many of these grandmothers and grandfathers, she was the incarnation of the words on our Roman stone house: God and Toil was engraved on her stories.

Many of my recollections of Tillie overlap other early memories. One of those is running wildly with small cousins at a Johnson family reunion. We darted behind trees and around the campground, all the while minding the stern warnings to stay clear of the rocky hillsides where rattlesnakes might lurk. Amidst all this energy, Grandma Tillie, then in her late seventies, sat peacefully on her chair, a content smile on her face. It was a posterity to be proud of: 12 children, 53 grandchildren, and 83 great-grandchildren by the time she turned 85.[50] When Tillie passed away I could count 23 living great-grandchildren, just among my grandmother's, Tillie's daughter Mayme's posterity.

This enormous family got together often in annual reunions and on other occasions. Describing such family gatherings, one of Tillie's children, Josephine, once wrote, *"When our families get together now we enjoy them so much and feel refreshed to see our brothers and sisters and the taste of the wonderful food and strong safe family feelings. There seems to be a good feeling of love and friendliness in just meeting together."*[51] At the reunions, there was always a program.[52]

Memories in Family Histories

The search for Matilda's and John's stories was a different kind of journey. There was no shortage of information. As I mentioned earlier, most of their children left typewritten one- or two-page histories stapled together in a family history entitled *"Reminiscences of the John Johnson and Matilda Ann Howard*

403

Johnson Family." They were probably inspired by a similar collection the children of Tillie's grandparents, Joseph and Ann Howard, left. Along my journey, I had found copies of both of these.

My mother Margie wrote and presented the life story at Tillie's large funeral where the crowd filled every seat in the church. I had forgotten Margie's part of the memorial until Tillie's granddaughter, Alice, sent me an audio recording of my young mother's voice eulogizing the adopted grandmother she loved. She left a thick file on Grandma Johnson as we grandchildren always called her.

Sometimes when gathering family stories of more recent grandparents we come across an abundance of source material left by family and friends. When searching for stories from medieval times, such as those of Queen Matilda (Chapter 1), we are usually forced to rely on secondary books about them and their times. However, the closer we get to today's family, the more apt we are to find contemporary primary sources ready to pour out we want to hear.

Of all the stories I had collected up to this point, I had more original material about Tillie than any other. Unlike Richard McGuire who lived not too many miles away from the Johnsons – and as far as I know they never met – Tillie realized the value of her legacy. She wanted it available to future generations. She penned her own short but revealing account of her life. Then, she designated my mother and others to write her stories, as well.

When I started going through Mother's family files, her collection on Tillie was a treasure trove of hand-written notes and papers, as well as a collection of several short life histories that had been written over the decades. One thing that caught my eye was that, though written with love and admiration, they rarely masked Tillie's frustrations and disappointments. Many personal histories try to leave only the happy memories and thereby remain two-dimensional. But that was not totally the case with these. Her disgruntlement with Idaho and her battle against homesickness feature in nearly every one of these histories, often adding a layer of color, sometimes humor, and always one of authenticity.

That is all good, but it presents some of its own challenges. I found that none of these short accounts, not even the newspaper obituary, was complete. Everyone recounted things that impressed their memories most. Everyone was unique in their own way, and so were their accounts. One thing often missing was sourcing, or footnotes. And something needed was a synthesis that pulled the various accounts into a whole, cohesive narrative. Just as a group of scattered leaves does not make a tree, so memories and family histories have to be joined into flowing and coherent narratives to get the most from them.

When compiling our family histories, it also makes them more powerful to set them in a time and place. Stories never occur in a vacuum but are conditioned by everything happening around them. For example, introducing World War I and the 1918 flu pandemic to the time Tillie ran the farm underscored her struggles and successes. Establishing context brought the stories alive. And this context brought a connection to the things we endure in the present.

Carefully "sourcing" via footnotes established a paper trail. It also made the stories authentic and verifiable. In the first draft of every story, I footnoted every new fact I found. All these footnotes were a little distracting when trying to read the passages, however, and in my final draft I aggregated many of them toward the end of a paragraph or section. I never hesitated to speculate, because that so often helped get closer to the "why" of things. But when I did, I identified it as speculation by using words such as, "maybe," "perhaps," "surely," or "must have," depending on how sure I was of the event I was describing.

Stories Behind the Stories

I also found that as I worked to integrate the various histories into a whole, there were the stories I found, and then sometimes the more obscure ones not discovered so easily. I was certain that I did not get Tillie's whole story, especially in light of comments I remember Mother occasionally made. There were parts of her and John's life together that no one seems to have wanted to write about. Nevertheless, I was glad that family members in their reminiscences

405

usually did little to sugar-coat what was obviously a life with many highs and lows. Perhaps they loved Tillie all the more for her openness. They knew how the remainder of her stories told of an admirable mother and grandmother, often heroic in what she faced and accomplished.

For example, Tillie's own words reveal how apprehensive she must have been when John left her in difficult circumstances for a voluntary ecclesiastical calling. However, nothing in her writings or from the histories written by others, spells out specifically what she said to John, or how much she might have resented the predicament. Family members who probably knew never said much about this, at least not in my hearing. However, I did find where my Grandmother Mayme alluded to those days: "I could write a book about when Dad was on his mission (but won't)," a saying she sometimes used with a gleam in her eye, hinting there was a lot to say about something, but it was impolite to say it.[53] It is easy to think that Tillie was not happy about John's departure.

In my mother's and grandmother's files, notes, and other memorabilia, I did not find a single correspondence between John and Tillie during the years he was away on his second mission to Sweden. Other relatives apparently have not found anything either. That is not to say I did not discover letters and cards he wrote from Sweden, but they were not addressed to Tillie. This time, it was John's turn to be homesick. In a card John wrote to 16-year old daughter Mayme, he complained, "Oh you can't imagine how I long to get home. I certainly will rejoice and I won't leave you any more if I can help it."[54]

In another letter to Mayme, John said, "...let me hear a few words from each one of you. I am so fond of those dear letters that tears come out and run down my cheeks." He added something interesting. "If you hear of any one coming on a mission I wish you would try and send me another pair of garments... Also send me a necktie and if Ma remembers get me a No 16 white shirt."

If things were well with Tillie, you would expect John to have asked her directly to get him clothes, and not his teenaged daughter. He continued, "Tell her [Tillie] to not worry so much but be contented," again, something you would expect him to write to Tillie, not their daughter.

John was also remorseful about the expense and problems his mission had caused Tillie. He asked Mayme to tell her mother, "I don't think I will need any more money now for a long time. I will try to make this $100 pay as far as I possibly can." He continues, "I feel that I ought to be with you. I am afraid that you need me home worse than I am wanted here."[55]

Several times Mother told me that Tillie's relationship with John was tense toward the last years of his life in the 1930s. My guess is that with his second mission to Sweden, Tillie's long and deep frustrations finally surfaced, never to completely subside. Mother confided that when John finally returned home, he made a mistake, one that may have doomed the possibility of ever rebuilding his marriage to what it once was.

All of this episode, of course, is sotto voce, *an undertone that flowed between the lines. It was not necessary for me to expound widely upon it. But understanding it was there added color to the stories of people who were human and real, as well as heroic, at least in my mind.*

Family Reunions

As always, I wanted to visit the places Tillie's and John's stories took place. When I heard that the Johnson family was planning another of their family reunions, not far from the old Johnson homestead, I was excited to go. It had been over 50 years since I had last attended one of those reunions. We planned a trip to Utah and Idaho to coincide with the reunion.

Family history was always an important part of the Johnson family reunions of the 1950s. Often held in a canyon picnic site, the get togethers normally had a genealogy table where people could share or network. Just like in older times, this reunion was a happy venue for sharing stories and distributing written updates on genealogy others had found. It is hard to replace a family reunion's potential for networking and preserving a family narrative.

407

We arrived at the Senior Citizens Center in Ririe, Idaho, on a hot Saturday afternoon. Inside, were relatives I had not met for years, cousins I knew as a child, and others, many of whom I had heard about over the years, but never met. The fried chicken was like I remembered from the get togethers when Tillie was still alive. But missing were the dozens of children who kept the old reunions lively. Many of us there were those children, and now we fit the category the Senior Citizens Center was meant to serve.

It was a warm and welcoming group of relatives, and there was a program with memorabilia from Tillie's and John's old stone home displayed on the table. I immediately felt a bond among us. We all descended from the same family we were commemorating. I did not want to leave when it was over. I realized ever more clearly how family reunions can bind families together.

One of those I met was Howard Johnson, Tillie's and John's grandson. He now owned their stone house, and his son's family lived in it. Howard asked if we would like a tour of the old residence, and my wife and I wasted no time accepting the kind invitation. We followed Howard's truck for a few miles and then drove up the lane to find a roomy, well designed stone home, now over 100 years old, with rows of trees surrounding it. Tillie finally got the trees she longed for when she first arrived from Bountiful.

The site of the original log cabin was off to the side, and across the road was a stately rock edifice that once was the church John, Tillie, and their Mormon neighbors had built. It no longer held services Sunday mornings. Howard's son still farmed 155 of the homestead's 160 acres. Just like most everywhere in the US today, no farmer in Idaho can make a living from just 155 acres. Farming was a part-time operation. Howard's son also worked as a mechanical engineer in nearby Idaho Falls.

A great deal of renovation had been done to the house over the years. It was beautifully preserved but modern and functional on the inside. The family had left a cross section of the wall open to exhibit the multiple layers of wallpaper. These layers chronicled the lives and stories of the four generations who had lived inside those walls

It was my first time inside Tillie's and John's old house, but I felt once again that this was a place never before visited, but very familiar. I felt like I knew it, and I even sensed some emotions of nostalgia, but for a memory I could not access.

Chapter 10

Where Two Rivers Joined
Seija Kaarina Heimala

In our lives we often look for Discovery...
And in this journey
There is nothing more pleasant
Than discovering with those you Love
Markus Cleverley (1997)

During the years I searched for family stories, my wife Seija was fervently on board as my constant companion. We traveled together on all but one of the trips I made. With every discovery, she was as excited as I was. We shared passage. We also shared stories. Her stories were my stories, too. When she and I wed, we adopted each other and the past that had made us who we were.

It was figuratively like two vast rivers from different pasts that arrived at a confluence. Their waters ran together to make a still broader channel that flowed into the new lands of the future. This was the river that carried the memories, stories, and traditions our children would inherit. They were heirs to the many families of the past, who lived along the river's tributaries.

I was captivated by her family's rich background, even though their stories were rarely easy. Her parents and grandparents knew war, loss, suffering, and grief. But they also knew redemption, reconciliation, and re-birth.

Returning to the Past (1997)
Our red Chevy Blazer with its diplomatic plates approached the border stations that separated Finland from its ofttimes troublesome neighbor Russia on a summer morning in 1997. The once impervious Iron Curtain that for decades separated Russia from the West had fallen only a few years earlier. We had had many previous adventures crossing this border – such as the time we smuggled iceberg lettuce in a diplomatic pouch, on a midnight train, to our

410

fresh vegetable-starved American Embassy colleagues in Moscow. The post-Cold War border was no longer what it once was. Still, Russia was Russia, and crossing its borders was never a simple formality.

The Finnish side was a model of modern efficiency. As we drew closer to the guard station, Finnish border guards took our license plate number from a distance. By the time we reached the control booth, they already knew who we were, and we were quickly waved through. The Russians were more suspicious, gave us pencil-scribbled slips of paper to carry to the next point along the complex crossing procedures. Nothing was streamlined.

We showed our diplomatic passports and valid diplomatic visas issued to us at the gray, communist-looking Russian embassy in Helsinki. We explained to the border control that we were traveling only a few miles to the city of Viipuri. We planned to return the next day. Finally, a Russian border guard waved us on. Seija, our college-student son Markus, and I pulled the Blazer forward, and we were in Russia.

We were on our way to find the home where Seija's family lived when she was born. Her mother always shared tales of the years of her earliest childhood: Russian planes dropping bombs over their neighborhood; racing with her baby to the potato cellar dug deep in the middle of their yard; Seija crawling under the table in the midst of the bombings to say, "Dear Russians, don't do anything to us, we did nothing to you."

Not quite two years old when they fled their home, Seija retained nothing from those frightful experiences. But the horror of the bombings left deep terror inside her. For years after we were married, she had me hold her tight whenever there was an unexpected clap of thunder.

We drove down the narrow two-lane highway toward Viipuri wondering how this adventure would end. Seija had never been back to the house of those bleak days, yet throughout her entire life she had heard from grandparents and parents about the glories of Viipuri. In their minds it was a paradise lost, and there was no end to the stories they told about their lives there. They even had a vial

411

of soil from the city hanging on the wall. When we drove into this place of family legends, however, Viipuri looked drab. It was only now repairing itself from the wounds suffered half a century earlier in the fighting between the Finnish and Soviet armies.

Before leaving Helsinki, Seija had hired a Finnish-speaking Russian guide who lived in Viipuri to show us around. The woman was an Ingrian from a Fenno-tribe that for centuries had lived in the area surrounding today's St. Petersburg. She spoke Ingrian, a language very close to Finnish, as well as Finnish, and Russian. When we pulled into the city, she met us outside her apartment building. Seija explained what she remembered from the many stories she had heard about the house's location and the landmarks around it. Congenial and friendly, our guide thought she could locate it.

She was right. We did not have to drive too long before we pulled onto a dirt road and parked before a detached wooden house with a large yard covered with grass, trees, shrubs, and bushes. To the side, a door opened to an old potato cellar dug into the ground. When we walked through the gate, a middle-aged man and an older teen-aged boy working in the yard looked up with unsettled expressions. It was clear from the man's glance that he had an idea who we were.

Seija spoke up quickly, asking our guide to translate that this had been her house before the war. We did not want to take it back, just a chance to see it. She gave a warm smile, and the ice immediately broke. The two smiled back, put down what they were doing, and slowly came over to shake our hands.

Following these greetings, the older man called into the house, and a woman close to 80 years old appeared in the doorway. He introduced her as his mother and the young man as his son. The babushka was charming, and we had an enjoyable conversation with her. She explained how her family had been loaded onto a train somewhere in the Ukraine during the summer of 1944. When they got off, they were in Viipuri and were taken to this house to live. The family had been there ever since.

It was quite remarkable to us. This family had been in the home since a few weeks after Seija's family had left it. Before us stood the three generations of Ukrainians who lived there, not because they chose to, but because the authoritarian Soviet state had assigned it to them. They were probably luckier than most of those transferees, for the home with its yard and plants was comfortable and roomy, especially for the Soviet Union.

The family showed us around. The house itself was a duplex where before the war erupted, Seija's grandparents had lived on one side, and her parents, on the other. Judging by the wood stove and other simple furnishings, the house was little changed from what it was decades earlier. In the yard were red and black currant bushes, perhaps once planted by her grandparents.

Seija shed a few tears, our son took photographs, and the Russians must have wondered about having Finns and Americans at their home. The family seemed to appreciate the emotion generated by my wife's return to a place she had always heard about. When Seija asked about the berry bushes, they brought out containers full of berries from their own yard and the surrounding woods. They wanted us to take the berries with us.

The entire visit may have lasted an hour or more. When it was over, a chapter was closed, and some old wounds began to heal. We took our guide back to her home, a small two-room apartment where she lived with seven other family members. Seija had asked what we could bring her from Finland, and she had responded "toilet paper." So, we left her a supply of what must have been a scarce commodity, at least in the quality that we in the West were used to. We also put an envelope in her hand. What we thought was a reasonable fee for a day's tour was equal to an entire month's salary.

Before leaving for home, we spent the night in a very basic hotel that was nevertheless the best in town. In the evening, Markus, Seija, and I ate at the Tower restaurant on Viipuri's old market square. The eyes of Seija's parents always sparkled when they told of the times they ate there. Now, the food was plain, but the excitement of being in this prominent spot from her family's memories overshadowed everything.

413

We had a chance to visit the home once more before my assignment in Helsinki ended. This time we traveled with another of our sons, a daughter and her fiancée, and Seija's New York cousin.[1] This time, we brought gifts for our new Russian friends, and we were welcomed graciously. Seija joked with the Russian man that she and he were brother and sister, since they shared the same childhood home, and we all laughed. The old Ukrainian babushka, sadly, had died since our first trip. We were glad we had had a chance to meet her. The visits validated many family stories transforming a place in our family memory into a real location, complete with walls, windows, gardens, laughter and kindness.

Perhaps as meaningful to us as the visits themselves was the reaction it had on our family. That year for Christmas, Markus, then a junior at Georgetown, gave us an exquisite album of photos he took in Viipuri. He prefaced it with a poem he had composed:

> In our lives we often look for Discovery
> To learn about who we are
> Where we came from
> And in this journey
> There is nothing more pleasant
> Than discovering with those you Love

Markus's thoughts perfectly expressed my own feelings of how valuable it was to include family in our efforts to discover our past.

From War to War (1917-1939)

Holding her tightly to her breast, Seija's mother Lempi and grandparents, two heavy trunks in their hands, fled the place they had always called home. When they reached the main road leading toward Helsinki, they looked behind one more time at the deserted house. Then, it all faded behind. It was early the summer of June 1944. Russian tanks would soon blast their way through the Viipuri suburb of Tienhaara. This was the second time in the war the family had lost everything.

Mamma and Pappa, mother Lempi, and baby Seija were alone. Seija's father, Manne, was in the Finnish army, stationed on the border, directly in front of the Russian attack. As they joined the

414

half million other Finns scrambling to evacuate this besieged eastern region of Finland, the family tried to suppress the thought that it would be hard for Manne to survive the onslaught. In fact, they soon received a notification that he was killed in battle, something her mother refused to accept.

The house remained empty, but only for a while. The peace treaty that ended hostilities later that summer gave Finland's second largest city, Viipuri, to the Soviet Union. Within months, the USSR was carting in families from Russia, the Ukraine, and elsewhere to populate the city's homes left behind, half in rubble.

But the family's stories of hardship began much earlier than this. In Finland, like in the rest of Europe, the 1930s were the eye of the 20th century storm. It was a looming catastrophe few on the continent realized until it was too late. The First World War, the Communist Revolution in Russia, and the Nazis' rise to power in Germany were not one-off events, but part of an intertwining stream of episodes that would soon crush the world with a new war that left tens of millions of people dead.

With its long border with Russia, and not far across the Baltic from Germany, Finland was geographically in the middle of two behemoth belligerent powers. Viipuri, was only a few miles from the Soviet border and just 90 miles from the USSR's important city of Leningrad, today known as St. Petersburg.

During the 1930's, Seija's parents and grandparents lived in the house we visited in Viipuri 50 years later. Aleksander and Selma Roos had only one child, Lempi, and she married Manne Heimala, a handsome, good natured young man with wavy blonde hair. Lempi was small and intense, stubborn but engaging, and had a large circle of friends. Manne was carefree, light, and teasing. Aleksander managed the warehouse for Starckjohann, Finland's largest hardware company.

Among the warehouse crew Aleksander supervised, was a teenager named Lauri Törni, a future war hero about whom I once wrote a bestselling biography. In fact, one of the things that caught my interest in Törni was that like Aleksander, Selma, Manne, and Lempi, he was from Viipuri. Viipuri was the capital of Karelia,

Finland's eastern province where the Karelian tribe spoke Finnish with its own dialect and enjoyed rich cultural traditions. The Heimalas and Rooses – and Törni – were proud Karelians.

The 20th century brought turbulent and dangerous times to Finland. Finland was a young country then, having got its independence from Russia in 1917 when Lenin led Russia into a revolution. In the aftermath of declaring independence, Finland erupted in its own civil war. Like in Russia, Finnish Communist Red Guards fought White Guards when the ideological battle between the Left and Right grew into a brutal war of fraternal rivalry. The civil war was violent with atrocities and executions on both sides.

Manne was only nine years old when the Red Guards hauled his father, Manu, from his job on the State Railways and forced him into their ranks, much like happened to Yuri in the movie Dr. Zhivago. With his father gone, Manne and his mother Ida struggled to survive the war. The two of them had little money for food or anything else.

Late one April afternoon in 1918, Ida's brother Eelis and a stranger banged on the door of her small cottage on the outskirts of Viipuri. Eelis was in his late thirties, eight years older than Ida. He appeared agitated and quickly asked if Ida would hide them in her cellar. Ida's ten-year old son Manne saw the two men were both in haggard shape, weak, apparently recovering from wounds.

Eelis was a Red Guard officer who had been in the Russian Czar's personal body guard before Nicholas II was overthrown. When the Finnish and Russian civil wars began, Eelis had returned to Finland to join the Red Guards whose working-class views he shared. The Reds had been in control of Viipuri until just a few days before. A White offensive had turned their fortunes.

Manne listened while Eelis told that he and his friend were trying to escape the city and urgently needed their help. He explained how they had been recuperating in the hospital after being wounded by machine gun fire in a battle near Viipuri. His Red colleagues had pulled both of them wounded from the battlefield. In the hospital in Viipuri the two met, shared a room, and became good friends.

416

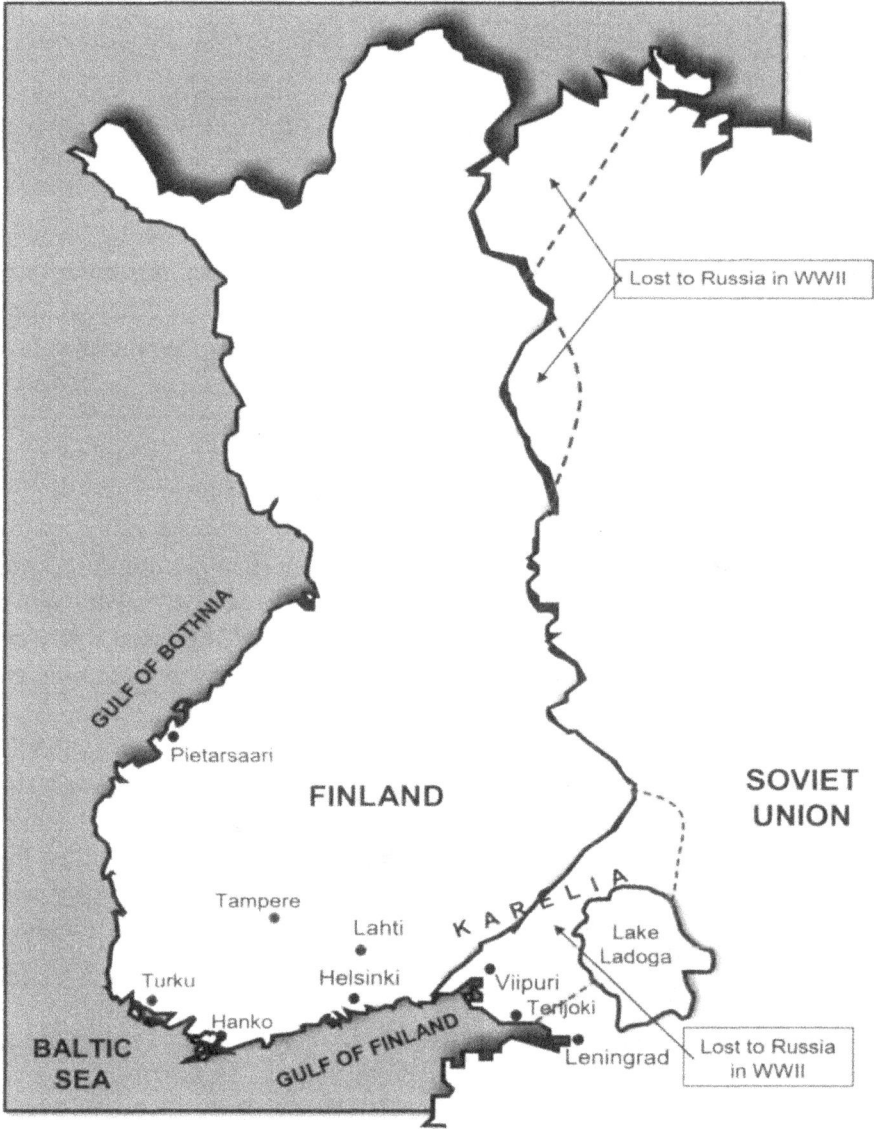

Map K – World War II Finland

Eelis continued, telling how recovering from their wounds, they were soon strong enough to have a day outside the hospital. While they were out, White partisans mounted the attack on the city. The two of them tried to get back to the hospital but had run into a roadblock on the outskirts of town. The White sentries, not knowing that Eelis and his companion were Reds, commanded them to move on. No one was allowed to enter the city.

In danger and having no other place to go, the two had finally come to Ida's home hoping to find refuge. It was a big favor they were asking. Ida could be arrested or suffer worse if the Whites found her harboring two Red soldiers. At first, she told the two men to get into the cellar. But Ida hardly had food enough for her own son. Pondering more, she realized that feeding two additional mouths was impossible. She told Eelis that his friend would have to find someplace else. The stranger left, as Ida asked.

What Eelis did not know was that his comrade was not a fellow Red Guard at all. Instead, he was a wounded White whom the Reds had mistakenly taken from the battlefield as one of their own. When he got to the hospital, then under Red control, he knew his best option was to pretend he was one of them. He had portrayed himself as a Red Guard since.

During the days Eelis hid in Ida's cellar, the Whites completely overtook Viipuri, achieving a final defeat of the Reds. With the victory, Ida faced a dilemma. Hiding Eelis grew more perilous every day. Yet she feared asking him to leave would result in his execution, imprisonment, or whatever was happening to so many Reds. One morning Manne and his mother were panic-stricken to see three White soldiers marching into their yard. One of them looked familiar, and when he got closer, Ida and her boy were alarmed to recognize him as Eelis's friend who had accompanied him that day they arrived seeking help.

The soldiers reached the door, knocked, and when Ida cracked it open, asked for Eelis. Terrified for what was coming next, Ida called Eelis to emerge from his hiding place. He slowly came forward, and the soldiers took him with them. Instead of marching Eelis to a prison, however, they escorted him back to the hospital. There, he

418

stayed and recovered from his wounds, while Manne and Ida brought food and visited him almost every day. When he was well, he was released. The friendship he had forged with his disguised enemy-friend had saved him.

Meanwhile, Manne's father Manu was still with the Red Guards who abducted him. The group plundered and expropriated property. If caught, they were likely destined for a firing squad. Throughout it all, Manu had somehow avoided deeds that eventually could be charged as war crimes. As the civil war came to an end, the rag-tag band of Reds mounted an escape eastward toward Russia where they hoped to find safety. Along their way, they passed through a town named Kotka. Transiting through the town's streets, they ran into a squad of German soldiers that had arrived from the World War I front to support the Whites.

The Germans captured all of them and shipped them to a White prison in Hennala, just outside the town of Lahti. With the other Reds, Manu was held imprisoned for months awaiting trial and the final reckoning it would likely bring. Fortunately for Manu, his employer, the State Railways, provided a letter that substantiated his story of being abducted involuntarily from his workplace. His refusal to participate in the Reds' crimes also saved him from the firing squad.

When Manu was released, he returned home to Ida and Manne. Prison life had been cruel. Manu nearly starved. When he finally reached his family, he was broken, weak, and in poor health. But he was alive, and back.[2]

Winter War (1939)

With the civil war over and his father home, Manne's life was easier. However, the family never had much. As he grew, he took part-time and full-time jobs to earn money and was unable to finish more than a few years of school. He met Lempi one day in the mid-1930s when they were both bicycling on roads near their homes.

Manne and Lempi lived about three miles from each other. Manne was working as a longshoreman in Viipuri's harbor and lived on his own. Lempi worked as a seamstress in a hat factory and was at home with her parents. They courted about two years and when they wed, in 1938, they moved into Lempi's parents' home to share the house together. The house had three rooms, and Manne built a fourth, giving both families two rooms in an arrangement that divided the house lengthwise into two sides. They bought 6,000 Finnish marks worth of furniture for their new home on a monthly time-payment and within a year had it paid off.

By Finnish standards of the 1930's, Manne and Lempi enjoyed a nice life, and these were happy times. They had a large yard where they planted berries, potatoes, rhubarb and many other vegetables and fruits that helped tide them over the winter. By summer's end, the potato cellar was brimming with homemade stores. Around them lived Karelian relatives and friends who enjoyed weekends with active social gatherings where everyone visited, laughed, and celebrated birthdays and other family events. All seemed tranquil and pleasant, a life most couples dream about when starting a family.

Everything was quick to change, however. During the months before their marriage, Hitler, to the south, took Czechoslovakia and annexed Austria. Just miles to the east, Stalin was in the midst of his purges and political cleansings that killed millions of Soviet citizens. All of Europe, knowingly or not, was on the verge of the greatest conflagration the world had ever known.

At first it appeared that the two ruthless dictators were independent evils who might even offset each other's designs – who hated communists more than Hitler's fascists? Or fascists, more than Stalin's communists? But when Manne and Lempi celebrated their first anniversary during the Midsummers celebration of 1939, Germany and the USSR were already secretly preparing to divide Europe between them.

Two months later, the Soviet and German Foreign Ministers, Vyacheslav Molotov and Joachim von Ribbentrop, signed a secret protocol that gave half of Poland and Lithuania to Germany, and the other half to the USSR along with Latvia, Estonia… and Finland. A month later, Germany invaded Poland. Almost simultaneously, Stalin put demands on its Baltic neighbors, and within a year it had annexed Latvia and Estonia into the Soviet Union. Finland, however, refused to buckle under the Soviet pressure.[3]

As tensions grew, Finland began calling reserve units to duty. Manne had already served his compulsory service in the Finnish army for fifteen months between 1929 and 1930. He was still in the reserves, though, as were almost all of Finland's younger men. At 31, he was somewhat old to be a soldier again, but he was mobilized with the rest of the Finnish reserves and sent to defend the long Finnish-USSR border. Lempi stayed with her parents. Hostilities had not yet begun when he reported for duty in October 1939, but weighing on their minds was the awful question of when, or if, they would see each other again.

The Finns were overwhelmingly outnumbered, but numbers are not everything. They cherished their young independence and had too much sisu – a Finnish term for guts and stubbornness – to cave into bullying. The words to a Finnish wartime song went, "Sisua riitää ja sitä tarvitaan," ("Sisu is needed, and there is plenty of it"). When the Soviets realized that Finland would not peacefully bow to their pressures, they settled things another way.

On the afternoon of November 26th, seven artillery shells exploded outside the Soviet border village of Mainila. Within hours, the USSR accused Finland of a provocation and demanded Finland withdraw all forces 18 miles from the border. The Finnish command mounted an immediate investigation. Through triangulated observations from three different posts, they pinpointed the source of the fire to be on the Soviet side of the border, about one mile from the target area. The shelling had been from the Russian side to the Russian side, a trumped-up excuse for the Soviet invasion that had been in preparation for several months.

Three days later, the Soviets' Red Army thundered hundreds of thousands of troops, thousands of tanks, and hundreds of planes over the Finnish border in an immense offensive. Stalin expected the Finnish line to collapse in days or short weeks. "All we had to do was raise our voice a little bit, and the Finns would obey. If that didn't work, we could fire one shot and the Finns would put up their hands and surrender. Or so we thought," Khrushchev wrote.[4]

So the Soviets thought, but that is not what happened. Finnish resistance was fierce, and within a few days the Soviet thrust hit a brick wall – or rather an ice wall – during what was one of the coldest winters in years. "White death" was the fate of hundreds of thousands in the infantry and tank divisions of the poorly clad and ill-prepared Russian army.

During the first hours of the invasion, an armada of Russian planes began dropping bombs over Helsinki, Viipuri, and other Finnish cities. When the first planes roared over Tienhaara, Lempi was at home visiting with her Aunt Emma[5] who lived nearby. In the middle of the conversation, a siren began its see-sawing blare in the distance. At first Lempi was unsure how to react. Emma quickly said, "We need to get into the cellar!" It suddenly dawned on them that they were under attack.

Lempi and Emma bolted from the house and across the yard as Russian bombers filled the sky directly overhead. Lempi pulled at the potato cellar door, and they jumped down into the dark earthen covered opening. Before they could slam the door completely, a rumbling explosion rocked everything around them. Snow flew up against the door and into their eyes, banging it shut just as fragments from the bomb blasted through both doors of the sauna shed and pounded into the cellar door behind it.

The two of them did not dare look outside to see what had happened. They waited a long while before they were certain the planes were gone. Lempi slowly opened the door and pulled herself from the cellar to see that a bomb had exploded in their yard next to the house. A good share of the wooden facade on one side of their home was now lying in shambles on the ground. All the windows were blown out. Their distress turned to anguish when they saw that their neighbors were not so fortunate as they. The family had not made it to their cellar on time. Their daughter was dead, and the mother and another lay badly wounded. The first day of war had arrived with all its horrors.

The Winter War with the Soviet Union continued for three months. Manne got a pass home from the front for Christmas. He spent his short leave trying to patch the windows and roof so the family would have better shelter from the harsh winter that had put the entire country into deep freeze. Meanwhile, the sub-zero cold and the Finnish army devastated the Russians. Khrushchev said they suffered a million casualties – the entire Finnish army was made up of only a fraction of that number. But as the spring thaw drew near, the Finns knew that with their inferior strength the war would turn against them during the warm days of spring and summer. They agreed with the Russians to a ceasefire.

After his Christmas furlough, Manne had returned to the front lines, and a few months later he received a letter from Lempi. She wrote that she and her parents were abandoning their house, leaving almost everything behind. As part of the peace agreement's harsh terms, Finland lost ten percent of its land to Russia, most of it from Karelia, including Viipuri. The entire Karelian population of, 450,000, evacuated rather than stay under communist rule.

From the day the treaty was signed, March 13, 1940, Finland had two weeks to remove everyone and everything not remaining. Lempi, Aleksander, and Selma packed what they could carry: the family silver, some clothing, and other small things went into a couple of trunks. Left behind was their home and its furnishings, their garden, sauna, berry bushes, potato cellar, clothing and possessions, and their beloved homeland. Many Karelians vowed to return, not knowing if, how, or when.

They went to Pietarsaari, a town on Finland's west coast, where Aleksander's company gave him work. Pietarsaari was a Swedish speaking town that in many ways must have seemed a world away from the Karelia they knew. When Manne was demobilized, he joined them there. He had no clothes but the military uniform he was wearing. Some total strangers on the street took him to a store and bought him something to wear.

Lempi and Manne were fortunate to get a small apartment with a table, wooden box, and a few cups. There was one bed, so one of them slept on the floor while the other was on the bed. At first, the lack of a bed was not too uncomfortable because Manne's job had him working night shifts while Lempi worked during the day. They sometimes passed each other on the way to and from work. It was an awkward life, but things could have been much worse.

The flux of displaced people into a small town like Pietarsaari in search of work and shelter presented a horde of dilemmas for everyone. How did you spread what was available equitably and productively? For the moment it was a zero-sum game: one's win was another's loss. Lempi's boss laid her off in order to take someone from a family without any income.

Lempi found another job working for a family with a 25-year-old invalid son wounded in the war. The family was kind and gave Lempi things for their empty home. In the fall, Aleksander's firm sent him to work in Lahti, a town in southern Finland. Manne and Lempi joined them there, and all four of them moved into a small home behind the railroad station. They had lost almost everything just a few months before, but had food, shelter, work, and each other. They felt fortunate.

War Continues (1941)

Viewing Europe from top to bottom, it was difficult for anyone in 1940 to imagine peace had come anywhere, including Finland. Hitler was rampaging across France, and by the time Manne and Lempi got to Lahti, Germany occupied most of Europe. Stalin had annexed two of the Baltic countries and had solidified his position in northern Europe. Even more ominously, Hitler had seen how poorly the Soviets fared in their war against small Finland. He mistakenly concluded that the vast USSR was a push over. Hitler began making plans for an invasion of the Soviet Union.

Wedged between the two, there was little possibility Finland could survive the duration of World War II without reaching an accommodation with one side or the other. Finland had to make its own calculations. When Hitler's general staff secretly told the Finns of their plan to attack Russia, Finland opted to get lost Karelia back by attacking the USSR simultaneously with the German invasion. They would not join Germany in an alliance, however. Their aims were confined to getting back their lost territory. The operation began in June 1941.

That month, Manne awoke early the morning of Midsummers Eve. It was already bright as midday. These were the longest days of the year, and here in the far north the sun was in the sky long before people were up. In the evenings, it hardly set. The next day was Lempi's and his third anniversary. Manne left for his new job at Raute, an iron-working company, but when he arrived, he was surprised to find no one in the workshop. On the wall was tacked a slip of paper. It read that anyone who had not received a notice in the mail should be aware that all men were immediately to join their reserve units that same morning.

Manne had not received the notice, but there was no confusion that it meant everyone. He urgently made his way to the mobilization point. There he found an officer and asked permission to return home to tell his wife what was happening. The officer granted the request, and Manne rushed home to find her.

When Lempi heard that Manne was again off to war, she was distressed but level-headed enough to ask him if he had taken his paycheck from Raute. That had not occurred to him, and she sent him after his pay. She knew she would need it. Paycheck in hand, Manne was soon home again, and, with a worried good-bye, he hurried once more to report for duty.

It was already afternoon when he got back to the mobilization point. Crowds of units were getting organized, but it seemed nothing would happen that day. So Manne decided to return home for the night. It was a big surprise for Lempi to see him again walk through the door. He spent the night and the next morning left another sad good-bye before scurrying to the mobilization point.

When he reached headquarters, his unit had already pulled out. An officer told him to hang around while another group of reservists gathered to await the next train. The mobilization was becoming more drawn out that he expected, and he saw little point in just sitting there all day. Manne once again returned home, and once again, he surprised Lempi at the door.

They talked for a while and then decided to walk together to the train station. Along the tracks, they found the train with Manne's unit still waiting to depart. He climbed aboard, waved good-bye to

Lempi one more time, and the locomotive's large steel wheels were soon rolling their way eastward toward the new Russian-Finnish border. The crowded cars were full of reservists talking, sharing war stories, speculating on how soon they would be home, laughing, and hiding their fears. Many, like Manne, were veterans of a war that had ended only the year before.

No one knew if these men would ever survive. But the moment was not one of total despair. Karelians, like Manne and Lempi, hoped that whatever happened, they might regain the homes they thought were lost. It was a teeter-totter mix of emotions: the hope of returning home balanced against the fear or likelihood they might not return at all from the conflict ahead.

A Home Lost Again (1944)

The second war between Finland and Russia was to last three years. There was a lot of sympathy in the West for Finland. Even though the United States was allied with the Soviets, the US never declared war on Finland for attacking the Soviet Union. Reeling from Germany's devastating thrust in the south, the Russian army at first did not fare well against the determined Finns. By the end of August, the Finns had regained Viipuri and even progressed beyond the lost parts of Karelia.

When Viipuri was again in Finnish hands, Lempi and her parents made preparations to return to the home they deserted a year and a half earlier. They packed the bed and the few chairs they had purchased in Lahti, boarded the train, and traveled home. When they pulled their things into the yard, they found the house still in need of repairs from the bombing two years earlier. Its recent Russian occupants, whoever they were, had tried to fix it using damaged material from the remaining rubble. But that was hardly adequate. The furniture was gone. Only a few articles the Russians left behind remained in the house. Still, they were happy to be back. Viipuri returned to life as its residents once again filled the streets and sifted into the city's shops.

Meanwhile Manne was assigned to the front as a forward artillery observer, spotting concentrations of fire against enemy

426

targets. The months ground on, and the heaviest fighting died down for a while. Both sides moved into static trenches opposing each other. The Finns did not have enough fire power to defeat the Russians, and the Russians were devoting most of their resources to fight the Germans in the south. If there were fewer big battles, however, there were regular skirmishes. Manne, a forward observer, was always close to the lines.

Months changed to years. It was a long time for the Finnish men to be continually on the front, and their families never ceased worrying about what was coming next. Lempi and Aleksander were back at their old jobs, and Manne occasionally came on leave to visit them. For better or worse, Viipuri was close to his unit, and in practice Manne could be home in only a few hours. By spring, 1942, Lempi was expecting their first child. In August, Seija was born. Manne was overwhelmed and did not know what to do with a baby. When he came to see his newborn for the first time, he brought a bag of apples for her!

Hitler's attack deep into the Russian interior eventually faltered, and finally the Germans started the long retreat across the Soviet steppes. It was only a matter of time before Russia could concentrate enough firepower in the north to break through the Finnish lines. With the arrival of summer 1944, the Red Army was ready. On June 9, the Russians launched a massed offensive with a colossal artillery bombardment of the Finnish lines – the largest artillery bombardment in northern Europe's history.

Manne was on the Soviet border when the barrage erupted. The booming artillery fire and aerial bombing was followed by hordes of Soviet troops storming through the woods. He was directly in front of the monstrous attack. In the confusion, horror, and gore that followed, he disappeared. In fact, his entire unit of 450 men was swallowed up by the Soviet blitzkrieg.

Back in Viipuri, it was the day every soldier's spouse dreads when Lempi was informed that Manne was gone, missing, and presumed dead. She and her parents were already evacuating along with everyone else. The Soviet offensive was so intense that the army could not ensure the defense of Viipuri. It was the total catastrophe everyone feared: loved ones lost at the front; everything else lost at home.

The families left in carts, with automobiles, by foot, and on trains that were continually strafed by the Soviet air force. Lempi, Aleksander, Selma, and little Seija, not quite two years old, hastily threw their things together, and once again rushed westward away from the fighting. They left their second set of furniture for whoever came to live there. The dispossessed grandparents, mother, and child eventually reached Lahti where they had resided a few months in 1941 before returning to Karelia.

By the end of June 1944, the Finnish army finally stopped the Russian advance, but not before it had overrun Viipuri. The war was nearing an end. Both sides were weary of battling, and the Soviet army was still engaging with Hitler's tough fighting divisions in the south. Prolonging the fighting made no sense to either side. Over the summer, Finnish and Soviet negotiators met in Stockholm to find an end to the hostilities, and on September 4th, a cease-fire brought an end to the fighting. As part of the agreement, the Soviet Union once again confiscated Viipuri and a good share of Karelia. This time there was little hope in the Karelians' minds of ever returning. But Finland had saved its independence.

It was the hardest of times for Lempi: no home, no possessions, no husband. She, her parents, and her toddler cramped into the small apartment of some distant family members. The refugees slept in the kitchen, one narrow folding bed to share. Lempi mourned Manne's loss, but refused to accept that he was gone. She had had a dream, she said, and in the dream, she learned Manne was alive.

In Blitzkrieg's Path (1944)

The night of the Soviet attack, Manne was on duty as an artillery spotter manning a position where he could see clearly to the Russian side. At about 5:30 in the dawn of a seemingly quiet morning, his duty ended, and he was on his way back, when suddenly the sky filled with low flying Russian aircraft soaring over him toward their targets. He looked again toward the Russian side to see waves of men emerging from the trees and sprinting across the fields.

Manne cranked up the radio to contact his artillery battery with a request for immediate shelling. He was ready to give the coordinates. The battery responded that they had no ammunition and could offer no support. Manne then called a long-range artillery unit to relay the same information. They returned that they only had five shells to spare. The battery let them fly, but when they crashed onto the onslaught, there were too few to make a difference.

Manne hurried along the path toward his unit. When he arrived, the men were lying low in their dugouts trying to make themselves invisible to the heavy air and artillery bombardment. When it finally paused, total confusion broke out. Men were running everywhere. They were too far forward to resist an invasion of this size. Everyone was looking for a way to get back to the Finnish force.

Manne, too, lost no time starting off in the direction of the main lines. One of his many virtues was a firm practical sense. If it was possible to get through, he would. But in the turmoil, he and a buddy named Väinö soon found themselves isolated and cut-off from everyone else. They kept moving with paths in one direction cut off, and then another.

When they felt they were far ahead of the Russians troops, the two stopped for a rest. Running through the forest swamps and bogs left them wet to the knees, and they pulled off their shoes to let them dry in the sun. While they were recuperating and drying off, a Finnish lieutenant appeared at the head of two companies. They looked haggard and beaten up. Manne asked him if he knew what was going on. The lieutenant responded by querying if they knew where the Russians were. Manne said they seemed to be coming from the direction of the shoreline. The two companies surrealistically disappeared in that direction.

Manne and Väinö pulled their shoes on and trudged off again through the woods and marshes toward Manne's artillery battery. When they found it and got to the placements, all the guns had been spiked and the tents were on fire. The battery company had left in a rush, leaving everything behind, destroying what they could.

By now, Manne and Väinö were on their own. In the distance, they saw enemy soldiers, but it was unclear whether the Russians had seen them. They were not sure where to go and decided to move back toward the lines they had just left. Maybe they could find others to group with. When the two men approached the camp, it was swarming with enemy soldiers. They leapt into the trees.

Väinö nervously was about to start sprinting as fast as he could in the opposite direction. Manne, more levelheaded, told him they should walk normally. The still distant enemy troops may not know they were Finns. The two men confidently stepped out of the trees, and matter-of-factly strode in the opposite direction, as if they were Russians on their way somewhere.

Manne was right. The enemy soldiers were too far off to make out their uniforms, but could see how they walked, and ignored the two lost Finns. Along the edge of a field, more Russian soldiers were marching in file winding their way toward them. Manne and Väinö again scrambled into the thick brush, firs, and birches, and started moving as quickly as possible away from the road. The dense foliage gave them cover, but the deeper they got into the woods, the more lost they were.

It simply was not clear which direction to move. Yet, choosing the right one was crucial if they were going to escape. Thinking things through, Manne and his companion decided their best hope was to orient in a northerly direction. Not sure which way was north, they tried to find it by looking at the trees. Roots were generally thicker on the south side, and with this crude method they started to make their way again. They kept moving and meandered through the woods for about three miles before they realized they were back to the place they started.

Each passing minute meant the Russians were closer, and they were less likely to find a way through the enemy troops surrounding them. Manne and Väinö had rifles and plenty of ammunition. The weapons, however, were not much use. Two well-armed men were helpless in any encounter. Manne had bread, butter, a few sugar cubes, and some pickled herring received in a package from Lempi. Väinö had no food. They sat down and shared what Manne had and then moved on.

Now, the trapped Finns began seeing Russian soldiers regularly. They crouched in the foliage alongside a road, watching them go by, and finally decided to hop across into the bushes on the other side. When they did, they found themselves looking into the eyes of a Russian soldier as he sauntered down the road. He stared back, but did not shoot, and just kept walking. The lone soldier was probably as afraid of the Finns as they were of him, perhaps calculating he would not have fared well in a fight. There were two of them.

It was already evening, although plenty light, and Manne and Väinö decided to get some sleep. They found a place in some rocks where they could hide. After curling up for a while to doze, they moved out again. They needed to get back from this spot behind enemy lines, and the road they were on had to lead somewhere.

Manne and Väinö suddenly came upon another Russian camp. The sentries saw them and fired warning shots before the two got away. They walked right by a Russian soldier, just a boy holding a sub-machine gun. Surprised, he just looked at them without raising his weapon. Finally, they rounded a bend to stumble into a group of soldiers putting gasoline into a stalled vehicle. Manne and Väinö again leapt into the roadside vegetation, but it was too late, they had been seen. Some of the soldiers grabbed their weapons and walked straight to their hiding place.

The Russians ordered Manne and Väinö to lie on the ground, and it seemed clear they intended to shoot them. Manne thought his only hope was to face the soldiers, and instead of obeying, he slowly stood to his feet and looked into their faces. The Russians hesitated for a moment, and just at that instant, a lieutenant arrived and ordered his men to hold their fire.

The immediate crisis passed. The soldiers loosened up and relaxed around their new prisoners. They sat Manne and Väinö at the edge of a clearing and built a fire. Their captors asked the Finns to take off their shoes to dry around the heat. They gave them some bread and soup to eat. Manne and Väinö were able to relax a little.

Their fear did not subside for long, however. When another lieutenant arrived, he and two riflemen grabbed Manne and Väinö and walked them into the forest. They both realized the situation was bleak. Väinö turned and said, "This is it, Manne."

Reassembling a Life (summer/fall 1944)

Seija turned two years old the summer her family evacuated Viipuri and penniless returned to Lahti. Although living was tight, she felt loved by the mother, grandparents, and relatives who surrounded her. She did not miss a father. In her mind, she had one: her Grandfather Aleksander. That was the only father she remembered. Aleksander resumed working in Starckjohann, the local store of the firm that employed him in Viipuri. Lempi also found work. Selma remained home tending the baby. Seija knew there was someone else who was supposed to be there. Among her first phrases were, "Isä häviää," (Father disappear), and "Isä karkaa," (Father gone away).

One day before the war ended, Lempi heard that "Moskovan Tiltu," a Tokyo Rose-type Russian radio propagandist, had broadcast that a man named Manne Heimala was among the Finnish prisoners in Soviet camps. Lempi was ecstatic. To her, this news confirmed what she already believed: Manne had not been killed and was still alive. Still, there was no official news, and the Soviets had not included anyone by that name on the lists of Finnish prisoners held in the Soviet Union.

Months later, in late November, a friend of Lempi's hurried to find her. She had been listening to the radio, she told, when the announcer read a list of the names of the first batch of Finnish prisoners of war to reach Finland. One of the names was "Manne Heimala." Lempi was overcome. She switched on the radio and eventually heard the same broadcast. The announcer went down a long list of the names and birthdates from the POW's who had arrived that day by train at the newly drawn Finnish-Soviet border. A "Manne Heimala" was on the list, but the birthdate he read was not Manne's.

Still, Manne Heimala was not a common Finnish name, and Lempi had her own reasons for believing this was her Manne. She rushed out the door to go as fast as she could to an office that supported military families. In her hurry, Lempi hit a patch of ice on the street, her feet slipped from under her, and she did a somersault landing on her back. Lempi got up, brushed herself off, realized she had no broken bones, and scurried off again to see if anyone could help her find if this Manne Heimala was who she thought he was.

The man on the prisoner train was, in fact, her Manne. In the confusion surrounding the first days of the Russian invasion, word of his fate had been lost. But Manne, though isolated and surrounded, had survived the Soviet blitzkrieg. And he was still alive after months of hellish, life-draining imprisonment in a Russian prison camp. "But what kind of shape could he be in?" Lempi asked herself.

People of a "Hard Destiny" (summer/fall 1944)

Instead of lining up the two prisoners among the trees to shoot them, Manne and Väinö soon realized the Russian lieutenant and his men were searching for other Finns hiding close by. After they found none, the Russians shipped their two prisoners to the rear. The next moment of pending doom came after Manne and his companion were taken by car to a town named Terijoki on the highway to Leningrad. Their transport dropped them off in front of a cellar and they were told to take off their shirts and stand before the door. Manne said he expected to be shot any moment, but instead his captors were simply searching for weapons before shoving them into the cellar.

Over the remainder of the day, more Finnish prisoners were brought to share the narrow cellar space with them. There were a lot of them. One-by-one, the Finns were interrogated by a Finnish-speaking Russian officer. Manne eventually learned that his entire unit of about 450 men had been killed or taken prisoner.

Finally, the Finns were marched off on a long hike to Leningrad where they were interrogated over and over again. Manne thought he was questioned about 20 times, with an officer regularly screaming at him that he was lying. This was the "easy" part of their imprisonment. After about a month in Leningrad, they were loaded onto a train and taken to a prison camp north of Moscow. In addition to the 400 Finns in the camp, there were thousands of German prisoners, and several hundred Spaniards from the famous, or infamous, Spanish Blue Division, as well as Romanians, and other nationalities.

The Finnish prisoners were held separate from the others. "The Finns had it quite well," Manne later recalled. He meant relative to the other prisoners. He and the Finnish prisoners worked hard pulling logs out of the nearby river. They were fed little. Often their entire food ration was 150 grams (about 5 oz.) of bread a day. When they were doing hard labor, they might get a kilogram (2.2 lbs.) of bread for the day.

Conditions in the camp, were harsh, though not necessarily cruel. Sometimes there was soup; sometimes they got sauerkraut with salted herring. Sometimes, they got nothing simply because no food had arrived at the camp. Many died, often the largest men first. When someone died, they wheelbarrowed his body to a trench that became a mass grave.

In November, a ray of hope that they might not all die in the camp brightened the bleak days. A Finnish-speaking Russian officer told the Finns that peace discussions were underway. When they were completed, this group of Finns would be in the first contingent to leave. By then, Manne had been a prisoner for about five months. The prisoners were anxious to hear more and asked for updates but did not get much.

The day of their release finally came, however, and when it did, the guards started calling out the names of each Finnish prisoner. Manne listened as they went down the list. Name after name was called, and the prisoners identified themselves. When they were done, his had not been mentioned. It had apparently been either misspelled or misplaced. A Russian officer told him to write it down, and with the rest, he was loaded onto a rail car that was soon rolling toward the Finnish border. Perhaps the name mix-up was why there was never an official notification to the Finnish government of Manne's capture and imprisonment.

The train of prisoners chugged westward for hours before it finally stopped at the Finnish-Soviet border station of Vainikkala. Women from a wartime service organization, Lotta, met the train on the Finnish side to give the haggard men pea soup, a true Finnish delicacy after what they had just been through. It must have been here that names were collected for the news broadcast that told Lempi a Manne Heimala was among the first contingent of prisoners.

The men then transferred to a Finnish hospital train and moved on toward Hanko, a Finnish military post on the country's south coast. When it pulled into the station, a military band was playing, and they were treated as heroes. There was more pea soup. The haggard men and boys were debriefed. And they had a sauna every day.

It is hard to describe how all this cheered men who a dozen times probably thought they would die before reaching home. Manne later wrote Lempi a letter where he laid bare his feelings on arrival: "At the border was a hospital train to meet us, and we were fed a lot of food, and in Hanko there was a band playing when we got off the train. Tears came to the eyes when we reached Hanko station."[6]

Many of the men were little more than skeletons. Manne, already a small man, had also lost a lot of weight. During the prison camp ordeal, he fell from 140 to a mere 100 pounds. He was weak, and not in great shape, but he was alive. In Hanko he learned about the treacherous evacuation of Viipuri. He did not know where his family was, or even if they had made it out alive.

Over his three weeks of internment in Hanko, Manne began looking for Lempi and Seija. The day after arriving, he wrote a card to his father-in-law, Aleksander, who he thought might be working at his old job in the Lahti Starckjohann hardware store:

November 24, 1944
From Private Manne Heimala
Mr. A. Roos
Lahti
Starckjohann

May my greetings reach you with this card. How have you been? And have you been healthy?

You probably thought I was dead. But this has not happened yet, rather I was a prisoner in Russia and arrived back on the 23rd. Write how you are and how Lempi is and whether Seija is even alive. I am a little weak, but this will soon get by now that I have reached this beloved Father Country.[7]

It took over a week to get any information about Lempi. When he finally learned she was in Lahti, he wrote to her:

Don't wonder when I write something like this. But we haven't received any money with which I could buy paper. These envelopes and cards were received from the government. I just got word that letters cannot be sent through military mail but must have stamps when the military mail was stopped the 4th day.

Greetings from our Pastor who wrote to you about my disappearance. He has received a transfer here to Hanko. He noticed my name and came to chat. He was very happy that I was alive. He said that the Russians had put my name in a flyer but they were not sure whether I was alive. I asked the Pastor your address, but he couldn't remember.

We will talk later my dear and sweet dreams.[8]

Lempi must have jumped for joy when she heard her husband was alive and back, not crippled nor an invalid. She quickly filled up a box with all the goodies she could find and sent it off to Hanko for Manne.

On December 7, he replied back in a warm letter telling how overjoyed he was to hear from her. But in a somber reflection, Manne wrote, "Of course all of our things remained there in Viipuri. We are certainly people with a hard destiny, but we will submit to our destiny, it is probably our lot."[9]

After three weeks in Hanko, Manne was transferred to a barracks in Hämeenlinna, a city not far from Lahti, to await out-processing from the army. A few days before Christmas, Lempi was scurrying around their tiny crowded apartment in Lahti. It would be a Christmas like they had not known for years. The war was over. Manne was coming home.

They told Seija that her father would be home soon, but it was beyond her understanding. She already had her pappa. When Manne finally knocked on the door, it was a joyous Christmas gift for everyone, except Seija. He walked in, Lempi cried with joy, and scared little Seija ran to hide behind the door. He looked like a skeleton. This moment is the first thing she remembers from her childhood.

If Another War Comes? (1950)

The following few years were hard ones. Manne got his job back at Raute. Lempi worked as a seamstress with a furniture making company. She upholstered pieces that became their third set of furniture, one they hoped never again to leave behind. They lived in small apartments, shared with others.

As part of the peace agreement, the Soviet Union saddled Finland with immense war reparations. The Finns feared the Soviets expected a default that could be used as justification for occupying its neighbor. To meet what seemed to be an unrealistic timetable for payment – in finished goods, just to make it even more impossible – everyone had to work hard and long. Manne reported for work Monday morning early and worked every day until nine or ten o'clock in the evening, not coming home again until Friday after work. There was no "impossible" to the Finns in those days. Finland paid its reparations on time and celebrated having done so the same year they hosted the 1952 Olympic games.

Manne and Lempi, too, eventually got back to their feet. With Lempi's parents, they were able to purchase a home in a suburb of Lahti, much like the one they lost twice in Viipuri. Seija grew up in this house, feeling loved and secure. Their memories furnished a

437

family narrative that unified them with a sense of self-esteem and confidence.

The new home had a large garden, covered with red and black currant bushes, strawberries and raspberries, furrows of potato plants, and plenty of vegetables. This time, the potato cellar was under the house and was filled with juices, jams, potatoes, onions, and anything else that would survive the long winter. They rarely threw anything away. "What if another war comes?" Seija's mother always asked.

Thy People shall be My People

I mentioned earlier that when talking of family history, the emphasis goes on the first word, "family." That is, not just family from the past, but family of the present, as well. I always found that the past is one of the important unifying bonds of the present within a family structure. When two people agree to join lives, their pasts, though distinct, can merge as well into a family identity. I discuss this more in the next chapter. In my family, a shared narrative helped us enjoy the good days and weather the poor ones.

In the spring of 1969, between our engagement and wedding, Seija sent me a reflective letter describing her feelings about our upcoming marriage. In her note she quoted a scripture from the Old Testament's Book of Ruth:

> *"And Ruth said, Entreat me not to leave thee, or to return from following after thee: for whither thou goest, I will go; and where thou lodgest, I will lodge: thy people shall be my people, and thy God my God."[10]*

It was an especially meaningful to me. By agreeing to marry me, she was once again leaving all behind. Like Ruth, she came to a new land to accept my people.

When Ruth voiced those immortal words, she was rejoicing not just for her new husband, Boaz, but also for the salvation she received by embracing his people and faith. In a fundamental way, however, our story was different from hers. Like Ruth, Seija gave herself to my land and roots, and she rejoiced in them. From the beginning, however, I was also glad to be part of her land and roots,.

Seija's and my lives and stories converged when we were married in Idaho in 1969. We both were studying at Ricks College in Rexburg and teaching Finnish to support our studies. We were only miles from where my parents, grandparents, and great-grandparents and great-great grandparents had lived for nearly 100 years. Seija was quickly aware of many of the stories she adopted through our union.

I was bothered, however, because I knew some of her history but had only met her parents for about 45 minutes one winter evening in Lahti. We also realized how painful it was for them to have an only child wed thousands of miles away without the possibility of seeing her walk the aisle in a beautiful wedding gown with her groom. Rheumatoid arthritis had confined Lempi to a wheelchair for over a decade. Traveling across the Atlantic to America was out of the question.

During our first year of marriage, we decided to resolve this problem. I applied and was accepted as an international student at the University of Helsinki. When we got to Finland, we spent every other weekend in Lempi's and Manne's Lahti home. It was a joyful thing to get to know them and others from their stories, such as the relatives who took them in as refugees when they fled penniless from Viipuri. Through our conversations, I learned details about the times of Seija's birth and early childhood. Their Karelian heritage was apparent just from the hangings on the walls. I developed a deep admiration for a brave family that had struggled to preserve their freedom and to give their daughter the life she had. After a year in Finland, we returned to my studies in the US.

In the summer of 1973, all of us traveled back for a holiday in Finland. By that time, we had three children, twin girls and a little boy one year younger, for practical purposes, triplets. The war had robbed Manne the chance to be around a baby, and now there were three of them. It was something totally fascinating for him. He cuddled and teased the three toddlers, his eyes full of excitement, especially when he looked at the youngest who was only a year and

439

a half. Lempi's eyes were full of tears when she first saw them. Times were so greatly different from the war years when she nursed her own baby among all the fearful unknowns the future held.

One morning, I saw a newspaper ad offering a weekend trip to Leningrad at a very nominal price. It was out of the question to go there with children along, and I was not interested in traveling alone. I asked Manne if the two of us might make a weekend of it. Manne was silent for a moment before coming back with an emphatic "No. I marched through Leningrad as a prisoner, with people spitting on me. I won't go there again," he said.

Manne was a minority of one on this question. We pointed out that the bus would travel through Viipuri. He might even have a chance to see their old house. He soon gave in, and on a Friday morning we climbed aboard a large tour bus filled with Finns, equally as curious as we were. Our group made its way to the border and passed through the long, involved formalities. After that, we followed a narrow windy highway, while a representative of the Finland-USSR Society fed us propaganda about how great everything was in the Soviet Union.

It was not long before we approached Viipuri and drove its streets. Manne was quiet and serious. This was the first time he had seen the city since his last furlough from the front, about two months before he was captured. It was almost 30 years since the Russians had taken Viipuri, and the once thriving city was still in wartime disrepair. Then he lit up. Manne remarked with a half-smile, "They haven't done anything to it since they took it from us!" he mused with a laugh. The bus pulled out of Viipuri toward Leningrad.

Somewhere along our drive through the dense Karelian forests, Manne caught my attention, pointed his finger, and murmured, "Over there." I looked through the window to see old Finnish bunkers in blown-out ruins from the Finnish-Russian wars. A few moments later, he said, "It was just about here that I was taken prisoner." We sat silently and watched the firs, birches, pines, meadows, and blown out ruins file by our window.

From there, it was only a short drive to Leningrad where we did the usual bus tour-type things, but at one point, Manne perked up

440

and was all eyes. His initial anxieties about returning to the city were long gone. "There!" he said as we went down a street. "That bridge... we marched over that bridge when they brought us here." Rather than reinforcing Manne's old bad memories of his months as a POW, I could see that the trip was almost therapeutic for him. Some old ghosts simply flew away as we toured the streets and sites.

Leningrad was a personality-lacking skeleton of what St. Petersburg was before the revolution. We listened in the background to more of our tour guides' propaganda while we looked at the worn-down buildings, bridges, and streets. Most of my Finnish fellow travelers were tolerant and expressed few objections to the political commentary, while through the windows of the bus they intently followed the street scenes.

However, a few, such as our Finnish driver, could hardly hold back their frustrations. The driver began to talk back to the guides with sarcasm, something that amused all of us passengers. On the second morning, the driver told us at breakfast how he awoke in the middle of the night to find someone in his room going through his things. Manne and I laughed, hardly surprised. The KGB was keeping track of him.

On Sunday afternoon we were on our way back to Finland. When we approached Viipuri, Manne went to the front of the bus to ask if we could make a short detour past Lempi's and his old home. It was only a couple blocks off the main Helsinki road. Without a pause, the guides said no. It was forbidden to wander off the established routes.

Our bus driver looked up at them with disgust. He knew from Manne's description exactly where the house was, and as we got to the right intersection, he announced in a loud happy voice, "We have time to stop by Manne's house."

With no further warning, he whipped the bus in that direction and kept going despite our guides' protests. Two blocks down the road, he stopped. "Is this it, Manne?" he yelled.

"Yes, that's it," Manne returned with an enthusiastic chuckle.

Then the smile left his face for a moment. He just looked out silently. Others on the bus were quiet, too. They knew perfectly well

441

the meaning of this moment. There was the house he had last seen when Lempi lived there, and Seija was a baby. He thought he would never see it again, but there it was. People were in the garden, perhaps working with the berry bushes and weeding the potatoes. The bus driver did not push his luck too far. He only stopped for 2-3 minutes and no one got off. He had made his point, and Manne had what he wanted to see.

We continued our trip to the border station where we all were told to get off the bus. We waited while Soviet border guards took it apart to make sure we were not smuggling anyone out. It was one of the few highly efficient operations that the Soviet Union ever managed. In about 15 minutes, we all climbed back on, and drove a hundred yards to the Finnish station. After a one or two-minute check, the Finnish guards waved us on.

The bus moved forward and down the highway into Finland. Everyone was once again on Finnish soil. The heavy weight of repression we all felt lifted perceptibly. The change in mood was measurable. The Finns spontaneously broke into song, one of their patriotic songs.

Manne was all smiles when we finally got home to Lempi, Seija, and the children. So was Lempi, sitting in her wheelchair on the porch overlooking their lush, well cared-for garden. On top of Manne's list to tell her was everything he could remember from that two-minute stop in Viipuri, in front of the home they had lost.

Over the years we had many laughs about the trip we made together to Leningrad. For me, the best thing about it, what remained most vividly in my memories, was traveling there with Manne. Many times since then, I have revered Seija's new stories that converged with mine into a wide river.

Preserving our Stories

Most of this chapter came from a source that should be our first stop when compiling a family history: the memories and family records of those of our family still alive. Discussing memories with parents, grandparents, or other family members in video and audio

442

recordings brings these people back to life, long after they are gone. Copies of their letters and other writings increase in value with age.

Today, unfortunately, our paper (as opposed to digital) trails are becoming scarcer, something I am sure future generations will regret. All the more reason to make sure paper does not disappear as a medium for telling our family stories. Paper has greater potential to endure decades and even centuries. I have concerns about the perishability of digital records, such as emails, messaging, digital photos, and videos.

Something my family has done to keep our stories on paper is to publish photos and writings in relatively inexpensive photo books-to-order, such as Blurb, Shutterfly, and many others. As mentioned earlier, each member of our family recently wrote three- to four-page reminiscences of homelife during their childhood. We sent the pages with digital and scanned photos, some already aging and fading, to be bound in a photobook we gave to our children for Christmas. Another holiday season we gave similar books that contained the year's entries on my wife's Facebook page. The books, full of pictures of family events and short explanations, were enduring records of that year. We hope generations of children and grandchildren will discover them with curiosity and fascination.

With digitalized memories, the objective is to get stories recorded and then transferred before they are lost. To do that it is essential the medium – film, email, MP3, whatever – is updated before we lose narratives on account of the obsolescence of the places we preserve our records. Some locations that seems to be durable are online family history sites, such as FamilySearch and Ancestry.com, that allow uploading records, memories, and photos. Preserving them through these sites has the added advantage of allowing others tracking the same ancestors to access what we have found. The bottom line is that we live in a fragile, ever-obsolescent society, and we must keep that in mind.

For example, the stories of how Manu and Eelis escaped firing squads barely survived. They had never been recorded until we first heard them. Seija knew nothing of her great uncle Eelis's adventures and had heard only sketchy stories of her grandfather

Manu's abduction. Her father, 70 years later, told them freely one afternoon when we chatted about his family's past in front of a tape recorder. That day we heard so many stories that these two slipped our minds completely for 30 years. What a loss it would have been not to learn how a friendship saved her uncle's life during the brutal days of Finland's civil war. Eelis's story belonged to Seija's collective stories and past. He apparently never married No children nor grandchildren remembered what Manne told us.

The lesson we learned from this experience is summarized in three words: interview, record, *and* preserve. *No matter where we are in collecting our family's history, no matter what barriers hinder passing backward on our familial lines, we usually have some living family members who can recount stories that will be colorful and valuable a few years hence. We want them to share their stories with us. And the corollary: record. We need to record the interviews one way or another, in front of a video or audio device, or simply by writing out the things we hear in the interviews.*

In 1984, when Manne related these stories to us, Lempi had suffered a serious stroke and was lying in the hospital, half of her paralyzed. We were visiting from London. Lempi was happy to see us and showed her warmth with a half-smile that she could barely manage. She would pass away a few months later after a life of ups and downs that never conquered her invincible spirit.

Later that day, we relaxed in the living room of the modest but comfortable apartment we had helped Manne find in the aftermath of Lempi's stroke. In front of us, a cassette recorder sat on the coffee table. For over two hours we talked about their lives. Manne was glad to have family at this lonely moment. He opened up and was detailed in his narratives, his memory as clear as ever.

Over thirty years after that afternoon, my wife and I sat before our computer and listened to Manne's voice once again. I had converted the old cassettes into MP3 files so that we could listen to him, our cassette recorder having been long before thrown out. Converting to an MP3 format also made it possible to preserve the discussion as a computer file and to send it to the rest of our family via the internet.

444

Hearing Manne speaking to us again impassioned our memories. Two and a half decades had passed since his death. It was as if he had never left. His spirit was alive as ever. Some of the stories he recalled were tragic and full of hardship, but he chuckled as he talked. It was an inspiration to realize that hardships need not leave lasting bitterness. He was balanced and happy, greatly because he could laugh at the past. We were glad that we had spent an afternoon recording Manne's recollections.

These and other interviews we did decades ago made it possible to share such stories as these with our children. Carrying what we find forward into the future is important. Just as we have a thousand family stories behind us, future generations should also be able to find their own thousand stories. We have a role to play in making that possible.

Getting the Meaning

When interviewing, it is beneficial to keep focused on why someone is telling the story: what is the story supposed to mean? Manne was always interested in telling us about his World War II days fighting on the Russian front. Those months and years fighting the Soviet Army were some of the most powerful experiences in his life. He was especially glad to relate his stories to me, a young American. I listened politely, and my enthusiasm mattered to someone who had put his life in danger for his family and country.

It was more than that, though. In retrospect, I think Manne was also telling me who his countrymen were – and who he was. He did not want me just to hear the stories. He wanted me to comprehend them, to know what they meant. He wanted me to understand that Finland was a patriotic place where people face all odds to keep their freedom and way of life. The Finns had been willing to go to war against the Soviet Union twice during World War II. Through fight and sisu, they succeeded in remaining an independent country after the war. Those boys shouldering up against Manne as they rushed down the tracks toward Russia that June day of 1941 were fierce in their refusal to be dominated.

445

I saw it again one day, decades later. I was turning 50, and on my birthday, we drove to a small Karelian town named Ilomantsi, deep in Finland's forests on the current Russian border. It was customary in Finland to celebrate big birthdays like this one. To avoid a big party and everything with it, I thought to visit Father Rauno, a friend who pastored the large Orthodox congregation there. I was then the Charge' d'Affaires at the American Embassy in Helsinki but expected that in a remote town like this one, I could avoid the protocol of my position and find time to relax about getting older.

Father Rauno and his lovely wife Anneli met us when we arrived and accommodated us in their cozy visitors' cottage. Surrounded with its authentic Karelian décor and handwork, my patriotic Karelian wife felt she was in heaven. Father Rauno said that if I really wanted to get away from everything, he had a suggestion. He had mentioned to the local border guard detachment that the head of the American Embassy would be staying a few days in Ilomantsi. Upon hearing this, the commander had extended an invitation to join one of their border patrols in a wilderness that was as far from civilization as any place in Europe could be. It was perfect, I thought.

The next morning, we were up early and after a Karelian breakfast, Seija stayed behind with Anneli and their children, while Father Rauno and I sped off across a lake toward the border guards' headquarters. Ever eastward, our speedboat slipped nimbly across another lake until we finally reached an inlet where the border patrol was waiting. There were about six or seven men commanded by a captain, plus Father Rauno and me. Perhaps the most important member of the team was their dog who was highly trained to sniff out incursions and to communicate what he found to members of the patrol.

The guards immediately made me feel welcome. We chatted for a few minutes, had a snack and something to drink. Our patrol then started out in single file along a wilderness path that eventually paralleled the high fence, sometimes in disrepair, located squarely along the border. Aside from the fence and an occasional deserted wooden block house on the Russian side, there were no other signs of people or celebrations, just the kind of birthday I was looking for. After about an hour and a half of eventless hiking, the dog's ears stood up, and his nose went to the ground. He wandered about the spot for a while and then returned to his keeper.

I asked the captain what the dog had found. He said that a bear had crossed from Finland into Russia at this spot a day before. "Don't worry," he joked, "when he finds where he has gone, he will be back." We all laughed, but I could see there was still an element of seriousness in the commander's voice.

We hiked all day. The once formidable fence, that only a few short years before kept Russia's citizens from escaping the oppressive Soviet Union, was now dilapidated. We did not see a single Russian border guard patrolling the other side. All the Russian watch posts were deserted. And yet the Finns patrolled this remote stretch without interruption. I finally asked the patrol commander why. "Why expend the effort if the Russians are no longer paying the same attention to the border as before?" I questioned.

The captain turned to me and now in a sober voice gave me his answer. It was just like sitting again across from Manne who a decade before told his war stories and wanted us to understand what they meant. "During the war," he began, "my grandfather fought for every meter of the land the Soviets tried to take from us." And then his point: "And I will do the same."

I enjoyed every minute of that patrol. Later, we again boated across another lake until we reached a camp where we planned to overnight. Some of the men threw out fish nets, and an hour later pulled them from the lake's chilly waters full of vendace, a small, tasty minnow-sized fish. They smoked their catch, and we chatted well into the night while we enjoyed it. At one point, the men said they had heard it was my 50th birthday. I laughed and said I was trying to keep that secret. Just the same, they wished me a happy birthday and pulled out a Finnish hunting knife with "Finnish Border Guards" engraved on it. They said it would remind me of the day I protected Finland along its Russian border.

447

What remained most in my mind, however, was the captain's comment, "And I will do the same." They had showed me their story – their life of daily patrols in the deep Finnish woods along the country's only closed border – but he wanted me to comprehend what their story meant. In a nutshell: Finland lives in a dangerous part of the world, even today, and their story was about protecting every inch of the soil that meant so much to them and to their grandfathers.

I learned that when people relate their stories to us, there is the story, itself, and there is often a meaning. As that meaning becomes clear, the narrative becomes richer, something we do not forget. Today, after years traveling and collecting my stories, I understand this point even better. It is one thing to gather stories from the past, but it is important to understand what we should take from them.

Something also worth considering: what do I want my stories to tell my grandchildren about the life I led? And: what am I doing to make sure they learn my stories?

History Surrounds our Family Narrative

The drama of losing, regaining, and losing almost everything again made a powerful story. Many of the previous ones I wrote about also told of resilient, strong, and never wavering people fighting against evils life threw at them. However, I discovered most of them, in one way or another, second hand. I got them from written materials that had survived the decades and sometime centuries.

However, Seija's Finnish stories were enormous, most of all because they were all around me. Seija was part of them: they framed her life. I did not have to go very far to find them. All I had to do was ask her, or her family. They were especially compelling because the narratives and adventures were set against the backdrop of a tragic world war whose horrors had haunted histories, books, and movies since it began.

Once after reading an article in a magazine about a John Wayne-esque Finnish war hero named Lauri Törni, I felt inspired to dig deeper into his life. As I mentioned earlier, my research eventually turned into a book. It was first a hobby, then an obsession, and finally a burden that took me five years. The book was a best-seller in Finland because it told a remarkable person's Finnish stories and some of his American stories, as well. It was also published in several other countries.

Törni's colorful adventures allowed me to understand better Seija's, Manne's, and Lempi's history. Conversely, unfolding the stories of what they endured and how they lived those dark days became a source of the passion that drove me to write the book in the first place. I subtitled it the "Times and Life of Lauri Törni"[11] rather than the other way around. His times – and Manne's and Lempi's times –defined their lives and stories.

Learning about the world where our forebearers and their families lived in any given era gives a boost to our efforts to learn their narratives. This approach was essential for the search for family stories, both for defining the context of those narratives, and for learning more about the meaning of the stories I discovered. I mentioned earlier how I spend time reading biographies and histories to understand the chapters of my family's everyday lives. Reading historical fiction was also an excellent way to learn feelings, frustrations, and thoughts they may have experienced. Authors of good historical fiction spend a lot of time researching the times as they attempt to bring their characters to life, true to history.

Bequeathing our Narrative

Manne lived a surprisingly healthy life despite what he went through during the war. There were scars, however. Sometimes when he was visiting, we woke up at night to horrific screams from his room. Manne saw dreams he could not remember when awakened. But during the daytime, his mind was clear, and his wit, sharp, always ready to tease the children. When in his seventies, doctors at a veterans' clinic found a piece of wartime shrapnel embedded in his head. He had never known it was there and had somehow survived perfectly well, in spite of it.

When Manne passed away in 1992, he left his papers neatly organized for us. It was as if he had a premonition. He died from a sudden heart attack in the town's market square, a place he spent afternoons visiting with old friends, most of them veterans like himself. It was a way and place to pass that he, himself, probably would have chosen if given an option.

Among the things we found in his boxes and files were the cards and letters he wrote from Hanko during the first days after his release from captivity in 1944. They were sincere and touching, and expressed his grateful feelings to be back, even as he reached out for news of his family. Had they survived the war? Where were they?

The letters not only revealed the wonderment and desperation of those first days of freedom, they also gave deep insight into Manne, himself. Fate had been hard on his family, he remarked, but they would survive their hardship. Even after he was gone, we were learning still more of his character.

How farsighted it was that he and Lempi had understood the importance of preserving these priceless letters. I was reminded that discovering family stories from the past is only half of the family history quest. Another part is to make sure our children and grandchildren are successful in their own quests to know their family narratives. We were grateful to Manne and Lempi for those letters, and much more.

How the Journey Ends

*"Genealogy is the backbone of human memory –
scaffolding upon which we can construct a sense of
how we came to being. At its heart, genealogy
springs from what is one of the most fundamental of
human impulses . . . a refusal to forget."*
Nathanael Philbrick, Prize-winning author
addressing the New England Historic
Genealogical Society's 170th anniversary

*"There is a moment when it is dysfunctional not to
look at the past"*
Bono

In my Prologue I related how this odyssey in search of my
family's past began. My stories were scattered over a thousand
years, an exhausting journey for even the indefatigable explorer. To
make it more manageable, I had decided to visit critical moments in
history – the Norman Conquest, Puritan New England, the
Revolutionary and Civil Wars, the great migration West – and to
experience them through the lives of my ancestors. Like Odysseus's
travel back to Ithaca, it was an adventurous journey that could easily
have taken a hundred detours and never ended. But any good trip
has to finish somewhere.

As my "island of Ithaca" began to appear on the horizon, its
harbor beckoning home, I was besieged with mixed feelings. On
one hand, with a sense of weariness and relief, I realized the voyage
was nearing its end. Anyone who has written a book knows that
such a project is possible only when you are infused with passion
and obsession. At some point, they begin to taper off, and you know
it is time for closure.

Another side of me did not want the journey ever to end. I had traveled over a vast swath of history, joining in new explorations at every turn. I had met fascinating people from both the past and present. Some of my ancestors had become so alive in my mind, that they could have lived next door, ready to greet me each morning when I went to the yard. They had stepped from their graves to tell their stories about things they wanted me to know and remember.

The insights I had gained from them were priceless. I continued to ponder the stories, long after I had written them down. From knights, with their battles and intrigues, to farmers, immigrants, and poor workers whose dream was to find more for their family than life had given them, they all kept my family history endorphins flowing, hungry for still more adventure.

I realized only too well that as rewarding and satisfying as the trip had been, I never succeeded in finding everything or everybody I sought. I wished for a better chance to break through the fogs of the past and to fill the gaps in the many stories I discovered. The more figures I saw in the distant haze, the more my wanderlust tempted me to explore further. Yet here was my destination where I needed to close my travels for now. There would be more trips.

The history I hoped to write encompassed the worlds of my grandmothers and grandfathers. It is easy for our everyday lives to seem inflexibly connected only to our current needs and wants. Our points of reference naturally feel attached to the present, rather than the past. We rush to work, school our children, face our obstacles, and strive towards our goals, everything apparently interconnected with today. But I wished to find today's connection with yesterday, in other words, how our roots mattered.

Once, when celebrating a landmark birthday, Seija and I stayed in a hotel at the foot of the Acropolis. It was a spot where at least 100 generations of people had lived, slept, worked, loved, fought, worshipped, and died. One evening with that thought in mind, we looked out across the roof terrace at the floodlit Parthenon radiating brightly against the dark behind it. On such a warm summer night as that, it was impossible not to feel immersed by the past. We understood ourselves as human beings, part of a long chain of people like ourselves. In that world, roots mattered, as did my grandmothers' and grandfathers' worlds and their journeys.

Nathanael Philbrick, the prize-winning author of such books as *Mayflower* and *Bunker Hill*, put it this way in a speech to the New England Historic Genealogical Society:

> "Genealogy is the backbone of human memory — scaffolding upon which we can construct a sense of how we came to being. At its heart, genealogy springs from what is one of the most fundamental of human impulses . . . a refusal to forget."[1]

The past matters to us, for our present well-being and sense of identity and belonging are conditioned by what happened before. Among the things many people dread most is the failure of memory, through senility and disease, for example. We rightly fear the loss of our connection to the past, and refuse to forget, if we can.

I once saw a movie in which the protagonist lost his short-term memory as the after-effect of a brutal attack. He realized that anything happening to him at any given moment would be forgotten within a few hours, or a day at most. It was a horrific state, and he fought to find ways to preserve his memories. If he wrote down his present, he could then have it available later as a history and reference point, after he had forgotten it.

However, he might also forget where he had written and placed his notes. The surest way to save a crucial memory was to write it down somewhere on his body with a pen, or a tattoo. Ensuring he had access to past events allowed him to deal more effectively with the realities of his present and future. He also found that lying to himself, by intentionally fudging one of his notes for example, would alter how he related to the future.[2]

The story was a graphic representation of how our past, and our understanding of it, affect our understanding of reality. It was an allegory demonstrating the connection of the past to our endeavors in the present. Family memories lost through the generations, when found, help us connect to our own realities. Just as we learn lessons for the future from our own experiences, so our grandparents' narratives, with their successes and failures, can be points of reference that help us more successfully navigate the lives we live now. U2 singing star Bono put in this way, "There is a moment when it is dysfunctional not to look at the past."[3]

Among the many things I learned from the stories I found was how it is possible to overcome the darkest of hours and afterwards resume happy lives. I admired the resiliency many of my ancestors possessed. One of the stories coming to mind is that of Obadiah Holmes. The brutal flogging he endured on the square before the Old Massachusetts State House did not irretrievably subdue his spirit, as the Puritan magistrates hoped it would. He rose from that moment to become one of the most respected clergymen in Rhode Island, praising the Almighty for his deliverance. The faith he expressed to his adult children when nearing the end of his life evidenced an optimism and hope that can benefit anyone.

Another similar example was Joseph Howard who tragically lost his wife and two daughters during their horrendous crossing of the American Plains. By all accounts, he rose from the depths of this loss to become a respectable and influential member of his civic and church communities. Then there was Tillie Johnson, who was left alone with twelve children in a place she never liked, to do something that did not fit her natural temperament. Rather than collapse into despair or depression, she rose and succeeded beyond what anyone could have expected. And, Manne Heimala, who was able to chuckle when relating the day he was caught and nearly executed behind Russian lines, and the desperate conditions of his detention in a Soviet prison camp.

Samuel Gorton and Dr. John Greene revealed the power of character. In their minds the difference between right and wrong was as clear as night and day. There was no equivocation like beset Sir Henry Greene, Jr., when he navigated the moral quagmire of Richard II's court. Samuel Gorton and Dr. John Greene were prepared to suffer anything in opposing oppression – Samuel, too, stood before the flogging post and spent months doing hard labor; John Greene lost his second wife on account of the Massachusetts oppression. Yet, they persevered, never gave up, and thought creatively about how to make justice win, even to the point of taking a perilous voyage back to London to argue successfully for Parliament's protection from their neighbors.

These were my people. Some of them set the bar high. Yet, because they were my lineage, it has made it easier for me to believe that I, too, have something inside that can produce resiliency, perseverance, character, and integrity in moments when they are needed. These stories offer inspiration not just to me, but to my own family, as well.

I saw this clearly during the last winter I worked on this project. Our adult daughter, Kristiina, was diagnosed with a brain tumor that over the years unbeknownst to anyone had grown to the size of a small pear. Over the months between December and April she underwent four surgeries and a life-threatening infection. She was the mother of five children, and the traumatic succession of procedures was the source of immense worry and stress for all of them, and us, too.

Just before the first of these surgeries, I emailed her a draft of the chapter I had just finished and named "Homesick." It recounted the stories of how Kristiina's Great-Great-Grandmother Tillie had conquered seemingly insurmountable challenges. The day before the initial surgery, Kristiina phoned to tell how after she started reading these stories, she called her entire family together. "We all read the chapter out loud. And we all cried together as we read," she told. Then Kristiina thanked me for sharing Tillie's stories at a moment her family needed fortitude and perseverance.

I was glad I sent Kristiina the chapter. Over the ensuing procedures and recoveries, she conquered the tumor that had invaded her life. Tillie's stories provided continual emotional support. As a writer in *Psychology Today* put it, our family stories provide "…context to our suffering, and the strength to persevere."[4]

Learning of our ancestors inevitably bolsters our sense of identity, belonging, and society. Today's lifestyle unfortunately does not always encourage communities as much as in the past. People too seldom live in close contact with extended families. Pursuing studies and jobs, we move away from our roots. Churches and their congregations no longer play as much a part of many people's everyday lives as they did in the past. We rarely do our shopping at small shops where we meet friends and know the shopkeeper. Often, we hardly know our next-door neighbors. If we lose a strong sense of identity, or wonder where we fit in, it is easy to feel anchorless.

Perhaps the search for identity and community is an important reason why family history has become so popular. According to articles in *Time* and *USA Today*, genealogy is the second most popular hobby in the United States. In fact, family history has become a big industry with online sites, such as Ancestry, making up the second most popular category of websites on the internet. Popular television series tell stories of tracing the roots of celebrities and others. And the number of people pursuing family history is growing year by year.[4] There obviously is a thirst for the things discovering one's family past does for you.

Of course, with the internet there is also an ironic juxtaposition of opportunities to reach out and tendencies for isolation. The same internet technology that enables the growing number of family researchers can also facilitate alienation, especially among young people. All coins have two sides. As parents know very well, our smartphones and computers can make it possible for young people, and adults, too, to draw into an inner world with little connection to what is outside. Computer games, movies, TV programming, pornography, messaging, and more can crowd out positive personal interactions that bolster this important sense of community and self-esteem.

One of my ecclesiastical leaders once told how he continually asks his children what is real and what is not in the things they do each day. It is a genuine, not an abstract question. Our digital playthings easily cloud the distinction between real and unreal. Finding our stories offers a chance to focus on the positive rather than negative aspects of the net that envelopes our lives. Knowing them allows us to transcribe the realities of the past onto our own lives as reference points for today, just as the protagonist in the movie I mentioned earlier learned to pen the past onto the backs of his hands and arms so as not to forget.

Families take many forms, but an aim most of them share is to enable a bond of love in a community that expedites an easier path through life. Often people fear that many forces are pulling at the seams of successful families. What makes some families effective and resilient, and others unhappy and turbulent, is a question many of us worry about.

Recent research suggests that an important and simple thing we can do to support success in the home is to develop a family narrative. A family narrative – the encapsulation of the "thousand stories behind us" – transfers memories, gives us an identity, and links us to those around us as well as those from the past. In short, our family narrative encourages bonds that replace those lost with the weakening of traditional neighborhoods.

An Emory University study shows that children who know more about their families perform better in the face of challenge. In their study, the researchers formulated 20 questions about a child's family – where grandparents grew up, where their parents met, what terrible thing once happened in the family, etc. – that they asked groups of children. The study found, "The more children knew about their family's history, the stronger their sense of control over their lives, the higher their self-esteem and the more successfully they believed their families functioned."

The "Do You Know?" quiz was the best single predictor of children's emotional health and happiness. Two months after the 9/11 attacks, for example, the Emory researchers assessed a group of children with these twenty questions. They found that whereas all Americans shared in the nation's trauma during those difficult days, "…the ones who knew more about their families proved to be more resilient, meaning they could moderate the effects of stress." [5]

The twenty "Do You Know?" questions were not a magic formula allowing parents to go down a list, teaching the right answers, so that everything would turn out fine. Instead, they were simply a metric that quantitatively demonstrated for sake of comparison which children knew something about their families and which did not. The ones with a family narrative answered the questions better than the others.

The family narrative itself was a product of both attitude and information. Families who had a knowledge of their past and who emphasized those stories among themselves were demonstrably happier and more successful. Children with a narrative had a "sense of being part of a larger family." They knew they belonged to something bigger than themselves. Even negative stories foster emotional resilience, sometimes even more than positive ones. As one therapist put it, "We all feel stronger if we are part of a tapestry. One thread alone is weak, but, woven into something larger, surrounded by other threads, it is more difficult to unravel."[6]

Knowing our stories is just as important for adults as for children. The military has known this for a long time. I learned it well during a year I once spent as a civilian student at the National War College at Fort McNair in Washington, DC.

General Dwight Eisenhower created the War College in the immediate aftermath of World War II to fill some gaps he perceived among his senior officers when he served as Supreme Commander of allied troops. Eisenhower noticed that British commanders had staffs composed of members of the various forces who understood the capabilities and vulnerabilities of their counterpart services. Army, navy, and air force officers had an appreciation of each other and their missions.

His American staff, on the other hand, did not do this quite so well, and Ike believed it made a difference in their general performance. When he returned to Washington, he created the War College to allow small groups of relatively senior officers and civilians – colonel- or lieutenant colonel-level commanders – to spend a year together studying national military strategy.

When I arrived as a State Department civilian to join the class of around 160 officers, I realized that General Eisenhower had been on to an important thing. Initially, we all informally divided into our various cohorts, army with army, foreign service with foreign service, and so on. There was a certain amount of discomfort and disorientation within the larger group when we first met for classes.

458

Over the year, however, that all changed. In the halls and classrooms, we got to know each other, what we had done in the past, and what we were expected to do now and in the future. We traveled together to observe naval air operations from the deck of an aircraft carrier. Flying high over the United States, we watched from the nose of an Air Force tanker as it refueled fighter aircraft. We visited embassies in different parts of the world. We explored the role of diplomacy as it related to military force.

In short, we were developing a unified narrative that bound us together as a team. This narrative augmented the *esprit de corps* that all services have tried to develop since armed forces were invented. It is this *esprit de corps* and the sense that we are part of a brotherhood, sisterhood, clan, or corps that glue people together in successful endeavors, whether in the military, the corporate world, or right in our own families. The sense of belonging gives us confidence to succeed along the paths we tread and to know we do not tread them alone.

Emory University's conclusions make sense. People with family narratives are surrounded with security and bulwarked against a sense of aimlessness or alienation. They more easily have a sense of being and a sense of identity. This is what the odyssey in search for one thousand stories is all about.

As I completed the journey to find my family's thousand stories, I knew I never found all of them, but my chests were full of tales and adventures. It was exhilarating to learn how I connected to my great-grandmother, or her grandfather, or to outspoken forefathers who favored freedom of expression and religion over the strictures of Puritan America. The boys who did not return from the Civil War and the extended family that took part in the first day of the American Revolution in Concord gave me an appreciation of how I fit into my family, culture, and country.

More than invigorating, the search was intoxicating. I found I wanted to find more and more. As my ship docked in Ithaca harbor, I was already wondering about the next trip and where it might take me. There was so much still to discover.

Family Trees

Note

These charts transport us back through time person-by-person until we get to the individuals and families whose stories I share. To be visually simple and brief, I have not added the usual genealogical facts of birth dates, death dates, and places. These are essential in family histories as markers that help us identify the people we are seeking. However, most of this information is available in the text and can also be found from the footnoted sources for each chart. With any good story, the dates and places are not the end of the research, but the means of doing it, settings that help us understand the people whose stories we find and tell.

Individuals shown in darker colored boxes are found in the various stories.

Five Generations from the Author

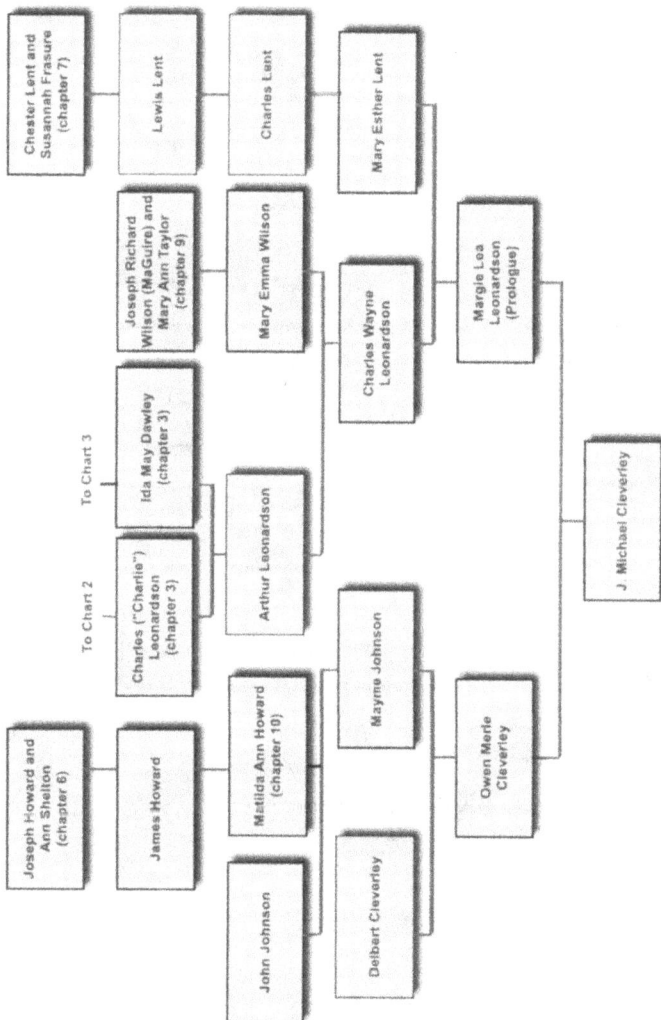

Family History Chart 2[2]
Charlie Leonardson to Benjamin Barrett, Jr

.

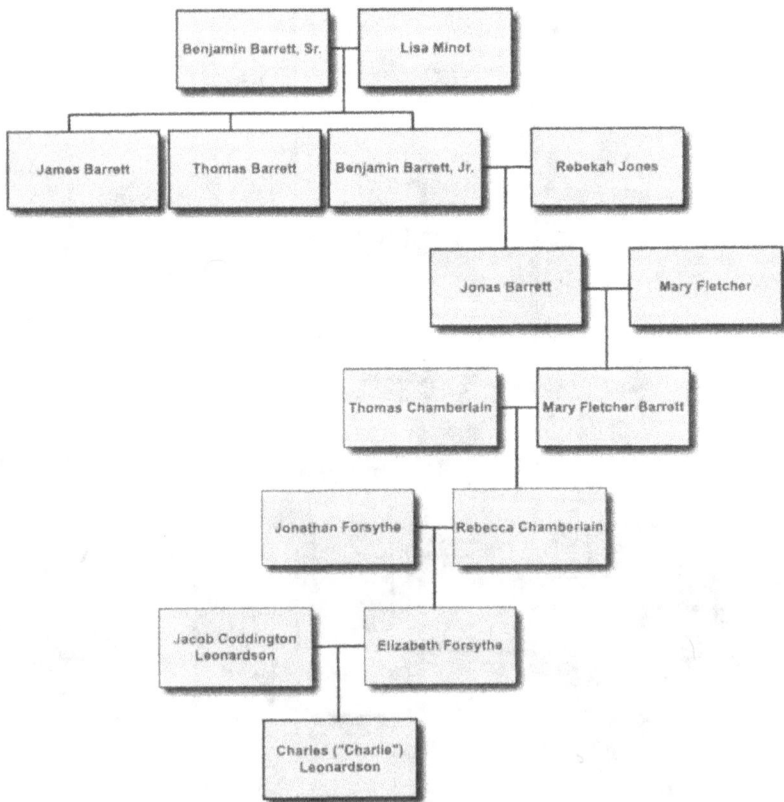

Family History Chart 3
Ida May Dawley to Great Migration Ancestors[3]

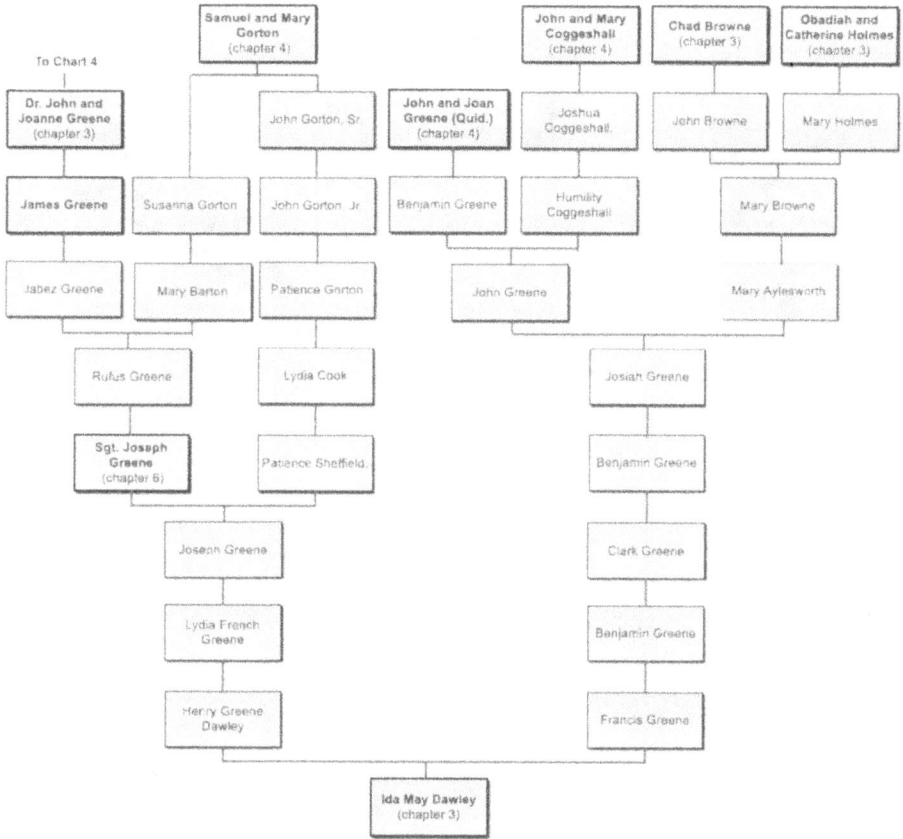

Dr. John Greene to Sir Henry Greene (Sr.)[4]

Family History Chart 5
Brothers and Cousins
in the Rebellion[5]

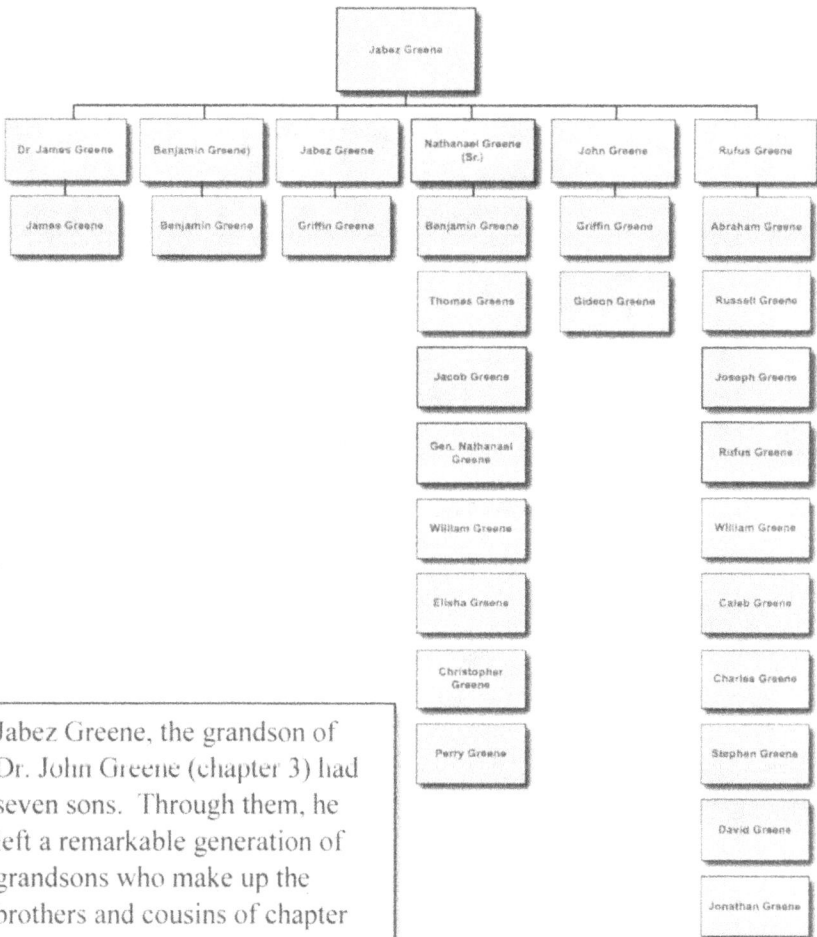

Jabez Greene

Dr. James Greene	Benjamin Greene)	Jabez Greene	Nathanael Greene (Sr.)	John Greene	Rufus Greene
James Greene	Benjamin Greene	Griffin Greene	Benjamin Greene	Griffin Greene	Abraham Greene
			Thomas Greene	Gideon Greene	Russell Greene
			Jacob Greene		Joseph Greene
			Gen. Nathanael Greene		Rufus Greene
			William Greene		William Greene
			Elisha Greene		Caleb Greene
			Christopher Greene		Charles Greene
			Perry Greene		Stephen Greene
					David Greene
					Jonathan Greene

Jabez Greene, the grandson of Dr. John Greene (chapter 3) had seven sons. Through them, he left a remarkable generation of grandsons who make up the brothers and cousins of chapter 5, "Road to Rebellion."

Family History Chart 6
Seija Kaarina Heimala[6]

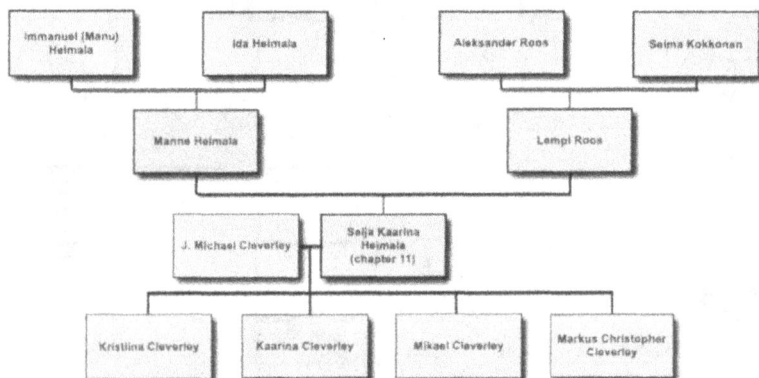

- Immanuel (Manu) Heimala
- Ida Heimala
- Aleksander Roos
- Selma Kokkonen
- Manne Heimala
- Lempi Roos
- J. Michael Cleverley
- Seija Kaarina Heimala (chapter 11)
- Kristiina Cleverley
- Kaarina Cleverley
- Mikael Cleverley
- Markus Christopher Cleverley

Bibliography

Prologue – The Inheritance

<u>Journals and Magazines</u>
Olson, Steve, "The Royal We," *The Atlantic Monthly*, 62 (May 2002).

Chapter One – Wife of a Conqueror

<u>Books</u>
Cuchemin, Catherine and Benoit Panozzo, *Falaise Castle William the Conqueror's Birthplace*, Cully, France: OREP Editions, 2008.

Fettu. Annie, *Queen Matilda*, Bayeux, France: OREP Editions, 2016.

Halstead, Robert, *Succinct Genealogies of the Noble and Ancient Houses*, London: 1685.

Hourquet, Michel, et. al., *William the Conqueror*, Bayeux, France: OREP Editions, 2015.

Mason, Patrick Q., *Planted, Belief and Belonging in an Age of Doubt*, Salt Lake City: Deseret Book, 2015.

Morris, Marc, *The Norman Conquest, The Battle of Hastings, and the Fall of Anglo-Saxon England*, New York: Pegasus, 2014.

Mortimer, Ian, *The Time Traveler's Guide to Medieval England*, New York: Touchstone, 2008,

Chapter Two – Two Knights and a Swordsman

<u>Books</u>
Armitage-Smith, Sydney, *John of Gaunt*, Kindle edition, Archibald Constable & Co., Ltd, 1904.

Bailey, Bruce, *Drayton House*, Drayton House, Northamptonshire, 1990.

Baker, George, *The History of Antiquities of the County of Northampton*, I, London: John Bowyer Nicols & son, 1822-1830.

Bennett, Michael, *Richard II, and the Revolution of 1399*, Stroud, UK: Sutton, 1999.

Ferling, John, *Almost a Miracle, The American Victory in the War of Independence*, New York: Oxford Univ. Press, 2007.

Greene, George Sears, T*he Greenes of Rhode Island, with Historical Records of English Ancestry, 1534-1902*, New York: 1902.

Halstead, Robert, *Succinct Genealogies of the Noble and Ancient Houses*, London: 1685.

Holinshed, Raphaell, *Chronicles of England, Scotland, and Ireland*, (1577), reprinted in Raphaell Holinshed, *Chronicles of England Scotland and Ireland*, II, London: J. Johnson et al, 1807.

La Mance, Lora Sarah Nichols, *The Greene Family and its Branches from A.D. 861 to A.D. 1904*, Floral Park, NY: Mayflower Publishing Co., 1904.

Mason, Patrick Q., *Planted, Belief and Belonging in an Age of Doubt*, Salt Lake City: Deseret Book, 2015.

Metcalfe, Walter A, Knights Banneret, *Knights of the Bath, and Knights Bachelor*, London: Mitchell and Hughes, 1885.

More, Sir Thomas, *History of King Richard III*, edited by J. Rawson Lumby, London: Cambridge University Press, 1883.

Mortimer, Ian, *The Time Traveler's Guide to Medieval England*, New York: Touchstone, 2008.

Mortimer, Ian, *The Perfect King, The Life of Edward III Father of the English Nation*, London: Vintage, 2008.

Shaw, Wm. A., *The Knights of England, A Complete Record from the Earliest Time to the Present Day of the Knights of all the Orders of*

Chivalry in England, Scotland, and Ireland and of Knights Bachelors, London: Sherratt and Hughes, 1906.

Somersby, Horatio, *The Greene Family in England and America: With Pedigrees*, Boston: 1901.

Stephen, Sir Leslie, ed., "Sir Henry Green," *The Dictionary of National Biography*, VIII, London: Oxford Univ. Press, 1917.

Walsingham, Thomas, *Historia Anglicana*, II, Henry Thomas Riley, ed., *Chronica Monasterii S. Albani*, London: Longman, Green, Longman, Roberts, and Green, 1864.

Weir, Allison, *The Princes in the Tower*, New York: Ballantine, 1992.

Weir, Allison, *The Wars of the Roses*, Kindle edition, New York: Ballantine, 1995.

Journals, Magazines, and Newspapers
Allaben, Frank, "Green of Greens-Norton," *The Journal of American History* 12:2 (April 1918).

Moriarty, G. Andrews, "Notes on the Greene and Turner Letters," *Rhode Island History* 6:1 (July 1947).

Washborn, Mabel Thacher Rosemary, Genealogical editor, "Loveland Ancestry" *The Journal of American History*, 12: 4 (Oct. 1918).

Websites
"Greene, Sir Henry (1347-1399)," *The History of Parliament: the House of Commons 1386-1421*,
(http://www.historyofparliamentonline.org/volume/1386-1421/member/green-sir-henry-1347-1399).

"John of Gaunt," *Shakespeare and History*,
(www.shakespeareandhistory.com/john-of-gaunt.php).

Summerson, Henry, "Green, Sir Henry, d. 1369," *Oxford Dictionary of National Biography*, (https://www.oxforddnb.com).

Chapters Three – Struggle for American Values, Struggle for American Values

Books

Anderson, Robert Charles, *The Great Migration Begins: Immigrants to New England*, 1620-33, I-III, New England Historic Genealogical Society: Boston, 1995.

Anon, *The Greene Family in England and America: With Pedigrees*, Boston: privately printed, 1901.

Armitage-Smith, Sydney, *John of Gaunt*, London: Archibald Constable & Co., 1904, reprinted in 2015 by Endeavour Press, Ltd., kindle edition.

Arnold, Samuel Greene, *History of the State of Rhode Island And Providence Plantations*, 1, New York: D. Appleton & Co., 1859.

Austin, John Osborne, *The Genealogical Dictionary of Rhode Island*, Albany, NY: Clearfield, 1887, reprinted as *The Genealogical Dictionary of Rhode Island*, Baltimore: Genealogical Printing Co, 1989.

Barry, John M., *Roger Williams and the Creation of the American Soul*, New York: Penguin, 2012.

Bicknell, Thomas Williams, *The History of the State of Rhode Island*, 3, New York: American Historical Society, 1920.

Bremer, Francis J., *The Puritan Experiment, New England Society form Bradford to Edwards*, Lebanon, NH: University Press of New England, NH, 1995.

Burrage, Henry S., *A History of the Baptists in New England*, Philadelphia: American Baptist Publication Society, 1894.

The Chad Browne Memorial, 1638-1888, printed for the Brown family in Brooklyn, NY, about 1888.

Conley, Patrick T., *Rhode Island's Founders, from Settlement to Statehood*, Charleston, SC: The History Press, 2010.

Dunray, Neil C., et. al., *Smith's Castle at Cocumscussoc, Four Centuries of Rhode Island History*, East Greenwich, RI: Meridian Printing Co., 2003.

The Early Records of the Town of Providence, I, Providence: Snow & Farnham, 1892.

Fisher, David Hackett, *Albion's Seed Four British Folkways in America*, New York: Oxford Univ. Press, 1989.

Gaustad, Edwin S., *Baptist Piety, The Last Will and Testimony of Obadiah Holmes*, Grand Rapids: Christian University Press, 1978.

Gorton, Adelos, *The Life and Times of Samuel Gorton*, Philadelphia: George S. Ferguson Co., 1907.

Gorton, Samuel, *Simplicities defence against seven-headed policy, or Innocency vindicated: being unjustly accused and sorely censured by that seven-headed church-government united in New-England: or that servant so imperious in his master['Js absence revived and...*, London: Jon Macock, 1646.

Greene, George Sears, *The Greenes of Rhode Island, with Historical Records of English Ancestry, 1534-1902*, New York: Knickerbocker Press, 1903.

Holmes, Col. J. T., *The American Family of Rev Obadiah Holmes*, Columbus, OH, 1915.

Howe, Charles, *Gylla's Hometown, How a Saxon Settlement became an English Country Town*, Gillingham, Dorset: Gylla Publishing, 1983.

King, Henry Melville, *A Summer Visit of Three Rhode Islanders to the Massachusetts Bay in 1651*, Providence: Preston and Rounds, 1896.

King, Henry Melville, *Historical Catalogue of the Members of the First Baptist Church in Providence, Rhode Island*, Providence, RI: Townsend printers, 1908.

La Mance, Lora Sarah Nichols, *The Greene Family and its Branches, from A.D. 861 to A.D. 1904*, Floral Park, NY: Mayflower Publishing Co., 1904.

Lodi, Edward, *Who, When, Where in King Philip's War*, Middleborough, MA: Rock Village Publishing, 2015.

McLoughlin, William G., *Rhode Island, A Bicentennial History*, New York: W.W. Norton, 1978.

Morris, Richard B., "Jezebel Before the Judges," Francis J. Bremer, ed., *Anne Hutchinson: Troubler of the Puritan Zion*, New York: Robert E. Krieger Publishing Company, 1981.

Mortimer, Ian, *The Time Traveler's Guide to Elizabethan England*, New York: Penguin, 2012.

Philbrick, Nathaniel, *Mayflower, A Story of Courage, Community, and War*, Penguin: New York, 2006.

Records of the Settlements at Providence, Portsmouth, Newport and Warwick, 1636-1647, I, Crawford Greene: Providence, 1856.

Richman, Irving Berdine, *Rhode Island Its Making and Its Meaning, A Survey of the Annals of the Commonwealth from the Settlement to the Death of Roger Williams 1636-1685*, New York: G. P. Putnam's Sons, 1902.

Savage, James, *A Genealogical Dictionary of the First Settlers of New England*, II, Boston: Little, Brown, and Co, 1860.

Shaw, Wm. A., *The Knights of England, A Complete Record from the Earliest Time to the Present Day of the Knights of all the Orders of Chivalry in England...*, London: Sherratt and Hughes, 1907.

H.E. Turner, *Greenes of Warwick in Colonial History*, Davis and Putman: Newport, RI, 1877.

Winthrop, John, *Winthrop's Journal, History of New England, 1630-1649*, Kindle edition, I and II, edited by James Kendall Hosmer, Charles Scribner and Sons, 1908.

Journals, Magazines, and Newspapers
Benny, Sally, "Preserving Your Family History in the Digital Age," *American Ancestors* 20:2 (Summer 2019).

"John Coggeshall," *The American Genealogist*, XIX, 131.

"Letter of Alice Daniell of Salem to Gov. John Winthrop at Boston," *The New England Historical and Genealogical Register* 35 (Oct. 1881), 318-320.

Leonardson, Gladys Laird, "Mary Emma Wilson Leonardson (of Dubois and Medicine Lodge)," *Snake River Echoes, A Quarterly of Idaho History* 11:1 (1982).

Porter, Kenneth W., "Samuel Gorton New England Firebrand," *The New England Quarterly* 7:3 (September 1934).

Websites
Cambridge University Alumni, 1261-1900 [database on-line], Provo, *Ancestry.com*.

"John Green," *Cambridge University Alumni, 1261-1900* [database on-line]. Ancestry.com, Provo, UT, USA: Ancestry.com Operations Inc, 1999,
(https://search.ancestry.com/cgi-bin/sse.dll?_phsrc=sdL155&_phstart=successSource&usePUBJs=true&indiv=1&dbid=3997&gsfn=John&gsln=Green&gsfn_x=NP_NN_NIC&msbdy=1590&new=1&rank=1&uidh=aic&redir=false&msT=1&gss=angs-d&pcat=37&fh=1&h=30550&recoff=&ml_rpos=2&queryId=65fda35b8f3e5f4ad57b885e31616167).

Johnson, Caleb, "Livestock," *Caleb Johnson's MayflowerHistory.com*, http://mayflowerhistory.com/livestock.

McBeth, Leon, "Baptist Beginnings," *The Baptist History & Heritage*, 1979, www.baptisthistory.org, accessed 2020.

Manuscripts
Cleverley, Margie Leonardson, "Sketches from the Life of the Charles H. Leonardson Family," type-written history in my possession.

Leonardson, Carl, "The Family of Charles H. and Ida M. Dawley Leonardson," type-written family history, in my possession.

Chapter Four – Road to Rebellion

Books
Carbone, Gerald M., *Nathanael Greene, a Biography of the American Revolution*, New York: Palgrave MacMillan, 2008.

"Deposition of Rufus Greene, Jr.," *The Royal Commission of the Commission of Inquiry*, found in John Russell Bartlett, compiler, *A History of the Destruction of His Britannic Majesty's Schooner Gaspee*, Providence: A. Crawford Greene, 1861.

Field, Edward, *State of Rhode Island and Providence Plantations at the End of the Century: A History*, II, Boston & Syracuse: Mason Publishing Company, 1902.

Greene, George W., *Life of Nathanael Greene, Major-General in the Army of the Revolution*, Boston: Charles Little and James Brown, 1846.

Hales, Virginia Dart Greene, *Greene and Greene, Their Ancestral Heritage, 1550-1900*, self-published, 2016.

Hawes, Alexander Boyd, *Off Soundings Aspects of the Maritime History of Rhode Island*, Chevy Chase: Posterity Press, 1999.

Johnson, William, *Sketches of the Life and Correspondence of Nathanael Greene*, Charleston, SC: A.E. Miller, 1822.

Park, Steven, *The Burning of His Majesty's Schooner Gaspee*, Yardley, PA: Westholme Publishing, 2016.

Rappleye, Charles, *Sons of Providence, the Brown Brothers, the Slave Trade, and the American Revolution*, New York: Simon and Schuster, 2006.

Raven, Rory, *Burning the Gaspee, Revolution in Rhode Island*, Charleston, SC: The History Press, 2012.

Journals, Magazines, and Newspapers
Allen, Col. Thomas, "Kentish Guards, a History," 1918, in The Kentish Guards, *The Kentish Guardsman & Fife and Drum Review* (August 2009).

Bryant, Samuel, "Rhode Island Justice – 1772 Vintage," *Rhode Island History* 26:3 (July 1967).

"Tory Mob," *Providence [Rhode Island] Gazette*, (September 17, 1774), printed in The Kentish Guards, *The Kentish Guardsman & Fife and Drum Review* (August 2009).

<u>Websites</u>
Gaspee Days Committee, *Gaspee Virtual Archives*, (www.gaspee.org).

Revolutionary War Pension and Bounty-Land Warrant Application Files, Roll 1124. From: Fold3: *Revolutionary War Pensions*, images, NARA M804.
(https://www.fold3.com/image/22090731?terms=war,us,joseph,revolutio nary,greene).

Chapter Five – Day of the Revolution

<u>Books</u>
Barrett, Amos, "Concord and Lexington Battle," in Rev. Henry True, *Journal of Letters*, Marion, Ohio, 1900.

Bell, J. L., *The Road to Concord, How Four Stolen Cannon Ignited the Revolutionary War*, Yardley, PA: Westholme, 2016.

Borneman, Walter R., *American Spring*, New York: Back Bay Books, 2014.

Chase, Ellen, *The Beginnings of the American Revolution, Based on Contemporary Letters, Diaries, and Other Documents*, 3, New York: Baker Taylor, 1910.

Fletcher, Edward, *Fletcher Family History, The Descendants of Robert Fletcher of Concord, Mass*, Boston: Rand, Avery, & Co, 1881.

Galvin, Gen. John R., *The Minute Men, The First Fight: Myths and Realities of the American Revolution*, Washington: Potomac Books, 2006.

Gross, Robert A., *The Minutemen and Their World*, New York: Hill and Wang, 1976.

Hodgman, Rev. Edwin R., *History of the Town of Westford, 1659-1883*, Lowell, MA: Morning Mail Co., 1883.

Hurd, D. Hamilton, *History of Middlesex County*, Massachusetts, 1, Philadelphia: J.W. Lewis, 1890.

Philbrick, Nathaniel, *Bunker Hill, A City, A Siege, A Revolution*, New York: Penguin, 2013.

Ripley, Rev Ezra, *A History of the Fight at Concord on the 19th of April, 1775*, Concord: Allen & Atwill, 1827.

Ryan, D. Michael, *Concord and Dawn of the Revolution, The Hidden Truths*, Charleston, S.C.: The History Press, 2007.

Shattuck, Lemuel, *A History of the Town of Concord, Middlesex County, Massachusetts From Its Earliest Settlement to 1832*, Boston: Russell, Odiorne, & Co., 1835.

Sidney, Margaret, *Old Concord Her Highways and Byways*, Revised and Enlarged Edition, Boston: D. Lothrop Co., 1893.

Swain, William, *Swain and Allied Families*, Milwaukee: Press of Swain & Tate, 1896,

Journals, Magazines, and Newspapers
"An Old House With Stories," [unnamed newspaper] (March 29, [1957]).

Websites
"Col. James Barrett Farm," *New England Landmarks for Save our Heritage*, Georgetown, MA, 2006, 9, (https://www.nps.gov/mima/learn/historyculture/upload/Barrett-Farm-HSR.pdf).

"Forge Village Historic District," *Westford Preservation Plan*, National Register (https://abbotmill.com/wp-content/uploads/NR_3.pdf)

Furness, Gregory T., "Crown Point, An Outline History," on *America's Historic Lakes*, (www.historiclakes.org/crown_pt.furness.html).

476

"Probate Records for Benjamin Barrett," *Probate Records 1648--1924 (Middlesex County, Massachusetts)*; Author: *Massachusetts. Probate Court (Middlesex County)*; Probate Place: *Middlesex, Massachusetts,* images. From: Ancestry.com: *Massachusetts, Wills and Probate Records, 1635-1991* [database on-line]. Provo, UT: Ancestry.com Operations, Inc., 2015,
(https://search.ancestry.com/cgi-bin/sse.dll?indiv=1&dbid=9069&h=2803800&tid=&pid=&usePUB=true &_phsrc=sdL173&_phstart=successSource).

Manuscripts
Shattuck, Lemuel, "Notes, Interview of Mrs. Peter Barrett," November 3, 1831, loose notes, *Lemuel Shattuck Papers*, Folder 46, Box 2, New England Historical and Genealogical Society, Boston.

Van Valkenburgh, Jim, "Charles Barrett Sr., His Life and Times," unpublished paper delivered before the New Ipswich Historical Society, September 14, 1989, in honor of Charles Barrett's 250th birthday.

Chapter Six – Soldiers, Survival, Sorrow

Books
Baker, James R., *Bushwhackers! A Civil War History of Vernon County Missouri*, Kindle edition, 2013.

Blackmar, Frank, ed., *Kansas, a Cyclopedia of State History*, I, Chicago, Standard Publishing Co, 1912.

Bird, Roy, *Civil War in Kansas*, Gretna, LA: Pelican, 2004.

Board for Certification of Genealogists, *Genealogy Standards*, 50th anniversary edition, Ancestry.com: Washington, DC, 2014.

Brophy, Patrick, *Bushwhackers of the Border*, VI, Nevada, Mo, Vernon County Historical Society, 1980.

Conard, Howard L, ed., *Encyclopedia of the History of Missouri*, 6, St. Louis: The Southern History Company, 1901.

Fry, Alice L., *Following The Fifth Kansas Cavalry, The Letters*, self-published, 1998.

Fry, Alice L., *Following the Fifth Kansas Cavalry, The Roster*, Independence, Mo.: Two Trails Publishing, 1998.

Publishing Co, 1912.

McPherson, James, *Battle Cry of Freedom*, New York: Oxford, 1988.

Mills, Elizabeth Shown, *Evidence Explained: Citing History Sources from Artifacts to Cyberspace*, 3rd ed., Baltimore: Genealogical Publishing Co., 2017.

Oliva, Leo E., *Fort Scott Courage and Conflict on the Border*, Topeka, Kansas State Historical Society, 1984.

Quammen, David, *The Tangled Tree, a Radical New History of Life*, New York: Simon & Schuster, 2018.

Robley, T. F., *History of Bourbon County, Kansas, to the close of 1865*, Ft. Scott, Ks: Monitor Book and Printing, 1894.

Scudder, Lt. Col. T. W., "The 5th Kansas Cavalry," in   Lt. Col. T. W. Scudder, "Military History of the Fifth Kansas Volunteer Cavalry," published in *Report of the Adjutant General of the State of Kansas, 1861-'65*, Topeka, Kansas: 1896 reprint, found on
www.arkansastoothpick.com/2007/12/civil-war-arkansas-5th   -kansas-cavalry-a-history/,
and included in Alice Fry, *Following the Fifth Kansas Cavalry, The Roster*, Independence, MO: Two Trails Publishing, 1998.

Supplement to the Officials Records of the Union and Confederate Armies, vol. 1, 246, September 4, 1861 account of Col. John T. Hughes., Wilmington, N.C: Broadfoot, 1994.

Supplement to the Official Records of the Union and Confederate Armies, Part II – Records of Events, vol 21, Serial No 33, Wilmington, NC: Broadfoot Publishing Co, 1996.

Schrantz, Ward L., *Jasper County, Missouri in the Civil War*, Carthage, Mo: The Carthage Press, 1923.

Report from Col. Powell Clayton, April 27, 1864, *The War of the Rebellion: A Compilation of the official Records of the Union and*

Confederate Armies, Washington: Government Printing Office, 1880-1901, Series I, vol. 34, pt. 2, 665.

Report of Lt. Col. Francis Drake, April 25, 1864, part 1, *The War of the Rebellion: A Compilation of the official Records of the Union and Confederate Armies*, Washington: Government Printing Office, 1880-1901, Series I, vol. 34, 712-713

Wood, Larry, *The Civil War on the Lower Kansas-Missouri Border*, Joplin, Mo: Hickory Press, 2000.

Journals, Magazines, and Newspapers
Kohl, Rhonda M., "Raising Thunder with the Secesh: Powell Clayton's Federal Cavalry at Taylor's Creek and Mount Vernon, Arkansas, May 11, 1863," *The Arkansas Historical Quarterly* 64 (Summer 2005).

Richards, Don, "The Engagement at Marks' Mills," *The Arkansas Historical Quarterly* 19:1 (Spring, 1960).

"The March of the Fifth Kansas Through Arkansas, Helena, Ark. July 14, 1862," *The Conservative*, newspaper, (July 26, 1862), in Fry, 31-33.

Websites
"Action at Marks' Mills, *The Encyclopedia of Arkansas History & Culture*, (http://www.encyclopediaofarkansas.net/encyclopedia/entry-detail.aspx?entryID=3222), accessed December 14, 2015.

Cutler, William G., *History of the State of Kansas*, "State History, Part 5, Fifth Regiment Kansas Volunteer Cavalry," (www.kancoll.org/books/cutler/sthist/milrec-p5.html), accessed on December 21, 2015.

"Formations and Ranks in Civil War Units," *Military Records Online*, www.angelfire.com/wv/wasec5/formations.html, accessed Dec. 19, 2015.

"Skirmishes at Taylor's Creek and Mount Vernon," *The Encyclopedia of Arkansas History & Culture*, (http://www.encyclopediaofarkansas.net/encyclopedia/entry-detail.aspx?entryID=3222), accessed December 19, 2015.

Documents

Kansas Adjutant General's Office, *Descriptive Roll, Fifth Regiment, Cavalry, Kansas Civil War Volunteers*, volume 4, 1861-1863, 38, image,

Kansas Historical Society, "Kansas Memory," Item Number: 227659, Call Number: Microfilm: AR 115, item 4 KSHS Identifier: DaRT ID: 227659, (https://www.kansasmemory.org/item/227659/page/38).

Kansas State Historical Society; Topeka, Kansas; *1865 Kansas Territory Census*; "Susanna Moyer," page 68, penned, dwelling 472, Roll: *ks1865_2*; Line: *12*. From: Ancestry.com. *Kansas State Census Collection, 1855-1925* [database on-line]. Provo, UT, USA: Ancestry.com Operations, Inc., 2009.

Missouri, Vernon County, *1860 U.S. Census*, population schedule, Little Osage page 99 (penned), dwellings 717, 718, and 732. From Ancestry.com: *1860*; Census Place: *Little Osage, Vernon, Missouri*; Roll: *M653_659*; Page: *99*; Family History Library Film: *803659*

Missouri, Vernon County, Deed Records, dated July 17, 1857, for purchase of 200 acres by Chester Lent from John Waldrop, copy in my possession.

Ohio, Holmes County, *1830 U.S. Census*, Salt Creek, (penned). From Ancestry.com: Year: *1830*; Census Place: *Salt Creek, Holmes, Ohio;* Roll: *64* page *577*, FHL *film 0337944.*

"Probate Records for Chester Lent," loose, Probate Records for Vernon County, Missouri, located in the Bushwhacker Museum, Nevada, Mo.

Vermont, Franklin County, *1810 U.S. Census*, Highgate, (penned). From Ancestry.com: Year: *1810*; Census Place: *Highgate, Franklin, Vermont;* Series *M19;* Roll: *133* page *303*, FHL *film 0218668.*

Manuscripts

Cleverley, Margie and Lavelle Cox Hogg correspondence, in my possession.

Cleverley, Margie and Ora Lent correspondence, in my possession.

Lent, Peggy Ann, "Lent Family Histories," written at various dates, copies in my possession.

Marsh, Freda F., "Robison Lent and the LENT family," family history written in 1963.

Diaries and Letters
Creitz, Capt. William, "Diary," printed in Alice L. Fry, *Following The Fifth Kansas Cavalry, The Letters*, self-published, 1998.

Flanders, Priv. George E. to "Dear Brother" [William Flanders], letter, August 2, 1862, printed in Fry, *Following The Fifth Kansas Cavalry, The Letters*, self-published, 1998.

Flanders, Priv. George E. to "Mother," letter, October 16, 1862, in Fry, *Following The Fifth Kansas Cavalry, The Letters*, self-published, 1998.

Flanders, George E. to "Dear Brother" [William Flanders], letter, November 2, 1862, in Fry, *Following The Fifth Kansas Cavalry, The Letters*, self-published, 1998.

Flanders, Priv. George E. to "Dear Father," letter, January 3, 1864, in Fry, *Following The Fifth Kansas Cavalry, The Letters*, self-published, 1998.

Flanders, Priv. George E. to "Dear Father," letter, March 14, 1864, in Fry, *Following The Fifth Kansas Cavalry, The Letters*, self-published, 1998.

Parmenter, Richard, to Mary Elizabeth Lent, letter, February 28, 1862, photocopy in my possession.

Trego, Alice M. to Lt. Joseph Trego, letter July 28, 1864, printed in Fry, *Following The Fifth Kansas Cavalry, The Letters*, self-published, 1998.

Trego, Alice M. to Lt. Joseph Trego, letter October 11, 1864, in Fry, *Following The Fifth Kansas Cavalry, The Letters*, self-published, 1998.

Trego, Mary to Alice M. Trego, letter, August 7, 1864, printed in Fry, *Following The Fifth Kansas Cavalry, The Letters*, self-published, 1998.

Trego, Lt. Joseph to "My Dear Little Wife," [Alice M. Trego], letter, Jan. 24, 1864, in Fry, *Following The Fifth Kansas Cavalry, The Letters*, self-published, 1998.

Chapter Seven – Promised Land

Books

Adams, Ethel Rose Howard Adams and Elias Harris, *A Map and Journal Story of the Joseph Howard Family and Their Journey to Utah*, self-published, 2014.

"Amelia Eliza Slade Bennion," Carol Cornwall Madsen, ed., *Journey to Zion*, Salt Lake City: Deseret Book, 1992.

Arrington, Leonard, *Great Basin Kingdom*, Lincoln: University of Nebraska Press, 1966.

Barker, Inez Foy, *The Joseph Howard Family Journeys 1861 and 1864 from Birmingham, England to the Great Salt Lake Valley via Sail, Rail, and Overland Trail*, self-published, available on "Joseph Howard," *FamilySearch*.

Bryson, Bill, *At Home*, Kindle edition, New York: Doubleday, 2010.

Cornwall, J. Spencer, *Stories of our Mormon Hymns*, Salt Lake City: Deseret Book, 1963.

Dickens, Charles, *The Uncommercial Traveller*, vol 4, *The Works of Charles Dickens*, New York, n.d.

Driscoll, John W., *The Joseph Howard Family*, Blackfoot, ID: Self-published, June 1998.

"John Shelton Howard," Daughters of the Utah Pioneers, *Pioneer Pathways*, Salt Lake City: Talon, 2005.

Marcy, Randolph B., *The Prairie Traveler, A Handbook for Overland Expeditions*, New York: Skyhorse, 2014, reprint of 1859 original.

The Perpetual Emigrating Fund, *Names of Persons and Sureties Indebted to the Perpetual Emigrating Fund Company from 1850 to 1877 inclusive*, Salt Lake City, 1877.

Plewe, Brandon S., ed., *Mapping Mormonism, An Atlas of Latter-day Saint History*, Provo, UT: BYU Press, 2012.

Sharpe, Michael, *Tracing your Birmingham Ancestors, A Guide for Family & Local Historians*, Kindle edition, Barnsley, So. Yorkshire: Pen Sword Books Ltd., 2015.

Svejda, George, *Castle Garden as an Immigrant Depot, 1855-1890*, US National Park Service, 1968.

The Historical Guide to North American Railroads, 3rd ed., Waukesha, WI, Kalmbach Books, 2014.

Thomson, David, *England in the Nineteenth Century*, New York: Penguin, 1982.

Journals, Magazines, and Newspapers Hulmston, John K., "Mormon Immigration in the 1860s: The Story of the Church Trains," *Utah Historical Quarterly* 58:1 (Winter 1990).

Kimball, Stanley B., "A Forgotten Mormon Trail and Settlements," *The Ensign* (February 1980).

Merrit, George K., and Richard Jensen, "Statistical Profile" *The Ensign* (July 1987).

Tobler, Douglas, "Truth Prevailing: The Significance of the Nineteenth-Century LDS Experience in Britain" *The Ensign* (July 1987).

Websites
Cannon, George Q., *Journal 1864*,
(https://churchhistorianspress.org/george-q-cannon/1860s/1864/05-1864).

"Death of John M. Kay, *Latter-day Saints' Millennial Star*, (November 19, 1864),
(https://history.churchofjesuschrist.org/overlandtravel/sources/9291/death-of-elder-john-m-kay-latter-day-saints-millennial-star-19-nov-1864-750).

England, Warwickshire, 1861 census of England, Aston, Warwickshire. Ancestry.com. *1861 England Census* [database on-line]. Provo, UT, USA: Ancestry.com Operations Inc, 2005.

Brigham Young University in collaboration with the Church of Jesus Christ of Latter-day Saints, *Saints by Sea, Latter-day Saint Immigration to America*, "London-New York, 3 June 1864 – 19 July 1874," (https://saintsbysea.lib.byu.edu/mii/voyage/169?netherlands=on&mii=on &sweden=on&keywords=Hudson&scandinavia=on&europe=on).
Saints by Sea is a compilation of diaries, autobiographies, newspaper articles, and other artifacts from people traveling from Wyoming, Nebraska, to Salt Lake City, Utah, with the Joseph and Ann Howard family.
— Aveson, Mary Ann Rawlings, "Reminiscence," Glady Rawlings Lemmon, *A History of the Richard Rawlings Family: Ancestors— Descendants*.
— Bird, Harriet, *Autobiography*.
— General Voyage Notes.
— Jenson, Andrew, *Church Chronology*, 2nd edition, Salt Lake City: Deseret News Company, 1899.
— Kay, John M. to George Q. Cannon, July 19, 1864, published *in Latter-day Saints' Millennial Star*, 26:34 (August 20, 1864), 539- 542.
— Kay, John M. to George Q. Cannon, June 8, 1864 published *in Latter-day Saints' Millennial Star*, 26:26 (June 25, 1864), 414-415.
— McCune, Michael, *Diary*.
— Nielsen, Peder Christian, *Journal*, from "London-New York, 3 June 1864 – 19 July 1874."
— "Our Immigration," *Deseret News* (14 Sep. 1864), 400.
— Smith, John Lyman, *Autobiography and Journals*, from "London- New York, 3 June 1864 - 19 July 1874.
— Smith, John L., *Journal*.
— Sutton, James T., *Autobiography*, Kate B. Carter. ed.. *Our Pioneer Heritage*, XVII, Salt Lake City: Daughters of the Utah Pioneers, 1974.
— Symons, Charles William, "Autobiography."

— Webb, Mary Ann Ward, "The History of Mary Ann Ward Webb and Her Diary of the Journey to Utah (1864)," in Robert R. King and Kay Atkinson King, *Mary Ann Webb: Her Life and Ancestry,* McLean, Virginia: America Society for Genealogy and Family History, 1996.

Measuring Worth Foundation, *Measuring Worth,* "Exchange Rates between the U.S. Dollar and Forty One Currencies," (http://measuringworth.com/datasets/exchangeglobal/result.php?year_so urce=1791&year_result=2007&countryE%5B%5D=United+Kingdom).

"Michigan Civil War History," *American Civil War Homepage,* (http://thomaslegion.net/americancivilwar/michigancivilwarhistory.html.

The Church of Jesus Christ of Latter-day Saints, *Pioneer Database,* "William Hyde Company (1864)," (https://history.churchofjesuschrist.org/overlandtravel/companies/166/wil liam-hyde-company). *Pioneer Database* is a compilation of diaries, autobiographies, newspaper articles, and other original artifacts from people traveling from London, England, to Wyoming, Nebraska, in the same company as the Joseph and Ann Howard family.
— Aveson, Mary Ann Rawlings, *Reminiscences,* in, Comp., *A History of the Richard Rawlings Family: Ancestors-Descendants,* 1986, 98-101.
— "Emma Howard Corbridge."
— Fletcher, Charles Eugene, *Autobiography,* 1911.
— Gerber, John T., *Journal.*
— "Home Items: Arrivals," *Deseret News* (2 Nov 1864).
—Hyde, William, *William Hyde Journal,* circa 1868-1873.
—Smith, Jesse N., *Autobiography and Journal, 1855.*
—Smith, John Lyman, *Diary* in John Lyman Smith Papers, 1845-1875, II, 102-117.
—Sutton, James T., *Reminiscences,* 2-4.

"Wages and Cost of Living in the Victorian Era," *The Victorian Web,* (http://www.victorianweb.org/economics/wages2.html).

Manuscripts
Howard, Joseph and Ann to Thomas and William Howard, February 20, 1862, handwritten, photocopy in my own files and a in Driscoll, 4.

Chapter Eight – "What was your Name in the States?"

Books
A Historical and Biographical Record of the Territory of Arizona, Chicago: McFarland & Poole, 1896.

Adams, Col. Gerald M., *The Post Near Cheyenne, A History of Fort D. A. Russell, 1867-1930*, Boulder, CO: Pruett Publishing, 1989.

Back to Backs Birmingham, Rotherham, UK: National Trust, 2004.

Bain, David Haward, *The Old Iron Road, An Epic of Rails, Roads, and the Urge to Go West*, New York: Viking, 2004.

Cleverley, J. Michael, "The Development of an Urban Pattern," Richard D. Poll, et al, eds., *Utah's History*, Provo, UT: Brigham Young University Press, 1978.

Chun, Clayton K S, *US Army in the Plains Indian Wars 1865-91*, Osceola, WI: Osprey, 2004.

Lubetkin, M. John, *Jay Cooke's Gamble, The Northern Pacific Railroad, the Sioux, and the Panic of 1873*, Kindle edition, Norman, OK: Univ. of Oklahoma Press, 2014.

May, Dean L., "Towards a Dependent Commonwealth," Richard D. Poll, et al, eds., *Utah's History*, Provo, UT: Brigham Young University Press, 1978.

Perpetual Emigrating Fund, *Names of Persons and Sureties Indebted to the Perpetual Emigrating Fund Company from 1850 to 1877 inclusive*, Salt Lake City: Star Book, 1877.

Peterson, Charles S., *Take Up Your Mission*, Tucson, AZ: Univ. of Arizona Press, 1973.

Sharpe, Michael, *Tracing your Birmingham Ancestors, A Guide for Family & Local Historians*, Barnsley South Yorkshire: Pen Sword Books Ltd, 2015,

Slaughter, Linda Warfel, *Fortress to Farm or Twenty-three Years on the Frontier*, Hazel Eastman, ed., New York: Exposition Press, 1972. The piece first appeared in *The Bismarck Tribune* and was later published in Anton Gartner, *History of Fort Rice North Dakota*, (1964).

Tanner, George and J. Morris Richards, *Colonization on the Little Colorado: The Richard City Region*, Flagstaff, AZ: Northland Press, 1977.

The Historical Guide to North American Railroads, 3rd ed., Waukesha, WI: Kalmbach, 2014.

Journals, Magazines, and Newspapers
American Ancestors, "Serendipity in Genealogy," *The Weekly Genealogist*, 19:59, Whole 832, (February 22, 2017).

"A Search for the Border Ruffian," *Outing and The Wheelman, An Illustrated Monthly Magazine of Recreation* V (October 1884-March 1885), 38.

Bishop, M. Guy, "Building Railroads for the Kingdom: The Career of John W. Young, 1867-91," *Utah Historical Quarterly* 48:1 (Winter 1980), 68-71.

"Obituary for Mary Ann Wilson," *Deseret News* (November 26, 1889), 5.

Lubetkin, M. John, "The Northern Pacific Railroad's 1872 Western Yellowstone Surveying Expedition," *Montana, The Magazine of Western History*, 56:2 (Summer, 2006).

Websites
Ancestry.com. *New York, Passenger and Crew Lists (including Castle Garden and Ellis Island), 1820-1957* [database on-line]. Provo, UT, USA: Ancestry.com Operations, Inc., 2010, (https://search.ancestry.com/cgi-

bin/sse.dll?indiv=1&dbid=7488&h=5262078&tid=&pid=&usePUB=true
&_phsrc=sdL215&_phstart=successSource).

Ancestry.com, "Meagry Family History,"
(https://www.ancestry.com/name-origin?surname=meagry).

Coombs, Isaiah M., *Diary*, Jan. 23, 31, Feb 4-11, 1876, Brigham Young
University in collaboration with the Church of Jesus Christ of Latter-day
Saints, *Saints by Sea, Latter-day Saint Immigration to America*,
"Liverpool-New York, 19 January 1876-1 February 1876,"
(https://saintsbysea.lib.byu.edu/mii/account/948?netherlands=on&mii=o
n&sweden=on&keywords=montana&scandinavia=on&europe=on).
Saints by Sea is a compilation of diaries, autobiographies, newspaper
articles, and other artifacts from people traveling from Wyoming,
Nebraska, to Salt Lake City, Utah, with the Joseph and Ann Howard
family

Dobson, G. B., *Wyoming Trails and Tales*,
(http://www.wyomingtalesandtrails.com/index.html)
    — "Cheyenne, Photos,"
        (http://www.wyomingtalesandtrails.com/cheyenne70s.html),
        accessed 9 February 2017.
    — "Fort Russell, Photos,"
        (http://www.wyomingtalesandtrails.com/cheyenne70s.html),
        accessed 9 February 2017.

Brigham Young University in collaboration with the Church of Jesus
Christ of Latter-day Saints, *Saints by Sea, Latter-day Saint Immigration
to America*, "Liverpool-New York, 14 October 1875-26 October 1875,"
https://mormonmigration.lib.byu.edu/mii/voyage/111?mii=on&account=
on&query=Eli+Taylor&passenger=on&dateTo=26+Oct+1875&voyage=
on&scandinavia=on&sweden=on&netherlands=on&europe=on&dateFro
m=14+Oct+1875).
    — "A Compilation of General Voyage Notes."
    — "Eardley, B. to A Carrington" October 15, 1875.
    — "Eardley, B. to A Carrington" October 24, 1875.

UtahRails.net, (https://UtahRails.net),

— Strack, Don, "John W. Young's Railroads," updated June 28, 2018, accessed, March 18, 2020, (https://utahrails.net/utahrails/john-w-young.php).

— "Utah & Northern Railway, 1878-1889)," (https://utahrails.net/utahrails/utah-and-northern-ry-1878-1889.php), updated July 21, 2014, accessed, March 19, 2020

U.S. Army Center of Military History, (https://history.army.mil/)
— "Lineage and Honors Information, 8th Infantry Regiment," 19 March 2014, (https://history.army.mil/html/forcestruc/lineages/branches/inf/0008in.htm), accessed, March 1, 2020

— Wilson, Lt. Richard H., "Eighth Regiment of Infantry," (https://history.army.mil/books/R&H/R&H-8IN.htm), accessed March 16, 2020.

Manuscripts
"Family Bible" of Mary Ann Taylor Wilson, Photocopies of the Bible's family history pages are in my possession.

Cleverley, Margie Lea Leonardson, "Richard Joseph MaGuire Wilson," typed history of Richard MaGuire's life, 3. This is one of several typed histories that Margie compiled and is noted "Margie Lea Leonardson – C." A copy in my possession.

Cleverley, Margie Lea Leonardson, "Richard Joseph Wilson McGuire," still another of the family histories Margie wrote. This is distinguished from the others as "Margie Cleverley A." Copy in my possession.

Cleverley, Margie Lea Leonardson," Richard Joseph McGuire (Wilson)," another typed history of Richard McGuire. Copy in my possession.

Jewett, Bonita, "Bonita Jewett Family History," dated Feb. 26, 2000, copy in my possession.

Documents
Arizona: Territorial Census Records, 1864-1882, [database on-line], From: Ancestry.com Operations, Inc., 2016, "1882 Arizona Territorial Census, **Census Enumeration, Apache County, Arizona**," *Arizona,*

489

Territorial Census Records, 1864-1882, Arizona History and Archives Division, Phoenix, Arizona, entries 2175, 2176; (https://search.ancestry.com/cgi-bin/sse.dll?_phsrc=sdL258&_phstart=successSource&usePUBJs=true&indiv=1&dbid=61064&gsfn=Mary&gsln=Wilson&gsfn_x=NP_NN_NIC&gsln_x=NP_NN&msrpn_ftp=joseph%20city,%20navajo,%20arizona,%20usa&msrpn=67541&new=1&rank=1&uidh=aic&redir=false&gss=angs-d&pcat=35&fh=2&h=43303&recoff=&ml_rpos=3&queryId=6249f45d3adb42f495ce34b7eb40af43).

Arizona,   Voter   Registrations,   1866-1955 [database   on-line]. Ancestry.com, Provo, UT, USA: Ancestry.com Operations, Inc., 2016. Original data: Great Registers (of Voters). Arizona History and Archives Division, Phoenix, Arizona. (https://www.ancestry.com/interactive/60875/43146_542780-00750?pid=279368&backurl=https://search.ancestry.com/cgi-bin/sse.dll?_phsrc%3DsdL277%26_phstart%3DsuccessSource%26usePUBJs%3Dtrue%26indiv%3D1%26dbid%3D60875%26gsfn%3DRichard%26gsln%3DWilson%26gsfn_x%3DNN%26gsln_x%3DNN%26msydy%3D1882%26msypn_ftp%3Darizona,%2520usa%26msypn_ftp_x%3D1%26msypn%3D5%26msypn_x%3DPAS%26msbdy%3D1855%26msbdy_x%3D1%26msbdp%3D10%26msrdy%3D1882%26msrpn__ftp%3Darizona,%2520usa%26msrpn_ftp_x%3D1%26msrpn%3D5%26msrpn_x%3DPAS%26new%3D1%26rank%3D1%26uidh%3Daic%26redir%3Dfalse%26gss%3Dangs-d%26pcat%3D35%26fh%3D3%26h%3D279368%26recoff%3D%26ml_rpos%3D4%26queryId%3D629e926e73b19e882daae5e71f883b57&treeid=&personid=&hintid=&queryId=629e926e73b19e882daae5e71f883b57&usePUB=true&_phsrc=sdL277&_phstart=successSource&usePUBJs=true).

Idaho, Fremont County, *1900 Census*, Dubois; Page: *2*; (penned), dwelling 27, Enumeration District: *0052*; FHL microfilm: *1240232*. From Ancestry.com. *1900 United States Federal Census* [database on-line]. Provo, UT, USA: Ancestry.com Operations Inc, 2004.

Utah, Salt Lake, *1880 US Census,* South Cottonwood, Page *23;* (penned), dwelling number: *195,* Enumeration District: *057;* Roll: *1337,* From:

Ancestry.com, Tenth Census of the United States, 1880. (NARA microfilm publication T9, 1,454 rolls). Records of the Bureau of the Census, Record Group 29. National Archives, Washington, D.C.

England, Birmingham, 1861 Census of England, St. Thomas, p 26, Elizabeth Nicholls; image, Ancestry.com, accessed 26 March 2020, citing Class: *RG 9*; Piece: *2135*; Folio: *39*; Page: *26*; GSU roll: *542923*.

England, Birmingham, 1871 Census of England, Ladywood, p 30, Eli Taylor; image, Ancestry.com, accessed 26 March 2020, citing The National Archives; Kew, London, England; *1871 England Census*; Class: *RG10*; Piece: *3094*; Folio: *18*; Page: *30*; GSU roll: *839568*.

General Register Office, London, UK, "Certified Copy of an Entry of Marriage," Eli Taylor and Elizabeth Nichols, 24 March 1864, a photocopy is in my possession.

"Post Infirmary Records," Davids Island, New York Harbor, Reg. No. 491, Hos. No. 2412, Page 81, June 21, 1872, photocopy in my possession.

"Post Infirmary Records," Fort Russell, Wyo., Reg. No. 59, Hos. No. 5638, March 9, 1873, photocopy in my possession).

"Oath of Enlistment and Allegiance, Richard Joseph McGuire," Davids Island, New York, 20 January 1872, R.G. 94, National Archives and Record Service, photocopy in my possession.

Records of the Adjutant General's Office, 1780's-1917, "Muster Roll of Captain William Worth's," National Archives Record Group 94, Muster Rolls, Regular Army Organizations, Co K, 8th U.S. Infantry, February 28-April 30, 1873, copy in my possession.

8th Infantry Enlistment Papers "Oath of Enlistment and Allegiance," Richard Joseph McGuire, Co. K, R.G. 94, January 20, 1872, National Archives, Washington, D.C.

U.S. Army Continental Commands, 1821-1920, Department of Dakota, loose, National Archives, Washington, DC, RG 393 Field Records/Yellowstone Expedition, 1872-1873.

— Hancock, General Winfield Scott to Col. T. J. Crittenden, telegram, Aug. 19, 1872, "Letters and Telegrams Received, July 1872-Oct.1872," 1334, Box no. 1, RG 393.

— "General Order No. 4," July 22, 1872, and "Circular," Aug. 6, 1872, "General Orders Issued" and "Circulars Issued," July 1872-Aug.1872," 1334, Box no. 1.

— "8th Infantry Sick Roll," Camp no. 27, Aug. 24, 1872, "Special Order No. 9,", "General Orders Issued" and "Circulars Issued," July 1872-Aug.1872," 1334, Box no. 1.

— Ft. D. A. Russell, Wyo., 1872, "General Orders, Special Orders, & Orders," RG 393, vol. II, Box no. 4.

— "Special Order no. 9," "General Orders Issued" and "Circulars Issued," July 1872-Aug.1872," RG 393, 1334, Box no. 1.

— Stanley, Col. D. T., commander, 2nd Yellowstone Expedition, to O. D. Greene, Assistant Adjutant General, telegram, July 25, 1872, "Letters and Telegrams Received, July 1872-Oct.1872," 1334, Box no. 1.

Diaries and Letters

Brooks, The Hon. James to W. W. Belknap, Secretary of War, April 22, 1872. Photocopy in my possession.

Belknap, Secretary of War William to the Hon. James Brooks, May 3rd, 1872, and marked number 3567. Photocopy in my possession.

Evans, Fern Leonardson to Margie Cleverley, May 8, 1980, photocopy in my possession.

Chapter Nine – Homesick

Books

Alexander, Thomas G. and James B. Allen, *Mormons & Gentiles A History of Salt Lake City*, Boulder, CO: Pruett Publishing, 1984.

Camp, Sarah A. Howard, ed., "Pioneer Memories," Shelton Idaho Chapter of the Daughters of the Utah Pioneers (DUP), 1940.

Cleverley, J. Michael, "The Development of an Urban Pattern," Richard D. Poll et al, eds., *Utah's History*, Provo, UT: Brigham Young Univ. Press, 1978.

Daughters of the Utah Pioneers, *Pioneer Pathways*, 8, Salt Lake City: International Society Daughters of Utah Pioneers, 2006.

Jenson, Andrew, "John E. Johnson, Jr.," *History of the Scandinavian Mission*, Salt Lake City: Deseret, 1927.

Manuscripts
"Addendum to Matilda Ann Howard Johnson Personal history," probably written by daughters, n.d., photocopy in my possession.

Blaylock, Zina, "Matilda Ann Johnson," typewritten biography from an interview with Matilda Ann Howard Johnson during the summer of 1959, photocopy in my possession.

Cleverley, Margie Lea Leonardson, "Life in the 1890s," typewritten manuscript written in the late 1950s, photocopy in my possession.

Cleverley, Margie Lea Leonardson, "Life Sketch of Matilda Ann Howard Johnson," typewritten manuscript based on interviews with Matilda Johnson and delivered at her funeral on June 3, 1962.

Cleverley, Margie Lea Leonardson, "Jons Johnsson," typewritten personal history of John Johnson's father, "as given to her by Matilda Ann Howard Johnson in about 1952." Photocopy in my possession.

Johnson, Matilda Ann Howard, "Personal History," typewritten manuscript written in her own hand, undated but probably written during the 1950s. Photocopy of in my possession.

Johnson, Matilda Ann Howard, "LDS Family and Individual Record," handwritten data sheet of family history information, original in my possession.

Ludwig, Dee Ann, "The Old Home," written for the James Howard Family Reunion held in Thayne, Wyo. July 26-27, typewritten, photocopy in my possession.

Ludwig, Eugene C., "James Howard History," Sons of Utah Pioneers Library, submitted July 17, 1977.

Moore, Florence, "History of James Howard," by Florence Moore (granddaughter), 1945," typewritten, photocopy in my possession.

Moore, Florence and Mayme Woolley, "History of Matilda Ann Howard Johnson," typewritten history, undated, written by two of Tillie's daughters. Photocopy in my possession.

Moore, Florence Moore, "Life of my Father John Johnson," typewritten manuscript, undated, photocopy in my possession.

"Reminiscences of the John Johnson and Matilda Ann Howard Johnson Family, an unpublished collection of memories written by John and Matilda Johnson's children after her death, photocopy in my possession.

"Ship News," the *S/S Oscar II,* dated Thursday, November 21, 1918.

Skinner, Delsa Jane, "James and Betsy Jane Fackrell, Howard," typewritten manuscript photocopy in my possession.

Journals, Magazines, and Newspapers
"Death Summons John Johnson," obituary probably from the [Idaho Falls] *Post Register* (October 1934), from "John Johnson," *FamilySearch,* (https://www.familysearch.org/tree/person/memories/KWC1-H5L).

Johnson, J. L., "The Shelton Road," *The Rigby [Idaho] Star,* (October 4, 1973).

Websites

"John E. Johnson, Jr.," The Church of Jesus Christ of Latter-day Saints, *Missionary Database*, (https://history.lds.org/missionary/individual/john-johnson-jr-1867?lang+eng), accessed March 20, 2020.

Johnson, John, "Missionary Journal," *FamilySearch*, accessed March 1, 1916-August 12, 1918, (https://www.familysearch.org/library/books/records/item/613541-john-johnson-missionary-journal-sweden-mission-january-1916?viewer=1&offset=0#page=1&viewer=picture&o=info&n=0&q=).

Documents

"Application for Registration – Native Citizen," for John Johnson, U.S. Consulate, Malmo, Sweden, dated July 30, 1918, original in my possession.

Diaries and Letters

Johnson, John to Mayme Woolley, postcard, sent from Sweden undated.

Johnson, John to Mayme Johnson Woolley, Oct. 11, 1916.

Videos

Brigham Young University-Idaho, "Wagon Box Prophecy," Video production, 2006.

Chapter Ten – Two Rivers Join

Books

Cleverley, J. Michael, *Born a Soldier, the Times and Life of Larry Thorne*, Booksurge, 2008.

Goodrich, Austin, *Study in SISU: Finland's Fight for Independence*, New York: Ballantine, 1960.

Manuscripts

Heimala, Manne to Lempi Heimala, December 5, 1944, original in my possession.

Heimala, Manne to Aleksander Roos, November 24, 1944, original in my possession.

Heimala, Manne to Aleksander Roos, no date, November 1944, original in my possession.

Heimala, Manne to Lempi Heimala letter, December 7, 1944, original in my possession.

Heimala, Manne. Lahti, Finland. Interview by J. Michael Cleverley, 11 July 1984; tape and MP3 file privately held by author.

Epilogue – How the Odyssey Ends

Journals, Magazines, and Newspapers
Copeland, Libby, "Genealogy Provides the Strength to Persevere," *Psychology Today* (April 13, 2020). (https://www.psychologytoday.com/us/blog/the-lost-family/202004/genealogy-provides-the-strength-persevere), accessed April 14, 2020.

Feiler, Bruce, "The Stories That Bind Us," *This Life, The New York Times*, (March 15, 2015).

Genealogy: the Second Most Popular Hobby in the US?" *Ancestry.com*, (https://blogs.ancestry.com/cm/genealogy-second-most-popular-hobby-us/).

Hardy, Rebecca, "Why children need to know their family history," *The Guardian, US Edition* (January 14, 2017), (https://www.theguardian.com/lifeandstyle/2017/jan/14/children-family-histories-tales).

Rodriguez, Gregory, "How Genealogy Became Almost as Popular as Porn" *Time*, (May 30, 2014), (https://time.com/133811/how-genealogy-became-almost-as-popular-as-porn/).

Rodriguez, Gregory, "Roots of Genealogy Craze," *USA Today*, (May 12, 2014), (https://www.usatoday.com/story/opinion/2014/05/12/genealogy-americans-technology-roots-porn-websites-column/9019409/), accessed March 21, 2020.

"How Popular is Genealogy?" *GenealogyInTime Magazine*, (http://www.genealogyintime.com/articles/how-popular-is-genealogy-page01.html), accessed March 21, 2020.

Films
Christopher Nolan, *Memento*, film, Summit Entertainment and Team Todd, March 16, 2001.

Guggenheim, Davis, *From the Sky Down*, documentary film, Universal Music Group: 2011.

Index

500

504

505

Lent, Peggy, vii, 268, 270
Lent, Robison, 236, 241-2, 259, 264, 266, 269, 481
Lent, Sarah, 236, 279-80,
Lent, Susannah Frasure, 234-47, 259, 262-72, 277, 280-1
Leonardson Arthur, 75-6, 360
Leonardson Ranch Company, 76
Leonardson, Charles Wayne, 73, 355, 361-2, 364
Leonardson, Charles ("Charlie"), v, 72-7, 190
Leonardson, Ida May Dawley, 72-9, 82-8, 101, 108-9, 120, 123, 129, 134, 145, 151, 163
Leonardson, Mary Emma Wilson, 76, 356-60, 366
Letters, 276, 320
Lexington, Massachusetts, 177, 179, 192-5, 205-6, 208-10, 212, 216, 221-23, 226-7
Library of Virginia, 275
lightning, 74
Lisle, Thomas, *See* Bishop of Ely
Little Colorado River, 351, 353
Little Colorado Colony, 350-4
Little Osage River, 235, 239
Little Rock, Arkansas, 253-4, 258, 264-5
Littlefield, Caty, 172-3, 180
Liverpool, England, 287-8, 340, 365
livestock, 43, 100, 117, 120, 141, 159, 204, 236, 242, 309, 312, 326, 330, 332, 359
Local Collections, 369
Local Histories, 225
Locke, Urania, 224
Long Island, New York, 113, 118, 144, 148-9, 152, 328
Lord Chief Justice, 45
Lords of Gillingham, 68

magistrates, 95-6, 98-9, 101, 110-1, 119, 122, 141, 454
maiming, 139, 141
malaria ("ague" or "brain fever), 264
Manchester, England, 112, 135-6
Manhattan, New York, 102, 149, 295, 321
Maps: Old and New, 315
Mark's Mill, Arkansas, 260
Marmaduke, Gen. John, 256-8
Massachusetts Bay Colony, 80-2, 84, 90-2, 94, 96-7, 106, 111, 113, 132, 136, 183, 138-9
Massachusetts General Court, 198-204
Massachusetts Provincial Congress, 178, 192, 194, 198, 204
Massachusetts State House, 148
Massasoit, 83
Matilda of Flanders, 7-8, 11-36, 39, 48, 404, coronation, 18, 22, 23; son's rebellion, 23-25; sons, 23
Mayflower, 81, 89, 453
McGuire, Richard, *See* Wilson, Joseph Richard McGuire
meaning, 150, 197, 372, 442, 448-9, 457
media obsolescence, 80, 443
Medicine Lodge, Idaho, 73, 75
medicine, 87, 91, 105, 170
Memories and Family Histories, 403
Miantonomi, 84, 97-8, 114, 118, 124-5, 153
Middlesex County, Massachusetts, 191, 209
Miles, Capt. Charles, 202, 222
Miles, Ruth Barrett, 218
Military Independent Company, *See* Kentish Guards

511

513

Footnotes

Prologue – The Inheritance

[1] Steve Olson, "The Royal We," *The Atlantic Monthly*, 62 (May 2002), 62.

Chapter One – The Wife of a Conqueror

[1] An account of Duke William's rough courting is found in *Chronicum Turonense*, quoted in Tracy Borman, *Queen of the Conqueror, The Life of Matilda, Wife of William I*, (New York: Random House, 2011), 35.

[2] Borman, 43-44.

[3] Michel Hourquet, et. al., *William the Conqueror*, (Bayeux, France: OREP Editions, 2015) 47. Annie Fettu, *Queen Matilda*, (Bayeux, France: OREP Editions, 2016), 7.

[4] Fettu, 7. Orderic Vitalis, *Gesta Regum Anglorum*, in Borman, 17. Borman, xxxi, 174.

[5] William of Malmesbury, Gesta Regum Anglorum, 477, in Borman, 29.

[6] Borman, 65.

[7] There has always been controversy over whether Edward the Confessor sent Archbishop Robert of Jumieges to designate Duke William of Normandy his heir. Norman chroniclers of the time claimed he did. Later Anglo-Saxon writers, who detested the Norman conquest, said he did not.

[8] If early English historians were unhappy with the idea that Edward the Confessor made William of Normandy his heir in 1051, they relentlessly rejected the Norman claim that Harold renewed the promise the day Harold knelt in William's court, as depicted in the Bayeux Tapestry. Whether or not the promise was made was obviously a politically charged issue that affected the legitimacy of William's Norman Conquest. Both sides naturally took opposing views. There is not enough evidence to prove it one way or the other, and it is not my purpose to resolve this age-old controversy, but it does seem strange that William would have needed to invent a justification for his conquest of England. Invaders, starting with the Anglo-Saxons, themselves, had for centuries attacked the Isles with little or no justification other than to assume its wealth and power. Credible justifications for aggression have not always been necessary in European history, before or since the Norman Conquest. I am persuaded to accept the Norman view. See Marc Morris, *The Norman Conquest, The Battle of Hastings, and the Fall of Anglo-Saxon England*, (New York: Pegasus, 2014), 69-70, 113-115.

[9] Morris, 133 ff.

[10] William of Poitiers, *Gesta Guillelmi*, 33, in Borman, 122.

[11] Borman, xxx, 99-100, 121-122, 131. Fettu, 12.

[12] Orderic Vitalis, *Ecclesiastical History* II, 125, quoted in Borman, 105-107.

[13] Fettu, 13. Borman, 111-113, 133-134. Morris, 216.

[14] Fettu, 17-18.

[15] Orderic Vitalis, *Ecclesiastical History*, 3, in Borman, 191.

[16] Vitalis, in Borman, 196.

[17] Vitalis, 103, in Borman, 197.

[18] Borman, 216.

[19] Borman 216-218. Fettu 26-27.

[20] Borman 219. Fettu, 18-19.

[21] Patrick Q. Mason, *Planted, Belief and Belonging in an Age of Doubt*, (Salt Lake City: Deseret Book, 2015), 71.

[22] L .P. Hartley, *The Go-Between*, (New York: New York Review Books Classics, 2002), 17.

Chapter Two – Two Knights and a Swordsman

[1] Boketon was a place name derived from the deer, the "bucks," that roamed the land the family received in the reign of King John (1203 AD) for their manorial lordship. The area was "memorable for the excellency of its soil and situation, as a spacious and delightful Green." Hence the later surname "Greene" is an allusion to the Boketon estate. Robert Halstead, *Succinct Genealogies of the Noble and Ancient Houses*, (London: 1685), 151. George Baker, *The History of Antiquities of the County of Northampton*, I, (London: John Bowyer Nicols & son, 1822-1830), 31-33. George Sears Greene, T*he Greenes of Rhode Island, with Historical Records of English Ancestry, 1534-1902*, (New York: 1902), 5.

[2] Halstead, 151. "Robert Halstead" was a pseudonym for the Henry Mordaunt, the 2nd Earl of Peterborough.

[3] Mabel Thacher Rosemary Washborn, "Loveland Ancestry," *The Journal of American History*, 12:4 (October 1918), 525. Washburn was the Journal's Genealogical editor. Knights had the title of "Sir," which was an abbreviated form of "Messire," French for "my lord."

[4] For a survey of Henry Greene's ancestry and descendants, see George Sears Greene, 22-29, and Frank Allaben, "Green of Greens-Norton," *The Journal of American History*, 12:2 (April 1918), 243. George Baker, 31-33.

[5] In April 1331 Henry, in the company of William Shareshull, Robert Sadington, and Roger Hillary, witnessed an indenture. Henry Summerson, "Sir Henry Green," *Oxford Dictionary of National Biography*, https://www.oxforddnb.com/. See Greene Genealogical Chart in Baker.

[6] Summerson. The surname "Greene," was variously spelled Grene and Green in old records.

[7] Alison Weir, *The Wars of the Roses*, Kindle edition, (New York: Ballantine, 1995), location 507. See Mortimer, *The Perfect King, The Life of Edward III Father of the English Nation*, (London: Vintage, 2008), 293 ff, 330-331, and especially 395-397 for an excellent summary of Edward III's many accomplishments.

[8] The *Oxford Dictionary of National Biography* states Henry was married twice. The oldest son, Thomas, was from his first wife, a woman named Amabilia, and the other children were Catherine's. This contrasts with Halstead's and some other genealogies that have Catherine as the mother of all. The basis for the *Oxford Dictionary's* different marriage information is not clear, and I suspect that it may be incorrect, another case where we suddenly pass through patch of fog rolling off the hills of time.

[9] Halstead, 83, 87. 157. George Sears Greene lists an additional son, Richard, who had no children and perhaps died in childhood, 6, 24.

[10] Words of the pope's physician, Guy de Chauliac, quoted in Ian Mortimer, *The Time Traveler's Guide to Elizabethan England*, (New York: Penguin, 2014), 201-202.

[11] Summerson. Mortimer, *Perfect King*, 318-319, 326.

[12] To distinguish between the two Sir Henrys, father and son, hereafter the elder will be referred to as Henry Sr. and the younger, Henry Jr.

[13] Sir Leslie Stephen, ed., "Sir Henry Green," *The Dictionary of National Biography*, (London: Oxford Univ. Press, 1917), . 12, 486-487, claims that Sir Henry Greene's home was on Silver Street, Cripplegate, London.

[14] Some genealogy histories have Henry Jr. born in 1352. However, the biography found in the quite thorough and authoritative *History of Parliament*, gives 1347 for the year of his birth. This earlier date seems to make more sense, given his marriage, inheritance, and the history surrounding his father's death in 1369. See "Green, Sir Henry (1347-1399)," *The History of Parliament: the House of Commons 1386-1421*,
 http://www.historyofparliamentonline.org/volume/1386-1421/member/green-sir-henry-1347-1399.

[15] "Green, Sir Henry," *The History of Parliament*...

[16] Maud was heiress to all of Sir Thomas Mauduit's many estates. Upon his father's death, Henry inherited not only the Drayton estate but also properties in Great Houghton (Northamptonshire), the manors of Chalton (Bedordshire), and Woolstone, Wavedon, and Emberton (Buckinghamshire}. Maud's inheritance included the lordships of Werminster, Westbury, Grately, Samborne, Dychurch, Buckworth, and more. "Green, Sir Henry," *The History of Parliament*... Halstead, 121.

[17] Allison Weir, *The Wars of the Roses*, Kindle edition, (Ballantine: New York, 1995), location 635.

[18] Quoted in Sydney Armitage-Smith, *John of Gaunt*, Kindle edition, (Archibald Constable & Co., Ltd, 1904), locations 3957-3994.

[19] At least one historian has claimed that neither King Richard nor John of Gaunt had foreknowledge of what happened the night of Friar John Latimer's torture and death. That is a little difficult to accept. They were the ones most interested in identifying the party or parties behind Latimer's false accusations, and the

torturers worked for them. See Sydney Armitage-Smith, locations 3957-3994. www.shakespeareandhistory.com/john-of-gaunt.php.
Thomas Walsingham, *Historia Anglicana*, II. Henry Thomas Riley, ed., *Chronica Monasterii S. Albani*, (London: Longman, Green, Longman, Roberts, and Green, 1864), 114. "Green, Sir Henry," *The History of Parliament...*   Raphaell Holinshed, *Chronicles of England, Scotland, and Ireland*, (1577) in a reprint, Raphaell Holinshed, *Chronicles of England Scotland and Ireland*, II, (London: J. Johnson et. al, 1807), 763, describes the torture Latimer endured in grisly detail, "...putting a cord about his necke, tied the other end about his priuie members, & after hanging him up from the ground, laid a stone upon his bellie, with the weight wherof and peise of his bodie withall, he was strangled and tormented, so as he verie backe bone burst in sunder therewith, besides the straining of his priuie parts: thus with three kind of tormentings he ended his wretched life."
[20] Michael Bennett, *Richard II, and the Revolution of 1399*, (Stroud, UK: Sutton, 1999), 88, 96. Weir, location 660, 712. According to "Green, Sir Henry (1347-1399)," *The History of Parliament*, the award from the King was a windfall for Sir Henry: manors in Wiltshire and Warwickshire as well as manors of Cosgrove and Preston Capes in Northamptonshire.
[21] Weir, location 751. "Green, Sir Henry (1347-1399)," "Green, Sir Henry (1347-1399)," *The History of Parliament*. Bennett, 119.
[22] Weir, locations 751-777. Holinshed, 853.
[23] Holinshed, 853-854. "Green, Sir Henry (1347-1399)," *The History of Parliament*. The poet called his piece, "Richard the Redeless." Bennett, 123.
[24] Lora Sarah Nichols La Mance, *The Greene Family and its Branches from A.D. 861 to A.D. 1904*, (Floral Park, NY: Mayflower Publishing Co., 1904).
[25] Bruce Bailey, *Drayton House*, (Drayton House, Northamptonshire, 1990). Halstead, 96-97.
[26] Germaine's unsuccessful micromanagement of the war in the Colonies was widely criticized in London during and after the war. See John Ferling, *Almost a Miracle, The American Victory in the War of Independence*, (New York: Oxford Univ. Press, 2007), 265-267, 566.
[27] La Mance, pp 35-36..
[28] Halstead,154. *The History of Parliament: the House of Commons 1386-1421*, www.historyofparliamentonline.org/volume/1386-1421/member/green-sir-henry-134. Halstead lists only five children from Sir Henry and Lady Maud, and omits the son Thomas that appears in many other genealogies such as those of La Mance and George Sears Greene. The authoritative *History of Parliament Online* entry for Ralph claims that Ralph had five siblings, six in all, thus making way for Thomas. La Mance, 33, see footnote.
[29] *The History of Parliament: the House of Commons 1386-1421*, www.historyofparliamentonline.org/volume/1386-1421/member/green-sir-henry-134. This Thomas is not to be confused with his father's brother, Thomas, who founded the Greenes Norton line of Greenes.

[30] La Mance, 34-37.

[31] Weir, *The Princes in the Tower*, (New York: Ballantine, 1992), 245. Sir Thomas More, *History of King Richard III*, ed. by J. Rawson Lumby, (London: Cambridge University Press, 1883), 81.

[32] Sir Thomas More, 81.

[33] Allison Weir, *The Princes...*, 147-148, 150, 156-157.

[34] Horatio Somersby, *The Greene Family in England and America: With Pedigrees*, (Boston: 1901), 91. G. Andrews Moriarty, "Notes on the Greene and Turner Letters," *Rhode Island History*, 6:1 (July 1947), 83.

[35] Walter A Metcalfe, *Knights Banneret, Knights of the Bath, and Knights Bachelor*, (London: Mitchell and Hughes, 1885), 3. Wm. A. Shaw, *The Knights of England, A Complete Record from the Earliest Time to the Present Day of the Knights of all the Orders of Chivalry in England, Scotland, and Ireland and of Knights Bachelors*, (London: Sherratt and Hughes, 1906), 14, 30, 163, 98.

[36] With the lack of concrete information regarding John the Fugitive's birth and death, the connection between the Greens of Bowridge Hill and the Greenes of Northamptonshire is not cast in iron if indeed the link must come through him. This has troubled some genealogists such as Moriarty (Andrews Moriarty, "Notes on the Greene and Turner Letters," *Rhode Island History*, 6:1 (July 1947)) who claims that even though generations of genealogists have accepted that the Gillingham Greenes were a branch of the Northampton Greenes, the connection is based on a "peculiar" pedigree made by Horatio Somersby. Somersby was an American who in the 19th century lived about 20 years in England and did considerable research on the Greene family. His work was published in *The Greene Family in England and America: With Pedigrees* and was accepted by La Mance. Moriarty outspokenly claims that Somersby's connection of the two families is "without one iota of truth and with much against it" (82-83), although he does not offer any of his own *truth* against it. Somersby's work in fact is not error-free, nor, for that matter, are many of the genealogies we usually accept totally error-free, but there is evidence that he did some proper research when you look at the sources he used and the details he provides. For example, it is clear he, too, found and used Halstead's extensive work on the Greene family. Unfortunately, hard and firm links between generations are not always as common in genealogy as we would like. So many of them are based, at some level or another, on our best judgments.

Sears (George Sears Greene, T*he Greenes of Rhode Island, with Historical Records of English Ancestry, 1534-1902)* in his exhaustive study of the family says he thinks the two families are the same (33-35). And so do I. For one thing, the families displayed an almost identical coat of arms, something not lightly done during the reigns of Henry VIII and Elizabeth I, unless the coats are from the same family. Even the early Rhode Island family used the Northampton family's coat of arms. John Greene, Deputy Governor of Rhode Island, in 1692 wrote a letter to one of the Secretaries of State to the Privy Council in London where he sealed the envelope with a red wax coat of arms displaying the three bucks of the Northamptonshire Greenes' coat of arms. (George Sears Greene, 49). For another, La Mance, who did her own research in England, records that in the late 1800's she interviewed an English genealogist, Henry K. Elliott, whose family had lived 300 years in the Greenes' family town of Greene's Norton. She wrote that Elliott told her that the Northampton Greene family had always accepted the Gillingham Greenes as a direct branch of their own. She added that Elliott produced charts and material to demonstrate it (La Mance, 33. See also footnote). I have not seen these sheets, but there is no reason to doubt La Mance's word on this. Some of this might seem circumstantial, but in the world of family history, especially when going back a half millennium, we do not always have the luxury of proving things beyond a shadow of a doubt. See the discussion about this in Chapter 6.

Chapter Three – The Struggle for American Values

[1] Margie Leonardson Cleverley, "Sketches from the Life of Ida May Dawley Leonardson," type-written history in my possession.

[2] Carl Leonardson, "The Family of Charles H. and Ida M. Leonardson," type-written history (1977) in my possession. Carl Leonardson was a son of Charles and Ida May Leonardson.

[3] Carl Leonardson.

[4] Margie Leonardson Cleverley, "Sketches from the Life of the Charles H. Leonardson Family," type-written history in my possession. Gladys Laird Leonardson, "Mary Emma Wilson Leonardson (of Dubois and Medicine Lodge)," *Snake River Echoes, A Quarterly of Idaho History*, 11:1 (1982), 37. Carl Leonardson.

[5] For more information on the digitalization of family history, see Sally Benny, "Preserving Your Family History in the Digital Age," in the New England Historic and Genealogical Society's *American Ancestors* 20:2 (Summer 2019), 27.

[6] Nathaniel Philbrick, *Mayflower, A Story of Courage, Community, and War,* (Penguin: New York, 2006), 7.

[7] John M. Barry, *Roger Williams and the Creation of the American Soul,* (New York: Penguin, 2012), 192-204.

[8] McLoughlin, 4-5. Barry, 217.

[9] Leon McBeth, "Baptist Beginnings," *The Baptist History & Heritage Society*, 1979, (www.baptisthistory.org). McLaughlin, accessed 2020.

[10] Henry Melville King, *Historical Catalogue of the Members of the First Baptist Church in Providence, Rhode Island*, (Providence, R.I.: Townsend printers, 1908), 23. Lora Sarah Nichols La Mance, *The Greene Family and its Branches, from A.D. 861 to A.D. 1904*, (Floral Park, NY: Mayflower Publishing Co., 1904), 46. The nomenclature for the two John Greenes is not my own, but has often been used by genealogists to differentiate them.

[11] During the period around John's birth, a Richard Greene, quite likely his father, was knighted in 1617, and Robert, perhaps his great-grandfather or great-great-grandfather, was knighted by Edward IV in 1471, for service in the Edward's big War of the Roses victory over the Lancastrians at Tewkesbury. See Wm. A. Shaw, *The Knights of England, A Complete Record from the Earliest Time to the Present Day of the Knights of all the Orders of Chivalry in England...*, (London: Sherratt and Hughes, 1907), 14, 163.

[12] George Sears Greene, *The Greenes of Rhode Island, with Historical Records of English Ancestry, 1534-1902*, (New York: Knickerbocker Press, 1903), 53. Anon, *The Greene Family in England and America: With Pedigrees*, (Boston: Privately Printed, Boston, 1901), 38. See my note at the end of Chapter 3 on the connection between the Bowridge Hill and Northampton Greene families.

[13] Ancestry.com. "John Green," *Cambridge University Alumni, 1261-1900* [database on-line]. Provo, UT, USA: Ancestry.com Operations Inc, 1999, (https://search.ancestry.com/cgi-bin/sse.dll?_phsrc=sdL155&_phstart=successSource&usePUBJs=true&indiv=1&dbid=3997&gsfn=John&gsln=Green&gsfn_x=NP_NN_NIC&msbdy=1590&new=1&rank=1&uidh=aic&redir=false&msT=1&gss=angs-d&pcat=37&fh=1&h=30550&recoff=&ml_rpos=2&queryId=65fda35b8f3e5f4ad57b885e31616167). The Cambridge and Oxford alumni lists include no other students named John Greene studying medicine during the time John would have studied, except this one. He was probably introduced to Puritanism during his time at Cambridge.

[14] *The Greene Family in England and America...*, 38-39, 123. George Sears Greene, 54.

[15] George Sears Greene, 55, 769. David Hackett Fischer, *Albion's Seed, Four British Folkways in America*, (New York: Oxford Univ. Press, 1989), 14, 28.

[16] John Osborne Austin, *The Genealogical Dictionary of Rhode Island, Comprising Three Generations of Settlers Who came Before 1690*, (Albany, NY: Clearfield, 1887), 88-89.

[17] Traditionally there has been some unclarity about when Joane died. Many family histories have erroneously dated her death to 1643, in Conanicut, as recorded in James Savage, *A Genealogical Dictionary of the First Settlers of New England*, 2, (Boston: Little, Brown, and Co, 1860), 302. However, as noted later in the chapter, this death date and burial place belong to Alice Daniels, John Greene's second wife. Austin's *Genealogical Dictionary of Rhode Island*, which in this case is more accurate than Savage's work, simply omits a death date. Joane boarded the *James* with her husband, and he remarried as a widower sometime after he reached Providence. Some genealogists have claimed she died aboard the *James* before reaching New England, but I have been unable to find a source to substantiate that, if it did happen. George Sears Greene, whose work on the Greene family (*The Greenes of Rhode Island...*, 1903) is more extensive and authoritative than any other Greene history, says Joane died "soon after his

removal to Rhode Island," 55. I take this as the best we know about it. The *Records of the Settlements at Providence, Portsmouth, Newport and Warwick, 1636-1647,* record Mrs. Daniels received her lot after paying two shillings, footnoting that "Alice Daniell, afterwards the wife of John Greene." 15. In May 1637, the records tell of John Greene's participation in the Verin trial in June 1637, and list him as getting an allotment of grass and meadow 17. From 1638 forward, all records mentioning the early inhabitants list Greene, but not Alice. It seems that sometime in late 1637 or early 1638, Greene and Daniels married, thus putting her property under her husband's name. This also suggests that Joane died sometime in late 1636 or during 1637. John Jr. eventually inherited Alice's lot and sold it after his father's death, reports George Sears Greene 61.

[18] *Records of the Settlements at Providence, Portsmouth, Newport and Warwick, 1636-1647,* I, (Crawford Greene: Providence, 1856). 15.

[19] "Letter of Alice Daniell of Salem to Gov. John Winthrop at Boston," *The New England Historical and Genealogical Register* 35, (Oct. 1881), 318-320.

[20] John Winthrop, *Winthrop's Journal, History of New England, 1630-1649,* . I, ed. by James Kendall Hosmer, Kindle edition, (first published by Charles Scribner and Sons, 1908), location 4246.

[21] *Winthrop Journal,* I, location 4246. *Records of the Settlements at Providence, Portsmouth, Newport and Warwick, 1636-1647,* 16. Samuel Greene Arnold, *History of the State of Rhode Island And Providence Plantations,* 1, (New York: Appleton & Co., 1859), 104-105. Austin, 212.

[22] *Winthrop Journal,* I, location 3870.

[23] Austin, 88. Adelos Gorton, *The Life and Times of Samuel Gorton,* (Philadelphia: George S. Ferguson Co., 1907), 35, *Winthrop Journal,* I., location 3870. Richman, 197, note 1.

[24] *Winthrop Journal,* II, loc. 1164.

[25] Adelos Gorton, 40. George Sears Greene, 46. Copies of the deeds for this purchase from Miantonomi and for the earlier Shawomet purchase are found in George Sears Greene, 745-746. Patrick T. Conley, *Rhode Island's Founders, from Settlement to Statehood,* (Charleston, SC: The History Press, 2010), 20-23. McLoughlin, 13-15. Barry, 169-171.

[26] Samuel Gorton, *Simplicities defence against seven-headed policy, or Innocency vindicated: being unjustly accused and sorely censured by that seven-headed church-government united in New-England: or that servant so imperious in his master[']s absence revived and...,* (London: Jon Macock, 1646), 10, 14, 19.

[27] Austin, 302. Adelos Gorton, 45. Arnold, 177 ff. *Winthrop Journal,* I, location 2037.

[28] That Dr. John Greene had a herd of livestock once again suggests his connection to family wealth that he derived from the Greenes in Dorset. Chad Browne's grandson James claimed that in 1638 a cow sold for the princely sum of 22 pounds silver. See Irving Berdine Richman, *Rhode Island Its Making and Its Meaning, A Survey of the Annals of the*

Commonwealth from the Settlement to the Death of Roger Williams 1636-1685, (New York: G. P. Putnam's Sons, 1902), 86, note 1. See also Caleb Johnson, "Livestock," *Caleb Johnson's MayflowerHistory.com*, http://mayflowerhistory.com/livestock.

[29] Letter from Capt. George Cooke and commissioners, in Samuel Gorton, *Simplicities...*, 38.

[30] See the discussion of Public Violence in Puritan Society in Fischer, 189-196.

[31] One of Greene's rivals in this sordid affair was Benedict Arnold, the ancestor of American Revolution arch-traitor Benedict Arnold, who wrote to Massachusetts' Governor John Winthrop that John Greene's wife died about the first week of January 1643. However, the attack occurred in October 1642, and that is the more accurate date of Alice's death. Adelos Gorton, 43, 46, 48-49, Arnold, 180, 184. Samuel Gorton, *Simplicities...*, 39. Kenneth W. Porter, "Samuell Gorton New England Firebrand," *The New England Quarterly* (September 1934), 7:3, 405, 424.

[32] Adelos Gorton, 49. Arnold, 184.

[33] Samuel Gorton describes the night John's second wife Alice died during during Shawomet attack, and later how John married Phillip in London. See Samuel Gorton, Simplicities...., 39. See also *The Early Records of the Town of Providence*, I, (Providence: Snow & Farnham, 1892), 92, for reference to Phillip as John's widow.

[34] Quoted in George Sears Greene, 56.

[35] Charles Howe, *Gylla's Hometown, How a Saxon Settlement became an English Country Town*, (Gillingham, Dorset: Gylla Publishing, 1983), 145-146.

[36] Adelos Gorton, 78.

[37] Adelos Gorton, 13.

[38] *Records of the Colony of New Plymouth in New England*, I, "Court Orders," (Boston: William White, 1855), dated 5 Nov. 1638, 100, 105-106.

[39] Adelos Gorton, 21. Porter, 405, 412-413.

[40] Adelos Gorton, 12.

[41] Adelos Gorton, 11-13. Porter, 408-409.

[42] John Winthrop, *Winthrop's Journal*, location 2875m 3537. Francis J. Bremer, *The Puritan Experiment, New England Society form Bradford to Edwards*, (Lebanon, NH: University Press of New England, 1995), 65- 66. Patrick T. Conley, *Rhode Island's Founders, from Settlement to Statehood*, (Charleston, SC: The History Press, 2010), 35.

[43] Conley, 37-38.

[44] Adelos Gorton, 22-23, 26. Porter, 415-417.

[45] George Sears Greene, 747. Adelos Gorton, 153.

[46] Porter, 418.

[47] Porter, 419.

[48] *Winthrop's Journal*, II, location 1164.

[49] Porter, 420.

[50] William Hubbard, *A General History of New England* [written in 1682], quoted in Porter, 419. Porter, 420. Adelos Gorton, 43.

[51] Adelos Gorton, 47-48. Porter, 423.

[52] Samuel Gorton, 39-40, 49. Adelos Gorton, 49.

[53] Adelos Gorton, 49-50.

[54] *Winthrop Journal*, vol II, location 2166 ff.

[55] *Acts of the Apostles*, chapter 19. Porter, 427-428. *Winthrop Journal*, II, location 2098 ff.

[56] *Winthrop Journal*, . II, location 2339.

[57] Porter, pp 430-431. Samuel Gorton, *Simplicities...*, 39.

[58] *Winthrop's Journal*, II, location 1969 ff.

[59] Adelos Gorton, 53.

[60] Samuel Gorton, *Simplicities...*, **80-81**.

[61] Adelos Gorton, 54-56.

[62] *Winthrop Journal*, II, location 4190.

[63] Porter, 433. Adelos Gorton, 71-77.

[64] Porter, 435-437.

[65] John M. Barry, 356.

[66] Samuel Gorton, *Simplicities...*, 100. Adelos Gorton, 93, 145-149.

[67] Adelos Gorton, 138.

[68] Austin, 103-104. Holmes, 44-47. Edwin S. Gaustad *Baptist Piety, The Last Will and Testimony of Obadiah Holmes*, (Grand Rapids: Christian University Press, 1978), 7 (also see his footnote # 9).

[69] Gaustad, 5, 9. Holmes, 47.

[70] Gaustad, 11. Austin, 104.

[71] Holmes, 16-18, 47. Austin, 104

[72] Gaustad, p 18. *Massachusetts Colony Records*, III, 174, quoted in Henry S. Burrage, *A History of the Baptists in New England*, (Philadelphia: American Baptist Publication Society, 1894), 26-27. Fischer, 203. Holmes, 16-18. Austin, 104. Gaustad, 18-20.

[73] Burrage, 26. Holmes 18. Gaustad, 23.

[74] Henry Melville King, *A Summer Visit of Three Rhode Islanders to the Massachusetts Bay in 1651*, (Preston and Rounds: Providence, 1896), 43 ff. Gaustad, 23-24.

[75] Gaustad, 25. King, A Summer Visit..., 52.

[76] Fischer, 193-194.

[77] Excerpts from a Holmes letter to friends in London, quoted in King, 92.

[78] King, 92.

[79] Ibid.

[80] Gaustad, 32-33.

[81] Holmes describes his trial and flogging in a letter to friends in London. Excerpts from the letter are found in King, 94-98, and Gaustad, 43-46.

[82] King, 61, 92 ff. Gaustad, 27, 32-33.

[83] Obadiah Holmes, "A letter to my dear wife, if she remain in the land of the living after my departure, as a true token of my love unto her," Gaustad, 95. Gaustad's work includes copies of Holmes's letters to his family.

[84] Holmes, 55-56.

[85] Neil C Dunray, et. al., *Smith's Castle at Cocumscussoc, Four Centuries of Rhode Island History*, (East Greenwich, RI: Meridian Printing Co., 2003), 1-2.

[86] Barry, 353. Dunray, 5-6, 10-12. The value equivalents are in 2003 dollars.

[87] Austin, 80-81. La Mance 66-67. There may be a question about the name of John of Quidnesset's wife. La Mance clearly mistakes his wife as "Joan Beggarly," a name, however, that is a combination of Dr. John Greene's first two wives' names. Austin, however, lists Dr. John Greene's three wives correctly, and gives only a first name, "Joan," for John of Quidnesset's wife, and places death as 1682. The *Find a Grave Index* locates her suspected grave and says it has only initials, "J.G." or "I.G." "Joan Greene," *Find A Grave*, (https://www.findagrave.com/memorial/102367576), accessed March 7, 2020.

[88] Dunray, 11-13. Arnold, 272.

[89] La Mance, 56-57.

[90] Philbrick, 205, 222-224, 237-238. Conley, p. 61.

[91] Philbrick, 245. Edward Lodi, *Who, When, Where in King Philip's War*, (Middleborough, MA: Rock Village Publishing, 2015), 71.

[92] McLaughlin, 42, Philbrick, 245, 252. Arnold, 395. Lodi, 83, 95.

[93] Philbrick, 265-279. Dunray, 16.

[94] Arnold, 408, 415. Adelos Gorton, 138. Dunray, 18. Lodi, 49, 71. Philbrick, 304.

[95] Philbrick, xiii, 332. Dunray, 11.

[96] Adelos Gorton, 143. La Mance, 58. Samuel Sears Greene, 64. Dunray, 10. Samuel Greene Arnold, 195.

[97] Austin, 87. La Mance, 47, 54. McLoughlin, 40.

Chapter Four – Road to Rebellion

[1] Samuel Bryant, "Rhode Island Justice – 1772 Vintage," *Rhode Island History*, 26:3 (July 1967), 65. Gerald M. Carbone, *Nathanael Greene, a Biography of the American Revolution*, (New York: Palgrave MacMillan, 2008), 3-4. Virginia Dart Greene Hales, *Greene and Greene, Their Ancestral Heritage, 1550-1900*, (self-published, 2016), 121. "Deposition of Rufus Greene, Jr.," before The Royal Commission of the Commission of Inquiry," found in *A History of the Destruction of His Britannic Majesty's Schooner Gaspee*, compiled by John Russell Bartlett, (Providence: A. Crawford Greene, 1861), 93-94. Gaspee Days Committee, *Gaspee Virtual Archives*, (www.gaspee.org).

[2] Rory Raven, *Burning the Gaspee, Revolution in Rhode Island*, (Charleston, SC: The History Press, 2012), 34-35.

[3] Carbone, 4, 9. Raven, 35.

[4] Carbone, 15-16. Rappleye, *Sons of Providence, the Brown Brothers, the Slave Trade, and the American Revolution*, (New York: Simon and Schuster, 2006), 102, 107. Raven, 42-43, 102, 107.

[5] A *privateer* was a private captain or owner commissioned by a government to use his armed vessel to attack, loot, and capture enemy ships. Many thought of them as officially sanctioned pirates. Privateers were common in Rhode Island and throughout the colonies during the days of the French and Indian Wars and the American Revolution.

[6] Rappleye, 108-110.

[7] Rappleye, 113-117, 124-125. Raven, 101. George W. Greene, *Life of Nathanael Greene, Major-General in the Army of the Revolution*, (Boston: Charles Little and James Brown, 1846), 22. Carbone, 8-9. Virginia Greene Hales, 124-125. Steven Park, *The Burning of His Majesty's Schooner Gaspee*, (Yardley, PA: Westholme Publishing, 2016), 62, 71.

[8] Rappleye, 124-125.

[9] Virginia Greene Hales, 130.

[10] "**Tory Mob,**" *Providence (Rhode Island) Gazette*, September 17, 1774, printed in The Kentish Guards, *The Kentish Guardsman & Fife and Drum Review*, (August 2009). Col. Thomas Allen, "Kentish Guards, a History," 1918, 1, quoted in The Kentish Guards, *The Kentish Guardsman & Fife and Drum Review*, (August 2009). Carbone, 15. Virginia Greene Hales, 131-132.

[11] Carbone, 15-17. Allen, 1.

[12] William Johnson, *Sketches of the Life and Correspondence of Nathanael Greene*, (Charleston, SC: A.E. Miller, 1822), 21-22. George W. Greene, 23-24. Carbone, 11.

[13] Johnson, 22. Carbone, 19-20.

[14] Rappleye, 196.

[15] George W. Greene, 29-31, 34.

[16] Edward Field, *State of Rhode Island and Providence Plantations at the End of the Century: A History*, I, (Boston & Syracuse: Mason Publishing Company, 1902), note 1, 539. Gil Troy, "The Black Regiment that Shocked the Redcoats." *The Daily Beast*, https://www.thedailybeast.com/the-black-regiment-that-shocked-the-redcoats?ref=scrollm, (May 29, 2018). Carbone, pp 79-81.

[17] Field, 423-431. Alexander Boyd Hawes, *Off Soundings Aspects of the Maritime History of Rhode Island*, (Chevy Chase: Posterity Press, 1999), 65, 97-101.

[18] "Joseph Greene," pensioner: "Patience Greene," (23 July 1838), NARA M804. *Revolutionary War Pension and Bounty-Land Warrant Application Files*, Roll 1124. From: Fold3, *Revolutionary War Pensions* (/title/467/revolutionary-war-pensions, accessed March 9, 2020), database and images, (https://www.fold3.com/image/22090731?terms=war,us,joseph,revolutionary,greene).

Chapter Five – Day of the Revolution

[19] Jonas and Mary Barrett → Mary Fletcher Barrett → Rebecca Chamberlain → Jacob Coddington Leonardson → Charles Harry Leonardson (See Appendix 2, Chart 2, "Charlie Leonardson to Benjamin Barrett, Sr.").

[20] Quoted in Lemuel Shattuck, *A History of the Town of Concord, Middlesex County, Massachusetts From Its Earliest Settlement to 1832*, (Boston: Russell, Odiorne, & Co., 1835), 100.

[21] "Jonas Barrett and Mary Fletcher," *FamilySearch,* includes extensive list of sources, (https://www.familysearch.org/tree/person/details/L4T7-C87).

[22] D. Hamilton Hurd, *History of Middlesex County, Massachusetts*, 1, (Philadelphia: J.W. Lewis, 1890), 210, 310-312, 324-325.

[23] Walter R. Borneman, *American Spring*, (New York: Back Bay Books, 2014) 136 ff..

[24] Hurd, 210, 310-312, 324-325. Shattuck, 99, 101. Robert A. Gross, *The Minutemen and Their World*, (New York: Hill and Wang, 1976), 118. Rev. Edwin R. Hodgman, *History of the Town of Westford, 1659-1883*, (Lowell, Mass: Morning Mail Co., 1883), 64-66. Edward Fletcher, *Fletcher Family History, The Descendants of Robert Fletcher of Concord, Mass*, (Boston: Rand, Avery, & Co, 1881), 189. Gregory T. Furness, "Crown Point, An Outline History," on *America's Historic Lakes*, www.historiclakes.org/crown_pt.furness.html. Gen. John R. Galvin, *The Minute Men, The First Fight: Myths and Realities of the American Revolution*, (Washington, D.C.: Potomac Books, 2006), 3-4, 65, 90. Rev Ezra Ripley, *A History of the Fight at Concord on the 19th of April, 1775*, (Concord: Allen & Atwill, 1827), 14-15.

[25] Ripley, 17. Galvin, 132. Gross, 119. Hurd, 311. Borneman 30-31, 179-181.

[26] Known in England as *The Massachusetts Government Acts*.

[27] Shattuck, 378-379. Borneman 141-142

[28] "Benjamin Barrett," *Probate Records 1648--1924 (Middlesex County, Massachusetts)*; Author: *Massachusetts. Probate Court (Middlesex County)*; Probate Place: *Middlesex, Massachusetts,* images. From: *Ancestry.com*: *Massachusetts, Wills and Probate Records, 1635-1991* [database on-line]. Provo, UT: Ancestry.com Operations, Inc., 2015 (https://search.ancestry.com/cgi-bin/sse.dll?indiv=1&dbid=9069&h=2803800&tid=&pid=&usePUB=true&_phsrc=sdL173&_phstart=successSource). Gross 77-80.

[29] Gross, 109-112. Borneman 33, 40, 101, 115, 118-119. William Swain, *Swain and Allied Families*, (Milwaukee: Press of Swain & Tate, 1896), 64. Shattuck, 36-37, 94-99. Galvin, 35-38, 45, 101. J. L. Bell, *The Road to Concord, How Four Stolen Cannon Ignited the Revolutionary War*, (Yardley, PA: Westholme, 2016) 5-67. Ripley, 17. "An Old House With Stories," [unnamed newspaper], March 29, [1957]. Hodgman, 352, 357. "Forge Village Historic District," *Westford Preservation Plan*, National Register. Jim Van Valkenburgh, "Charles Barrett Sr., His Life and Times," unpublished paper delivered before the New

Ipswich Historical Society, September 14, 1989, in honor of Charles Barrett's 250th birthday

[30] See: "Benjamin Barrett (1681-1726)," *FamilySearch*, (https://www.familysearch.org/service/tree/tree-data/pdf/family-group/LLSR-3K6/spouse/DEFAULT?locale=en&showOrdinances=true) for extensive list of sources).

[31] Gross, 94, 96, 151.

[32] Van Valkenburgh, "Charles Barrett Sr....."

[33] Bell, 140.

[34] Shattuck, 91, 97-98, 110. Ellen Chase, *The Beginnings of the American Revolution, Based on Contemporary Letters, Diaries, and Other Documents*, 3, (New York: Baker Taylor, 1910), 6. D. Michael Ryan, *Concord and Dawn of the Revolution, The Hidden Truths*, (Charleston, S.C.: The History Press, 2007), 42-43. Ripley, 9, 43. "Col. James Barrett Farm," *New England Landmarks for Save our Heritage*, Georgetown, MA, 2006, 9. Borneman, 121. Swain, 71.

[35] Gross,115. Borneman,131 ff. Galvin, pp 101-103. Bell, pp x-xi.

[36] Borneman, 151-160. Galvin, 128.

[37] Amos Barrett, "Concord and Lexington Battle," in Rev. Henry True, *Journal of Letters*, (Marion, Ohio, 1900), 31, 31.

[38] Barrett, 31. Chase, 7.

[39] Shattuck, 105-106. Chase, 7. Shattuck 13. Swain, p 71. Gross, 115.

[40] Lemuel Shattuck, "Notes, Interview of Mrs. Peter Barrett," November 3, 1831, loose notes, *Lemuel Shattuck Papers*, Folder 46, Box 2, New England Historical and Genealogical Society, Boston. Galvin, 137-138. Barrett, 31.

[41] Chase,11, 13.

[42] Galvin, 131-132, 137-138. Nathaniel Philbrick, *Bunker Hill, A City, A Siege, A Revolution*, (New York: Penguin, 2013), 132. Barrett, 31. Chase, 12-13. Ryan, 44. Ripley, 16.

[43] Ripley, 17-18. Galvin, 131-132.

[44] Chase, 6.

[45] Galvin, 143-144 Ripley, 19, 21. Margaret Sidney, *Old Concord Her Highways and Byways*, Revised and Enlarged Edition, (Boston: D. Lothrop Co., 1893), 18-23. Chase, 28. Borneman, 123. "Lemuel Shattuck interview with Mrs. Peter Barrett," Nov 3, 1831, loose, located in New England Historical and Genealogical Society. Shattuck, 109-110.

[46] Ripley, 20.

[47] Barrett, 33.

[48] Galvin, 4, 53, 62, 65. 70, 143-144. Borneman, 175, 197-198. Ripley, 19-21. Shattuck, 108.

[49] Ripley,23.

[50] Shattuck, 25.

[51] Barrett, 33.

[52] Galvin, 148-151. Ripley, 23, 25. Ryan, 46. Shattuck, 111-112. Borneman, 183. Barrett, 33. Gross, 125.

[53] Barrett, 33.

[54] Ryan, 45.

[55] Borneman, 223-24.

[56] Ripley, 37. Chase, 56.

[57] Barrett, 33. Galvin, 152, 161, 164, 166, 178 ff. Ryan pp 45-46. Borneman 188, 191. Gross, 127-128, 131, 147, 158. Ripley, 32. Shattuck, 116-118, 353, 363. *Massachusetts Soldiers and Sailors*, 681. New England Landmarks, 7-8.

[58] **"An Old House With Stories."**

[59] Hurd, 313.

[60] Shattuck, iii.

[61] **"An Old House With Stories."**

Chapter Six – Soldiers, Survival, Sorrow

[1] Patrick Brophy, *Bushwhackers of the Border*, (Nevada, Mo: Vernon County Historical Society, 1980), 6-36. James R. Baker, *Bushwhackers! A Civil War History of Vernon County Missouri*, Kindle edition, download from Amazon.com, location 379.

[2] **"Chester Lent and Susannah Frasure,"** *FamilySearch*, (https://www.familysearch.org/tree/person/details/KNWX-FLR), for extensive list of sources.

[3] Howard L. Conard, ed., *Encyclopedia of the History of Missouri*, VI, (St. Louis: The Southern History Company, 1901), 296-297.

[4] **All livestock mentioned in "Property Appraisal, Probate Records for Chester Lent,"** loose, February 14, 1859, *Probate Records for Vernon County*, Missouri, located in the Bushwhacker Museum, Nevada, Missouri, photocopies in my possession. *Deed Records,* dated July 17, 1857, for purchase of 200 acres from purchased from John Waldrop in Vernon County, MO, copy in my possession.

[5] Family Records of Margie Lea Leonardson Cleverley and Peggy Ann Lent.

[6] Baker, Chapter 2.

[7] From a family history in possession of Peggy Lent and also recorded in a family history entitled "Robison Lent and the LENT family," by Freda F. Marsh, written in 1963.

[8] *1860 U.S. Census, Vernon County, Missouri*, population schedule, Little Osage page 99 (penned), dwellings 717, 718, and 732. From Ancestry.com: Year: *1860*; Census Place: *Little Osage, Vernon, Missouri*; Roll: *M653_659*; Page: *99*; Family History Library Film: *803659*.

[9] Family Records of Peggy Ann Lent. Roy Bird, *Civil War in Kansas*, (Gretna, LA: Pelican, 2004) 20. T. F. Robley, *History of Bourbon County, Kansas, to the close of 1865*, (Ft. Scott, KS: Monitor Book and Printing, 1894) 155.

[10] I have yet to find a birthdate for Maria's and James' son but the 1880 Census, taken on June 1, 1880, listed him born in Bourbon County, Kansas, and 19 years

old. This indicates that he was born in late spring 1861, about the time other evidence suggests they left Missouri for Kansas.

[11] Bird., 13, 21. Larry Wood, *The Civil War on the Lower Kansas-Missouri Border*, (Joplin, Mo: Hickory Press, 2000), 3-5, 16-17, 88-89. T. F. Robley, 150.

[12] Wood., 11-15, 20-22. Bird, 23, 28.

[13] Wood, 17. T. F. Robley, 173. Bird, 30, 34. Leo E. Oliva, *Fort Scott Courage and Conflict on the Border*, (Topeka: Kansas State Historical Society, 1984), 64-68.

[14] "Fort Lincoln," *Kansas, a Cyclopedia of State History*, ed. by Frank Blackmar, I, (Chicago: Standard Publishing Co, 1912), 666-667.

[15] Kansas Adjutant General's Office, *Descriptive Roll, Fifth Regiment, Cavalry, Kansas Civil War Volunteers*, volume 4, 1861-1863,38, image, Kansas Historical Society, "Kansas Memory," Item Number: 227659, Call Number: Microfilm: AR 115, item 4 KSHS Identifier: DaRT ID: 227659, (https://www.kansasmemory.org/item/227659/page/38).

[16] Bird, 32. Richard Parmenter to Mary Elizabeth Lent, letter, February 28, 1862, photocopy in my possession.

[17] Wood, 20. Bird, 12.

[18] Bird, 41.

[19] Wood, 27-28.

[20] Robley, 177.

[21] Lt. Col. T. W. Scudder, "Military History of the Fifth Kansas Volunteer Cavalry," published in *Report of the Adjutant General of the State of Kansas, 1861-'65*, Topeka, Kansas: 1896 reprint, found on (www.arkansastoothpick.com/2007/12/civil-war-arkansas-5th-kansas-cavalry-a-history/), and included in Alice Fry, *Following the Fifth Kansas Cavalry, The Roster*, (Independence, MO: Two Trails Publishing, 1998), 2-8. Lt. Col. Scudder served in the Fifth Kansas Cavalry during the Civil War.

[22] Richard Parmenter to Mary Elizabeth Lent, dated February 28, 1862, photocopy in my possession.

[23] "Formations and Ranks in Civil War Units," *Military Records Online*, (www.angelfire.com/wv/wasec5/formations.html), accessed Dec. 19, 2015. Scudder.

[24] Scudder. Ward L. Schrantz, *Jasper County, Missouri in the Civil War*, (Carthage, Mo: The Carthage Press, 1923) 64.

[25] Bird, 50-51.

[26] Capt. William Creitz, "Diary", printed in Alice L. Fry, *Following The Fifth Kansas Cavalry, The Letters*, (self-published, 1998), 27. Capt. Creitz was commander of the Fifth Kansas Company A. Fry's book is a compendium of diaries and letters written by members of the Fifth. Bird., 58.

[27] Priv. George E. Flanders to "Dear Brother" [William Flanders], letter, August 2, 1862, printed in Fry, *The Letters*, 155.

[28] Scudder. Creitz, 27-30. "The March of the Fifth Kansas Through Arkansas, Helena, Ark. July 14th, 1862," from *The Conservative*, newspaper, July 26, 1862, printed in Fry, 31-33.

[29] Creitz, 29. Alice L. Fry, *Following the Fifth Kansas Cavalry, The Roster*, (Independence, MO: Two Trails Publishing, 1998), 178. James McPherson, *Battle Cry of Freedom*, (New York: Oxford, 1988), 791. Priv. George E. Flanders to "Dear Brother" [William Flanders], letter, November 2, 1862, printed in Fry, *The Letters*, 162.

[30] Rhonda M. Kohl, "Raising Thunder with the Secesh: Powell Clayton's Federal Cavalry at Taylor's Creek and Mount Vernon, Arkansas, May 11, 1863," *The Arkansas Historical Quarterly*, 64, (Summer 2005), 146-170. Priv. George E. Flanders to "Dear Mother," letter, October 16, 1862, in Fry, *The Letters...*, 161.

[31] Priv. George E. Flanders to Dear Brother [William Flanders], letter, March 25, 1863, in Fry, *The Letters...*, 169.

[32] Scudder. "Skirmishes at Taylor's Creek and Mount Vernon," *The Encyclopedia of Arkansas History & Culture*, (http://www.encyclopediaofarkansas.net/encyclopedia/entry-detail.aspx?entryID=3222). Kohl, 160-164.

[33] Scudder. "State History, Part 5, Fifth Regiment Kansas Volunteer Cavalry," in. William G. Cutler, *History of the State of Kansas*, (www.kancoll.org/books/cutler/sthist/milrec-p5.html), accessed December 21, 2015.

[34] Scudder. Cutler. Priv. George E. Flanders to "Dear Father," letter, January 3, 1864, in Fry, *The Letters...*, 189.

[35] Lt. Joseph Trego to "My Dear Little Wife" [Alice Trego], letter, Jan. 24, 1864, in Fry, *The Letters...*, 91.

[36] Scudder. Cutler. "Action at Marks' Mills, *The Encyclopedia of Arkansas History & Culture*. Don Richards, "The Engagement at Marks' Mills," *The Arkansas Historical Quarterly*, 19:1, (Spring, 1960) 51-60. Report of Lt. Col. Francis Drake, April 25, 1864, *The War of the Rebellion: A Compilation of the official Records of the Union and Confederate Armies*, (Washington: Government Printing Office, 1880-1901), Series I, . 34, pt. 1, 712-713.

[37] Cutler. Scudder. "Action at Marks' Mills." Report from Col. Powell Clayton, April 27, 1864, *Official Records*, . 34, pt. 2, 665.

[38] George E. Flanders to "Dear Father," letter, March 14, 1864, in Fry, *The Letters...*, 193-194.

[39] Alice M. Trego to Lt. Joseph Trego, letter, July 28, 1864, printed in Fry, *The Letters....* 112.

[40] Bird, 42, 84-86, 105-107, 118. Wood, 88-89, 102-103. Alice M. Trego to Lt. Joseph Trego, letter, July 28, 1864, printed in Fry, *The Letters....* 112.

[41] Mary Trego to Alice M Trego, letter, August 7, 1864, printed in Fry, *The Letters....* 117.

[42] Alice M. Trego to Lt. Joseph Trego, letter, October 11, 1864, printed in Fry, *The Letters*.... 135.

[43] From a Family History of Bernice Clayton in letter dated November 9, 1971. The *1865 Kansas State Census* taken June 28, 1865, showed Susannah living in Franklin Township and listed as Susan Moyer. Xenia was the largest town in Franklin Township, and not to be confused with the modern Franklin, Kansas, an unincorporated community about 20 miles south of Fort Scott in Crawford County. Living in John Moyer's and Susannah's home at the time of the census was John Moyer (aged 18), Lewis Lent (16), Nancy Jane Lent (13), Amos Lent, male (14), and Ralison Lent [Robson Lent] (age 11). Kansas State Historical Society; Topeka, Kansas; *1865 Kansas Territory Census*; "Susanna Moyer," page 68, penned, dwelling 472, Roll: *ks1865_2*; Line: *12*. From: Ancestry.com. *Kansas State Census Collection, 1855-1925* [database on-line]. Provo, UT, USA: Ancestry.com Operations, Inc., 2009.

[44] George E. Flanders to "Dear Father," letter, March 14, 1864, in Fry, *The Letters...*, 193-194. Lt. Joseph Trego to "My Dear Little Wife" [Alice Trego], letter, August 22, 1964, in Fry, *The Letters...* 124.

[45] Capt. William Creitz, "Diary", printed in Alice L. Fry, *The Letters*, (self-published, 1998), 15. T. F. Rowley, 188-193. Bird, 125-128.

[46] T. F. Robley, 200.

[47] *Encyclopedia of the History of Missouri*, 298. Probate Records Chester Lent, Vernon County, Missouri, loose, located in the Bushwhacker Museum, Nevada, Mo. Vernon County, Missouri. Deed Records dated July 17, 1857, for purchase of 200 acres from purchased from John Waldrop in Vernon County, Missouri, copy in my possession.

[48] Letter from Peggy Lent Goudeau dated October 15, 2015.

[49] *Ohio, County Marriage Records, 1774-1993*, image, Film Number 000477144 [database on-line]. Lehi, UT, USA: Ancestry.com Operations, Inc., 2016.

[50] On the census it was spelled "Hercules Lint," a variation on the last name that he sometimes used. For example, this was the spelling recorded in the Albany Dutch Church records when he was married in 1789. *1810 U.S. Census*, Highgate, Franklin County, Vermont, (penned). From Ancestry.com: Year: *1810*; Census Place: *Highgate, Franklin, Vermont;* Series *M19;* Roll: *133* page *303*, FHL *film 0218668.*

[51] *1830 U.S. Census*, Salt Creek, Holmes County, Ohio, (penned). From Ancestry.com: Year: *1830*; Census Place: *Salt Creek, Holmes, Ohio;* Roll: *64* page *577*, FHL *film 0337944.* The summary page for the 1830 entry has sometimes spelled the name "Herenley." This is a transcriptional or other error. When you look at the original census document, you see "Hercules" clearly handwritten Before that entry is another Lent that on Ancestry.com's summary sheet is written "John Leatz." Looking at the original, however, you read "John Lent" with some type of a scribble, perhaps inadvertent, at the end. John Lent lived next door to Hercules and was their son, who Lavelle's research had shown

was born in 1805. The census document places him as a head of a family and in the age group, 20-29, which is right. Hercules and Elizabeth's children John and Charity both listed Vermont as their place of birth, as did Chester, on the 1850 census.

[52] Even this is not a 100% proof that Chester was their sibling, because perhaps these living descendants could have errors on their own family trees linking them to Hercules. However, if there were just one of them related to me, that is one thing. When there are three separate individuals of Hercules's children (marked on ThruLines as distant uncles and an aunt) who have descendants DNA-related to me, it is difficult to believe Chester was not their brother, especially in light of the combined evidence.

[53] Elizabeth Shown Mills, *Evidence Explained*, 3rd ed., (Baltimore: Genealogical Publishing Co., 2017), 17.

[54] Board for Certification of Genealogists, *Genealogy Standards*, 50th Anniversary Edition, (Ancestry.com: Washington, DC, 2014), 3. The GPS sets five criteria for establishing "proof." This definition of *proof* is a flexible and usable one that maintains a strict discipline for doing research.

[55] See David Quammen, *The Tangled Tree, a Radical New History of Life*, (New York: Simon & Schuster, 2018).

[56] Oliva, 66-67, 80.

Chapter Seven – Promised Land

[1] Charles Dickens, *The Uncommercial Traveller*, vol 6 of *The Works of Charles Dickens* (New York, n.d.), 635-638.

[2] *1861 census of England*, Aston, Warwickshire, 36, Howard, Joseph; image, Ancestry.com, (https://www.ancestry.com/ accessed March 11, 2010) citing Class: *RG 9*; Piece: *2185*; Folio: *36*; Page: *27*; GSU roll: *542932*.

[3] George K. Merritt and Richard Jensen, "Statistical Profile," *The Ensign*, (July 1987). *2007 Church Almanac*, (Salt Lake City: Deseret Morning News, 2006), 635.

[4] John W. and Deanne Driscoll, eds. *The Joseph Howard Family*, (Blackfoot, ID: self-published, June 1998), 1-5. *The Joseph Howard Family* holds a compilation of family histories written about each of the Joseph and Ann Howard children. "Thomas Howard," Driscoll, 16. "Joseph and Ann Howard to Thomas and William Howard," February 20, 1862, a copy of which is in my own files as well as in Driscoll, 4.

[5] *Names of Persons and Sureties Indebted to the Perpetual Emigrating Fund Company from 1850 to 1877 inclusive*, (Salt Lake City: Star Book, 1877), 68, 73, shows that both Thomas and William in 1877 still owed at least some of the loan from 1861.

[6] Initially, debts were forgiven the most needy. As church president John Taylor put it, "The rich can always take care of themselves – that is, so far as this world is concerned. I do not know how it will be in the next." Arrington, 355-362.

[7] Michael Sharpe, *Tracing your Birmingham Ancestors, A Guide for Family & Local Historians*, Kindle edition, (Barnsley South Yorkshire: Pen Sword Books Ltd, 2015), locations 335, 342, 619, 655, 2200. David Thomson, *England in the Nineteenth Century*, (New York: Penguin, 1982), 13-14. Douglas Tobler, "Truth Prevailing: The Significance of the Nineteenth-Century LDS Experience in Britain," *The Ensign*, (July, 1987). "Life Sketch of Thomas Howard as written by his daughter Sarah Ann Howard Tuttle" in Driscoll, 16. Leonard Arrington, *Great Basin Kingdom*, (Lincoln: University of Nebraska Press, 1966), 98-99, 101. "Wages and Cost of Living in the Victorian Era," *The Victorian Web*, (http://www.victorianweb.org/economics/wages2.html), accessed March 11, 2020. Driscoll, 7. Brandon S. Plewe, ed., *Mapping Mormonism, An Atlas of Latter-day Saint History*, (Provo: BYU Press, 2012), 102, 105. Andrew Jenson, *Church Chronology*, 2nd edition, (Salt Lake City: Deseret News Company, 1899), found on "London-New York, 3 June 1864 – 19 July 1874: A Compilation of General Voyage Notes," *Saints by Sea, Latter-day Saint Immigration to America*, (https://saintsbysea.lib.byu.edu/mii/account/563?netherlands=on&mii=on&sweden=on&keywords=Hudson&scandinavia=on&europe=on). *Saints by Sea* is an online database of journals, newspaper articles and other original artifacts related to the 19th century LDS immigration to Salt Lake City, Utah. "Emily (Emma) Howard," in Driscoll, 43.

[8]: Journal of John L. Smith," May 18, 1864 in *Saints by Sea, Latter-day Saint Immigration to America. Journal of George Q. Cannon*, May 11 and 31, 1864, (https://churchhistorianspress.org/george-q-cannon/1860s/1864/05-1864).

[9] See Joseph Howard and Ann Shelton," on *FamilySearch* for sourced family details, https://www.familysearch.org/tree/person/details/KWJH-RGT.

[10] Journal of John L. Smith," June 2, 1864. John M. Kay to George Q. Cannon, July 19, 1864, *Latter-day Saints' Millennial Star* 26:34, August 20, 1864, 539-542, *Saints by Sea...* "Joseph Howard" in Driscoll, 29. John Kay writes that Joseph was the president of the 6th ward, whereas counselor John Lyman Smith in his detailed journey has James in that position.

[11] Charles Dickens, *The Uncommercial Traveller*, vol 6 of *The Works of Charles Dickens* (New York, n.d.), 635-638.

[12] *Diary of Michael McCune*, June 3, 1864, *Saints by Sea...* Diary of Michael McCune," *Saints by Sea...*

[13] *Autobiography of Harriet Goble Bird, Saints by Sea... George Q. Cannon Journal*, 3 June 1864.

[14] Dickens.

[15] *Journal of John Lyman Smith*, June 5, 1864. John M. Kay to George Q. Cannon, June 8, 1864, *Latter-day Saints' Millennial Star* 26:34, June 25, 1864, 414-415, *Saints by Sea...*

[16] J. Spencer Cornwall, *Stories of our Mormon Hymns*, (Salt Lake: Deseret Publishing, 1963), 264-265. Mary Ann Rawlings Aveson, "Reminiscence," in *A History of the Richard Rawlings Family: Ancestors—Descendants*, pp 98-101,

from *Saints by Sea... Autobiography and Journals of John Lyman Smith*, June 7, 1864, from *Saints by Sea...* Mary Ann Ward Webb, "The History of Mary Ann Ward Webb and Her Diary of the Journey to Utah (1864)," in Robert R. King and Kay Atkinson King, *Mary Ann Webb: Her Life and Ancestry* (McLean, Virginia: America Society for Genealogy and Family History, 1996), 107, 109, *Saints by Sea...*, "London-New York, 3 June 1864 – 19 July 1874, Autobiography of Mary Ann Ward Webb."

[17] Joseph Howard, in Driscoll, 29.

[18] *Autobiography ... of John Lyman Smith*, June 17, 1864 and June 27, 1864. John M. Kay to George Q. Cannon, July 19, 1864. *Journal of John Lyman Smith*, June 29, 1864, *Saints by Sea...*

[19] Kay to Cannon, July 19, 1864.

[20] Diary of Michael McCune, July 8, 1864.

[21] Charles William Symons, "Autobiography," in Carley Budd Meredith and Dean Symons Anderson, *The Family of Charles William Symons and Arzella Whitaker Symons* [privately printed, 1986) 4-6, from *Saints by Sea...*

[22] *Autobiography and Journals of John Lyman Smith*, entries for July 18-19, 1864. *Michael McCune Diary*, entry for July 19, 1864, *Saints by Sea...*

[23] Unfortunately, their records and most of the rest from Castle Garden were lost in an 1897 fire.

[24] *Autobiography and Journals of John Lyman Smith*, entries for July 21, 1864, *Saints by Sea...*

[25] James T. Sutton, *Autobiography* in *Our Pioneer Heritage*, comp. by Kate B. Carter, XVII, (Salt Lake City: Daughters of the Utah Pioneers, 1974), from *Saints by Sea...*, "London-New York, 3 June 1864 – 19 July 1874, Autobiography of James T. Sutton," *Saints by Sea...*

[26] *Autobiography and Journals of John Lyman Smith*, Wednesday, July 22-24, 27, 1864. Kay to Cannon, July 19, 1864. *The Historical Guide to North American Railroads*, 3rd ed., (Waukesha, WI: Kalmbach Books, 2014), 84. "Mary Ann Howard," in Driscoll, 33. *Autobiography of Mary Ann Ward Webb.* "Michigan in the American Civil War," *American Civil War Homepage*, (http://thomaslegion.net/americancivilwar/michigancivilwarhistory.html.). *Journal of John L. Smith*, July 27, 1864, *Saints by Sea...*

[27] *Autobiography of Mary Ann Ward Webb, Saints by Sea....*

[28] *Autobiography of Mary Ann Ward Webb. Autobiography and Journals of John Lyman Smith*, Wednesday, July 28, 1864. Peder Christian, *Journal*, 27-30, *Saints by Sea...*

[29] *Autobiography of Mary Ann Ward Webb. Journal of John Lyman Smith*, July 29, 1864. *Autobiography and Journals of John Lyman Smith*, July 28-August 2, 8,1864.

[30] Plewe, 83. John K. Hulmston, "Mormon Immigration in the 1860s: The Story of the Church Trains," *Utah Historical Quarterly*, 58:1 (Winter 1990), 33-37.

[31] Charles Eugene Fletcher, *Autobiography*, 145-52, from: The Church of Jesus Christ of Latter-day Saints, *Pioneer Data Base*, "William Hyde Company (1864): Fletcher, Charles Eugene Autobiography 1911 pp 149-152." (https://history.churchofjesuschrist.org/overlandtravel/sources/5408/fletcher-charles-eugene-autobiography-1911-145-52). Hulmston, 37. Jesse N. Smith, *Autobiography and Journal, 1855*, August 9, 1864, from *Pioneer Database*,

[32] John T. Gerber, "Journal," in *Journal History of the Church of Jesus Christ of Latter-day Saints*, 26 Oct., 1846, 3-9, *Pioneer Database*. "Ann Shelton," in "Find a Grave Memorial." Hulmston., 44. "Amelia Slade Bennion," in Carol Cornwall Madsen, *Journey to Zion*, (Salt Lake: Deseret Book, 1992), 568-569. "Joseph and Ann Shelton Howard," Driscoll, 5. Randolph B. Marcy, *The Prairie Traveler, A Handbook for Overland Expeditions*, (New York: Skyhorse, 2014) reprint of 1859 original, 29.

[33] Madsen, 314, *Pioneer Database*.

[34] Fletcher, *Pioneer Database*. John T. Gerber, *Pioneer Database*, 26 Oct. 1864, 3-9.

[35] John Lyman Smith, "Diary in John Lyman Smith Papers, 1845-1875," II, 102-117. James T. Sutton, "Reminiscences," 2-4, *Pioneer Database*.

[36] See Stanley B. Kimball, "A Forgotten Mormon Trail and Settlements," *The Ensign*, (February 1980). Inez Foy Barker, *The Joseph Howard Family Journeys 1861 and 1864 from Birmingham, England to the Great Salt Lake Valley via Sail, Rail, and Overland Trail*, (self-published, available on FamilySearch "Joseph Howard"), 33. Hulmston, 40. Mary Ann Rawlings Aveson, "Reminiscences," in Glady Rawlings Lemmon, Comp., *A History of the Richard Rawlings Family: Ancestors-Descendants*, 1986, 98-101, *Pioneer Database*. Fletcher, *Pioneer Database*. William McNiel, "Autobiography," Marjorie Scott Peterson, McNiel family information, *Pioneer Database*. William Hyde, "William Hyde Journal," circa 1868-1873, 186-188, *Pioneer Database*. "John Shelton Howard," in Daughters of the Utah Pioneers, *Pioneer Pathways*, (Salt Lake: Talon, 2005), 345-346. Madsen, 318, *Pioneer Database*. Marcy, 326. "Ann Shelton Howard," *Find a Grave Memorial*.

[37] *George Q. Cannon Journal*, October 7, 1864.

[38] "Stories and Genealogical Information of Mary Lowe Howard," quoted in Inez Foy Barker, 67.

[39] Emma Howard Corbridge, "Family histories, ca. 1932", *Pioneer Database*. "Emily (Emma) Howard," in Driscoll, 44. Inez Foy Barker, 67.

[40] "Our Immigration," *Deseret News*, 14 Sep. 1864,400. "Home Items," "Arrivals," *Deseret News*, 2 Nov 1864, 37. *Deseret News*, 9 Nov 1864, 44.

[41] "Death of John M. Kay," *Latter-day Saints' Millennial Star*, November 19, 1864, 750. Plewe, 83. Emily (Emma) Howard, in Driscoll, 45.

[42] Bryson, Bill, *At Home*, Kindle edition, (New York: Doubleday, 2010), location 109.

[43] Joseph and Ann Howard to Thomas and William, February 20, 1862. Copy in my possession.

[44] Joseph and Ann Howard to Thomas and William, February 20, 1862.

[45] George Svejda, *Castle Garden as an Immigrant Depot, 1855-1890*, (US National Park Service, 1968), Appendix L. The City of New York Department of City Planning, "The Newest New Yorkers," December 2013, 2, 46-47.

Chapter Eight – "What was your Name in the States?"

[1] Old American folk song best known for being sung by Debbie Reynolds in *How the West was Won* in 1962. However, the lyrics go much farther back. For example, see "A Search for the Border Ruffian," *Outing and The Wheelman, An Illustrated Monthly Magazine of Recreation*, 5 (October 1884-March 1885), 38.

[2] Linda Warfel Slaughter in, *Fortress to Farm or Twenty-three Years on the Frontier*, Hazel Eastman, ed., (New York: Exposition Press, 1972), that first appeared in *The Bismarck Tribune*, and was later published in Anton Gartner, *History of Fort Rice North Dakota*, (1964), 24. Clayton K S Chun, *US Army in the Plains Indian Wars 1865-91*, (Osceola, WI: Osprey, 2004), 67.

[3] Telegram from Col. D. T. Stanley, commander, 2nd Yellowstone Expedition, to O. D. Greene, Assistant Adjutant General, July 25, 1872, located in the National Archives, Washington, DC, RG 393 U.S. Army Continental Commands, 1821-1920, Department of Dakota, Field Records/Yellowstone Expedition, 1872-1873, "Letters and Telegrams Received, July 1872-Oct.1872," 1334, Box no. 1.

[4] Linda Slaughter, 24

[5] "Richard Wilson" told the 1900 United States census-taker that he had emigrated to the United States in 1863. He also claimed he was born in Ireland in 1858. That would make him about five-years old when he arrived at Castle Garden, New York. He also called himself "Richard Wilson," although when he died two years later, they wrote on his tombstone, "Joseph Wilson," the name by which he must have been known among his neighbors. As described below, he gave different birth years on different occasions. *1900 Census* Place: *Dubois, Fremont, Idaho*; Page: *2*; (penned), dwelling 27, Enumeration District: *0052*; FHL microfilm: *1240232*. From Ancestry.com. *1900 United States Federal Census* [database on-line]. Provo, UT, USA: Ancestry.com Operations Inc, 2004.

[6] Ancestry.com. *New York, Passenger and Crew Lists (including Castle Garden and Ellis Island), 1820-1957* [database on-line]. Provo, UT, USA: Ancestry.com Operations, Inc., 2010, (https://search.ancestry.com/cgi-bin/sse.dll?indiv=1&dbid=7488&h=5262078&tid=&pid=&usePUB=true&_phsrc=sdL215&_phstart=successSource). Family histories from those close to Richard's wife and daughter tell that Richard McGuire traveled as a boy to the United States from Ireland to New York with his older sister Mary Ann to live with their uncle and aunt. On the 1900 census he stated he immigrated to the U.S. in 1863. A search of immigration arrivals shows only three people named Richard

or R McGuire arrived in 1863, and none of them was in the right age range. On the other hand, "Maria Ann Meagry" (age 18) and "Richard Meagry" (age 14) arrived in New York from Liverpool on July 13, 1863. "Meagry" was an almost nonexistent name in the U.S – only one was found on the 1880 census in the entire country, in Oregon. And name is not Irish. (See "Meagry Family History," Ancestry.com, https://www.ancestry.com/name-origin?surname=meagry). The handwritten "Meagry" on the *Great Eastern's* passenger list is most certainly a transcription error. Margie and other family historians have concluded the listing records Richard McGuire's and his sister's passage to America.

[7] Richard Joseph McGuire, Co. K, 8th Infantry Regiment, Enlistment Papers, R.G. 94, "Oath of Enlistment and Allegiance, Richard Joseph McGuire," Davids Island, New York, 20 January 1872, R.G. 94, National Archives and Record Service, photocopy in my possession

[8] The Hon. James Brooks to W. W. Belknap, Secretary of War, April 22, 1872. Secretary of War Belknap to the Hon. James Brooks, May 3rd, 1872, and marked number 3567. Photocopies in my possession.

[9] Infirmary records noted that Richard McGuire, Pvt, Co. K, 8th Infantry Regiment was admitted June 19, 1872, with "Acute Diarrhea." He was released June 21, 1872. ("Post Infirmary Records," Davids Island, New York Harbor, Reg. No. 491, Hos. No. 2412, Page 81, June 21, 1872, photocopy in my possession). Before the Eighth Regiment transferred to Ft Russell, four of its companies were sent to Chicago to protect property following the great Chicago Fire of October, 1871. In May 1872, these four companies left for Utah where they established Fort Cameron, and in 1874 they moved to support Army camps in Arizona. See Lt. Richard H. Wilson, "Eighth Regiment of Infantry," U.S. Army Center of Military History, (https://history.army.mil/books/R&H/R&H-8IN.htm), 522, accessed March 16, 2020. The 8th Infantry has a long proud tradition in the US Army. Formed in 1838, it served in the Mexican War, in nearly every campaign the Army of the Potomac fought during the Civil War, in Indian wars on the northern plains and in the American Southwest, in the Spanish American War, in World War I and World War II (where it landed in Normandy), and in Vietnam and the Gulf Wars. U.S. Army Center of Military History, "Lineage and Honors Information, 8th Infantry Regiment," 19 March 2014, (https://history.army.mil/html/forcestruc/lineages/branches/inf/0008in.htm), accessed, March 1, 2020.

[10] M. John Lubetkin, *Jay Cooke's Gamble, The Northern Pacific Railroad, the Sioux, and the Panic of 1873*, Kindle edition, (Norman, OK: Univ. of Oklahoma Press, 2014), location 2635.

[11] Quoted in Lubetkin, *Jay Cooke's Gamble...*, location 2867.

[12] Lubetkin, *Jay Cooke's Gamble...*, location 2950-2969.

[13] General Winfield Scott Hancock to Col. T. J. Crittenden, telegram, dated Aug. 19, 1872, National Archives, Washington, DC, RG 393 U.S. Army Continental Commands, 1821-1920, Department of Dakota, *Field Records/Yellowstone*

Expedition, 1872-1873, "Letters and Telegrams Received, July 1872-Oct.1872," 1334, Box no. 1.

[14] Lubetkin, *Jay Cooke's Gamble...*, 3626, 1335.

[15] Chun, pp 20, 73, 93. Linda Slaughter, 24. "Eighth Regiment of Infantry," 522. "General Order No. 4," July 22, 1872, and "Circular," Aug. 6, 1872, National Archives, Washington, DC, RG 393, U.S. Army Continental Commands, 1821-1920, Department of Dakota, *Field Records/Yellowstone Expedition, 1872-1873*, "General Orders Issued" and "Circulars Issued," July 1872-Aug.1872," 1334, Box no. 1. Lubetkin, *Jay Cooke's Gamble...*, locations 2628, 2650, 2804, 2808, 2814, 2817, 2844-2853, 2892 3331-3409, 3453, 3480, 3618. "8th Infantry Sick Roll," Camp no. 27, Aug. 24, 1872, National Archives, Washington, DC, RG 393, U.S. Army Continental Commands, 1821-1920, Department of Dakota, *Field Records/Yellowstone Expedition, 1872-1873*. "Special Order No. 9," National Archives, Washington, DC, RG 393 U.S. Army Continental Commands, 1821-1920, Department of Dakota, *Field Records/Yellowstone Expedition, 1872-1873*, "General Orders Issued" and "Circulars Issued," July 1872-Aug.1872," 1334, Box no. 1. M. John Lubetkin, "The Northern Pacific Railroad's 1872 Western Yellowstone Surveying Expedition," *Montana, The Magazine of Western History*, 56:2 (Summer, 2006), 29, 34-35, 41.

[16] 1861 Census of England, St. Thomas, Birmingham,26, Elizabeth Nicholls; image, Ancestry.com, (https://search.ancestry.com/cgi-bin/sse.dll?db=uki1861&indiv=try&h=20942905). accessed 26 March 2020, citing Class: *RG 9*; Piece: *2135*; Folio: *39*; Page: *26*; GSU roll: *542923*.

[17] See "Eli Taylor, Mary Elizabeth Nicholls, and Mary Ann Stringer," *FamilySearch*, (https://www.familysearch.org/tree/person/details/KWJ4-F6C.) for well sourced details on the family. For Joseph Howard's story, see the chapter "Promised Land," earlier in this book. 1871 Census of England, Ladywood, Birmingham, 30, Eli Taylor; image, Ancestry.com (https://search.ancestry.com/cgi-bin/sse.dll?_phsrc=sdL227&_phstart=successSource&usePUBJs=true&indiv=1&dbid=7619&gsfn=Eli&gsln=Taylor&gsfn_x=NN&gsln_x=NN&msrpn__ftp=birmingham,%20warwickshire,%20england,%20united%20kingdom&msrpn__ftp_x=1&msrpn=1652385&msrpn_x=1&new=1&rank=1&uidh=aic&redir=false&gss=angs-d&pcat=35&fh=0&h=2846791&recoff=&ml_rpos=1&queryId=675ae7278cbafd5f0d72c88023f1837f): accessed 26 March 2020, citing The National Archives; Kew, London, England; *1871 England Census*; Class: *RG10*; Piece: *3094*; Folio: *18*; Page: *30*; GSU roll: *839568*.

[18] General Register Office, London, "Certified Copy of an Entry of Marriage," Eli Taylor and Elizabeth Nichols, 24 March 1864, a photocopy is in my possession.

[19] The 1871 British Census entry for the Eli Taylor family lists Mary Ann and her sister Elizabeth as "scholars," noting their enrollment in school. Eli's occupation

was a "Boot and Shoe Maker," but nothing was listed for Mary Elizabeth, perhaps indicating that she was now home, hands full with three small children. They were living on the courtside of a back-to-back in the Ladywood District, about 20 minutes' walk from the spots where they dwelled in the 1861 census before they were married. Their neighbors were solid working-class tradesmen.

[20] Possibly there was another child named Alma who was perhaps even a twin to Eli, Jr. Alma apparently died young; sometime before or after their emigration to Utah. See *FamilySearch* entry for Eli Taylor. Perpetual Emigrating Fund, *Names of Persons and Sureties Indebted to the Perpetual Emigrating Fund Company from 1850 to 1877 inclusive*, (Star Book: Salt Lake City, 1877), 177. See Chapter 8 "Promised Land" for a discussion of the Perpetual Emigrating Fund (PEF). "Liverpool-New York, 14 October 1875-26 October 1875: A Compilation of General Voyage Notes," *Saints by Sea, Latter-day Saint Immigration to America,,* https://mormonmigration.lib.byu.edu/mii/voyage/111?mii=on&account=on&query=Eli+Taylor&passenger=on&dateTo=26+Oct+1875&voyage=on&scandinavia=on&sweden=on&netherlands=on&europe=on&dateFrom=14+Oct+1875.

[21] "B. Eardley to A Carrington" October 15, 1875, in *Saints by Sea...*

[22] "B. Eardley to A Carrington" October 24, 1875, in *Saints by Sea...*

[23] "Liverpool to New York, 14 October – 26 October 1875," *Saints by Sea...* Michael Sharpe, *Tracing your Birmingham Ancestors, A Guide for Family & Local Historians*, Kindle edition, (Barnsley, South Yorkshire: Pen Sword Books Ltd, 2015), location 2200, 2656. *Diary of Isaiah M. Coombs Diary*, Jan. 23, 31, Feb 4-11, 1876, "*Saints by Sea, Latter-day Saint Immigration to America*, "Liverpool-New York, 19 January 1876 – 1 February 1876, (https://saintsbysea.lib.byu.edu/mii/account/948?netherlands=on&mii=on&sweden=on&keywords=montana&scandinavia=on&europe=on). Coombs was part of the LDS party that departed from Liverpool on the *Dakota's* sister ship, the *Montana*, three months after the Taylors' voyage. Their route was the same and there were many similarities in the two parties' experience. "B. Eardley to A. Carrington" October 15, 1875, in *Saints by Sea*, printed in *"Latter-Day Saints' Millennial Star*, 37:43 (October 25, 1875), 686, 734.

[24] G. B. Dobson, "Cheyenne, Photos," *Wyoming Trails and Tales*, (http://www.wyomingtalesandtrails.com/cheyenne70s.html), accessed 9 February 2017.

[25] Richard MaGuire's name was not on the long list of those disciplined between Nov 1, 1872 and March 15, 1873. See "Ft. D. A. Russell, Wyo., General Orders, Special Orders, & Orders," *Records of U.S. Army Continental Commands, 1821-1920*, National Archives, Washington, DC, RG 393, Ft. D. A. Russell, Wyo., 1872, II, Box no. 4.

[26] A band of Sioux in fact did attack a ranch just south of Cheyenne in April 1873. Col. Gerald M. Adams, *The Post Near Cheyenne, A History of Fort D. A. Russell, 1867-1930*, (Boulder, CO: Pruett Publishing, 1989), 37, 45, 49-50.

[27] Richard was admitted on March 6 and released on March 8, 1873 for "Piles." "Post Infirmary Records," Fort Russell, Wyo., Reg. No. 59, Hos. No. 5638, March 9, 1873, photocopy in my possession).

[28] Chun, 45-47. Adams, 34.

[29] Over the years people have sometimes spelled his surname McGuire as "MaGuire." However, when Richard enlisted he gave the name of "Richard Joseph McGuire," and "Richard J. McGuire" is how the records usually carried him. Interestingly, in the letter from Secretary of War Belknep to the Hon. James Brooks, dated May 3, 1872, Belknep gives his name as "Richard McGuire, Jr.," suggesting Richard's father's first name may also have been Richard. I have chosen to use the "McGuire" surname in conformance with the spelling used in what official records we have. See "Oath of Enlistment and Allegiance, Richard Joseph McGuire," Davids Island, New York, 20 January 1872, R.G. 94, National Archives and Record Service, photocopy in my possession.

[30] "Muster Roll of Captain William Worth's," *Records of the Adjutant General's Office*, 1780's-1917, National Archives Record Group 94, Muster Rolls, Regular Army Organizations, Co K, 8th U.S. Infantry, February 28-April 30, 1873, copy in my possession.

[31] David Haward Bain, *The Old Iron Road, An Epic of Rails, Roads, and the Urge to Go West*, (New York: Viking, 2004), 133-134. "Fort Russell, Photos," *Wyoming Trails and Tales*, http://www.wyomingtalesandtrails.com/cheyenne70s.html), accessed 9 February 2017. Adams, 34, 42, 45. J. Michael Cleverley, "The Development of an Urban Pattern," in Richard D. Poll, et al, *Utah's History*, (Provo, UT: Brigham Young University Press, 1978), 687.

[32] *US Census*, 1880, Census Place: *South Cottonwood, Salt Lake, Utah*; Roll: *1337*; Page: *23*; (penned) Enumeration District: *057*, Dwelling number: *195*. *From: Ancestry.com*, Tenth Census of the United States, 1880. (NARA microfilm publication T9, 1,454 rolls). Records of the Bureau of the Census, Record Group 29. National Archives, Washington, D.C. In one of her several histories of her great-grandfather, Mother claimed he was working in the same area where the Taylors lived, and in still another, she wrote he was working for Eli Taylor. The 1880 Census has Mary Ann living with the John and Mary Ann Tullidge family in Salt Lake's 7th Ward.

[33] Photocopies of the Bible's family history pages are in my possession. Cleverley, 687. "Bonita Jewett Family History," dated Feb. 26, 2000, a photocopy in my possession.

[34] Mary Ann Taylor Wilson's entry in their family's New Testament.

[35] 1882 Arizona Territorial Census, from Ancestry.com, "Census Enumeration, Apache County, Arizona," *Arizona, Territorial Census Records, 1864-1882*, entries 2175, 2176, [database on-line]. Provo, UT, USA; Ancestry.com Operations, Inc., 2016. Territorial Census Records. Arizona History and Archives Division, Phoenix, Arizona.

(https://search.ancestry.com/cgi-bin/sse.dll?_phsrc=sdL258&_phstart=successSource&usePUBJs=true&indiv=1&dbid=61064&gsfn=Mary&gsln=Wilson&gsfn_x=NP_NN_NIC&gsln_x=NP_NN&msrpn_ftp=joseph%20city,%20navajo,%20arizona,%20usa&msrpn=67541&new=1&rank=1&uidh=aic&redir=false&gss=angs-d&pcat=35&fh=2&h=43303&recoff=&ml_rpos=3&queryId=6249f45d3adb42f495ce34b7eb40af43).

[36]Charles S. Peterson, *Take Up Your Mission*, (Tucson, AZ: Univ. of Arizona Press, 1973), 63 ff, 134 ff. George Tanner and J. Morris Richards, *Colonization on the Little Colorado: The Richard City Region*, (Flagstaff, AZ: Northland Press, 1977), 18 ff, 84. **Don Strack, "John W. Young's Railroads,"** *UtahRails.net*, updated June 28, 2018, accessed, March 18, 2020, (https://utahrails.net/utahrails/john-w-young.php). M. Guy Bishop, "Building Railroads for the Kingdom: The Career of John W. Young, 1867-91," *Utah Historical Quarterly*, 48:1 (Winter 1980), 68-71. *The Historical Guide to North American Railroads*, 3rd ed., (Waukesha, WI: Kalmbach, 2014), 29. Ancestry.com. *"1882 Arizona Territory Census,"* Territorial Census Records, 1864-1882, [database on-line]. Provo, UT. From: Ancestry.com. *Arizona, Voter Registrations, 1866-1955* [database on-line]. Provo, UT, USA: Ancestry.com Operations, Inc., 2016. Original data: Great Registers (of Voters). Arizona History and Archives Division, Phoenix, Arizona.

(https://www.ancestry.com/interactive/60875/43146_542780-00750?pid=279368&backurl=https://search.ancestry.com/cgi-bin/sse.dll?_phsrc%3DsdL277%26_phstart%3DsuccessSource%26usePUBJs%3Dtrue%26indiv%3D1%26dbid%3D60875%26gsfn%3DRichard%26gsln%3DWilson%26gsfn_x%3DNN%26gsln_x%3DNN%26msydy%3D1882%26msypn__ftp%3Darizona,%2520usa%26msypn__ftp_x%3D1%26msypn%3D5%26msypn_x%3DPAS%26msbdy%3D1855%26msbdy_x%3D1%26msbdp%3D10%26msrdy%3D1882%26msrpn__ftp%3Darizona,%2520usa%26msrpn__ftp_x%3D1%26msrpn%3D5%26msrpn_x%3DPAS%26new%3D1%26rank%3D1%26uidh%3Daic%26redir%3Dfalse%26gss%3Dangs-d%26pcat%3D35%26fh%3D3%26h%3D279368%26recoff%3D%26ml_rpos%3D4%26queryId%3D629e926e73b19e882daae5e71f883b57&treeid=&personid=&hintid=&queryId=629e926e73b19e882daae5e71f883b57&usePUB=true&_phsrc=sdL277&_phstart=successSource&usePUBJs=true).

[37] Once they had completed the line across Arizona, it was possible to travel into California to connect to the line running from Sacramento via Salt Lake City to Omaha.

[38] Murray Cemetery, Salt Lake City, Lot 93 Block 4. Next to her are the graves of her mother, step-father, brother, sister, and some of their families.

[39] "Obituary for Mary Ann Wilson," *Deseret News*, November 22, 1889.

[40] An entry in the family bible shows Eli Taylor died on January 1, 1879. Cleverley, 556. **Margie Lea Leonardson Cleverley, "Richard Joseph MaGuire**

Wilson," typed history of Richard MaGuire's life, 3. This is one of several typed histories that Margie compiled and is noted "Margie Lea Leonardson – C.".

[41] Margie Cleverley C, 4-5. One of Mother's scribbled notes from a conversation with Emma Louise stated Emma Louise told her that they were married in the Mormon South Cottonwood Ward meeting house and that he was an "Elder" at the time. "Elder" is a position in the lay priesthood of the Church of Jesus Christ of Latter-day Saints, one most actively involved adult male members are granted. This note caught my eye, for it is the only reference that Richard may have joined the Mormon faith sometime during his years in Utah and Arizona. It might explain why he and Emma Louise were married in a Mormon meeting house. She, too, in later years accepted the Mormon faith, but long after he was gone. If he were *not* a member when they married, one wonders why they chose a Mormon wedding instead of a civil ceremony. It may well be that Richard was at some moment before or after his marriage with Mary Ann baptized into the LDS church. If so, this was still another secret that his later family never knew, or at least shared.

[42] Margie Cleverley C, 3. Fern Leonardson Evans to Margie Cleverley, May 8, 1980, photocopy in my possession. Fern was Richard's granddaughter.

[43] Margie Cleverley," Richard Joseph McGuire (Wilson)," another typed history of Richard McGuire.

[44] Margie Cleverley C, 4. Discussions with Bonita Jewett, granddaughter.

[45] Margie Cleverley A, "Richard Joseph Wilson McGuire," still another of the family histories Margie wrote. This is distinguished from the others as "Margie Cleverley A."

[46] Ida Fern Leonardson Evans to Margie Cleverley, May 8, 1980.

[47] For words to the folksong, see "A Search for the Border Ruffian," *Outing and The Wheelman, An Illustrated Monthly Magazine of Recreation*, 5 (October 1884-March 1885), 38.

[48] Dean L. May, "Towards a Dependent Commonwealth," in Poll, 220-223. "Utah & Northern Railway, 1878-1889)," www.*UtahRails.net* .

[49] "Serendipity in Genealogy," *The Weekly Genealogist*, 19:59, Whole #832, February 22, 2017.

[50] National Trust, *Back to Backs Birmingham*, (Rotherham, UK: 2004).

[51] *A Historical and Biographical Record of the Territory of Arizona*, (Chicago: McFarland & Poole, 1896). Charles S. Peterson, *Take Up Your Mission*, (Tucson, AZ: Univ. of Arizona Press, 1973). George Tanner and J. Morris Richards, *Colonization on the Little Colorado: The Richard City Region*, (Flagstaff, AZ: Northland Press, 1977).

[52] The man who deserted the 8th Infantry with Richard McGuire was "Charles H. Gallagher." He was a "musician" who enlisted in New York a few months before Richard McGuire, according to the Muster Roll. It listed Richard as a "Private," and his enlistment papers of a year earlier called him, too, a musician. The Gallagher with Richard and Mary Ann in St. Joseph was named James Gallagher,

from Ireland, aged 28. The James Gallagher later noted in the 1882 Voter Registration was 29 years old and gave New York as his "Country of Nativity." If he had stated his nativity outside the U.S., he probably would have had to offer proof of his naturalization in order to vote. By saying "New York," he avoided that. Richard Wilson also gave the "U.S." as his country of nativity on the Voter Registration.

Obviously, the two Gallaghers have different first names, but it is difficult to know how much meaning to put into that. As with Richard MaGuire, aka Joseph Wilson and Richard Wilson, deserters normally changed their names if they hoped not to be caught. They both probably altered their names one way or another. Richard and James were both at one end of the Atlantic and Pacific Railroad construction in early 1882 and apparently at the other end when it reached Kingman. There is not 100% certainty that they worked their way across the territory together, but in genealogy one rarely finds 100% certainty in anything. It is not unreasonable to think they worked as part of the railroad construction nor to suspect the connection between Gallagher and Wilson.

[53] "Utah & Northern Railway (1878-1889)," www.Utah.Net, 5.

Chapter Nine - Homesick

[1] Margie Lea Leonardson Cleverley, "Life in the 1890s," typewritten manuscript written in the late 1950s, copy in my possession.

[2] Margie Lea Leonardson Cleverley, "Life Sketch of Matilda Ann Howard Johnson," based on interviews with Matilda Johnson and delivered at her funeral on June 3, 1962. Hereafter referred to as "Matilda Howard Life Sketch." Typewritten copy in my possession.

[3] Technically she was the fourth child, but her older brother William lived only a few months. Another younger brother, Owen, lived only a year.

[4] Florence Moore, "History of James Howard, by Florence Moore (Granddaughter), 1945," copy of typed manuscript in my possession.

[5] Delsa Jane Skinner, "James and Betsy Jane Fackrell, Howard," copy typewritten manuscript in my possession.

[6] Matilda Ann Howard Johnson's personal history written in her own hand in the 1950s, copy of typewritten manuscript in my possession and hereafter referred to as "Matilda Howard's Personal History." Addendum to Matilda Ann Howard Johnson's personal history probably written by her daughters (hereafter referred to as "Addendum to Matilda Howard's Personal History."). Handwritten loose notes taken by Margie Cleverley during her interviews with Tillie, originals in my possession. Zina Blaylock, "Matilda Ann Johnson," a typewritten bio based on Blaylock's interview with Tillie during the summer of 1959, photocopy in my possession. Dee Ann Ludwig, "The Old Home," written for the James Howard Family Reunion held in Thayne, Wyo., July 26-27, 1974, typewritten manuscript, a copy in my possession.

[7] Skinner.

8 "Matilda Howard's Personal History..." "Matilda Howard Life Sketch...". "LDS Family and Individual Record," handwritten manuscript kept by Matilda Johnson, original in my possession. *Reminiscences of the John Johnson and Matilda Ann Howard Johnson Family,* an unpublished collection of memories written by John and Matilda Johnson's children after her death, hereafter referred to as "Reminiscences..." "Application for Registration – Native Citizen," for John Johnson, U.S. Consulate, Malmo, Sweden, dated July 30, 1918, original in my possession.

9 "Matilda Howard Life Sketch..."

10 "Matilda Howard Life Sketch...". Daughters of the Utah Pioneers, *Pioneer Pathways*, 8, (Salt Lake City: International Society Daughters of Utah Pioneers, 2006), 344-345.

11 "A Brief Sketch..." in "Reminiscences...".

12 Thomas G. Alexander and James B. Allen, *Mormons & Gentiles A History of Salt Lake City*, (Boulder, CO: Pruett Publishing, 1984), 107. J. Michael Cleverley, "The Development of an Urban Pattern," Richard D. Poll et al, eds., *Utah's History*, (Provo, UT: Brigham Young Univ. Press, 1978), 545 ff.

13 *Pioneer Pathways*, 312-318. "Matilda Howard's Personal History..."

14 Ed Brown was John's sister's brother-in-law.

15 *Pioneer Pathways*, 345-346.

16 "A Brief Sketch of the Lives..." in "Reminiscences...". "Matilda Howard's Personal History...". Handwritten notes taken by Margie Cleverley in an interview with Matilda Johnson, originals in my possession.

17 Handwritten notes taken by Margie Cleverley in an interview with Matilda Johnson. "Matilda Howard's Personal History..."

18 "Matilda Howard's Personal History."

19 J. L. Johnson, "The Shelton Road," in *The Rigby Star*, Thursday, October 4, 1973. Handwritten notes taken by Margie Cleverley in an interview with Matilda Johnson.

20 "Matilda Howard's Personal History..."

21 Idaho's headstrong winters obviously were so stubborn that it took another apostolic blessing before crops could be continually raised. As described in "Wagon Box Prophesy," a video by BYU-Idaho, 2006, church leader Wilford Woodruff in 1884 stood on the back of a wagon box also to give a blessing that the valley's climate would be tempered.

22 Florence Moore and Mayme Woolley, "History of Matilda Ann Howard Johnson," typewritten history written by two of Tillie's daughters, photocopy in my possession. "Matilda Howard's Personal History..." "A Brief Sketch of the Lives...," in "Reminiscences..."

23 "Matilda Howard's Personal History..." "A Brief Sketch..."

24 "Matilda Howard's Personal History..." "Addendum to Matilda Howard's Personal History..."

[25] Sarah A. Howard Camp, ed., "Pioneer Memories," Shelton Idaho Chapter of the Daughters of the Utah Pioneers (DUP), 1940. Tillie was Captain of this section of the DUP when this publication was put together. "Matilda Howard's Personal History..."

[26] Florence Moore, "Life of my Father John Johnson," typewritten personal history. Andrew Jenson, *History of the Scandinavian Mission*, (Salt Lake City: Deseret, 1927), 361. "John E. Johnson, Jr.," from The Church of Jesus Christ of Latter-day Saints, *Missionary Database*, (https://history.lds.org/missionary/individual/john-johnson-jr-1867?lang+eng), accessed March 20, 2020. "Matilda Howard's Personal History..."

[27] Zelma Storer, in "Reminiscences...". "Matilda Howard's Personal History..." "Addendum to Matilda Howard's Personal History..." Notes from Mayme Johnson Cleverley, daughter.

[28] Wayne Johnson in "Reminiscences..." Geneve Jenson and Ellen Johnson in "Reminiscences...". Moore and Woolley, "History..."

[29] Zelma Storer, in "Reminiscences..."

[30] Florence Nelson in "Reminiscences..."

[31] Wayne Johnson in "Reminiscences..."

[32] Blaylock.

[33] Geneve Jensen, in "Reminiscences..."

[34] Florence Nelson, "Reminiscences..."

[35] Josephine Howard, Maud Green, Florence Nelson, Geneve Jenson, in "Reminiscences..." Camp, *Pioneer Memories*. Not long after John's death Tillie was chosen head, or "Captain," of the local Daughters of the Utah Pioneers chapter for four years, 1939-1942.

[36] "Matilda Howard's Personal History..." One family tradition is that John, Jr., was to be called on a mission, but when he broke his leg, his father John offered to take his place. This may be true, although I have not been able to substantiate it. In correspondence between John and the church's First Presidency, found in the LDS Church History Library, the case of taking his son's place is not mentioned. It may be likely that the church wanted to call John, Sr., to Sweden as a result of its missionary drawdown there after the outbreak of World War I. With many fewer missionaries than earlier, more mature and experienced missionaries, like John, Sr., would be valuable in shepherding the church's isolated flock during the war years.

[37] Mayme Woolley, in "Reminiscences..."

[38] "Matilda Howard Life Sketch..." John Johnson, "Missionary Journal," *FamilySearch*, accessed March 1, 1916-August 12, 1918, (https://www.familysearch.org/library/books/records/item/613541-john-johnson-missionary-journal-sweden-mission-january-1916?viewer=1&offset=0#page=1&viewer=picture&o=info&n=0&q=). "Application for Registration – Native Citizen," for John Johnson, U.S.

Consulate, Malmo, Sweden, dated July 30, 1918, original in my possession. Andrew Jenson, 464, 486.

[39] Mayme Woolley in "Reminiscences..."

[40] Mayme Woolley in "Reminiscences...".

[41] "Matilda Howard Life Sketch..." Mayme Woolley in "Reminiscences..." "Matilda Howard's Personal History..."

[42] "A Brief Sketch of the Lives..."

[43] Mayme Woolley in "Reminiscences..." "Ship News," *S/S Oscar II*, November 21, 1918.

[44] The accusation about "Mr. Henry," as all called him even decades later, was one of those stories that was always left untold. I had heard several times that when John lay in the hospital after the accident with his team and load of timber, Tillie refused to go to him. Many times, I asked about this, never to receive a convincing response. One day, during the months just prior to Mother's death, I asked again. She looked at me, paused, and in a voice barely stronger than a whisper, finally answered, "When John returned home from his second mission, he accused her of being unfaithful with Mr. Henry." Incredulously, I repeated her words back, and she looked me in the eyes and nodded with a "Yes, you heard right." This obviously was one of those topics no one ever discussed or wrote about. I would have wanted to pursue the matter for more details. But from the look on Mother's face, there was no more to be said. She agreed with the family that there were things you did not talk about, especially when they were not pretty.

There was another issue that was generally known, but rarely discussed. John had a drinking problem. Consuming alcohol, though frowned upon in his time, was not considered as big an issue then as it is now in Mormon culture. The church's "Word of Wisdom" which denies alcohol and tobacco – a signature practice among Mormons – was stressed more sometimes than others but was not considered a commandment barring priesthood advancement and temple entrance until 1930. (See James B. Allen and Glen M. Leonard, *The Story of the Latter-day Saints*, (Salt Lake City: Deseret Book with the LDS Church Historical Department, 1976), 524 ff.)) Commandment or not, however, alcohol abuse had its own social and family consequences, and it may have been a significant issue in John's and Tillie's relationship. I have even wondered whether the accident that took his life may have had an alcohol component. If it did, it could have further infuriated Tillie, helping to explain her refusal to see him in the hospital. As she would have seen it, his negligence not only injured him but could have also taken their youngest son, who was riding next to him when the accident happened.

[45] Blaylock. "Matilda Howard's Personal History..." "Death Summons John Johnson," obituary probably from the [Idaho Falls] *Post Register*, October 1934, from "John Johnson," *FamilySearch,*
(https://www.familysearch.org/tree/person/memories/KWC1-H5L).

[46] Wayne Johnson, in "Reminiscences..."

[47] Margie L. Cleverley, "Jons Johnsson," typewritten personal history of John Johnson's father, "as given to her by Matilda Ann Howard Johnson in about 1952." Photocopy in my possession.

[48] "Matilda Howard Life Sketch..."

[49] "Addendum to Matilda Howard's Personal History."

[50] Mentioned in an undated article in the Idaho Falls *Post Register* that I found attached to an addendum (hereafter referred to as "Addendum to Matilda Howard's Personal History."), probably written by daughters. "Matilda Howard's Personal History.". Matilda Ann Howard Johnson's personal history written in her own hand and hereafter referred to as "Matilda Howard's Personal History.".

[51] In *Reminiscences of the John Johnson and Matilda Ann Howard Johnson Family,* an unpublished collection of memories written by Tillie's children after her death, hereafter referred to as "Reminiscences...".

[52] There was not just a program, but a detailed typed program distributed to everyone present. One preserved from the 1960 Johnson Family Reunion read:

> Program of the Day
>
> 10:00 Ball Game (Soft Ball)
>   Badminton
> 11:00 Sewing-Cooking Demonstration
> 12:00 Prepare Lunch & Eat
> 12:30 Eat
> 1:30 Program
> 2:30 Men's Fish Casting Contest
> 3:00 Women's Fish Casting Contest...

And so on. The program ended with an admonishment: "Make yourself known to everyone and make sure you know everyone."

[53] Mayme Woolley in "Reminiscences..."

[54] John Johnson to Mayme Woolley, postcard, sent from Sweden undated.

[55] John Johnson to Mayme Johnson Woolley, Oct. 11, 1916.

Chapter Ten – Where Two Rivers Joined

[1] Seija's cousin, Ebba, and her husband, John, traveled with us. When they were young, Ebba's mother, Rosa, and Seija's mother, Lempi, were close. The two of them wanted to leave for the United States in the early 1930's, but Lempi's father was not keen on letting her go. She stayed behind, and Rosa left in 1933, first to Canada and then the United States where she married Gust, another Finnish immigrant. Rosa would eventually become a chef for Rose Kennedy, John F. Kennedy's mother. But Rosa never forgot her cousin and good friend, Lempi. One of Seija's fondest memories from her childhood was the day Rosa and Gust drove into their yard a few years after the war, in the early 1950s. These were the New York cousins, and all the neighborhood watched as they got out of the cab and walked to Seija's house with packages in their arms. It was better than

Christmas amidst the poor post-war years. The doll they brought Seija was her first doll. She named it "Ebba" after the American cousin who gave it to her.

[2] Manne Heimala, (Lahti, Finland), interview by J. Michael Cleverley, 11 July 1984; tape and MP3 file privately held by author. This story and many of those that follow are attributable to this interview and others done during the 1980s.

[3] The source for this narration of Finland in World War II is my book: J. Michael Cleverley, *Born a Soldier, the Times and Life of Larry Thorne*, (Booksurge, 2008).

[4] Cleverley, 22-23.

[5] Emma Auvinen was Ebba Sayre's grandmother – see footnote 2.

[6] Manne Heimala to Lempi Heimala, December 5, 1944, original in my possession.

[7] Manne Heimala to Aleksander Roos, November 24, 1944, original in my possession.

[8] Manne Heimala to Aleksander Roos, no date, original in my possession.

[9] Manne Heimala to Lempi Heimala, December 7, 1944, original in my possession.

[10] Ruth 1:16

[11] Cleverley, *Born a Soldier: The Times and Life of Larry Thorne,* and in Finnish: *Lauri Törni, Syntynyt Sotilaaksi*, (Helsinki: Otava, 2003). In addition to Finland, the book was published in the United States, Greece, Sweden, Norway, Poland, and Romania.

Epilogue – How the Journey Ends

[1] Philbrick address at the New England Historic Genealogical Society's 170th anniversary gala October 22, 2015.

[2] Christopher Nolan, *Memento*, March 16, 2001, movie, Summit Entertainment and Team Todd.

[3] Davis Guggenheim, *From the Sky Down*, 2011, documentary film, Universal Music Group.

[4] Libby Copeland, "Genealogy Provides the Strength to Persevere," *Psychology Today*, April 13, 2020, accessed April 14, 2020, https://www.psychologytoday.com/us/blog/the-lost-family/202004/genealogy-provides-the-strength-persevere

[5] "Genealogy: the Second Most Popular Hobby in the US?" *Ancestry.com,* (https://blogs.ancestry.com/cm/genealogy-second-most-popular-hobby-us/). Gregory Rodriguez, "How Genealogy Became Almost as Popular as Porn," *Time,* May 30, 2014, (https://time.com/133811/how-genealogy-became-almost-as-popular-as-porn/), accessed March 21, 2020. Also, Gregory Rodriguez, "Roots of Genealogy Craze," *USA Today*, May 12, 2014, (https://www.usatoday.com/story/opinion/2014/05/12/genealogy-americans-technology-roots-porn-websites-column/9019409/), accessed March 21, 2020. See also, "How Popular is Genealogy?" *GenealogyInTime Magazine,*

(http://www.genealogyintime.com/articles/how-popular-is-genealogy-page01.html), accessed March 21, 2020.
[6] See Bruce Feiler, "The Stories That Bind Us," *This Life, The New York Times*, March 15, 2015.
[7] Rebecca Hardy, "Why children need to know their family history," *The Guardian*, US Edition, January 14, 2017, (https://www.theguardian.com/lifeandstyle/2017/jan/14/children-family-histories-tales), accessed March 21, 2020.

Family Trees

[1] Sources Chart 1 Margie Lea Leonardson Cleverley, "Family History Files, Records and Documentation." Margie knew and interviewed the majority of those on this chart. For those not interviewed, she compiled their information from family records and interviews with spouses, children, and grandchildren.
[2] Sources Chart 2 Margie Lea Leonardson Cleverley, "Family History Files, Records and Documentation." Entries for individuals are also well sourced on *FamilySearch.com*. More information is included in: Rev Ezra Ripley, *A History of the Fight at Concord on the 19th of April, 1775*, (Concord: Allen & Atwill, 1827); Lemuel Shattuck, *A History of the Town of Concord, Middlesex County, Massachusetts From Its Earliest Settlement to 1832*, (Boston: Russell, Odiorne, & Co., 1835); Rev. Edwin R. Hodgman, *History of the Town of Westford, 1659-1883*, Lowell, MA: Morning Mail Co., 1883; and Hamilton D. Hurd, *History of Middlesex County*, Massachusetts, 1, Philadelphia: J.W. Lewis, 1890.
[3] Sources Chart 3 Margie Lea Leonardson Cleverley, "Family History Files, Records and Documentation." Entries for these individuals are well sourced on *FamilySearch.com*. The following sources provide additional material:
Chad Browne: John Osborne Austin, "Chad Brown," *The Genealogical Dictionary of Rhode Island, Comprising Three Generations of Settlers Who Came Before 1690*, (Albany: 1887), 258. *The Chad Browne Memorial*, 1638-1888, Printed for the Brown family in Brooklyn, NY, about 1888.
John Coggeshall: Austin, 49.
Samuel Gorton: Austin, 302.
Dr. John Greene: Austin, 88. George Sears Greene, *The Greenes of Rhode Island with Historical Records of English Ancestry, 1534-1902*, (New York, 1902). La Mance, Lora Sarah Nichols, *The Greene Family and its Branches, from A.D. 861 to A.D. 1904*, (Floral Park, NY: Mayflower Publishing Co., 1904).
John Greene of Quidnessett: Austin, 80. La Mance, Lora Sarah Nichols, *The Greene Family and its Branches, from A.D. 861 to A.D. 1904*, (Floral Park, NY: Mayflower Publishing Co., 1904).
Obadiah Holmes: Austin, 103. Holmes, Col. J. T., *The American Family of Rev Obadiah Holmes*, (Columbus, OH, 1915).
[4] Sources Chart 4 See comments regarding the connection between the Northampton and Dorset Greene families in Chapter 2.

[a] Sir Henry Greene, Sr.: Robert Halstead, *Succinct Genealogies of the Noble and Ancient Houses*, (London: 1685).

[b] Sir Thomas Greene: Halstead.

[c] Sir Henry Greene, Jr.: Halstead.

[d] Ralph Greene: Halstead.

[e] John Greene: Halstead.

[f] Thomas Greene: Halstead did not have this Thomas listed as a son of Sir Henry Greene, Jr., but others have listed him, including George Sears Greene who bases this on other writers, among them, the normally authoritative Baker's *History of Northamptonshire*. Greene, George Sears, T*he Greenes of Rhode Island, with Historical Records of English Ancestry, 1534-1902*, (New York: 1902), 33-35.

[g] John Greene: George Sears Greene,33. An estimated birthdate could be between 1405 and 1425.

[h] Thomas Greene: George Sears Greene, 33.

[j] John Greene: Otherwise known as "John the Fugitive," from Lora Sarah Nichols La Mance, *The Greene Family and its Branches from A.D. 861 to A.D. 1904*, Floral Park, NY: Mayflower Publishing Co., 1904), 36. WikiTree gives 1452 as his birthdate. If we accept that John Greene was a descendant of the Northampton Greene family, as I and a great number of other Greene family historians do, and La Mance's claim that John was a descendant of Sir Henry Greene, Jr. through his son Thomas, he would very likely have to connect into the generation shown on this chart. George Sears Greene traced three generations down from Thomas, and chronologically John would fit as son of Thomas [h]. Nevertheless, there is no proof of the linkage of Thomas and John, hence the dotted line, and he could have descended from a brother somewhere else along the line.

[k] Robert Greene: According to La Mance, Robert was son of John Greene the Fugitive, La Mance, 36. Robert was already elderly with grandchildren when listed on subsidy rolls in 1543. La Mance, 36. WikiTree gives 1490 as his birthdate.

[l] Richard Greene: Sears. WikiTree gives 1527 as his birthdate.

[m] Richard Greene II: Sears. WikiTree gives his birthdate as 1550.

[n] Dr. John Greene: George Sears Greene.

[5] Sources Chart 5 From *FamilySearch.com* data.

[6] Sources Chart 6 Personal information and family records of Seija Kaarina Cleverley.

www.ingramcontent.com/pod-product-compliance
Lightning Source LLC
Chambersburg PA
CBHW070621270326
41926CB00011B/1769